Europe, 1890–1945

Europe, 1890–1945 is a new approach to teaching and learning early twentieth-century European history at A-level. It meets the needs of teachers and students studying for today's revised AS-level exams.

In a unique style, *Europe, 1890–1945* focuses on the key topics within the period. Each topic is then comprehensively explored to provide background, essay-writing advice and examples, source work and historical skills exercises.

From 1890–1945, the key topics featured include:

- The Origins and Impact of the First World War
- The Russian Revolution and the Rise of Stalin
- The Weimar Republic and the Rise of Hitler
- Mussolini and Fascist Italy
- Stalin and the Soviet Union, 1928–41

Using essay styles and source exercises from each of the exam boards, AQA, Edexcel and OCR, this book is an essential text for students and teachers.

Stephen J. Lee is Head of History at Bromsgrove School. His many books include *The European Dictatorships, 1918–1945* (2nd edition, 2000), *Hitler and Nazi Germany* (1998) and *The Weimar Republic* (1998).

Spotlight History

Britain, 1846–1919
Jocelyn Hunt

Europe, 1890–1945
Stephen J. Lee

Forthcoming titles:

Britain in the Twentieth Century
Ian Cawood

The United States, 1763–2000
John Spiller, Tim Clancey, Stephen Young and Simon Mosley

Stephen J. Lee

Europe, 1890–1945

Routledge
Taylor & Francis Group

LONDON AND NEW YORK

£19·99

First published 2003 by Routledge
11 New Fetter Lane, London EC4P 4EE

Simultaneously published in the USA and Canada
by Routledge
29 West 35th Street, New York, NY 10001

Routledge is an imprint of the Taylor & Francis Group

Typeset in Minion and Helvetica Neue Light by
Florence Production Ltd, Stoodleigh, Devon

Printed and bound in Great Britain by
St Edmundsbury Press, Bury St Edmunds, Suffolk

British Library Cataloguing in Publication Data
A catalogue record for this book is available from the British Library

Library of Congress Cataloging in Publication Data
Lee, Stephen J., 1945–
    Europe, 1890–1945/Stephen J. Lee. – 1st ed.
      p. cm.
    1. Europe – History – 1871–1918.   2. Europe – History – 1918–1945.
    3. World War, 1914–1918.   4. World War, 1939–1945.
    5. Communism – Soviet Union.   6. Germany – History – 1918–1933.
    7. Germany – History – 1933–1945.   8. National socialism.   I. Title.
    D397.L36 2003
    940.2′8–dc21   2003005353

ISBN 0–415–25454–X (hbk)
ISBN 0–415–25455–8 (pbk: alk paper)

For Margaret
and Charlotte

Contents

Illustrations

Acknowledgements

The author and publishers would like to thank the following for permission to reproduce material:

Hulton Archive/Getty Images (illustrations 3.1, 3.4, 3.5, 4.2, 4.6, 4.7, 5.1, 5.2, 5.8, 6.1, 6.4, 7.1, 8.1, 8.2); Corbis (illustrations 2.2, 2.5, 6.3, 7.4, 8.3); Atlantic Syndication (illustrations 5.6, 5.9); Novosti Photo Library (illustration 3.6); David King Collection (illustration 7.6)

While every effort has been made to trace and acknowledge ownership of copyright material used in this volume, the publishers will be glad to make suitable arrangements with any copyright holders whom it has not been possible to contact.

Series Introduction

The aim of this book is to help prepare you for the papers in AS History. It is written very much with the AS specifications in mind, although it is clearly desirable to use other books as well. It is also hoped that the advice given in this book will be valuable to students preparing for courses other than AS.

Each chapter is divided into standard parts, the purpose of which is to combine essential knowledge and the various skills necessary to achieve the highest grade in line with the AS specifications.

The first page of each chapter takes the form of a 'map' or outline of the chapter. The purpose is to enable the reader to 'navigate' through each topic, and to see which aspects of the subject form the focus of each part.

Part of the chapter	Purpose	Method
Part 1: Historical background	To provide the basic, factual backgrounds and issues related to each topic. This may also be relevant to some questions of the simpler format.	The factual narrative is structured to include all the key themes. A chronological summary is also provided to give perspective at a glance.
Part 2: Essays	To provide worked answers to the major aspects of each topic. These provide examples of interpretation and factual support.	The wording of the question varies to allow for different types of examination response. Further questions are provided for term-work and examination practice; these can be prepared through the further reading recommended.
Part 3: Source analysis	To provide a selection of some of the key sources – primary and secondary – for each topic and to examine the different types of questions which can be asked about these.	Each set of sources has two sets of questions: one with worked examples and one without. The worked examples are accompanied by a brief explanation of the approach used. The questions without worked examples allow for class discussion or for individual practice.

| Part 4: Historical skills | To provide some suggestions about how the topic can be used as a focus for selected skills not already covered in Parts 2 and 3. | The types of skills covered vary from chapter to chapter: they include discussion and presentation. |

The rest of this Series Introduction deals with essays, source analysis, and key skills as general concepts and briefly explains the essential meaning of each. The explanations are developed in each chapter by the use of specific examples.

 Part 1: Historical background

A good understanding of the topic in each chapter is essential before any meaningful analysis can be done. This involves three main approaches.

Type of approach:	Reason for this:	How it is accomplished:
1. Outline perspective	An ability to visualise the structure of the topic covered in the chapter and the way in which components of the topic fit together.	Through the chronological summary, the headings and sub-headings, and the introductory paragraphs of each section.
2. Knowledge in depth	An ability to focus on parts of the topic in depth.	Through careful and systematic development of details. These are grouped within an overall structure.
3. Integrating perspective and depth	An ability to combine the overall perspective with a focus on specific selected details.	By relating the details to the interpretations in the essays.

Part 2: Essays

What is an essay?

An essay is a formal attempt to answer a question or to provide a solution to a problem; the term derives from the French '*essayer*' and the Latin '*exigere*', the latter meaning 'to weigh'. The better the attempt, the higher the mark will be. There is usually no right or wrong solution. But there can be a solution which is presented well or badly, or which makes good or poor use of supporting material.

An essay should always be written in full sentences and paragraphs and should not normally include notes or bullet points. Appropriate lengths vary considerably, but some idea can be gained by the worked answers in Part 2 of each chapter. Relevance is vital throughout. This means keeping exactly to the confines of the question asked. The answer should be direct and should start within the first sentence or two. You should also keep the question in mind throughout the essay, answer all parts of it and include nothing which is not relevant to it. Think in terms of '*The question, the whole question and nothing but the question*'.

Instruction	Meaning of instruction	Examples
Outline . . . Describe . . . What is meant by . . .? How did . . .? What were . . .?	Provide a coherent summary of the topic or issue in the question. It is important to include at least some specific factual references. ('Outline', does not mean 'be vague about'.) This type of instruction is less common than the others and, if it does appear, is more likely as a short question.	Ch. 2: 1a, 2a; Ch. 3: 1a, 2a, 3a, 5a, 7a, 11a, 13a; Ch. 4: 1a, 1a, 3a, 8a, 15a; Ch. 5: 3a, 5a, 7a, 8a, 10a, 11a; Ch. 6: 4a, 5a, 8a, 9a, 11a, 13a, 16; Ch. 7: 1a, 2a, 3a, 4a, 7a, 11a, 12; Ch. 8: 10, 15, 17
Examine . . . Why. . .? Explain why . . .	The, emphasis switches from 'describing' to 'providing reasons for'. This means looking at the question as a problem to be solved by a direct answer based on an argument which selects relevant factual information to support it.	Ch. 2: 1b, 2b, 3, 11, 15, 19; Ch. 3: 1b, 2b, 3b, 5b, 6, 7b, 11b, 13b, 17, 21; Ch. 4: 1b, 2b, 3b, 6b, 8b, 14a, 15b, 18; Ch. 5: 1, 2b, 3b, 5a, 7b, 8b, 10b, 11b, 14, 17; Ch. 6: 1b, 4b, 5b, 9b, 11b, 14; Ch. 7: 1b, 2b, 3b, 4b, 6, 7b, 11b, 14, 15; Ch. 8: 3, 11, 14
Identify . . . and explain TWO . . .	In addition to the previous instruction, this involves choosing two areas to 'explain'. Make sure that they are relevant to the question and that they can both act as a base for argument. This is common as a second question in a two-part structure.	Ch. 5: 18; Ch. 7: 18, 19
To what extent . . .? How far . . .? How far do you agree . . .? How valid is the view that . . .? How successful was . . .? How serious were . . .? How important was . . .? With what justification . . .?	This group of instructions involves more directly the notion of 'weighing'. It is therefore essential to have a clear idea of the 'extent' to which you 'agree' with the proposition put in the rest of the question. The extremes are 'entirely' or 'not at all'. If you adopt one of these, you need to explain why the alternative is not acceptable. More likely are 'to a very limited extent' or 'to a large extent, but not entirely.' In 'weighing' two arguments you need to explain: why one is 'heavier' or 'lighter' than the other. In terms of style, it is better to avoid using 'I' in the answer even if there is a 'you' in the question.	Ch. 2: 5, 6, 16, 18, 20; Ch. 3: 1c, 2c, 3c, 5c, 7c, 9, 11c, 13c, 16, 18, 19; Ch. 4: 1c, 2c, 3c, 4, 6c, 7b, 9, 10, 12, 15c, 17, 19; Ch. 5: 4, 5b, 6, 7c, 8c, 9, 10c, 11c, 12, 16, 20; Ch. 6: 1c, 2, 3, 4c, 5c, 8b, 9c, 11, 12c, 13b, 15, 17; Ch. 7: 7c, 10, 11c; Ch. 8: 1, 2, 4, 5, 9, 13, 16, 18, 19

Assess . . .
Assess the reasons
   for . . .
Assess the effects
   of . . .
	These are very similar to the previous set in that they involve 'weighing'. They also have a substantial element of 'Why?' and 'What were . . . ?', although with a more conscious comment on the relative importance of the 'reasons' or 'effects'. Some comment is needed on why one is more important and why another is less important.	Ch. 1: 8. 9. 12. 13. 14;
		Ch. 3: 8, 12, 14, 15;
		Ch. 4: 5, 11, 14b, 16;
		Ch. 5: 15, 19; Ch. 6: 2, 6, 7, 18; Ch. 7: 8; Ch. 8: 6, 7, 8, 12

Compare . . .
Compare and
   contrast . . .
Compare the
   importance of three
   reasons . . .
Assess the relative
   importance of . . .
How similar were . . . ?
How different were . . . ?
	The approach will involve the process of 'weighing', as with the previous set of questions. There are, however, two or more specific items to 'weigh'. These may be policies, or they may be arguments about policies. They may be named in the question, or you may be asked to select your own. Whatever the case, you need to consider the two against each other; at all costs avoid a description of the two separately. 'Compare and contrast' (or 'compare' by itself) involves finding similarities and differences between items, as do 'how similar were' and 'how different were'.	Ch. 1: 10; Ch. 3: 4, 10;
		Ch. 4: 13; Ch. 5: 18;
		Ch. 6: 10

Argument and support

Since most essays involve an attempt to solve a problem, the solution should be clearly presented and well supported. The structure should be argument backed up by factual examples. This is much more effective than factual narrative followed by deduction. For most types of question you should argue then support; do not *narrate then deduce*.

Appropriate essay technique	**Inappropriate essay technique**
Argument	Narrative
Factual detail supporting the argument	Argument deduced from narrative

To become accustomed to writing in this way it can be helpful to outline or highlight *argument* in red and *factual detail supporting the argument* in blue; there will, of course, be some overlapping between the two. For each issue covered in the essay the red should come *before* the blue.

Stages in the essay

Stages	**Appropriate development**
Introduction	Mostly argument: considering the meaning of the question and offering an outline answer without detail.

Each subsequent paragraph	A part of or stage in the argument. The first sentence of each paragraph is based on argument. The rest consists of argument supported by factual detail. It should not normally be factual detail followed by deduction.
Conclusion	Need not repeat the arguments already provided, but may pull together any threads. The final sentence should be a generalisation.

The introductory paragraph is vital since it will usually provide the direction for the rest of the essay; it will also provide the initial impression for the person reading or marking it. It should be a single paragraph and of immediate relevance to the question rather than leading gradually to the point. It should be largely argument, attempting to consider *all* the key words and concepts in the question and to provide a brief outline answer to it. This can then be developed in the rest of the essay. All this means that the introductory paragraph can and should be quite short.

The main section of the essay (about 90 per cent) will consist of several paragraphs that will develop the issues raised in the introduction. Ideally, each paragraph should start with a stage in the argument, with the rest of the paragraph comprising a combination of the argument in more detail and relevant factual support. Paragraphs therefore need to be seen as units within the answer. The reason for starting another paragraph is usually to move on to another unit. A sequence of very short paragraphs usually shows a disjointed argument, and a complete absence of paragraphs makes it difficult to follow the stages in the argument at all.

It is important to have some sort of conclusion and not to stop suddenly. This should round the essay off by pulling threads together and giving a final assessment in any 'to what extent?' essays. It might also be a fitting place for a quotation, especially one which complements or contradicts any quotation included in the question. Never write 'unfinished'; in the event of mistiming, use a rounding off sentence rather than a full conclusion.

The different styles of essay question

The examining boards provide differing essay styles, which are reflected in the various chapters.

Board	Style of essay question, choice and time allowed	Example of style of essay question
OCR	One-part essay question in 45-minutes, testing all essay skills. (90)	How effective were the SS and Gestapo as instruments of the Nazi regime? (90)
AQA	Brief quotation, followed by three-part essay question in 60 minutes, testing: (a) Contextual knowledge (3) (b) Background knowledge (7)	'The Crimean War forced Alexander II to show his credentials as a great reformer and as the "Tsar Liberator"'. (a) What influence did the Crimean War have on the intentions of Alexander II on his accession in 1855? (3)

(c) Interpretation, discussion. (15)

(b) Explain why Alexander II introduced a range of reforms *after* the emancipation of the serfs (1861). (7)

(c) Does the emancipation of the serfs (1861) justify the description of Alexander II as the 'Tsar Liberator'? (15)

Edexel — Two-part essay in 60 minutes, testing:
(a) Knowledge of issues. (30)
(b) Causation. (30)

(a) What were the origins and meaning of 'Italian Fascism'? (30)

(b) Why was Mussolini appointed Prime Minister of Italy in 1922? (30)

Part 3: Source analysis

Questions are set on primary sources, secondary sources or both. There are different styles of source-based questions (see p. xviii). Despite contrasts in wording, however, they do have certain common features (see below).

Type of question	Examples of question structure	General advice on the answer
The source used for information and inference.	• What can you learn from this source about . . .? • What evidence is there in Source 1 to suggest that . . .?	Identify implications as well as information. This means inferring, not describing.
The source used as a stimulus for further knowledge. Usually this means explaining a particular sentence or phrase in the source: this will involve further material outside the source.	• Using Source A and your own knowledge, explain the meaning of '. . .' [a phrase in quotation marks]. • Using your own knowledge, explain briefly, why '. . .' [an event or development in quotation marks].	Identify precisely what is required and confine the use of 'your own knowledge' to explain the words in the quotation marks. This will, however, need accurate detail rather than vague generalisation.
Questions on a source's 'usefulness' and 'reliability'.	• How useful is Source A about . . . ? • How reliable is Source A about . . .? • How useful are these sources to the historian studying . . . ?	For usefulness distinguish between internal criteria (i.e. content) and external criteria (i.e. the type of source). Reliability can also be assessed by referring to whether the content is accurate and the circumstances in which the source was produced. A source may be unreliable but still useful.

Questions asking for comparisons between sources. These may concern similarities, or differences, or both. They may involve an explanation of the reasons for similarities or differences.

- Compare . . . according to Sources A and B.
- How would you explain the differences?
- What evidence in Source 1 supports the view in Source 5 that . . . ?
- Explain how the judgement in Source A challenges the judgement in Source C that . . .

'Compare' or 'compare and contrast' mean finding similarities and differences. These may involve details or general arguments. In either case precise references are needed, using brief quotations from the sources. Reasons for differences in the content of sources usually involve a comment on the differences in the type of source.

Questions which provide a viewpoint that needs to be tested against the sources and against additional knowledge beyond the sources.

- Use Sources A to D, and your own knowledge, to explain whether the view that '. . .' is accurate.
- Study Sources A, B and C and use your own knowledge. How important . . .
- Refer to Sources A, B and C and use your own knowledge. Explain . . .
- Do you agree that '. . .' Explain your answer, using the sources and your own knowledge.

The answer needs two dimensions.

- The content and your own knowledge of the sources should be 'used' to test the viewpoint in the question. At the same time, the reliability of this content should be briefly assessed: does the source apparently support . . . and does it really support . . .?
- 'Own knowledge' should have the same amount of time and space as the 'use of sources' and should include material beyond the sources.

As with the essays, the Boards have different styles of questions on sources, even though they are testing very much the same skills.

Board	Style of source-based questions and time allowed	Example of style of source-based questions
OCR	4 primary sources, 3 questions in 60 minutes. (a) Explanation of context of an issue mentioned in a source. (20) (b) Comparison between sources. (40) (c) Testing a viewpoint against all the sources and own knowledge.(60)	(a) Study Source A. From this source, and from your own knowledge, explain . . . (20) (b) Study Sources B and C. Compare . . . according to Sources B and C and explain the difference. (40) (c) Use all the sources. Use all the sources and your knowledge to explain . . . (60) Total (120)
AQA	1 primary source, 2 secondary sources; 3 questions in 45 minutes. (a) Explanation of context of an issue mentioned in a source. (3)	(a) Study Source A. Using your own knowledge, explain briefly . . . (3) (b) Study Sources B and C.

(b) Comparison between sources. (7)

(c) Explanation of importance of issue 'in the relation to other matters'; use of sources and own knowledge. (15)

With reference to your own knowledge, explain how the judgement on . . . expressed in Source C, challenges the judgement put forward in Source B. (7)

(c) Refer to Sources A, B and C and use your own knowledge.
Explain the importance, in relation to other factors, of . . . (15)

Total (25)

Edexcel 4 primary sources, 1 secondary source; 5 questions in 90 minutes.

(a) Explanation of context of an issue in the source. (3)

(b) Use of own knowledge to describe or explain an issue related to the sources. (5)

(c) Comments on usefulness of sources for the historian studying . . . (5)

(d) Comparison between sources. (5)

(e) Comments on a viewpoint, using 2 specified sources and own knowledge. (12)

(a) Study Source 1.
What does this source reveal about . . .? (3)

(b) Use your own knowledge.
Use your own knowledge to explain . . . (5)

(c) Study Sources 2 and 3.
How far does Source 3 support the statement in Source 2 that . . . (5)

(d) Study Sources 4 and 5.
Compare the value of these two sources to the historian studying . . . (5)

(e) Study Sources 1 and 5 and use your own knowledge.
Do you agree that . . .?
Explain your answer, using these two sources and your own knowledge. (12)

Total (30)

Combined essay and source-based questions

Two Boards have a combination of essay questions and one source. Here the source is intended as a stimulus for the essays.

Board	Style of essay and source question, and time allowed	Example of style of essay and source question
AQA	Brief quotation from a secondary source, followed by three-part essay question in 60 minutes, testing: (a) Contextual knowledge. (3) (b) Background knowledge. (7) (c) Interpretation, discussion. (15)	'The Crimean War forced Alexander II to show his credentials as a great reformer and as the "Tsar Liberator"'. (a) What influence did the Crimean War have on the intentions of Alexander II on his accession in 1855? (3) (b) Explain why Alexander II introduced a range of reforms *after* the emancipation of the serfs (1861). (7) (c) Does the emancipation of the serfs (1861) justify the description of Alexander II as the 'Tsar Liberator'? (15) Total (25)

Edexcel 1 or 2 primary sources, followed by three-part essay question in 60 minutes, testing:
(a) Contextual knowledge. (5)
(b) Background knowledge. (7)
(c) Interpretation discussion. (18)

(a) Study Sources 1 and 2. What do the two sources reveal about Hitler's attitude to the working class in Germany? (5)
(b) Use your own knowledge In what ways did the Hitler regime try to promote greater social equality among Germans? (7)
(c) Use your own knowledge. Were Nazi economic policies in the years 1933 to 1939 aimed primarily at preparing Germany for war? Explain your answer. (18)

Total (30)

How does this book combine the different approaches of the Boards to essays and source questions?

The use by the Boards of different styles is an opportunity to see common objectives from slightly different angles. It is very likely that an approach used by a Board you are not following will clarify at least one approach used by the Board that you are. At the very least, you will learn a great deal about what essay and source skills mean by comparing the ways in which they are approached. This is because you will be doing the most important thing you can do: you will be thinking about what the skills actually *mean*.

This book attempts to use all the approaches of the Boards in a way in which they relate to each other and reinforce each other. At the same time, it intends to give precise examples of how the questions of specific Boards can best be approached.

The basic principles behind the essays in this book are as follows:

(a) The single-essay approach of OCR is used as the basis, since this is similar in terms of length (45 minutes) to the second essay in the Edexcel questions (30 minutes) and the third essay in the AQA questions (36 minutes). The material covered relates to the whole of the OCR period specifications, but overlaps substantially into the period specifications for Edexcel and AQA; in this case, the answers provided should cover all the topics and skills needed and require little adjustment to meet the different style of question.

(b) Each chapter also contains a proportion of essay styles which relate specifically to Edexcel (in two parts) and AQA (in three parts). There is much in common between the length and style of the first Edexcel essay (30 minutes) and the second AQA essay (18 minutes). Where the subject specifications overlap, they would therefore be interchangeable. Any subject area which is not represented in a Board's specifications contains no essays in that Board's question style.

(c) In this way it is intended that all the topics are covered for all the subject specifications in a way which develops the skills required by each Board. Good essay-writing is a skill which crosses all the boundaries and an awareness of the variety of skills expected can only help to sharpen them in practice.

The differences in the source-based questions are more in terms of style than of skills. The common approaches are summarised on pages xvi–xvii. The main principles in covering the sources are as follows:

(a) The styles of AQA and Edexcel are used as the basis. AQA features in Chapters 2, 3, 4, 5, 6 and 7; Edexcel in Chapters 3 and 5; and OCR in 3, 4 and 8.

(b) Edexcel has an additional essay-source combination in certain topics. Examples of these feature in the Sources sections of Chapters 4 and 8.

Question styles of the Boards and where they are located in this book

Board	Styles of answers	Where located in chapters (essay/source number)
OCR	Essays (one-part)	Ch. 2: 3–20; Ch. 3: 4, 6, 8–10, 12, 14, 15; Ch. 4: 4, 5, 9–13, 16–19; Ch. 5: 1, 6, 9, 12–20; Ch. 6: 2, 3, 6, 7, 10, 11, 14–18; Ch. 7: 5, 6, 8–10, 12–19; Ch. 8: 1–19.
	Sources (3 questions)	Ch. 5: 1; Ch. 6: 1; Ch. 7: 2.
AQA	Essays (three-part)	Ch. 2: 1, 2; Ch. 3: 1–3, 5, 7, 11, 13; Ch. 4: 1–3, 6, 7, 15; Ch. 5: 7, 8, 10, 11; Ch. 6: 1, 4, 5, 9, 12; Ch. 7: 7, 11.
	Sources (3 questions)	Ch. 2: 1; Ch. 3: 1; Ch. 4: 1; Ch. 8: 1.
Edexcel	Essays (two-part)	Ch. 4: 8, 14; Ch. 5: 2, 3, 5; Ch. 6: 8, 13; Ch. 7: 1–4.
	Sources (5 questions)	Ch. 2: 2; Ch. 3: 2; Ch. 4: 2.
	Essay/source combination (3 questions)	Ch. 5: 2; Ch. 6: 2; Ch. 7: 1.

Part 4: Historical Skills

History is a diverse subject with wide-ranging skills. There is also much more emphasis on academic skills within the context of the sixth form. The two can be closely connected and the purpose of Part 4 of each chapter is to suggest how specific skills can be developed both within the History course and with a close connection to more general sixth-form courses. The intention is to enhance techniques already developed in essay-writing and source-analysis – but also to go beyond them in anticipating the needs of students of higher education. The focus of Part 4 of the various chapters is summarised below. These overlap – but are not intended to duplicate – the various patterns of key skills.

Each chapter considers the development of a different skill. The historical context may not be directly relevant to what you are studying, but the skill will be transferable to the area that is. This has the added benefit of making you think about the process of transferring ideas from one context to another and, in the process, changing and refining them. This, as much as anything else, is what History is about.

Type of skill	What it is covered	Where it is covered
1. Essay-writing	• Purpose of essay. • Preparation and structure; analysis and factual support. • Precise coverage of the requirements of different styles of question.	Chapters 2–8, Part 2

2. Source-analysis	• Types of sources and techniques of analysis. • Different types of question. • Contextual knowledge. • Comparison between sources. • Usefulness and reliability of sources. • Use of sources and own knowledge in an overall assessment.	Chapter 2–8, Part 3
3. Effective note-taking and filing	• Adapting to the different styles of notes required in class (or lectures); making the most of handouts; and note-taking from books and the Internet. • Different types of filing systems for notes.	Chapter 2, Part 4
4. Oral contributions	• Developing the confidence to contribute orally in class. • Being aware of the different skills required for speeches, interviews, discussions and debates. • Suggestions for specific class situations covering each type of oral skill – and a combination.	Chapter 3, Part 4
5. Numerical skills in History	• Different types of data used in History and how to interpret them. • The most effective way of using ICT to convert statistics to charts. • The most appropriate style of chart for each type of data. • Questions relating to numerical data.	Chapter 4, Part 4
6. Presentation skills: using an overhead projector	• Effective methods of making a presentation to a group. • Presenting a topic based on interpretation and maintaining a balance between argument and detail. • Using the OHP to provide the focus of the presentation and to integrate several images. • Example of an OHP presentation.	Chapter 5, Part 4
7. Presentation skills: using ICT through PowerPoint	• Effective communication to a group (see 6 above). • Techniques of setting up a PowerPoint presentation.	Chapter 6, Part 4

- Advice on inclusion of text, preparation of diagrams and insertion of images from the Internet.
- Example of PowerPoint presentation.

8. Research skills: coursework or individual study
- Explanation of the purpose of coursework.
- Advice on preparation, reading, planning, writing.
- Detailed advice on style, paragraphing, footnoting, Bibliography.
- How everything fits together.

Chapter 7, Part 4

9. Concentration and learning skills
- Meaning of concentration, problems associated with it and suggestions for overcoming them.
- Time-management.
- Revision for examinations.

Chapter 8, Part 4

10. Anticipating the skills required for A2
- Historiography and the study of different interpretations.
- Synoptic approaches to a period of about 100 years.
- How the study of AS History leads conceptually to A2 History.

Chapter 9, Part 2

Chapter 1

An Introduction to the Period

Introduction

Contrary to what some historians have argued, the twentieth century really did begin around 1900 and not in 1914. All the influences which affected the first half of the century were clearly emerging by 1900. The roots of twentieth-century ideologies are recognisable some years in advance of 1914, as are the strains experienced by structures of the older regimes. The war did, however, accelerate the process, compressing into a decade what might otherwise have taken half a century or, arguably, might not have happened at all. In this way, war and revolution were closely connected.

The main ideological development in the period covered by this book was the shift from **autocracy** to **dictatorship**. By 1900 Tsarist Russia was already being threatened by revolutionary movements on the left. Eventually one of these – **communism** – filled the gap, left by the collapse of autocracy, with a dictatorship of the far left. Alexander III and Nicholas II therefore gave way to Lenin and Stalin. France, meanwhile, had become a seedbed for a different type of ideology, which started as a merging of revolutionary socialism and extreme nationalism. This was transplanted into Italy where, by the time of the First World War, Mussolini and D'Annunzio were shaping it into **fascism**. This was also to influence post-war Germany, which had its own roots back into the nineteenth century – racism, **anti-Semitism** and struggle; the combination became known as national socialism, or Nazism. These new ideologies were similar to the older autocracies in having an **authoritarian** approach to political power but, unlike them, also sought to mobilise the masses behind them. However, despite their claim to a popular base, the dictatorships were as far removed from the liberal democratic regimes of France, Britain or the United States, as the autocracies had ever been.

It is appropriate to open this book with the First World War to show the strength of war as a catalyst, converting the trickle of earlier developments into a revolutionary torrent. A major theme is the initial confidence of the late nineteenth-century regimes giving way to fear and suspicion. Established powers like Russia sought additional strength in rapid industrialisation, while newly united countries like Germany and Italy aimed to become world powers. But diplomacy gradually became fearful and gave way to considerations of defence. The way to preserve the peace, as everyone knows, is to prepare for war. By 1914, however, such preparations had become so complex that they exerted their own influences and prevented the use of diplomacy to solve crises without conflict. The problem was that the outcome of the war was beyond everyone's expectations.

In no country was the impact of war so dramatic as in Russia. Chapter 3 deals with the last years of the tsarist regime and its overthrow. To give this greater coherence, the starting point is taken back to 1855. The period as a whole saw swings between reform and **reaction**, between backwardness and economic growth. Gradually, two trends emerged to threaten autocracy – the demand for a constitutional system and the development of revolutionary movements. War made tsarism vulnerable to both: there was a close connection between the Russo-Japanese War (1904–5) and the Revolution of 1905, and even more so between the First World War and the Revolutions of 1917. The outcome was the emergence of the world's first communist regime under the leadership of Lenin. In this case Trotsky was correct in his view that 'war is the locomotive of history'.

Meanwhile the other great continental power had also been thrust into crisis by the First World War. Chapter 4 starts with Germany as a recently united country becoming increasingly confident in its military strength and assertive in its foreign policy. At the same time, it was beset by internal complications and international problems. Confident in its military preparations, it made no attempt to avoid war through diplomacy. The result, however, was totally unexpected, as success on the eastern front was followed by defeat in the west. In the process Germany experienced internal transformation from a semi-autocratic empire to a democratic republic. But the stability of this new democracy was undermined by a combination of internal and external problems and crises, which produced the ideal breeding ground for Nazism. By 1933 the situation had become so serious that Hitler was offered the chancellorship.

When this happened, Italy had already been under a dictatorship for just over ten years (Chapter 5). Again, the First World War was a crucial factor. Although theoretically one of the victors, Italy had been seriously destabilised by the experience of economic and political dislocation, while further fuel was added by popular resentment at Italy's meagre territorial gains in 1919. Post-war governments lost their struggle to maintain Italy's liberal institutions and eventually had to give way to Mussolini in 1922. The new regime was the first experience of fascist power anywhere in Europe. Mussolini claimed to have established the first truly **totalitarian** regime and he gave Italians the illusion of military prowess. In reality, however, Italy lacked the economic infrastructure to support a belligerent foreign policy and, in 1943, fascism was the first of the three systems to be overthrown.

Figure 1.1 **Map of Europe, 1914**

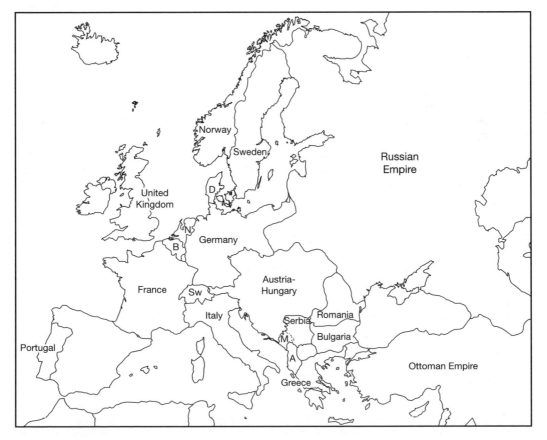

Figure 1.2 **Map of Europe, 1919–39**

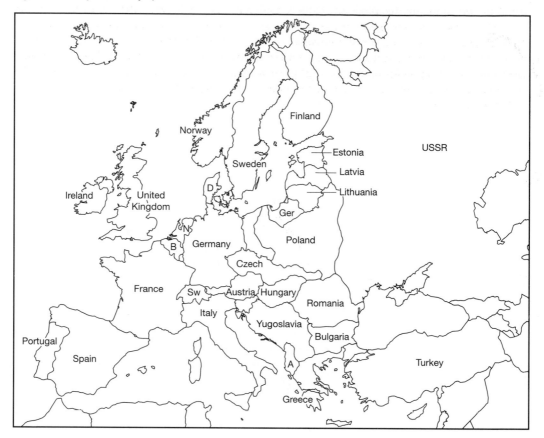

Nazi Germany (Chapter 6) was much more powerful than Fascist Italy because Hitler was able to mobilise Germany's huge economic and military potential. At first he aimed to consolidate his position through a strategy of 'legal revolution' but, from 1935 onwards, the regime became more **radical** as anti-Semitic policies were intensified, rearmament introduced and propaganda and coercion both extended. A second and more intensive radicalisation occurred during the Second World War, which saw the rapid spread of the power and influence of the **SS** and the introduction of a policy of genocide. From 1942 onwards the regime had to gear itself to total war but, by 1945, the overwhelming strength of its external enemies brought total defeat and collapse.

One of these opponents was the Soviet Union (Chapter 7). At first basic survival was the key issue as the **Bolsheviks** had to fight a civil war between 1918 and 1921 and consolidate their regime. The implementation of communism required the introduction of political dictatorship but there were still many economic issues left unsettled by 1924. Stalin's regime placed the focus on rapid industrialisation and rearmament, reinforced by a huge apparatus of terror. The result was a new military power, which was cumbersome but sufficient to overwhelm Nazi Germany. After 1945 Stalin converted it into a world force, one of the two poles of the Cold War. In the longer term, however, the economic infrastructure created by Stalin was too inflexible to support the expanding aspirations of a superpower. Hitler's Germany may have been brought down by war – but Stalin's Soviet state eventually fell apart in the peace which followed.

The First World War had been the 'war to end wars'. Actually, it brought in regimes and created problems which led rapidly to the Second. International relations between 1919 and 1939 (Chapter 8) reflected the tensions between the newly released ideologies of communism, fascism and Nazism, each of which aimed at domination and expansion. They were also complicated by unfinished business arising from the peace settlement of 1919–20, over which Britain and France were initially intransigent during the 1920s but increasingly accommodating in the 1930s. The outbreak of war in 1939 was more predictable than it had been in 1914 and eventually settled into a clash of ideologies.

Chapter 2

The Era of the First World War, 1890–1919

This chapter will consider the relationship between the powers between 1890 and 1914, the outbreak of the First World War, the effects of the conflict on the countries involved and the peace settlement which followed between 1919 and 1920.

 ## Historical background

The European powers and the growth of
    the alliance systems, 1871–90
The policies of the powers
Irritants: imperialism and the Balkans
The outbreak of war in 1914
The impact of war
The end of the war and the peace
    settlement

 ## Sources

1. Germany and the outbreak of war
2. The impact of the First World War
    on Russia

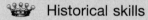 ## Historical skills

Note-taking and filing

 ## Essays

The policies of the powers
Irritants: imperialism and the Balkans
The outbreak of war in 1914
The impact of war
The end of the war and the peace
    settlement

Chronology

1878		Congress of Berlin
1879		Dual Alliance (Germany and Austria-Hungary)
1882		Triple Alliance (Germany, Austria-Hungary and Italy)
1894		Franco-Russian Alliance
1898		Fashoda Crisis
1902		Anglo-Japanese Alliance
1904		Anglo-French Entente
1907		Anglo-Russian Convention
1908		Bosnian Crisis
1911		Agadir Crisis
1912–13		Balkan Wars
1914		Assassination of Franz Ferdinand at Sarajevo (28 June)
		Austrian declaration of war on Serbia (28 July)
		Russian mobilisation in support of Serbia (30 July)
		German declaration of war on Russia (1 August)
		German declaration of war on France and invasion of Belgium (3 August)
		British declaration of war on Germany (4 August)
		Defence of the Realm Act (Britain)
1915		Battle of Verdun
1916		Battle of the Somme
		Lloyd George became Prime Minister
		Dublin Easter Uprising
1917		Battle of Paschendaele
		Revolutions in Russia
		Military dictatorship in Germany: *Oberste Heeresleitung* (OLH)
1918		Entry of the United States
		Surrender of Bulgaria, Austria-Hungary, Turkey and Germany
1919		Treaty of Versailles (Germany)
		Treaty of St Germain (Austria)
		Treaty of Neuilly (Bulgaria)
1920		Treaty of Trianon (Hungary)
		Treaty of Sèvres (Turkey)
1923		Treaty of Lausanne (Turkey)

Part 1: Historical background

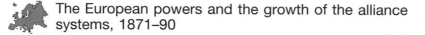

The European powers and the growth of the alliance systems, 1871–90

The decade between 1861 and 1871 had seen major changes in Europe. Italy had been largely united in 1861, a process completed by the addition of Venetia in 1866 and Rome in 1870. The Austrian Empire, forcibly evicted from the German Confederation in 1866 by Prussia, had reconstituted itself as a dual state, Austria-Hungary. Meanwhile, under the leadership of Bismarck, Prussia had replaced the German Confederation with a much tighter North German Confederation. Between 1870 and 1871, Bismarck completed German unification by military victory in the Franco-Prussian War. Russia was a vast empire alternating between crisis, such as defeat in the Crimean War (1854–6) and the Russo-Japanese War 1904–5), and internal reform, such as the abolition of serfdom by Alexander II (1855–81) and the development of heavy industry under Alexander III (1881–94) and Nicholas II (1894–1917). Britain was, after its involvement in the Crimean War, the most detached of the powers, withdrawing into self-imposed isolation until after 1900.

The diplomacy of the period 1871–90 was dominated by Bismarck, now Chancellor. His main concern was to preserve the security of the newly formed German **Reich** by preventing the emergence of a coalition centred on France. During his chancellorship he managed to keep France in isolation while drawing up the Dual Alliance between Germany and Austria-Hungary in 1879, which was expanded into the Triple Alliance (1882) with the inclusion of Italy. He also managed to maintain diplomatic connections with Russia, including the Reinsurance Treaty of 1887. After Bismarck's resignation in 1890, however, Germany had to face the emergence of a counter-alliance system. The first stage was the Franco-Russian Military Convention of 1892, which was expanded into a full alliance in 1894. Subsequent developments were the Anglo-French **Entente** (1904), the Anglo-Russian Convention (1907) and the Triple Entente (1907). At first Britain had no military obligations in Europe, although she had formed an **alliance** with Japan in 1902. Nevertheless, by 1914, the Entente had tightened into a close military and naval co-operation between Britain and France. With the exception of Italy, the powers had, by 1914, established their allies for the period of the First World War.

The policies of the powers

The emergence of the alliances reflected the different policies of the individual powers. The most active throughout the period 1871–1914 was Germany. Bismarck had been content with a European role for the new Reich, but Kaiser Wilhelm II, who assumed personal direction of Germany's foreign policy in 1890, envisaged a world role in the form of **Weltpolitik**. This meant a rapid expansion of Germany's navy and overseas empire (see Essay 1a). The reasons for this (dealt with in Essay 1b) were a new and predictable phase in Germany's rapid growth as a major power, as well as an attempt to put pressure on Britain and also to divert domestic opposition into more patriotic channels. The expanding scale of German foreign policy, however, brought its own problems. It provoked France and Russia into forming an alliance in 1894 and, far from making Britain more amenable to Germany, forced her into forming an Entente with France in 1904 and a Convention with Russia in 1907. Bismarck had managed to avoid the emergence of a counter-alliance, whereas Wilhelm II seemed to accelerate it. Although seemingly a confident and forceful figure it is valid to ask whether he was fully in control of Germany's foreign policy, especially in the months immediately before the outbreak of war in 1914 (Essay 1c).

In 1871 it was widely assumed that France was set on revenge for defeat by Prussia and, more specifically, for the loss of Alsace and Lorraine to the new German Reich. This is why Bismarck tried to divert French attention from Europe into a burst of colonialism in Africa while, at the same time, building a defensive alliance round Germany. French attempts to emerge from isolation were unsuccessful until after 1890, when French investments in Russia and a common interest in outflanking Germany on two sides produced the 1894 Franco-Russian Alliance. It was not until after the turn of the century that France abandoned its traditional rivalry with Britain; indeed, the Fashoda Crisis of 1898 brought the two countries close to war. By 1904, however, it had become clear to France that Germany was a greater threat than Britain to French security. As a result, France was willing, in the Entente, to accommodate British interests in Egypt in return for a similar undertaking by Britain concerning French interests in Morocco. The bond tightened as a result of two German attempts to undermine the French position in Morocco – in 1906 and 1911. On each occasion France requested – and secured – British diplomatic support. By 1914 France was also looking to the British navy for the defence of her northern coastline.

Russia, meanwhile, was following a more erratic course. Defeated in the Crimean War, Russia withdrew for a decade from European diplomacy, before reappearing strongly as victor in a war against Turkey (1877–8). This indicated a revival of her interests in the Balkans and brought her into direct rivalry with Austria-Hungary for influence over the Christian **Slav** states which were breaking away from the Ottoman Empire. At first the rivalry was controlled by Germany, Bismarck managing to resolve two major confrontations between Austria and Russia in 1878 and 1885–7: the latter crisis was so serious that it needed the Reinsurance Treaty to calm Russia's fears (Essay 2a). But, after the resignation of Bismarck in 1890, Russia had to look elsewhere for its security. Since Germany was moving more obviously behind Austria's interests, Russia hastened to form the 1894 Alliance with France (Essay 2b). During the following decade Nicholas II followed a policy of rapid industrialisation, largely with French capital. The success of this encouraged the Russian government to pursue expansionist aims in the Far East, the result of which was defeat in the Russo-Japanese War of 1904–5. This, along with the 1905 Revolution, caused the Russian government to follow a more cautious policy in Europe, although rivalry with Austria reasserted itself from 1908 onwards, largely over the futures of Bosnia-Herzegovina and Serbia. It was this area which brought Russia directly into the crisis following the assassination at Sarajevo, which resulted in the outbreak of war. Throughout the whole period between 1871 and 1914, therefore, Russia seemed to alternate between aggression and preoccupation with defence (Essay 2c).

Throughout the period 1871–1900 Britain had avoided specific military commitments and alliances, preferring to concentrate resources on the empire. In fact, during the 1890s, Britain's diplomatic relations with all the major powers were equally poor. Gradually, however, Britain emerged from this 'Splendid Isolation', through the Anglo-Japanese Alliance (1902), the Anglo-French Entente (1904), the Anglo-Russian Convention (1907) and the joint Anglo-French naval manoeuvres from 1912. Which of these stages was the turning point in pulling Britain into European involvements is discussed in Essay 3, along with the main reason for this change – the German challenge to British interests.

After losing its dominance over the German Confederation, Austria now had to adjust to a different role. By the **Ausgleich** of 1867 the one-quarter German portion agreed to share power with the one-quarter Hungarian element, with two capitals, two governments and a new name to reflect the overall duality: Austria-Hungary. The remaining half of the population, however, consisted of minority Slav groups. Austria-Hungary's policy was based partly on finding a new role in Eastern Europe to fill the gaps left by the collapsing Ottoman Empire and partly on preventing external Slav pressures from encouraging dissent from its own Slavs. This led to a number of crises involving Austria-Hungary and Russia in one of the main flashpoints of Europe – the Balkans.

Irritants: imperialism and the Balkans

The development of alliances does not inevitably lead to war nor necessarily lead to deteriorating relations between major powers. They can actually increase international stability. During the period 1871–90, however, rivalries were often inflamed by two issues which, directly or indirectly, affected all the powers: imperial rivalries overseas or developments in the Balkans.

Imperialism (dealt with in Essay 4) had been exploited in a more or less controlled way by Bismarck, who had deliberately encouraged colonial rivalries to divert tensions away from Europe. After 1890, however, these returned to roost. A key factor in Britain's emergence from isolation was Germany's switch from a European emphasis to *Weltpolitik*; it is significant that both of Britain's commitments to European powers were in the form of colonial agreements – the 1904 Entente and the 1907 Convention. Similarly, Germany's threats to Morocco in 1906 and 1911 were a major reason for Britain's eventual decision to transform the agreement with France into a *de facto* alliance.

The Balkans were a particularly unstable part of Europe between 1871 and 1914. The Ottoman Empire was failing in its attempts to maintain control over its Christian provinces, which emerged as the independent states of Bulgaria, Romania and Serbia. This resulted in three forms of tension. The first was rivalry between two of the major powers, Austria-Hungary and Russia, for ascendancy over the new states. This peaked in the periods 1877–9, 1885–7 and 1908–14, and played a key role in the formation of the Dual Alliance (1879) and Reinsurance Treaty (1887), as well as influencing the drift to war in 1914. The second occurred between the successor states themselves, especially between Bulgaria, which eventually aligned itself with Austria-Hungary and Germany, and Serbia, which looked to Russia. The third, and potentially most dangerous problem, was the specific area of Bosnia-Herzegovina. Lost to the Ottoman Empire by 1877, it was set aside by the Treaty of Berlin (1878) for future Austrian occupation. When this eventually took place in 1908 it antagonised the Bosnian Serbs, neighbouring Serbia (which had direct ethnic connections with Bosnia) and Russia, which was by this stage behind Serbia. From this tangle emerged the fears which produced the situation leading to war in 1914. Austria-Hungary was convinced that Serbia was trying to destabilise Bosnia-Herzegovina and therefore moved towards military action to contain the threat. Serbia saw this as a direct threat to its own sovereignty, while Russia perceived an Austrian attempt, with German backing, to establish ascendancy over the entire area. All these issues are covered in Essay 5.

At certain periods there was an overlap of imperial and Balkans issues (Essay 5). The main example is the Italian invasion in 1911 of Libya, the Ottoman Empire's last remaining province in Africa. This encouraged Bulgaria, Serbia and Greece, in the First Balkan War (1912) to extract Turkey's remaining territory, mostly in Macedonia and Thrace. This was followed by the Second Balkan War (1912–13) in which the victors fought each other for the spoils. This was particularly dangerous since Turkey, which lost the first war, and Bulgaria, loser in the second, strengthened their links with Austria-Hungary and Germany, while Serbia was now in virtual alliance with Russia.

In this way, overseas and Balkans rivalries helped both to establish the alliance systems and to move them into direct confrontation with each other.

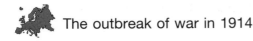 ## The outbreak of war in 1914

The sequence of events leading to the outbreak of war is covered in Essay 6. These were set in motion by the assassination, on 28 June 1914, of the Archduke Franz Ferdinand, heir to the throne of Austria-Hungary, by a Bosnian Serb in Sarajevo, the regional capital of Bosnia-Herzegovina. Backed by Germany, Austria-Hungary issued an ultimatum to Serbia. When this was rejected, Austria declared war on Serbia on 28 July. Russia mobilised in support of Serbia on 30 July. Germany declared war on Russia on 1 August and, two days later, on France. To implement the Schlieffen Plan, Germany invaded Belgium, which caused Britain to declare war on Germany on 4 August. Later additions to the central powers (Germany and Austria) were Bulgaria and Turkey while, in 1915, the Allies received the support of Italy. The way in which war actually broke out does not seem to have had much of a bearing on the terms of the various alliances. But the patterns of **mobilisation**, which dictated the declarations of war, were based on war plans intended to make the alliances work. These issues are also dealt with in Essay 6.

The reasons for the involvement of each of the powers is covered separately. Essay 7 considers the debate on Germany's responsibility for the outbreak of hostilities. Did it deliberately provoke the war in pursuit of expansionist aims? Or did the Schlieffen Plan, devised to offset Germany's strategic vulnerability, remove the possibility of a diplomatic settlement? A similar question arises over Austria-Hungary (Essay 8). Was the July ultimatum a specific attempt to deal with Serbia's apparent threat to Austria-Hungary's ethnic stability? Or was it part of a more general aim to destroy, with Germany's backing, the state of Serbia? Turning to the Allies, were France and Russia in any way responsible for the outbreak of war in 1914? Were they the victims of a German and Austro-Hungarian conspiracy, or did Russia set the wheels in motion, encouraged by France (Essay 9)? Britain's reason for entering the war was attributed to the German invasion of Belgium. Was this the real issue – or an excuse to justify going to the help of France, with which Britain had no formal alliance (Essay 10)? Italy refused to honour the commitment of the Triple Alliance (1882), claiming that it had been released from its obligations by German aggression. In 1915, however, it proceeded to join the Allies. The reasons for this switch are covered in Essay 11.

 ## The impact of the war

The two main fronts saw very different types of campaigns – and results. German intentions were to inflict a swift defeat on France and end the war in the west in order to concentrate on the longer and more difficult campaigns envisaged in the east. As it turned out, the western front became the sector of stalemate and immobility, while the eastern front was much more open to the expected strategies. The somewhat strange result was that, although Germany defeated Russia in the east (Essay 14), it lost the war as a whole because it could not break through in the west. The reasons for the stalemate on the western front are analysed in Essay 12.

War is nearly always a catalyst for political and social change amongst its participants. The First World War was a prime example of this. Three empires collapsed under the strain of defeat. The tsarist regime was brought down by revolution in March 1917 (Essay 14), the direct result of political and economic dislocation caused by military defeat. Its successor, the **Provisional Government**, was overthrown in October 1917 and the war would also have brought down the Bolshevik regime had Lenin and Trotsky not made peace with the Germans in March 1918. In Germany, war was initially a unifying experience, but the military stalemate and heavy losses in the west resulted in a military dictatorship in 1917. When this failed in its bid for victory, the dictatorship was replaced by a more representative government to negotiate an armistice. The Kaiser's regime collapsed in November 1918, to be replaced by a republic (Essay 13). Austria-Hungary, the third of the empires, folded up internally. With defeats on the eastern front by Russia, the two governments in Vienna and Budapest were unable to prevent their Slav subjects from establishing or joining new states based on the principle of national self-determination. With the loss of the Poles, Czechs, Slovaks, Serbs and Croats, Austria and Hungary collapsed into two separate rumps. Hungary faced additional pressure from Romanian armies which seized Transylvania (see Essay 19).

Even the so-called 'victors' experienced political upheaval. The one exception was France; although it paid dearly in loss of life, destruction and economic dislocation, political catastrophe was deferred until the fall of France to Germany in 1940. Italy was even more stretched by the conflict, experiencing economic collapse and immediate post-war political instability which assisted the rise of Mussolini and fascism (Essay 17). By contrast, Britain is normally considered to have emerged from the war politically secure. If the perspective is Great Britain itself, this is perfectly true. A series of emergency measures produced an effective government under Lloyd George (Essay 15) while the longer-term political impact was concerned mainly with changes in the balance of power among the political parties. But the focus should be on the United Kingdom, in which case the war was directly instrumental in bringing about the independence of Ireland, the nearest Britain has come to a revolution for three centuries. The impact of the war on society and the economy was also extensive and is assessed in Essay 16.

The end of the war and the peace settlement

Two key developments occurred early in 1918. One was the withdrawal of Russia from the war by the Treaty of Brest-Litovsk with Germany. This gave the latter the opportunity to make a final effort to break through on the western front. This, however, was offset by the entry of the United States into the war. President Wilson's Fourteen Points also provided a series of objectives for a post-war settlement.

Armistices were signed with Bulgaria, Turkey, Austria-Hungary and, on 11 November 1918, with Germany. The victorious Allied leaders assembled in Paris to draw up a settlement, most of the decisions being taken by President Wilson, Lloyd George and the French premier, Clemenceau. Germany was dealt with by the Treaty of Versailles (June 1919), Austria by the Treaty of St Germain (1919), Bulgaria by the Treaty of Neuilly (1919) and Hungary by the Treaty of Trianon (1920). Turkey was initially the subject of the Treaty of Sèvres (1920), although this was subsequently redrawn as the Treaty of Lausanne (1923).

Four issues were particularly important for the future. The first was the establishment of a new international order in the form of the League of Nations. Chapter 8 shows how this fared in the future. The second was the treatment of Germany, which caused huge resentment; whether the terms of the Treaty of Versailles were unduly harsh is discussed in Essay 18, while its effects on the newly formed Weimar Republic are assessed in Essay 20 and form one of the strands for Chapter 4. The third was the redrawing of boundaries throughout Europe to accommodate the principle of national self-determination. Although a great deal of positive thought went into this, the collapse of Austria-Hungary and the huge loss of territory by Russia created a comparative power vacuum in central and eastern Europe – later to be filled by the revived power of Germany and Russia. Finally, one country combined the experience of victory with a sense of deprivation. Italy's resentment at receiving so little from the Treaty of St Germain helped produce Europe's first major political backlash in the form of fascist dictatorship (Essay 21 and Chapter 5).

Part 2: Essays

The policies of the powers

1. **'The main decision made by Kaiser Wilhelm II in the 1890s was to pursue *Weltpolitik*.'**

    a) **What is meant by *Weltpolitik* in relation to German foreign policy between 1890 and 1914?** (3 marks)

Weltpolitik is a term used to describe the expanding scope of Germany's foreign policy after 1890. While Bismarck and Kaiser Wilhelm I had considered Germany to be a European power, with continental objectives, Wilhelm II aimed to transform Germany into a world power with maritime as well as European aims. *Weltpolitik* had two main components. One was the rapid expansion of overseas colonisation, already started during the Bismarck era; this eventually produced the world's third largest colonial empire The other was the development of a navy; the 1898 Navy Law signalled the intention to rival Britain's naval supremacy.

    b) **Explain the reasons for *Weltpolitik* and its effects on Germany's relations with Britain.** (7 marks)

There are three main reasons for the development of *Weltpolitik*. First, the most obvious is that it was a logical stage in Germany's growth as a major power. Prussia had absorbed the rest of the German states to produce the German Reich, an empire within Europe. For Bismarck this was enough but his successors sought further expansion and 'a place in the sun' by transforming the Reich into a maritime empire. Second, on the advice of Tirpitz, Wilhelm II aimed to put pressure on Britain. The theory was that the expansion of the German navy would force a large part of the British navy into home waters, thereby exposing British colonies. Britain would therefore have to come to accommodate Germany, possibly by joining the Triple Alliance to form a new Quadruple Alliance. Third, some historians have also advanced domestic reasons for *Weltpolitik*. Colonial expansion was an attempt to encourage German nationalism, especially within the working and middle classes, as a diversion from industrial and constitutional conflicts.

The result of *Weltpolitik* was not quite what the German government had intended. Although there were negotiations for an Anglo-German agreement between 1899 and 1902, nothing materialised since Britain had no reason at this stage to become involved in the European commitment which would be required by an alliance with Germany. After 1902, in fact, *Weltpolitik* succeeded only in pushing Britain out of isolation towards accommodation with France in the 1904 Entente and with Russia by the 1907 Convention. Germany's vulnerability was further increased by the acceleration of British dreadnought construction and by the joint military and naval manoeuvres carried out with France from 1912. Bismarck's more limited objectives had their advantages after all.

c) 'Kaiser Wilhelm II was not fully in control of Germany's foreign policy between 1890 and 1914.' Explain why you agree or disagree with this view. (15 marks)

At first sight, this argument seems incorrect. After all, Wilhelm II played a much more direct role in foreign policy than had either of his predecessors, Wilhelm I (1871–87) and Frederick III (1887). Indeed, he was the only one to make full use of his powers under the 1871 Reich Constitution. He also made clear changes in the direction of German foreign policy, abandoning the Euro-centric approach and introducing *Weltpolitik*. Finally, he added a powerful military dimension, approving the Schlieffen Plan and using Germany's military preparedness to stiffen the resolve of Austria-Hungary in dealing with the crisis of June 1914. Right he may not have been, but in control he certainly was.

This approach is, however, simplistic. There are at least three factors which provide a different perspective on the term 'control'. The first is the extent to which Wilhelm II was influenced by others. He may have dominated his chancellors, especially Caprivi (1890–94) and Chlodwig-Hohenlohe (1894–1900). But he was notoriously secretive and inclined to accept the views of advisers and personal friends operating behind the political scenes. Baron Holstein, for example, persuaded him to reject Russia's application to renew the Reinsurance Treaty in 1890, while the whole grand strategy of using *Weltpolitik* to force Britain into compliance came from Admiral von Tirpitz. Between 1907 and 1914 Wilhelm was also manoeuvred by the general staff: first into accepting the Schlieffen Plan and then into letting military considerations dominate diplomacy.

If, despite this, the Kaiser had at least some direct input into specific policies, did he exert control by acting responsibly? Not according to the **Reichstag** and, more significantly, his ministers. On at least two occasions Wilhelm took unwelcome initiatives which had to be unpicked by officials who must have considered him very much 'out of control'. One was the Treaty of Björko between Germany and Russia signed by Kaiser Wilhelm and Tsar Nicholas II on a private yacht in 1905. This was subsequently rejected by both the German and Russian governments, who feared compli-cations with their respective allies, Austria-Hungary and France. The German Chancellor, Bülow, threatened to resign over the issue. He did so again in 1908 as a protest against another gaffe committed by the Kaiser in the *Daily Telegraph* affair and there was a more concerted effort by officials to try to prevent unwelcome surprises in the future.

Finally, the Kaiser was far from being in full control over the most crucial diplomatic phase of all – in June and July 1914. Although he appears to have been the most decisive of all the European leaders in the aftermath of the Sarajevo assassination, he was actually the most constrained. France, Russia, Austria-Hungary and Britain all appeared more hesitant – but this was because they were still influenced by diplomatic considerations. Wilhelm, on the other hand, was under the strongest pressure from the military, especially von Jagow and von Moltke, to take the decision which would enable them to operate the Schlieffen Plan. The final turn of the ratchet was that the success of the military option depended on *immediate* action. Wilhelm could not even exert temporary control through a 'wait-and-see' approach.

2. 'After 1890 Russian foreign policy underwent a major change. When the Kaiser refused to renew the Reinsurance Treaty in 1890, the Tsar looked instead to France.'

   a) What is meant by the 'Reinsurance Treaty'? (3 marks)

By the Reinsurance Treaty, drawn up in 1887, Germany agreed to remain neutral if Russia were attacked by Austria-Hungary, while Russia would not assist any French invasion of Germany. This treaty followed a deterioration in relations between Russia and Austria-Hungary, which made Alexander III fearful of joint action from Germany and Austria, while Bismarck was concerned about the possibility of an alliance between Russia and France *against* Germany. In the event, the Reinsurance Treaty temporarily allayed the fears of both countries.

b) Explain why France and Russia formed a military alliance. (7 marks)

The main reason for the Franco-Russian Alliance was the concern both countries had about growing German power and influence, whereas each felt capable of dealing with any other threat alone. This is shown by the terms of the Military Convention, which eventually became the Alliance of 1894: Russia would assist France if the latter were attacked by Germany, or by Italy plus Germany, while France would support Russia against an attack by Germany or by Austria-Hungary plus Germany.

French antagonism towards Germany had existed ever since the Treaty of Frankfurt (1871) and the forcible surrender of Alsace-Lorraine to Germany. Russian resentment was more recent, dating from 1890. Until then, Russia's main rival had been Austria-Hungary, especially in the Balkans. While Bismarck was in power Germany had restrained Austria and, through the 1887 Reinsurance Treaty, secretly undertaken not to assist any Austrian attack on Russia. The latter had also been given German investment to assist Alexander III's industrialisation programme. By 1890, however, German credits had been withdrawn and an application for the renewal of the Reinsurance Treaty was turned down. It was obvious to Russia that Wilhelm II wanted to tighten the Dual Alliance with Austria-Hungary. Despite the ideological differences between a democratic republic and an autocratic empire, Russia and France had a great deal to offer each other. The industrialisation carried out by Vyshnegradski and Witte was now based on French capital, while military co-operation appeared to overcome the vulnerability of Russia and France, transferring it instead to Germany which was now outflanked.

c) 'Russian foreign policy between 1890 and 1914 was based more on aggression than on considerations of defence.' Explain why you agree or disagree with this statement. (15 marks)

'Aggression' and 'defence' usually overlap and depend on the perspectives from which they are viewed. It is therefore sensible to consider the proportions in which they combined rather than try to separate them entirely. Using this approach, Russian policy in the East seemed to be more aggressive than defensive, while in the West defensive criteria were usually paramount.

Russian aggression in the Far East was certainly apparent in its diplomacy during the 1890s. This was calculated to minimise Japanese gains from the war with China in 1895. More blatantly, one of Japan's losses, the Liaotung peninsula, was subsequently leased to Russia by China, along with Port Arthur, which was used as a naval base for the Russian Pacific fleet. The Russian government pursued a policy of deliberate expansion in Korea and Manchuria, confident that the industrial reforms of Witte (Finance Minister between 1893 and 1903) had given Russia overwhelming military superiority over Japan. It was even argued by Plehve, one of the Tsar's key ministers, that external expansion would be a useful way to divert internal social tensions. There was certainly a great deal of racist propaganda about the Japanese. Although Japan struck first, in a pre-emptive attack on Port Arthur, the subsequent performance of Russia suggests that defence had been a low priority because it had been felt to be unnecessary.

In the West, by contrast, there was a sharper focus on defence because the threat was considered more serious. This can be seen in the attempt to renew the Reinsurance Treaty in 1890 and in the formation of the Franco-Russian Alliance in 1894. The terms of the latter were worded in defensive terms; France and Russia agreed to support each other only if they were *attacked by* Germany, which removed the option of a first strike by Russia. After the shock of military defeat by Japan, Russian diplomacy after 1905 was also geared to security rather than aggression. There are several examples of Russian attempts to reduce external threats through diplomacy. The 1907 Anglo-Russian Convention, drawn up by Izvolsky, resolved the clash of imperial interests in Tibet, Afghanistan and Persia. In the same year, an approach was made to Austria-Hungary to settle rivalries in the Balkans; the fact that this never materialised was due to the Bosnian Crisis of 1908, which followed the Austrian occupation of Bosnia-Herzegovina. And, in 1910, Russia negotiated with Germany a settlement over the Baghdad Railway. Even the outbreak of war in 1914 does not readily support a case for Russian 'aggression'. There is no evidence that Russia looked to military conflict to solve diplomatic and strategic problems. In fact, provoking war at this stage would have made little sense since Russia's plans for strengthening its military defences were not due for completion until 1917 at the earliest. Unlike the Kaiser, the Tsar was faced with a genuine dilemma in his reaction to the Austrian declaration of war on Serbia in July 1914. He preferred partial mobilisation for a war against Austria alone. Since, however, this would leave Russia defenceless against an attack by Germany, he was obliged to opt for general mobilisation. Taking the offensive was therefore dictated by defensive considerations.

The one area in which Russia *could* be accused of showing consistent aggression was in support for Slav aspirations in the Balkans. Russia had long been criticised by Germany, Austria-Hungary and even Britain for its policy of pan-Slavism. This tended to work in pulses. It had been strong in the 1880s, when Alexander III had sought to control Bulgaria, eased off during the 1890s but reasserted itself after the 1908 Bosnian Crisis. To complete the destruction of Turkish power in the Balkans, Russia encouraged an alliance between Serbia, Bulgaria and Greece in 1912. When this turned into a second Balkan war, mainly between Bulgaria and Serbia, Russia backed the latter and also sympathised with Serbia's continuing campaign against Austria's occupation of Bosnia-Herzegovina. This, more than anything else, confirmed Vienna's view that Russia was a dangerous threat which needed, with German help, to be stopped. Of course, the Russian perspective on this was that Russia was providing support to a small fellow-Slav state which had been served with an impossible ultimatum in July 1914.

3. When, and why, did Britain emerge from 'Splendid Isolation'? (90 marks)

'Splendid Isolation' is a term used to describe the policy of the British governments at the end of the nineteenth century, especially the 1886–92 and 1895–1902 ministries of Lord Salisbury. Since British priorities were imperial and maritime, there was no reason to become involved in what Harcourt called 'permanent or entangling alliances' in Europe. Britain's involvement in the First World War, however, shows the reversal of such a policy in the early years of the twentieth century, although the actual turning point for this has always been a matter of controversy.

The first possibility is the attempt to come to an agreement with Germany at the turn of the century, which was seen by Colonial Secretary Chamberlain as the most effective way of reducing Germany's threats to Britain's imperial interests. Specific treaties were not difficult, and included the Anglo-German agreement on Portugal's colonies (1898) and the Anglo-German China agreement of 1900. But Chamberlain's efforts to secure a stronger connection between the two powers failed in the negotiations of 1898, 1899 and 1901. The basic problem was that the two countries had different expectations: Britain wanted a guarantee of German support against Russia in the Far East, while Germany hoped that Britain would become a full member of the Triple Alliance. Since nothing emerged from the talks it is clear that they were not the crucial factor in Britain's emergence from isolation.

A second, and much stronger, case for the turning point could be put for the Anglo-Japanese Alliance (1902), in which the two powers promised neutrality if either were at war with one power and mutual support if against two. As the first military commitment Britain had made to any state since the Crimean War, this must surely indicate a move away from isolation. A.J.P. Taylor, however, argued that the alliance did not end British isolation; 'rather it confirmed it' by making it easier for Britain to remain detached from European commitments.[1] This is probably an oversimplification, for the Anglo-Japanese Alliance soon brought a closer relationship between Britain and France. A powerful influence here was the need for Britain and France to avoid any action which might involve them in a conflict on the side of their respective allies, Japan or Russia. The most likely irritant, colonial rivalry, was therefore removed by the 1904 Anglo-French Entente.

This agreement is normally seen as the stage at which Britain emerged from European isolation. But was it? The Anglo-French Entente was not an alliance, merely an imperial agreement by which Britain agreed to recognise French interests in Morocco in return for a similar French undertaking over British Egypt. It was a standard device of the type which Britain had already used with Germany in 1898 and 1900. But there was one major difference between the Entente and those earlier agreements. By Article 9 of the Entente, Britain and France would 'afford to one another their diplomatic support'[2] to ensure that the provisions concerning Egypt and Morocco were carried out. This opened the way for closer co-operation between Britain and France in the future, resulting in a gradual tightening of the Entente. It also brought growing contacts with Russia, and the Anglo-Russian Convention of 1907 resolved imperial disputes between the two countries over Afghanistan, Persia and Tibet. The same year even brought formal recognition of a relationship in the form of the Triple Entente.

Yet there was still no British military obligation to any major power in Europe and the term 'Splendid Isolation' continued to be used, even if less frequently than before. By 1911, however, the situation had changed and the Foreign Secretary, Grey, announced in parliament that 'That policy is not a possible one now'. Perhaps this should be seen as the decisive point at which Britain threw in its lot with a European alliance. The key factors had been the arms race with Germany, especially in the building of dreadnoughts, and the support given to France over the two Moroccan crises, especially over the *Panther* incident at Agadir in 1911. What followed indicated that there was no going back. Britain increased its military co-operation with France, instituting joint Anglo-French fleet manoeuvres and agreeing to spheres of responsibility: France for the Mediterranean and Britain for the Channel and North Sea. This decision created a military obligation which effectively removed any remaining freedom of diplomatic action. In August 1914, therefore, the decision Grey and the Prime Minister, Asquith, had to take was not whether to go to war on the side of France but how to present the decision to ensure the agreement of the whole Cabinet.

If emergence from 'Splendid Isolation' means putting Britain's commitment to France beyond recall, then the most appropriate date is probably as late as 1911. But clearly this decision was related directly to the initiative taken in 1904 with France and extended in 1907 to Russia: these had, after all, been the result of Britain's decision to establish closer links with the continent. These, in turn, were made necessary by the diplomatic complications following the Anglo-Japanese

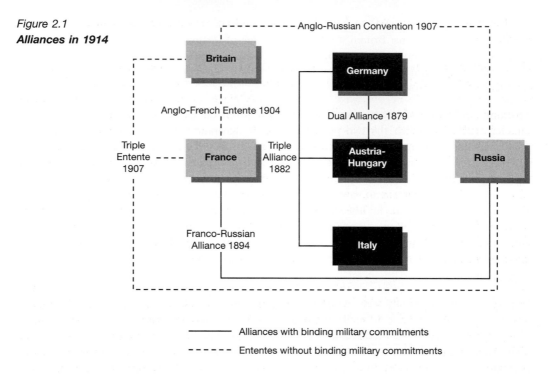

Figure 2.1
Alliances in 1914

Alliances with binding military commitments
Ententes without binding military commitments

Alliance of 1902, which had been drawn up partly as a result of the failure to come to terms with Germany between 1899 and 1901. The whole process of ending isolation therefore comprised a series of interlinked stages, each decision revealing further complications and leading to further obligations.

Irritants: imperialism and the Balkans

4. How did the imperial policies of the great powers affect international relations between 1890 and 1914? (90 marks)

The impact of imperial policies on international relations changed noticeably from 1890 onwards. During the two decades before that, imperialism in Africa and the Pacific had been seen as a safety mechanism. Bismarck, for example had used Africa as a means of projecting European rivalries on to a safer screen. During the 25-year period before the First World War, however, imperial issues became much more directly involved in European tensions and often made them worse.

In the first place, during the 1890s colonial problems caused widespread anti-British feeling in Europe, which could well have been the reason for Britain's isolation. Crises occurred between Britain and Germany over the Kruger Telegram of 1896 and between Britain and France over the Fashoda Incident (1898), while the Boer War (1899–1902) made Britain universally disliked in Europe. Yet, paradoxically, imperial issues also helped bring Britain back to involvement in Europe. The key factor here was the pursuit of *Weltpolitik*, a more explicit global strategy by Germany under Kaiser Wilhelm II. This involved challenging Britain's imperial interests and naval power from the coastlines of Africa to the islands of the Pacific. Britain's reaction was to seek greater security, first through abortive negotiations with Germany between 1898 and 1901, then through an alliance with Japan in 1902, and finally through imperial agreements with France (1904) and Russia (1907).

The Anglo-French Entente was, therefore, an attempt by Britain to resolve one set of imperial problems (with France) in order to focus on another (with Germany). But the imperial focus had major complications in Europe. One was the rapid acceleration in the race between Britain and Germany to build dreadnoughts, seen by both sides as vital in the protection of trade routes, sea lanes and colonies. Another was the tightening of the Entente between Britain and France as a result of German pressure on the French colony of Morocco. Britain supported France at Algeçiras in 1906 and over the Agadir Crisis of 1911; this actually arose from an obligation in Article IX of the 1904 Entente for Britain and France to uphold each other's interests in Morocco and Egypt respectively. A direct link was therefore established between the colonies and Europe. When the Moroccan crises combined with the arms race, the direct result was the development of Anglo-French military and naval co-operation from 1909. This meant that, by 1914, there was a *de facto* alliance between the two countries. It is difficult to see anything other than imperial and naval factors having such an influence on this momentous development.

Another imperial development also had an impact on European diplomacy, if more indirectly. This was the failure of Russia's bid for territory and economic concessions in Korea and Manchuria, both of which ended in defeat in the Russo-Japanese War (1904–5). The option for expansion in Tibet, Afghanistan and Persia was also voluntarily relinquished in the Anglo-Russian Convention of 1907. This transferred the focus of Russian foreign policy westwards – into south-eastern Europe. The tsarist regime actively involved Russia in the Balkans at the very time that this area was embroiled in the Bosnian Crisis (1908). The result was intensified rivalry between Russia and Austria-Hungary, a dangerous counterpart to that between Britain, France and Germany.

The Balkans became particularly dangerous from 1912, with two regional wars threatening at any moment to draw in the major powers. But these were actually precipitated by another burst of imperialism between 1911 and 1912. The Italian invasion of Libya, Turkey's only remaining territory in North Africa, diverted Turkey from effectively defending its vulnerable Balkan possessions in Macedonia. This encouraged Serbia, Bulgaria and Greece to declare war on Turkey in 1912. Once these countries had ended Turkish rule over Macedonia, they became involved in another conflict, this time with each other. The two Balkan wars of 1912–13, further sharpened the rivalry between the major powers by establishing connections between Serbia and Russia and between Bulgaria and Germany. This was particularly dangerous in 1914. In this instance colonial rivalries had acted as a catalyst for dangerous regional conflicts. These, in turn, interacted with tensions between alliances which had been tightened by imperial issues.

Overall, therefore, imperial rivalries after 1890 acted in two ways. In the West they were often directly related to confrontations between the major powers and eventually played a significant part in the alienation of Britain and Germany and the co-operation between Britain and France. In the Balkans they acted more as a catalyst to revive or accelerate tensions which were already there; in this case the influence of imperialism was more indirect – but no less deadly.

5. **To what extent were the Balkans a reason for the growing tension between the great powers between 1890 and 1914?** (90 marks)

Developments in the Balkans were one of several reasons for the growth of tension between the powers. Others included imperial rivalries and rearmament. Without the existence of an alliance system, reinforced by war plans, it is unlikely that the Balkans would have endangered the European peace in the way they did. The Balkans crises affected the members of both alliance systems and ultimately destroyed their real purpose, which was defensive rather than offensive.

The Balkans were less dangerous between 1890 and 1907 than between 1908 and 1914. The earlier period saw the development of the ingredients for crisis but without immediate impact; at this stage imperial, military and naval rivalries were more important. Britain was preoccupied with issues in Africa such as the Jameson Raid (1896), the Fashoda Crisis (1898) and the Boer War (1899–1902). Germany was actively pursuing a policy of *Weltpolitik* and challenging British naval supremacy, while Russia's interests focused on the Far East, especially Manchuria and Korea. Compared with the tensions stirred by these issues, the Balkans were relatively quiet. Yet the 1890s saw the hardening of rivalries which were to become dangerous later. There was continued pressure for the independence of the remaining Balkan peoples under Turkish rule, especially in Macedonia and Bosnia-Herzegovina, and growing tension between Bulgaria and Serbia. Serbia, in turn, gradually fell foul of Austria-Hungary, accused of fomenting disturbances among Austria-Hungary's southern Slav population; between 1906 and 1908 Austria and Serbia were also involved in a prolonged dispute over agricultural tariffs known as the Pig War. Although it was not immediately obvious at the time, all the ingredients were in place for the Balkans to become the most dangerous part of Europe. These comprised unfinished business between the Balkan peoples and Turkey, growing dependence of Bulgaria on Germany and Serbia on Russia and, above all, increased tension between Austria and Serbia.

The year 1908 proved to be the turning point between the Balkans acting as a latent threat to international stability and their sudden emergence as the actual focus of great-power rivalry and conflict. Although imperial crises over Morocco (1906 and 1911) were of more direct concern to Britain and France, the Balkans became the focus of Russian and Austrian attention and soon drew in their respective allies as well. Several developments occurred which suddenly activated the combustible ingredients which were already in place.

The first was the annexation of Bosnia-Herzegovina by Austria-Hungary in 1908. This had been agreed to in principle by the Congress of Berlin in 1878 but was delayed for 30 years, with Bosnia remaining nominally under Turkish rule. Austria's action antagonised neighbouring Serbia, which claimed the territories, along with Russia, which now backed Serbia more openly. The Serbs were ready to resist Austria's annexation, and Russia was willing to help the Serbs. In the event, both Britain and France restrained Russia and the threat of immediate war subsided. Even so, the potential for crisis remained. Serbia saw Austria-Hungary as the oppressor of fellow Serbs in Bosnia, while Austria now feared that Serbia would destabilise the large Slav population within the southern part of the Empire. Russia remained resentful of her diplomatic humiliation and intensified her support for Serbia, while Germany was equally willing to take any measures necessary to support Austria-Hungary against both Serbia and Russia.

The second factor which intensified the dangers in the Balkans was the upheaval within the Ottoman Empire. In 1908, Turkey seemed to have been given a revival of national purpose by the Young Turks, only to face renewed crisis and imperial loss with the Italian invasion of Libya in 1911. This was a disastrous combination of circumstances. The possibility of Turkish revival alerted the Balkan states, Austria and Russia, while the prospect of sudden collapse in 1911 provided an incentive for swift action. The victory of Bulgaria, Serbia and Greece over Turkey in the First Balkan War (1912–13) deprived Turkey of almost all her remaining territories in Europe. As a direct result, Turkey turned to Germany and Austria-Hungary. The Second Balkan War (1913) saw Serbia, Greece and Romania enlarge themselves from spoils of the First Balkan War – at the expense of Bulgaria. This had two particularly dangerous results. One was the drift of a resentful Bulgaria into the same sphere as Germany, Austria-Hungary and Turkey. The other was the enhancement of Serbia: the growth of her population by 50 per cent now enabled her to support an army of 400,000 men. In effect, the Balkans states were now divided in their loyalties between the Central Powers and the Entente Powers. To make matters worse, one of the powers, Austria, considered that one of the Balkans states, Serbia, had become impossible to live with.

These conditions contained all the ingredients for an explosion. The assassination of the Archduke Franz Ferdinand at Sarajevo on 28 June 1914 ignited all the tensions mentioned. Serbia was accused of complicity and, according to the Austrian Prime Minister, Berchtold, 'must be eliminated as a power in the Balkans'. Germany gave Austria unconditional support for any action which might be considered appropriate, while Russia stood firmly by Serbia. The Balkans were no longer the main reason for tension between the powers: they had become the reason for war.

 ## The outbreak of war in 1914

6. **How did war break out between the major powers in the summer of 1914? To what extent were the alliances between the great powers the key factor in this outbreak?** **(90 marks)**

General conflict broke out in the summer of 1914 as a chain reaction of mobilisations and declarations of war between the major powers. The initial impetus was provided by Austria-Hungary's actions against Serbia following the assassination of Archduke Franz Ferdinand at Sarajevo on 28 June. When the Belgrade government partially rejected Vienna's ultimatum, Emperor Franz Joseph declared war on Serbia on 28 July.

This, in turn, provoked the mobilisation of all armed forces in Russia in defence of Serbia on 30 July. Faced with the choice of partial mobilisation against Austria alone, or total mobilisation involving Germany as well, Tsar Nicholas II chose the latter. He had no alternative, as to concentrate his forces against Austria-Hungary would have left his Polish frontier open to a later invasion by Germany. The latter's response was immediate. Kaiser Wilhelm II demanded the immediate reversal of the Tsar's decision and, when this did not happen, declared war on Russia on 1 August. On 3 August Germany followed this with a declaration of war on France, after President Poincaré had called up French troops. Since the Schlieffen Plan meant that a German attack on France would involve passage through Belgium, the latter was invaded by German forces on the same day. Britain's reaction was crucial. The Prime Minister, Asquith, and Foreign Secretary, Grey, agreed to assist France with the defence of her Atlantic coast but it was the German invasion of Belgium which brought the British declaration of war on 4 August. This was on the grounds that Germany had violated Belgian independence and neutrality guaranteed by the 1839 Treaty of London.

The connection between this sequence of events and the alliance system involves two perspectives. One is that there was no direct overlap between the declarations of war and the specific terms of the alliances between the great powers. The other, however, is that the alliances had been given military scope by the development of complex war plans. It was these plans which influenced the way in which war broke out, not the wording of the treaties themselves. By the first perspective, the alliances were not responsible; by the second, they were.

Figure 2.2 **Assassination of the Archduke Franz Ferdinand at Sarajevo, 28 June 1914**

ASSASSINAT DE L'ARCHIDUC HÉRITIER D'AUTRICHE
ET DE LA DUCHESSE SA FEMME A SARAJEVO

The existence of the alliances was not, in itself, sufficient explanation for the outbreak of war. Indeed, their main purpose was defensive. The 1879 Dual Alliance had committed Germany and Austria-Hungary to mutual support only if either were attacked *by* Russia; there was no such obligation should Germany or Austria-Hungary launch an invasion *on* Russia. In the Triple Alliance of 1882, a similar obligation covered Italy and Germany in relation to France. Italy would assist Austria-Hungary only in the event of a war between the Dual Alliance and two powers and, in any case, Italy specified that it would not become involved in a war against Britain. The Franco-Russian Alliance of 1894 also made mutual assistance dependent on aggression by either Germany or Austria-Hungary.

Such terms could not, in themselves, have led to war and were clearly not intended to do so. The way in which war actually broke out in August 1914 bore little direct relation to treaty obligations between the major powers. Under the terms of the Dual Alliance, Germany had no need to give Austria-Hungary a 'blank cheque' to deal with Serbia after the Sarajevo assassination. Russia had no treaty commitment to assist Serbia, which had not even been mentioned in the Franco-Russian Alliance. And, if her quarrel was with Austria, why did she mobilise on 30 July against Germany as well? There was nothing in the Dual Alliance of 1879 to require Germany to declare war on Russia – and certainly not against France and Belgium. France, on the other hand, was committed by the Franco-Russian Alliance to assist Russia in the event of an attack by Germany; yet she did not do so immediately. Britain had a moral, although not a legal, obligation to assist the Entente powers, but actually chose to enter the struggle after the German invasion of Belgium, a state which was entirely outside the Entente.

A legalistic interpretation of their terms therefore shows that the alliances could not have led to the outbreak of war. If anything, war occurred because the specific terms of the alliance treaties were ignored. Yet this is too simple a view of the alliance systems. As documents, they were open to interpretation by politicians and military leaders and were subject to unforeseen events. The alliances became rival networks and were interconnected with dangerous areas of tension. Hence links were established between remoter issues and great-power rivalries. The best example of this was the Balkans, where local conflicts involving Serbia, Bulgaria and Turkey linked up with the opposing strategic interests of Russia and Austria-Hungary. Alliances were not, therefore, merely pieces of paper: they had a diplomatic purpose and were bound to be adapted to specific circumstances. They had also stated the *minimal* conditions for mutual support. There was nothing to prevent the powers from adopting a more *generous* interpretation, as Germany did with Austria over Serbia. Although the 'blank cheque' was not *required* by the Dual Alliance, it was not actually in *violation* of it.

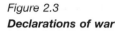

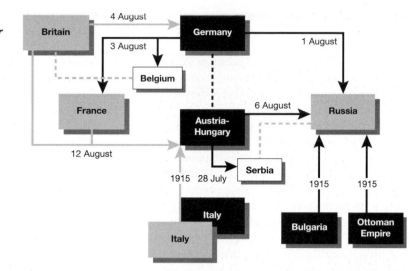

Figure 2.3
Declarations of war

Treaties of alliance are insufficient by themselves. They require guaranteed armed support to be fully effective. The outbreak of the First World War was heavily influenced by the war plans of the different powers which were, in turn, adapted to alliance obligations. Russia prepared two plans – one for partial mobilisation against Austria-Hungary, the other for total mobilisation against Austria and Germany. The Tsar decided in favour of total mobilisation, given the likelihood of German support for Austria under the Dual Alliance. The German High Command had developed the Schlieffen Plan as a means of dealing with the problem of a war on two fronts. The bulk of Germany's armies would be sent against France first and, after a swift conquest, would be switched to deal with Russia. In 1914 the German government therefore declared war on France as well as on Russia to bring the Schlieffen Plan into operation and in the certain knowledge that the Franco-Russian Alliance would come into effect anyway. The key problem was the inflexibility of the war plans. They were geared up to the assumption that a war between two major powers would inevitably involve respective allies, whereas an area like the Balkans could conceivably have produced a more limited and localised conflict. Unfortunately the method of mobilisation was also inflexible. Since it involved complex timetabling of railway transports, it was impossible to reverse or change mobilisation, once it had started, without causing total chaos.

The outbreak of a European war in August 1914 could not have occurred without the existence of two armed alliances. The key factor, however, was not so much the alliances themselves as the military planning used to make them effective.

7. How valid is the view that Germany provoked war in 1914? (90 marks)

Germany's role in the outbreak of war in 1914 was pivotal. It provided Austria-Hungary with a 'blank cheque' and actively encouraged a military solution against Serbia. Then, when Russia mobilised, it became the first of the major powers to declare war on another. This was swiftly followed by an apparently unprovoked declaration of war on France and an invasion of Belgium. It is clear that Germany carried substantial responsibility for the outbreak of the First World War and this is now widely accepted by historians. There are, however, two versions of this responsibility, over which there is still controversy concerning the degree of 'provocation'.

One version involves the premeditated and unprovoked aggression on the part of Germany, the other a desperate attempt to escape from dangerous encirclement.

During the 1960s the German historian Fritz Fischer put the case for almost total and premeditated German aggression. Germany, he argued, was being driven deliberately towards long-term expansion. The influence behind this were internal factors. The ruling German elites – the traditional agriculturalists and the new industrialists – were finding it difficult to adjust to the massive social and economic changes taking place within Germany. Particularly worrying were the growth of the urban **proletariat** and the middle classes, one pressing for mass political participation and the latter for more active constitutionalism. The solution was to externalise any conflict so that class interests would be replaced by nationalist loyalties. The Kaiser's regime was already actively pursuing *Weltpolitik*; therefore, expansion, especially into eastern Europe, would be a logical next step. With such a total vision, it is hardly surprising that Germany should have reacted so forcefully to events in Europe between 1911 and 1914. From 1912 onwards Germany became increasingly assertive and, during the period immediately following the assassination at Sarajevo, put pressure on Austria to deal with Serbia – in the certain knowledge that this would result in the outbreak of war. The crisis of July 1914 was therefore an opportunity for Germany to press ahead with a preconceived aim; there can be no question that the war was deliberately provoked by Germany.

This line of argument can, however, be challenged. Although it is common to see a connection between domestic problems and an aggressive foreign policy, this does not inevitably lead to active provocation of war. After all, war always brings with it a risk of extensive social change, while the aim of the German elites was to maintain the status quo. It is quite possible that part of the pattern of assertive diplomacy was a calculated risk that it might result in war, but this is not the same as arguing that way was the *intended* outcome. The calculated risk could equally have been the result of fear.

There was actually good reason for this. Germany's strategic vulnerability, of which Bismarck had always been aware, was intensified by the development of a counter-alliance system which he had always managed to avoid. The Franco-Russian Alliance of 1894 meant that Germany was outflanked from both east and west, while the Anglo-French Entente (1904) and Anglo-Russian Convention (1907) suggested a powerful maritime threat from Britain. To make matters worse, all three Entente powers were rapidly upgrading their military strength. Britain was, by 1914, opening a gap with Germany in dreadnought construction, and France had introduced conscription. Russia, however, had the greatest potential for change, having launched a programme to strengthen her army by 1917. According to Jagow: 'In a few years, according to expert opinion, Russia will be ready to strike. Then she will crush us with the weight of her soldiers.'[3] The effect of encirclement was made worse by the Agadir Crisis (1911), which had led to the tightening of the Anglo-French Entente into close military and naval co-operation. Another dangerous scenario for Germany was the Balkan Wars (1912–13) which had led to an *enlarged* Serbia with a capacity to destabilise the southern Slav population within Austria-Hungary. Even more worrying was that Serbia had, since the 1890s, clearly fallen under Russian influence. Time therefore seemed to be against Germany. Its rivals were growing in strength, while its ally was, if anything, growing weaker. Some sort of action was clearly necessary.

One way in which Germany could respond to this accumulation of pressures was by using the approach to war which had always been part of the Prussian tradition. This had been articulated by the Prussian military strategist von Clausewitz, who believed that 'war is the continuation of diplomacy by other means.'[4] Faced with a deteriorating diplomatic situation after 1911, the German government therefore hoped that a rapid military response would remove the threat to Germany. The key point was that such a victory was still possible, through the Schlieffen Plan, which had been drawn up to deal with the strategic threat. Rather than dividing into two defensive units, the German high command would send the bulk of its forces against France, via Belgium, in a rapid offensive. After victory had been achieved in the west, the main thrust would then be transferred to the east to deal with the Russian advance. A complex series of railway timetables would maximise the speed of the initial mobilisation and attack. By using this strategy, the military guaranteed the Kaiser a rapid victory.

This did not, however, mean that a conflict should be deliberately 'provoked'. The German Chancellor, Bethmann Hollweg, adopted a tough policy which operated as a calculated risk, poised between war and diplomacy. A diplomatic victory would make war unnecessary, while diplomatic failure would bring about a war which could then be won. Provocation in this sense was not to move deliberately towards war; it was not to try very hard to maintain peace. This has often been referred to as a 'diagonal policy', poised as it was between war and peace.

In the final analysis, provocation can be direct and premeditated or indirect and sudden. The former depends more on the influence of domestic factors which, on reflection, seem less immediately dangerous than the external crises. When the military went to war in 1914, it was seeking a way to deal with the threat of France and Russia, not of the German working classes.

8. **Assess the reasons for Austria-Hungary's determination to invade Serbia in 1914.**   (90 marks)

Austria-Hungary's ultimatum to and invasion of Serbia in 1914 are an immediate reaction to the assassination at Sarajevo, the longer-term problem of security within the Empire, the opportunity offered by German support, and the reduction of opposition within Hungary. These were interlinked, the driving force being the feeling of insecurity.

The immediate reason for intervention was the assassination of the Archduke Franz Ferdinand at Sarajevo. This produced a radical reaction in Vienna, resulting in a harsh ultimatum being sent to Serbia on 23 July, following close consultation with the German government. When Serbia rejected a crucial clause, which would have given Austria-Hungary control over its security forces, Austria declared war and invaded Serbia. Clearly the assassination was the spark – but this would not by itself have led to war had there not been a longer-term volatility to bring about the eruption of war. Indeed, the time lapse between the assassination (28 June) and the declaration of war on Serbia (28 July) suggests a deliberate aggression and the use of Sarajevo as an excuse.

This was affected by a profound feeling of insecurity which dominated the policy of the Austrian government towards Serbia. The Empire had always comprised a mixture of ethnic groups and was therefore vulnerable to internal pressures. The *Ausgleich* of 1867 had granted parallel status to the Austrian Germans and the Hungarian Magyars, setting up separate governments within a **Dual Monarchy**. The Slavs, however, had been excluded from this arrangement and the authorities became increasingly aware of their demands for a degree of self-determination. The situation was further aggravated by the annexation of Bosnia-Herzegovina in 1908. This introduced Serbia as an external catalyst for internal unrest. Serbia claimed possession of Bosnia-Herzegovina in order to complete its own unity and the Bosnian Serbs became the most difficult to govern of all of Austria's subjects. The assassination at Sarajevo was blamed (although incorrectly) on Serbia. Unless swift action was taken, rebellion could be expected among all the Empire's southern Slavs in Slovenia and Slavonia, as well as in Bosnia and Herzegovina. The impact would be devastating. Unrest would spread to the Empire's northern Slavs – the Czechs, Slovaks, Ruthenes and Poles – and threaten the whole structure of Austria-Hungary. The Slavs could bring the entire system crashing down since they actually formed over half the total population, outnumbering the Germans and Hungarians combined. Under these circumstances, the Austrian Foreign Minister Berchtold, and the Chief of Staff Conrad, wanted to settle once and for all the perceived threat from Serbia before it could spread subversion through the Empire and open up a channel for Russian influence. The Sarajevo incident seemed to offer the appropriate excuse to draw Serbia's sting. It was, however, subordinate to longer-term considerations.

The third reason for Austria's action was the extent of the diplomatic support provided by Germany. This, more than anything, affected the *timing* of the ultimatum and served to stiffen Vienna's determination to enforce it. Here the Austrian government was acting under a strong external influence. The German government had its own problems in 1914 and was being hard pressed by the High Command to prepare for a war 'sooner rather than later' and certainly before the rearmament programmes of France and Russia had been completed. The German government was also determined to avoid any diplomatic concessions to the Entente powers. Vienna therefore received unconditional support from Berlin to pursue any action it considered appropriate to deal with the Sarajevo assassination. This meant that Austria was guaranteed success in its undertaking against Serbia and could expect full military support from Germany should Russia intervene. There was, therefore, nothing to impede the decisive action which Berchtold and Conrad, Foreign Minister and Minister of War, really wanted. On the other hand, German pressure would not have stood much chance of success without this willingness.

The remaining obstacle was the possibility that the Hungarian part of the Dual Monarchy might refuse to co-operate. But this gradually fell into line with Vienna. The final factor was therefore the gradual erosion of moderating influences from Budapest; in this case Austria was itself exerting the influence. The Hungarian Prime Minister, Tisza, was more inclined to caution and negotiation, and, for a time, it seemed possible that indecision might allow the assassination to slip into the past without reply. But the Vienna government persisted with its view that the security of the whole country was threatened – and that Hungary would be as badly affected as Austria by any future Slav uprisings. The clinching argument was that, with German support, the Serbian threat could be neutralised swiftly. The Hungarian government therefore moved reluctantly behind Austria and the ultimatum was delivered to Serbia on 23 July. This gave the appearance of unanimity to Vienna's decision, although it was hardly the key factor in the decision itself.

In descending order of importance, therefore, the Austrian government feared for the future survival of Austria-Hungary, given the perceived aggression of Serbia. Hence it seized the opportunity, provided by the assassination at Sarajevo, to settle the issue once and for all – especially since Germany, acting for its own reasons, provided full backing. This, in turn, enabled Vienna to put pressure on Budapest to take collective action.

9. Assess the roles of France and Russia in the outbreak of the First World War.
(90 marks)

In 1919 the Allied Commission on War Guilt cleared both the French and Russian governments of responsibility for the outbreak of the First World War. This was, of course, a politically loaded interpretation. In retrospect it is clear that both countries actually did very little to try to avoid war, seeming willing and prepared to take up the challenge presented by Austria-Hungary and Germany. Both responded forcefully to the actions of others.

It may seem that Russia's responsibility was greater than that of France. It was, after all, the Tsar who, on 30 July, ordered the first mobilisation of any of the major powers. He had been encouraged to do this by the High Command, which was convinced that Russia was able to defeat both Germany and Austria-Hungary. France had been drawn in after the German declaration of war on Russia which, in turn had necessitated further declarations on France and Belgium in order to implement the Schlieffen Plan. From this perspective, France was the victim of Russia's over-reaction to the Austrian ultimatum to Serbia and the inflexibility of German war planning.

This is, however, an oversimplification. France was by no means merely the helpless victim of the confrontation between other powers. French militarism was very much in evidence in 1914 and confidence had been greatly increased when, in 1913, the high command under Joffre had developed a new strategy to deal with a German invasion. But the main problem was the prospect that France would have to take the main impact of any German attack. It had always been the purpose of the Franco-Russian Alliance of 1894 to engage Germany in a two-front war. The primary aim of French diplomacy since 1911 had therefore been to persuade Russia to launch the fastest possible invasion of Germany if war broke out. Hence France gave Russia a 'blank cheque' during the 1912 Balkan Crisis and then put pressure on Russia to mobilise in July 1914. France was a willing military partner and was no more drawn into the War by Russia than was Germany by Austria-Hungary.

There is, in fact, much in common between the influences on and fears behind the diplomacy of the two countries. Both were motivated partly by **revanchism**, France by the humiliation of her defeat by Germany in 1870–1 and Russia by the diplomatic reverses at the hands of Austria-Hungary and Russia since 1908. Both feared a war against the whole military strength of Germany – France because of the proximity of Paris to the frontier, Russia because it would also have to take on Austria-Hungary. On the other hand, both were confident of success if Germany could be engaged simultaneously on both fronts. After all, France had lengthened the period of conscription to increase the size of the army, while Russia had instituted a series of military reforms for completion in 1917. France and Russia therefore needed each other against Germany, and this was transmitted into military commitment.

10. Compare any two reasons for Britain's entry into the First World War in August 1914. (90 marks)

Two main reasons are normally given for Britain's declaration of war on Germany on 4 August 1914. One is the need to support France, upon which Germany had declared war on 3 August. The other, and more openly stated, reason was the objection to Germany's violation of Belgian neutrality. Clearly the two are complementary, but it is possible to argue that one was used a means of giving greater credibility to the other. This can work in two ways. On the one hand, the defence of Belgian integrity can be seen as the decisive issue bringing Britain into the war, making the support of France a practical necessity. Alternatively, Britain was moving towards supporting France and used the German invasion of Belgium as a means of uniting domestic support behind this.

The first argument may initially appear the stronger, since Britain had more definite obligations to Belgium than to France. By the Treaty of London (1839) Britain, along with other major powers, had guaranteed the independence and neutrality of the newly independent Belgian state. The German invasion violated the Treaty, a document to which the Kaiser famously referred as a 'scrap of paper'. The Prime Minister, Asquith, and Foreign Secretary, Grey, were therefore reacting to the invasion by carrying out Britain's treaty obligations, old though these obligations were. France, by contrast, could claim no such legal commitment from Britain. The key document defining Anglo-French relations was the 1904 Entente. But this fell far short of an alliance, or any undertaking of military support, being concerned mainly with resolving colonial disputes in Morocco and Egypt. In honouring an existing legal commitment to Belgium, Britain was therefore creating a new commitment to France.

But this argument could be seen as too restricted and too legalistic. It is true that Britain had no formal treaty obligations to France – but there were connections which were just as strong. The important thing was that the Entente of 1904 had been tightened up by 1914, going well beyond its original intention. Britain had drawn closer diplomatically to France as a result of the Algeçiras Conference (1906) and the Agadir Crisis of 1911. In both cases the common threat had come from Germany, which was also engaging in a naval race against Britain. As a result of this, Britain and France agreed to troop concentrations and to naval deployments which made the French responsible for the Mediterranean and the British for the Channel and North Sea. This amounted to a military alliance in every respect short of an actual document. With an impending German attack on France in August 1914, Asquith and Grey therefore felt honour-bound to assist the French. They had to persuade the Cabinet to give an undertaking which transcended the narrow obligations of the 1904 Entente. Otherwise, the defeat of France would lead to Britain's dishonour and isolation in Europe.

The situation was therefore urgent even before the German invasion of Belgium. At this stage, a domestic problem arose in the form of a Cabinet split. Grey's proposal to assist France was supported by a small group which included Churchill and Haldane but opposed by the majority of the ministers. This is where Belgium provided a solution. Whereas Grey and Asquith could not guarantee unanimous support for entering a war on behalf of France, they could be sure of concerted action in defence of Belgium. The dissidents in the Cabinet may have been able to question the legality of Britain's 'alliance' with France, but they could hardly refute Britain's obligation to Belgium under the Treaty of London. The Prime Minister and the Foreign Secretary therefore chose to make the violation of Belgium their reason for declaring war on Germany, knowing full well that this would achieve what they most wanted: intervention on the side of France.

It is possible to downgrade the importance of the Belgian issue even further. Some historians have shown that the Liberal dissidents were actually looking for a cause which would save their face – and the government. Grey had threatened on 1 August to resign if the Cabinet continued to adopt a policy of non-intervention at all costs. When the Conservatives made it clear that they were behind France, it seemed that the Liberal dissidents could do little good by holding out. But how could they be persuaded to change their mind? The answer was the noble cause of supporting Belgium in its struggle for survival against brutal violation. Thus it would be more accurate to say that Belgium saved the British government rather than that the British government saved Belgium. The invasion of Belgium was therefore the stated reason for war – but it is highly probable that Britain would have supported France even if it had not happened.

11. Why did Italy enter the First World War in 1915 rather than in 1914?   (90 marks)

Italy entered the First World War on the side of Britain, France and Russia in April 1915. In doing so, the Italian government reversed its decision to remain neutral in August 1914 and to ignore a commitment it then had to support Germany and Austria-Hungary. In each case government policy was influenced by internal and external factors, most of which changed during the intervening eight months.

Italy's involvement on the side of the Allies was the result of the secret Treaty of London, signed with Britain and France on 26 April 1915. The Italian Prime Minister, Salandra, and Foreign Minister, Sonnino, were influenced in this decision by two key factors. One was their mistaken view that the war would end within months, with an Allied victory: this was deduced from the apparent exhaustion of the German offensive at the Marne on the western front and the early Russian victories over the Austrians in the Carpathians in the east. The other was their view that Italy would have to become involved at this point if any gains were to be made from the general peace settlement which would soon follow. The Treaty of London guaranteed Italy territorial acquisitions from Austria, including Trentino, Trieste, south Tyrol, Istria and a large part of Dalmatia. These lands would complete the unification of Italy by bringing within its national boundaries the substantial number of Italians who still lived beyond them. A military victory would also be a sign that the Italian state had developed an expansionist dynamic. Intervention would therefore fulfil Italian **irredentism** and Italian prestige. The Italian government had some difficulty in winning over public acceptance, but decided to press ahead anyway. It was the determination, especially of Salandra and Sonnino, which secured Italian involvement. They were prepared to ignore the opposition of socialists, republicans, Catholics and businessmen. They also gave effective publicity to the pro-war demonstrations organised by nationalists like D'Annunzio and syndicalists such as Mussolini. In other words, they decided on a course and won the argument over implementing it.

Figure 2.4 **Map showing the sides in the First World War**

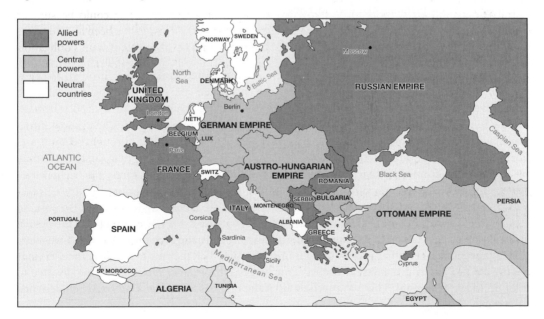

This was all very different to the situation in 1914. For Italy, the First World War had broken out at the worst possible time and over the worst possible issue. In the summer of 1914 Italy was experiencing a wave of strikes and disturbances which culminated in 'red week' and the declaration of a republic in the Romagna. Troops were called up, and uniforms and munitions issued, to control domestic riots, not to fight an external enemy. In any case, Italy had little sympathy with the way in which her allies at that time – Austria-Hungary and Germany – had got themselves into the conflict. Austria's ultimatum to Serbia had contravened the Triple Alliance, the 1891 version of which had guaranteed Austrian consultation with Italy before any action was taken in the Balkans; no such contact took place in 1914 and Italy felt that its own interests and security were threatened. The original Triple Alliance (1882) had also stipulated that support should arise if the members of the Alliance were attacked 'without direct provocation on their part'; this hardly covered the Austrian invasion of Serbia or the German declaration of war on Russia, France and Belgium. Finally, the original Alliance had also specified that Italian involvement would not be 'directed against Britain'. This was partly through longstanding friendship between these two countries and partly through fear of the enormous damage the British fleet could inflict on a country with such a long and vulnerable coastline. When Britain declared war on Germany over the latter's invasion of Belgium, the Italian government had another reason for not immediately supporting its allies.

The same Prime Minister, Salandra, took both decisions. He clearly saw huge opportunities with a new set of allies in 1915 which replaced his fears about the dangers involved in Italy's old commitments in 1914. While he was probably right about the latter, events showed that he exaggerated the former.

12. Assess the reasons for the existence of stalemate on the western front for most of the First World War. (90 marks)

The First World War was widely expected to be over more quickly than any of its predecessors. Yet, for all the war planning and ever-increased speed of mobilisation, the conflict on the western front ground to a halt within weeks of its start. The reasons were initial military problems, technological deficiencies and unimaginative strategy.

Swift mobility on the western front depended on an immediate German breakthrough, as envisaged by the Schlieffen Plan. This, however, did not occur, with the result that the Anglo-French forces had time to prepare an effective defensive system. The result was a prolonged stalemate. The reason for this is that the Schlieffen Plan was not properly implemented. The original intention had been for the main thrust of the German army to push rapidly through Belgium and north-eastern France, to scythe round Paris and trap the French armies against another German force advancing from the Rhineland. Everything depended on the main force, the 'right wing', being strong enough to carry out such a bold stroke. In the event, the German right was weakened by von Moltke, who drew off troops to send against the advancing Russians in the east. As a result, the advance faltered well short of Paris and, in September 1914, was stopped by the French at the Battle of the Marne. By this stage both sides were constructing complex systems of trenches, which prevented any further possibility of a breakthrough. For the rest of the war, the Germans simply did not have the manpower to revive the original thrust since men were being diverted to fight on the eastern front. This was precisely what the original Schlieffen Plan had been designed to prevent.

It could be argued, therefore, that the crucial factor in the stalemate was the failure of the German offensive in the West. This, in turn, highlighted the technological deficiencies which caused whole armies to pile up against each other within a confined space. Railway networks were geared up for rapid mobilisation and movement of troops to the frontier – but then what? Further advances would have to be by more traditional forced marches and supplies would be carried by horse. There was therefore plenty of time to dig trenches and fortify them to withstand heavy artillery bombardment. There were, of course, major attempts by both sides to break through – the French at Verdun (1916) and the British at the Somme (1916) and Paschendaele (1917). In all cases, however, advances were stopped by the lethal combination of barbed wire and machine guns, neither of which had been used on a large scale in any previous European war. This was less of an issue on the eastern front – but this was because of the success and speed of the German break-through. Trenches followed failed offensives as much as they prevented successful ones.

The field was therefore given to unimaginative strategies born of desperation rather than of insightful calculation and planning. The slaughter increased as both sides strove to 'break through'. The measures used by Moltke, Falkenheyn, Joffre, Foch and Haig were all based on the same premise: heavy artillery bombardment, followed by a heavy concentration of troops on so-called vulnerable sectors of the enemy defences. These strategies did not, however, have the desired effect. For one thing the network of trenches was not broken by continuous artillery pounding; the only real effect was to increase the obstacles faced by advancing infantry, adding deep craters to the existing obstacles of barbed wire and machine guns. The figures show the extent of the stalemate. The British army fired 1.7 million artillery shells in 8 days at the Somme, the French 2.7 million at the Aisne in April 1917 and the British 4.3 million at the third Battle of Ypres. On each occasion the Germans were pushed back by less than 5 miles. Thus the western front was not unfrozen by any military breakthrough. At any point in its history warfare tends to be dominated by technology which is ahead in either the offensive or defensive sectors. In the case of the First World War it was definitely the latter. It is significant that the German surrender was taken at Compiegne, near Paris, with the German armies still on French soil.

The impact of these three factors was broken only in 1918, indicating how strongly they had been linked. In each case something new was required. The military stalemate was cancelled by the arrival of huge numbers of US troops, while the introduction of the tank broke the immobility of the trenches.

 ## The impact of the war

13. Assess the effect of the First World War on Germany. (90 marks)

When war broke out the German people united behind the common effort. When things began to go wrong, however, it increased the social tensions and divisions which had always been there. By the end of 1918, therefore the war was a catalyst for revolution.

The initial unity was the result of the enormous popularity of the war. Most people believed that Germany was involved in a 'just' war and that its participation was defensive. This brought a truce, known as the 'Burgfriede', between the normally antagonistic classes and parties. The upper classes and the Conservative Party, which represented the social elites, welcomed the war as a crusade which would focus the priorities of the other classes on patriotism rather than on the pursuit of their domestic interests. Working-class organisations, who had been expected to oppose the war, in fact welcomed it. For the Social Democratic Party (**SPD**), patriotism became the main priority and there was also a hope that service by the working class in the war effort would enhance its status in society. The middle classes expected the war to be a liberalising force, increasing the power of the Reichstag. Each sector of the population therefore believed that its long-term objectives would be fulfilled by the war: the elites hoped that the rest of the population would be quietened by the experience, the working masses looked for an improvement in their conditions and status, and the middle classes hoped for greater constitutional input in the future. The only dissenting voice came from the radical left wing of the SPD, which opposed the war in principle. But even they felt that war would serve a useful purpose in destabilising the regime and preparing the way for revolution.

Within two years all the early optimism and apparent unity was being undermined. While the thought of war had been beneficial, prolonged experience of war was to prove very destructive. German losses were heavy, with 2.4 million deaths and even more wounded or permanently disabled. Civilians suffered badly from food shortages in 1917. These were partly the result of the British naval blockade and partly because of a cold winter in 1916–17 and a bad harvest in the summer of 1917. Civilian casualties were 293,000 in 1918, largely from starvation and disease. Deprived of vital imports of raw materials and food, the economy was dislocated. There seemed to be no alternative to total mobilisation – which eventually brought a severe internal backlash. At first total mobilisation was confined to the economic sector, with the establishment of the Raw Materials Department (KRA), which distributed key raw materials to where they were most needed. The War Ministry also introduced the conscription of labour.

Eventually the war also exerted a strong political impact as military failure in the west brought a change to the government within Germany. The reputation of the Kaiser declined considerably and he no longer exerted his full power. Constitutional government was also weakened as the Chancellor, Beythmann Hollweg, had to give way to a military dictatorship under Hindenburg and Ludendorff, the *Oberste Heeresleitung* (OHL). By June 1917 the high command had therefore come to dominate the political system.

By 1918 it had become clear that German victory in the east could not be repeated in the west. The various groups within the population, previously reconciled, became disillusioned. The elites found that war without swift victory had only made internal dissension worse, while the lower and middle classes saw in military dictatorship the very reverse to the democracy they sought. It is true that the governments of Britain and France had also become more authoritarian under the impact of war. But they were still democracies, operating a temporary state of emergency and retaining full civilian control over the military. In Germany, by contrast, the army had ultimate control over the government, which had ceased to function normally.

Under these conditions the initial unity disintegrated and a revolutionary situation emerged under the direct impact of a war going badly. By August 1918 the situation was desperate. Classes and political groups once again polarised and were made more confrontational by impending military defeat. The middle classes now hated the regime which had a narrower base even than before 1914. The working class was again radicalised and the SPD targeted the military dictatorship of the OHL. This pressure soon told. In October 1918 the OHL, realising that the Allies would sign an armistice only with a civilian government, stepped aside in favour of Prince Max of Baden. But the new constitutional government was soon overtaken on the left by the proclamation of a republic on 9 November by the SPD. This was shortly to be followed by an attempt by the radical left, the Spartacists, to imitate the Russian experience of the previous year and to establish a communist regime.

From the cauldron of military defeat and political revolution emerged the Weimar Republic, which contrasted with the old Kaiser Reich in being a democracy with an elected president and a chancellor accountable to the Reichstag. Yet, despite the dislocation brought by the war, there was much continuity between the two regimes in terms of class influences and expectations. In this sense the First World War had sharpened existing divisions within Germany without producing a system capable of resolving them.

14. Assess the reasons for and effects of Russia's defeat on the Eastern Front. (90 marks)

See Chapter 3, Essay 12

15. Examine the impact of the First World War on the type of government in Britain. (90 marks)

Before 1914 the normal peacetime process of government in Britain had been a parliamentary democracy with the **executive** accountable to parliament. Governments had been based on single parties, whether Conservative (1895–1905) or Liberal (1905–1914). The First World War had a direct impact on the composition of the government, on the powers it exercised, on the parties which competed to run it and upon the **constitution** which circumscribed it. Some of these changes were long-term, others were more immediate and soon wore off.

The composition of the government was directly affected. The war acted as a catalyst for change in four distinct phases. At first there was direct continuity, based on the assumption that normal party-based government could lead Britain in war as well as in peace. Before long, however, it had become clear that Asquith lacked the skill for military co-ordination and he became subject to increasing criticism. This persuaded him, in the second stage, to transform the Liberal government into a coalition; the catalyst for this was the shells scandal of 1915. Again, however, there were deficiencies. In the third stage, between 1916 and 1918, Asquith was replaced as leader by Lloyd George, who extended the inter-party scope of the coalition government and made extensive use of an Imperial War Cabinet. The final stage was perhaps the most radical of all. After seeing Britain through to victory, Lloyd George sought support from the electorate to continue his coalition government into peacetime. The short-term transformation was complete. The Prime Minister at the beginning of the war had possessed a Liberal majority but lacked the confidence of other parties; at the end of the war he possessed widespread support – but had no party base. Yet, by 1922, the appeal of coalition had worn off; with the fall of Lloyd George, Britain reverted to party-based government.

As a direct result of the war the government widened its executive powers and became more directly involved in the lives of the people. In some cases the measures were short-term, based on the emergency. The Defence of the Realm Act (DORA) of August 1914 gave the government powers which ranged from censorship to the nationalisation of industries vital to the war effort. Other measures followed, including conscription (1916), the prosecution of conscientious objectors, a series of licensing acts, the regulation of imports by the McKenna Duties, a ban on strikes, and the introduction of summer time to reduce fuel consumption. The government also sought to influence people's minds through propaganda, establishing in 1916 the Department of Information and the National War Aims Committee. Many of these measures were modified or relaxed after the war. But some changes were more permanent. For example, the war influenced the decision to extend the franchise to all men over 21 and some women over 30 in the 1918

Representation of the People Act, which had a profound political impact on the entire period between 1918 and 1939.

This, in turn, combined with other influences to change the party political scene. Labour gained its first experience of government in a coalition government and also increased its electoral support through the 1918 Representation of the People Act. The impact on the Liberals was primarily negative, causing a major split between Asquith and Lloyd George and bringing about terminal decline as a party of government. A combination of the two processes enabled Labour to achieve the breakthrough which had been impossible in 1914. The Conservatives, in turn, benefited from the prolonged rivalry between a stronger Labour Party and the weakening Liberals, the remaining split gave the Conservatives unprecedented predominance between the wars.

Finally, the war accelerated a basic change to the constitutional structure of the United Kingdom, profoundly affecting the connection between Britain and Ireland. After the abandonment of the Third Home Rule Bill in 1914, Irish politics became more radical – the Irish Nationalists giving ground to Sinn Fein and the IRA on one hand and the Irish Unionists on the other. The war, far from calming the differences as had been hoped, made them worse. The Easter uprising (1916) and the British response made it more difficult than ever to settle Britain's biggest constitutional crisis, the eventual result being that Home Rule was replaced by independence and partition.

16. To what extent did the First World War affect the British economy and society? (90 marks)

The most immediate impact of the war on both the economy and society was in terms of the damage and destruction caused. Britain lost some 750,000 men, or about 9 per cent of the age group between 18 and 45, while similar numbers were disabled. Given the effect of this on families, the entire population was exposed to a degree of shock and trauma. More impersonal criteria, however, indicate that the war had an uneven effect.

The most serious economic consequences were felt in finance and trade. Before 1914 Britain had been a major creditor. Her balance of payments (the balance between payments made for imports and payment received through exports and services) had been very healthy. But this had been due mainly to 'invisible earnings'; brought in through overseas investments and insurance, these had actually concealed a deficit in the balance of trade. The First World War had, however, severely depleted British reserves and investments. These were rapidly used up in the quest for victory, thus changing the whole basis of Britain's international role. After the war, Britain had fewer invisible earnings and began to experience overall deficits. Similarly, Britain found it impossible to maintain the pre-war strength of sterling. Returning to the gold standard in 1925 proved a severe strain and had to be reversed in 1931. Before 1914 Britain had been the leading financial power in the world. Between the wars Britain was rapidly overtaken by the United States.

The impact of the war on industry was more varied. The traditional, or staple industries, received a temporary boost during their long-term decline. War created an enlarged demand for coal, steel, shipbuilding and textiles but during the early years of the peace these industries had to confront all their original problems of inadequate infrastructure, under-investment and lack of competitiveness on world markets. The main consequences of continued decline in the inter-war period were increased industrial unrest and rising unemployment. New industries, especially motor manufacturing, experienced the reverse of this trend. The First World War depressed consumer demand and temporarily undermined the car industry. During the 1920s, however, these effects rapidly wore off. By the 1930s the new industries had become the healthiest sector in the economy.

The war also had a mixed impact on social issues and society. It had a generally negative impact on government policy, often interrupting schemes which had been projected before 1914. One example of this was the suspension of Pease's Education Bill on the outbreak of war. When the measure was finally reactivated as the Fisher Education Act, it had lost some of its more progressive proposals. Another example was the slowing of the government impetus on health. Despite the high profile given by the war to health issues, the coalition government was unable to allocate the resources which would have been needed for the extension of the pre-war reforms of the Liberals. Overall, the First World War did not see a concerted government effort to extend welfare schemes. This was in contrast to initiatives taken by the coalition government in the Second World War, which produced an early outline for the welfare state and National Health Service.

More directly influential was the impact of the war on the role of women in society, as they were involved in a wide variety of occupations crucial for the war effort. Examples included battlefield nursing, munitions manufacturing, transport driving and agricultural work. There were also important consequences for women's representation in parliament. Before 1914 the Liberal government had resisted the demands of the Women's Social and Political Union (WSPU) for the extension of the franchise. Using as a reason women's service during the war, Lloyd George's coalition government extended the vote, in the 1918 Representation of the People Act, to women over 30 who were householders or married to householders. There is always the suspicion that Lloyd George got in first before the Suffragettes' campaign could start up again – but at least the war gave him that choice.

17. What effect did the First World War have on Italy? (90 marks)

See Chapter 5, Essay 2a.

The end of the war and the peace settlement

18. With what justification can the Treaty of Versailles be considered a 'harsh settlement' for Germany? (90 marks)

Ever since the signing of the Treaty of Versailles in June 1919, there has been a controversy amongst politicians, economists and historians about the harshness of its terms. With the passage of time it is now possible to establish a clearer perspective and to show that there are two sides to most of the clauses involved.

There were certainly valid reasons for the territorial changes and Germany suffered fewer losses than those she had already inflicted on Russia by the Treaty of Brest-Litovsk in March 1918. Most of the changes were logical. The return of Alsace-Lorraine to France was simply reversing the Prussian annexation of 1871, while the incorporation of northern Schleswig, after **plebiscite**, into Denmark undid the Prussian conquest of the area in 1864. Posen and West Prussia were given to Poland because the vast majority of their population was Polish, and the non-German population of southern Silesia opted for Poland and Czechoslovakia. The surrender of the German port of Danzig might be considered harsher, but this was needed to make the new state of Poland

Figure 2.5
The signing of the Treaty of Versailles, 1919

economically viable and, in any case, was placed under the League of Nations. The strongest case for harshness was the removal of Germany's entire overseas empire, comprising the colonies of Togo, Kamerun, South West Africa, East Africa, New Guinea, the Solomon Islands and the Mariana Islands. There was some justification to the argument that Germany had mistreated the populations of these areas; on the other hand, Belgium, one of the beneficiaries, also had a poor colonial record.

Strong criticism was made of the Treaty's military clauses on the grounds that they deprived Germany of any effective means of self-defence against France, Czechoslovakia and Poland, all of whom now had much larger armies. By contrast, the German army was restricted to 100,000 volunteers and the navy to six battleships; there was to be no airforce and the Rhineland was to be demilitarised. On the other hand, such measures have to be considered within the context of the huge threat which German military power had posed. During the war the combined forces of Britain, the Empire, France, Russia and Italy had been unable to bring down the Second Reich; United States intervention had been necessary to ensure Allied victory. It was therefore logical to remove this threat by limiting the possibility of rebuilding Germany's military capacity in the future. The reasoning of the Allies was that 100,000 volunteers would provide for a highly professional army which would be capable of dealing with any internal disturbances without posing an external threat to neighbouring states. In fact, this same clause worked to Germany's long-term benefit since the high quality of military provided a core upon which subsequent military recovery could be constructed.

Article 231, in which Germany and her Allies were forced to admit responsibility for the outbreak of the First World War, has been seen as particularly harsh and the whole concept of 'war guilt' was to be bitterly resented by the German people. The financial provisions of the Treaty of Versailles were also seen at the time as harsh. J.M. Keynes, for example, considered the transfer of iron, coal and rolling stock from Germany to the Allies as 'inexpedient and disastrous'.[5] The final bill for **reparations**, fixed in 1921 at 136,000 million gold marks, was to be a vital factor in destabilising the German economy and therefore the political support for the new democratic republic. Yet even these criticisms can be partly countered. The 'War Guilt clause' was, it is true, politically motivated; but historians, particularly German, have recently produced considerable evidence to demonstrate Germany's actual responsibility for the outbreak of war in 1914. As for the financial provisions, there was a not unreasonable expectation that Germany, largely un-damaged by war, should transfer at least some resources to Belgium and France to offset the enormous destruction caused on their territory.

Perhaps the greatest mistake made by the Allies – and the clearest case for harshness – was their decision not to involve Germany in any of the discussions leading to the Treaty. This meant that the German government had no part-ownership of the settlement and was bound to react to it as a *diktat* conceived in the spirit of hostility rather than of compromise. This was to poison the whole political atmosphere of the Weimar Republic.

19. Why had Austria-Hungary disappeared from the map of Europe by 1919? (90 marks)

Austria-Hungary was a heterogeneous empire comprising a dozen ethnic groups. Two of these, the Germans of Austria and the Magyars of Hungary, dominated the dual administration, while the majority of the population, consisting of Slavs, had long pressed for similar status or for independence. This is the fundamental reason for the end of Austria-Hungary. The First World War brought the collapse of the centralising influences of the empire and the task was completed by the peace conferences, which formalised the new regimes which had emerged.

The catalyst for collapse was sustained military pressure. From 1915 onwards the Russians threat-ened Bukovina and Galicia, while the Italians, who entered the war by the Treaty of London in the same year, threatened Austria's southern frontier. As a result, the empire's survival became inextricably entwined with Germany's military performance. In the meantime, the unity of the empire was fracturing internally. The new emperor, Karl, failed to win the confidence of the Hungarian part of the empire and his introduction of military zones and martial law in the Austrian half of the monarchy alienated all the Slavs – Czechs, Slovaks, Poles, Ruthenes, Serbs, Croats and Slovenes. Even the economic arguments for imperial unity were disappearing. The Danube basin, previously an area where trade had been fully integrated, now broke up into smaller units of economic self-sufficiency under the impact of Allied blockades. This development, in turn, under-mined the argument for political unity.

Since Austria-Hungary had strong centrifugal tendencies, it needed external as well as internal constraints. The internal ones had stopped working by 1916, while the external influences ended in the last 18 months of the war. The March Revolution of 1917 removed the threat of Russian aggression, thus releasing the Slavs of Austria-Hungary from one of their greatest fears. Indeed, Russia's new Provisional Government seemed to strengthen the case for breaking up the Habsburg Empire by openly recognising the 'right of the nations to decide their own destinies'. The Bolshevik Revolution (October 1917) seemed to confirm this policy. In any case, the pressures of the civil war forced Lenin's regime to sign the Treaty of Brest-Litovsk in March 1918. The sudden emer-gence of independent states like Estonia, Latvia, Lithuania, Poland and Ukraine from the western provinces of the former Russian Empire exerted a powerful influence on separatist movements within Austria-Hungary. These rapidly moved beyond the control of the Vienna and Budapest governments, while Germany, confronted by imminent defeat from September, could no longer provide assistance. By this stage there really was nothing to hold together the different national-ities of a discredited and increasingly artificial empire.

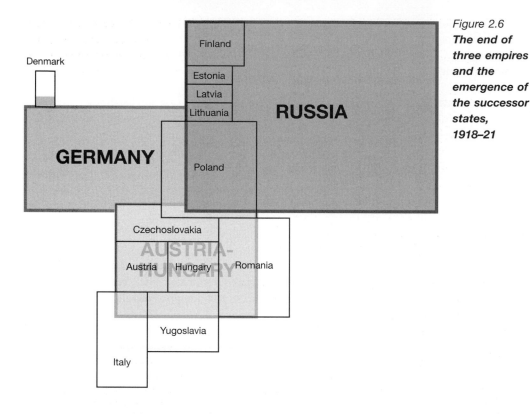

Figure 2.6
The end of three empires and the emergence of the successor states, 1918–21

By the time the emperor surrendered in October 1918, the various ethnic groups had therefore taken matters into their own hands. Following widespread desertions from the imperial armies, a new military threat emerged. Ethnic Poles occupied parts of Galicia, Czechs campaigned in Bohemia and Bosnian Serbs prepared the way for union with neighbouring Serbia. Hungary also came under pressure as the Romanians of Transylvania made common cause with the invading forces of Romania, the largest of the independent Balkan states and now one of the victorious Allies. To complicate matters further, Hungary was soon in the throes of a communist revolution in Budapest. More than any other state, Russia included, Austria-Hungary was brought to total chaos by the final stages of the war.

The leaders of the Allied powers, who assembled in Paris to draw up a peace settlement, decided not to try to reverse events or restore the old system. They had a number of compelling reasons for accepting the inevitable and sanctioning what had already been done. The first was a matter of practicality. It would take military intervention by the powers to reverse the collapse of the Empire and this would have been entirely unjustifiable – both to governments and their electorates. In any case, there were strong political arguments in favour of national self-determination; President Wilson of the United States had incorporated the principle directly into his Fourteen Points. There was also a widely held belief that, since the First World War had been brought about by autocracies, future peace would be best guaranteed by free peoples living in their own states under democratic constitutions. Thus international recognition was readily accorded to new creations such as Czechoslovakia and Yugoslavia, to revivals like Poland and to extensions such as Romania. Since their political stability would depend on their economic viability, they were generously provided with land and economic resources from the former Empire.

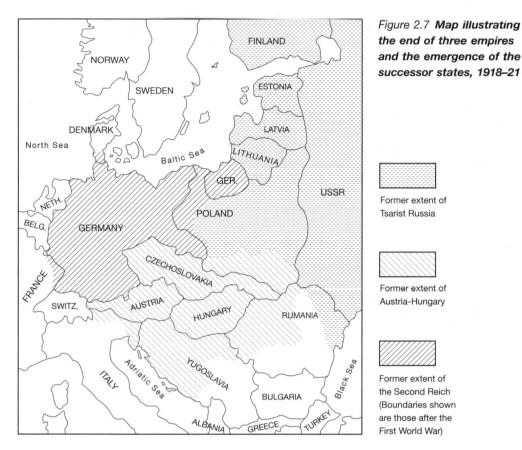

Figure 2.7 **Map illustrating the end of three empires and the emergence of the successor states, 1918–21**

These principles underlay the two peace treaties which confirmed the new order in central Europe. Between them, the Treaties of St Germain (1919) and Trianon (1920) confirmed the cession of Galicia to Poland, Transylvania to Romania, Croatia and Bosnia-Herzegovina to Serbia, and the South Tyrol and Trentino to Italy. As a result, Poland, Czechoslovakia and Yugoslavia all emerged as larger and more populous states than either Austria or Hungary, which were the dwarf states from a collapsed great power.

There were, of course, many anomalies in the Treaties of St Germain and Trianon. German and Magyar minorities were unfairly treated and there were to be future problems of political instability in all the new states except for Czechoslovakia. Even so, there has always been a resigned acceptance of the inevitable. King Albert of the Belgians said of the decisions of the statesmen of Paris: 'What would you have? They did what they could.' More recently, the historian A.J.P. Taylor succinctly summarised the long-term dilemma: 'The dynastic Empire sustained central Europe as a plaster cast sustains a broken limb; though it had to be destroyed before movement was possible, its removal did not make movement successful'.[6]

20. How serious was the effect of the Treaty of Versailles on Germany? (90 marks)

See Chapter 4, Essay 10

21. **Why and with what results were Italians so resentful of the peace settlement of 1919?** (90 marks)

See Chapter 5, Essay 2b

✎ Additional essay questions (with advice)

Each of these questions can be tackled as a single essay or as one of the answers to a question in several parts. Additional reading and research is desirable for each one.

22. **Assess the reasons for the emergence between 1890 and 1914 of a combination of powers against Germany and Austria-Hungary.**

   Advice: *Consider 'combination' in a broad sense and include alliances and ententes. Find three or four main reasons for its formation. One might be the threat perceived from Wilhelm II's policies, a second the lessening tensions between Britain, France and Russia, and a third the increasing overlap between imperial and Balkans issues. Try to connect these and to prioritise their importance.*

23. **To what extent was the existence of rival alliances responsible for the outbreak of war in 1914?**

   Advice: *The key phrase is 'to what extent?' The answer should therefore deal with the ways in which the alliances contributed to the war – but should also see whether their terms could have been responsible for the way in which the war broke out. Look at both sides, but come to a conclusion based more heavily on one side than on the other.*

24. **How valid is the view that Austria-Hungary provoked war in 1914?**

   Advice: *Consider what is meant by 'war'. Was it 'war with Serbia' or 'general war'? The answer might be 'yes' to the first (consider Austria-Hungary's concern about Serbia in 1914) but 'no' to the second (look at Germany's motive and at Hungary's hesitancy). You could conclude with this split verdict.*

25. **Why did Germany win the war in the east but lose the war in the west?**

   Advice: *Avoid narrative at all costs. You could either answer the question in two parts (winning in the east, then losing in the west) or look for common factors and integrate east and west into these. The second method is probably better. Think in terms of the extent of the front, the amount of support on each front, and the relative strength of the opposing powers.*

26. **'The First World War brought revolution to Russia, Germany and Austria-Hungary.' How far do you agree with this view?**

   Advice: *Rather than a straight 'yes' or 'no' approach, try to establish a variety of views. For example, you might argue that the strongest case for revolution (in fact, for two) was in*

Russia; these were clearly accelerated by the war, although there was already instability before 1914. Germany is a more debatable case: defeat brought internal changes in 1918 – but were these part of a 'revolution'. Austria-Hungary folded up internally – was this a revolution, or many revolutions, or simply internal collapse?

27. Which was treated more harshly by the peace settlement after the First World War: Germany or Austria and Hungary?

Advice: *Avoid writing half the essay on Germany and half on Austria and Hungary. Look for common criteria and make direct comparisons between them.*

Essay plan

Para 1: Overall approach.
- *Direct comparison of Treaty of Versailles (1919) with Treaties of St Germain (1919) and Trianon (1920).*
- *To be based on the use of specific criteria: territorial losses; ethnic considerations; economic losses; military measures.*

Para 2: Both suffered heavy territorial losses.
- *In terms of total area overall: Germany lost most – colonies (names).*
- *In terms of area in Europe: Austria and Hungary lost more than Germany (comparative details).*

But it is arguable that the losses of Austria and Hungary were a fait accompli brought by the collapse of Austria-Hungary before the peace treaties were drawn up. In this case, the settlement had a greater effect on Germany.

Para 3: Ethnic terms of the treaties more complex.
- *National self-determination for Slav groups meant German minorities affecting Germany and Austria about equally (details, including Sudetenland from Austria).*
- *But Hungary more severely treated than either Germany or Austria – reduced to one-third the size of historic Hungary: large Magyar minorities in Romania, Yugoslavia.*

Para 4: Economics were different for Germany, Austria and Hungary.
- *The economic impact of territorial loss was more serious for Austria and Hungary than for Germany (supporting detail).*
- *The amount of reparations and the concept of 'War Guilt' were more damaging to Germany than to Austria and Hungary (supporting detail).*

The basic difference was that Austria and Hungary lost much of their infrastructure to the new states. Germany kept most of its infrastructure, but this was affected by subsequent economic problems associated with reparations.

Para 5: Military measures.
- *Austria and Hungary suffered fewer direct military constraints than Germany, which was bound by extensive losses (supporting detail).*

> • *On the other hand, fewer constraints were needed for Austria and Hungary since these were now smaller than the new 'successor' states. Germany, however, was still in a position to threaten them, which makes the military measures seem less harsh.*
>
> *Para 6: Integrated conclusion.*

Part 3: Sources

1. Germany and the outbreak of war

This exercise consists of three questions on three sources, with a time allocation of 45 minutes.

Source A: A report from the Austrian ambassador in Berlin to the Austrian Foreign Minister, 5 July 1914. This is a summary of a conversation he had had with Kaiser Wilhelm II.

The Kaiser authorised me to inform our gracious majesty that we might in this case, as in all others, rely on Germany's full support. He did not doubt in the least that Herr Bethmann Hollweg would agree with him, especially as far as our action against Serbia was concerned. But it was the Kaiser's opinion that this action must not be delayed. Russia's attitude will no doubt be hostile, but for this he had for years prepared, and should a war between Austria-Hungary and Russia be unavoidable, we might be convinced that Germany, our old faithful ally, would stand at our side.

Source B: Adapted from A.J.P. Taylor, *How Wars Begin* (1979)

One essential part of the Schlieffen Plan was to go through Belgium. The other essential part which was equally important was that there could be no delay between mobilisation and war, because if there were delay then Russia would catch up and the Germans would get the two-front war after all. The moment the Germans decided on mobilisation, they decided for war, or rather war followed of itself. The railway timetables in the Schlieffen Plan brought the troops not to their barracks but into Belgium and Northern France. The German mobilisation plan actually laid down the first forty days of the German invasion of France and none of it could be altered because if it did all the timetables would go wrong. Thus the decision for mobilisation which the Germans announced on 1 August was a decision for a general European war.

Source C: G. Layton, *From Bismarck to Hitler: Germany 1890–1933* (1995)

When one looks at the evidence it is difficult to escape from the conclusion that the German leadership must shoulder the major responsibility both for the worsening international atmosphere in the five years or so before 1914 and also for the escalation of the July crisis into a continental war.

German *Weltpolitik* and the ham-fisted diplomacy which accompanied it had contributed to a marked increase in international tension and to a dangerous deterioration in Germany's strategic position by about 1907. However, more significantly, in the following years there was no concerted attempt by Germany to overcome this – no preparedness to compromise as a way to engender conciliation and trust. Instead, German foreign policy was generally typified by a hawkish mentality of bluster and brinkmanship and by an increased determination to stand by Germany's one remaining reliable ally, Austria-Hungary. This policy and approach came to a head in the German response to and direction of events in the July crisis. From early July Bethmann adopted a strategy of calculated risk in the hope of winning a diplomatic victory which would decisively weaken the Entente. To achieve this end the crisis was deliberately escalated and attempts at constructive mediation were torpedoed. All this was done because it was also believed that the failure of diplomacy would lead to a war with the Entente powers, which, according to the assessment of the generals, Germany at that time could win. Thus, when Russia did mobilise, Germany willingly accepted the challenge and implemented the Schlieffen Plan.

QUESTIONS WITH WORKED ANSWERS

a) Study Source A and use your own knowledge. Explain briefly the reference in Source A to 'Germany, our old faithful ally'.   **(3 marks)**

The word 'ally' refers to the Dual Alliance between Germany and Austria-Hungary, drawn up, at Bismarck's instigation, between Kaiser Wilhelm I and the Emperor Franz Joseph. Originally a defensive alliance to deal with the threat of a Russian invasion, this had gradually tightened up so that, from the time of the 1908 Bosnian Crisis, Germany was giving open and unqualified backing to whatever action Austria considered necessary to deal with threats to her security from the Balkans. This dependability explains the term 'faithful'.

b) Study Sources B and C. With reference to your own knowledge of the outbreak of the First World War, explain the differences in interpretation between Source B and Source C over Germany's war plans.   **(7 marks)**

The arguments of the two historians are similar in one respect but differ on points of interpretation. Both show Germany to be the power which was most directly involved in the sequence of events leading to the outbreak of war: according to Source B, German mobilisation 'laid down the first forty days of the German invasion of France', while Source C blames the 'German leadership' for the 'escalation of the July crisis into a continental war'.

The differences between the two sources are, however, more obvious. The main implication of Source B is that the outbreak of war was accidental, while Source C refers to longer-term calculation. Hence Taylor's thesis is that the Schlieffen Plan was the means by which Germany could if necessary transform defensive vulnerability into military success. The problem was that the 'railway timetables' involved in implementing the Plan could not be reversed once mobilisation had taken place. It was therefore a *military* problem, over which Germany lost control. Layton reflects the more recent view that Germany had been pursuing longer-term *diplomatic* aggression in the form of 'brinkmanship'. This was not so much a loss of control as a 'calculated risk' since German policy would lead either to a 'diplomatic victory', which would 'decisively weaken the Entente', or to a war, which 'according to the assessment of the generals' Germany could win. By this analysis, the Schlieffen Plan was the opportunity for converting aggressive diplomacy into military victory, and not, as Taylor suggests, the point at which Germany stumbled into war.

c) **Study Sources A, B and C and use your own knowledge. Explain the ways in which German foreign policy after 1890 contributed to the outbreak of war in 1914.** (15 marks)

Total (25 marks)

The sources provide some insight into the contribution made by German foreign policy to the outbreak of war in 1914, although these need to be supplemented by additional knowledge. The earliest trends contribute to the strengthening of an alliance system against Germany, while policies after 1907 were an attempt to prepare for this system's defeat.

Contributing to the emergence of a counter-alliance does not make Germany responsible for the outbreak of war in 1914. Nevertheless it created a problem which Germany eventually tried to resolve militarily, in contrast to Bismarck's dependence on diplomacy (at least after 1871). The two key developments of the 1890s were Wilhelm II's decision to abandon the Reinsurance Treaty and hence Germany's connection with Russia (not mentioned in any of the sources) and his departure from Bismarck's European constraints in pursuit of *Weltpolitik* (Source C). These alienated the two powers likely to give Germany strategic problems in the future and pushed both towards France – in the Franco-Russian Alliance of 1894 and the Anglo-French Entente (1904). This gave Germany the dual problem of contesting maritime supremacy against the world's largest naval power and defending Germany against two continental powers which outflanked her.

The abandonment of diplomacy meant that solutions had to be military. The whole purpose of the Schlieffen Plan (Source B) was to defeat both France and Russia without having to fight a prolonged two-front war to which Germany seemed to have been condemned. Even this is not direct evidence of Germany's complicity in the outbreak of war since all the powers developed plans for mobilisation. Two things, however, made Germany's position unique. One was the vulnerability of Austria-Hungary, Germany's closest ally, to Serb agitation which, from 1907 onwards, was supported by Russia. The other was an awareness that time was not on Germany's side. Britain was opening up an unassailable lead in dreadnoughts, France was closing the gap with Germany in the size of her army and Russia was undergoing military reforms which were due for competition in 1917.

Faced with this scenario, the German military became ever more influential, urging a pre-emptive strike while Germany still held the lead. To its credit, the German government did not directly succumb to this pressure. Instead, Chancellor Bethmann Hollweg pursued a 'diagonal policy' between peace and war, using the predicament of Austria-Hungary as the decisive issue. This is described in Source C as a 'calculated risk'. After the assassination at Sarajevo, Austria-Hungary was encouraged to take vigorous action with full German support (Source A). A.J.P. Taylor argues in Source B that the outbreak of war was made inevitable by German mobilisation and the implementation of the Schlieffen Plan. It could, however, be argued that inevitability preceded this. Germany was determined to force the issue in June and July 1914 by pressing as hard as possible for victory. This could be either diplomatic, if the Allies backed down, or military if they did not. This argument restores the importance of personal decisions (unlike Source B) while, at the same time, seeing these decisions as an attempt to get out of a desperate situation caused by the collapse of earlier diplomatic solutions (not mentioned in Source C).

PARALLEL QUESTIONS WITHOUT WORKED ANSWERS

a) **Study Source A and use your own knowledge. Explain briefly the
    reference in Source A to 'our action against Serbia'.**   **(3 marks)**

    Advice: *Use additional knowledge to explain what the phrase means in the context of the
    source.*

b) **Study Sources B and C. With reference to your own knowledge of the
    outbreak of the First World War, explain the differences in interpretation
    between Sources B and C over the importance of the decisions of
    Germany's leaders in the outbreak of war.**   **(7 marks)**

    Advice: *'Explain the difference' at two levels: (1) explain the different arguments within
    the two sources and (2) explain the differences in terms of historians' approaches to inter-
    pretation.*

c) **Study Sources A, B and C and use your own knowledge. Explain the
    ways in which German relations with Russia deteriorated between
    1890 and 1914.**   **(15 marks)**

                                                                        Total (25 marks)

    Advice: *Try starting with a paragraph on what light the sources throw on deteriorating
    relations. Then choose criteria in the subsequent paragraphs, based on your own knowledge,
    but bringing in the sources, where possible, for agreement or disagreement.*

2. The impact of the First World War on Russia

This exercise consists of five questions on five sources, with a time allocation of 60–75 minutes.

Source A: A warning from the Minister of the Interior, Durnovo, in a memorandum
to Nicholas II, about the possible effects of war on Russia

Certainly Russia, where the masses without doubt instinctively profess to socialist principles, represents an especially favourable soil for social tremors. If the war ends in victory, the suppression
of the socialist movement will not pose any difficulties. But in the case of defeat, the chance of
which in a struggle with such an opponent as Germany it is impossible not to foresee, social revolution will inevitably manifest itself in its most extreme forms and Russia will be plunged into
hopeless anarchy, the end of which cannot even be foreseen.

Source B: The views of Trotsky on the influence of war

Revolution directs its blows against the established power. War, on the contrary, at first strengthens
the state power which, in the chaos engendered by war, appears to be the only firm support – and
then undermines it. Hopes of revolutionary movements are utterly groundless at the outset of a
war. But this is only a political delay, a sort of political moratorium.

Source C: Extracts from letters from the Empress Alexandra to Nicholas II in 1915

Never forget you are and must remain autocratic Emperor – we are not yet ready for a constitutional government. God anointed you at your coronation. He placed you where you stand.

Dearest, I heard that that horrid Rodzianko and others beg the **Duma** to be at once called together – oh please don't; it's not their business. They want to discuss things not concerning them and bring more discontent. They must be kept away.

No, hearken to our Friend. He has your interest at heart – it is not for nothing God sent him to us – only we must pay attention to what he says.

Source D: Adapted from Michael Karpovich, *Imperial Russia 1801–1917* (1932)

On the eve of the World War, Russia was profoundly different from what she had been in the beginning of the nineteenth century. In spite of the deadweight of the past and the acute contradictions of the present, it was a steadily and rapidly progressing country. In view of this progress it would be hardly correct to assert that the revolution was absolutely inevitable. Russia still had to solve many complicated and difficult problems but the possibility of their peaceful solution was by no means excluded. To this hope of peaceful evolution the war dealt a staggering blow. It caught Russia in the very process of internal reorganisation.

Source E: Adapted from Edward Acton, *Rethinking the Russian Revolution* (1990)

In the light of recent research the traditional view of the revolution as the fortuitous product of war is unacceptable. Before 1914, neither peasant land-hunger nor working-class militancy were abating. Middle-class pressure for liberal reforms was ineffectual. At the same time the gradual erosion of the regime's social base and its repressive power pointed firmly towards a revolutionary upheaval likely to be fatal to tsarism and liberalism alike.

QUESTIONS WITH WORKED ANSWERS

a) **Study Source B. What does this source reveal about the expectations which Trotsky had in 1914 for opposition to the tsarist regime?** (3 marks)

Opposition in Russia aimed at changing or replacing tsarism, the latter by revolution. As a **Marxist**, Trotsky firmly believed that war would act as a catalyst to bring this about since, as he said elsewhere, 'war is the locomotive of history'. Revolutionaries should not, however, expect to benefit immediately, since at the outset war 'at first strengthens the state power' (Source B). Opposition would therefore have to survive this early setback and prepare to take advantage of the end of the 'political moratorium', when war at last 'undermines' the regime.

b) **Study Source C and use your own knowledge. Explain the reference in Source C to 'our Friend' who has 'your interest at heart'.** (5 marks)

'Our Friend' is a direct reference to Rasputin, a *moujik* who had acquired enormous influence over the royal family. Despite his coarse manners and sexual appetites, he was greatly admired by the Empress Alexandra, who considered that 'God had sent him to us'. She was convinced that Rasputin had healing powers (although he was probably a hypnotist) since he brought relief to the Tsarevich Alexis, a haemophiliac.

Having 'your interest at heart' really referred to the expansion of Rasputin's talents. After insinuating himself into the court, he established himself as a political adviser, a sort of low-grade Pobedonostsev. His views on autocracy accorded exactly with Alexandra's own – that Nicholas should stand resolutely against any pressure, especially from the Duma, to share power.

c)   **Study Sources D and E. Compare the arguments in Sources D and E as to the effect of the First World War on the development of Russia. How would you explain the differences between them?**   **(5 marks)**

Sources D and E have in common a long-term perspective on the collapse of Tsarist Russia. This is possible since, as secondary sources, they are both based on a variety of other sources, both primary and secondary, and present a considered analysis.

Beyond that they differ widely. The essence of Karpovich's view is that the First World War disrupted a positive period in which 'Russia was a steadily and rapidly progressing country' (Source D). Acton, by contrast, argues that the whole system was vulnerable to 'peasant land-hunger', to 'working-class militancy', resulting in the 'gradual erosion of the regime's social base' (Source E). Hence, while Karpovich maintains that, without the war, revolution cannot be considered to have been 'absolutely inevitable' (Source D), Acton implies strongly that the war made little difference to the onset of 'revolutionary upheaval'.

The differences can be seen as part of the whole process of historiography. Historians present interpretations as part of their trade: whether other historians agree or disagree is entirely up to their own reading of the material available. In this instance there is also a more general difference in perspective. Karpovich is following a more traditional approach of viewing events from the perspective of those in power and he concludes that since they were introducing reforms the situation must have been improving. Acton, on the other hand, has contributed to modern research into radicalism from below, which has been attributed much greater significance even before 1914.

d)   **Study Sources A and B. Compare the value of these two sources to the historian studying the expected impact of the First World War on Russia.** **(5 marks)**

Both have the value usually attributed to primary sources – a particular slant representing a contemporary viewpoint and a sense of the immediate situation. Although they lack any retrospection, which is the main advantage of the secondary sources, A and B both attempt to give a longer-term perspective, based on predictions or likely outcomes. As it happened, both were proved right by subsequent events.

They are also valuable as an insight into the concerns felt at the time by the two extremes of the political spectrum. Source A shows that there was a growing awareness within the government itself about the strength of the 'socialist revolution'. Since this is likely to have been a confidential memorandum, it had no reason to be anything but a frank assessment of the dangers. These were so considerable that the memorandum is implicitly advising the Tsar against provoking them through a declaration of war. In Source B Trotsky is equally frank about the trials faced by revolutionaries at the beginning of war. Although Source B is largely theoretical, it is deduced from his own experience of revolution, as well as from Marxist principles. It also gives an insight into his growing commitment to structured revolutionary organisation to prepare for the opportunity offered after the end of the 'political moratorium'. Perhaps this is why he eventually switched from the **Mensheviks** to the Bolsheviks during the course of 1917.

e) **Study Source C, and any of the other sources, and use your own knowledge. Explain how the First World War undermined the tsarist regime.** **(12 marks)**

Total (30 marks)

The First World War contributed much to the collapse of tsarism in Russia. Military defeat destabilised the political system and provided the revolutionary activists with their experience, while social and economic dislocation directly encouraged the intervention of the masses.

The main effect of the First World War on Russia was to discredit the political system. Trotsky was right to assume that there would be initial support for the regime but that the war would eventually undermine this. Source A, in a warning to the Tsar, adds the extra dimension of defeat, warning of the dire social consequences. What actually happened first was political dislocation. The poor performance of the Russian armies induced the Tsar to replace Grand Duke Nicholas as commander-in-chief at the front, leaving a political vacuum in Petrograd which was filled by Alexandra. This proved disastrous since her intransigent approach ('Never forget you are and must remain autocratic Emperor') alienated the Duma and its hitherto cautious element, including 'that horrid Rodzianko'. Rasputin reduced autocracy to farcical levels and earned universal ridicule and resentment. The war was therefore a catalyst for the isolation of tsarism, which meant that there was pressure for his abdication in March 1917 from the Duma and even from the commanders in the army and navy.

But a discredited tsar was nothing new in Russian history. What made it different this time was that the war had weakened one of the means whereby tsarism was able to control social and political dissent. A destabilised army, the vast majority of which was composed of peasant conscripts, hastened the events of March 1917. They refused to put down the popular demonstrations and, after the first few days, the Petrograd Garrison and the Cossacks joined the demonstrators. The fears of Durnovo (Source A) that 'defeat' would bring 'social revolution' were therefore realised. As for the crowds themselves, the driving force was the food shortages caused by difficulties with transport, the direct result of the dislocation caused by military defeat.

Whether or not the collapse of tsarism was inevitable is the subject of a debate represented here by the alternative viewpoints of Sources D and E. Karpovich maintains that it was not, and that the war dealt a 'staggering blow' to a reforming system. In this case, the war acted as a catalyst which reversed a previous trend. Even Acton's argument that previous developments 'pointed firmly towards a revolutionary upheaval' (Source E) has a place for the war as a catalyst – this time as an accelerator.

PARALLEL QUESTIONS WITHOUT WORKED ANSWERS

a) **Study Source A. What does this source reveal about the advice given to the Tsar about the possible consequences of mobilising the Russian army for war?** (3 marks)

   Advice: *'Reveal' can mean what is directly stated and what can be inferred from the wording.*

b) **Study Source C and use your own knowledge. Explain the reference in Source C to 'that that horrid Rodzianko' and his reason for wanting 'the Duma to be at once called together'.** (5 marks)

   Advice: *Refer directly to both extracts. Explain who Rodzianko was and why Alexandra considered him 'horrid'. Possibly in a separate paragraph, explain why Rodzianko wanted the calling of the Duma.*

c) **Study Sources A and B. Compare the arguments in Sources A and B as to the expected impact of the First World War on the tsarist regime.** (5 marks)

   Advice: *'Compare' means finding similarities and differences. Try to integrate these and to avoid simply summarising each source in turn. Use your own sentences with words or phrases from the sources in quotation marks.*

d) **Study Sources D and E. Compare the value of these two sources to the historian studying the impact of the First World War on Russia.** (5 marks)

   Advice: *'Compare' means finding advantages and disadvantages for each source. Think in terms of content and reliability.*

e) **Study Source C, and any of the other sources, and use your own knowledge. Did the First World War destroy tsarism?** (12 marks)

   Total (30 marks)

   Advice: *Consider the points made in Source C and other sources you select. Then make your own criteria from your own knowledge, integrating the sources where possible.*

Part 4: Historical skills

♛ Note-taking and filing

This section covers the problem most frequently encountered by any A-level or university student – how to take and organise an effective set of notes.

WHY TAKE NOTES?

Note-taking is one of the most basic of all requirements for the historian, both in the sixth form and beyond. It is virtually impossible to avoid it. It can be dreary and unproductive, or it can be meaningful and stimulating, depending on the approach.

There are two quite distinct reasons for note-taking, both of which are equally important. The first reason is to assist the memory. Most people retain information for only a short period and therefore need a reminder, for both the short term and the long term. Notes prevent the need to do the spadework all over again. The second reason is to focus the mind on the material being studied. Note-taking involves thinking and can lead to analysing and questioning; it is much more difficult to achieve this while simply listening.

FIVE SITUATIONS IN WHICH NOTES ARE TAKEN OR PROVIDED

1. Notes in class or in lectures

Description   Most subjects involve a certain amount of note-taking in class. At university this is usually done more formally in lectures, so it is essential to master now the technique of making good notes on what is said in class. These should not be called 'dictated notes', which means writing down everything verbatim, a technique now rarely used and, in any case, pointless.

Purpose   They are specially adapted to the needs of the particular class. Therefore a record needs to be kept both of the content of the subject and of techniques related to it.

Writing notes sharpens concentration on what is being said.

Filed notes provide the basis for future revision.

There are several common problems with note-taking in class. One concerns quantity – writing either too much or too little. Many students have said: 'I try to write too much and miss the important points. I wish I could take shorthand.' This would only make matters worse since revising the topic would involve repeating all the original work. The answer is to make selective notes and to think about what is being said.

The reverse problem is writing too little. 'My notes end up looking like a telegram. They seem to have no useful purpose.' This is probably because there is insufficient involvement in what is being said. The answer is to follow both the argument and the examples, concentrating first on the structure of what is being said in class and then gradually extending the focus to the details. It helps to take a more active part in discussion or ask questions: these methods could direct the lesson more along the lines you will be able to follow. It may also help to listen carefully for clues given in the lesson or lecture:

- Stress on a particular point should indicate its importance; the same applies to repetition.
- 'First', 'Second' etc. can be converted into numbers.
- Certain key phrases indicate supporting argument ('for example', 'this is shown by' etc.) or a different angle ('on the other hand' etc.).

It is important to get a visual impression of what is being said; this is really a matter of habit and will become automatic after a while. It might also help to use two or more different colours and to have a predetermined system of underlining.

2. Handouts

Description   These are provided by the teacher or tutor. They can be:

- a set of notes covering the whole topic
- a summary of the topic
- a focus on a specific part of the topic
- advice on essay or source technique.

Purpose   Handouts involve time and effort on the part of the teacher or tutor. They are used:

- to provide a well organised survey of the topic, with an emphasis on the particular skills and techniques required.
- to save the necessity of spending time making own notes; this releases time for further reading and supplementary note-taking.

The one major problem with handouts is that the student may take them for granted. It is tempting simply to file them and assume that they have been dealt with. What is actually needed is personalisation through several readings, selective highlighting and summarising in the margin. It is also important to accept the main reason for handouts – to divert the time which would be spent on routine note-taking into further reading.

3. Notes from books

Description   Notes from books represent a more direct intellectual relationship between the student and the various works and authors recommended for the course.

Notes from books can

- summarise the main ideas of the author and
- contain comments by the student on these ideas.

Purpose   History students come of age only when they engage directly with books and are able to take their own notes from them. The main priorities are:

- To gain more extensive knowledge.
- To have a wider understanding of ideas and any controversy surrounding a subject.
- To think more actively by having to grapple with the material. Intellectual development is like physical development in that it needs appropriate exercise.
- To gain confidence. This will result in more adventurous and therefore original work.
- To improve English style by familiarity with vocabulary, phrases and sentence structure used by authors.

Many books appear daunting at first sight – but there are certain preliminary procedures which can make things easier. The first is to take a few minutes to become familiar with the basic layout of the book:

- Use the table of contents to narrow down the area of the book required. Look also at any subheadings in a chapter.
- Use the index to see what type of coverage there will be on specific topics. Start with the key word and follow through with others. Either jot down page references on a piece of paper or put removable sticky tags on the pages themselves.

This process is known as scanning. It will help define the general area needed – perhaps 20 to 30 pages – and will take about 5 minutes. You are not quite ready to start making notes, as you may include unnecessary detail. The next stage is therefore to take a rapid look through the pages to be read to get an idea of:

- the structure of the section (clues are often provided in the opening sentence of each paragraph)
- the amount of argument
- the types of examples.

This process is known as skimming. It helps define the overall approach to the area needed. You should then jot down in rough a few words on the overall structure plus any questions you think the extract will answer. Deduce these questions from your preliminary skim or start out with questions related to an assignment you have been set.

This approach may be criticised as a waste since it will increase the total time spent taking notes. In fact, it should reduce the time spent by ensuring that 30 pages will be summarised in 3 pages, not 15. Another objection might be that it will make slow readers even slower. Again, this is not true. The preliminary skim should speed up the whole reading method. When skimming, keep your eyes moving forward quickly and focussing mainly on the centre of the page. Do not go back to re-read a phrase or sentence: this is probably what slows you down at the moment. You will in any case be having another look at the whole section in a few minutes time. After a while you will find that you are looking back much less frequently.

Making notes should now be much easier. You know what you are looking for and have an outline idea of what the material comprises. You may even have your main headings. What comes next?

- Start with the title of the subject. Add in brackets (From Author: Title of book). If you are doing the reading for a project which will require footnotes, include page references in the margin of your notes; this will save you having to go back later.
- Use plenty of headings and subheadings: be guided by the structure of the paragraphs.
- Indicate arguments and examples. Be guided by clues in the text. Look also for clues on stages (for example, 'First . . . second', 'on the one hand . . . on the other', 'furthermore . . . finally' etc.).
- Spread the notes out to allow for later additions.
- Add any comments of your own (in a different colour).
- Try pacing yourself. Set yourself a target of making notes on a section within a particular time and put your watch in front of you. This is very effective if you are working in a library.
- If the notes are for coursework or an individual study, make sure that quotation marks are used when you copy original sentences or phrases: otherwise, you are in danger of plagiarising.

- When you have completed making notes on the section, allow a few minutes to read through what you have written. This should set what you have just written more firmly in your mind and enable you to judge how much further reading needs to be done.

4. Notes from the Internet

Description   The Internet is the most recent of all the sources uses for note-taking. It comprises a wide variety of websites:

- Educational (organised by professional associations, schools and colleges, and publishers).
- Individual – provided by a wide range of people including established authors and students publicising their work.
- Documents, consisting of published primary sources.

Purpose   Notes from Internet sites are a valuable supplement to those from other sources:

- They offer a stimulating and eye-catching approach.
- They can be useful for introductions or revision.
- They might offer detail on more technical areas.
- They are immediately accessible; this applies especially to primary sources.

The problem with using the Internet is recognising that it is not, at present, the most important source of ideas and materials for the academic historian; this role is for the time being still fulfilled by books in libraries (although books may in the future be published on the Internet). For the moment websites should be used as valuable, but supplementary, sources for notes.

Note-taking from the Internet has its problems. Downloading an article or essay is not in itself a form of note-taking; it is equivalent to printing or photocopying. Downloading and then using the delete key on the computer to shorten produces a more selective approach. There remains, however, the possibility of plagiarism if any of the original text is transferred to an essay or piece of coursework.

The answer is to make a brief summary on paper either from the article on screen or from a printed version. Selected printouts can provide a valuable addition to any file but too many can swamp the core notes and material from books.

5. Revision notes

Description   Revision notes are a summary of the more detailed notes taken throughout the course, focusing on two dimensions:

- The outline and the way in which all the topics relate to each other.
- The details of each topic.

Purpose   The purpose relates to the description. There are two priorities in any exam question:

- To identify quickly all the material relevant to the question.
- To identify the detail needed to support the argument given in the answer.
- Revision notes have to be able to fulfil these – or they will have been pointless.

Revision notes should be minimalistic and act as a trigger for further recall. This means using as few words as possible to put across the arguments and detail needed. This can be done in the form of linear notes, cards or summary charts. These are covered in more detail on pages 358–60.

GENERAL TECHNIQUES OF NOTE-TAKING

Notes should be graded carefully so that they are easy to follow. It is best to develop a simple overall technique, for your own needs, which you can carry out automatically without having to think about it. This will enable you to concentrate on what you are making notes on.

There are many different formats, including the one suggested on the facing page. Experiment until you find something which works – then stick with it.

GENERAL HEADING

Main side heading. Followed by introductory point.

1. Subsidiary heading. Followed by introductory point. Then: further breakdown into specifics, grouped as follows:

a. (i)   Specific point
    (ii) Specific point
    (iii) Specific point

b. (i)   Specific point
    (ii) Specific point
    (iii) Specific point

1. Subsidiary heading. Followed by introductory point. Then: further breakdown into specifics, grouped as follows:

a. (i)   Specific point
    (ii) Specific point
    (iii) Specific point

b. (i)   Specific point
    (ii) Specific point
    (iii) Specific point

Main side heading. Followed by introductory point.
    etc.

FILING

Note-taking has to be accompanied by regular filing. This prevents gaps and discontinuity which make revision so difficult. Dividers help to keep the sections apart and therefore make it much quicker to locate what you need or to add the latest notes in exactly the right place.

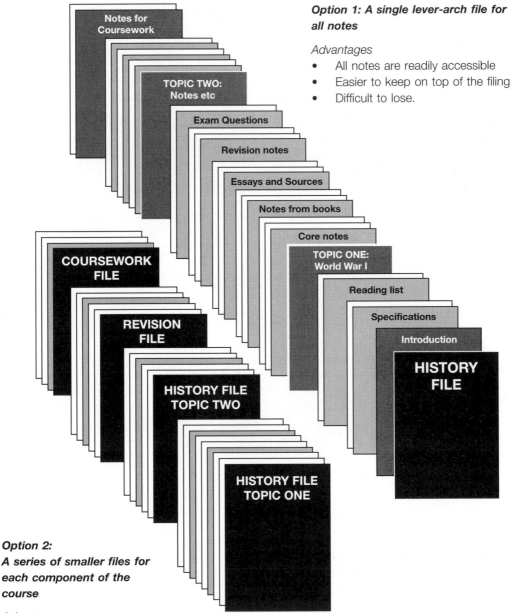

Option 1: A single lever-arch file for all notes

Advantages
- All notes are readily accessible
- Easier to keep on top of the filing
- Difficult to lose.

Option 2:
A series of smaller files for each component of the course

Advantages
- Easier to transport the component needed
- Less disastrous if lost

References

1. A.J.P. Taylor, *The Struggle for Mastery in Europe 1848–1918* (Oxford 1954)
2. M. Hurst (ed.), *Key Treaties for the Great Powers 1814–1914* (London 1972), Document 165
3. See H.-U. Wehler, *The German Empire 1871–1918* (Leamington Spa 1985)
4. See W.J. Mommsen, *Imperial Germany 1867–1918* (London 1995)
5. See J.M. Keynes, *Economic Consequences of the Peace* (London 1919)
6. A.J.P. Taylor, *The Habsburg Monarchy 1809–1918* (London 1948), Epilogue

Sources

1A. G. Martel, *The Origins of the First World War* (Harlow 1987), document 11
1B. A.J.P. Taylor, *How Wars Begin* (London 1979)
1C. G. Layton, *From Bismarck to Hitler: Germany 1890–1933* (London 1995), p. 53
2A. Adapted from R. Kowalski, *The Russian Revolution 1917–1921* (London 1917), p. 18
2B. Leon Trotsky, *My Life* (1971), extracts quoted in N. Rothnie, *Documents and Debates: The Russian Revolution* (London 1990), p. 25
2C. Adapted from A.F. Kerensky, *The Road to the Tragedy* (London 1935), pp. 61–3
2D. Adapted from Michael Karpovich, *Imperial Russia 1801–1917* (1932)
2E. Adapted from Edward Acton, *Rethinking the Russian Revolution* (London 1990), p. 82

Chapter 3

Russia, 1855–1917

This chapter will consider the climax and the collapse of imperial Russia. Between 1855 and 1917 Russia experienced a series of changes and upheavals. Reform alternated with attempted revolution, war acted as a catalyst for both, and reaction was the fallback for a system in search of underlying security. The period is therefore full of contradictions. There are pointers to the ultimate collapse of tsarism – but also hints that it was capable of survival through modernisation. Much depended on the attitudes of each of the last three Tsars.

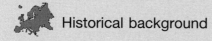 ## Historical background

Alexander II (1855–81) and Alexander III
   (1881–94)
Nicholas II and the crisis of Tsarist
   Russia, 1894–1917
Revolutionary movements, 1855–1917
   and the 1917 revolutions

Sources

1. Russia before the First World War, 1870–1914
2. The Bolshevik Revolution, October 1917

 ## Historical skills

Oral contributions

Essays

Alexander II (1855–81) and Alexander III
   (1881–94)
Nicholas II and the crisis of Tsarist
   Russia, 1894–1917
Revolutionary movements, 1855–1917
   and the 1917 revolutions

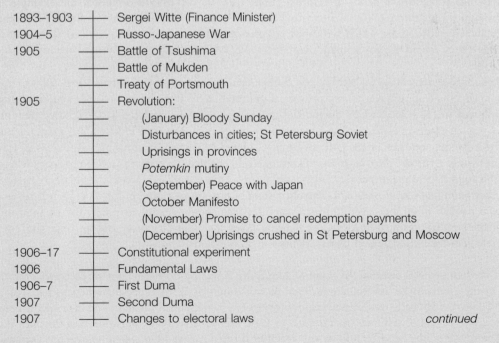

Chronology

Alexander II 1855–81

1856	Manifesto for the liberation of the serfs
1861	Edict of Emancipation
1863	University reforms
	Polish revolt
1864	School reforms
	Reform of the judicial system
	Establishment of zemstva
1866	Attempted assassination of Alexander II
1870	Establishment of city dumas
1874	Military reforms
1881	Loris-Melikov's proposed consultative assembly
	Assassination of Alexander II

Alexander III 1881–94

1881	Statute of State Security
1882	Tightening of censorship
1887	Limitation of university freedoms
	Attempted assassination of Alexander II

Nicholas II 1894–1917 (March)

1893–1903	Sergei Witte (Finance Minister)
1904–5	Russo-Japanese War
1905	Battle of Tsushima
	Battle of Mukden
	Treaty of Portsmouth
1905	Revolution:
	(January) Bloody Sunday
	Disturbances in cities; St Petersburg Soviet
	Uprisings in provinces
	Potemkin mutiny
	(September) Peace with Japan
	October Manifesto
	(November) Promise to cancel redemption payments
	(December) Uprisings crushed in St Petersburg and Moscow
1906–17	Constitutional experiment
1906	Fundamental Laws
1906–7	First Duma
1907	Second Duma
1907	Changes to electoral laws

continued

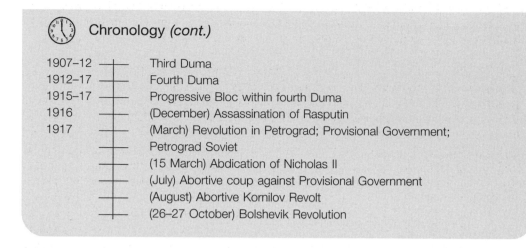

Chronology *(cont.)*

1907–12	Third Duma
1912–17	Fourth Duma
1915–17	Progressive Bloc within fourth Duma
1916	(December) Assassination of Rasputin
1917	(March) Revolution in Petrograd; Provisional Government;
	Petrograd Soviet
	(15 March) Abdication of Nicholas II
	(July) Abortive coup against Provisional Government
	(August) Abortive Kornilov Revolt
	(26–27 October) Bolshevik Revolution

Part 1: Historical background

Alexander II (1855–81) and Alexander III (1881–94)

Alexander II came to the throne in 1855, in the middle of the Crimean War between Russia and an alliance of Britain, France, Turkey and Piedmont. The conflict had shown up all the deficiencies of Russia's political, economic and social structure and Alexander felt that there was enough evidence to launch a series of reforms (Essay 1a). In his 1855 **Manifesto**, for example, he announced his intention of emancipating the serfs. This he carried out in his **Edict** of Emancipation of 1861, under which serfs were granted personal freedom and provided with land for which they repaid the government over a period of 49 years.

This crucial reform was a catalyst for further changes (Essay 1b). Reforms were, for example, carried out in local government: provincial **zemstva** were introduced in 1864, and city dumas followed in 1870. Meanwhile, the judicial system had also been updated in 1864, based on a new system of magistrates, district and regional courts, trial by jury and independent judges. Under the university reforms of 1863, the freedom of higher education institutions was increased, while the School reforms (1864) introduced gymnasia and enabled the zemstva to open primary schools. In recognition of the impossibly harsh conditions within the armed forces, a series of changes was made to military service in 1874. The old system of peasant recruitment for 25 years was replaced by a liability of all men over 20 to six years' service. These reforms, especially the emancipation of the serfs has resulted in Alexander II being called the 'Tsar Liberator' and his reign the 'era of great reforms'. These are, of course, debatable propositions (Essay 1c).

It is often pointed out that the reign of Alexander II was by no means one of consistent reform. On the contrary, he was equally inclined to reactionary policies, especially when he felt that his rule was being challenged by national minorities (as in the Polish revolt of 1863) or by the emergence of revolutionary movements such as Land and Liberty, Black Partition and People's Will. The dividing line between reform and reaction is often put at 1866, when an attempt was made on his life (Essay 2a). Repressive policies were certainly in evidence during the late 1860s and the 1870s (Essay 2b) and, by 1879, most large cities were under virtual military law. Even so, the distinction between reform and reaction can be seen as an artificial one, since there was plenty of evidence of reaction in the 'era of reforms' and of reforms in the 'era of reaction' (Essay 2c).

From 1880, however, there is little doubt that the regime was prepared to take further liberalising steps. Loris-Melikov, appointed by Alexander II, proposed a policy of conciliation. In March 1881 he recommended the establishment of a consultative assembly, which the Tsar was willing to accept. Whilst on his way to sign the necessary papers, however, Alexander II was killed by a bomb hurled at his carriage by conspirators from People's Will (Essay 3a). This had a profound impact on Alexander III, whose reign was devoted to restoring autocracy to its fullest extent (Essay 3b). He was particularly influenced by the ideas of Pobedonostsev, **procurator-general** of the Holy Synod, who argued strongly against making any political concessions, especially parliamentary represen- tation. Alexander III therefore reversed the trend of the previous reign by making repression the norm. The secret police of the Third Section were fully reinstated, the **judiciary** was brought under tighter control by the 1881 Statute of State Security, censorship was tightened in 1882 and univer- sity freedoms were severely curtailed by the 1887 Statute. Measures were also introduced to reduce the powers of the zemstva and dumas set up in the previous reign and also to impede the freedom of the peasantry to migrate from the land to the urban areas. More sinister were the discrimina- tory measures against minority groups, especially the Jews; the government was also suspected of condoning some of the vicious *pogroms*, especially in the Ukraine. Such measures were bound to have a profound effect on the next reign (Essay 3c).

Nicholas II and the crisis of Tsarist Russia, 1894–1917

The reign of Nicholas II divides into four main phases. The first decade (1894–1904) saw rapid economic development without, however, any corresponding political change. The result was the more forceful assertion of autocracy which culminated in a second phase – the Russo-Japanese War of 1904–5 and the 1905 Revolution. This was followed, between 1906 and 1914, by a period of constitutional, social and economic reforms; but, since these were not properly implemented and only partially effective, there was an intense accompanying frustration. The fourth phase (1914–17) saw the regime weakened by the First World War and overthrown by the Revolution of March 1917.

The economic reform of the first decade was largely the work of Sergei Witte (Finance Minister 1893–1903), who renewed Russia's industrial and railway infrastructure, deriving the capital from French loans and investments, domestic taxation and protective tariffs. Although there were defi- ciencies in his reforms, Witte played a crucial role in the greatest bout of modernisation in Russia since the reign of Peter the Great. The regime did not, however, accompany economic change with political reform (Essay 4). Nicholas II resisted all calls for liberalisation, instead using the industrial infrastructure to strengthen autocracy; he had in common with Alexander III the contin- uing influence of Pobedonostsev. His focus was firmly on an enhanced personal role in foreign policy. Nicholas II therefore used Witte's industrialisation in pursuit of expansion in the Far East (Essay 5a), thereby associating it directly with militarisation. In the meantime, industrialisation had also created an enlarged urban proletariat with an increasing grudge against the regime's lack of social and political reform.

The result of this combination was war and revolution. The Russo-Japanese War (1904–5) fol- lowed a steady deterioration in relations between the two countries over their claims in Manchuria and Korea; the reasons for this rivalry are examined in Essay 5b. The initiative was taken by the Japanese who torpedoed the Russian fleet in Port Arthur in 1904. The Russian Baltic fleet was subsequently defeated in the Straits of Tsushima (1905) and Russian land forces at Mukden. The reasons for these disasters are covered in Essay 5c. Although no foreign troops set foot on mainland Russia, the defeats came as a profound shock and were a major factor in the intensification of the Revolution of 1905 (Essay 6). This really started in January 1905 with Bloody Sunday, the massacre of demonstrators outside the Winter Palace trying to petition the Tsar for reform (Essay 7a). Disorder spread rapidly through St Petersburg and Moscow, where **soviets** of workers' and soldiers' deputies were established. Meanwhile, the Black Sea fleet was affected by a mutiny on board the battleship *Potemkin*, while a number of provinces experienced peasant uprisings (Essay 7b). Faced with this combination of threats, the government was forced in September 1905 to draw up the Treaty of Portsmouth with Japan and to make sufficient concessions to the revolutionaries to save the regime (Essay 7c). He promised a constitution in the **October Manifesto**, which neutralised the middle class activists, and pacified the peasantry by promising the cancellation of their redemption payments in September. This enabled the army to take action against the remainder of the revolutionaries – the urban workers in the key cities, especially Moscow. By the end of 1905 the regime had clearly survived, although it had been badly shaken.

Quite how badly Nicholas failed to grasp. Although he fulfilled his promise of introducing a new constitution, he remained reluctant to concede any real power (Essay 8). The Fundamental Laws of 1906 established a new bicameral **legislature** comprising the State Duma and State Council and legalising a range of parties which included the Social Democrats, **Socialist Revolutionaries**, **Constitutional Democrats**, **Octobrists**, Union of Russian men and Union of Russian People. But the franchise was narrow and there was little the Duma could do to control the policies of the Tsar's government, especially since the Fundamental Laws emphasised the continuation of 'the autocratic power'. A series of disputes followed between the government and the first two Dumas between 1906 and 1907. The third Duma (1907–12) was elected on a narrower roll, but the fourth Duma (1912–17) developed within it a **Progressive Bloc** which acted as a focal point for constitutional opposition to the Tsar. The period after 1906 is, therefore, often seen as a missed opportunity for a successful constitutional experiment (Essay 8).

Although it made as few concessions as possible to liberal democracy, the tsarist regime did, from 1906, introduce a series of economic and social reforms. The period 1906–14 saw rapid industrial growth, reviving the progress made by Witte's earlier policies between 1893 and 1903. An industrial boom between 1906 and 1913 produced an annual growth rate of 6 per cent, an increase in foreign trade and the growth of consumer industries. Many contemporaries thought the regime had done enough to prolong its existence indefinitely – although in retrospect there are clearly many discernible faults which increased its vulnerability (Essay 9). A major influence during the period was Stolypin, who tried to accomplish for the agricultural sector what Witte had earlier achieved for industry. The two therefore invite direct comparison (Essay 10).

 Revolutionary movements (1855–1917) and the 1917 revolutions

Yet, for all the attempted reforms, the crucial issue by 1914 was whether the population had been sufficiently pacified to prevent future disturbances. Some historians have argued that Tsarist Russia was doomed even before the outbreak of the First World War and that the radical movements and parties had gained rapid headway (Essay 11a) to consolidate their growth between 1870 and 1905 (Essay 11b). The key issue, however, is whether the bulk of the Russian people were revolutionary, one which has always divided historical opinion (Essay 11c). Whether or not Tsarist Russia could have survived was rendered hypothetical by the defeat of Russia's armies on the eastern front between 1915 and 1917. The reasons were a combination of inadequate preparation and poor leadership; the effects were economic and military collapse (**Essay 12**). The turning point was probably the Tsar's decision to take personal command of the army in 1915, leaving a political vacuum at the centre of government in Petrograd (the new name for St Petersburg) which was filled by the most irresponsible examples of despotism under Alexandra and Rasputin. This alienated all sections of the Russian population and the Tsar refused to heed the warning signals until it was too late.

The events of the Revolution of March 1917 are dealt with in Essay 13a and Essay 13b. They were the result of the alienation of all sectors of the Russian population, from the aristocrats who assassinated Rasputin in December 1916, to the constitutionalists in the Duma who tried to pressurise Nicholas into introducing immediate reforms, and the urban workers who took matters into their own hands in Petrograd. The desertion of parts of the army settled the issue and, on 15 March, the Tsar was forced to sign papers of abdication. His regime was succeeded by two alternatives – the Provisional Government, established by the Duma, and the Petrograd Soviet, set up by the revolutionaries – although not by the Bolsheviks (Essay 13c). There is a certain irony that they came into existence in the same building, and yet after the first few weeks found it difficult to communicate with each other. The Provisional Government tried hard to establish the type of liberal democratic regime for which the Duma had been pressing. It achieved much between March and October 1917 – but it was to be overtaken by events (Essay 14).

Russia experienced two main forms of revolutionary activity between the beginning of the reign of Alexander II and the end of that of Nicholas II (Essay 11a).

The first was the emergence of Populism (Essay 11b), a movement for peasant-based socialism in the rural areas. Strongly influenced by the ideas of Lavrov, various **Populist** groups sought radical changes in the pattern of land ownership, especially after the emancipation of the serfs by Alexander II in 1861. The first formal organisation, Land and Liberty, was set up in 1874 by Plekhanov. Within two years, however, this had split into two factions. The activists, known as *Norodniya Voliya* (People's Will), operated through political violence and assassination, while Black Partition, the more moderate group considered that the most effective method was propaganda. People's Will maintained much the higher profile, assassinating Alexander II in 1881 and making several attempts on the life of Alexander III. By 1900 the two main wings reunited as a new political party, the Socialist Revolutionaries, which played an active part in the 1905 Revolution and successfully contested the elections for the Duma in 1906. Its methods gradually moderated and it maintained a broad level of popularity with the peasantry throughout the period between 1905 and 1907. Socialist Revolutionaries played an active part in undermining the tsarist war effort from 1915 and were extensively involved in the Revolution of March 1917 and the formation of the Petrograd Soviet. Thereafter the party's paths began to diverge. The leadership, especially Kerensky, became too closely identified with the policies of the Provisional Government, with the result that much of the peasantry became temporarily disillusioned. The more radical members of the party, the left SRs, sensed the general drift of popular opinion and joined up with the Bolsheviks, who seized power from the Provisional Government in October 1917. Between 1918 and 1921, however, the Bolsheviks lost ground to the right SRs, who regained their credibility with the peasantry because of Bolshevik attempts to requisition grain supplies. By 1921 the right SRs had been driven to extinction by the new communist dictatorship.

This regime had roots going back, as far as the 1880s, to Russia's first Marxist groups (Essay 11b). These owed their origins partly to Western infiltration and partly to Populist defectors, such as Plekhanov and Axelrod, who were converted to Marxist ideas and established the league of Combat for the Liberation of the Working Class. This united with the other groups in 1898 to form the Russian Social Democratic Labour Party (**RSDLP**), under the leadership of Plekhanov, Lenin and Martov. Deriving most of its support from the urban workers, this aimed to remove the autocracy of tsarism and move, via a temporary period of liberal democracy, to the Marxist goals – first of the '**dictatorship of the proletariat**', then of the '**classless society**'. By 1903, however, the RSDLP had been rent by internal disputes as to the most effective method of achieving their aims. The party divided, as a result of the Congress held in 1903 in Brussels and London, into Bolsheviks and Mensheviks. The Bolsheviks, under the leadership of Lenin, pressed for a closed system of professional revolutionaries and a rapid move towards the 'dictatorship of the proletariat'. Less radical were the Mensheviks, under Martov, who argued for a more broadly based party which was prepared to co-operate with all opponents of tsarism and to take as long as necessary to move towards an agreed socialist alternative. The Mensheviks were initially more popular, playing a greater role than the Bolsheviks in the Revolutions of 1905 and March 1917; they were also willing to collaborate with the Socialist Revolutionaries and with non-socialist parties such as the Constitutional Democrats. But, like the Socialist Revolutionaries, the Mensheviks became discredited during the course of 1917 because of the involvement of their leadership in the Provisional Government. A left-wing splinter-group, the **Menshevik Internationalists**, made common cause with the Bolsheviks and left SRs, helping them to victory in October 1918. The remainder of the Mensheviks joined with the right SRs in trying to resist the emergence of Bolshevik dictatorship until they, too, were eliminated in 1921.

This brings us to the role of the Bolsheviks in 1917 (Essay 15). They played very little part in the March Revolution, Lenin being in exile in Switzerland. With the help of the German government, however, he transferred to Russia, where he promised in his *April Theses* an immediate end to the war, the transfer of land to the peasantry and elections to a constituent assembly. This programme (part of which was subsequently repudiated) was sufficient to attract widespread popular support so that, by September 1917, the Bolsheviks had attained a majority in the Petrograd Soviet, which then elected Trotsky as its President. The Bolsheviks were then able to seize power on the night of 24–25 October (6–7 November) and to oust Kerensky's Provisional Government. The Bolsheviks were almost immediately involved in a struggle for survival, partly against the right SRs and the majority Mensheviks, and partly against the White counter-revolutionaries. The outcome was Bolshevik victory, but the bloody civil war spawned a political dictatorship which had no room for other revolutionary movements.

The Revolution of October 1917 therefore has two perspectives. One is that it completed the task begun in March; the Bolsheviks argued that the achievements of March had been taken over and distorted by the Provisional Government. The other perspective is that the regime established by the Bolsheviks in October eventually turned out to be a counter-revolution, a return to the tyranny and despotism which March 1917 had supposedly driven out of Russia.

Part 2: Essays

Alexander II (1855–81) and Alexander III (1881–94)

1. 'The Crimean War forced Alexander II to show his credentials as a great reformer and as the "Tsar Liberator"'.

   a) **What influence did the Crimean War have on the intentions of Alexander II on his accession in 1855?** (3 marks)

It was an important coincidence that Alexander II succeeded Nicholas I in the middle of the Crimean War (1854–6). Russia's poor military performance had pointed to the need for extensive military, administrative and economic reforms. Alexander II was more willing than Nicholas I to give these absolute priority. He therefore learned the lesson of Prussia which, after being defeated by Napoleon in 1806, launched a series of reforms starting with the emancipation of the serfs.

   b) **Explain why Alexander II introduced a range of reforms *after* the emancipation of the serfs (1861).** (7 marks)

When Alexander II emancipated the serfs in 1861 he created an impetus for further reform. There were two reasons for this. The first was the continuing impact of the Crimean War on Russia's need to update its antiquated superstructure. It was most unlikely that one reform would suffice: one was bound to lead to others. A second, and closely linked, reason was that emancipation meant a massive legal change to the position of the peasantry. This, in turn, had a major social, economic and political impact on Russia's future. Hence most of the reforms from 1862 were either related to the needs of the newly liberated peasantry or intended as some sort of balancing compensation to the nobility.

This can be seen in the specific measures. Local government reform (1864) gave the peasantry an indirect voice in the choice of delegates to the new zemstva, although the nobility retained the key influence. The reform of the judicial system (1864) also acknowledged the redefined social balance; since the nobles had lost their role as local law enforcers, a new system of magistrates, district and regional courts was established. The establishment of dumas in 1870 was a logical extension of the principle of representative institutions to the urban areas. Meanwhile, the School reforms of 1864 were a conscious attempt to reduce peasant illiteracy by enabling the zemstva to make primary school provision. Finally, there was also a logical need for the reform of the armed forces (1874), by which 25-year recruitment was replaced by more extensive 6-year conscription. As in the other cases, emancipation would have been illogical without at least some improvement in the harshest of environment of all.

   c) **Does the emancipation of the serfs (1861) justify the description of Alexander II as the 'Tsar Liberator'?** (15 marks)

Two quite distinct arguments are possible. One is that 'Tsar Liberator' is fully deserved as a plaudit for Alexander II, considering the extent of his achievement on behalf of the serfs. The alternative, however, is that any change was designed not to liberate the serfs but to strengthen traditional social structures; hence 'Tsar Regulator' might be a more appropriate description.

There is much to support the first view. The scale of the reform was massive, affecting the most of Russia's population. According to M.S. Anderson,[1] 'the grant of individual freedom and a minimum of civil rights to 20 million people previously in legal bondage was the greatest single liberating measure in the whole modern history of Europe'. If the size of the act and the depth of vision are taken as the key factors, then the 1856 Manifesto and 1861 Decree can be seen as a 'turning point' by comparison with what went before; indeed, the Manifesto explicitly referred to the need to 'liberate the serfs from above'. The terms, affecting the state and privately owned serfs, created a new landed peasantry. They were able to buy their land, repaying government assistance of up to 80 per cent of the total value over 49 years. This effectively ended the feudal system which had survived in Russia longer than any other country in Europe. The Edict of Emancipation was also a turning point in that it released a series of other reforms during the reign, many directly related to the needs of a newly liberated peasantry.

There are, however, reservations about all this. Even in the context of its time, Alexander II's measure of emancipation was not particularly radical. The 1856 Manifesto had, after all, shown that the purpose of measures from above was to prevent the serfs from 'liberating themselves from below'. Nor was Alexander forcing through a new idea entirely on his own initiative. He had been warned by the Third Section that continuing the existing system unchanged carried the risk of ever-increasing peasant revolts which would eventually threaten the empire and his regime. It would, Alexander felt, be far better to restore social stability by redefining the obligations of the largest sector of the population. He therefore 'liberated' the serfs in order to regulate their successors, the peasantry. Certainly there was little acknowledgement from below for his efforts; his reign was to see a rapid increase in revolutionary movements which, in its Populist form, established roots within the peasantry.

Nor can it be argued that Alexander had made the peasantry significantly better off than the serfs. According to Edward Acton, 'the peasantry as a whole remained in a position of extreme economic and political weakness.' The terms of the 1861 Decree meant that the average redemption payments were significantly higher than the market value of the land. This caused impoverishment which, in turn, meant that the time-limits for payments had to be extended in 1896 and then abolished in 1906. In addition, land ownership was complicated by the control of the communes – both hereditary and **repartitional** – which were clearly intended to form a new layer of authority within the social hierarchy. In many areas the peasantry became victims of the 'double burden', being obliged to sell their labour to supplement their own subsistence agriculture. Ultimately the most important liberating aspect of Alexander's measures was that individual peasants now found it easier to leave the land to swell the urban workforce.

In many ways, Alexander II was a traditionalist. He aimed not to liberate Russia but to make it more secure. He recognised that it would be dangerous to perpetuate serfdom in its existing form but certainly did not intend to transform the network of authority and social obligations on which Russian society was built.

2. **'The first half of Alexander II's reign was an "era of great reforms", the second half an "era of reaction". The dividing line between the two was the threat to his life in 1866.'**

   a) **What is meant by 'the threat to his life in 1866'?** (3 marks)

On 4 April 1866 Dimitry Karakozov fired a pistol at Alexander II at close range – but missed. He was a member of a radical Populist group which considered that all reforms from above were futile and that the only true alternatives were the overthrow of the government followed by social revolution. As the personal representative of autocracy, Alexander II was considered the prime target for assassination.

b) **Explain which of Alexander II's policies might be considered 'reactionary'.** (7 marks)

Reactionary policies were partly based on long-term objectives, the most important of which was to maintain autocracy and the social hierarchy. They were, however, also more immediate reactions to the threat from political dissidents and conspirators. These two trends can be seen in a variety of measures introduced during the reign.

There was, for example, a tightening of control over student activities. The University Regulations of 1861 forbade 'absolutely any meetings without permission of superiors'. In 1867 this was taken further with the order that academic authorities should provide information to the police about any political activities by students. Restrictions were also placed on publications: censorship was gradually extended in scope, while the 1872 Press Law transferred authority for dealing with offences by journalists from the courts to government ministers. Underlying these measures was a disturbing trend towards executive dictatorship. In 1879 came the appointment of 'regional military governors' for St Petersburg, Moscow, Kiev, Karkhov, Warsaw and Odessa, with extensive military powers for maintaining order. In 1880 dictatorship also emerged at the centre, with Loris-Melikov's Supreme Executive Commission.

Meanwhile there had been, from the mid-1860s, a significant change in government personnel. Progressives, like Golvnin were replaced by conservatives such as Tolstoy and Shuvalov, leading Milyutin to comment in 1873 on the 'devastating and disgusting contrast with the atmosphere in which I entered the government thirteen years ago'.

c) **Do you agree with the view that the reign can be divided into eras of 'reform' and 'reaction' – separated from each other by the year 1866?** (15 marks)

There has always been a widely held view that Alexander II's reign comprised 'reforming' and 'reactionary' eras and that there must have been a point of transition from one to the other. What could have been a stronger motive for such a change than an attempted assassination?

Supporting this argument is the impressive list of reforms before 1866, which contrasts with their apparent absence in the late 1860s and 1870s. The earlier measures covered a wide range of social, economic and political changes. The 1856 Manifesto made a declaration of intent to liberate over 20 million serfs, while the 1861 Edict of Emancipation carried this through. The momentum continued well into the 1860s with the establishment of zemstva by the local government reforms of 1864, the reform of the judicial system (1864), and educational improvements for universities (1863) and schools (1864). Compared with these, the actual reforms after 1866 look somewhat limited. The introduction of dumas in the towns in 1874 was, arguably, simply a completion of the process already started with the zemstva in the provinces, while the reform of the armed forces in 1874 was a practical necessity and had more to do with security than with liberalisation. The year 1866 could easily have been the turning point in the transition from reform to reaction, since the attempted assassination tied in with the growth of revolutionary movements, which were seen by the regime as a barometer of public security. Alexander II could well have come to realise that he was going too far too quickly. This explains the rapid increase in reactionary measures like the 1872 Press Law, the appointment of regional military governors (1879) and the creation of the Supreme Executive Commission in 1880.

And yet this division into two eras is too simple – and too convenient. It also ignores some of the facts. Although there were changes in government personnel during the mid- and late 1860s, these did not necessarily mean that the whole base of the regime shifted from enlightened reform to unyielding reaction. There were instances of reaction before 1866 and examples of reforms after 1866. The terms of the 1861 Edict of Emancipation, for example, were essentially very conservative and were to result in widespread discontent with the actual conditions of freedom. The same applied to the limitations imposed on the reforms of 1864: the zemstva were entirely dominated by the nobility and wealthy classes, while legal changes such as trial by jury were often not applied in practice. Nor should it be assumed that the reforming impetus completely dried up after 1866; the counterpart to reaction in the so-called era of reforms was reform in the phase of reaction. The 1870 Municipal Statute may have been intended to settle unfinished business – but it was to have a vital influence on Russia's constitutional future. It is also likely that Alexander II was on the point of agreeing to a proposal by Loris-Melikov for a limited consultative assembly of elected representatives of public opinion. This, in fact, was cancelled only because of Alexander II's assassination and the imposition of a far more reactionary regime by Alexander III.

A reasonable synthesis would be that the reign did see changes of emphasis, although there was also striking continuity. But the reason for the changes was not necessarily the assassination attempt of 1866. Such events were common in Tsarist Russia and could well have had less psychological impact than other upheavals. A much more likely possibility is the Polish Revolt of 1863. This would have been seen as a challenge to the integrity of the Russian Empire as well as a negative response to concessions already granted. Alexander II's reaction to this would have been to complete his current programme (up to 1864), but to be more selective in the future. This would explain why the early stage of the reforms seems to stop in 1864 (not 1866) and why there was a partial revival of the reforming initiative after 1870.

3. 'The dramatic end to Alexander II's reign convinced both Alexander III and Nicholas II that reaction was preferable to reform.'

     a) What is meant by 'the dramatic end to Alexander II's reign'?   (3 marks)

Alexander II was mortally wounded when his carriage was blown up by a bomb thrown by activists in **Narodnaia Voliya** (People's Will). The event had a special irony because Alexander II was at the time on his way to approve proposals made by Loris-Melikov for the establishment of a central consultative assembly. For some historians this gives the assassination a special significance.

     b) Explain how Alexander III made Russia more 'reactionary' between 1881 and 1894.   (7 marks)

In this case, 'reactionary' means ultra-conservative, based on both theory and practice. Alexander III strengthened reaction through a combination of political autocracy, religion and ultra-nationalism.

Autocracy was based on a combination of divine right and opposition to any form of constitutionalism; indeed, parliamentary institutions were 'the great lie of our time'. These were the words of Konstantin Pobedonostsev, procurator-general of the Holy Synod and the political head of the Russian Orthodox Church. The established religion reinforced autocracy in return for a position of privilege by comparison with all other Christian and non-Christian sects. Russian nationalism gave the system its drive. Taking the form of **Russification**, it attempted to weaken the identity of all other ethnic groups and cultures. According to Alexander III, 'We can have no policy except one that is purely Russian and national'. At times this spilled over into extreme measures of persecution, including anti-Semitic *pogroms*.

The specific measures of reaction were implemented with the help of ministers such as Dmitri Tolstoy, Katkov and Durnovo. By the 1881 Statute of State Security, government powers were increased in relation to law, order and justice. For example, government-controlled courts dispensed administrative justice outside the normal scope of the legal system. Judges and magistrates could also be removed from office if shown to be sympathetic to liberal ideas, while the powers of the secret police, or **Okhrana**, were considerably extended. Meanwhile, the reaction also involved the University Statute of 1887, which brought universities under government control and made university rectors the appointees of the Ministry of Education. The local government reforms of Alexander II were systematically undermined by the Zemstva Act of 1890, which reduced the power of the local councils. These have been described by Florinsky as a series of 'administrative counter-reforms', intended to return to the earlier despotism of Nicholas I (1825–55).

c) **'During the first ten years of his reign, Nicholas II seemed to have learned more from Alexander III than from Alexander II.' Explain why you agree or disagree with this opinion.** **(15 marks)**

The usual perspective on Nicholas II (1894–1917) is that he was instinctively autocratic, lacking any leanings towards progressive reform. This seems to place him far more in the tradition of Alexander III (1881–94) than of Alexander II (1855–81).

Nicholas II was always conscious of Alexander III's legacy, asserting at the outset that 'I shall uphold autocracy as firmly and unflinchingly as it was upheld by my unforgettable dead father'. In this he continued to depend on the official support of the Orthodox Church, especially of its political head – Konstantin Pobedonostsev – who had been appointed procurator-general of the Holy Synod by Alexander III. This defined the overall momentum of the first ten years of his reign, a period in which there was no political change and comparatively little in the way of social improvement. Instead, Nicholas II placed the emphasis firmly on economic change, especially on rapid industrialisation. This was in apparent contrast with Alexander II, who had given priority to political and social reform, but very much in line with the policies of the second half of Alexander III's reign. The latter had started the process though his Finance Ministers, Vyshnegradskii (1886–92) and Witte (appointed in 1892). With Witte's continuing help, Nicholas II maintained the same focus on heavy industry, state subsidies and foreign loans. There was also a common purpose to all of this. Like Alexander III, Nicholas II was using industrialisation to strengthen his autocratic base, not to develop a more open society based on middle-class economic liberalism.

It would, however, be a mistake, to rule out any connections between Nicholas II and Alexander II. In terms of personality, Nicholas II probably had more in common with his grandfather than with his father. Like Alexander II, he was often hesitant and likely to change his mind, whereas Alexander III had been strong-willed to the point of extreme obstinacy. In an autocracy such traits have a special significance. In terms of ideological belief there is a direct connection between the three – personified by the influence of Pobedonostsev. After all, it was Alexander II who had begun the political elevation of Pobedonostsev; Alexander III completed the process and Nicholas II inherited him as a fixture within his government. It was also Alexander II who had made Pobedonostsev the official tutor and mentor to the future Alexander III, the latter maintaining the tradition by giving him the same responsibility for Nicholas. Although, it is true, Alexander III gave Nicholas II the means of associating autocracy with industrialisation, Alexander II provided another precedent. As Witte's industrialisation strengthened Russia's infrastructure during the 1890s, Nicholas II looked beyond the relatively quiet reign of Alexander III to try to re-establish a connection between autocracy and successful militarism. The nearest approximation to this was Alexander II's Russo-Turkish War (1877–8), the success of which was a factor in enticing Nicholas into further expansionism, although this time eastwards against China.

Overall, Nicholas II was a flawed combination of his two predecessors. He had Alexander III's dislike of progressive change but without the latter's strength of character. Or, to put it the other way round, he was as indecisive as Alexander II without the flexibility to introduce reform. This was not a promising combination, given the ever-increasing complexity of circumstances Nicholas II had to face during his reign.

Nicholas II and the crisis of Tsarist Russia 1894–1917

4. **Compare the political and economic policies of the first part of Nicholas II's reign (1894–1904). What impact did they have on each other?** **(90 marks)**

The period started with the accession of Nicholas II and ended with the outbreak of the Russo-Japanese War, which completely changed the reign's momentum. These ten years saw two very different types of momentum. One was political continuity, even inertia. The other was rapid economic change, leading to industrial transformation. They were bound to affect each other.

The political structure of Russia barely changed between 1894 and 1904, following the reactionary policies of Alexander III. The main influence behind autocracy was Pobedonostsev, Procurator-General of the Holy Synod between 1880 and 1905, who had tutored both Alexander and Nicholas. Pobedonostsev had consistently maintained that 'The secret of order lies at the top, in the supreme authority of the tsar.'[2] Nicholas II remained totally committed to this line. Hence there was no attempt to introduce a central legislature and Alexander III's restrictions on the local zemstva remained fully in force. This was very much in contrast with the development of economic growth, with its emphasis on acceleration and change.

In one respect, economic developments mirrored the political. There was also continuity in Russian agriculture where, again, official policy was to avoid change and to maintain the system of redemption payments made by the peasantry, along with the repartitional and **hereditary land tenures**. The result, as in government, was stagnation and a failure to address the growing pressure for change from revolutionary movements like the Populists.

On the other hand, the main economic development of the early part of the reign was in clear contrast to the lack of political momentum. During the 1890s Russia went through a rapid expansion of industries and communications, directed largely by Sergei Witte, Minister of Finance between 1893 and 1903. Here was an example of government policy aiming explicitly at change rather than continuity, at reform rather than reaction. The role of the state was to force the pace of economic growth through official sponsorship, the capital being derived from loans abroad (especially from France) and from taxation at home. Protective tariffs would regulate imports, while placing the rouble on the gold standard would ensure Russia's stability in the international markets. The key to industrialisation was the development of the iron and steel industries in the Urals: production of iron increased from 0.89 million tons in 1890 to 2.66 million by 1900. Also of vital importance was the increase in the railway mileage from 32,000 kilometres in 1891 to 53,000 by 1900, giving Russia the second largest rail network in the world.

Political autocracy and industrial expansion may, at first, appear to have been working in opposition to each other. In actual fact, they exercised a considerable influence on each other. In the first place, a stagnating autocracy helped shape the type of industrial change which took place. Witte's reforms were impeded by the underlying state control of the process, which meant that the roots of industrial growth were shallow. No large entrepreneurial class developed, in contrast to Britain, Germany and the United States. This meant that capital was hard to come by, which increased Russia's dependence on foreign loans; this, in turn, increased Russia's vulnerability to the type of recession which hit it in 1900. It might even be argued that industrialisation was shaped by autocracy as a means of preserving autocracy and that economic growth was accelerated to secure the political status quo.

At the same time, industrialisation helped shape the political responses of autocracy, especially in tsarist foreign policy at the turn of the century. In other circumstances industrialisation might have been a liberalising agent, acting as a catalyst for political modernisation and the inclusion of the middle classes in the governing system as had happened elsewhere in Europe. But it was not. Instead, industrialisation confirmed the Tsar's belief that autocracy had been strengthened to the point where it could seek an outlet in a more expansionist and assertive foreign policy. This was particularly apparent in the Far East, where Russian ambitions in the Liaotung Peninsula and Korea clashed with those of Japan and resulted in the outbreak of war in 1904. Russia's eventual defeat in 1905 came as a major blow to tsarism precisely because it was so unexpected. Industrialisation had meant to strengthen autocracy through external victory.

What actually happened was that the misuse of industrialisation in war did more than anything else to shake the foundations of autocracy in the Revolution of 1905. And this revolution was organised by sectors of society which had increased in size and concentration because of the industrialisation of the previous decade. Thus, for all the intended overlap between the two, the changes brought by industrialisation were bound to upset the uncertain equilibrium which autocracy had to try to maintain.

5. **'In 1904 Russia's growing interests in the Far East involved her in a war with Japan which resulted in unexpected defeat.'**

    a) **What is meant by 'Russia's growing interests in the Far East'?** **(3 marks)**

Russia's growing interest was partly the result of industrialisation in the 1890s. Witte saw the trans-Siberian railway as replacing the Suez Canal as Europe's link with the Orient which Russia now aimed to dominate. Two areas were particularly important. One was Manchuria, through which the last stretch the trans-Siberian railway would run towards Vladivostok and Port Arthur. The other was Korea, which would be dangerous for Russian strategic security should it ever fall into Japanese hands.

b)   Explain why war broke out between Russia and Japan in 1904.   (7 marks)

Russia's war with Japan (1904–5) followed a steady deterioration in relations between the two countries over their claims in China and Korea. Military conflict was the result of provocative Russian diplomacy and a Japanese military system which allowed itself to be provoked.

Unfortunately for Russia, there were two strategies for Russian penetration. One, advanced by Witte, was economic expansion, pursued by diplomatic agreement with China. The other, which eventually prevailed, was based on the views of Berobrazov and Plehve that territory should be acquired and economic penetration be reinforced by military action. By 1903 Witte had been dismissed and the Plehve approach was favoured by the Tsar. This was bound to increase the chances of conflict, especially when associated with Russian diplomacy. Over the previous decade the Japanese government had been willing to recognise Russian interests in return for a similar recognition of a Japanese sphere of influence. Russia's response was inflexible. In 1895, for example, Russia had joined a combination of powers to remove some of the territorial gains made by Japan in the war with China (1894–5): the humiliation was rubbed in when, in 1898, Russia secured its own 25-year lease on one of these territories – the Liaotung Peninsula. Although infuriated, Japan offered a compromise on two occasions, in 1898 and 1903: Russia should recognise Japanese interests in Korea in return for Japan agreeing to Russian predominance over the whole of Manchuria. On each occasion Russia presented major obstacles.

Domestic factors were involved in all this. It has been argued that the Tsar fell under the influence of advisers who sought to strengthen autocracy by using industrialisation to pursue victory in a successful war. This would be an outlet for internal pressures and would help to develop a new patriotism. Plehve is believed to have remarked that Russia needed 'a little war to stem the revolutionary tide'[3] It is quite likely that the government was pursuing a course in the certain knowledge that war would result – and in the expectation that this war would be easily won. The reward of victory would, in turn, be a strengthened regime.

In actual fact, the initiative was taken by the Japanese who abandoned diplomacy for the pre-emptive strike preferred by the military. Thus war actually broke out with the totally unexpected destruction of the Russian Far Eastern fleet in Port Arthur.

c)   'Russia was defeated by Japan in 1905 because of the poor state of its preparations for the war.' Explain why you agree or disagree with this statement.   (15 marks)

Russian defeat was a complete surprise to the tsarist regime, which had expected to crush Japanese forces in the Far East and end Japan's presence on the mainland. The nature and speed of the defeat showed that Russia's expectations had been built on a series of inadequate preparations and faulty judgements based on them.

The Tsar's government had been repeatedly warned from 1903 onwards about impending war but had refused to take these seriously. In any case, Russian attitudes to Japan were contemptuous and comparisons were made with '*makaki*' (little apes). The most obvious contrast was in the readiness of transport and communications. The war started before the completion of the trans-Siberian railway link, including a gap round Lake Baikal, which meant that supplies had to be transported across the Lake throughout 1904 and 1905. The rest of the line was single-track only, which inevitably slowed down the transportation of supplies and men. For this reason, the Russian commander, Kuropatkin, had urged the postponement of hostilities on the grounds that it would take four months to concentrate sufficient numbers of troops in the Far East and sixteen months to complete the entire railway network. In complete contrast, Japan's immediate proximity to the war zone meant that troops could be landed troops in Korea within 24 hours of their embarkation in Japanese ports.

Russian strategy and weaponry were also behind those of the Japanese. Again, there was a major clash over Russian intentions. Kuropatkin preferred delaying action and strategic withdrawal to allow Russian forces to be built up sufficiently to ensure eventual victory. Alekseev, by contrast, wanted to maintain all lines of communication with Port Arthur and put his faith in the Russian fleet, being despatched from the Baltic, to inflict early defeat on the Japanese. The result was delay, confusion and serious Russian defeats on the Yalu and at Mukden. The Japanese commander, Oyama, was much more decisive, planning and executing a pincer movement. This was devastatingly successful at Mukden, costing the Russians 90,000 casualties and prisoners out of a total force of 310,000 troops.

An even greater contrast developed in terms of naval strength. In terms of numbers, the navies were more or less evenly balanced in 1904. But Russia's Far Eastern bases were 900 miles apart – at Port Arthur, where facilities had still to be completed, and at Vladivostok, where the sea was frozen in the winter. The Russians lost the initiative with Japan's surprise attack on their fleet in Port Arthur – and never regained it. This meant that the Japanese could use their own ports with impunity and build up their military presence on the mainland. Russia's only answer was to despatch the Baltic fleet to Japan. But this took eight months to arrive and was promptly ambushed and destroyed by Admiral Togo in the Straits of Tsushima. It became clear during the battle that older design, thinner hulls and lighter armament meant that the Russian warships were no match for the Japanese fleet, based as it was on the latest naval technology from Britain and Germany. The significance of the engagement was such that it was immediately known as the 'Trafalgar of the East'.

Finally, the Russian regime had no option but to withdraw from the war at the earliest opportunity, thus giving up its only remaining card of wearing Japan down through attrition. The reason was a particularly close connection between external and internal events in 1904 and 1905: war led to the outbreak of revolution and revolution contributed to military defeat. Troops were required to save the tsarist regime, which meant that there was a real sense of urgency in the signing the Treaty of Portsmouth in 1905. Thus, uniquely in Russian history, Russia agreed to terms even though no enemy troops had entered its mainland territory.

6. Examine the effects of the Russo-Japanese War   (90 marks)

The impact of the Russo-Japanese war was mixed, producing a combination of results. In terms of territorial loss, it was actually quite limited. By the Treaty of Portsmouth, Russia ceded to Japan the lease on the Liaotung Peninsula, together with Port Arthur and Dalny and the section of the Manchurian railway which served it. Russian troops were pulled out of Manchuria, which was returned fully to Chinese sovereignty, while Korea was to come within the Japanese sphere of influence. The only territory actually belonging to Russia which was handed over to Japan was the southern half of the island of Sakhalin. Compared with the losses which Russia incurred in other wars, these were mild indeed.

an essential means of ending the redemption payments and changing the system of land tenure. Where there were mutinies, as on board the *Potemkin*, representation and democracy suddenly became the key inspirational concepts. All this meant that there could be co-operation between the lower levels of society and the professional sectors of the middle classes or the more progressive members of the nobility. It was the variety of classes represented which entitles this to be called a 'revolution' rather than a more limited 'coup' or '**putsch**'.

c) **'The 1905 Revolution failed because the tsarist regime knew how to save itself.' Explain why you agree or disagree with this statement.** **(15 marks)**

This statement is true to the extent that the tsarist regime made the necessary concessions to save itself from collapse. It would, however, be going too far to suggest that it remained in full control of its response throughout the crisis. Many of its actions were the result of desperation rather than forethought; the fact that they succeeded was in part due to luck.

The revolution certainly fell apart piece by piece; it is arguable that it was unpicked as the Tsar resorted to a series of hasty but effective measures carried out on Witte's advice. First, he saved the army from disintegration by agreeing in September 1905 to the Treaty of Portsmouth with Japan. Military disruption was therefore partial, and mutinies tended to be isolated to specific areas like Tashkent and Odessa. There were at this stage few examples of troops deserting to demonstrators and strikers and there was sufficient military discipline to overcome the soviet in St Petersburg and break through the barricades in Moscow. The following month he conceded the October Manifesto. This persuaded the liberals to pull out of the revolution, won over by the promise of a representative assembly; this seemed to them preferable to continuing the struggle for a different type of regime altogether. Their withdrawal was, of course a crucial factor in weakening the rest of the revolutionary impetus. The peasantry followed in November, pacified by the government's announcement that their redemption payments would be cancelled. This meant an end to the violence in the provinces, organised by the Socialist Revolutionaries, and allowed troops to be targeted more precisely at the remaining centres of trouble, especially in Moscow and St Petersburg. The headquarters of the St Petersburg Soviet was stormed by troops in December and Trotsky was arrested. Moscow experienced greater violence and bloodshed before the barricades were finally pulled apart.

Of course, the regime was able to take these measures because it still had choices which could be made. It had the option of signing an armistice with Japan before experiencing invasion and further disruption. Then, with the military infrastructure still intact, it could make concessions to two social classes in order to isolate the third. A more extreme scenario was to occur between 1916 and 1917 when such options no longer existed because of the more drastic nature of military defeat.

8. **Assess the reasons for the failure of the Russian constitutional experiment between 1906 and 1917.** **(90 marks)**

Three factors were particularly important in the failure to make effective use of Russia's new constitution. These were the obstructive policy of the Tsar, the frustration of the members of the Duma and the effect of military defeat. These were interrelated and had a direct impact on each other.

Figure 3.2 **Russian political parties from 1906**

Radical left	Moderate left	Moderate right	Reactionary right
Social Democrats	Constitutional Democrats	Octobrists	Union of Russian Men
Socialist Revolutionaries			Union of Russian People

The attitude of Nicholas II was crucial in determining whether the experiment would succeed or fail. It soon became evident that the October Manifesto, which guaranteed the population 'inviolable foundations of civic freedom', had been granted under pressure and was really a tactic designed to neutralise the revolutionaries of 1905. The Fundamental Laws of 1906, which were supposed to give effect to the October Manifesto, actually ended up undermining the concessions through the reassertion of the Tsar's authority. Hence, although a new legislature was established in the form of the Imperial Council and the State Duma, the Tsar retained the power to approve or veto laws, to declare war and make peace, and to issue decrees. He also appointed half of the Council of Ministers, over which the Duma had no direct influence. It was clear from the outset that the Tsar was determined to make full use of the 'supreme autocratic power', emphasised in Article 4 of the Fundamental Laws. It was on the initiative of the Tsar and Stolypin that, for example, the first Duma was dissolved prematurely in 1906 and the second in 1907 – both for questioning government policy. A new electoral law in 1907 substantially altered the composition of the third and fourth Dumas (1907–12 and 1912–17). In effect, Nicholas II was attempting to snatch back concessions which he felt had been extorted from him as a result of one revolution, without realising that this attitude was helping to prepare the way for another.

This led to the second reason, the alienation of all those participants who might just possibly have saved the experiment. In theory the new constitution was based on a multi-party system, comprising the Socialist Revolutionaries, Social Democrats, Constitutional Democrats (Cadets), Monarchists and the Union of Russian People. Given that substantial parts of the more radical parties were not sympathetic to the aims of constitutionalism, any meaningful role for the Duma would depend on close co-operation with the moderates. This did not happen. By closing the first and second Dumas in 1906 and 1907 the Tsar alienated the left-wing Mensheviks as well as the moderate Cadets, while the Octobrists became sufficiently disillusioned to join the Progressive Bloc in the Duma from 1915 onwards. Virtually the whole Duma united in its condemnation of the Tsar's refusal to allow it to meet at the height of the crisis of February/March 1917. By this stage the Tsar had very little personal support or allegiance left, even from the upper levels of the social hierarchy. This alienation was the key factor in his abdication – which the Duma demanded. But would this have occurred without the long record of tsarist obstruction?

Or would it have occurred without the untimely intervention of the First World War? This determined the outcome of the conflict between the Tsar and the Duma by placing the entire political system under intolerable pressure through the threat of military defeat. Conversely, victory could well have reprieved autocracy and further undermined the Duma. The turning point was probably the switch in the role of the Tsar from head of government to commander-in-chief of the armed forces in 1915. This created a political vacuum in Petrograd, which was filled by Alexandra, herself under the influence of Rasputin. The result was that autocracy became increasingly capricious, interfering with the functioning of government ministries and alienating the bureaucracy as well as the Duma. Any sign of ministerial stability collapsed, with a rapid succession of premiers between 1915 and 1917. All this added urgency to the Duma's criticism of the conduct of government so that, by the end of 1916, normally cautious politicians like Rodzianko, Miliukov and Guchkov were prepared to take part in a conspiracy to unseat the Tsar. The result was the preparation of papers of abdication which were signed on a train at Pskov on 15 March 1917.

The failure of constitutional monarchy was therefore predictable, given the monarch's reluctance to be constitutional. This was bound to provoke those who were genuinely interested in giving the Duma a meaningful role – and it was the Duma which effectively ended the experiment in March 1917. These two factors were interlinked, although the second would have been unlikely without the first. The third factor, the impact of war from 1915, acted as a catalyst for the other two. Victory would have enabled the Tsar to override the Duma, while defeat forced the Duma into removing the Tsar.

9.   Would you agree that 'The tsarist regime had by 1914 made rapid progress with economic and social reform, thereby making itself secure'?   (90 marks)

Before 1914 Russia experienced a period of rapid change, largely introduced from above. In economic terms this meant that Russia was catching up with the rest of Europe, while socially it was beginning to address some of the problems experienced by the workers in the towns and the peasants in the countryside. This much needs to be acknowledged. On the other hand, the whole process was too deeply flawed to guarantee the security of the tsarist regime. If anything, raising expectations and then failing to fulfil them, made revolution more, not less, likely.

That economic development was rapid is undeniable and there is plenty of evidence that Russia was narrowing the gap with the Western powers by 1914. The whole process had been given a boost by Witte's policies during the 1890s, and, following a period of recession between 1900 and 1905, Russia experienced a second boom from 1906 to 1913, which produced an annual growth rate of 6 per cent. This fed through to an increase in foreign trade and to the wider availability of capital. There was also a further acceleration in industrialisation. Coal production, for example, increased from 16.1 million tons in 1900 to 35.4 million by 1913, and iron from 0.42 million tons to 4.12 over the same period. Overall, industrial output grew in index terms from 100 in 1900 to 163.3 by 1913. This was the fastest rate of growth in Europe. The fact that Russia had industrialised later than other European powers was actually an advantage in that it could learn from the mistakes of others and adapt already modern technology to its own use.

Yet there were shortcomings within this process which made the regime vulnerable to destabilising pressures. The main initiative came from the government, which meant that Russia produced a smaller entrepreneurial class than elsewhere: this made industrial growth difficult to sustain. Another result was that there was extensive bureaucratic interference. The Congress of the Representatives of Industry and Trade, set up in 1906, applied pressure for more say in the decisions of the Department of Finance. Finally, there was never any possibility of industrialisation leading to political liberalism and, in turn, to economic **laissez-faire** and competition (the normal pattern in other industrial states). Reinstituting autocracy seemed at the time a safer and more logical device. But this was, of course, a dreadful fallacy. Within the rigid constraints imposed by an autocratic regime, intensive industrialisation acted as a political time bomb.

It has been said that the regime made real progress in dealing with the social problems of the working classes. There are several examples of real progress, from the increase in factory legislation to measures allowing basic trade union rights in 1906. Between 1900 and 1913 expenditure on state education quadrupled, while health insurance was introduced in 1912. These may not have been spectacular reforms, but at least they took the edge off discontent and, given a longer period of peace, might well have worked. The expanding economy enhanced living standards and promoted consumerism. There was, between 1905 and 1914, simply too much to lose from revolutionary activism. There are, however, several problems with this approach. The most direct indicator for assessing the standard of living of the urban working class is distinctly unfavourable. While the rate of inflation rose by 40 per cent from 1908 to 1914, wages increased by less than 0.3 per cent, a substantial decline in real wages. In these conditions it is hardly surprising that the number of strikes increased from 222 in 1910 to 2,032 in 1912 and, despite the outbreak of war in August, to 3,574 in 1914.

The regime's changes involving the peasantry have also been seen in a positive light. In the period after the 1905 Revolution, Stolypin introduced a series of reforms aimed at improving the efficiency and status of the peasantry. Between 1906 and 1910, his Peasant Land Bank encouraged the purchase of land to create a peasant elite which would act as a stabilising force for the rest. At the same time, his changes to land tenure and the abolition of redemption repayments cleared away some of the obstacles to consolidating units for more effective farming. The whole basis of the argument is that Stolypin's reforms, although flawed, were improving the system and may have worked in time. Because of the sudden upheaval of 1914, however, they were not given a proper chance.

This line of argument has, however, been strongly questioned. Gatrell, for example, maintains that improvements in farming methods were already taking place in the 1890s, resulting in greatly improved harvests for which peasant cultivators were largely responsible. Furthermore, the position of the peasantry was actually improving before the reforms of Stolypin and the commune system was not as much of an obstacle to progress in agriculture as was once believed. Even Stolypin's attempts to create a strong sector within the peasantry were overstated, since such a sector already existed. The revisionist conclusion is therefore that Stolypin's reforms were far less significant than was previously believed. Indeed, they merely went with a trend which was already occurring. This had implications for the future. The peasantry had *not* come to accept the concessions of the pre-1914 regime and were becoming more and more assertive. This was partly because the concessions were minimal and partly because expectations were rising rapidly.

There remains a split verdict among historians on the record of the pre-1914 tsarist government. The 'optimists' maintain that the reforms were beginning by 1914 to show benefits and that, given time, they could have ensured the survival of the regime. The 'pessimists', by contrast, argue that the regime was doomed by its inability to adjust to change and that the war merely accelerated its inevitable demise. Although it is impossible to prove or disprove either case, the balance of probability is that the system was moving too slowly to bring about a full recovery from the shock of 1905. There were reforms but progress was too slow to ensure security.

10. Compare the aims and achievements of Witte and Stolypin. (90 marks)

Sergei Witte and Peter Stolypin were the most important of all the ministers of Tsar Nicholas II. Both served in high office, Witte as Minister of Finance (1892–1903) and Stolypin as Prime

Minister (1906–11). In this capacity they directly influenced Russia's economic and political developments, 1905 being the watershed between the two.

Their common aim was to modernise the economic infrastructure of imperial Russia, although they targeted different sectors. As Minister of Finance, Witte hoped to extend Russia's industries, while Stolypin, as Prime Minister, intended to create a more efficient agricultural base. To an extent, their visions were obviously complementary and can be seen as an integrated approach to modernisation. Reform in one sector would be held back without a comparable advance in the other. Stolypin was perhaps more aware of the connection, since he followed on from the initial changes made by Witte.

Yet there was a difference in the method used to achieve modernisation in the two sectors. Witte stressed the need for direct government action through 'state capitalism'. Since, he said, there was 'neither capital nor knowledge nor spirit of enterprise', the whole process would have to be state-driven. He said, in his 1899 Report, that capital had to be advanced by the state, and derived by foreign loans and investments. Stolypin, by contrast, considered that the role of the government should be indirect, creating an environment for the emergence of a new peasant elite. This, according to a report prepared by Stolypin in 1904, would be based on the very spirit of enterprise which Witte found lacking. It would be done through education and self-interest, the result being the natural growth of a capitalist sector, or upper layer of '**kulaks**'. They, in turn, would increase the consumer demand which would sustain industrial growth.

These approaches were bound to affect the timescale involved in the reforms. Witte envisaged a rapid change: 'We cannot wait for the natural accumulation of capital.' He was looking for immediate results in terms of railway infrastructure and heavy industrial production. Stolypin took the longer view. It would take a considerable time for a new peasantry to emerge. Stolypin gave the rather arbitrary – and probably optimistic – figure of 20 years. The process could not be rushed; in any case, it was unlikely that the peasantry would reorganise 'its land habits by order and not by inner conviction'.

The contrasting approaches and timescales influenced the results. With state funding and drive, it is not surprising that industrial growth was more immediate and measurable, seeming to show a rapid increase in production: coal, for example, increased from 5.9 million tons in 1890 to 16.1 million in 1900 and 35.4 million in 1913. The comparable figures for iron were 0.89 million, 2.66 million, and 4.12 million; for oil they were 3.9 million, 10.2 million and 9.1 million. Railway mileage, meanwhile, had increased from 31,219 kilometres in 1891 to 53,234 in 1900 and 70,156 in 1913. In agriculture the main production figures were for grain, which showed an increase from 36 million tons in 1890 to 56 million in 1900 and 90 million in 1913; it is, however, very difficult to equate the rate of growth to the Stolypin reforms since the upward curve preceded them. The main measurable achievement of the Stolypin reforms was the change in land tenure rather than productivity. Out of a total of 12 million peasant households, the number becoming independent gradually declined from 508,344 in 1908 to 342,245 in 1910 and 122,314 in 1912. This raises questions about whether the impetus of change could actually have been maintained for Stolypin's 20-year target period.

Both Witte and Stolypin had a direct involvement in the key political decisions made in Russia, especially between 1905 and 1907. They shared a strong preference for conservatism and both inclined towards maintaining autocracy where possible. At the same time, both recognised the need to be pragmatic when necessary. Both were connected with the constitutional experiment from 1905, although in different ways: Witte helped set it up, while Stolypin tried to control it. Witte advised the Tsar to set up the Duma by the October Manifesto (1905). He had come to realise that the transition to a limited form of constitutional monarchy was essential if the tsarist system was to be saved from overthrow in 1905 and economic modernisation was to continue. Stolypin was involved in the aftermath of the 1905 Revolution and his role was more complex. As governor of Saratov, he had already acquired a reputation for firm anti-revolutionary measures. Like Witte, he could be pragmatic and, for a while, co-operated with the moderate Octobrists in the first Duma; indeed, the Octobrist leader, Guchkov, had 'absolute confidence' in him. Gradually, however, he reverted to his more conservative views and undermined the independence of the Duma, altering its composition by the 1907 electoral laws. From 1906 he also increased the coercive powers of the governors of the provinces, which resulted in the widespread use of courts martial and exemplary executions. Although neither Witte nor Stolypin was a friend to democracy and both strongly opposed radicalism, it was Stolypin who came to be seen as the agent of repression.

In their aim to strengthen and modernise the tsarist system, Witte and Stolypin did, to an extent, pursue complementary roles. There was also a certain logic to their different methods: it is easier to centralise the drive for industrial growth than for agricultural change, as Stalin was to discover after 1929. Yet in the last years of his life, Witte felt that Stolypin was slowing down the impetus he had started, while Stolypin came to see Witte's 'solutions', both economic and political, as his own 'problems'. The Tsar, in the meantime, saw only the contradictions, not the connections. This was, however, entirely in keeping with the regime in its final years.

Revolutionary movements 1855–1917 and the 1917 revolutions

11. 'After decades of influence from radical movements and parties, the Russian people were, by 1914, on the verge of revolution.'

   a) What is meant by 'radical movements and parties'?   **(3 marks)**

By 1914 there were two main radical movements in Russia. One was Populism, representing the interests of the peasantry. The other, Marxism, was more influential in the industrial and urban areas. The Populist groups had united in 1900 to form the Socialist Revolutionaries, while the Marxists had established the Russian Social Democratic Labour Party in 1898; in 1903 the latter separated into Bolsheviks and Mensheviks.

   b) Explain the growth of the main revolutionary movements and parties in Russia between 1870 and 1905.   **(7 marks)**

Two main strands of revolutionary activism developed in Russia. The earlier form was Populism, based largely on indigenous Russian aspirations and influences. There were, however, tactical differences between those who argued for a campaign of persuasion and those who preferred violence and revolution. The latter formed two organisations which were dedicated both to land redistribution and to a campaign of political assassination: they were Land and Liberty (1876) and People's Will (1879), which was directly responsible for the death of Alexander II in 1881. The more moderate variant of Populism set up Black Partition in 1879, which focused on trying to re-educate the peasantry and achieve their objectives by long-term propaganda. By 1900 most

Populist groups had come together to form a more united party in the form of the Socialist Revolutionaries.

The other strand of revolutionary activism was imported from the West, especially from Germany. A series of Marxist groups developed during the 1880s, based on the urban working class which began to expand quickly as a result of the growth of industrialisation in the 1890s. These were given a start by an injection of support from several ex-Populists, such as Axelrod and Plekhanov, who converted to Marxism. By 1898 the various groups, which focused on the cities and the urban proletariat, united to form the Social Democrats. Like the Populists, they also had a moderate and radical wing. Unlike the Socialist Revolutionaries, however, the difference emerged within the Social Democrats after the formation of the united group. Between 1903 and 1905 different strategies emerged on achieving the Marxist programme and on matters of organisation. The Mensheviks pursued a gradualist strategy, while the Bolsheviks aimed at accelerating the revolution. In terms of organisation, the Mensheviks under Martov favoured a broad base and open membership, while the Bolsheviks under Lenin preferred limited membership and conspiratorial measures.

By 1905, therefore, there were three major revolutionary movements, all claiming to represent different forms of socialism. The Socialist Revolutionaries were the traditional populist response to peasant grievances; the Mensheviks hoped for gradual reform to enhance the conditions and political power of the working class; and the Bolsheviks sought to implement Marxist revolution. All three groups were involved in the 1905 Revolution, along with constitutional opposition to the regime, provided by the bourgeoisie.

c) **Would you agree that the Russian people were 'revolutionary' by 1914?**   **(15 marks)**

Being 'revolutionary' depends on two factors. One is the existence of widespread discontent with the status quo. The other is a means of converting discontent into radical change. The potential for both existed in Russia before 1914.

Widespread discontent certainly provided fuel for revolution: this applied across most of the social structure. Most of the peasantry had not come to accept Stolypin's reforms, as was shown by an increasing trend of peasant disturbances and uprisings, especially between 1911 and 1914. This was despite the good harvests between 1909 and 1913. Similarly, the industrial workers had not been won over by factory and trade union legislation, educational reforms, and health insurance. Far from declining between 1906 and 1914, the number of strikes actually increased, especially amongst the metal workers. Most of these strikes were politically motivated and many workers' committees supported Bolshevik deputies, rather than the more moderate socialist parties, whenever they had the chance. It is true that they were unlikely to gain much support from the middle classes, who preferred a peaceful coexistence with the regime. But even the non-revolutionary Cadets and Octobrists were by 1914 becoming impatient with the constant constitutional obstacles being placed by the Tsar in the way of progressive reform. It seems, therefore, that there was a growing revolutionary tide which the post-1905 reforms had been unable to check.

Discontent provides a motive for revolution. But it remains inert unless it is transformed into action by revolutionary movements. There were, it is true, obstacles here. The revolutionary trends of Populism and Marxism competed actively with each other, while the Marxists themselves split in 1903 between Bolsheviks and Mensheviks; both developments probably weakened the impetus of any united protest. And yet the masses remained volatile and a danger to the regime; recent

Figure 3.3 **Russian revolutionary movements**

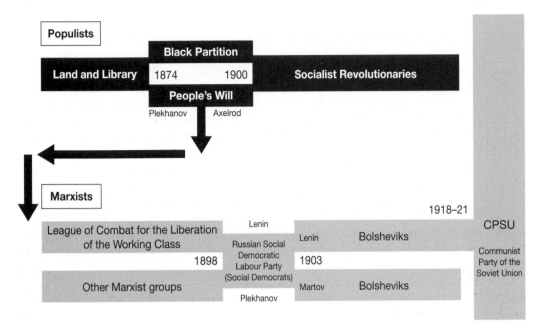

historians have shown that both discontent and radicalism were widespread before the outbreak of war in 1914. Nor did all the influences come from above, from the educated intelligentsia. Equally significant was the rapid growth in the rank and file membership of unions and committees. The ideas of the various movements were heavily influenced by the needs of the grass roots. According to revisionist historians, Lenin's conversion of Marx's basic ideas to the Russian situation was not so much a conscious policy as a response to the pressures exerted by Russian workers. What the intelligentsia did was not to bring the Russian masses to revolutionary activism but, rather, to provide some of the ideas from abroad which gave this activism an outlet. They did not create a revolutionary energy but channelled one which already existed.

Revolutionary feeling was therefore widespread in Russia before 1914 – with or without formal party leadership. Because of its steady growth the tsarist regime faced pressure from two directions. One was the ever-contracting support of its base, which was made increasingly apparent by the failure of the constitutional experiment. The other was its growing dependence on the army, which was destabilised as a result of defeat in the First World War.

12. Assess the reasons for and effects of Russia's defeat on the Eastern Front.

(90 marks)

Russia's failure in the First World War was the result of its strategic disadvantage, inadequate military infrastructure and defective leadership. The impact of defeat was devastating; the war brought down not one – but two – regimes.

From the first year of the war, Russia had to fight three countries simultaneously along a front which was at least four times the length of that in the West. Germany and Austria-Hungary had to be engaged simultaneously, while Turkey placed a stranglehold on supply routes through the Straits which even the British-inspired Gallipoli campaign of 1915 failed to break. This placed Russia at a fundamental disadvantage. Although not in itself decisive, it placed intolerable pressure on Russia's limited military resources and infrastructure.

This was even more important, since Russia was inadequately prepared militarily for such an undertaking. Although Russia had been going through a process of modernisation and rearmament, this had clearly not yet had much influence. The army was poorly supplied, the training of the higher officer corps had been seriously defective and there was a grave lack of co-ordination between the Ministry of War and the Front. The inadequate defences were apparent by 1915: Russian trenches lacked the depth and back-up facilities of those of the British and French, while Russian artillery soon ran desperately short of shells. There was also serious disruption of communications and supply lines; even the railway system, the pride of Russia's new industrial infrastructure, failed to operate effectively because it became clogged up with the huge amounts of fodder needed to supply the Russian armies' horses. It is difficult to see how Russia could have succeeded against three enemies simultaneously without the infrastructural capacity which existed, for example, in the Second World War.

Unless, of course, such disadvantages could be compensated by inspirational leadership. This, however, Russia did not possess in the First World War. Grand Duke Nicholas, Yanushkevich and Danilov, lacked the necessary military experience and expertise, while the Tsar's decision to take command in 1915 made matters even worse. The collapse of the tsarist government in March 1917, followed by the futile decision of the Provisional Government to struggle on with the war, only served to increase popular discontent and to prepare the way for the success of the Bolshevik Revolution in October 1917. They, of course, had most to lose from perpetuating the war – and most to gain by ending it. In March 1918 Lenin and Trotsky ended the struggle with a now irrelevant external enemy in order to focus their attention on impending civil war. Thus the final reason why Russia lost the war is that its new leaders no longer considered it necessary to win it.

Between 1915 and 1918 the First World War acted as a catalyst which brought about the collapse of the tsarist system and of the Provisional Government. Particularly affected were Russia's political institutions, economic viability and military security.

Russia's political institutions were fatally damaged by the military collapse in the early stages of the war. The difficulties really started with Nicholas II's decision in 1915 to lead the Russian army in person. This left a political vacuum in the centre of the administration in Petrograd which was, in turn filled by the more irrational and arbitrary despotism of the Empress Alexandra under the influence of Rasputin. This incurred the bitter opposition of the Duma, which formed a Progressive Bloc from the Constitutional Democrats and Octobrists to agitate for more direct legislative influence over the process of government. The response of the government was to increase the scope of its dictatorship by issuing special decrees under Article 87 of the Fundamental Laws. The bureaucracy, normally a reliable supporter of tsarist government was also alienated by the interference of Rasputin. This increased the resentment of the Duma to the point that it was prepared to become involved in the Revolution of March 1917 and insist on the Tsar's abdication. The Provisional Government fared no better. Because of its determination to win the war, it postponed urgent land reforms and the establishment of a permanent Constituent Assembly. Its loss of political credibility was a key factor in the growing isolation of Kerensky and the success of the Bolsheviks in October 1917.

Political change through revolution was therefore the most spectacular effect of military defeat. But this was hastened by the impact of the war on Russia's economy. This was so widespread that discontent reached the point of spontaneous eruption in March 1917. The problem was started by inappropriate government policies to deal with wartime emergencies and priorities. At a time when the British and German governments were imposing extensive state control, the Russian administration adopted only half measures relying, in effect, on a dual system of both state monopolies and private enterprise. This caused extensive confusion and massive shortages which, in turn, fuelled hyperinflation. Particularly serious was the inadequate supply of raw materials and foodstuffs; this was largely a problem of distribution and reflected badly on the decision, taken before 1914 by the Minister of Transportation, Rukhlov, to slash government expenditure on the railways. The deteriorating standard of living inevitably fuelled popular discontent and was directly responsible for the timing of the Revolution in March 1917. Similar shortages alienated the peasantry and urban workers from the Provisional Government and the moderate socialist parties which had participated in it.

The demonstrations and strikes of 8–13 March would not normally have led to the Tsar's overthrow. He had, after all, experienced worse violence in 1905. The war, however, made a decisive difference. It swelled the numbers of those who were prepared to take to the streets, thus making impossible the task of enforcing law and order. In 1905 the Tsar had owed the survival of his regime to the backing of the army. By 1917, however, this had been severely weakened by a series of defeats by the Germans. In this respect the impact of the First World War was far greater than that of the Russo-Japanese War, which had left the army intact as an anti-revolutionary force. A parallel situation occurred later in 1917 as the disintegration of the army left the Provisional Government helpless in the face of the more highly organised Bolshevik **Red Guard**.

Overall, the main impact was the collapse of two political systems. Economic disruption and military chaos undoubtedly accelerated this process – but it was the change of regime which most affected Russia's future.

13. **'The Revolution of March 1917 arose spontaneously. That is why it replaced the tsarist system with two governments, not one.'**

    a) **What is meant by 'two governments'?**   **(3 marks)**

The two governments established in March 1917 were the Provisional Government and the Petrograd Soviet of Workers' and Soldiers' Deputies. The former started as the Provisional Committee of the Duma, while the latter was elected by those directly involved in the strikes and mass demonstrations.

    b) **What were the main events of the revolution of March 1917?**   **(7 marks)**

Waves of unrest occurred in March 1917, a combination of industrial unrest, popular demonstrations, military mutinies and action from the Duma. When, on 7 March, striking workers were locked out of the Putilov steel works, other factories took strike action in their support. By 8 March, fifty factories had closed in Petrograd and 90,000 workers were on strike. On the same day popular demonstrations were conducted by thousands of socialist women commemorating International Women's Day; there were also bread riots and shops were looted. By 9 March the strikers had increased to 200,000 workers and the streets were full of people hostile to the regime and the entire transport system had been paralysed. When, on 10 March, troops were called to restore order, the Cossacks mutinied and joined the strikers and demonstrators. Similar developments were by now taking place in Moscow and other key cities.

By this time it had become clear to the Duma that the government had lost all control. On 11 March, therefore, the President of the Duma, Rodzianko, sent a telegram to the Tsar urging him to appoint a new government capable of ending the crisis. The Tsar's response was a direct order for the Duma to stop meeting. Events had, however, gone too far for this type of resoluteness – or obstinacy. On 12 March the Volinsky regiment of the army mutinied and the high command feared the total disintegration of army discipline. The Duma's solution was to establish a provisional committee to take over the government, if necessary, at a moment's notice. On the same day, a soviet of workers' and soldiers' deputies was set up by the revolutionaries themselves. Now realising the seriousness of the situation, the Tsar sent a message to the Duma on 13 March announcing that he was ready to share power. It was, however, too late since the army renounced its support for Nicholas. When the latter attempted to return to Petrograd to take control, his train was halted at Pskov and he was presented by representatives of the Duma with his abdication papers: these were dated 15 March.

c) 'The March Revolution was spontaneous, leaderless and Bolshevik-free.' Do you agree with this statement? (15 marks)

By comparison with the October Revolution, the events of March may well seem spontaneous and lacking in central leadership. It is certainly true that the popular strand of the March Revolution contained minimal input from the Bolshevik organisations. Lenin was in Switzerland at the time and there had been no direct evidence of Bolshevik influence behind the waves of strikes which had affected Russia in 1915 and 1916. Nor had the Bolsheviks destroyed the Tsar's armies: most mutinies were spontaneous eruptions organised by troops radicalised by experience and trauma rather than by ideological conviction.

The Bolsheviks had even less to do with the immediate collapse of the tsarist regime. This was far more related to the 'broad opposition' approach than to 'professional conspiracy'. Indeed, it could be said that all the main ingredients of the February/March revolution were Bolshevik-free. The strikes in the Putilov steel works were largely spontaneous, the only significant organised group being the *Mezhraiontsy*, Social Democrats who were neither Bolsheviks nor Mensheviks. These issued proclamations and placards on 23 and 24 February urging strikes and revolt. Even these did no more than contribute to the outbreak of strike action. The hunger marches were more closely related to demonstrations on the occasion of International Women's Day, and the desertion of the Petrograd Garrison was an on-the-spot decision.

What turned these events into a change of regime again had nothing to do with the Bolsheviks. It was due much more to the broadening of opposition through co-operation across classes and parties – exactly the opposite of what the Bolsheviks advocated. The Cadets and Octobrists in the Duma, sensing the inevitability of the collapse of Nicholas II, took steps to form a provisional committee which, in turn, forced the Tsar's abdication. Meanwhile, the Socialist Revolutionaries and Mensheviks were moving in two directions. One was involvement in the Petrograd Soviet alongside the non-party delegates who had set up the soviet in the first place. The other was a broader willingness to establish links between the soviet and the provisional committee.

At this point, leadership and party structures became more important, although not in the tightly conspiratorial sense. Rodzianko became the spokesman for the Cadets and Octobrists in the Duma, Plekhanov for the Mensheviks and Kerensky for the Socialist Revolutionaries. Their aim was to shape the revolution into something more meaningful and permanent. After all, all the components had become interdependent. The Progressive Bloc in the Duma could not have acted against the Tsar without the spontaneous uprising in the streets. The spontaneous uprising would have lacked any structure in the Petrograd Soviet without the involvement of the Mensheviks and Socialist Revolutionaries. And the Socialist Revolutionaries and Mensheviks needed the Duma as a means of establishing a broader-based regime.

The March Revolution was therefore spontaneous in its origin but was gradually pulled into line with objectives of the different organisations affected by it. In the absence of Bolshevik conspiracy, these groups at first found that they had much in common and could at first think in terms of co-operation between the two new institutions they had established. By this stage, however, spontaneity was giving way to organised leadership under Lvov, Miliukov, Chernov and Kerensky.

14. Assess the achievements and weaknesses of the Provisional Government between March and October 1917. (90 marks)

The boundary between success and failure is often very narrow. This is particularly the case with the achievements of the Provisional Government, which ruled Russia between February/March and October/November 1917.

Its initial achievements were considerable, showing strong promise for the future. It rescued Russia from the spontaneous chaos of the March Revolution and provided a moderate constitutional structure for the future. The Programme of the Provisional Government, drawn up on 3 March 1917, implemented the types of reform which had been envisaged by the Progressive Bloc during the last years of the tsarist regime. Literally overnight Russia became one of Europe's more democratic regimes, with guarantees for freedom of the press, association and movement, and promises of land reform. Yet behind all this there was a fatal flaw. The Provisional Government postponed until the 'successful conclusion of the war' any permanent constitution. This, in turn, would have to be ratified by a Constituent Assembly, the election to which was also deferred. As it turned out, his was a fatal error since Lvov, Miliukov and Kerensky were tying together reform and victory. Military failure therefore ended the prospect of reform and increased the chances of political collapse.

Despite this, it could be argued that another achievement was survival until October 1917. At several stages in the months following March, Russia could have lapsed into chaos or dictatorship. Instead, Prince Lvov showed the way to a liberal and constitutional democracy until July while, from that stage onwards, Kerensky tamed the Socialist Revolutionaries (no mean achievement considering their inclination to terrorism in the past) and showed a willingness to co-operate with the Mensheviks. With the single exception of the Bolsheviks, therefore, the Provisional Government had within it all political backgrounds and viewpoints. In the early days, it was even able to collaborate with the Petrograd Soviet on some areas of policy. Other revolutions have descended much more quickly into terror and dictatorship. But ultimately the Provisional Government did collapse, which meant that its weaknesses must have been more marked than its achievements. Four of these were particularly important.

One was the inability of the Provisional Government to secure the long-term loyalty of the Petrograd Soviet. The result was a dual power base between March and October 1917; Russia was, in effect, ruled by two separate institutions, each reflecting a different tradition of opposition to the Tsar. Early attempts at co-operation between the two institutions fell apart and even Kerensky, a member of both, could not hold the Provisional Government and the Soviet on the same course. They disagreed on fundamental issues. The Provisional Government gave absolute priority to fighting a war which the Soviet opposed. From this sprang other conflicts. The Provisional Government decided to postpone any elections for a constituent assembly until after the conclusion of the war. This deprived it of any permanent legitimacy and enabled the Soviet to claim that it was the real representative of the people's wishes. Similarly, the Provisional Government was in favour of postponing the reallocation of the nobles' land to the peasantry, while the Soviet preferred to do this immediately. Despite the promise of advanced constitutional change, there was no social or economic equivalent.

The second weakness was the internal dissension within the Provisional Government itself. Although the Provisional Government did broaden in July into a coalition, the political base quickly contracted from August onwards as the Cadets and Octobrists pulled out in the wake of the Kornilov revolt. This did not by itself cause the collapse of the Provisional Government, since Kerensky remained in power. He was, however, isolated and vulnerable, presiding over a mere rump separated by an ever widening gap from the Soviet. The end of the coalition governments served to strengthen the support for the Soviet, the confidence of which grew as the power of the Provisional Government contracted.

The third weakness amounted to an error of judgement on the part of Kerensky. During the Kornilov revolt he issued arms to the Bolsheviks to try to resist the threat of right-wing military dictatorship. In the process, however, he was actually providing the means whereby power could, in the longer term, be seized by the radical left. The Bolsheviks retained their weapons and rapidly gained a majority within the Soviet, which Lenin and Trotsky used to front the October Revolution. Without the parallel weakening of the Provisional Government and strengthening of the Soviet it is unlikely that Kerensky would even have needed to call for Bolshevik assistance. As it was, his decision provided to be the point at which vulnerability deteriorated into collapse.

Underlying all of these developments was Russian military performance in the First World War, the fourth and arguably greatest problem of the Provisional Government. Just as it had been the catalyst for the collapse of the old system of tsarism, it also made it impossible for the new democratic system to find its feet. The Provisional Government's determination to achieve victory was unrealistic and a distraction from the more immediate task of reform. It also widened the gap between itself and the Soviet, providing the opportunity for the Bolsheviks to infiltrate the latter. As a microcosm of society, the army was also destabilised by military defeat. The result was the threat of right-wing revolt from the leadership and of left-wing desertion and subversion by the rank and file.

The special circumstances of 1917 therefore meant that the constitutional phase of the Revolution, with all its considerable potential for the future, gave way to radical alternatives. Unable to deliver its promises because of its overriding commitment to the war, it lost support to the Soviet, fell apart internally and, in an act of desperation, armed the conspirators who were eventually to replace it.

15. Assess any three reasons for the success of the Bolshevik Revolution in October 1917. (90 marks)

The Bolshevik Revolution of October 1917 was successful for interrelated reasons, each of which depended on the other two. The first was the organisation of the party under the leadership of

Figure 3.4
The Bolshevik Revolution, October 1917

Lenin and Trotsky; the second was the popularity of the Bolsheviks with the population at large; and the third was the weakness of the alternatives to Bolshevik rule.

The organisational strength of the Bolsheviks has long been seen as a crucial factor in their success in October/November 1917. Ever since the 1903 split with the Mensheviks, Lenin had emphasised the importance of absolute control by the Party Central Committee, which should consist of professional revolutionaries. In October 1917 this organisation was able to move quickly into action from its headquarters in the Smolny Institute. At the same time, the party was able to adapt its structure so that it could be seen to be acting in the name of the Petrograd and Moscow Soviets. Lenin realised the importance of legitimising the Bolshevik conspiracy when he said on 22 October: 'If we seize power today, we seize it not against the soviets but for them'. Effective organisation had to be accompanied by a clear overall strategy. The Bolsheviks tended to combine a fixed long-term objective with a flexible short-term approach to it. The long-term aim was ideological. Lenin's *April Theses* described it as the 'transition from the first stage of the revolution, which gave power to the bourgeoisie . . . to the second stage, which should give the power into the hands of the proletariat'. The short-term approach was pragmatic and would involve the right degree of force at the right time. Lenin had been reluctant to endorse the attempted July coup but, by early October, he judged the situation to be right for immediate action. He calculated that circumstances had changed sufficiently to warrant immediate action. He therefore urged: 'We must not wait! We may lose everything!' From this point the organisational and tactical initiative passed to Trotsky who used the Revolutionary Military Committee of the Petrograd Soviet to take over the key installations in the capital.

The second factor was the extent of popular support for the Bolsheviks. It was once thought by historians that the Bolsheviks had seized power in a coup which was not necessarily approved by the population. More recent views have, however, emphasised that the Bolsheviks were very much in tune with the aspirations of the people and that they were actually revising their policies and programme to meet them. Organisation was therefore combined with consent. There were three

Figure 3.5 **Lenin and Trotsky**

particularly influential groups, to which the Bolsheviks adapted their programme. One, previously much underestimated, was the peasantry, who agitated openly for the possession of land previously belonging to the aristocracy. They made their point through several rural uprisings in 1917 and the Bolsheviks took advantage of the failure of the Provisional Government to do anything positive by promising the immediate transfer of land to the peasantry. Lenin was also more in tune with the needs of the urban workforce, especially the skilled workers who dominated the local soviets and factory committees. The army, too, had pro-Bolshevik elements who demanded the democratisation of the command and an early end to the war.

Finally, the Bolsheviks succeeded because of the weakness of the various alternatives. This was cumulative: the Bolsheviks strengthened their organisation and increased their support as the other possibilities began to fade. The Provisional Government, for example, began to struggle from July onwards in the face of a deteriorating military situation, the Kornilov revolt and the defection of the liberal ministers from Kerensky's coalition. This was the very period that the Bolsheviks were increasing the base of their support, especially in the Petrograd Soviet, in which they secured a majority in October. By the time that the Bolsheviks were ready, through their organisation, to seize power, the Provisional Government had lost all ability to defend itself. This explains why the transfer of power was effected overnight, with remarkably few casualties involved. Outside the Provisional Government, the Socialist Revolutionaries, normally much more popular than the Bolsheviks, had not prepared themselves as an alternative regime; this gave the Bolsheviks a clear field.

Secure in their organisation and confident in their support, the Bolsheviks could therefore focus on one enemy – one which had become so weak that the October Revolution could be seen as a coup, and the coup as a *coup de grace.*

Additional essay questions (with advice)

Each of these questions can be tackled as a single essay or as one of the answers to a question in several parts. Additional reading and research is desirable for each one.

16. 'Alexander II was no less autocratic than Alexander III.' How far do you agree with this view?

Advice: Avoid writing the first half of the essay on Alexander II and the second half on Alexander III. Establish criteria and make direct comparisons. You could, for example, consider the term 'autocratic' in two ways: (1) as a basic system of government and (2) as a barrier to reform. The overall argument might be (1) that autocracy was very similar as a style of government but (2) that Alexander II used it in a more progressive way than Alexander III.

17. Explain why Alexander III and Nicholas II were convinced that autocracy was the best form of rule for Russia.

Advice: *As for Question 16, avoid a straight split for the two reigns. Establish criteria which cover both rulers. These might be: (1) tradition plus the influence of Pobedonostsev; (2) the growth of revolutionary movements; and (3) the experience of Alexander II.*

18. To what extent were the outbreak and the outcome of the 1905 Revolution linked to the Russo-Japanese War?

Advice: *'To what extent' needs to be quantified (i.e. 'partly' or 'largely' rather than 'entirely' or 'not at all'). 'Outbreak' and 'outcome' also need full coverage. Ask yourself: (1) was the outbreak of revolution due more to war than to the growth of revolutionary movements over a period of time?; and (2) was the collapse of the revolution due more to the survival of the regime, despite its defeat, than to the problems of the revolutionaries?*

19. How secure was the tsarist regime by 1914?

Advice: *Consider this question using criteria, which might be: (1) was the regime strengthening itself through reform after the experience of 1905?; and (2) were the revolutionaries growing stronger after their experience of 1905? Consider the two main possibilities that (1) collapse was inevitable (the 'pessimist' approach); and (2) survival was possible (the 'optimist' view). Come to a definite conclusion.*

20. Why did the First World War have such an impact on Tsarist Russia?

Advice: *Be careful. This is not a straight question on 'what the impact was'. Instead you need to consider: (1) how Russia was already vulnerable; and (2) how the war made this worse. Consider this, using criteria such as 'political', 'economic' and 'social'.*

21. Explain why there were two revolutions in 1917.

Advice: *At all costs avoid a straight description of the March Revolution and then the October Revolution. Instead, focus on 'why' there were 'two revolutions'. Establish criteria which can be applied to both. For example: (1) the war destabilised both regimes; (2) this made them both vulnerable to revolutionary movements because both failed to deal with growing dissatisfaction; and (3) different revolutionary groups were involved in the two revolutions.*

Essay plan

Para 1: Overall approach. The First World War destabilised first one regime, then the other. This made each regime vulnerable to revolutionary movements. These movements were different – resulting in two separate revolutions.

Para 2: The war was the common factor in destabilising both regimes.
- *It was the catalyst for the collapse of the tsarist military, political and economic systems (supporting detail).*
- *It destabilised the Provisional Government by pushing all of its proposed reforms into the background (supporting detail).*

Para 3: In each case it provided the opportunity for the emergence of an alternative regime.
- *The March Revolution was a combination of spontaneous action and pressure on the Tsar from the Duma (supporting detail).*
- *The October Revolution was carried out by the Bolsheviks who appealed to the population, via the April Theses, on the basis of the unkept promises of a preoccupied Provisional Government (supporting detail).*

Para 4: The revolutions were sufficiently different to be considered two rather than one in two stages.
- *The March Revolution was more moderate – a reaction to the crisis of the tsarist system from all parts of the population (supporting detail). It therefore reflected a variety of previous influences: Socialist Revolutionary, Menshevik, constitutionalist, etc. (details).*
- *The October Revolution was more specifically a radical Marxist phase, the purpose and organisation of which were more directly influenced by its leadership – Lenin and Trotsky (supporting detail).*

Para 5: Completing the connections. The year 1917 saw three regimes and two revolutions.
- *The Bolsheviks had been unable to bring down the tsarist system, which was more vulnerable to the widespread opposition shown in March.*
- *But the Bolsheviks were more effective in overthrowing the divided system which replaced tsarism.*

Part 3: Sources

1. Russia before the First World War, 1870–1914

This exercise consists of three questions on three sources, with a time allocation of 45 minutes.

Source A: A socialist cartoon, produced in 1900, showing the social classes in Russia (see facing page)

Figure 3.6 **Social classes in Russia, 1900 (Source A)**

Source B: M. Lynch, Reaction and Revolutions: Russia, 1881–1924 (1992)

It is a remarkable feature of the 1905 Revolution how minor a role was played by the revolutionaries. Hardly any of them were in St Petersburg or Moscow when it began. Revolution occurred in spite, rather than because of them. With the exception of Trotsky, none of the SDs made an appreciable impact on the course of events. This has led many historians to doubt whether the events of 1905 merit being called a revolution. They further point to the fact that in a number of important respects tsardom emerged from the disturbances stronger rather than weaker. In spite of its disastrous failure to win the war against Japan, which occasioned massive protest throughout Russia and united the classes in opposition, the tsarist regime survived 1905 relatively unscathed.

Source C: E. Acton, *Russia: The Tsarist and Soviet Legacy* (second edition 1995)

The drama of 1905 left a profound imprint upon Russian public life. Both leaders and rank and file at all levels of society – nobility, middle class, workers, and even some peasants – had taken part in open political struggle. They had established new institutions, new parties, soviets, and unions. Radicals and conservatives alike had become politically mobilized. The process had been crowned by the Tsar's undertaking to set up a State Duma, a permanent forum for public participation in the affairs of government. Yet the moment this promise was made, the polarized structure of society was fully exposed. Deep social divisions, briefly overshadowed by the chorus of demands for constitutional reform, came to the fore. On the Left, the effect in political terms was fragmentation. Among the more militant workers, the sense of defeat at the end of the year gave rise to bitter disillusionment with what was seen as betrayal by liberal leaders and professional groups. Fresh credence was given to the class analyses of socialist activists and their warnings that workers must keep 'the bourgeoisie' at arm's length.

QUESTIONS WITH WORKED ANSWERS

a) **Study Source A and use your own knowledge. Explain briefly what point is being made by the cartoonist.** (3 marks)

The cartoonist depicts the rigid hierarchical structure of Russian society, set on tiers of privilege and authority. The apex is the **Romanov** eagle, symbolising tsarist autocracy, perched on the current ruler, Nicolas II and his consort Alexandra. They, in turn, are supported by the three main institutions of tsarism – the bureaucracy, the church and the army which are designed, respectively, to maintain political control, ideological conformity and security. The exploiting classes, the nobility and the bourgeoisie, bear no part of the cost of this apparatus, since their tier and the tiers above them are all supported on pillars. Instead, the burden of the entire structure is on the shoulders of the working classes, or proletariat. It is therefore a hierarchy which bears down heavily on the majority of the Russian people.

b) **Study Sources B and C. With reference to your own knowledge of the 1905 Revolution, explain how the interpretation of the scale of the revolution in Source B differs from that in Source C. How would you explain these differences?** (7 marks)

Sources B and C offer entirely different interpretations of the scale of the 1905 Revolution. Source B acknowledges that there was a 'massive protest throughout Russia' but argues that only a 'minor role was played by the revolutionaries'. Spontaneous uprising, therefore, could be no real threat to the system without the involvement of experienced leaders and organisation. By contrast, Source C refers to the importance in 1905 of 'both leaders and rank and file at all levels of society'. Far from there being no revolutionary activism, there was actually extensive political mobilisation. The conclusions are also different. Source B, quite logically in view of what it has already said, questions whether the 'events of 1905 merit being called a revolution'. Source C, on the other hand, attaches much more importance to the scale of 1905. In particular, the revolution produced new institutions, especially the soviets, along with sharper 'class analyses' by 'socialist activists'.

The reasons for the differences between the two sources concern the nature of historical debate. In the absence of any evidence which can be considered infallible, historians are entitled to interpret events in the way which, to them, best fits the known facts. In the process, some types of evidence will be given more attention than others, depending on the historical viewpoint. The main difference between Sources B and C is the issue of where the revolutionary drive originates. The assumption in Source B is that there cannot be one without leadership and organisation from above. Source C reflects a new interpretation, based on more detailed research, that revolutionaries existed at all levels.

c) **Study Sources A, B and C and use your own knowledge. Explain whether Tsarist Russia was on the verge of collapse even before the outbreak of war in 1914.**

(15 marks)

Total (20 marks)

The documents as a whole return a split verdict on this. Source A could be interpreted either way – that the tsarist system was for the moment secure in its structure or that it was so inflexible that it was bound to collapse. Source B puts the argument clearly for tsarist survival and recovery after 1905, while Source C emphasises the vulnerability of the entire tsarist system and the strength of the opposition to it. These views fall within the overall historical debate which this issue has always attracted.

As a comment on the tsarist system Source A is hostile, emphasising the exploitation of the working people by successive layers of privilege resting on their shoulders. The implication is clearly that the system should be changed and that any such change would have to be revolutionary to sweep the whole structure away. This would certainly be in line with socialist thought in 1900, whether Populist or Marxist. By itself, however, the cartoon does not give any clue as to whether the collapse was imminent; it would therefore have to be examined in the context of other socialist sources. Sources B and C, by contrast, provide a clear perspective – and opinion – on the stability of Tsarist Russia by 1914. They are, of course, able to do this since, as secondary sources, they are a retrospective analysis which can consider the whole period down to 1914 in the light of the 1905 Revolution and of the First World War. Both are carefully presented and based on systematic research. They do, however, tend to present their argument strongly so as to exclude the alternative; it would be difficult to combine them.

This is in line with the conflict of opinion between historians considered to be 'optimists' and those more accurately seen as 'pessimists'. The former argue that, given time, Tsarist Russia might have survived because of the more progressive policies it pursued after 1905. What actually brought about its collapse was military defeat *after* 1914. Source B is very much in line with this view since it stresses the way in which the regime survived the upheaval of 1905. Objectively, there are certain points in favour of this view. It is true that Trotsky was the only prominent revolutionary actually involved in the revolution and that after 1905 the Bolsheviks entered a period of internal crisis. It also seemed that the constitutional experiment, if limited, offered a channel for future reform and that the agrarian reforms of Stolypin might, in time, have created a stable peasant base against revolution. Yet the reference to the regime being 'relatively unscathed' is really going too far; the 1905 Revolution widened the gulf between the Tsar and his subjects, strengthening the former's belief in autocracy and the latter's total distrust of any reforms he might concede.

This seems to point us more in the direction of Tsarist Russia being fundamentally unstable by 1914 and in danger of collapse irrespective of subsequent defeat in the First World War. The argument of the 'pessimists' is boosted by Source C's emphasis on the depth of Russia's revolutionary influence; this was not so much developed as revealed by 1905. This meant that whatever the Tsar tried to do to save the regime he would meet growing popular resistance. Hence Stolypin's reforms did not prevent an increase in peasant violence and the measures to maintain economic growth provoked an unprecedented wave of strikes in 1912 and 1913. Nor would the Tsar have been unaware of the alienation of his people. He became more determined than ever to use what was left of his personal authority which, in turn, undermined the new Duma in its first two years and antagonised moderates like the Constitutional Democrats. Tsarist Russia was nearing collapse by 1914 because, in the words of Source C, 'the polarized structure of society was fully exposed'. This, of course, brings us full circle to Source A.

PARALLEL QUESTIONS WITHOUT WORKED ANSWERS

a) **Study Source A and use your own knowledge. Explain briefly why the cartoonist has depicted Russian society in the form of a pyramid.** **(3 marks)**

Advice: *Focus on the pyramid in the source and use specific examples from your own knowledge to relate it to Russia's hierarchy.*

b) **Study Sources B and C. With reference to your own knowledge of the 1905 Revolution, explain how Source C's interpretation of the effects of the Revolution differs from that in Source B.** **(7 marks)**

Advice: *Avoid summarising Source B and then Source C. Find issues to contrast between the sources.*

c) **Study Sources A, B and C and use your own knowledge. Explain whether the 1905 Revolution was a 'turning point' in the 20-year period between 1894 and 1914.** **(15 marks)**

Total (25 marks)

Advice: *Define 'turning point' and give a brief summary of what the sources seem to show as a set. Then introduce your own criteria, linking these with the sources in more detail. The occasional comment on the usefulness of the sources should be built in if relevant to your argument.*

📖 2. The Bolshevik Revolution: October 1917

This exercise consists of five questions on five sources, with a time allocation of 60–75 minutes.

Source A: An extract from a letter from Lenin to the Central Committee of the Bolshevik Party, 6 November 1917

Comrades, I am writing these lines on the evening of November 6th. The situation is critical in the extreme. It is absolutely clear that to delay the insurrection now will inevitably be fatal.

I exhort my comrades with all my heart and strength to realize that everything now hangs by a thread, that we are being confronted by problems that cannot be solved by conferences or congresses (even Congresses of Soviets) but exclusively by the people, by the masses, by the struggle of the armed masses. We must at all costs, this very evening, this very night, arrest the Government. We must not wait! We may lose everything! History will not forgive revolutionaries for procrastinating when they can be victorious today (will certainly be victorious today), while they risk losing much, in fact, everything, tomorrow!

Source B: *A Short History of the Communist Party of the Soviet Union*, officially approved by the Soviet Government. (This extract is from the 1970 edition.)

The Bolshevik Party led by Lenin inspired and organised the October Revolution. Lenin had studied the revolutions that had taken place in a number of countries and summed up the vast experience of insurrection gained by the proletariat and other working people. Lenin characterised the attitude of Marxists to an armed uprising and defined the conditions under which it was possible as follows: 'To be successful, insurrection must rely not upon conspiracy and not upon a party, but upon the advanced class. That is the first point. Insurrection must rely upon a *revolutionary upsurge of the people*. That is the second point. Insurrection must rely upon that *turning-point* in the history of the growing revolution when the activity of the advanced ranks of the people is at its height, and when the *vacillations* in the ranks of the enemy ... are strongest. That is the third point.'

The situation in Russia on the eve of the October Revolution satisfied all these conditions. Since these conditions obtained it was necessary to approach insurrection as an art, i.e. to prepare for it thoroughly. Lenin demanded and demonstrated this art in his leadership of the uprising. He made sure that once the revolution got under way the Bolsheviks would see it through.

Source C: Christopher Hill, *Lenin and the Russian Revolution* (1947)

In pleading for haste Lenin was obsessed by two fears. The first was that the army command would open the front and surrender Petrograd, together with the Baltic fleet, to the Germans, as a lesser evil than surrendering it to the Soviet ... Lenin's other fear was that the rising peasant revolt might get completely out of hand, and that when the Bolsheviks ultimately took over power, they might be faced with a situation of utter economic collapse and 'a wave of real anarchy may become stronger than we are'. This anxiety was, I believe, at the back of Lenin's mind from the day of his return to Russia, and that was one reason why the spinelessness and ineffectiveness of the Provisional Government enraged him so much: he feared that – as so often in nineteenth-century revolutions – it would play into the hands of a military dictator who would restore 'order'.

Source D: Robert Wolfson, *Years of Change* (1978)

During the last weeks of October, plans for the coup were carefully made and 6–7 November fixed as the date. On the evening of the 6th, Lenin arrived at the party's headquarters, the Smolny Institute in Petrograd, to find everything carefully organized and ready. Early the next morning sailors on the battleship 'Aurora' opened fire on the Winter Palace across the river Neva. This was the signal for action. More than 20,000 troops were committed to the Bolsheviks. They now occupied the important strategic points of the city – stations, electrical power stations, main roads, the banks – almost without opposition. Only the Winter Palace remained untaken that day, guarded as it was by 100 cadet officers. During the night of 7–8, Bolshevik troops moved up to surround it and got into the grounds. Early the next morning they moved in, again without a struggle and arrested the ministers of the Provisional Government, apart from Kerensky, who had already fled.

Source E: Adapted from Edward Acton, *Rethinking the Russian Revolution* (1990)

The upsurge in Bolshevik popularity was confirmed by explosive growth in the party's membership. Indeed, the party was virtually recreated by a mammoth influx of new recruits … an expansion from some 10,000 in February to some 250,000 or even 300,000 by October is not unlikely.

Yet the impact of the party's agitation and propaganda must not be misconstrued: it evoked so powerful a response precisely because it so accurately articulated the masses' own goals. But it did not create either these goals or the mass radicalism which went with them.

QUESTIONS WITH WORKED ANSWERS

a)   **Study Source A. What does this source reveal about Lenin's attitude to his colleagues in the Bolshevik Party Central Committee in November 1917?   (5 marks)**

This appeal combines persuasion with veiled threats, showing that Lenin was aware of serious shortcomings within the Central Committee. He feared that a number of his colleagues would prefer to sit back and to justify their inaction by their dependence on 'conferences and congresses'. This is almost certainly a reference to colleagues like Kamenev, Zinoviev and Bukharin, who wanted to wait until the Congress of Soviets had met to sanction a military takeover. He was deeply concerned that they would persuade the rest of the Central Committee to do nothing and, to prevent this, Lenin was 'exhorting' the rest with all his 'heart and strength'. Since they were 'comrades' rather than subordinates, this approach would be more effective than a direct command. But they needed to be shaken out of their complacency and to be made aware that the situation was 'critical in the extreme' and that they had to take action 'this very night'. In all this, he considered them open to reason and therefore held over them the threat of the verdict of History.

b)   **Study Source C and use your own knowledge. Explain the reference in Source C to 'the rising peasant revolt'.**   **(3 marks)**

This is a reference to the growing impatience of the peasantry with the policies of the Provisional Government over the land issue. Both Lvov and Kerensky had promised to consider the redistribution of land from the nobility to the peasantry – but only after the settlement of the main priority, the war. From August onwards the peasantry began to take matters into their own hands, seizing estates and defying attempts by the Provisional Government to maintain order. The situation favoured the Bolsheviks for the moment, since some of the peasantry had abandoned their normal allegiance to the Socialist Revolutionaries. There was, however, no way of knowing how far the revolt would go in the future, unless the Bolsheviks leashed it.

c) **Study Sources B and D. How far does a study of Sources B and D offer support to the view that October 1917 was a 'popular uprising'?** **(5 marks)**

These two sources have fundamentally different approaches: Source B presents a broad historical sweep, Source D a detailed description. The notion of a 'popular uprising' is central to the interpretation of Source B, which justifies the events of October 1917 in the light of Lenin's own theories. Hence the focus is very much on the 'revolutionary upsurge of the people', as interpreted, prepared and carried through under the leadership of Lenin. While, however, this supports the view contained in the question, it does not actually prove it; the purpose of the source was to confer legitimacy on the soviet regime rather than to produce a balanced historical assessment.

Source D contains no direct reference to popular uprising, only of planned takeover carried out by disciplined groups ('sailors on the battleship "Aurora"' and 'more than 20,000 troops'). But the emphasis on the absence of any resistance could indicate that the Bolsheviks came to power because there was so little to oppose them. The uprising was more 'popular' than the Provisional Government in that it took 'almost without opposition' the key parts of the city and the Winter Palace ('again without a struggle'). The underlying assumption of Source D, however, is that everything was planned as a 'coup'. This seems to weigh against the view in the question but cannot be considered decisive in the light of more recent research into grass-roots support for Bolshevism in 1917.

d) **Study Sources A and C. Compare the value of these two sources to the historian studying Lenin's reasons for carrying out the October Revolution.** **(5 marks)**

Two very different perspectives can be provided in response to this question.

The first shows the advantages of A, as a primary source, over C. Source A has all the advantages of immediacy. As a letter it contains a direct statement of Lenin's intent and reveals his concerns about the attitudes of his colleagues. It also suggests a dismissive attitude to 'congresses and conferences'. Such a document will always be referred to by historians, whether their motive is to use it as an icon for propaganda (as in soviet histories) or as evidence within a more balanced context. By contrast, Source C has no immediacy. The author is not the originator and has no direct contact with the situation he discusses. His work may, or may not, be of use to other historians and they will probably pay it less attention than they would one of Lenin's letters.

But reverse the approach and a different set of priorities emerge. Source A, like any primary source, will probably conceal as much as it reveals. All documents acquire true significance only as the lapse of time clarifies the perspective in which they are placed – and this clarification is the work of historians. Hence Source C provides a considered insight into Lenin's motives, quite possibly in the light of other primary sources read by the author. Since the author's view is controversial, it will stimulate other interpretations and perspectives. These are as much part of the process of history as are the events and sources themselves.

e) Study Sources A, B and E and use your own knowledge. Assess the personal importance of Lenin in the October Revolution. (12 marks)

Total (30 marks)

The role of Lenin in the October Revolution is now one of the most controversial of all historical issues. Sources B and E provide examples of the two main alternatives, while A can be interpreted either way.

There has always been an argument that Lenin was essential for the success of the Bolshevik revolution. Source B is typical of this. Lenin 'inspired and organised' the Revolution; he was its overall strategist, drawing on his study of other revolutions, and was able to define in detail 'the conditions under which it was possible'. He directed the 'revolutionary upsurge of the people' and took advantage of 'vacillations in the ranks of the enemy'. There is much evidence, in his writings, for the theoretical contributions of Lenin, especially in *What is to be Done?* (1902) and *The State and Revolution* (1917). He also managed to increase support for the Bolsheviks through his *April Theses*. Yet there are problems with the interpretation in Source B, not least the nature of the source: as an official publication it was clearly designed to boost Lenin's contributions to mythical proportions. Detailed study shows that Lenin's leadership was never decisive at any stage between 1903 and April 1917. Did he suddenly change during the second half of 1917 – or was he actually pushed into action by changing circumstances?

This is very much the line taken by Source E, which attaches great importance to the 'explosive growth in the party's membership' from '10,000 in February' to perhaps '300,000 by October'. But the party was simply responding to the 'goals' of the 'masses', rather than leading them. Although this view reverses most previous assumptions about Lenin, there is much to be said for it. Sections of the population had become disillusioned with parties, like the Socialist Revolutionaries, which they had previously supported, because of their connection with the Provisional Government. They were taking matters into their own hands with, for example, the seizure of land or factories, and were putting pressure on the Bolsheviks to seize power on their behalf. Rather than the masses following Lenin's leadership, Lenin's leadership was following the masses.

This brings us to Source A, which could be used in support of either B or E. On the one hand, Source A seems to show great resolution and foresight. Since 'the situation' was 'critical in the extreme' he was 'exhorting' his 'comrades' to action in case they should 'lose everything!' On the other hand, Lenin had spent much of his time since July 1917 in internal exile in Finland, while other Bolsheviks were beginning to make the running. Kamenev and Zinoviev, for example, placed their hope in a future Congress of Soviets, while Trotsky, as President of the Petrograd Soviet, had set up the Revolutionary Military Committee and emerged as the supreme *tactician* of revolution. Could it actually be that Lenin was urging action before the 'situation' became 'too late' for *him* – or, alternatively, before the Bolsheviks were swamped by the masses in pursuit of their own changes?

PARALLEL QUESTIONS WITHOUT WORKED ANSWERS

a) **Study Source A. What does this source reveal about Lenin's views of
    the prospects of a successful revolution?**   (3 marks)

    Advice: *Sources 'reveal' in two ways: directly and by inference.*

b) **Study Source C and use your own knowledge. Explain the references in
    Source C to 'the Provisional Government' and to its 'spinelessness' and
    'ineffectiveness'.**   (5 marks)

    Advice: *Be precise: define the meaning of Provisional Government but avoid writing a long
    essay on its history. Instead, relate your knowledge to the context of the source – by giving
    specific examples of the Provisional Government's weaknesses.*

c) **Study Sources B and D. How far does a study of Sources B and D offer
    support to the view that Lenin himself planned and led the Bolshevik
    Revolution?**   (5 marks)

    Advice: *'How far' needs to be addressed: go for 'to an extent but . . .' rather than 'not at all'
    or 'entirely'. Consider the question in the light of the different approaches of the two sources
    (one is propaganda, the other narrative). You will also need to comment on the reliability
    of each source as 'support to the view . . .'.*

d) **Study Sources C and D. Compare the value of these two sources to the
    historian studying the October Revolution.**   (5 marks)

    Advice: *'Value' needs to be addressed in terms of content and reliability. Avoid at all costs
    being dismissive about secondary sources simply because they were not produced 'at the time'.
    Instead, say something about the different approaches used by two historians in the light of
    their research and what they add to the debate on the October Revolution. You might also
    express a preference.*

e) **Study Sources A, B and E and use your own knowledge. Do you agree
    that the Bolshevik Revolution was more a minority coup than a popular
    revolution?**   (12 marks)

                                                          Total (30 marks)

    Advice: *Explain 'revolution' and 'minority coup' as you come to the terms. Start with a
    general impression of what the three sources show as a set. Then set criteria from your own
    knowledge and bring in the sources as relevant.*

Part 4: Historical skills

👑 Oral contributions

This section provides an introduction to the various forms of oral participation in class. (The emphasis is 'oral' rather than 'verbal' since the latter can also mean 'written'.) It covers the different skills related to speeches, interviews, discussions and debates.

Why is oral participation important?

(1) Participation is expected in the Sixth Form. Modern teaching methods are less didactic than they once were. The average lesson is therefore geared to student response.

(2) In higher education, seminars and other discussion groups are essential to the course. Unless you get some practice in the Sixth Form you could find these difficult.

(3) Being involved in discussion helps you focus the mind, sustain your interest and question your material. This is bound to increase your understanding.

(4) Discussion develops interview skills – upon which future university courses and jobs partly depend.

What impediments are there to taking part in discussion? How can these be overcome?

Problem

(1) 'I am better expressing myself in writing than in discussion.'

(2) 'I contributed once and made a fool of myself.'

(3) 'I can't be bothered.'

(4) 'I am always on the point of saying something but someone else gets in first and makes precisely the same point.' *or* 'I hold back so long that by the time I finally get round to making my point the discussion has moved on. No one has said what I had in mind, but by now it is too late.'

Solution

(1) The latter is a skill which has to be developed through practice. Some people are more quick witted than others: this does not mean that their contributions are better.

(2) Who hasn't? This should be a good reason for increasing contributions and gradually increasing your standard.

(3) This might mean that you are bored with the subject: put something into it. Or you don't think much of the level of discussion: raise it.

(4) The solution in both cases is to get in first, or as early as possible. By doing so, you control the direction of the discussion at the outset. You then have the choice of contributing further or sitting back and letting others take over. This is very good practice for group discussions which feature in almost every job. You will not impress by remaining silent, but you will by contributing first.

Oral contributions consist of four main types: speeches, interviews, discussions and debates. We frequently come across all of these, whether through our own direct experience or through the media, especially radio and television.

Similarities and differences between speeches, interviews, discussions and debates

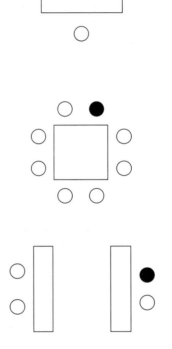

Type	Situation
Speech	Typically, a speech involves one person addressing an audience, which can be of any size. The speaker usually stands apart from the audience.
Interview	All experiences involve more than one person. The standard pattern of the interview is two people: an interviewer and an interviewee. Many situations, however, involve several interviewers and, less commonly more than one interviewee. The process can be formal, in which case there is normally a table, or informal.
Discussion	Discussion by definition involves at least two people and can involve ten, twenty or more. It can be conducted round a table or, less formally, in easy chairs. Some situations, usually televised programmes, have two related groups involved in discussion – a selected panel and a wider audience whose views are also sought.
Debate	Debates generally need the speakers to be more formally organised into two sides; in the case of competitions each of these may comprise two or three, while political debates in the House of Commons can involve dozens of speakers.

● = you as a participant
○ = other participants

The purpose of speeches, interviews, discussions and debates in History

Type	Purpose	Image
Speech	A speech provides an opportunity to present a topic which you have researched to an audience. You should be able to hold their attention through a clearly presented argument. Afterwards you should be able to answer questions on your topic.	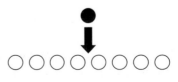

Interview   There are two possibilities for an interview:

- As a historian, you answer questions about your views on a particular issue, using the normal historical skills and perspective.

- You re-enact a situation or historical character to answer questions – either based at the time or in retrospect.

Discussion   Discussions on historical issues involve the interchange of ideas between individuals within a group. A good discussion will have opportunities for everyone to take part. Different ideas are encouraged and arguments will develop as a matter of course. The purpose of a discussion is *not* to have one argument ending up triumphing over the others. Instead, it is to understand the topic more completely as a result of seeing it through different perspectives.

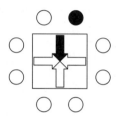

Debate   Debates generally need the speakers to be more formally organised into two sides; in the case of competitions each of these may comprise two or three speakers, while political debates in the House of Commons can involve dozens of speakers.

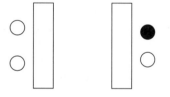

● = you as a participant
○ = other participants

THE ACADEMIC USE OF SPEECHES, INTERVIEWS, DISCUSSIONS AND DEBATES IN SCHOOLS AND UNIVERSITIES

Schools and universities have a different structure to their teaching methods. Universities have three main teaching styles in a subject such as History – the lecture, tutorial and seminar. These involve a combination of the four methods already covered.

The lecture is delivered as a speech by one of the university teachers to a group of students. It is usually an hour in length and can take place in venues ranging from a lecture theatre to class-rooms. It may also involve the use of visual material, in which case the lecture is a presentation as well as a speech. The tutorial is a one-to-one or one-to-small-group discussion to ensure that the student is on top of the topic. It is therefore a combination of an interview and a discussion. The seminar involves the delivery of one or more short papers (similar to a speech), after which various aspects of the topic are discussed fully. Some students will hold firmly to their views, in which case the seminar will also have a strong element of debate.

In schools the approach is much more integrated. In most History lessons there will be a combination of the lecture (which will consist of a certain amount of didactic teaching), the tutorial (with an emphasis on individual work) and the seminar (an opportunity for the contribution of the whole class to discussion). From time to time, however, whole periods may be given over to specific skills. These need to be carefully thought about and prepared in advance.

SETTING UP A CLASSROOM SITUATION, BASED ON RUSSIA 1855–1917

Setting up a speech

Either: Considering the period retrospectively, as an historian, give a ten-minute talk on 'Why the tsarist system collapsed'. The main argument needs to be clearly established in the opening sentences. The rest of the speech should be clearly divided into stages, each one already referred to very briefly in the introduction. The conclusion should pull the themes together and – perhaps – end with a quotation or a question. For further details on the speech as a presentation, see pages 205–7.

Or: Considering the period from the perspective of 1914 and through the eyes of one of the main characters, prepare a case for:

- Why Russia needs a revolution.
- Why Russia can reform.

The first set of topics can be the starting point for a discussion, the second set can be in the form of a debate.

Setting up an interview

Either: As an historian, answer questions put by an interviewer on whether Alexander II deserves his reputation as a 'great reformer'. The interviewer's questions should have a definite development, but should also react to the answers given. The interviewee should answer the questions as fully as possible.

Example of an extract from an interview on Alexander II

Q   You said a few minutes ago that Alexander II brought major changes to a system which was in crisis in 1855. Do you think he *intended* these changes to be so sweeping?

A   In one way, perhaps not. Like his father, he believed in autocracy. Therefore . . . On the other hand, he felt that reforming Russia's various institutions was the only way to preserve autocracy. This explains why he . . .

Q   All right; I accept your distinction between two types of 'major change'. But when it really comes down to it, can *any* of his changes be considered successful in practice?

A   Clearly there were failures. But if you compare his achievements with the situation he inherited, he made huge progress. Let me give two examples . . .

Or: As Alexander III, explain why you were so determined to resist further reform after 1881. This involves more of a one-sided approach and may well move more towards a debate than a discussion.

Example of an extract from an interview of Alexander III

Q   I think what most people would want to know is why you have suddenly turned against your father's policies and tried to undermine the work of a lifetime.

A   That is not at all what I am trying to do. Far from it. My father made many changes – most of them necessary to update Russia – and I have not reversed these. For example . . . But we must not underestimate the dangerous forces which were set in motion during his reign. What gratitude was shown to him by People's Will, for example, when they murdered him in 1881? When the answer to reform is deliberate terrorism, the time has come to take a strong line.

Q   Does this mean slowing down the pace of reform, or even stopping it altogether?

A   For a time, yes. We have to concentrate on where the dangers are coming from. I have received official advice from my Procurator General, Pobedonostsev, and I accept his views that . . .

Q   That's all very well, but are you not storing up even more trouble for the future?

Setting up a discussion

Example: Why the Bolsheviks were successful in October 1917. Several speakers should start by giving slightly different perspectives on the October Revolution. For example, one could focus on the conspiratorial approach, another on the popular support behind the Bolsheviks, a third on the weakness of the Provisional Government – and so on. A good discussion should see some give and take. Sometimes it will seem necessary to hold a position, sometimes to concede it. It is also more important to keep the discussion flowing smoothly with other people contributing than it is to dominate it yourself. The right balance is explained below in the criteria for Level 3 of the Key Skills for discussion.

Extract from A-level Key Skills: Level 3 on Communications (Discussion)

(i)   Make clear and relevant contributions in a way that suits your purpose and the situation.
(ii)   Listen and respond sensitively to others, and develop points and ideas.
(iii) Create opportunities for others to contribute when appropriate.

Here is an example of how a discussion on the Bolshevik Revolution might be developing after about five minutes.

Extract from a discussion on the Bolshevik Revolution

Speaker 1:   Taking all that into account, I am not convinced that the Bolsheviks actually planned the October Revolution. There was a huge element of luck – not least the crisis faced by the Kerensky government.

Speaker 2:   I agree with that. I would actually go further and point out that the Bolsheviks owed their success to the support of the Russian people. The peasants realised that the Bolsheviks were more likely than the Socialist Revolutionaries to deliver the land ownership they wanted.

Speaker 1: Yes, and the left wing of the other parties – the left SRs and the Menshevik Internationalists – were prepared to go along with the Bolsheviks because they thought the Provisional Government had sold them out.

Speaker 3: I certainly wouldn't deny the popular support behind the Bolsheviks. But let's retrace a few steps. Who set up the conditions for gaining that support? After all, Lenin's *April Theses* said that . . .

Speaker 4: Sorry, I'm not convinced. You are all making the Bolsheviks out to be a democratic force which was swept to power by the will of the people. Yet we all know that they proceeded to establish a repressive dictatorship as soon as they had come to power . . .

Speaker 2: It's possible that they changed their whole approach between 1917 and 1918 because of the situation they faced . . .

Setting up a debate

Example: 'The collapse of Tsarist Russia was inevitable – with or without the First World War.' Two speakers on each side could address the key arguments, each with a particular emphasis.

For the Proposition, Speaker 1 could focus on the underlying instability of Tsarist Russia – and its inability to reform. Speaker 2 could emphasise the strength of the revolutionary movements and the growing popular support for the overthrow of the tsarist regime. Both speakers might emphasise that the First World War may have accelerated a collapse which would have happened anyway.

The Opposition would adopt the reverse approach. Speaker 1 could concentrate on the inherent strengths of the tsarist regime, especially the rapid growth of the economic infrastructure and the scope for future constitutional reform. Speaker 2 might focus on the vulnerability of the revolutionary parties before 1914. The common theme for both speakers would be the transformation brought by the First World War – through the collapse of credible political leadership and the unexpected opportunity provided to widely divergent revolutionary organisations.

Setting up a combination

There are several possibilities for combining the various styles of oral contribution. A combination would be particularly useful in covering the different types of historical analysis. For example, a debate (which consists of several speeches) could be followed by an interview or by a discussion.

Try this as an integrated approach:

* Begin with a debate, possibly with one speaker on each side instead of two: 'The collapse of Tsarist Russia was inevitable – with or without the First World War.'
* Follow this with a discussion with the wider involvement of the whole class. In academic terms, the debate could be equivalent to presenting historical 'schools of thought' as clearly and distinctly as possible. The discussion would be an investigation of the strengths and weaknesses of each.
* Conclude with an essay which could use the ideas from both the debate and the discussion. This will confirm the connection between the 'oral' and 'written' forms of 'verbal' communication.

References

1. M.S. Anderson, *The Ascendancy of Europe 1815–1914* (London 1972), p. 119
2. Quoted in Arthur E. Adams, *Imperial Russia after 1861: Peaceful Modernization or Revolution?* (Boston 1965), p. 44
3. B. Dmytryshyn, *Imperial Russia. A Source Book, 1700–1917* (Hinsdale, IL 1974), Document 49: The Fundamental Laws of Imperial Russia, 1906

Sources

1A. Novosti Picture Library
1B. M. Lynch, *Reaction and Revolutions: Russia 1881–1924* (London 1992), p. 48
1C. E. Acton, *Russia: The Tsarist and Soviet Legacy*, second edition (London 1995), p. 119
2A. V.I. Lenin, *Collected Works* (London 1960), Vol. XXVI, pp. 234–5
2B. *A Short History of the Communist Party of the Soviet Union* (Moscow 1970), p. 124
2C. Christopher Hill, *Lenin and the Russian Revolution* (London 1947)
2D. Robert Wolfson, *Years of Change* (London 1978), p. 329
2E. Adapted from Edward Acton, *Rethinking the Russian Revolution* (London 1990), p. 193

Chapter 4

Imperial and Weimar Germany, 1890–1933

This chapter opens with the last two decades of the German Reich and deals with the impact of the First World War. It looks at the formation of the Weimar Republic and its subsequent crises and achievements. The last section discusses the rise of Hitler and the Nazis.

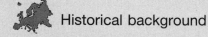 ## Historical background

Imperial Germany, 1871–90
The domestic and foreign policies of
    imperial Germany, 1890–1914
War and revolution, 1914–18
The Weimar Republic and the first crisis,
    1919–23
The Republic's recovery and second
    crisis, 1924–33
The rise of the Nazis
The achievements of the Weimar
    Republic

Sources

1. The Weimar Republic in crisis,
    1919–23
2. The rise of national socialism in
    Germany to 1933

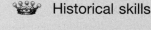 ## Historical skills

The use of numerical data in History

Essays

The domestic and foreign policies of
    imperial Germany, 1890–1914
War and revolution, 1914–18
The Weimar Republic and the first crisis,
    1919–23
The Republic's recovery and second
    crisis, 1924–33
The rise of the Nazis
The achievements of the Weimar
    Republic

Chronology

1871–1918	German Reich
1888	Accession of Wilhelm II
1890	Resignation of Bismarck
1917	Military dictatorship under Hindenburg and Ludendorff
1918	Handover to civilian government
	Proclamation of Republic (9 November)
	Armistice with Allies (11 November)
1919	Spartacist uprising
	Treaty of Versailles
	Constitution of Weimar Republic
1920	Kapp Putsch
1921	Announcement of final reparations figure
1923	French invasion of the Ruhr
	Peak of hyperinflation
	Rentenmark and *Rentenbank*
	Munich Putsch
1924	Dawes Plan
	Two Reichstag elections
1925	Locarno Pact
	Hindenburg elected President
1926	German admission to the League of Nations
	Treaty of Berlin
1928	Reichstag election
1929	Young Plan
	Wall Street Crash
1930	Reichstag election
	Collapse of Grand Coalition
1931	Collapse of *Kreditanstalt*
1932	Two Reichstag elections and presidential election
1933	Hitler appointed Chancellor (30 January)

Part 1: Historical background

 ### Imperial Germany, 1871–90

The German Reich was established in 1871 after the Franco-Prussian war had involved the southern German states on the side of Prussia and the North German Confederation. The new constitution was a semi-constitutional monarchy; the Kaiser possessed extensive executive powers but there was also a broadly based legislature comprising an elected Reichstag and a **Bundesrat** which represented the different German states. The chief minister was the Chancellor, to whom the first Kaiser, Wilhelm I (1871–88) delegated much of his authority. As a result, Bismarck (Chancellor between 1871 and 1890) continued to dominate Germany as he had Prussia between 1862 and 1870.

During his chancellorship, Bismarck engaged with the various parties and interest groups in Germany, either in co-operation with them or in direct conflict. His most consistent ally was the Conservative Party (K), which represented the interest of the Prussian Junkers and the great industrialists. He was less fortunate with the Centre Party (**Z**) and failed in his attempts in the *Kulturkampf* to reduce the influence of the Catholic Church which the Centre strongly supported. The National Liberals (NLP) were committed to free trade, a policy which Bismarck supported until 1879, when he introduced protection instead. This meant abandoning the NLP and, by dropping the *Kulturkampf*, gaining the support of the Centre instead. The one party with which

Figure 4.1 **Map of Germany, 1871–1918**

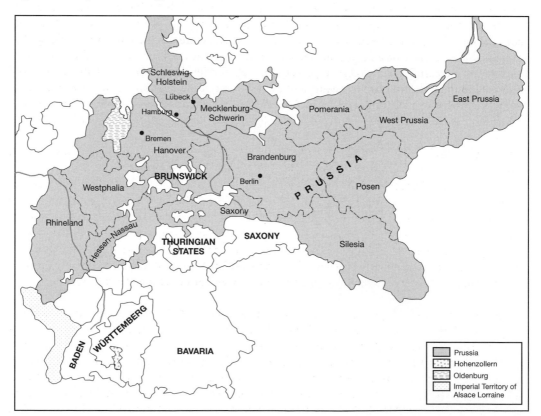

Bismarck never attempted any deal were the Social Democrats (SPD), which he tried unsuccessfully to eliminate, first by repression and then by competing with them for the support of the working classes.

Bismarck was also in control of Germany's foreign policy. His main priority was to establish permanent security for the new Reich by isolating France, the power which was most likely to upset it. This he achieved by making Germany the centre of an alliance system, forming the Dual Alliance with Austria-Hungary in 1879 and expanding this into the Triple Alliance in 1882 with the inclusion of Italy. He also managed to prevent Russia from establishing a connection with France, first by means of a looser connection with Austria-Hungary and Germany known as the *Dreikaiserbund*, then by a more specific agreement with Germany – the Reinsurance Treaty of 1887. During the 1880s Germany also became a colonial power, although Bismarck always regarded imperialism as a useful means of projecting European rivalries overseas: hence he encouraged French imperialism to divert France from revanche for the loss of Alsace-Lorraine in 1871.

The period 1871–90 saw the emergence and consolidation of a united Germany. It was, however, dominated by a Prussian whose view of Germany's role was confined to Europe. Between 1890 and 1914, however, Germany established itself as a world rather than a European power.

 ## The domestic and foreign policies of imperial Germany, 1890–1914

Between 1890 and 1914 Germany forged ahead to develop the largest industrial base in Europe (Essay 1a), the reasons for which are covered in Essay 1b. The effects of this transformation were considerable (Essay 1c), especially on Germany's social structure. As the industrial working class expanded and learned how to defend their interests through trade unions and the SPD, other sectors felt increasingly vulnerable, especially the ruling elite which comprised the agricultural interest and the industrial entrepreneurs and cartels. The middle classes, caught between the two, found themselves equally under pressure. Overall, Germany had become a fractured society with many unresolved conflicts. These were to affect both domestic and foreign policy after 1890.

The four chancellors of the period were Caprivi (1890–4), Choldwig-Hohenlohe (1894–1900), Bülow (1900–09) and Bethmann Hollweg (1909–17), who were overshadowed by the power exercised by Kaiser Wilhelm II (Essay 2a). Their domestic achievements were extensive (Essay 2b). Social reforms were introduced by Caprivi, as part of his 'New Course' from 1890, and by Posadowski from 1900; some of these, especially social insurance measures, were well ahead of developments in Britain at the time. The economy also developed rapidly, as did the flow of funding for rearmament and naval growth. There is, however, some question as to the effectiveness of the Kaiser's overall management of domestic policy, the extent to which he was influenced by economic and social pressures and the wisdom of some of his actions (Essay 2c).

Foreign policy went through a period of rapid change after 1890. Reversing Bismarck's European emphasis, Wilhelm II introduced a policy of *Weltpolitik*, providing Germany with a world role through colonial and naval expansion (Essay 3a). Although this was a logical development in Germany's rise to prominence, it was also the result of a decision to put Britain under pressure by threatening its overseas interests. This, the Kaiser and his advisers hoped, would force Britain into an agreement with Germany. It actually had the reverse effect. In 1904 Britain signed an Entente with France and in 1907 a Convention with Russia, while the German Navy Laws provoked

Britain into a massive increase in dreadnought building (Essay 3b). The Kaiser's personal role in foreign policy has been subject to even more scrutiny than his domestic influence. Not all of this is positive (Essay 3c).

By 1914 Germany was certainly under a great deal more pressure than she had been in 1890. Instead of being at the centre of the only alliance system in Europe, Germany was now confronted by an alternative network which comprised the Franco-Russian Alliance (1894), the Anglo-French Entente (1904) and the Anglo-Russian Convention (1907). War was beginning to appear the way out of a crisis of foreign policy as well as a solution to internal disunity.

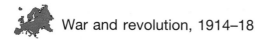 ## War and revolution, 1914–18

Germany declared war on Russia on 1 August 1914, following Russian mobilisation on 30 July. This was followed by a declaration of war on France on 3 August, along with the invasion of Belgium to enable the German general staff to implement the Schlieffen Plan. This was countered by Britain's declaration of war on Germany on 4 August. All these developments are covered in Chapter 2. Whether or not the outbreak of war was actually provoked by German diplomacy is considered in Essay 4. It appears, at the very least, that the general staff had developed a military answer to Germany's strategic vulnerability (outflanked as she was by France and Russia) which greatly reduced the diplomatic options available in the crisis following the assassination at Sarajevo.

The experience of war was a very mixed one (Essay 5). Germany achieved military victory against Russia, forcing the Russian government to sign the Treaty of Brest-Litovsk in March 1918 and to give independence to Finland, the Baltic states, Poland and (temporarily) the Ukraine. But German armies failed to break through on the western front, even when reinforcements became available after the withdrawal from Russia. The stalemate in the west produced an internal crisis which resulted in the establishment of military dictatorship under Hindenburg and Ludendorff in 1917 (Essay 6a). This folded up in 1918 following the failure of the final German offensive and a series of military and naval mutinies. Facing defeat in France and starvation on the home front – the result of the British naval blockade – the Kaiser reintroduced constitutional government under Prince Max of Baden in October.

By 9 November, however, this too had collapsed. The Kaiser and the other German rulers abdicated and, on the same day, Germany was proclaimed a republic by one of the leaders of the SPD, Philipp Scheidemann (Essay 6b). Over the following weeks this was challenged by a Soviet Republic in Bavaria and in Berlin by an uprising organised by the **Spartacus league**, or German communists. Both of these were put down by the remnants of the German army as a result of a deal between the government of the new Republic, under Ebert, and the commander-in-chief, Groener. For a few months, at the height of the crisis, the Weimar became the centre of government. Even after its transfer back to Berlin, the name 'Weimar Republic' remained.

The changes in 1918 and early 1919 were certainly dramatic. But did they amount to a 'revolution'? This has strong implications for the type of regime which actually emerged in 1919 and is examined in Essay 6c.

The Weimar Republic and the first crisis, 1919–23

The permanent constitution of the Weimar Republic was drawn up in 1919. In some ways, the Republic was an advanced democracy, with a Reichstag elected by universal suffrage according to the principle of proportional representation, a chancellor who was dependent on the support of a Reichstag majority, and an elected president. On the other hand, there was a great deal of continuity with more authoritarian patterns from the past, including a specific article allowing the president to rule by decree in emergencies. All this is considered in Essay 7. The Republic also permitted a complete range of political parties. The four moderate parties, which supported the Republic and took part in most of the coalition governments, were the Social Democrats (**SPD**), Democrats (**DDP**), Centre (Z) and People's Party (**DVP**). The Republic was, however, opposed by the extreme left, comprising the Communists (**KPD**) and Independent Socialists (**USPD**), as well as by the far right – the Nationalists (**DNVP**) and the National Socialists (**NSDAP**) (Essay 7b).

In its opening years the Republic experienced one crisis after another – or perhaps a single crisis with several strands (Essay 8a). One was the collapse of the mark in the most serious hyperinflation Germany had ever experienced: by November 1923 there were 42,000 million marks to the dollar. Another was the threat of revolution. Several attempts were made against the Republic by communists and there were two putsches from the right – by Kapp in 1920 and Hitler in 1923. Both problems were exacerbated by the Treaty of Versailles (1919), which had imposed penalties on Germany in terms of territory, disarmament and reparations. Whether this was in reality a harsh settlement (Essay 9), the important thing is that it was perceived by the German public to have been so. The way in which the reparations clauses affected Germany were somewhat complex, as is explained in Essay 10.

Serious though the crises were, the Republic had survived by 1923 (Essay 8b). This was due to three main factors. One was the decisive use of emergency powers by President Ebert and the intervention of Chancellor Stresemann to end the currency crisis in November 1923. A second was the comparative weakness at this stage of the alternatives to the Republic: neither the far left nor the far right commanded sufficient support to bring about a change of regime. Finally, the international situation began to change in favour of a more diplomatic solution to the Republic's problems. There was therefore an apparent upsurge in the Republic's fortunes from 1924.

 The Republic's recovery and second crisis, 1924–33

Between 1924 and 1929 there was a marked improvement in the political stability of the Weimar Republic. There were no more attempted putsches and in the Reichstag elections of 1924 and 1928 the radical parties, especially the Nazis, did not do well. The economy grew rapidly, assisted by American investments and Germany entered a period of positive diplomacy with Britain, France and Italy, signing the Locarno Pact in 1925 to guarantee Germany's western frontier and entering the League of Nations in 1926. The catalyst for some of these improvements was Gustav Stresemann, Chancellor in 1923 and Foreign Minister between 1923 and 1929 (Essay 11).

Yet the extent of the recovery can be questioned (Essay 12). Germany's dependence on foreign loans may have stimulated industry in the short term, but the method established by the Dawes Plan to deal with the problem of reparations ultimately proved very dangerous. It only required a sudden recall of American loans to bring about an instant crisis. Political stability was also illusory since a substantial gap was opening up between the two main coalition partners, the SPD, which was moving further to the left and the Centre, which was being pulled to the right. These two problems combined to produce a second economic and political crisis from 1929.

Economic collapse was the direct result of a unique combination of circumstances (Essay 13). To some extent German economic recovery had been based on the misuse of short-term American loans, which had been invested in long-term projects and industrial infrastructure. The imme-diate withdrawal of these brought a crisis to German industry, which led to a rapid increase in unemployment. As Essay 13 shows, this was a very different situation to that of 1923 and it proved far more difficult to deal with depression than it had with inflation.

Economic collapse led inexorably to political crisis. The coalition broke up as the SPD refused to adopt the Centre policy of cuts in the dole to try to balance the budget. Deprived of anything like a majority in the Reichstag, successive chancellors (Brüning, Papen and Schleicher) had to rely on the use of the presidential decree. In this way, the Republic turned its back on democracy after 1931 and had begun to look like a political dictatorship even before the appointment of Hitler as Chancellor in January 1933. Essay 14a explains this in more detail and Essay 14b considers the relative responsibility of Brüning, Papen and Hindenburg for the collapse of democracy and the emergence of dictatorship.

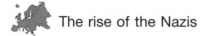 ## The rise of the Nazis

The party which dominated Germany by 1933 began in obscurity in 1919 as the German Workers' Party (DAP), as shown in Essay 15a. Hitler moved rapidly up the party until, in 1921, he supplanted Drexler as leader. The new name, National Socialist German Workers' Party (NSDAP) was adopted, along with a 25-Point Programme, in 1920. The Party also gained a propaganda outlet in the *Völkischer Beobachter* and a paramilitary base in the form of the *Sturm Abteilung* (**SA**) (Essay 15b). In 1923 Hitler felt sufficiently confident to make a bid for power. The Munich Putsch, however, was an abject failure, for reasons explained in Essay 15c.

While serving a prison sentence in Landsberg prison, Hitler reformulated his approach. Instead of trying to seize power in a putsch, it would be necessary to adopt a 'strategy of legality' and try to win the support of the masses in Reichstag elections. The NSDAP was extensively reorganised and became more flexible in its policy, targeting each class with a specific policy (Essay 16). At first these changes had little effect, the 1928 Reichstag election producing fewer seats for the NSDAP even than the two elections of 1924. It was proving impossible to disturb the apparent equilib-rium of the Republic during its years of prosperity.

The situation changed dramatically after 1929. The collapsing economy and rising unemployment increased the vote in the 1939 Reichstag election both for the communists and for the Nazis, while the latter became easily the largest party in the Reichstag in July 1932. Despite – or possibly because of – a slight drop in the Nazi vote in November 1932, Hitler was appointed Chancellor by President Hindenburg on 30 January 1933. The reasons for these developments, and a comparison with the lack of Nazi success in the 1920s, are provided in Essay 18.

The achievements of the Weimar Republic

Despite the collapse of democracy after 1930 (Essay 17) and the success of the Nazis by 1933, the Weimar Republic can still be credited with major achievements – political, social and economic. These are covered in Essay 19.

Part 2: Essays

The domestic and foreign policies of imperial Germany, 1890–1914

1. 'Between 1871 and 1914 Germany developed Europe's leading industrial base. The social and political side effects after 1890 were considerable.'

a) What is meant by 'Europe's leading industrial base'? **(3 marks)**

In this context the term refers to Germany's capacity to produce key industrial materials, such as coal, steel and chemicals, and to its production of engineered goods, both for the domestic market and for export. By 1900 Germany's GDP and industrial production figures had overtaken Britain's.

b) Explain why this base had developed since 1870. **(7 marks)**

Between 1867 and 1914 Germany's overall industrial production increased eight times, by comparison with that of France which increased three times and that of Britain which doubled. The rapidity of this overall growth-rate was due to a number of interrelated factors.

The first was the long-term influence of Prussia on the rest of Germany. This had taken the form of the *Zollverein*, which had not only provided the infrastructure for political unification but had also set in motion the rapid expansion of trade and industry in central Europe. Prussia had also seen considerable changes and progress in agriculture, which acted as a stimulus for industrial growth with, for example, a growing demand for threshing machines and steam threshers. Prussia also had considerable advantages in terms of natural resources, especially in the enormous coal and iron deposits in the Rhineland and the salt deposits near Halle, upon which was built Germany's chemical industry, which included such giants as Bayer at Leverkusen.

Economic progress and widespread resources were enhanced by massive investment in research. The excellence of Germany's education in technology and science ensured that industry was led by highly qualified people. It is often said that Germany had fewer individual industrial entrepreneurs than Britain. This is probably not the case: rather they stood out less because they tended to be part of a research team. Possibly the best example of an individual's achievement with the support of a research team was Siemens, whose dynamo boosted the electricity industry, especially combines like *Elektrizitäs-Gesellschaft Allgemeine* (AEG) and *Siemens-Schukert*. Of vital importance to all companies and combines was Germany's extensive banking system, which included the *Deutsche* Bank, *Commerz-und-Disconto* Bank and *Dresdner* Bank.

The final factor was the highly efficient organisational structure of German industry. This was based partly on the co-operation between individual enterprises within the new structure of cartels, the number of which increased from eight in 1875 to 673 by 1910. Employers were also able to rely on a semi-military discipline to maintain high levels of efficiency and commitment from the workforce, the size of which was steadily increasing. Of course, the degree of discipline imposed had social side-effects, which ultimately threatened Germany's internal stability.

c)   Explain why you agree or disagree that 'the social and political side effects after 1890 were entirely positive.'   **(15 marks)**

This opinion contains some elements of truth but does not take into account a number of negative pressures. Social and political opportunities were therefore counterbalanced by ever-increasing tensions between the social classes.

The benefits were certainly apparent. Despite the existence of concentrations of poverty, the new working class in Germany was one of the most affluent in Europe. The attraction of higher wages in the urban areas than in the countryside explains why the proportions of population employed in agriculture and industry had changed from 41 per cent to 31 per cent in 1875 and from 35 per cent to 40 per cent by 1907. The new working classes had also been accorded basic welfare services such as old age pensions and sickness or accident insurance, started by Bismarck and finished by Posadowski. Since they had been enfranchised by the 1871 Constitution, they could also vote for the newly formed Social Democratic Party (SPD) in Reichstag elections and were permitted limited involvement in trade union activity. Industrialisation had therefore been accompanied by political concessions as well as social reform.

Yet the complications accompanying Germany's rapid industrialisation were probably more important in the long term than the opportunities. This applies especially to the growth of conflict between the social classes. The concentration of ever-increasing numbers of workers in the cities created a hardening in the attitudes of the social elites which tried to defend the traditional system from social and political change. The workforce became heavily involved in trade unionism, grass-roots organisations and pressure groups, while the main outlet – the SPD – became increasingly vocal in its demand for social and political reform. The elites, meanwhile, did whatever they could to slow these down and divert their attention. The Junkers, or pre-industrial landed nobility, had most to fear. They felt particularly vulnerable since the proportion of agriculture to industry within the total economy was in steady decline. Also on their guard, however, were the newly developed class of industrialists, who sought to defend the class system by co-operating with the Junkers. Class boundaries were therefore tightened, not loosened, by industrialisation. Political developments reflected this, especially after 1890, with fairly regular collaboration between the Conservatives (who represented the interests of the Junkers) and the Free Conservative and National Liberals (based more on industrial wealth). The result was regular confrontation in the Reichstag with the SPD and the Free Democrats.

This hardening of social and political divisions had serious implications. According to some historians, the elites sought to externalise the social pressures within Germany by supporting an increasingly active foreign and colonial policy. The intention was to rally the lower orders and to channel their attention into nationalism through patriotism rather than socialism through internationalism. The result of this was a social fracturing, which was to be of vital importance for the future. The working class became increasingly divided between those who were inclined to revolution and those who preferred to adapt to the political system and to seek reforms within it. This dilemma was represented within the SPD, which developed revolutionary and reformist wings, later producing a split between Social Democrats and Communists. The middle class was similarly fractured, with a substantial section seeking political outlet in the fringe movements of the right: by the turn of the century there was already an incipient fascist movement which developed into Nazism during the 1920s. Germany's future politics of extremism were therefore directly connected to the negative impact of industrialisation.

2. **'None of Bismarck's successors succeeded in using the powers of Chancellor as he had. The result was the ever-increasing influence of Kaiser Wilhelm II, often with disastrous results.'**

    a) **Explain the reference to 'Bismarck's successors' as Chancellor.**   **(3 marks)**

As German Chancellor between 1871 and 1890, Bismarck had set the pace for Germany's domestic and foreign policies. His successors were given much less chance to do so; they were Caprivi (1890–4), Chlodwig-Hohenlohe (1894–1900), Bülow (1900–09) and Bethmann Hollweg (1909–17).

    b) **Explain what Germany's chancellors achieved in social and economic policy between 1890 and 1914.**   **(7 marks)**

The achievements of the chancellors of this period are probably clearer when grouped in categories rather than itemised under individual terms of office. Each category carries a mixed record but with identifiable achievements in each case.

The first achievement was a reasonable level of social reform, although this was intermittent between the chancellorships. Certainly attempts were made to come to terms with the problems resulting from rapid industrialisation. Caprivi, for example, made factory legislation an integral part of his 'New Course', limiting the hours for women and children working in factories and enforcing Sunday as a day off. The following year Caprivi followed up with a system of arbitration over disputes between employers and workers. More extensive social reforms were introduced by Chancellor Bülow (1900–09), or rather by his Minister of the Interior, Posadowski. Accident insurance and pensions were extended to a larger part of the workforce in 1900, while the duration of sickness benefits was lengthened in 1903. These changes were highly regarded in Britain and Asquith's Liberal government based many of their measures on sickness and accident insurance on them. Conversely, within Germany, the Social Democrats considered the reforms inadequate and a defensive response to pressure from the trade unions.

The chancellors also gave a high priority to economic growth and improving commercial contacts with other states in Europe. Caprivi's New Course established specific agreements with Italy, Austria-Hungary, Russia and various Balkan states. The basic principle was to increase external markets for Germany's manufactures and reduce the price of imported food. It is true that such measures were resented by the landowners who now had to compete on harsher terms; when they complained through the Agrarian League, Bülow's government responded in 1902 with the re-imposition of partial tariffs. This may seem inconsistent, but it has been argued that it was a means whereby governments were trying to balance the demands for cheap food with those of stable agricultural prices.

Finally, the chancellors maintained a consistent flow of funding for Germany's main political priority – rearmament and naval growth. This was done by careful management of the Reichstag. All the chancellors were able to play on the patriotic appeal of the new navy. Chlodwig-Hohenlohe and Bülow, in particular, secured the funding necessary to implement the Navy Laws of 1897, 1900 and 1906. There was, however, greater difficulty financing the expansion of the army (which was associated more narrowly with Prussia) as Caprivi discovered between 1890 and 1894.

c) **'Kaiser Wilhelm II became increasingly powerful and irresponsible in Germany's domestic policy between 1890 and 1914.' Explain why you agree or disagree with this view.** (15 marks)

There is no question that Kaiser Wilhelm II increased the personal intervention of the monarchy in political issues after 1890. What is more debatable is whether he did so on his own initiative and whether this intervention was 'irresponsible'.

Unlike his two predecessors, Wilhelm II was unwilling to delegate any of his authority to his chancellor. Instead, he was determined to reactivate the full powers inherent in the Prussian monarchy and confirmed by the 1871 Constitution of the German Reich: under this the Kaiser could appoint and dismiss ministers and, when he wished, block legislation passed by the Reichstag. In his determination to avoid being dominated by the Chancellor, Wilhelm dismissed Bismarck in 1890 and undermined the positions of Caprivi (1890–4) and Chlodwig-Hohenlohe (1894–1900) by preferring the counsel of Holstein and Tirpitz, neither of whom were official government ministers. To reinforce his political authority Wilhelm set up direct channels between each government department and the relevant section of the German army. He also used press offices within the central administration to promote a favourable image of his leadership and the policies of his government. In this respect the projection of his authority through the media was much more modern than the methods used by his predecessors.

Figure 4.2 **Kaiser Wilhelm II**

Yet, although there is considerable evidence to support the Kaiser's personal exercise of power, it cannot be claimed that his motive was entirely personal. Recent German historians have shown that Wilhelm II was, more often than not, expressing the underlying needs of Germany's social elites, such as the Junkers, the industrial leadership and the military establishment. It is true that he made the lives of his chancellors difficult; ultimately, however, he sided with them against the real enemy, which was perceived to be the Reichstag. There was therefore a common identity of interest between the Kaiser and his government officials, which is a strong argument against any lack of responsibility on his part. 'Responsibility' also remained in a constitutional sense in that the Kaiser was unable to break the financial constraints imposed by the Reichstag on military expenditure: every army bill therefore had to be negotiated. There were limits beyond which Wilhelm II could not go.

The Kaiser's contribution to policy was also mixed. In some ways it was very positive, showing a high level of 'responsibility' in the sense of awareness of what was needed. At the outset, he showed progressive tendencies and refused Bismarck permission to revive earlier measures against the Social Democrats. He was also a direct influence behind the social reforms in Caprivi's New Course. Yet there are also two examples of the more negative aspects of the Kaiser's personal rule. The first concerns his own personal eccentricities. In addition to being influenced by widely disliked advisers (such as Eulenberg and Holstein), he was disconcertingly unpredictable in his public announcements. He caused particular embarrassment in the *Daily Telegraph* Affair (1908), when he maintained that the German people were hostile towards Britain – and that he was the only restraining influence upon them. This provoked condemnation from all quarters in the Reichstag. Second, he also showed a lack of judgement when working *with* the establishment: in the Zabern Crisis (1913) he refused to take action against the military even after it had been clearly established that civilians had been subjected to abuse and physical violence.

Wilhelm II was strikingly different to Wilhelm I and Frederick III. But Germany, too, was changing rapidly after 1890. There was inevitably a strong mutual influence between the two – both positive and negative.

3. 'The main decision made by Kaiser Wilhelm II in the 1890s was to pursue *Weltpolitik*.'

   a) What is meant by *Weltpolitik* in relation to German foreign policy between 1890 and 1914?   (3 marks)

   b) Explain the reasons for *Weltpolitik* and its effects on Germany's relations with Britain.   (7 marks)

   c) 'Kaiser Wilhelm II was not fully in control of Germany's foreign policy between 1890 and 1914.' Explain why you agree or disagree with this view.   (15 marks)

See Chapter 2, Essay 1.

War and revolution, 1914–18

4. How valid is the view that Germany provoked war in 1914?   (90 marks)

See Chapter 2, Essay 7.

5. Assess the effect of the First World War on Germany.   (90 marks)

See Chapter 2, Essay 13.

6.   'The emergence of a German Republic was a political revolution, brought by the collapse of the Kaiser's military dictatorship as a direct result of the First World War.'

    a)   Explain the reference to the 'Kaiser's military dictatorship'.   (3 marks)

Germany had entered the First World War under the civilian government of Bethmann Hollweg. By 1917, however, Germany was facing the real prospect of defeat and internal upheaval; the Kaiser therefore gave way to pressure from the two leading commanders, Ludendorff and Hindenburg, to form a military government. This was widely criticised as a 'dictatorship' by the left within Germany and by the Allied governments outside.

    b)   Explain the changes which occurred between 1918 and 1919 to make Germany a republic.   (7 marks)

A new Republic was proclaimed on 9 November 1918 by Philipp Scheidemann to replace the previous regime of imperial Germany, which had been under the rule of Kaiser Wilhelm II. It became more permanent with the establishment of a constitution in 1919.

The Kaiser's government was severely undermined by the threat of military defeat on the western front, by the entry of the United States into the war and by a crippling blockade imposed by the Royal Navy. One development led to another, until the whole system fell apart. The military dictatorship of Ludendorff and Hindenburg, which had underpinned the government from July 1917, suddenly stepped aside and, in October 1918, advised the Kaiser to appoint a new Chancellor, Prince Max of Baden, and to negotiate an armistice with the Allies. President Wilson made it difficult for the new administration by insisting that the Allies would negotiate only with a democratic Germany. Not surprisingly, Max of Baden and the Kaiser lost control and, as the political power weakened, the armed forces began to disintegrate with naval and military mutinies. When the state of Bavaria erupted in open revolt, the Kaiser expected the same to happen elsewhere and fled to Holland. This forced the hand of the moderate leaders of the SPD. To maintain some sort of political order, therefore, they proclaimed an immediate replacement. In the absence of a monarch, this had to be in the form of a republic.

The proclamation did not in itself guarantee anything and there was considerable tension over Germany's political future over the next few months. There was, however, no credible alternative to the new republic. The right-wing Nationalists (DNVP) would have preferred the reinstatement of the empire, but any attempt to do this would certainly have brought the occupation of Germany by the Allies. The far left, comprising the Spartacists (later the KPD) and the Independent Socialists (USPD), were probably a greater threat and their leaders – Liebknecht and Luxemburg – did try to overthrow the republic and install a soviet-style regime in imitation of Bolshevik Russia. The republic was, however, able to survive, partly because its leaders withdrew the government from Berlin to Weimar during the Spartacist revolt in January. At the same time, Ebert was able to do a deal with the armed forces, now under Groener, to put down the Spartacists and eradicate the communist threat both in Berlin and in Munich; this was carried out mainly by the *Freikorps*. Although Ebert and Scheidemann could not have approved of the brutality used, they could at least claim to have saved the republic from a soviet takeover. Their work was subsequently confirmed by the establishment of a permanent constitution.

c) 'Germany experienced a political revolution between 1918 and 1919.' Explain why you agree or disagree with this view. (15 marks)

The term 'revolution' has a variety of meanings in this context, each producing a different interpretation and approach. The first development, it has been argued, was a revolution 'from above', when the military dictatorship of Ludendorff and Hindenburg gave way in October 1918 to constitutional government under Prince Max of Baden. This, however, rapidly gave way to revolution 'from below', which started, as a direct result of impact of the war, with naval mutinies at Wilhemshaven, Kiel, Hamburg, Bremen and Lubeck and army disaffection in Frankfurt, Cologne, Stuttgart and Leipzig. The revolution 'from below' then divided into two conflicting strands, sometimes described as 'moderate' and 'radical' respectively.

The 'moderate' strand was dominated by the Social Democrats. It involved the proclamation of the Republic on 9 November by Scheidemann, the signing of the armistice on 11 November and the installation of the SPD leader, Ebert, as the first Chancellor. It ended the Kaiser Reich and, by the 1919 Constitution, confirmed that Germany was a permanent republic. In this way, war acted as a catalyst for the destruction of autocracy and the emergence of democracy through the agency of a *controlled* revolution.

This was, however, threatened by an alternative revolution 'from below', which aimed at nothing less than the creation of a soviet-style regime based on that established in Russia in October 1917. This occurred in Berlin at the turn of 1918 as the Spartacists under Liebknecht and Luxemburg tried to seize the capital through a German version of the Bolshevik revolution. The influence of Russia was direct since both were in direct contact with Lenin and, even after their deaths in January 1919, the remainder of the Spartacists became the core of a new German Communist Party, or KPD. The moderates, meanwhile, had taken action to preserve their own strand of 'revolution' against a communist version which would destroy it altogether. This explains Ebert's use of the army under Groener – not only against the Spartacists but also against Eisner's soviet republic in Bavaria. Ebert saw his role as preserving the interim democracy until a more permanent version could be established. What happened in Germany was therefore the reverse of Russia's experience the previous year. In Russia, the moderate Provisional Government had fallen to the radical Bolsheviks; in Germany the Provisional Government defeated the communists.

This categorisation shows that 'revolution' can be a relative as well as an absolute term. It is, however, possible to challenge it. Arguably, the only 'revolution' as such was the one which failed – launched by the Spartacists in Berlin and Eisner in Bavaria – because these alone would have transformed the political system of Germany. The other developments were certainly major changes, but they had too many links with the past to warrant the description 'revolution'. The Kaiser's 'revolution from above' in October 1918 was merely the ending of an emergency military dictatorship and the restoration of the constitutional power of the Chancellor: Prince Max possessed no authority which had not been used by Bethmann Hollweg before 1917. Even the emergence of the Republic was not really a 'revolution'. The Constitution of 1919 altered as few of the institutions of the Reich as possible (even referring in places to the Republic *as* the 'Reich'). The Reichstag was retained, the *Bundesrat* became the **Reichsrat**, the parties either retained their existing identity, or were recast under another name. What really changed was not so much the institutions as the way in which they related to each other. But even here the conservative forces in the civil service, the judiciary and army ensured that there was a strong continuity with the past.

The Weimar Republic and the first crisis, 1919–23

7. **'The democratic features of the Weimar Constitution were a triumph for moderate political influences in Germany in 1919.'**

   a) **Explain the reference to 'moderate political influences in Germany in 1919'.** **(3 marks)**

'Moderation' is a relative term. Political moderation in 1919 contrasted with the revolutionary attempt of the Spartacists and Independent Socialists to set up communist regimes in Berlin and Bavaria, and also with the conservative influences which remained from the old Reich. The political parties exercising 'moderate influences' were the SPD under Ebert and Scheidemann, the DDP, the Centre and the DVP. The Constitution was framed by Hugo Preuss, a prominent lawyer in the DDP.

   b) **To what extent did Germany's political parties contribute to 'democracy' in the Weimar Republic?** **(7 marks)**

This question can be addressed in two ways. The first involves the basic attitudes and policies of the parties towards democracy in the Republic. The second is more concerned with the active contributions of the parties to the Republic's survival and demise.

Four of the major parties were consistent supporters of the principles of liberal democracy. Ranging from moderate left to moderate right, these were the SPD, the DDP, the Centre and the DVP. The SPD had lost its radical Marxist wing, which meant that any socialism it adopted was no longer revolutionary; the DDP provided many of the more classical liberal ideas which appeared within the 1919 Constitution; and the Centre and DVP emphasised the balance between tradition and progress, between authority and rights. By contrast, liberal democracy was strongly opposed by the USPD and, more especially, the KPD, which aimed for the soviet style of 'democracy' introduced by the Bolsheviks. On the right, the DNVP were instinctively opposed to the erosion of traditional authoritarianism, while the newly emergent NSDAP projected a strongly anti-democratic form of populism.

The actions of the parties affected democracy in different ways. The KPD and NSDAP both attempted to bring the Republic down, in 1921 and 1923 respectively, before switching to a more legal strategy. Both continued to campaign against the Republic and the KPD eventually refused to co-operate with the moderate parties to prevent the NSDAP from gaining power. The DNVP damaged the cause of democracy after 1928 through their close collaboration with Hitler. The SPD, DDP, Centre and DVP all upheld democracy and were the mainstay of most of the coalitions which kept the Republic in existence. On the other hand, they also contributed to the Republic's problem. For example, the rift between the SPD and Centre in 1930 saw the end of the Grand Coalition and the emergence of an authoritarian regime dependent on Presidential decrees.

   c) **How 'democratic' was the Weimar Constitution?** **(15 marks)**

The Weimar Constitution contained examples of an advanced democracy while, at the same time, maintaining several authoritarian links with the past. The contradiction between the two was eventually to lead to democracy's irreversible decline.

Figure 4.3 **The German constitutions of 1871 and 1919**

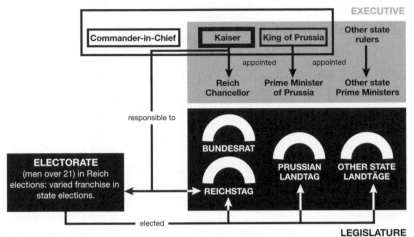

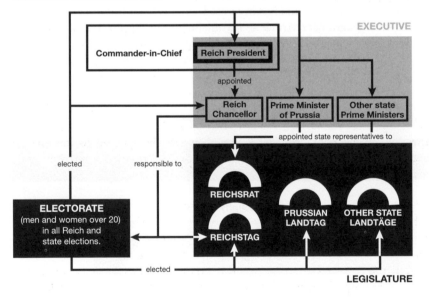

There was certainly evidence of those features most commonly associated with democracy. One of these was popular representation – by Article 1, 'Political authority emanates from the people'.[1] The electoral system was based on 'universal, equal, direct, and secret suffrage by men and women over twenty years of age, according to the principle of proportional representation.'[2] This related the number of votes cast to the size of party representation in the Reichstag, with the result that smaller groups could be included alongside the major parties. The president was elected by the people every seven years whereas, of course, the former Kaiser's authority had been hereditary.

Another component of a democratic system is the responsibility of the executive to the legislature, which had been largely missing in the Second Reich. According to Article 54, the chancellor now required the 'confidence of the Reichstag'. Third, some democratic systems also include provision for rights of individual states in the form of federalism. Section IV of the Constitution guaranteed the autonomy of the German Länder and for the representation of their interests in the *Reichsrat*. Fourth, the population as a whole needs to be assured of basic rights. The Constitution guaranteed equality before the law, 'liberty of travel and residence' and freedom of expression and speech.[3] Finally, democracy has to be guaranteed against threats to destroy it. Article 48 provided for the use of emergency powers by the president, should these be needed. The Reichstag could, however, refuse these powers through a majority vote.

In theory, therefore, the Weimar Constitution was one of the most democratic in Europe. In practice, however, it did not work well. Some of the clauses distorted the others and worked in ways which were not foreseen. The inevitable casualty was democracy itself.

The main problem was the operation of proportional representation within the German context of splintered parties. Every government was, by definition, a coalition. These were initially based on the parties of the moderate left to the moderate right (the SPD, DDP, Centre and DVP). In 1930, however, the divergent policies of the SPD and Centre, largely over the issue of unemployment benefit, caused the collapse of consensus politics. The Constitution had no mechanism for dealing with this – except through presidential intervention. Article 48 allowed the president to issue decree laws in an emergency, bypassing the normal legislative process. This had been intended to make democracy more secure and had been used selectively for this purpose by Ebert. But, with the end of coalition government, Article 48 became the means by which chancellors like Brüning, Papen and Schleicher remained in power without a popular mandate. Thus the clause which was intended to save democracy from a revolution of the left eventually undermined it more insidiously by giving the initiative to the political right.

*Figure 4.4 **The political parties of imperial and Weimar Germany***

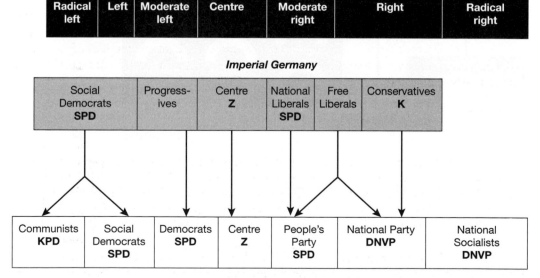

8. (a) What crises faced the Weimar Republic between 1919 and 1923? (15 marks)

The newly formed German Republic faced a variety of crises, both internal and external. Two examples of these were economic, in the form of hyperinflation, and political, in the form of revolts.

The economic crisis was best shown by the decline in the value of the mark from 8.9 to the dollar in 1918 to 42,000,000,000 to the dollar by November 1923. The reasons are controversial but can be seen as a complex interaction between various influences. The long-term cause was the First World War, which brought about creeping inflation, halving the value of the mark against the dollar between 1913 and 1918. The Berlin government accelerated this by introducing from 1919 onwards a policy of deficit spending, based on heavy printing of notes. At first this was an attempt to finance reconstruction without increasing taxation, which would have been the only other possibility. But when the Reparations Commission announced in 1921 the final bill of 132,000 million marks the government became much less concerned about the consequences of its policy; after all, financial collapse would demonstrate to the Allies in the strongest possible terms the injustice of the reparations terms. Once the French had invaded the Ruhr, there was little incentive to put a stop to the printing presses and the hyperinflation merged with the government policy of passive resistance. As events turned out, this proved effective in bringing the Allies to their senses.

The political crisis was caused by revolutionary activity from the extreme left and the extreme right to replace the newly established system of democracy with one of several radical alternatives. The far left showed, in the Spartacist uprising of January 1919, their preference for a communist system, based on that of Soviet Russia. The Kapp Putsch of 1920 was the exact opposite to the communist revolt: it was to have been the means whereby Germany could return to the more conservative system of the old Reich, possibly with the restoration of the Kaiser. Hitler's Munich Putsch (1923) had something in common with both. Unlike the Kapp Putsch, it envisaged a new regime rather than a revived one; on the other hand, this would be a system of the radical right, not of the communist left.

There was inevitably some interaction between the economic and political crises – and between the strands of the political upheaval. The Spartacist uprising and the Kapp Putsch both impressed on the government the need to avoid antagonising any more of the population through increasing taxation. This was a factor in the inflationary spiral which, by 1923, convinced Hitler that he could launch a putsch in Munich.

b) Why did the Weimar Republic manage to survive the crises of 1920–3? (15 marks)

According to Kolb, it was 'almost a miracle that the Weimar democracy succeeded in maintaining its existence during these years of extreme tribulation'. At first sight, this is an attractive proposition. There are, however, feasible explanations for the survival of the Republic, based on the actions of the government, the weaknesses of the opposition and the favourable influence of external factors.

The actions of the government were surprisingly resilient and pragmatic. On the one hand, it was prepared to follow the line of least resistance by printing money as an alternative to raising taxation. On the other hand, it was able to act decisively to end the economic crisis in November

1923. Gustav Stresemann, the Chancellor, managed to deal remarkably quickly with the threat of economic collapse by cutting government expenditure and instructing Schacht and Luther to substitute the **Rentenmark** for the devalued *Reichsmark*. This proved highly successful in winning the Western powers round to the view that Germany deserved their support and resulted in the signing of the Dawes Plan in 1924. The government also took firm action against the political threats; President Ebert, for example, used the emergency powers allowed to him by Article 48 of the Constitution to overcome the various threats to the Republic from the Kapp Putsch and from the Ruhr and Saxon uprisings.

Although the response of the government had to some extent been effective, even more important to the survival of the Republic was the shortcomings of its enemies. This applied to both the far left and the far right. The far left, mainly communists, lacked popular support and effective organisation. The KPD never became a mass movement and, even when combined with the USPD, were never able to win more than 15 per cent of the vote in the Reichstag elections before 1924. Nor did they have the structure and leadership of the Bolsheviks, which Lenin had used to compensate for a similar lack of popularity in Russia. The Republic benefited from a similar weakness on the far right, which consisted at this stage of small *völkisch* groups competing with each other for a tiny part of the electorate. As yet, the radical right had none of the support of the conservative right which later gave it respectability. Although the DNVP shared the hatred of the NSDAP for the Republic, they were not prepared to be drawn into premature putsches. Hence, in the early 1920s, the Nazis and similar *völkisch* groups were even less popular than the communists.

Finally, the Republic benefited from a sudden change of external circumstance in 1924. The right-wing government of Poincaré, which had ordered French troops into the Ruhr in March 1923, was succeeded by a moderate one which reversed the action. The year 1924 also saw the formation of the first British Labour government. The new Prime Minister, Ramsay MacDonald, had a particular interest in foreign policy and, as a renowned pacifist, was determined to restore harmony in Europe. Meanwhile, because of the extent of the economic crisis in Germany, the United States were also prepared to make an exception to their policy of non-involvement in European affairs. The overall result of these developments was the Dawes Plan (1924). This made possible a rapid recovery by Germany from the crisis of 1923 by ensuring the evacuation of French troops from the Ruhr, the rescheduling of reparations payments and the introduction of loans by the United States. These terms provided the basis for Germany's period of recovery between 1924 and 1929.

9. With what justification can the Treaty of Versailles be considered a 'harsh settlement' for Germany? (90 marks)

See Chapter 2, Essay 18.

10. How serious was the effect of the Treaty of Versailles on Germany? (90 marks)

The Treaty of Versailles has been widely blamed for inflicting mortal damage on Germany, and for fuelling its two main crises of 1919–23 and 1929–33. It could, however, be argued that, while the damage inflicted was considerable, it was indirect. The Republic recovered from the immediate consequences of the Treaty but not from the long-term problems which the Treaty helped set in motion. The most destructive effects were therefore when the Treaty acted as a catalyst for other forces.

The economic situation which undermined the Weimar Republic did have a connection with the Treaty of Versailles. But the nature of this connection needs to be precisely identified.

At first it was direct. When, in April 1921, the Allied Reparations Commission finalised the bill at 132,000 million gold marks, the immediate result was the acceleration of hyperinflation between 1921 and 1923. The latter might perhaps have been prevented had the German government opted for raising taxation instead printing notes. But such a course would have alienated still further a public already deeply hostile to the whole notion of reparations as a punishment for 'war guilt'. It is also possible that the government let things get out of hand to show the Allies that the Versailles settlement was too harsh.

The rescheduling of reparations after 1923 may, at first sight, appear to have reduced the potential for damage to Germany. After all, the Dawes Plan of 1924 enabled Germany to make reparations payments in proportion to an 'index of prosperity', while the Young Plan of 1929 extended the deadline by fifty-eight years. Furthermore, the economic stability of Germany was to be guaranteed by the accessibility of huge amounts of American investment. Yet the new economic order, designed to make reparations more bearable at the time, actually made Germany more vulnerable to economic crisis in the future. A new chain of dependency was set up, by which Germany provided reparations payments to Britain, France and Italy who, in turn were enabled to pay off their war debts to the United States. These returned as loans to Germany. The famous triangular pattern was therefore firmly set.

It might be thought that this alleviated Germany's economic problems. Actually, it intensified them. The German economy was damaged – not by the future payment of reparations but by the new economic system which made this payment possible. During the period 1924–9 American loans had a positive impact: Germany received 16,000 million marks, whereas she paid 7000 million in reparations. This substantial gain made possible the expansion of industrial production which, in turn, resulted in full employment. Unfortunately, the nature of this expansion made Germany highly vulnerable to any fluctuation in the world markets. The Wall Street Crash, which occurred in October 1929, resulted in a sudden withdrawal of the American loans from Germany. The key problem was that the loans had been short term and repayable on demand. In the optimistic climate of the mid-1920s these were constantly renewable – and invested in long-term projects. The sudden recall therefore precipitated a rapid collapse in German industry and a spectacular increase in unemployment. These events were not related to reparations themselves. They were the direct result of the way in which Germany had become dependent on the triangular relationship, developed to deal with the original reparations problem. The irony is that reparations themselves no longer counted for much: they had been further rescheduled by the 1929 Young Plan and were virtually cancelled at the Lausanne Conference. If, therefore, economic catastrophe occurred, it was the result of the loans engendered by reparations rather than by the reparations themselves.

With economic crisis came the collapse of the political democracy of the Weimar Republic and the rise of Hitler and the Nazis. This was made possible by growing popular support for the right and the increased co-operation after 1929 between the Nazis and the conservative elements in Germany. Both trends were indirectly accelerated by the impact of Versailles. This was important in undermining German democracy – not because it acted directly in the rise of Hitler but because it produced several key influences which continued to grow long after the Treaty itself had ceased to be critical. In this way, the Treaty was itself a catalyst for, rather than a direct cause of, the collapse of the Republic. This operated as follows.

The territorial and financial terms of Versailles and, above all, the 'War Guilt Clause', caused widespread resentment. The unfortunate target of this was the Republic's government, condemned by the media for having signed a 'disgraceful' document. Even though the government of Scheidemann had tried to negotiate more moderate terms, the Republic faced an ultimatum from the Allies to sign the Treaty – or support an Allied occupation. In this way, the Republic was the hapless victim of external circumstances. This was made worse by the attempt of the government, through a symposium of German historians, to disprove Germany's responsibility for the outbreak of war in 1914. This had the unintended side-effect of reviving support for the former German Reich and enabling Hindenburg to foster the legend of the German army being 'stabbed in the back' by the government in November 1918. This phrase became one of the major criticisms of the Republic once Hindenburg had been elected President in 1925.

The reaction against 'war guilt' also helped the rise of Hitler – by associating the Nazis with the conservative right. Hitler's extreme views were given greater credibility and popular appeal by his use of conservative terms like 'stab in the back' and the 'Versailles *diktat*'. These gave the radical Nazis a common ground with the more respectable conservatives within the DNVP, the army and business which, in turn, widened Hitler's appeal at a vital time in the development of the Nazi movement. They also gave Hitler more credibility as a politician and assisted the political manoeuvres which resulted in his appointment as Chancellor in January 1933. Thus, although over a decade had passed since the signing of the Treaty of Versailles, 'war guilt' had become, in the words of Heiber, 'a dangerous explosive charge'.

The Republic's recovery and second crisis, 1924–33

11. Assess Stresemann's contribution to Germany's domestic and foreign policies between 1923 and 1929. (90 marks)

Gustav Stresemann occupied two main offices during this period: Chancellor (1923) and Foreign Minister (1923–9). His importance transcended both and he became the leading German statesman of the 1920s; indeed the period 1923–9 is often referred to as the 'Stresemann era'. There are, however, also criticisms which can be levelled at his record.

Stresemann's domestic achievements were limited in number because of his short time in office as Chancellor (August to November 1923). He showed nevertheless the importance of decisive policy making and reversed the previous tendency to drift and political evasion. His one crucial contribution during the period was the introduction of the *Rentenmark*, issued by a new *Rentenbank*, to re-establish the value of the old *Reichsmark*. This was a major influence in bringing hyperinflation under control. It could, however, be argued that he was the political catalyst rather than the policy maker; the ideas behind these changes really came from Luther and Schacht (Finance Minister and President of the *Reichsbank* respectively). The fact that he was only Chancellor for a few months indicates a weakness in his personal power base – and possibly insecurity in high office. His real political role was as a bridge in the Reichstag, which he best fulfilled as a minister rather than as Chancellor. He served in all the coalitions between 1923 and 1929 and used his considerable experience to keep these together and to negotiate Reichstag majorities for individual political machines: as leader of the People's Party (DVP) and before that of the National Liberals (NLP) he was experienced in the difficult art of parliamentary diplomacy.

Paradoxically he had this domestic impact while serving as Foreign Minister. But Stresemann's diplomatic skills were used to even greater effect in Germany's foreign policy; he clearly considered

Figure 4.5 **The triangular economic relationship following the Dawes Plan (1924) – reparations and loans, 1924–9**

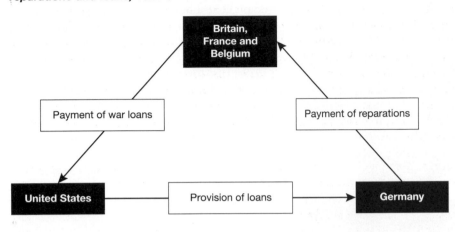

himself more at home as Foreign Minister than as Chancellor. He made two major contributions, although each tended to provide short-term rather than long-term solutions to Germany's problems.

The first was to resolve the issue of reparations. The Dawes Plan of 1924 rescheduled payments and set up the channels for American investment into Germany, while the Young Plan (1929) postponed the deadline for completion by a further 58 years. These, however, had a mixed impact. In the short term, they provided the impetus for Germany's economic recovery and prosperity, American investment helping the revival of manufacturing and foreign trade. Unfortunately, the prosperity of the period 1924–8 was illusory since the course taken created excessive dependence on American loans. This had disastrous implications between 1929 and 1931 as the onset of depression meant that Germany was faced with the prospect of having to repay short-term loans which had been invested in long-term projects. It is true that German recovery had been swift, but how sound was Stresemann's infrastructure for this recovery?

Stresemann's second achievement in foreign policy was the rehabilitation of Germany in Europe through the Locarno Pact (1924) and membership of the League of Nations in 1926; Germany was also integrated into the world-wide Kellogg–Briand Pact (1928). His personal importance in bringing about this reconciliation was recognised through the award of a Nobel Peace Prize in 1926. He was one of the architects of **collective security**, the means whereby the European powers would reconcile their differences in western Europe by negotiation where possible and, where necessary, collective action against an aggressor after consultation with the League of Nations. Again, however, there were deficiencies. Collective security did not cover eastern Europe, where Germany's boundaries with her neighbours posed major problems in the future. There was also a strand of Stresemann's policy which was secretive and opportunistic. For example, the Treaty of Berlin, formed with the Soviet Union in 1926 had the additional – and controversial – motive of enabling the German army under von Seeckt to begin secret rearmament. Stresemann was thus a diplomat with two faces. One was the reconciler aiming, in his words, to make Germany 'the bridge which would bring East and West together in the development of Europe'. The other, however, was the revisionist, who sought a means of gradually undermining the Treaty of Versailles. His strength was that he could do the two things at once. But he could not assume that those who succeeded him could do likewise.

Figure 4.6 **Gustav Stresemann**

Which is the greatest of Stresemann's achievements depends on the criteria used. His economic contributions were all cancelled out by the depression – and the dependence of Germany on US loans which he helped promote weakened Germany's capacity to weather the storm after 1929. His foreign policy re-established Germany's influence in Europe, although the regime to benefit from this was the Third Reich, not the Weimar Republic. The precedent of political co-operation was perhaps his most creditable contribution to Germany's future, even though it was interrupted by the Republic's descent into dictatorship and by the Nazi regime which followed.

12. How real was Germany's internal stability between 1924 and 1929?   **(90 marks)**

It is usually argued that the Weimar Republic underwent a complete recovery after the economic and political crises of 1921–3, and that its stability recovery lasted until late in 1929. This was then reversed by the Wall Street Crash and the onset of depression. Although this view is still tenable, it is more likely that the stability of the Republic during these years was more apparent than real: there were major flaws in this 'stability' which made the Republic all the more vulnerable to future crisis.

The case for economic stability is, at first sight, compelling. Hyperinflation had been ended by Schacht, by means of the *Rentenmark* and the *Rentenbank,* while the Dawes Plan (1924) removed the worst effects of the reparations payments and gave the German economy a boost through the inflow of investments from the United States. The foundations were therefore laid for six years of economic prosperity and growth. German industries doubled their overall production between 1923 and 1929, benefiting from American investment and also from the new production techniques of 'Fordism'. Industrial efficiency was also increased by the development of the cartel system and by increasingly harmonious relations between workers and managers. These developments produced an underlying stability which could be destroyed only by external crisis.

A similar stability, it has been argued, existed in the political sphere. This showed itself in two ways. First, there was no repetition of the Spartacist uprising (1919), the Kapp Putsch (1920) and the Munich Putsch (1923). Second, the electorate seemed to have become more moderate, which resulted in the decline of the parties of the far right and far left in the Reichstag elections; between 1924 and 1929, the combined seats of the NSDAP, DNVP and KPD fell from 187 (1924) to 149 (1928). By contrast, the moderate parties prospered, the combined seats of the DVP, Centre, DDP and SPD increasing from 237 seats to 285. There was also a revival of consensus politics, often used as a barometer for political stability, including the Grand Coalition of the SPD, Centre, DDP and DVP, under the leadership of Müller. The coalition might well have continued into the 1930s but for the catastrophe of the depression, which wrecked the consensus between Müller and Brüning and tempted future governments to make dictatorial use of Article 48 of the Constitution.

By this argument, the Weimar Republic was genuinely stable between 1924 and 1929. Economic well-being was guaranteed by steady growth and prosperity, while political consensus replaced government crisis. The fact that the Republic collapsed within four years of the end of the period must, therefore, be attributable to external, not internal, influences. But this view is too simplistic. Recovery, it can be argued, was temporary because it was badly flawed; these flaws, in turn, made it vulnerable to external crisis. Stability seemed to exist, but it was partly an illusion.

This certainly applies to the economic situation. Dependence on external credit was dangerous: the short-term loans from the United States were invested inappropriately in long-term projects and infrastructure, making Germany vulnerable to any sudden change on the US stock market, as happened in 1929. But it should not be assumed that the German economy was sound apart from this one fatal flaw. There were other destabilising influences at work. Although German industrial production rose, thus giving an illusion of stability, there was no corresponding increase in the volume of foreign trade. This meant that the main market for industrial expansion would have to be inside Germany itself. Yet, from 1928 to 1929 consumer goods production actually decreased by 3 per cent – even though total production rose by 2 per cent. Since the industrial drive was not consumer-based, it was therefore inherently vulnerable. Even agriculture was unstable. German farmers were affected by the increase in competition from other countries without being able to modernise their production techniques.

Thus two related propositions are possible. The first is that there was a degree of economic recovery from 1924 to 1929 – but that this recovery was inherently fragile. The second is that external forces in 1929 did not suddenly bring down a healthy economy; rather, they further weakened one which was already failing to find its own balance. Hence the German economy was living on borrowed time as well as on borrowed money.

Political stability was also flawed: the 'positive' period between 1924 and 1929 can actually be seen as a negative one. Although there were coalitions, the real difficulty was to establish stable ones. The aims and policies of the individual parties made it difficult to achieve continuity. The SPD, for example, refused to join any coalition containing members of the DNVP. This meant that any coalition hoping for an overall majority would have to comprise the parties of the moderate left to moderate right (the SPD, DDP, Centre and DVP) or those from the centre to the right (DDP, Centre, DVP and DNVP). Even during the period of so-called economic prosperity, these coalitions were inherently unstable and fractured on the fault lines of either domestic or foreign policy. The only man who could make the system work at all was the Foreign Minister, Gustav Stresemann – but he died in 1929.

To add to the long-term instability, the differences between the parties were actually widening throughout the so-called period of recovery. The SPD, for example, were moving further to the left, the Centre more to the right. The liberal parties – the DDP and DVP – were so vulnerable that they were on the point of breaking up, which explains the suddenness of their collapse in 1930. Parliamentary democracy was therefore in trouble before 1929.

How do these trends combine? The traditional argument is that this coalition broke up in 1930 on the issue of cutting unemployment benefits; this, in turn was the direct result of the externally imposed depression. Germany was stable up to the time of that depression. But this is not entirely true. The parties of the Grand Coalition were already divided over economic and social policies which, in turn, reflected increasing tensions between sections of the economic infrastructure. The depression did not, therefore, create a crisis where none had previously existed; it exacerbated one which was already there.

13. Compare the causes and effects of the economic crisis of 1929–31 with that of 1921–3.

(90 marks)

A crisis is the point of balance between two possible outcomes: recovery or collapse. During the years from 1921 to 1923, and again from 1929 to 1933, the future of the Weimar Republic was poised. Despite certain similarities between the two occasions, there were fundamental differences which explain why the Republic survived the first crisis – but not the second.

One of the main similarities between the causes of the economic crises of 1921–3 and 1929–31 is that both were started by external influences. In the case of the first crisis the key stimulus was the final demand, drawn up in 1921 by the Reparations Commission, for a total of 136,000 million gold marks. This had a significant and immediate effect on the decline of the value of the *Reichsmark* since foreign currency had to be purchased to make the payments. The inflation accelerated when, in 1923, the French invaded the Ruhr in response to the German government's default on the latest payments. From that point onwards, inflation became hyperinflation. The 1929–31 economic crisis was also started by an outside impulse – again in two stages. This time, the Wall Street Crash of November 1929 resulted in the recall of all the American loans which had done so much between 1924 and 1929 to stimulate Germany's economic recovery. The situation was exacerbated by a second crash – this time the collapse of *Kreditanstalt* in Vienna, which resulted in the collapse of the German banking system.

Another similar cause was the interaction between external and internal influences: in both cases, the former were compounded by the latter. For example, the French invasion of the Ruhr resulted in a government policy of printing banknotes. This fuelled the most rapid period of inflation between March and August 1923 until plans were drawn up to replace the inflated mark with a new *Rentenmark*. Similarly, the recall of American loans after October 1929 was made more traumatic by the way in which these had been used within Germany since 1924. In effect, short-term investment had been channelled into long-term projects, which meant that repayments could only be made by serious damage to industrial infrastructure.

There were, of course, major differences in the origins of the two economic crises. One is the scale. The 1921–3 crisis affected Germany alone since it resulted from a combination of circumstances following the treatment of Germany by the Versailles Settlement of 1919. By contrast, the 1929–31 crisis was on a global scale, starting in the United States and spreading to all countries. Similarly, the collapse of *Kreditanstalt* in 1931 affected other European states in addition to Germany, helping to accelerate the depression in Britain. There is also a fundamental difference in the way in which reparations worked to fuel the crises. Their impact on the inflation of 1921–3 was direct. On the other hand, their influence on the crisis of 1929–31 was indirect, the result of the sudden malfunctioning of the new channel for investment set up by the Dawes Plan to deal with reparations.

There were certain similarities between the effects of the two crises. Both brought social dislocation and the threat of political upheaval. Rising prices between 1921 and 1923 caused a rapid decline in the standard of living, in many respects similar to the impact of growing unemployment after 1929. There was also insecurity of personal savings in 1923 and of personal bank deposits in 1931. Governments faced added difficulty in sustaining coalition governments as Cuno's administration collapsed in 1923 and Müller pulled out of the Grand Coalition with Brüning in 1930. There was additional pressure from radical groups such as the Nazis and communists: their violent rivalry intensified in 1923 and 1930 as on each occasion both sensed the impending collapse of bourgeois democracy.

Despite these similarities, what is most striking about the effects of the two crises was their contrasts. In the first place, their economic impact was literally poles apart. The crisis of 1921–3 was one of short-term hyperinflation, characterised by increases in prices but not in unemployment. The 1929–31 crisis, on the other hand, brought long-term depression, in which prices and earnings fell and unemployment rose. Germany's industrial base was much more severely affected by the second than by the first and the working class more badly dislocated by the experience of heavy unemployment. There was also a sharp contrast in the political consequences. The 1921–3 crisis was followed by recovery and the greater political stability of the so-called 'Stresemann era', whereas the crisis of 1929–31 started a series of events which by 1933 produced a complete change of regime. Two further differences counted here. One was that President Ebert was more careful in his use of Article 48 of the Constitution during and after the first crisis than President Hindenburg during the second. Ebert guided Germany back to a functioning democracy, while Hindenburg transformed parliamentary democracy into presidential dictatorship. This admirably suited Hitler. Nazis seats in the Reichstag, only 32 in May 1924, rose suddenly to 107 in 1930 and 230 in July 1932. This showed the very different effect of the two crises on support for the Nazi Party. In 1924 they were a lunatic fringe ignored by a coalition government; by 1931 they were a major force who had to be taken into account by the conservative right.

Economic crises normally have political effects. The result of the 1921–3 crisis was a political effort to solve the problems which had led to the economic crisis in the first place. It was the Republic's misfortune that the nature of this solution was, however, to create a very different and more serious problem in the future. In this sense, the effect of the first economic crisis was one of the causes of the second.

14. (a) Explain the way in which Hitler and the Nazis came to power between 1929 and January 1933. **(15 marks)**

The key developments in Hitler's rise to power between 1929 and January 1933 were, first, the dramatic increase in the support for the Nazis and, second, the way in which Hitler sought one of the key offices of state.

Hitler's quest for power was greatly strengthened by the growth in support for the Nazis. Hitler took full advantage of the Republic's crisis in 1929, arranging mass rallies and a flood of material from the propaganda department. The Reichstag election of 1930 was a triumph for the NSDAP which secured 6.5 million votes and increased its representation from 12 to 107 seats, thus becoming the second largest party in the Reichstag. The trend continued in the election of July 1932, when the NSDAP became easily the largest party, with 230 seats and 37.3 per cent of the popular vote. These figures dropped back slightly in November 1933 to 196 seats in the Reichstag and 33.1 per cent of the vote. At the same time, Hitler was capitalising on his electoral success by cultivating connections with the traditional right, including the DNVP, the army, industrialists like Thyssen, and agriculturalists. He drew up the Harzburg Front of October 1931 and, in January 1932, made a direct appeal to German industrialists in his Dusseldorf speech.

The success in the Reichstag elections enhanced Hitler's image and popularity but it did not by itself guarantee him political power. This was because it occurred, ironically, at a time when parliamentary democracy no longer counted in Germany. Hitler therefore had to use his popularity to gain office in some other way. His preferred option was head of state. In the presidential elections of 1932 he therefore challenged Hindenburg but lost on the second ballot by 13.8 million votes to Hindenburg's 19.4 million. The only other possibility was now to try for the second most important office – the chancellorship.

This proved more successful because of the use of back-door methods of diplomacy and intrigue involving Hindenburg, Schleicher and Papen. When Hindenburg dismissed Brüning's government in May 1932, the new Chancellor, Papen, offered Hitler a cabinet post. Hitler declined, holding out for the chancellorship itself; his decision was vindicated by the increase in Nazi support in the Reichstag election of July 1933, although this dipped in November. Then events swung in Hitler's favour. Papen proved incapable of holding power for very long and the chancellorship went to Schleicher, Papen's deadly rival. Schleicher tried to attatch individual Nazis to his government, but tempted only Strasser. Papen and Hitler now combined against Schleicher and, on 30 January 1933, Hindenburg was persuaded to appoint Hitler as Chancellor in a coalition government which would contain only three Nazis and with Papen as Hitler's Vice-chancellor.

Hitler had therefore achieved power more or less through the constitutional process. Almost immediately, however, he started to dismantle that process to ensure that it could not work against him in the future.

b) **Assess the relative importance of Brüning, Hindenburg and Papen in undermining democracy in the Weimar Republic.** (15 marks)

The contributions of Brüning, Hindenburg and Papen to the decline of democracy in the Weimar Republic were different in emphasis but complementary in their overall effect.

Heinrich Brüning was the first Chancellor of the Republic to attempt to govern permanently without majority support in the Reichstag. After the resignation of Müller and the collapse of the Grand Coalition, Brüning survived between March 1930 and May 1932 largely through the use of presidential decrees under Article 48 of the Constitution. As leader of the moderate Centre Party, Brüning was not an enemy of the Republic as such. But he inflicted great damage to the fabric of democracy. His was actually the longest chancellorship of the entire Republic and was therefore a gradual transition in the drift to the right.

Figure 4.7 *Paul von Hindenburg*

Paul von Hindenburg was more openly anti-democratic than Brüning. He was largely responsible for the 'stab in the back' myth aimed at the Republic and, after his election as President, he showed little sympathy for the Republic's complex system of party politics and coalition governments. His preference for authoritarian leadership came out into the open after 1930 and he used Brüning as a front for his own power; after all, Article 48 was authorised by the president and could have been denied at any time. His motive was always to replace the party politics of the Republic with a more cohesive political system more akin to the old Reich in which he had spent his early military career.

Franz von Papen was more ruthless than either Brüning or Hindenburg. He lacked Brüning's moderation or Hindenburg's sense of service, pursuing instead his own ambitions. As Chancellor between May and November 1932 he had no party base in the Reichstag and became involved in a series of intrigues – first to maintain his power, then to regain it after he had been displaced by Schleicher. This produced the agreement in January 1933 by which Hindenburg was persuaded to appoint Hitler as Chancellor, with Papen as his 'keeper'.

Of the three, Hindenburg was the most consistent danger to democracy in that his use of presidential powers went well beyond what had originally been intended by the Constitution. The other two, however, also served important roles. Brüning blurred the transition to dictatorship in the name of stability, gradually undermining the ability of the Reichstag to resist the trend. Papen concocted the specific plot which destroyed democracy altogether and helped unleash Nazism.

 The rise of the Nazis

15. 'Between 1919 and 1923 the Nazi movement grew from insignificance to prominence as the DAP developed into the NSDAP. In the process, it acquired a leader, a structure, a policy and a paramilitary movement.'

a)   What is meant by 'DAP' and 'NSDAP'?   (3 marks)

The DAP was the German Workers' Party, founded in Munich in January 1919 by Anton Drexler. In 1920 it was renamed the National Socialist German Workers' Party (Nazis) and given a 20-Point Programme to emphasise its nationalist and socialist policies.

b)   Explain how, between 1919 and 1923, the NSDAP acquired 'a leader, a structure, a policy and a paramilitary movement'.   (7 marks)

Within the first three or four years of its existence the party went through major changes. Under its original leader, Anton Drexler, the DAP was nothing more than a fringe discussion group with a tiny membership. It was, however, transformed by Hitler. Initially in charge of propaganda, he supplanted Drexler in 1921, converting a collective leadership into the *Führerprinzip*, which remained at the core of Nazism until 1945. From the start, Hitler developed a sense of irresistible power and overwhelming confidence based on the belief that 'history does not make men, but men history'.

The organisation was in the meantime extensively restructured and the party was renamed, in 1920 becoming the National Socialist German Workers' Party (NSDAP). The main focus of the organisation was on the spread of propaganda, to which Hitler gave priority in 1920 and 1921; a key acquisition was the *Munich Observer*, which was renamed the *People's Observer* (*Völkischer Beobachter*) and became the party's official mouthpiece.

The party's new identity was confirmed by the 25-Point Programme. This contained principles which could be seen as both nationalist and socialist. The former predominated, demanding for example 'the union of all Germans in a Greater Germany' (Article 1), the 'revocation of the peace treaties of Versailles and St Germain' (Article 2), and the acquisition of 'land and territory to feed our people and settle our surplus population' (Article 3). There was also a strong anti-Semitic component, with the demand for the exclusion of the Jews from German nationhood (Article 4).

Finally, the party was given teeth by the formation, in July 1921, of the *Sturm Abteilung* (SA), a violent paramilitary organisation intended, in the words of the *Völkischer Beobachter*, 'to develop in the hearts of our young supporters a tremendous desire for action'.[4] The SA proceeded to intimidate opponents, disrupt other meetings and engage in bloody clashes in the streets. With the addition of the SA, the party became a movement.

c) **'The failure of the Munich Putsch was due to the unexpected opposition to it from Kahr's Bavarian government.' Explain whether you agree or disagree with this view.** **(15 marks)**

This view contains the truth about the failure of the Munich Putsch – but not the whole truth. Other factors were of equal importance, although Kahr's opposition to Hitler's scheme destroyed any remote chance that Hitler might have managed to pull it off against all the odds. It is also likely that Kahr, an astute politician, refused to support Hitler's putsch because he saw through its weaknesses.

Without Kahr's support the whole idea of the putsch was doomed to failure. Hitler was undoubtedly influenced by Mussolini's March on Rome in 1922, when the threat of a mass takeover of the capital had led to King Victor Emmanuel III offering Mussolini the premiership. Hitler clearly hoped to repeat the advance from Naples to Rome by a similar march from Munich to Berlin. The situations were, however, very different. Italian fascism had widespread support which transcended any one city or region, whereas Nazism in its early years was totally dependent on the favourable environment of Bavaria – and especially of Munich. Kahr had been responsible for this, showing some sympathy for the far right ever since he had made himself commissioner of Bavaria in 1920. But in assuming that Kahr would automatically support him in a major bid for power, Hitler went too far. Kahr refused, even at gunpoint, to support Hitler's mobilisation of Bavarian support for the overthrow of the Weimar Republic. After escaping capture by the SA, he called out the Bavarian police, who dispersed the Nazi marchers the following day. Kahr was therefore instrumental in stopping the march at its very outset. As the key witness at Hitler's trial, Kahr was also responsible for Hitler's subsequent term of imprisonment in Landsberg Castle.

Kahr reacted as he did not because he disagreed with Hitler's hatred of the Republic, but because he knew that Hitler would fail. He could either stop the putsch immediately and retain some control over the methods used, or he could let matters take their course, in which case, his own regime in Bavaria would be targeted by the Berlin government which would make full use of the presidential power under Article 48, as it had already done against a left-wing administration in Saxony. There was no question of Kahr lending his support to the Nazis since the prospects of the far right seizing power in Berlin had already been discredited by the failure of the Kapp Putsch in 1920. Quite simply, Kahr disagreed with Hitler's prognosis of the Republic's vulnerability. Although it was unpopular because of the Treaty of Versailles (1919), economically destabilised through hyperinflation (1919–23) and humiliated by the French occupation of the Ruhr (1923), the Republic still had the advantage of reasonably consistent political consensus among the moderate parties, especially the Centre, DDP and SPD. The central government also had the loyalty of the **Reichswehr** and an affective strategy for dealing with threats to the capital; in 1919, for example it had withdrawn to Weimar and in 1920 to Dresden. On both occasions it had survived with little difficulty. Kahr could not, of course, have known that Hitler's power would grow in the future; as far as he was concerned, Hitler in November 1923 was little different to Kapp in 1920.

There was another crucial point recognised by Kahr. Any attempt by the right to seize power in Germany would need the support of the conservatives, whether in the army or industry or in the DNVP. At this stage the conservative right distrusted the radical right almost as much as it did the far left. After all, a substantial part of the 1920 Nazi Party Programme was based on socialist policies and there was profound suspicion over the violence, thuggery and indiscipline shown by the SA.

For all these reasons, Kahr decided to stand firm and to adopt the approach which Facta had recommended in 1922 to deal with Mussolini. As it happened, Kahr was right about Hitler's chances of success, even though he totally underestimated Hitler's capacity to learn from experience and plot a different course to power.

16. Assess the lessons learned by Hitler from the failure of the Munich Putsch of 1923. (90 marks)

The failure of the Munich Putsch in November 1923 came as a profound blow to the Nazi movement and to Hitler's own quest for power. Nevertheless, he used his time in Landsberg Prison both to write *Mein Kampf* and to rethink his whole approach. The period after his release in 1925 showed that he had learned a series of lessons from the events of 1923. One was a fundamental change of strategy. The others were refinements to enable the Nazi movement to meet it.

The first, and most important, lesson was that a completely different strategy was necessary to achieve power. Until November 1923 Hitler had assumed that the Weimar Republic could be overthrown directly; the whole purpose of the Munich Putsch was to launch a march on Berlin in imitation of Mussolini's march on Rome the year before. The failure of the putsch showed that democratic government was at this stage more resilient than in Italy. Hence Hitler would have to settle for a constitutional or 'legal' path to power. This did not mean a fundamental conversion to the principles of constitutional democracy; on the contrary, parliamentary politics would be the means, not the end. Revolution was still the ultimate aim, but would now be the result of achieving power rather than the means by which power would be achieved. For the time being it would be necessary, in Hitler's words, 'to hold our noses and enter the Reichstag alongside Marxist and Catholic deputies'. At the same time, he saw a continuing need for the SA and paramilitary influences. In fact, Hitler now led the Nazis at two levels. On the surface they were a parliamentary party, aiming at gaining electoral support at the expense of their rivals. Below the surface they remained a mass movement, committed to gaining mass support. Their chance would come in the future, after the victory of the 'legal' approach.

To accomplish this change of strategy it was necessary to extend the party's appeal. A second lesson therefore was that the Nazi Party had to move away from its narrow working-class base. It could not hope to compete effectively for the working-class vote with a moderate SPD and a revolutionary KPD. Instead, Hitler decided to reformulate parts of the 1920 party programme so as to appeal to different parts of the population as they became alienated from the Republic. This meant that he moved away from socialism. In the process, he became involved with Strasser in an ideological battle – which Hitler won. By attacking socialism and the left, Hitler began to exercise more of an appeal to the middle classes and the right.

This involved a third lesson. For the time being, at least, the Nazis had to co-operate with the conservative–traditionalist right, especially the DNVP, and use its weapons to attack the Republic. This meant that Hitler increased the emphasis on nationalism, on the 'stab in the back' and 'November Criminals' myths of 1918 and on the Versailles 'diktat' of 1919. By the end of the 1920s, Hitler and the Nazis were openly co-operating with Hugenberg and the DNVP. It was not difficult to develop a broader consensus with industrialists, big business and army leaders in the Harzburg Front of 1931. Conservative politicians, including Hindenburg, were eventually persuaded that Hitler could be useful to them, which, of course, opened up a channel to power in 1932–3.

At the same time, Hitler became more aware of the need for a more adaptable policy, a fourth lesson from 1923. The NSDAP became more flexible and pragmatic; Hitler was able to appeal directly to each class and sector within the electorate by making specific pledges calculated to it individually. This was in addition to the more general policies based on nationalism and race. This dual approach to party policy meant that the NSDAP became the only party in the Weimar Republic able to project an appeal to all sectors of the population.

The strength of the Nazi appeal would depend very much on how persuasively it could be put across. The fifth lesson of the Munich Putsch was that propaganda should be given the highest priority. Hitler reflected on this at length in *Mein Kampf*, arguing that 'Propaganda works on the general public from the standpoint of an idea and makes them ripe for the victory of this idea'. He argued that, to work on the collective emotions of crowds, his message to them had to be kept simple, striking and memorable. It was also vital to make the individual feel important only in the context of the crowd and to establish stereotyped enemies and targets by means, if necessary, of 'the big lie'.

All these developments depended on effective organisation, the final lesson of the Munich Putsch and its immediate aftermath. Again, *Mein Kampf* contained Hitler's observations based on experience. He aimed particularly to integrate organisation with propaganda. 'The function of propaganda,' he argued, 'is to attract supporters, the function of organization is to win members.' Even more important, however, was the style of leadership within the party. In the period immediately after the Munich Putsch, the Nazi Party had disintegrated for want of active leadership. This had actually suited Hitler since it had shown that he was indispensable. After 1925, therefore, the *Führerprinzip* was strengthened – and was never fundamentally questioned until 1945. This underlay the reorganisation of the party and its subdivision into regional units, each under a **Gauleiter**.

Of all the lessons learned from the failure of the Munich putsch, the most fundamental was the change in strategy, without which the others would not have been possible – or even relevant. The change was essential to enable the Nazis to extend their appeal to all sections of the population and to gain the support of the conservative right. To mobilise this support it was, of course, vital to reorganise the party and focus its propaganda more sharply. But the way in which this was done was itself acceptance of revolution as the consequence, not the cause, of power.

17. How valid is the view that Germany was a dictatorship even before Hitler's appointment as Chancellor in January 1933. (90 marks)

The answer to this question depends on the meaning given to dictatorship. One definition might be the decline of democracy through the encroachment of the executive, or government, on the powers of the legislature, or parliament. Often justified by an emergency, this can be seen as 'creeping dictatorship' and is certainly what Germany had experienced by January 1933. The other definition would be the permanent destruction of all alternative forms of power and the centralised control of society. This was to occur after January 1933, not before.

There is plenty of evidence for 'creeping dictatorship' occurring between 1930 and January 1933. The change began with the narrowing of the political base. The Weimar Constitution had tried to ensure democracy through a combination of universal suffrage and proportional representation. This needed to be translated into practical power through coalition governments with a majority in the Reichstag. Democracy was kept afloat by ten coalitions between 1919 and 1930 but the turning point came with the collapse of Müller's Grand Coalition under the impact of the depression in 1930. The difference was now that Brüning formed a minority government, based on the Centre Party alone, without any real attempt to secure Reichstag consent for his legislation. The next stage saw a further narrowing of the political base as Papen, Chancellor between May and November 1932, and Schleicher (November 1932–January 1933) dispensed with party support altogether. The result was to remove the competition between political parties to transmit popular votes into political power, one of the key safeguards against dictatorship.

Instead, power became confused with authority. The Constitution had provided for an elected president as head of state, with certain reserve powers under Article 48 to safeguard democracy as necessary. Creeping dictatorship involved the regular use of these emergency powers to bypass normal constitutional procedures for passing laws. Thus the governments of Brüning, Papen and Schleicher were kept afloat by Hindenburg, whose use of decree laws under Article 48 increased from 5 in 1930 to 44 in 1931 and 60 in 1932. In the same period the Reichstag became less and less involved in legislation, its sessions declining from 94 in 1930 to 41 in 1931 and a mere 13 in 1932. In this situation the role of the head of state, far from using his power to safeguard the constitution, was using the constitution to safeguard his own power and the position of his chancellor's government.

This conversion of authority into authoritarianism was seen increasingly as a positive rather than a negative development. Instead of defending democracy against dictatorship, politicians of the right sought to use dictatorship as a defence against democracy. There had always been an undercurrent of anti-democratic feeling within the army, the judiciary and the civil service, while Hindenburg and other conservative figures had been suspicious of the unwieldy operation of party politics. During the period 1930–3, therefore, various suggestions were put forward about the future; conservative constitutional theorists argued that the party system would eventually fracture and be replaced by a broad front. For this reason the DNVP were prepared to co-operate closely with the Nazis in the electoral campaigns of 1930 and 1932 and the conservatives saw the Nazis as the means of sweeping away the inefficiencies of Weimar democracy. Thus, by appointing Hitler as Chancellor in January 1933, Hindenburg accepted that 'creeping dictatorship' was about to move into a different stage.

Yet in January 1933 this stage had not yet been reached. Despite having many of the appearances of dictatorship, Germany still had a Constitution which maintained certain guarantees of democracy. It still had a multi-party system, in which the SPD and Centre continued to attract support, even if the DDP and DVP had collapsed. Despite the collapse of party politics at the centre, they did continue at local level: the state administration of Prussia continued to be run by a coalition between the Centre Party and the SPD and there was always a faint hope that this combination might be revived nationally. There were even occasions when the Reichstag was able to fight back. For example, the Constitution enabled it to challenge the president's use of Article 48, provided that it could summon up a majority. This it did on two occasions in 1932 and forced Hindenburg into calling for two sets of elections. Although these resulted in a swing to the right, they were evidence that the Constitution was still intact. It is also true that, for all his anti-democratic views, Hindenburg still considered himself bound to uphold the existing state system. His dictatorship resulted from abusing the Constitution, not from destroying it.

Nor did Hindenburg and his chancellors seek to impose any of the restrictions normally associated with dictatorship. No political parties were banned. Even the KPD, who were becoming increasingly revolutionary and were openly loyal to Stalin and the Soviet Union, were allowed to contest the 1932 elections and take up their seats. It is true that Brüning banned the SA, but this was for their excessive violence. There was no government censorship on the media or political pamphlets and no attempt to stop or control political meetings. The central government took no measures to spread propaganda or to use education for the process of indoctrination – largely because there was no official ideology, or even policy, to enforce. All these were to be features of Hitler's totalitarian dictatorship, not of Hindenburg's authoritarian rule.

By January 1933, therefore, the Weimar Republic was experiencing 'creeping' dictatorship through regular use of emergency powers. This impeded and weakened the normal operation of the democracy but did not destroy the democratic process itself, since this remained intact within the Constitution. Nor had there been any attempt to introduce a totalitarian regime which would make dictatorship permanent. It is, however, difficult to see how the Nazi dictatorship could have come to exist without the 'creeping dictatorship' of the last years of Weimar.

18. Why did Hitler come to power in 1933 but not in the 1920s? (90 marks)

Hitler came to power in 1933 through a combination of factors which had not existed in the 1920s. The three most important were widespread support for the Nazis, a collapsed democracy, and a close co-operation between the Nazis and the conservative right.

Widespread support was an essential precondition for the Nazis to gain power. This had been shown by the failure of the 1923 Munich Putsch to put together any sustained support for Hitler's proposed march on Berlin. The Nazis were at this stage a local party, based in Bavaria and with little contact with other areas. By 1932 they had become the party with the largest and most widespread following in Germany. The transformation can be explained partly by a change in Hitler's political strategy after 1924, and partly by the impact of the Great Depression on German society after 1929. Hitler's 'legal' approach to power ended the initial appearance of the Nazis as a 'lunatic fringe' and substituted an image of a genuine political party prepared to contest Reichstag elections with other parties. The depression delivered the votes for this party in a way which had not happened in the 1920s, increasing the number of Nazi seats from 12 in 1928 to 107 in 1930 and 230 in July 1932. For all his preparation and party reorganisation in the 1920s, Hitler could not have shot to prominence without the sudden cataclysm of the depression. On the other hand, success in the 1930s depended considerably on his preparation in the 1920s.

The huge swing to the Nazis showed that major changes had taken place in the political allegiance of the German electorate between the 1920s and 1930s. All this took place within the context of a collapsing democracy after 1930. This was crucial to Nazi success, since functioning democracy was the strongest safeguard against the triumph of extremism of any kind. During the period 1924–9 the Nazis had been reorganised and redirected: yet the operation of relatively stable coalition governments had kept the majority of the German population loyal to the moderate parties – the SPD, Centre, DDP and DVP. There was never a chance of any breakthrough for Hitler before 1930. The Wall Street Crash and the consequent increase in bankruptcies and unemployment transmitted a major blow to the whole democratic process by destroying the basis of coalition government; the withdrawal of Müller from the Grand Coalition in 1930 was followed by the minority governments of Brüning, Papen and Schleicher. These circumstances brought a change in the will of the electorate: whereas it had flowed through democratic channels in the 1920s, it now became profoundly anti-democratic and anti-Republican. This was most evident in the 1932 presidential election, which was contested between two candidates of the anti-democratic right (Hitler and Hindenburg) and one of the anti-democratic left (Thälmann). The electoral upheaval was also clear in the Nazi surge in the Reichstag elections of 1930 and 1932. The rise of Hitler therefore depended upon the collapse of the Weimar Republic.

On the other hand, the collapse of Weimar did not have to result in the rise of Hitler. This is where the close association between the Nazis and the conservative right provided the actual channel to power between 1930 and 1933. Nothing could have been further from the situation in the 1920s. Until 1928 the conservative right, especially the DNVP, had despised Hitler as an upstart and, although the Nazis had flourished in the right-wing environment of Bavaria, Hitler had completely failed to win over Kahr in the Munich Putsch of 1923. After 1929, however, there was a much closer collaboration between the Nazis and DNVP and their new leader, Hugenberg. In the light of economic chaos and political disintegration, the radical and conservative right began to make common cause. Landowners, businessmen and industrialists saw in Hitler the prospects of safety from the threat of communism and socialism on the left. This explains the formation of the Harzburg Front in 1932. Hitler also benefited from the belief of conservative constitutional theorists that the Weimar party system would eventually fracture and be replaced by a broad front. For this reason, the DNVP therefore aimed to create a broad 'movement' of the right which would also include the NSDAP. The Nazis could, in fact be used to destroy the Republic and then, once that had been achieved, they would be brought into line with the more conservative objectives of the DNVP. This explains why Papen and Hindenburg were prepared to place Hitler in power as Chancellor in January 1933; after all, Papen was the Vice-chancellor, who would selectively direct Hitler's destructive capacity. There was a huge contrast between this and the situation in 1923. Then Hitler had tried unsuccessfully to intimidate the conservative right in Munich and he was up against President Ebert in Berlin who was committed to maintaining democracy and party politics, not replacing them.

Hitler therefore failed to seize power by conspiracy in 1923, only to be given power by conspiracy in 1933. He failed to overthrow democracy in the 1920s when he had little popular support. However, he acquired that support from the collapse of democracy. This gave him credibility with the conservative right who helped him into power.

The achievements of the Weimar Republic

19. How much did the Weimar Republic achieve? **(90 marks)**

The Weimar Republic is usually seen in a negative overall light. This is because it eventually failed to provide a transition to democracy, instead being only an interlude between an authoritarian regime and a dictatorship. Yet, while admitting that this was the overall trend, the Republic achieved a great deal that was positive between 1919 and 1933 in terms of political structure, economic growth, foreign policy and social development.

The main political achievement was the establishment of one of Europe's more advanced democracies. The Constitution explicitly stated that 'authority emanates from the people' (Article 1); this was in contrast to the *Kaiserreich*, which had been based on an authoritarian combination of monarchy and social and military elites. The Republic also allowed for the development of the widest range of political parties anywhere in the world, ranging from the KPD on the radical left through the SPD and DDP on the moderate left, the Centre, the DVP and DNVP on the right and, finally, the NSDAP on the extreme right. Proportional representation (Article 22) ensured that each of these parties was genuinely representative of the votes cast. The Republic also introduced legislative control over the executive, Article 54 insisting that the chancellor should have the support of the Reichstag. Although Article 48, giving the president emergency decree powers, was later to prove a means for undermining democracy, it was used with restraint by President Ebert before 1925 to see off threats to the new regime from the revolutionary left and right. It is true that the whole system eventually malfunctioned. But the positive side of the political experiment was that the German Federal Republic, formed in 1949, used a large part of the political structure, although with a weaker president and a modified form of proportional representation. It also adopted the same flag, acknowledging that modern Germany is descended from Weimar, not from the Third Reich – or even the Second.

The economic achievement of the Weimar Republic was to adapt to a particularly severe reparations demand which stripped Germany of part of her industrial infrastructure and imposed a bill of 136,000 million marks. Admittedly the governments of Wirth and Cuno lost control over the inflationary trends between 1921 and 1923, but Stresemann (1923) helped stabilise the currency with the new *Rentenmark*. The Republic also achieved a major rapport with the United States and, as a result of the Dawes Plan (1924), received more in the form of investments before 1929 than it actually paid out in reparations. As a result, Germany experienced four years of rapid industrial and consumer growth, becoming for a while the world's second economic power. Although this achievement was undermined by the depression from 1929 onwards, the living standards experienced before that date were never restored by Hitler. This was in contrast to most other advanced economies which had, by 1936, recovered sufficiently to overtake their 1929 index of prosperity.

In terms of international relations, the Weimar Republic achieved reconciliation with Europe, at least in the 1920s. Stresemann, particularly, saw Germany as 'the bridge which would bring East and West together in the development of Europe'. The rehabilitation of Germany was actually very rapid, resulting in its inclusion in the Locarno Pact in 1925, the League of Nations (1926) and the Kellogg–Briand Pact (1928). Although the darker side to the Republic's activity was secret rearmament, conducted by General von Seeckt, probably with the government's connivance, it is arguable that even this was an achievement since it laid the foundations for Germany's future military resurgence.

The social achievements of the Weimar Republic were extensive. Civil rights were given official sanction in the 1919 Constitution, with guarantees of 'equality before the law' and 'liberty of travel and residence'.[5] The regulation of economic life 'must be compatible with the principles of justice', with the aim of 'attaining humane conditions of existence for all'. A comprehensive system of social insurance was guaranteed, along with regulations on the working environment and industrial arbitration. The Republic gave social and economic advancement to various different groups. One was women, who benefited greatly from a more progressive and egalitarian climate: Weimar led Europe in advances in women's fashions. Another group was the Jews, who were able to contribute greatly to the economic and intellectual achievements of the period.

Finally, there was a major cultural resurgence in the Weimar Republic which spread across all the arts. Artists were particularly prominent. George Grosz, for example, commented on social problems in works such as *Grey Day*. Others developed new approaches and techniques: Hannah Hoech belonged to the Dada school, which cultivated the 'absurd'. The Bauhaus movement, inspired by Walter Gropius, brought major changes to architecture and design. There were also major developments in drama, led by Berolt Brecht, and literature, which was dominated by Arnold Zweig, Hermann Hesse, Stefan George, Thomas Mann and Erich Remarque. Throughout the 1920s the Republic thrived on an unprecedented freedom which allowed widespread debate. Thomas Mann claimed that Germany had replaced France as the cultural centre of Europe. He might also have added that Berlin had replaced Paris.

The Republic's real achievement was therefore its diversity, incorporating all the areas mentioned. Of these the most directly influential was the political achievement, since this defined the influence of the others. At least until 1929 it promoted more positive economic policies and improved relations with other states – which would have been impossible without the base of official policy. The multi-party nature of Weimar democracy also created an atmosphere which promoted social and intellectual change. Unfortunately, the political system also became the channel for the rise of dictatorship after 1930: again, none of the other developments, whether economic or social, could have brought about the collapse of democracy without the sudden collapse of coalition politics. This development ultimately destroyed the Republic – but not its actual achievements.

Additional essay questions (with advice)

Each of these questions can be tackled as a single essay or as one of the answers to a question in several parts. Additional reading and research is desirable for each one.

20. Which of the chancellors between 1890 and 1914 achieved the most in Germany's domestic policies?

Advice: *Avoid writing the essay on a chronological approach to the chancellors. Instead, select criteria and consider all four for each one. Come to a conclusion in each case, although your overall conclusion may well be a mixed one. Criteria may include: (1) reform; (2) effective management of the finances; and (3) management of Wilhelm II.*

21. **How far do you agree with the view that 'Kaiser Wilhelm II achieved his objectives in foreign policy'?**

Advice: *Establish what these objectives were and, in each case, provide arguments for and against his having achieved them. Do this by slanting each argument in a particular way; the combination of arguments may, however, provide a mixed conclusion. Objectives could include: (1) making Germany a world rather than a European power; (2) supporting Austria-Hungary (see Chapter 2, Essay 8); and (3) making use of Germany's military advantage in 1914.*

22. **To what extent was the political structure of the Weimar Republic different to that of the German Reich?**

Advice: *'To what extent' needs to be quantified (i.e. 'partly' or 'largely' rather than 'entirely' or 'not at all'). Avoid at all costs writing the first half of the essay on the Reich and the second half on the Republic. Choose three or four criteria and, in each case, show the continuity and change between the two systems. These criteria might include: (1) The legislature and electoral system; (2) the government and head of state; (3) the political parties; and (4) overall attitudes – progressive or conservative?*

23. **How secure was the Weimar Republic by 1924?**

Advice: *Avoid writing a straight account of the Republic's early years. Instead, find some criteria to illustrate 'secure' and give some views for and against. The overall conclusion might be: (1) that the Republic had been secure enough to survive the threats against it between 1919 and 1923; but (2) that certain weaknesses which had shown up in these early years were still present in 1924.*

24. **Why did the Weimar Republic collapse in 1933 but not in 1923?**

Advice: *Avoid writing an account of the two periods and ending 'Thus it can be seen that . . .'. Instead, select a broad criteria for survival by 1923 turning into collapse by 1933. These could be: (1) that depression was a more serious problem than inflation; (2) that presidential dictatorship was a feature of the second period but not of the first; and (3) that the radical right had extensive popular support by 1933 but not by 1923. Putting these points together will provide an integrated conclusion.*

25. **How far do you agree that Hitler had been 'given' power by January 1933?**

Advice: *Avoid a straight account of the rise of Hitler, followed by a deduction. Instead, consider the three main possibilities: (1) he was 'given' power as a result of the support of the conservative right; (2) he won power by extending his electoral support; and (3) a combination of the two – he made himself indispensable through his popular support and the conservative right conspired to use him.*

Essay plan

Para 1: Overall approach. Hitler's 'power' began with his appointment as Chancellor in January 1933. This was partly 'given', partly 'earned': the two existed in combination, although one was arguably predominant.

Para 2: The case for being 'given' power is based on the sudden elevation of Hitler for reasons not necessarily connected with Hitler's own position:

- *Hitler's appointment by Hindenburg as a result of the intrigue of Papen against Schleicher (supporting detail).*
- *This was part of a broader intention of the conservative right to use the Nazis, going back via the Harzburg Front to the agreement between the Nazis and DNVP (supporting detail).*

Hitler was therefore 'given' a second chance of power after his failure to defeat by Hindenburg in the 1932 presidential election.

Para 3: On the other hand, Hitler would not have been 'given' power had he not developed a strong political base and widespread appeal. Importance of:

- *his change of strategy after the failure of the Munich Putsch (supporting detail).*
- *his widespread appeal from 1929 and its translation into electoral support in 1930 and 1932 (supporting detail).*

If Hitler was 'given' power, it was because he had 'earned' sufficient importance to be targeted for the gift.

Para 4 (Possibility 1): Of the two approaches:

- *the first was more important than the second since the conservative right were in strong position, having converted the Weimar Republic into a dictatorship (supporting detail); hence,*
- *the second was less important than the first because the collapse of democracy meant that the growth of Nazi support in the Reichstag elections mattered less constitutionally (supporting detail).*

Para 5 (Possibility 1): Hence Hitler needed the conservative right more than the conservative right needed Hitler. He was, on balance, 'given' power.

Para 4 (Possibility 2): Of the two approaches:

- *the first was less important than the second since the conservative right were able to implement a dictatorship only through emergency powers (supporting detail); hence,*
- *the second was more important than the first because Nazism represented a major change occurring within Germany from 1929 onwards (supporting detail).*

Para 5 (Possibility 2): Hence the conservative right needed to harness Hitler before Hitler swept the conservative right away. He was not, therefore, 'given' power.

Part 3: Sources

📖 1. The Weimar Republic in crisis, 1919–23

This exercise consists of three questions on three sources, with a time allowance of 45 minutes.

Source A: From a Proclamation by Wolfgang Kapp, 13 March 1920

> The Reich and nation are in grave danger. With terrible speed we are approaching the complete collapse of the State and of law and order. The people are only dimly aware of the approaching disaster. Prices are rising unchecked. Hardship is growing. Starvation threatens. The Government, lacking in authority, impotent and in league with corruption, is incapable of overcoming the danger.
>
> The Reich Chancellor
> Kapp

Source B: Adapted from E. Kolb, *The Weimar Republic* (translated from German 1988)

The conclusion of the peace treaty and the adoption of the Weimar constitution did not usher in a period of internal consolidation. On the contrary, during the first few years the very existence of the political system created in 1918–19 was more than once threatened. Successive governments were confronted by a multitude of political, economic and social problems that seemed almost insoluble; they had to resist fierce attacks from the opponents of parliamentary democracy, and were under massive pressure from outside. It is almost a miracle that the Weimar democracy succeeded in maintaining its existence during these years of extreme tribulation.

Source C: Adapted from G. Layton, *From Bismarck to Hitler: Germany 1890–1933* (1995)

Weimar's survival in 1923 was in marked contrast to its ignominious collapse a decade later. Why was this? It could be argued that popular resentment was channelled more towards the French and the Allies than towards Weimar itself. It has also been suggested that, despite the effects of inflation, workers did not suffer to the same extent as they did when there was mass unemployment. Similarly, employers tended to show a less hostile attitude to Weimar in its early years than in its final phase of deflationary economic depression. If these assumptions about popular instincts towards Weimar are valid, then it seems that, although there was distress and disillusionment in 1923, disaffection with Weimar had not yet reached critical proportions. Moreover, in 1923 there was no clear political alternative to Weimar.

QUESTIONS WITH WORKED ANSWERS

a) Study Source A and use your own knowledge. Explain briefly the origins and outcome of the Kapp Putsch.   **(3 marks)**

The Kapp Putsch was an incident which occurred in March 1920. One of the *Freikorps* units which had refused to disband advanced on Berlin, where it was supported by a senior civil servant, Wolfgang Kapp, and General Luttwitz, who hoped to establish a new right-wing government. President Ebert withdrew to Dresden and then to Stuttgart. There he made an appeal for a general strike. With full support from trade unions several cities, including Berlin, came to a standstill. Deprived of essential services and unable to form an alternative government, Kapp and Luttwitz fled from Berlin.

b) Study Sources B and C. With reference to your own knowledge of the problems faced by the Weimar Republic between 1919 and 1924, explain the difference in views between Source B and Source C.   (7 marks)

The approaches in Sources B and C differ in their overall slant: the first is more pessimistic than the second about the Republic's prospects for survival. This is apparent from several phrases used. There was, for example no 'period of internal consolidation', with the political system 'more than once threatened' by a 'multitude' of problems which were 'almost insoluble'. Source C, although acknowledging that there was 'distress and disillusionment' states that there was less suffering than 'a decade later'. According to Source B, the Republic had to resist 'fierce attacks' on democracy and 'massive pressures from outside'; survival was therefore 'almost a miracle'. Source C, however, emphasises the viability of the Republic, rather than its vulnerability. Compared with later events, 'popular resentment' was at this stage 'channelled' against external enemies, while employers showed 'a less hostile attitude'; 'disaffection' had not yet become 'critical' since there was no 'political alternative'. The inference is that survival was predictable rather than miraculous.

It seems strange that two historians can address the same period in such a different way. There are two possible explanations. One is that history as a discipline is based on controversy, different viewpoints leading to a welcome variety of approach and interpretation. The other is the perspective on which the arguments are based. Source B is looking forward from the bleak period between 1918 and 1923, whereas Source C is viewing this period retrospectively from the even bleaker one of 1929–33. Views are inevitably affected by viewing points.

c) Study Sources A, B and C and use your own knowledge. How far had the political and economic threats to the Weimar Republic been overcome by 1924?   (15 marks)

Total (25 marks)

In some respects a major recovery had occurred by 1924. Political stability had been restored, in contrast with Source A's prediction of 'a complete collapse of the State'. The Republic did, in the words of Source B, 'resist fierce attacks from the opponents of parliamentary democracy'. It had overcome political threats from the far left in the form of the Spartacist uprising (1919), the Bavarian Soviet Republic (1919) and attempted communist coups in Saxony and Thuringia (1921). It had also dealt successfully with attempts from the right in the Kapp Putsch (1920) and Hitler's Munich Putsch (1923). In these cases the president or state leadership had taken decisive action. The ease with which the threats were overcome does seem to support Source C's conclusion that there was 'no clear political alternative to Weimar'.

Similarly, the 'multitude' of 'economic and social problems' appear to have been largely resolved by 1923. Prices, 'rising unchecked' from 1920 (Source A) had, by November 1923, been brought under control during Stresemann's brief chancellorship. The mark had been stabilised by the issue of the *Rentenmark* by Schacht, President of the *Reichsbank*, while the destabilising impact of reparations was largely resolved in 1924 by the Dawes Plan. This all led to a much more prosperous period between 1924 and 1929.

Yet this recovery was only temporary and, as Source C shows, worse was to follow in 1929. This means that the underlying problems before 1923 must somehow have remained. Source B may, therefore, have a point in considering the survival of the Republic at this time as 'almost a miracle'. There was only a temporary respite from political problems, as the far left and far right both revived after 1929. The underlying problem which was not resolved by 1923 was the need for constant coalition government, which had managed up to that time but was to collapse in 1930. Economic problems were also to recur. The threat of inflation was dealt with by an agreement on reparations which created German dependence on US loans and made it vulnerable to future crisis. It could be argued that the financial solution of 1924 helped set up the financial problem of 1929. From this emerged the political crisis of 1931–3, which resulted in the replacement of the Weimar Republic by the Third Reich.

PARALLEL QUESTIONS WITHOUT WORKED ANSWERS

a) **Study Source A and use your own knowledge. Explain briefly how the Government was able to deal with the danger posed by Kapp.**   **(3 marks)**

Advice: *Avoid a straight account of the Kapp Putsch. Focus on the effectiveness of government measures, the support of the workforce for these and the shortcomings of the Putsch.*

b) **Study Sources A and B. With reference to your own knowledge of the problems faced by the Weimar Republic between 1919 and 1924, compare the views in Source A with those in Source B.**   **(7 marks)**

Advice: *'Compare' means finding similarities and differences. Use your own knowledge to make further inferences about what to compare.*

c) **Study Sources A, B and C and use your own knowledge. Examine the different types of threats confronting the Weimar Republic between 1919 and 1924.**   **(15 marks)**

Total (25 marks)

Advice: *Start with a brief summary of what the sources seem to show as a set. Then introduce your own criteria, linking these with the sources in more detail. The occasional comment on the usefulness of the sources should be built in if relevant to your argument.*

2. The rise of national socialism in Germany to 1933

This exercise consists of five questions on five sources, with a time allowance of 60–75 minutes.

Source A: Percentage of the vote won in the Reichstag elections by Germany's main parties between 1924 and 1932

	KPD	SPD	DDP	Centre	DVP	DNVP	NSDAP	Others
1924 (May)	12.6	21.6	5.7	16.6	9.5	19.5	6.5	8.3
1924 (Dec)	9.0	26.0	6.3	17.3	10.1	20.5	3.0	7.8
1928	10.6	29.8	4.8	15.2	8.7	14.2	2.6	13.7
1930	13.1	24.5	3.5	14.8	4.9	7.0	18.3	14.4
1932 (July)	14.3	21.6	1.0	15.7	1.2	5.9	37.3	3.2
1932 (Nov)	16.9	20.4	1.0	15.0	1.8	8.5	33.1	4.7

Source B: Hitler's comments while in prison in 1924, recorded in K. Ludecke, *I Knew Hitler* (London 1936)

When I resume active work it will be necessary to pursue a new policy. Instead of working to achieve power by armed conspiracy, we shall have to hold our noses and enter the Reichstag against the Catholic and Marxist deputies. If outvoting them takes longer than outshooting them, at least the results will be guaranteed by their own constitution! Sooner or later we shall have a majority and after that we shall have Germany.

Source C: P. Salmon, *The Weimar Republic: Could it have Survived?* (an article in *Modern History Review*)

If Weimar had some chances of survival before 1929, it had very little chance afterwards, not just because of the Slump but also because of the attitude and actions of the German electorate and their political leaders. This does not mean that Nazism was its inevitable replacement. Nazism came to power as a result of a miscalculation by conservative politicians and the military after a large number, but by no means a majority of the electorate, had put it in a position to contend for power. Those who intrigued Hitler into power were opposed to Weimar democracy and favoured a return to authoritarianism, but they neither nor expected the triumph of Nazism.

Source D: From a speech made by Hitler in 1928

There are only two possibilities in Germany: do not imagine that the people will for ever go with the middle party, the party of compromises: one day it will turn to those who have most consistently foretold the coming ruin and have sought to dissociate themselves from it. And that party is either the Left: and then God help us! For it will lead us to complete destruction – to Bolshevism, or else it is a party of the Right.

Part 1: Historical background

For much of the nineteenth century, Italy had been a 'geographical expression', consisting of a series of smaller states. These were the Kingdom of Piedmont and Sardinia (linked in 1815), the Kingdom of Naples or the 'Two Sicilies', the Papal States, the Duchies of Parma, Modena and Lucca and, finally, the Austrian provinces of Lombardy and Venetia. The first stage of unification, or *Risorgimento*, had been accomplished by Cavour, Prime Minister of Piedmont, and Garibaldi, a guerrilla leader. In 1861 the Kingdom of Italy was formally proclaimed, to which Venetia was added after the defeat of Austria in the war with Prussia in 1866. The final part to be included was Rome, removed from the political control of the pope in 1870.

The First World War and the peace settlement

Shortly before his death Cavour had said: 'We have made Italy; now we have to make Italians'. The problem was partly the huge material gulf between north and south and partly the tradition of local politics which made effective central government particularly difficult. Nevertheless, Italy had pretensions to become a major power. Thus it involved itself in European diplomacy, joining the Triple Alliance with Germany and Austria-Hungary in 1882, and acquired an overseas empire based on Eritrea and Libya; attempts to conquer Ethiopia, however, failed in 1895. On the outbreak of the First World War in 1914, Prime Minister Salandra at first maintained Italian neutrality, only to denounce the Triple Alliance in 1915 and to switch to supporting the Allies by the Secret Treaty of London (see Essay 1). Italian expectations of a swift end to the war did not materialise and there were serious military, economic and political complications (Essay 2a). The peace settlement proved a major disappointment and Italy's gains of South Tyrol and Trentino, by the Treaty of St Germain (1919), were so disappointing that Prime Minister Orlando was accused of betraying the nation and creating a 'mutilated victory' (Essay 2b).

The rise of Mussolini and fascism to 1922

Born in 1883, Benito Mussolini began his career as an elementary teacher in 1902, before being conscripted into the *Bersaglieri* light infantry in 1906. He subsequently became a journalist and editor of the socialist newspaper *Avanti!*. Before 1915 his views were strongly influenced by the radical left, especially by the **syndicalism** of Georges Sorel, the French socialist (Essay 3a); he hoped for revolution, took an active part in Italy's 'red week' in June 1914, and opposed Italy's adventures abroad. By October 1914, however, he had come to favour Italy's involvement in the First World War. He left *Avanti!* and founded another paper, *Il Popolo d'Italia*, before serving in the Italian army until he was wounded in 1917. By the end of the war, Mussolini's far-left syndicalism had joined up with the far-right nationalism of Gabriel D'Annunzio, the conjunction being named 'fascism'.

At first fascism was primarily an activist movement, based on the squads of the *Fascio di Combattimento*, established in 1919. In 1921 Mussolini also set up the *Partito Nazionale Fascista* (**PNF**). Between them, the squads and the party exerted growing influence on Italian politics and contributed greatly to the chaos which was endemic in Italy by 1921 (Essay 2b). While the fascist squads created the violence, Mussolini projected himself, with some skill, as the only politician capable of controlling it (Essay 3b and Source 2b). This strategy paid off in October 1922. King

Victor Emmanuel III gave way before the threat of a fascist 'March on Rome' and invited Mussolini to form a coalition government as Italy's Prime Minister (Essay 3b). This showed Mussolini's success in personalising a movement which had not been his creation alone (Essay 4). His appointment was a popular move, as fascism had begun to appeal to at least part of every sector and class within Italy (Essay 5a).

 ## Mussolini in power, 1922–43

Once appointed, Mussolini moved from a restricted power base in 1922 (Essay 5b) to a full personal dictatorship (Essay 6). This involved measures such as the Acerbo Electoral Law (1923), which gave any party gaining a 25 per cent poll an automatic two-thirds majority in the Chamber of Deputies. Mussolini was, however, severely embarrassed by the involvement of members of the fascist movement in the kidnap and murder of the socialist deputy, Matteotti. The resulting scandal threatened to bring down Mussolini's government, but the latter took full advantage of the withdrawal of the opposition parties in protest (the Aventine Secession) by preventing their return and banning them altogether. In 1928 he introduced a new electoral law to create a voting system en bloc. Meanwhile, he had increased his own powers: from 1926 he was able to govern by decree, he became personally responsible for all eight of Italy's key ministries, and he surrounded himself with the aura of the Cult of the **Duce**. Whether or not these changes were fully effective is dealt with in Essay 6.

Having strengthened his own position, Mussolini attempted to convert Italy into a totalitarian state. His political changes were to be strengthened through the development of the personality cult (Essay 7a). He also made extensive use of indoctrination. Education was reorganised from 1925 and the Fascist School Charter standardised all teaching in 1939. Youth groups consisted of the Sons of the She-Wolf, the *Balilla*, the *Avanguardisti* and the Fascist Levy. Controls were also placed on the press by the Exceptional Decrees of 1926, while music, art, literature and the cinema were all controlled by the Ministry of Popular Culture. If such measures failed to prevent the revival of opposition, coercion was used, through the secret police, or **OVRA**, founded in 1926, and the Special Tribunal for the Defence of the State. These are covered in Essay 7b; whether they worked is discussed in Essay 7c.

In addition to imposing controls, Mussolini also sought to transform Italy through a series of targeted policies. One of his first priorities was to come to terms with the Catholic Church, despite his own agnostic views (Essay 8a). The papacy had been antagonistic to every Italian government since unification. This was largely because unification had cost the pope his political status and also his secular rule in central Italy. Mussolini produced a compromise with Pope Pius XI in 1929 in the form of the **Lateran** Treaty. This consisted of a **Concordat**, guaranteeing the role of the Catholic Church in the fascist state, the Lateran Treaty, which restored the Vatican City to the pope's political sovereignty, and a financial agreement which compensated the church for its earlier losses. The details of the settlement are dealt with in Essay 8b and the extent to which future policies were related to it in Essay 8c. The effects on Mussolini's regime and on Italy are covered in Essay 9.

A more controversial change introduced by Mussolini was a policy of racism and anti-Semitism. During the earlier part of his rule he had tended to avoid both (Essay 10a) but, in 1938 he issued the Manifesto on Race, to provide a 'scientific' basis for a new fascist racial doctrine. He followed this with a series of decrees banning inter-marriage between Jews and non-Jews, removing Jews

Figure 5.1 **Mussolini in civilian clothes in the 1920s**

from most forms of employment and placing restrictions on Jewish property. After 1943 Jews were also deported to the **extermination camps** in Germany. Why Mussolini changed his policies is covered in Essay 10b and the attitudes of the Italian people in Essay 10c. A key issue is the growing influence of Hitler on Mussolini's whole approach to race.

Meanwhile, Mussolini had also been trying to transform the Italian economy and to improve the social conditions of the Italian people. The main method he used was the **Corporate State.** This was a new structure, intended to replace Western democracy and capitalism without moving to socialism or communism; in some ways, this represented a return to the original policy of fascism (Essay 11a). The Rocco Law of 1926 created syndicates for the seven branches of economic activity. By 1934 there were also twenty-two more specialised corporations. New institutions included the Ministry of Corporations (1926) and two new political organisations: the National Council of Corporations made its appearance in 1930, which supervised the voting system, and the Chamber of Fasces and Corporations which replaced the Chamber of Deputies in 1938. The rather complex structure of the Corporate state is explained in Essay 11b and its impact in Essay 11c. At first, Mussolini's economic policies were relatively cautious but, from 1925 became more sweeping and ambitious. In 1929 he tried to reflate the Italian currency, for reasons of national prestige rather than sound economic principles. There were some improvements. Industry, for example, expanded, largely through the IRI (*Istituto per la recostruzione industriale*), set up in 1933. But the dominant trend was negative. The structure of the Corporate State caused confusion and a further problem was added by Mussolini's wars of the 1930s. These forced a policy of **autarky**, or self-sufficiency, and the military demands wrecked any chance of a full recovery from the Great Depression. These points are covered in Essay 12, as are the measures taken by Mussolini to try to improve living conditions; these included the Battle for Grain, launched in 1925, to promote agricultural self-sufficiency, and the Battle for Births, which stimulated improvements in medical care for children and mothers and a decline in infant mortality. Yet the benefits of Mussolini's policies varied widely according to social class: generally the industrialists and landowners received far more from Mussolini's system than did the peasantry, landed labourers and working classes.

Mussolini's efforts to expand Fascist Italy, 1922–39

The aims and priorities of Mussolini's foreign policy are covered in Essay 13. These included making Italy 'great, respected and feared', seizing the initiative in European diplomacy and expanding Italy's frontiers and colonies in order to offset the 'mutilated victory' of 1918–19. During the 1920s, however, he was relatively cautious, alternating pacific diplomacy such as participation in the Locarno Pact (1925) with limited but targeted aggression like the seizure of Corfu in 1923 and Fiume in 1924 (Essay 14). He also assisted the forces of Noli in the Albanian Civil War and formed agreements with Czechoslovakia and Yugoslavia in 1924. By 1929 he had earned the respect of other European leaders as a relatively moderate and reliable statesman (even if subject to occasional acts of aggression). During the period 1930–4 he seemed to commit Italy more to Britain and France than to Germany; his main reason for signing the Stresa Front against Germany was his resentment of Nazi pressure on neighbouring Austria and the assassination in 1934 of his close friend, the Austrian Chancellor, Dollfuss. From 1935 the momentum of Mussolini's foreign policy changed dramatically. In 1935 he launched an invasion of Ethiopia with the largest army ever sent by Europe to Africa. Even before this campaign was completed, he sent troops, tanks, aircraft and naval ships to assist Franco's Nationalists in the Spanish Civil War (1936–9). The reasons for his change of approach, both domestic and foreign, are analysed in Essay 15. The impact on Italy's economy of such extensive commitments proved disastrous (Essay 16). Any hope of a full economic recovery from the depression was destroyed and Italy's military resources had been virtually used up within three years. This meant that the conquest of Albania in 1939 was accomplished only with difficulty. Meanwhile, Mussolini had been moving away from France and towards Germany, largely as a result of the Ethiopian and Spanish

Figure 5.2 **Mussolini in uniform in the 1930s**

Civil Wars (Essay 17). The first stage was the formation of the Rome–Berlin Axis (1936); this was followed by the Anti-Comintern Pact with Germany and Japan (1937) and the Pact of Steel, a full-scale military alliance with Germany, in May 1939.

The decline and fall of Mussolini and fascism, 1940–5

By 1939, therefore, Mussolini had committed Italy to three wars and his new connection with Germany carried with it the growing possibility of a fourth. When, however, Hitler invaded Poland in September 1939, Mussolini was unable to take the next step of honouring the Pact of Steel. He therefore informed Hitler that Italy would not be able to join unless huge supplies of war material were made available by Germany. Hitler accepted Italy's neutrality with surprising equanimity and then proceeded to conquer not only Poland but also Denmark, Norway, the Low Countries and France. By the summer of 1940 the war in Europe appeared to have been won by Germany and Mussolini felt obliged to enter in order to extract concessions for Italy. The change of Mussolini's policy from 1939 to 1940 is covered in Essay 17. This was to prove a costly error, as Italy was totally unsuited to the conflict which followed, in terms either of strategy or of military infrastructure (Essay 18). By the end of 1941 Italian troops had been defeated in the Balkans by the Greeks, by the British in North Africa and by empire and commonwealth contingents in Ethiopia. German replacements were sent by Hitler to recapture the Balkans and North Africa and Italy had become little more than a German satellite. Italy was also seen by the Allies as the most accessible entry into the Axis bloc; hence the first Anglo-American landings in Europe came in 1943 in Sicily and the Italian peninsula.

The threat of military defeat completely destabilised Mussolini's political position as a plot developed against him within the Fascist Grand Council in July 1943. He was then dismissed as Prime Minister by Victor Emmanuel III, who installed Marshal Badoglio in his place. In the event, it all proved remarkably simple, for reasons explained in Essay 19. After some weeks of hesitation, the new government surrendered in September to the Allies. The delay gave the Germans a chance to rescue Mussolini from Gran Sasso, where he had been imprisoned, and to install him as a puppet ruler in northern Italy, which had not yet been conquered by the British and Americans. Mussolini's new regime, the Salo Republic, was based on Lake Garda and was seen as a second chance to establish fascism (Essay 20). A new programme was drawn up at Verona in November 1943, followed by the nationalisation of key industries, the introduction of land reform and a general focus on syndicalism. Unfortunately for Mussolini, the Salo Republic was entirely dependent on the German army, under Kesslring, and the SS, under Wolff. The majority of the Italian population hated the regime and a large proportion took part in active resistance. By April 1945 the Allies had broken the Gothic Line into northern Italy and the Germans were forced to withdraw. Mussolini fled with them but was intercepted by communist partisans and shot alongside his mistress, Clara Petacci. Their bodies were displayed in the *Piazzale* Loreto in Milan. Mussolini received as much execration in death as he had ever received adulation in life.

Part 2: Essays

The First World War and the peace settlement

1. Why did Italy enter the First World War in 1915 rather than in 1914? (90 marks)

See Chapter 2, Essay 11.

2. a) What effect did the First World War have on Italy? (15 marks)

The military, political and economic effects of the First World War pushed Italy from uneasy co-existence with constitutional democracy towards acceptance of authoritarianism and dictatorship.

The military effect of the war proved worse than anything that had been imagined. Although Italian troops fought bravely, they were equipped with obsolete weapons and badly led by officers using outdated tactics. The Austrians proved a far more obdurate enemy than had been imagined and Italian defeat at Caporetto came as a major blow. It was not until Austria-Hungary was in the process of collapse that the Italian army was able to avenge the humiliation of Caporetto through a victory at Vittorio Veneto. For much of the time soldiers suffered conditions in the trenches which were even worse than those on the western front; these proved ideal conditions for the spread of radical ideas – both from the extreme left and the extreme right, and it is no coincidence that this was the period in which fascist ideas developed. The trenches were also a breeding ground for communism, after 1919 the main target for fascism. Far from uniting Italians, therefore, the experience of military conflict created a deep rift between two greatly strengthened extremes.

Parliamentary democracy fell into this chasm as a direct result of the war. The problem was that, ever since unification, Italy had struggled to maintain stable governments, experiencing no fewer than twenty-two ministries between 1860 and 1900 and nine between 1900 and 1914. Until 1915 at least some continuity had been maintained by the use of *trasformismo*, but the experience of war marked, in the words of De Grand, 'a rupture in Italian political development'. After 1918, *trasformismo* was out of the question, which meant that Italy could not sustain the moderate centre at the very time that the extremes were growing in importance. War acts as a powerful political catalyst, accelerating underlying trends and exploiting weaknesses. It so weakened the fabric of 'liberal Italy', created by the Risorgimento of the nineteenth century, that this was to be torn apart by new forces of fascism after 1921.

The economic impact of the war was also disastrous. The cost of Italy's involvement was over twice the total government expenditure of the previous fifty years. All parts of the economy were affected through a combination of massive debt, declining industries and disrupted trade. Postwar recovery was slower in Italy than in any of the other Allied countries, leading to a steady rise in unemployment and a quadrupling of inflation. Part of the population, however, profited from the war, either through providing supplies or through speculation. This accentuated political instability. By becoming a ready target for communists they swung behind the fascists, thus establishing the eventual connection between the radical right and the 'moneyed' right. This provided fascism with the image of respectability it needed to gain power.

Overall, the First World War exaggerated the frailty of Italy's political and economic base by removing earlier stabilising influences and exposing the people to extremist movements. Unemployment soared, with demobilisation mainly responsible for the total of 2 million by the end of 1919. Inflation had also become a fact of life, with the cost of living in 1919 about four times that of 1913. At the same time, there were some who benefited from the war, making profits through supplies or playing the stock exchange. These contributed greatly to the post-war instability; by providing a ready target for communists, they bought their support of fascism and established the eventual connection between the radical right and the 'moneyed' right. This provided fascism with the image of respectability it needed to gain power.

b) Why and with what results were Italians so resentful of the peace settlement of 1919? (15 marks)

Although on the 'winning side' in the First World War, Italy was disillusioned by the limited fruits of victory. Territorially the peace settlement proved very disappointing. The Treaty of London (1915) had guaranteed Italy possession of Trentino, Trieste, south Tyrol, Istria and Dalmatia. What Italy actually received by the Treaty of St Germain in 1919 were Trentino and south Tyrol.

Italian nationalists considered that Italy had been cheated. The rules had been changed – without Italy's consent – and were being applied against it. President Wilson insisted, where possible, that the new nation states of Europe should be given boundaries which reflected national self-determination. If Italy were to receive all the territories claimed, the new state of the Serbs, Croats and Slovenes (later called Yugoslavia) would be deprived of much of its coastline. Orlando realised that Italy had limited influence in 1919 and therefore looked to Lloyd George and Clemenceau to put pressure on Wilson to moderate his ideas. They, however, were more concerned with the question of Germany. In any case, they argued, Italy's security had been greatly enhanced by the break-up of Austria-Hungary and the reduction of Austria itself to a size not much larger than Switzerland, the population reduced from 51 million to 6 million. In actual fact, there was much to this argument. Italy's frontier was now stronger than at any time in its history and there were certain advantages to not having large minorities of Slovenes, Serbs and Croats to destabilise it.

Few Italians, however, saw the rationale of limited territorial gain. Instead, the peace settlement had a profound and collective psychological impact. The Treaty of St Germain simply did not satisfy national aspirations; after all, Italy had entered the First World War quite deliberately in pursuit of extra territory. As we have seen it received only a small part of what it had been promised. This played a significant role in the development of Italian nationalism after the war and, in particular, it enhanced the profile of fascism. Terms such as the 'mutilated victory' and 'treachery in high places' were widely used. No doubt these allegations were exaggerated but the disappointment of 1919 gave rise to the sensational occupation of Fiume by Gabriel D'Annunzio, who, in turn, provided a precedent for the fascist squads which were soon to be so prominent throughout northern Italy. The government was also hamstrung by the settlement. Although supposedly on the winning side, it was as much affected by the legacy of the Treaty of St Germain as was the government of the Weimar Republic by the Treaty of Versailles. For post-war Italian Prime Ministers like Giolitti (1920–1), Bonomi (1921–2) and Facta (1922), the task of effective and stable government was complicated by unresolved issues from the settlement, which greatly assisted the rise of fascism. Above all, the obsession with the 'mutilated victory' drew attention away from more urgent issues such as stable government and economic recovery.

The rise of Mussolini and fascism to 1922

3. a) What were the origins and meaning of 'Italian fascism'?   **(15 marks)**

As an ideology, Italian fascism resulted from the meeting of the two extremes of the political spectrum. These were the far left, developed by Mussolini's revolutionary syndicalism, and the far right, driven by the ardent nationalism of D'Annunzio. The experience of the First World War fused the two into one movement, the ideas of which were spread by Mussolini's newspaper *Il Popolo d'Italia* through concepts like 'Revolution is an idea which has found bayonets'.

Figure 5.3 **The origins of fascism**

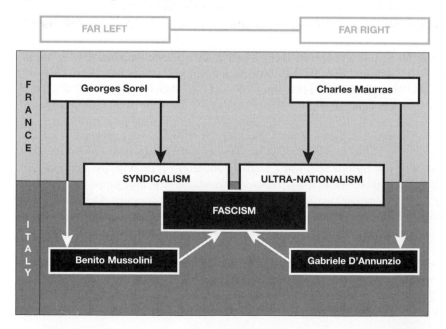

As a movement, fascism developed in two main stages. In 1919 the **Fasci di Combattimento** were set up; these organised a series of attacks on the socialist and communist left throughout northern Italy, especially in Milan, Ferrara and the Romagna. As violent activists, these squads were the primitive undercurrent of fascism. In 1921 fascism was given a more legal appearance with the establishment of the *Partito Nazionale Fascista* (PNF), which contested the 1921 general election and took part in parliamentary activity. Thus by 1921 fascism had developed two broadly different strategies to achieving power.

The term 'fascism' derives from the 'fasces' emblem which symbolised authority in ancient Rome. The axe-head protruding from the bundle of rods bound round the axe-haft represented ordered discipline and allegiance created among disparate groups by centralised power. Mussolini himself considered the key components to be opposition to the principles of liberal democracy, socialism and communism. Fascism was strongly **etatist** in that it 'conceived of the state as an absolute'. Indeed, 'Outside the state no human or spiritual values can exist.' Fascism was also militaristic and expansionist, aiming to extend Italy's boundaries in Europe and acquire an overseas empire through conquest. War was necessary to fascism as an 'essential manifestation of vitality'.[1]

But historians have shown that fascism was less ordered than Mussolini's definition implies. Far from being a simple statement of *etatist*, militarist and anti-communist objectives, fascism was actually a loosely connected series of appeals directed towards different groups of the population. De Grand, for example, identifies five such components. 'National syndicalism' was to bring together workers and industrialists by replacing trade unions. 'Rural fascism' would similarly unite peasants and landlords through a new agricultural focus; 'technocratic fascism', by contrast, stressed modernisation and industrialisation. 'Conservative fascism' reassured the Church, the monarchy and the aristocracy that traditional values would be retained, while 'national fascism' pointed to a more radical future based on mobilisation and conquest.[2]

Fascism was therefore **eclectic**. It emerged from opposite ends of the political spectrum, developed a dual strategy and had different ideas and appeals which were only loosely combined.

b) Why was Mussolini appointed Prime Minister of Italy in 1922? (15 marks)

The immediate reason for Mussolini's appointment was that King Victor Emmanuel III gave way to the threat of the fascist levies gathering on the outskirts of Rome in October 1922. This, however, occurred within the broader perspective of violence and political chaos as a result of which the king assumed that he had no alternative.

The so-called March on Rome presented the existing government with a direct ultimatum. Preparations were made at a fascist conference in Naples to seize power unless Mussolini was granted at least five cabinet ministries. The official response was divided, which gave Mussolini a major advantage. Although the Prime Minister, Facta, urged the King to declare martial law, the latter refused. He felt that the fascist contingents, now gathering outside Rome, could plunge Italy into civil war. Instead, Victor Emmanuel made Mussolini a conciliatory offer of a place in a coalition government. Sensing that he could now set his own terms, Mussolini demanded nothing less than the premiership. The King capitulated and invited Mussolini, now in Milan, to form his own government.

The March on Rome was therefore enough of a threat to the establishment to bring about the transfer of power that the fascists wanted. But the threat seemed so great because of the political circumstances between 1918 and 1922. Two major factors interacted to give the impression that the Mussolini and the fascists held the key to the future. The first was the wave of violence unleashed all over Italy by the *squadristi* of the *Fasci di Combattimento*. The main cities affected were Milan, Bologna and Ferrara, while rural areas included Emilia, Tuscany, Umbria and parts of Lombardy and Venetia. The second factor was the impression that Mussolini was the only politician in Italy capable of controlling the violence and preventing a descent into chaos. This was because of the instability of the governments of Giolitti (1920–1), Bonomi (1921–2) and Facta (1922). The proliferation and fragmentation of political parties made it increasingly difficult to operate an effective coalition government. In this situation Mussolini exerted more of an influence than the thirty-five PNF seats suggested, as he was able to manoeuvre and deal between other parties and politicians in the Chamber. In the process he gradually established himself as a credible alternative.

Fascist influence was greatly enhanced by the personal skills of Mussolini. To a large extent the internal situation favoured his appointment in 1922, but there is evidence that he also earned it. He had proved to be a flexible pragmatist: he had avoided any ideological commitment and, in his own words, had pursued 'a doctrine of action'. He had also ensured that the appeal of fascism should vary as widely as possible in order to include different groups within the population. This made the PNF possibly the only truly nationwide party in Italy. He knew how to gain popular attention and support and, above all, made full use of the political instability in 1921 and 1922. He made it apparent that fascism could disrupt the existing system. Alternatively, it could offer the only real alternative and provide a means of reconciling and uniting Italy.

Within this context, Victor Emmanuel's reaction to the March on Rome is understandable. If Mussolini were refused government power, he could well signal an increase in the violent

Figure 5.4 **The significance of the fasces symbol**

The symbol of fascism was an adaptation of the *fasces*, originally carried by the lictors in ancient Rome. Under Mussolini, the bundle of rods symbolised the different classes and sectors within Italy, bound by the thongs of discipline around the axe-head of authority and power. This was very much in line with the fascist emphasis on totalitarian control by a state aiming at militarism and expansion.

activities of the *Fasci* and the Italian army could not be relied upon to deal with these effectively. On the other hand, offering Mussolini the premiership could undermine the *Fasci* and strengthen the influence of the party. Power would therefore bring moderation and responsibility; in any case, the political system would prevent Mussolini from gaining a parliamentary majority, which meant that the King would have the option of dismissing him at any time in the future. He was not, at this stage, aware that Mussolini would seek to change the political system.

4. To what extent was Italian fascism the creation of Mussolini? (90 marks)

Fascism and Mussolini were not, as historians like A.J.P. Taylor have claimed, one and the same thing. It is true that Mussolini played a vital role in the development of fascism. But his role was really to co-ordinate influences occurring around him and to use his own skills to promote new forms of activism. He did not create fascism out of nothing; nor did he create the conditions in which fascism flourished. He did, however, respond creatively to these conditions and developed the organisation and leadership which enabled fascism to grow and flourish. This can be seen in a number of ways.

Mussolini was once seen as the 'creator' of fascism as an ideology. The seedbed of fascism was not, however, Italy but France. There, at the turn of the century, the left-wing syndicalism of Georges Sorel linked with the far-right nationalism of Charles Maurras. Mussolini's role was as a channel for the arrival of syndicalism in Italy. His initial contribution to Italian fascism was to provide the far-left ingredient through his journalism on the socialist paper *Avanti!*. The far-right component of Italian fascism, again under the influence of France, was D'Annunzio. Thus the origins of Italian fascism both preceded and bypassed Mussolini. This means that he could not have been its 'creator' in the sense of its 'originator'. Nor was his the only individual influence behind its development. In addition to D'Annunzio, the early history of Italian fascism was shaped by the likes of Farinacci, Balbo and Grandi, all committed leaders of the fascist squads.

Mussolini did not create the symbols, emblems and paraphernalia which are always associated with Italian fascism. The 'fasces' itself was borrowed from the lictor's mace of authority in ancient Rome. The black uniforms, the death head insignia, the salute of the raised daggers, and even the fascist war cry, were all taken directly from the followers of D'Annunzio during the latter's attempted occupation of Fiume between 1919 and 1920. If fascism, as Taylor has maintained, was based essentially on slogans and show, these did not come from Mussolini's repertoire.

Nor was Mussolini directly responsible for the special conditions upon which Italian fascism depended: political and economic crisis. Although these had been endemic to Italy since the completion of unification in 1870, they had been aggravated by the First World War. There was widespread disillusionment with the unstable governments of Giolitti (1920–1), Bonomi (1921–2) and Facta (1922), with the apparent failure of parliamentary democracy and with a failing economy which at the end of the war had quadrupled the cost of living and increased the level of unemployment to 2 million. Fascists were drawn from Italy's fractured classes and occupations: they came from a demobilised army, from industrialists who feared socialism, from workers disillusioned with capitalism, and from the lower middle classes who felt trapped between the two. This fracturing process, without which fascism would have had few recruits, was not created by Mussolini.

Nevertheless, the transfer of allegiance involves attraction as well as repulsion. This is where Mussolini made creative use of the circumstances operating in his favour. He was above all a flexible pragmatist who was able to adjust his policies and to avoid any ideological strait-jacket. The best example of this was his formation of the *Partito Nationalista Fascista* in 1921 once it had become clear that the *Fasci di Combattimento* (1919) could not succeed alone. This created the highly successful strategy of taking part in parliamentary politics above the surface while stirring up public disorder below the surface. In this way Mussolini could claim that the fascist squads were the only bodies capable of maintaining order and that they were under the control of a legal parliamentary party. It was this type of ruse which made King Victor Emmanuel III reject Facta's advice to declare martial law and, instead, to invite Mussolini to form a government on 29 October 1922.

The period between 1918 and 1922 showed another facet of Mussolini's creativity: the way in which he projected a popular image and made a direct appeal to all parts of the Italian population. He used all his journalistic skills to project simple and effective messages and to offer specific promises to specific classes and economic interests. His oratory, although well rehearsed, appeared spontaneous and was calculated to stir the emotions of the crowd. In this respect he was probably the first leader of the twentieth century to understand and exploit the psychology of the masses.

On balance, Mussolini cannot be considered creative in the sense of a designer or an architect. Unlike communism, Italian fascism had no theoretical plan or blueprint. Mussolini was, however creative in the sense of a builder using materials to hand. But because these materials were themselves fragments, fascism was ultimately to prove both flawed and unstable.

5. a) Which sections of the Italian people had come to support fascism by 1922 and why? (15 marks)

Fascism claimed to represent all classes and sectors within the Italian population. This was in contrast to the other parties, such as the **PSI** and **PCI** which had the support of specific sectors of society.

The armed forces, for example, were broadly sympathetic to fascism. Demobilised veterans, fiercely patriotic and now unemployed, made up a new ***lumpenproletariat*** which, as in Germany, turned to the far right rather than to the far left. Their ardour was also fired by D'Annunzio's occupation of Fiume. Troops who continued to serve after the end of the war generally responded with enthusiasm to the fascist rallies and diverted considerable amounts of military equipment and arms. The officer class had less reason to be radical or unstable but they had to be careful not to provoke mutinies amongst their men. While trying to keep discipline within the army, they therefore refrained from taking counter-measures against fascist supporters. In this way they allowed fascism to penetrate the army.

From the various social classes, by far the most consistent support for fascism was provided by the lower middle class, comprising small shopkeepers, artisans and clerical workers. Normally a moderate sector of society, they had been destabilised partly by the rapid industrialisation of Italy before 1914 and partly by the impact of the war itself. Caught between the rival forces of the working class and socialism on the left, and business and capitalism on the right, they saw fascism as a genuine alternative to both. To them it appeared a moderate alternative, a 'third way' between two extremes. Fascism, they hoped would end the industrial disruption of revolutionary socialism while also controlling the power of big business.

In the countryside, fascism also made considerable headway. At first it was supported mainly by the landlords and estate owners, who welcomed the attacks by the fascist squads on peasant strikers between 1920 and 1922. Gradually, however, fascism also succeeded in winning over some of the peasantry, especially those who preferred the fascist policy of small land grants to individual cultivators rather than the socialist alternative of collectivised cultivation.

In the urban and industrial centres fascism was supported, for its stand against communism, by leading industrialists such as Alberto Pirelli, the tyre magnate, and Giovanni Agnelli of Fiat. At first, the vast majority of workers were hostile to fascism. From 1921, however, many were won over, largely because the split on the left and the separation between the PSI and PCI weakened the left-wing alternative.

Finally, there were sectors within Italy which assisted fascism indirectly, although they withheld total support. The aristocracy were partially won over by Mussolini's decision to end the attack made by fascism on the monarchy. Indeed, Margherita, the queen mother, and the Duke of Aosta, were both admirers of Mussolini. The Catholic Church took its cue from Pope Pius XI who, from the time of his election in 1922, remained on good terms with Mussolini. The reason was that the Church considered that the main threat came from communism and, since Mussolini was prepared to do a deal with Catholicism, he was seen as a guarantor of Catholic liberties against atheism.

Overall, the appeal of fascism was so widespread because it was so diverse. As an ideology, it was flexible enough to appeal to all individuals and groups within all classes and sectors, although it was probably the lower middle class which provided the most cohesive support. The fasces emblem genuinely reflected the diverse strands – shortly to be bound together by fascist authoritarianism.

b)   How strong were the obstacles standing between Mussolini and political dictatorship when he came to power? (15 marks)

The appointment of Mussolini as Prime Minister in October 1922 is often seen as the first step in the development of his personal dictatorship in Italy. This was not inevitably the case, since Mussolini was, in 1922 and 1923, surrounded by a range of initially strong obstacles. Nevertheless, since most of these obstacles were eventually removed, they must have contained flaws which allowed them to be eroded over time.

Mussolini had no constitutional base for dictatorship in the first year of his power. He led a coalition, not a fascist, government and of the fourteen members of his cabinet, only three were from the Fascist Party. There seemed little likelihood that this situation would change since, as a result of the 1921 parliamentary election, the PNF had only thirty-five seats, or about 7 per cent of the total in the Chamber. Parties with a larger representation included the Socialists (PSI), the Populists (PPI) and Communists (PCI), all of which were confident that the fascist experiment would fail; at this stage there was certainly no indication that these would give way to a one-party state characteristic of dictatorship. Above all, there appeared to be an ultimate safeguard against the emergence of personal dictatorship. As Prime Minister, Mussolini was not even head of state, a position reserved for Victor Emmanuel III. The King was commander-in-chief of the armed forces; any special powers used by the government were in his name and with his consent; and he could replace Mussolini at any time. Apart from the fascists themselves, other right-wing influences in Italy – the Church, the army, the civil and diplomatic service – all tended to be conservative and anti-radical.

If there was any indication of dictatorship in 1922 and 1923, therefore, it was the type which was allowed to deal with a temporary emergency, not one which was seen as permanent. The problem,

and PCI from contention. He also altered the voting system by the electoral law of 1928, by which all parliamentary candidates were selected by the Fascist Grand Council and the final list voted on as a whole. The process was completed by the replacement in 1939 of the Chamber of Deputies by the Chamber of Fasces and Corporations. Meanwhile, Mussolini gathered to himself all major political powers, governing by decree from 1926 and popularising his personal control through the Cult of the *Duce*. He used this power to pursue a series of policies intended to maintain support from all sectors of the population. These included reconciliation with the Catholic Church through the Lateran Agreements of 1929, the development of syndicates and the Corporate State from 1926, the promotion of industry through the IRI (1933) and the Battles for Grain (1925) and Births (1925). Elements of Mussolini's foreign policy also proved popular, especially the Locarno Pact (1925) and the conquest of Ethiopia (1935–6).

Another layer of support was provided through the process of indoctrination; these were intended to mobilise support and prevent it from drifting away if Mussolini's policies failed in any way. Hence education was reorganised by Fedele in 1925 and Bottai from 1936. Textbooks became a state monopoly and the Fascist School Charter standardised all teaching in 1939. This was enhanced by the growth of youth groups, which, for boys, comprised the Sons of the She-Wolf (4–8), the *Balilla* (8–14), the *Avanguardisti* (14–18) and the Fascist Levy. Ideas and beliefs were also heavily influenced through the state-controlled press; alternative newspapers were suppressed by the Exceptional Decrees of 1926 and all journalists were compulsorily registered. Music, art, literature and the cinema were all mobilised in support of fascism, dominated by the Ministry of Popular Culture. All forms of indoctrination and propaganda were to focus on Mussolini. This was a recognition that Mussolini remained more popular than the fascist movement. Hence, through the Cult of the *Duce*, propaganda enabled Mussolini to transcend fascism.

When such measures failed to prevent the revival of opposition, coercion was used. This was intended partly as a corrective and partly to reinforce the support of the rest of the population by showing them that dissent would certainly be punished. The two major institutions were the OVRA, founded in 1926 and the Special Tribunal for the Defence of the State. These acted as a secret police force and as a summary form of justice to deal with offenders. Less ruthless, but effective, were the patterns of promotion in all forms of employment, where the key factor was loyalty to fascism, not efficiency.

c) **'The controls by the totalitarian state on Italian society and culture were not particularly effective'. Explain why you agree or disagree with this view.**

(15 marks)

Mussolini always intended Fascist Italy to be the model totalitarian system, in which the individual would be subject in all areas to the needs and dictates of the state. In theory this was very extensive, as shown by the slogans '*credere, obbedire, combattere*' and 'nothing outside the state, nothing beyond the state, nothing against the state.' Such grandiose schemes, however, met with mixed success, depending on their target, their aims and their timing.

Control over education, youth movements and employment carried certain advantages. Fedele and Bottai were able to close the minds of much of Italy's youth to liberal influences, while the activities of the *Avanguardisti* and Balilla would have had a cumulative effect in creating a more aggressive spirit in line with fascist militarism. But the impact was far less than intended. Something like 40 per cent of the age group between 8 and 18 avoided membership of the youth groups, preferring more traditional, possibly Catholic, alternatives. Similarly, the attempts to redefine the role of women seemed dramatic in theory but were limited in practice. The Battle for Births, launched in 1925, was at first an important factor in reducing the number of women in the work-force; this was, however, reversed during the 1930s as women were required in larger numbers because of the absence of over a million men on regular campaign in Italy's foreign wars.

Control over the press was probably one of the most effective of all of Mussolini's measures. The 1926 Decrees gave the regime a virtual monopoly over the reporting of all events and prevented negative images interfering with the Cult of the *Duce*. Yet it proved much more difficult to promote a positive commitment to the ideas of fascism. The efforts of the Ministry of Popular Culture were often ridiculed by a population with a sophisticated appreciation of its cultural heritage. It was also extremely difficult to develop a total commitment to a new ideology. All that Mussolini could reasonably hope for was coexistence between fascism and Catholicism. Although this was intro-duced by the Lateran Agreements of 1929, there was never any question about the population's ultimate allegiance. From 1931 onwards Catholic Action developed rapidly as a group aiming to undermine the secular and militaristic components of the youth movements. Italians therefore had no difficulty in turning against fascism from 1943 onwards, since under Aldo Mori and De Gasperi a powerful political alternative was emerging in the form of Christian Democracy.

The area in which the regime had the least influence over the population was race. The attempts to introduce a policy of anti-Semitism in Italy was never popular. The 1938 Manifesto on Race failed as a propaganda device and the anti-Jewish decrees were always less likely to be enforced with the complicity of the rest of the population than in Germany. Indeed, it took the German occupation of northern Italy from 1943 and the involvement of the SS to bring the Jewish deportations into effect.

Totalitarianism was therefore flawed in Italy. Mussolini had the political means to attempt social and cultural control and, for a while, to succeed. Ultimately, however, two factors undermined the totalitarian state. One was the continuation of the monarchy, which meant that Mussolini could be dismissed in 1943. The other was the deep roots of the Catholic tradition in Italy, which fascism could not hope to supplant.

8. **'Mussolini's relations with the Catholic Church show that he was able to conceal his own personal preferences for the sake of Italian unity.'**

   a) **What is meant, within the religious context, by 'his own personal preferences'?** (3 marks)

During his school days Mussolini had drawn attention to himself through his open atheism. An act of defiance became a more permanent conviction as Mussolini harmonised his dislike of reli-gion with the ideology of the far left, especially syndicalism. As he moved to the far right and came to represent the new force of Italian fascism, he continued to distrust religion as a poten-tial restraint on the martial spirit he wished to create. Nevertheless, since fascism did not require atheism as a part of its ideology, he adopted a more pragmatic approach and decided to form an alliance of interest with the Catholic Church. There is no evidence that his personal beliefs ever changed as a result.

   b) **Explain why and how Mussolini came to terms with the Catholic Church.** (7 marks)

Mussolini had good reasons to come to an agreement with the Catholic Church, which had been in conflict with the Italian state since the completion of Italian unification. His main method was the Lateran Treaty of 1929.

Although he saw himself as an atheist, Mussolini soon realised that fascism could not succeed in confrontation with Catholicism. Instead, he saw an opportunity to end the problematic relations between Church and state which had existed since the loss of the Papal States to Italian unification in 1861 and 1870. Besides, fascism needed the goodwill of all sectors of society which, in Italy, had one common factor – the Catholic religion. Mussolini also needed to confirm himself as the permanent political power within the state after the stormy developments of the mid-1920s. Although he had emerged successfully from the Matteotti Crisis, Mussolini still needed to confirm his credibility. What better way of doing it than by securing the sanction of the pope?

The way in which Mussolini went about this reconciliation was also pragmatic. He moved right away from the anti-religious stance of early fascism and, from 1921 onwards, began to play the anti-communist card to show that the real enemy of the church was the far left, not the far right. By 1929 he felt that it was necessary to provide a permanent structure for their reconciliation. This was done through the Lateran Agreements, which comprised three distinct settlements, each intended to deal with a major problem. The Concordat re-established a role for the church in the state: Catholicism would be recognised as the official state religion, Catholic instruction would be allowed in schools and church marriages would have restored validity. The Lateran Treaty restored a small part of the pope's former power as a ruler by returning the Vatican City. The third component settled the issue of compensation for earlier losses by payment of 750 million lire in cash and 1000 million in state bonds.

> c) 'Mussolini used his agreement with the Catholic Church as the foundation for his policies during the 1930s.' Explain why you agree or disagree with this view. (15 marks)

This quotation is partly true, although with considerable reservations. Mussolini did make the most of the goodwill created by the 1929 Lateran Agreements to seek a common interest between fascism and Catholicism. But fascism, not Catholicism, remained the real basis of his intentions and actions.

It is certainly the case that Mussolini publicised the *support* provided by the Catholic Church and that his domestic and foreign policies had a common objective with Catholicism. Hence he secured papal approval for the Battle for Births, which overlapped the Catholic emphasis on family values. He also enlisted the support of the upper clergy for Italy's involvement in a 'crusading' foreign policy abroad – especially the invasion of Ethiopia in 1935 and the involvement of Italy on the side of Franco's Nationalists in the Spanish Civil War (1936–9). He could even rely on the official sanction for the Corporate State as an alternative to the former system of trade unions influenced by socialists and communists.

It is, however, difficult to see any way in which Catholicism directly *influenced* Mussolini's policies. The decision to involve Italy in foreign ventures was due more to fascist expansionism and militarism, together with a need to divert Italian public opinion from prevailing economic crisis. The Battle for Births and the adjustment of women's role in society were fascist in conception, even if compatible with Catholic values. And the Corporate State was based on Mussolini's own ideas of syndicalism.

Even if Catholicism did not influence the regime's policies, could it not be argued that the regime at least adjusted its policies by taking *heed* of Catholic opinion? This is partly true. Mussolini curbed any openly atheistic tendencies in the fascist movement and did what he could to keep Catholics on board. Yet, where fascism followed a separate course, he made little attempt to compromise. There were two examples of this. One was Mussolini's determination to 'fascistise' Italy's youth, which incurred the protest in Pius XI's 1931 **encyclical** *Non abbiamo bisogno*. The other was the 1938 Manifesto on Race, which was condemned by Pope Pius XII.

Overall, Mussolini certainly used his agreement with the Catholic Church in the 1930s. Where possible, he did so to seek approval and sanction for his actions; he even tried to demonstrate that there was a broad common ground between fascists and Catholics. But there is no evidence that he adjusted fascism to fit Catholic principles.

9. **How valid is the view that Mussolini's reconciliation with the Catholic Church was 'an unqualified success'?** (90 marks)

There was no natural or ideological affinity between fascism and Catholicism; even so, the 1929 Lateran Agreements cleared up the conflict between the papacy and the state which went back to 1861. In this respect, the reconciliation between Mussolini and the Church must be considered a success. On the other hand, this success was far from 'unqualified'. The Church was never completely subordinated and elements within it continued to oppose fascist policy.

That the reconciliation had its success is readily apparent. Mussolini succeeded in gaining for his regime the sanction of a power which had been hostile to all previous governments for a period of fifty years. For the first time the Vatican recognised the secular Italian state and even urged the electorate to vote for the fascist list in the new electoral system. The Church also approved many of Mussolini's social policies, especially on family and divorce. Of particular value to Mussolini was the support provided by Pope Pius XI and Cardinal Shuster for ventures abroad: the 1935 invasion of Ethiopia was likened to the 'Crusades' and Italian intervention in the Spanish Civil War was applauded as a campaign against 'atheistic communism'. Overall, Pius XI believed that the Lateran Accords had 'brought God to Italy and Italy to God'.[4]

It is also clear that the official sanction of the Church for the regime stabilised the attitudes of other sectors within the population. This was especially important after the turbulent politics of the mid-1920s arising from the Matteotti murder. The leadership of no other group had been so readily converted. Royalty, for example, remained divided about Mussolini. King Victor Emmanuel III offset the Duke of Aosta's enthusiasm for Mussolini by a more cautious and occasionally hostile approach; he was particularly suspicious of the Cult of the *Duce*. The army had also been incompletely brought over to fascism. Its leadership remained responsible to the King, not to the *Duce*, and the latter lost considerable respect from the disasters of war after 1939. Industrial leaders, perhaps the natural allies of fascism, also had reason to distrust Mussolini after the Corporate State had failed to solve the problems thrown up by the Great Depression. In securing the support of the Catholic Church Mussolini was, therefore, able to rely upon the most influential group in Italy as a catalyst for political and social cohesion.

On the other hand, there were two main complications which prevented the reconciliation between fascism and the Catholic Church from being considered an 'unqualified' success. One was that the initial confidence placed by the Catholic leadership in fascism was not necessarily shared by other levels of the Church hierarchy. Many of the lower clergy and much of the laity remained suspicious of fascism and a conflict gradually developed over Mussolini's educational policies. Catholic Action, an organisation for laymen, was prepared to take on the government, while its youth wing actively competed with the *Balilla*; by 1939 Catholic Action was winning its battle for the soul of the younger generation, which goes some way towards explaining the absence of fanaticism in most units of the Italian army during the Second World War. Catholicism also developed an anti-fascist tone within the universities, based on the FUCI, for students and staff, and the *Movimento Laureati*. Along with Catholic Action, these gradually developed into a potential opposition and, from 1939 onwards, began to develop political groups, led by Aldo Mori and De Gasperi. These formed the basis of the post-war Christian Democratic Party.

There is a second reason for questioning Mussolini's 'success'. Although the authorities of the Church initially upheld the fascist regime, they eventually became disillusioned and the Vatican began to fall into line with the lower levels of the hierarchy in voicing its criticism. In 1931, for example, the Pope issued an encyclical *Non abbiamo bisogno*, which criticised fascist policies towards youth movements and education; as a result, Mussolini was forced to concede Catholic influences which actually undermined the impact of state indoctrination. Second, the Pope's opposition to part of Mussolini's racial legislation in 1938 struck a chord with the majority of the Italian population, who regarded anti-Semitism as alien to Italian traditions. In this way the Church was an impediment to Mussolini's attempts to radicalise fascist ideology.

Mussolini's reconciliation with the Catholic Church was never more than a tactical compromise. For a while it succeeded in giving his regime recognition and stability which fascism by itself could not. But the Church remained a separate institution which, for all the fascist sympathies of its leadership, was never fascistised. Lay organisations showed the way for effective opposition which the Church itself followed as the regime began to come apart. 'Unqualified success' does not turn into failure; Mussolini's more limited success did.

10. **'Fascist Italy was not originally racist. It adopted racism as an open policy only during the 1930s – and the Italian people found it alien.'**

   a) **What is meant by the sentence 'Fascist Italy was not originally racist'?** (3 marks)

In the early days of the fascist movement, there was little, if any explicit racism. There were, for example, many Jewish members of the fascist *squadristi*. Even when Mussolini had established himself in power, there was no initial attempt to follow a policy of anti-Semitism. Indeed, as late as 1933, Mussolini was referring in his public speeches, to 'certain unscientific doctrines' being practised 'beyond the Alps'. This was probably his most subtle and moderate performance, even if delivered in typically ebullient style.

   b) **Explain how and why Fascist Italy pursued racist policies during the 1930s.** (7 marks)

Mussolini introduced policies of anti-Semitism late in his political career; for the first sixteen years, indeed, there was no official discrimination against the Jews. The switch of policy was sudden and the reaction of the Italian people one of either indifference or resentment, which goes some way to explain the lack of success.

In 1938 Mussolini rushed through new and sweeping measures. The Manifesto on Race, drawn up by Mussolini and ten professors, provided a 'scientific' basis for fascist racial doctrine. Its main point was that the population of Italy was 'of **Aryan** origins and its civilization is Aryan', that there 'now exists a pure Italian race' and that 'Jews do not belong to the Italian race'.[5] This was followed by Mussolini's decrees which, like Hitler's Nuremberg Laws of 1935, prevented marriage between Jews and non-Jews; they also banned Jewish participation in medicine, education, politics and finance. Restrictions were placed on the ownership, bequest and inheritance of property, while all Jews who had entered Italy since 1919 were to be expelled. These measures were later intensified, during the Salo Republic, to cover the transportation of Italian Jews to the Nazi extermination camps.

Racism was not an inherent component of early fascism; rather, it developed during its later stages. This seems to have emerged for two reasons. The first was the conquest of Ethiopia (1935–6), which exposed Italians to extreme views on racial 'inferiority'; a brutal war, which included the use of mustard gas, was justified on the basis of race. Hence there was a growing parallel between the preparation of Italians for a future domination over 'inferior' peoples in Africa and Hitler's projections for Aryan expansion into eastern Europe. The second, and related, reason for growing racism in Italy was the diplomatic connection between Mussolini and Hitler from 1935 onwards. By 1938 Mussolini needed Hitler's support in Europe and the Rome–Berlin Axis (1936) was moving steadily towards a military alliance. Anti-Semitism was an extension of this vision. Although the connection was influenced by developments within Germany, Mussolini was also building up a case for the existence of a Jewish 'conspiracy' within Italy. This was partly because Italian Zionists, whose ultimate aim was the establishment of a Jewish state in Palestine, opposed his intention to take over from Britain the League of Nations **mandate** of Palestine. But a more immediate factor was the criticism by Jewish leaders of the conquest of Ethiopia. Hence the changing direction of Italian foreign policy, associated with the 'conspiracy' theory, drew Italy into the mainstream of anti-Semitism.

From 1935, therefore, Mussolini moved Italian fascism into a more dynamic, expansionist and racist phase. In the process he found reasons to turn against Italian Jews and therefore adapted Hitler's ideas and methods to Italy.

c) **'Mussolini's anti-Semitic policies failed largely because the Italian people were not inclined to racism.' Explain why you agree or disagree with this statement.** (15 marks)

The anti-Semitic measures failed largely because of the reaction of the Italian people. Italy had always been less affected than other parts of Europe by anti-Semitism. The Jews were a smaller proportion of the total population and had fully assimilated. Immediately after the First World War individual Jews had even joined the Fascist Party. When they were introduced, anti-Semitic measures were therefore perceived as being out of place in Italy. There were no outbursts of public opinion as occurred on *Kristallnacht* in Germany in 1938. Authorities were reluctant to enforce the full rigour of the law and the OVRA was not sufficiently intimidating to terrorise the population into denouncing Jews or those who befriended Jews. The Catholic Church, too, questioned the need for such measures. Pope Pius XI, who had in 1929 been prepared to collaborate with fascism, was by 1939 criticising Mussolini: 'Why, unfortunately, did Italy have to go and imitate Germany?'[6] Anti-Semitism therefore disturbed the Catholic conscience which was still a strong influence in Italy. It also acted as a catalyst for the growing unpopularity of the regime which, by 1943 had also produced secular misgivings of those who saw the creeping influence of Nazism in Italy. When Mussolini authorised the deportation of Jews to the extermination camps from 1943, he depended entirely on the German occupying authorities and the initiative was taken largely by the SS. The Italian army was far more reluctant to co-operate than the German army in the same circumstances. As for the population, many had been provoked into active resistance.

Mussolini had hoped to make fascism more dynamic by converting nationalism into racism. In this he made a profound mistake. Nationalism exerted a powerful appeal in Italy but there was no historic connection with racism, let alone anti-Semitism, as there was in other parts of Europe. Ultimately it was constrained by the revival of traditional Italian values, which the regime was insufficiently ruthless to prevent.

11. 'Mussolini's Corporate State was a partial return to his original ideas. It was, however, far too complicated ever to succeed in practice.'

    a)   What is meant by 'a partial return to his original ideas'?   **(3 marks)**

Mussolini's early ideas had been strongly influenced by the syndicalism of Georges Sorel. These were based on the far-left notion that trade unionism could be used as a political weapon through the general strike. Mussolini had departed permanently from this strategy in his move towards the right but he did eventually reverse the process. Instead of the trade unions reshaping the state, the state would reshape the unions in the form of syndicates.

    b)   Explain the meaning of the term 'Corporate State'.   **(7 marks)**

The 'Corporate State' was Mussolini's attempt to use the monopoly of power which the fascists gained in Italy during the 1920s to redesign Italy's economic and political structure. His intention was to destroy Western parliamentary democracy and *laissez-faire* capitalism without replacing it with a communist system like that of the Soviet Union. Some of the ideas, and most of the terms, derived from Mussolini's earlier commitment to syndicalism, although the conjunction of syndicalism and nationalism gave the actual institutions an authoritarian structure more appropriate to fascism.

The Corporate State involved, first of all, a decision to change the existing structures of Italian economic activity. Influenced partly by the ideas of Georges Sorel and partly by an imperfect knowledge of medieval guilds and corporations, Mussolini intended to bring to an end the conflicts between labour and capital by replacing the trade unions and employers organisations. Hence the 1926 Rocco Law officially recognised seven branches of economic activity: industry, agriculture, internal transport, merchant marine, banking, commerce and intellectual work; each of these was formed into a syndicate. Then, in 1934, economic activity was further reorganised into twenty-two specialised corporations. In theory, corporativism would end the conflict between socialism on the left and undiluted capitalism on the right. It would enhance state control over the economy without destroying private enterprise. It would, in other words, offer the best of both worlds and seemed ideally suited to help Italy tackle the pressures of unemployment and declining production brought by the Great Depression.

The political components of the Corporate State were really an adjustment of the institutions of democracy in line with economic corporativism. These emerged more gradually. Hence the Ministry of Corporations was set up in 1926 to co-ordinate the syndicates and the much larger National Council of Corporations made its appearance in 1930. It addition to supervising the syndicates and corporations, the National Council was also the means whereby the block-voting system was carried out in parliamentary elections: it scrutinised names presented to it by the corporations and prepared a final list. By 1938 the last vestige of parliamentary democracy gave way to the Corporate State when the old Chamber of Deputies was replaced by the new Chamber of Fasces and Corporations.

c) 'The Corporate State was a total failure.' Explain why you agree or disagree with this statement. (15 marks)

At first sight the structure of the Corporate State appears logical enough. Each part of the workforce was allocated its role within a rationally segmented economic structure, while the overall emphasis was on harmony and co-operation. It should, therefore, have been the means whereby fascism increased its efficiency as well as its control.

But the real significance of the Corporate State was not its rationale in theory but its failure to deliver results. When applied in practice the system became far too unwieldy. It also failed to provide a consensus between employers and workers and was usually excluded from any real decision-making on the economy. Historians have always been critical of its practical applications. Cassels remarks that 'the corporative state was a true child of Mussolini: the great poseur brought forth an organism which was a travesty of what it purported to be'.[7] According to Pollard, 'In reality, in the corporations and other new government agencies fascism had created a vast, largely useless apparatus'.[8] The Corporate State has been seen largely as an agreement reached by the fascist regime with the landowners and industrialists. It was more about creating a subservient labour force than about proving a structure capable of undertaking genuine economic change. Hence, in the words of Tannenbaum, 'Fascist Italy had complete control over the labour force and very little control over the nation's economic structure'.[9] Increasingly, the whole structure of corporativism was ignored and policies pursued outside its scope. This meant that economically and politically the Corporate State merely provided another layer of administration which promoted confusion rather than order.

There is another perspective as well. Even if the Corporate State had been administered as intended, it would still have experienced the gravest difficulties. This was because of the growing economic crisis of the 1930s. The initial problems caused by the depression were exacerbated by the impact of war on Italy's limited industrial base from 1935 onwards, which no amount of structural efficiency could have offset.

12. With what justification can it be said that Mussolini's economic policies were 'a failure'? (90 marks)

Italy had the smallest and most unstable economy of all the major powers in inter-war Europe. Mussolini had some of the most elaborate ambitions of all the inter-war dictators. The two did not match. When Mussolini adopted a cautious and restrained approach to exploiting the economy he was often successful. When, however, his ambitions took over the economy all but collapsed under the severe strains imposed upon it. All this was compounded by more fundamental structural problems relating to the divisions between industry and agriculture and between north and south. Mussolini had some impact on these but, it has to be said, it was minimal.

For the first three or four years the fascist regime established for itself a reputation of careful financial management. This was largely because the Finance Minister, Di Stefani, pursued virtually unchanged the economic policies of previous governments based on the simple expedients of balanced budgets and allowing maximum free enterprise within a *laissez-faire* economy. Italy's experience during this period was similar to that of much of Europe – a general recovery followed the pattern of post-war boom and recession. Unemployment began to fall, consumerism expanded and the balance of trade deficit narrowed for a while. It has to be said, however, that during this period Mussolini was content to delegate economic responsibilities. His priority was political survival and any economic success was due to restraint from direct interference rather than to any carefully formulated policy.

The same could not be said of the second half of the 1920s and of the 1930s. Moderation and pragmatism gave way to more direct involvement, the style of which became more and more radical. The results, too, were more negative. One example was Mussolini's decision in 1929 to reflate the Italian currency to the level of 90 lire to the pound sterling. This was entirely inappropriate to Italy's economic needs. Mussolini was influenced as much on the dictates of national prestige as by sound economic thought, declaring 'I shall defend the Italian lira to my last breath'. In fact, his decision undermined Italy's competitiveness as an exporter and probably brought on recession even before the impact of the Great Depression. From the mid-1920s, also, Mussolini attempted unsuccessfully to drive the economy forward by the institutional changes of the Corporate State. Far from rationalising any economic planning, the syndicates, corporations and National Council added another layer of bureaucracy. By 1934 the Corporate State gave way to the even more inappropriate policy of autarky, the purpose of which was to prepare Italy's economic base for a series of wars over Ethiopia (1935–6), Spain (1936–9) and Albania (1939). The result of four years of constant warfare with a restricted economic base was such intolerable pressure that in September 1939 Mussolini had to warn Hitler that he could not immediately honour Italy's military obligations to Germany. This was the closest Mussolini ever came to an admission that his economic objectives had failed.

Clearly military priorities wrecked any positive work that might have been done. There was at least some evidence of progress in industry before the shattering effect of war. With the onset of the depression the government had a marginal effect on the levels of unemployment by introducing schemes for job-sharing and for rescuing those industries in particular difficulty. It also tried, sensibly enough, to channel state investment into those industries which were considered most vital; this was done through the IRI (*Istituto per la recostruzione industriale*), set up in 1933. In some ways industry recovered from the impact of the depression. Between 1936 and 1940 it overtook agriculture for the first time in Italian history as the largest single contributor to the GNP, industrial production increasing by 9 per cent. But this trend was offset by permanent underlying weaknesses in the industrial sector. Mussolini entirely failed to deal with the huge inequality between northern and southern Italy, while the economy as a whole continued to experience low productivity and a declining domestic consumer market. Italy took longer than any other power to recover from the depression, a trend which was exacerbated by the pressures of military conflict throughout the second half of the 1930s.

Agriculture is often cited as a success for Mussolini, at least in terms of statistics. He aimed at achieving self-sufficiency in grain production to improve Italy's balance of trade with the rest of Europe and with North America. The Battle for Grain, launched in 1925, increasing grain production by 50 per cent between 1922 and 1930 and by 100 per cent between 1922 and 1939. In the process, Mussolini avoided the disruption and chaos which attended the Stalinist agricultural policies. Nevertheless, his vision was obsessive and narrow. The focus on grain had a serious effect on other crops like fruit and olives, which would have been more suited to the land given over to grain. As elsewhere, excessive interference created an imbalance in agriculture which belied apparently favourable statistics.

It is difficult to avoid a negative overall assessment of fascist economic policy. The 'third way' of corporativism proved obstructive and irrelevant; Italy was better off under the more traditional liberal economic policy. There might, even so, have been some progress in industry but for the distortion of a limited economic base through autarky imposed by an overactive foreign policy. With this as the overriding influence any specific economic gains had to be magnified by propaganda into the 'victories' of 'Battles' accomplished. This became ever less convincing.

Mussolini's efforts to expand Fascist Italy, 1922–39

13. What were the main aims of Italian foreign policy between 1923 and 1940? (90 marks)

See Chapter 8, Essay 10.

14. Examine the successes and failures of Mussolini's foreign policy between 1922 and 1940. (90 marks)

See Chapter 8, Essay 11.

15. Assess the reasons for Mussolini's invasion of Ethiopia in 1935 and for his intervention in the Spanish Civil War (1936–9). (90 marks)

See Chapter 8, Essay 12.

16. 'For Italy, the negative effects far outweighed the positive.' To what extent do you agree with this view of Mussolini's invasion of Ethiopia (1935) and involvement in the Spanish Civil War (1936–9)? (90 marks)

See Chapter 8, Essay 13.

17. Why did Italy enter the Second World War on the side of Germany – but in 1940 rather than in 1939? (90 marks)

See Chapter 7, Essay 14.

The decline and fall of Mussolini and fascism, 1940–5

18. Compare the importance of any three reasons for the military defeat of Italy by 1943. (90 marks)

Three key factors in the military defeat of Italy by 1943 are: first, Mussolini's defective strategic decisions; second, the inadequacy of Italy's armed forces; and third, the limited extent of Italy's industrial base. The first brought Italy into the Second World War in 1940 and determined the style of war to be fought. Once these decisions had been taken, however, it was the inadequacy of Italy's armed forces which was responsible for Italy's rapid defeat. These, in turn, were due to

Figure 5.5 **Map of Italian expansion, 1919–40**

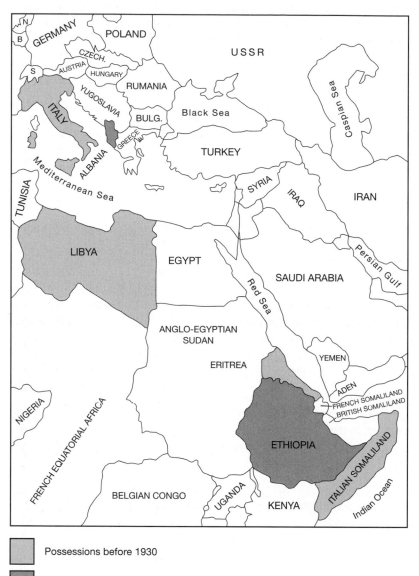

◻ Possessions before 1930

◼ Acquistions during the 1930s

Italy's having the smallest industrial infrastructure of all the major European powers. The first factor was therefore completely inappropriate for the second, while the third meant that the second ensured the failure of the first.

Mussolini made a series of disastrous decisions between 1940 and 1943 which made absolutely no sense when related to Italy's inadequate military infrastructure. The first was to commence hostilities in June 1940 despite the warning from the Commission on War Production that Italy could not sustain a single year of warfare until 1949. Mussolini then committed Italian forces not to a limited engagement but to fullscale partnership with Germany which would produce what he called a 'parallel war'. He aimed to expand Italian power in the Mediterranean, the Balkans and North Africa to re-establish the power of the Roman Empire: this was his equivalent of Hitler's vision of **Lebensraum** for Germany. This was entirely out of keeping with Italy's limited military base. It was always unlikely that Germany would provide forces to assist Mussolini's quest for further expansion in Africa. It also went directly against all of Italy's traditional military strategy to go to war with Britain; the latter had the means to control the Mediterranean, to threaten Italy's vulnerable coastline and to destroy its foothold in North Africa. Mussolini's decision to expand into the Balkans was also out of keeping with Italy's military capacity. This was one of the most difficult areas of Europe to conquer and the Germans soon had to intervene to rescue Italy from humiliation by the Greeks. Even with this disastrous experience behind him, Mussolini proceeded to another blunder. He committed Italy against the world's two industrial and military giants, the United States and the Soviet Union. The former played a vital part in rolling back the Axis occupation of North Africa in 1942 and 1943, while the latter drained off the Axis troops needed to prevent this.

The weakness of Italy's armed forces meant that Mussolini's elaborate schemes to pursue a 'parallel war' and revive the Roman Empire could not logically succeed. As a result of pre-war expansion, the Italian army was already exhausted. Instead of being able to mobilise 8 million men, as Mussolini boasted, the Italian army in 1940 comprised a total of 3 million men, who were inadequately supplied with 1.3 million rifles (of 1891 design). The army's obsolete tanks and armoured cars were entirely inappropriate to Mussolini's 'parallel' war. The navy was also unequal to the demands of 'parallel war', especially when confronted by the British fleet in the Mediterranean. Italy possessed no aircraft carriers and only 8 battleships, none of which inflicted any damage. Although there was a substantial submarine fleet, these suffered heavy losses. Even the air force was defective. Italian production was smaller than that of Germany and Japan and the main designs – the Fiat CR 42 and Macchi MC 200 – had little success against British and American aircraft. Matters were made even worse by the refusal of the air force leadership to co-ordinate its plans with the army and navy. Unlike the **Luftwaffe** and the RAF, the Italian air force always demanded, and received, special autonomy. This was part of a long-term rivalry between the three services, which made combined operations virtually impossible. Hence, according to Whittam, 'Military weakness had been built into the regime from the very start.'[10]

An ambitious military strategy was therefore impossible to fulfil because of totally inadequate military resources. This, in turn, was due to a limited economic and industrial base, which was entirely inadequate to the demands placed upon it. The losses already incurred in the Ethiopian War (1935–6) and the Spanish Civil War (1936–9) had been particularly disruptive. Mussolini had attempted to compensate for these through an emergency policy of autarchy. But this had proved unsuccessful and Italy had had to appeal to Germany for extensive aid in September 1939. Italy's capacity for steel production was particularly small: in 1939 she produced 2.4 million tons, compared with Britain's 13.4 million and Germany's 22.5 million. This meant that Mussolini was bound to have serious problems in converting Italy's limited industrial infrastructure into sustained warfare. It has been estimated that Italy's military capacity was less than one fifth of that of Nazi Germany or the Soviet Union and about one quarter of that of Britain. Even in war, Italy could not be made to yield extra military resources: her infrastructure was simply too small.

Italy's military defeat was, therefore, always very likely in any war involving powers with vastly greater industrial and military capacity, such as the United States and Britain. Defective infrastructure must be seen as the most important long-term impediment, but actual defeat came as a direct result of Mussolini's folly in committing Italy's already depleted armed forces to attempt the impossible.

**19. Assess the reasons for Mussolini's dismissal as Prime Minister
  in 1943.** (90 marks)

Mussolini was dismissed by King Victor Emmanuel III in July 1943 as a direct result of a conspiracy against him. The reason for this was impending military defeat which had undermined Mussolini's whole claim to power. He was also vulnerable because of the incomplete hold which he had over fellow fascists and over Italy's institutions.

The conspiracy was the immediate factor behind the dismissal. It was unintentionally started by Mussolini himself: in February 1943 he sacked Grandi, Bottai and others for insubordination in the Fascist Party. They, in turn, collaborated with several military leaders and with disillusioned moderate fascists, who hoped to dump Mussolini and replace him with Caviglia. At a session of the Fascist Grand Council in July 1943, therefore, Grandi, Bottai and Ciano secured a majority of 19 votes to 7 for the full restoration of the legal organs of the state and the dismissal of Mussolini himself. The King then exercised his constitutional powers in replacing Mussolini as Prime Minister with Marshal Badoglio.

These events did not, however, occur spontaneously. They were driven by a key factor: military disasters. Italian armies had been defeated in the Balkans by the Greeks and had to be rescued by the Germans in North Africa. The defeat of the Germans at El Alamein and the Anglo-American invasion of Sicily and Italy brought more immediate danger, provoking a wave of disillusionment with Mussolini's leadership. There was also resentment at the rapid fall in living conditions: Italians had to put up with some of the worst hardships suffered by civilians anywhere in Europe. And, further, there was pressure for peace from industrialists and military leaders. Even the Church tried to disentangle itself from the regime, and now swung its support behind the King rather than Mussolini. The Fascist Party, now incapable of rallying the population to face adversity, split asunder and hastened to get rid of its leader before the Allies reached Rome. Throughout the critical first half of 1943 there was increasingly powerful anti-German feeling; explaining his plot against Mussolini, Grandi said: 'You believe you have the devotion of the people. You lost it the day you tied Italy to Germany.'[11]

Although it was the crucial influence behind Mussolini's decline, military defeat does not explain the apparent ease with which he was actually removed. This brings us to the third factor – Mussolini's failure to safeguard his own position. Quite simply, he had no means of preventing this coup. He had never promoted close unity within the Fascist Party, preferring to encourage the growth of cliques in order to pursue a policy of divide and rule. But this backfired on him in 1943 when he was supported in the Grand Council only by a group led by Farinacci. The other members accused him of having disrupted the party's development. Hence, according to Pollard, 'The overthrow of fascism when it came was essentially a "palace revolution".'[12] Crucially, Mussolini had no means of preventing it. He had never made himself head of state; that role had been reserved by the King, whose position had been strengthened in 1943 by the support of army leaders desperate for an armistice with the Allies. These had never been 'fascistised' in the way that the German high command had been 'Nazified' and had continued to owe ultimate allegiance to the monarch, not to the Duce. Mussolini had concentrated so much on neutralising the potential for opposition within the party that he had entirely overlooked the possibility of trouble from his generals. Even his intelligence service was defective, for he was taken completely by surprise by the July coup. All this was in direct contrast to Hitler, who maintained his leadership of the Nazi regime until the very end and had no superior who was able to dismiss him.

Finally, there was no fundamental attachment between the Italian people and fascism. Mussolini had never succeeded in implanting a new ideology in the popular mind, which meant that it was not difficult to revert to more traditional loyalties once the occasion arose. The occasion itself offered the prospect not so much of unconditional surrender as of a change of government, and an armistice leading to a change of sides. In this situation, the removal of Mussolini was seen not just the end of an adventure but also the rediscovery of commonsense. Weary of war, Italy was ready to be jolted back into its pre-fascist course. But the key was weariness with military *failure*; victory would have covered up the deficiencies of fascism and prevented the population from deserting it.

Overall, the most important reason for the collapse of the regime was military defeat. This provided an incentive for other fascist leaders to launch a coup, which secured Mussolini's dismissal by the King. The ease with which this was accomplished was a reflection on Mussolini's own complacency and the shallowness of the attachment of the Italian people to the ideology of fascism.

20. With what justification can it be said that 'the Salo Republic (1943–5) was Mussolini's second chance to establish a fascist regime, which was doomed because it depended on German rather than Italian support'?   (90 marks)

Broadly speaking, this is an acceptable summary of the origins and fate of the *Repubblica Sociale Italiana* (**RSI**), which lasted from September 1943 until April 1945. It is clear that Mussolini did try to rediscover his ideological roots by introducing an earlier form of fascism, although the result was a pale imitation which lacked the support and impetus it needed. It is also true that the Salo Republic was dependent on German occupation, which was fiercely resisted by a variety of Italian groups.

The new regime, based on headquarters at Lake Garda, was designed by Mussolini with Hitler's support. It was to be staffed by those fascists who had not been involved in the July plot against Mussolini, men like Pavolini, Ricci, Farinacci and Preziosi, who were pro-Nazi, and those, like Graziani and Pini, who had no military future under the new royal government in Rome. Mindful of the way in which the establishment had turned against him, Mussolini decided from the outset that the new fascist regime would be a purer, more radical version, which would no longer try to compromise with other authorities. In this way, Mussolini genuinely had a second chance to revive some of his early ideological preferences. As a 'republic', the regime was able reverted to the original anti-royalist views of fascism. Mussolini could also rediscover his original preference for revolutionary syndicalism. No longer dependent on the great industrialists, Mussolini was once again free to attack capitalism rather than having to appease it. He could now target 'the parasitic plutocracies and make labour the object of our economy and the indestructible foundation of the state'. Under the Verona programme (1943) and the socialisation law (1944), the main industries were nationalised, workers were included in industrial management and land reforms were introduced. In this way Mussolini intended to cut the fascist connection with conservatism and rediscover its radicalism.

But one thing was missing. Throughout his period in power in Rome, Mussolini had emphasised the national power of a mobilised Italian nation. During the 1930s, especially, fascism had also meant Italian expansionism and the recreation of empire. There was, therefore, no 'second chance' for the nationalist and *etatist* conceptions of fascism. The revival of the radical left was therefore probably due to the end of the early conjunction with the nationalist right. The new fascism was therefore a mockery of the version which had ruled Italy from 1923 to 1943. Instead of ruling an Italian empire, Mussolini was now confined to a small republic which owed its existence entirely to German support. There was therefore no chance that Mussolini would now be able to revive his career as an autonomous dictator. The Salo Republic had, in effect, become a Nazi rather than a fascist regime. Most of the power was held by SS General Wolff and eight provinces were detached from the Republic to be put under German administration. Mussolini had now become virtually identical to the German-controlled 'puppets' in Hungary, Slovakia and Romania.

Whether or not it was a genuine 'second chance' the new fascist regime was certainly doomed because of the German connection. This worked in two ways.

First, it became the target of Allied troops attempting to breach the German defences on the Gothic Line and in the Argento Gap. The Salo Republic had to be overthrown if Germany was to be defeated in southern Europe as well as in the west and the east. Hence Mussolini's fate was bound up with the military decisions of the German officers in Italy such as Kesselring and Wolff.

Second, the German occupation alienated much of the Italian population and meant that the Salo Republic held none of the attractions of the earlier fascist regime. Workers and peasants, who had once deserted the left for fascism, now abandoned fascism to return to the socialist and commun-ist left. They took part in strikes and demonstrations and joined the Italian resistance movement. Industrialists saw no advantages in Mussolini's new radicalism and did everything in their power to prevent the implementation of the 1944 Decree Law. Even the mainstay of fascism, the lower middle class, became resentful at the decline in living standards caused by prolonging the war against the Allies. They, too, switched their allegiance and once more craved parliamentary poli-tics. Italians had been jolted back into their pre-fascist course and saw the Salo Republic as an enemy. Many participated in extensive patriotic resistance against the German occupation. Others targeted both German occupiers and Italian fascists. The extent of the resistance was massive and was not broken even by its 100,000 deaths.

The Salo Republic therefore proved to be a practical impossibility. It could not survive because of German control, but would have fallen even sooner without it. The death of Mussolini shows how dependent he had become on foreign support and how much he had to fear from Italians. As the German army retreated from the last occupied areas of the north, Mussolini was caught by communist partisans on Lake Como, where he was arrested, shot and displayed in Milan.

Additional essay questions (with advice)

Each of these questions can be tackled as a single essay or as one of the answers to a question in several parts.

21. Assess the impact of economic and social problems on Italy before 1922.

Advice: *Avoid a straight description of the problems. Try to group them into categories. You could, for example, deal with 'longer-term' problems apparent since unification and 'imme-diate' problems created by the First World War and its aftermath. Bear in mind that 'social' problems can arise as a result of 'economic'. Consider which was the most important problem – and why others were less important.*

22. **Explain the development of Mussolini's ideas between 1900 and 1922.**

Advice: *Concentrate on Mussolini's ideas and cover his career only insofar as it relates to these. The overall pattern was his early belief in the ideas of the far left, especially syndicalism, which eventually converged with the nationalism of the far right to form fascism. But there was also a strong tendency towards pragmatism and opportunism.*

23. **How far do you agree with the view that 'Mussolini rose to power by 1922 by his own devices'?**

Advice: *Quantify 'How far?'. The answer is likely to be 'to an extent', even to 'a large extent' – but 'not entirely'. You might distinguish between 'subjective factors', over which Mussolini had control, and 'objective factors', circumstances which worked in his favour but for which he was not responsible. In each case, argue first, then support. At all costs avoid straight narrative on his rise to power.*

Essay plan

Para 1: Overall approach. Mussolini's rise was dramatic, indicating the importance of his own contributions. But these would have counted for nothing without the exceptional circumstances of the time. Hence the importance of subjective and objective influences.

Para 2: Objective factors created the situation in which Mussolini was able to develop his ideas and leadership:
- *Political instability preventing continuity in government (supporting detail).*
- *Economic crisis and its radicalising social impact (supporting detail).*
- *The catalytic impact of the First World War (supporting detail).*

Para 3: Subjective factors were vital for the emergence of a movement of the radical right emphasising authoritarian leadership:
- *Mussolini's personal qualities (supporting detail).*
- *Mussolini's pragmatic approach to organisation and strategy (supporting detail).*
- *Mussolini's development of fascist ideology (supporting detail).*

Para 4: Subjective and objective factors interacted in different ways, in varying degrees of importance. For example:
- *Mussolini's exploited political stability and developed fascism into a movement which promoted it and offered solutions for it (supporting detail).*
- *Mussolini developed fascist ideology to suit the needs of the different classes destabilised by economic collapse (supporting detail).*

Para 5: Integrated conclusion with a considered opinion as to which were the more important factors overall.

24. **How far would you agree with the view that by 1922 fascism appealed to all of Italy?**

Advice: *Quantify 'How far?' 'All of Italy' needs careful consideration. Does it mean a majority of the population? Or all regions? Or all members of all sectors and all classes? Or, as is more likely, substantial numbers in all sectors and classes. If you opt for the last, you need to explain the diversity of fascist appeal which made this possible.*

25. **How successful was Mussolini in making fascists of the Italian people?**

Advice: *Focus on the impact of propaganda and indoctrination in their various forms. 'How successful?' has to be quantified. Generally you can deduce a degree of success from each of the measures used but you need to explain that traditional loyalties often resulted in resistance to fascism. You should also introduce the failure of the experiment in militarism and the way in which Italians turned against Mussolini and fascism from 1943. This can therefore be a wide-ranging essay.*

26. **Assess the motives of Mussolini in coming to terms with the Catholic church in Italy.**

Advice: *Try to infer three or four 'motives' by thinking (before you start writing) about what he actually did. You might decide on (1) a change of his personal attitude to religion (unlikely), (2) the need to extend the support for fascism by winning over all sections of the population, (3) healing the historic rift between Church and state. Base these on specific factual support and make sure you prioritise the importance of the reasons (1) might be least and (2) the most important, while (3) could define the decision within a broader context.*

27. **What were Mussolini's economic priorities for Italy between 1922 and 1939?**

Advice: *From your knowledge of what Mussolini actually did in terms of economic policy, you need to deduce his intentions; the most important of these will be his 'priorities'. You might consider self-sufficiency, industrialisation, state controls, etc.*

28. **Which had the more serious effect on the Italian economy: the Ethiopian War (1935–6) or Mussolini's involvement in the Spanish Civil War (1936–9)?**

Advice: *The answer is obviously that both helped bankrupt the Italian economy and distort any industrial development into rearmament. In terms of scale, you might argue that the Ethiopian War was the larger commitment in terms of men and resources, but that involvement in the Spanish Civil War prevented Italian recovery – and lasted longer.*

29. **How far was Mussolini's fall from power in 1943 due to military failure in the Second World War?**

Advice: *Consider the fall of Mussolini in the 'short term' (due directly to military defeat) and in the longer term (due to his inability to prevent himself from being ousted). Hitler survived until the end: why not Mussolini? There is obviously a difference in the base of their power which means that defeat in war is the key factor – but not the only one.*

30. Why did the Salo Republic (1943–5) fail?

Advice: *Avoid an account of what happened between 1943 and 1945 and provide an argument grouping key reasons for the failure of the Salo Republic. You might consider the limited base of the Republic, its dependence on German domination, the Italian resistance and the Allied military offensive. A suggested conclusion: Mussolini was transformed by the Salo Republic from 'Roman genius in person' to 'a German puppet'. The Italians and Allies reacted accordingly.*

Part 3: Sources

1. The fascist movement: support and violence

This exercise consists of three questions on four sources, with a time allocation of 60 minutes.

Source A: Membership of the PNF (Fascist Party) November 1921

Profession	Number	Percentage
Industrialists	4,269	2.8
Agrarians*	18,094	12.1
Free professions	9,981	6.6
Tradesmen/artisans	13,979	9.3
Private employees	14,989	9.8
Public employees	7,209	4.8
Teachers	1,668	1.2
Students	19,783	13.2
Workers	23,410	15.6
Agricultural workers	36,874	24.6
Total	150,256	100.0

* Large, medium and small landowners

Source B: A telegram from the deputy of Budrio (province of Bologna) to the Prime Minister, Bonomi, 1 October 1921

Must report to your Excellency the very grave situation which has been created in the town of Budrio. Terrorised by an unpunished fascist band using clubs, revolvers, etc. Union organisers and municipal administrators forced to leave for fear of death. Workers forced to lock themselves at home because of continuous threats of beatings. Unions and socialist club ordered to dissolve themselves within 48 hours or face physical destruction. Life of the town is paralysed, authorities impotent. Mass of the workers request energetic measures to protect their freedom of association and personal safety.

Source C: An extract from the Fascist Party Programme, November 1921

The state should be reduced to its essential function of preserving the political and juridical order. The National Fascist Party will take steps to discipline the disorderly struggles between classes and occupational interests.

Source D: Extract from A. Rossi, *The Rise of Italian Fascism* (1938). 'Rossi' was the pseudonym used by A. Tasca, a communist at the time he was writing about, but was expelled from the Communist Party in 1929.

In the Po valley, the towns were on the whole less red than the country, being full of landowners, garrison officers, university students, officials, professional men and tradespeople. These were the classes from which fascism drew its recruits and which officered the first armed squads. Thus the expedition would usually set out into the country from some urban centre. The blackshirts would ride to their destination in lorries. When they arrived they began by beating up any passer-by who did not take his hat off to the colours, or who was wearing a red tie, handkerchief or shirt. They would rush to the buildings of the Chamber of Labour, the Syndicate, or Co-operative, or to the People's House, break down the doors, hurl out furniture, books or stores into the street, pour petrol over them, and in a few moments there would be a blaze. Anyone found on the premises would be severely beaten or killed, and the flags were burnt or carried off as trophies.

QUESTIONS WITH WORKED ANSWERS

a)   **Study Source B and use your own knowledge. Explain why the fascist band in Budrio would have been 'unpunished'.** **(20 marks)**

The fascist band referred to in Source B would have been 'unpunished' for a number of reasons. Budrio was only one of the many areas experiencing violence through 1921. Terror tactics were widespread, especially in Emilia and the Romagna, and the 'continuous threats of beatings' by the *Squadristi* would have taken a major concerted effort from the authorities. This would have been difficult: the squads were strengthened by demobilised officers and NCOs with whom the domestic police forces had some sympathy. In any case, the main targets of the *Squadristi* were socialists and trade unions. Since most of the authorities responsible for maintaining law and order were generally anti-left, they were unlikely to take action against the fascists.

b)   **Study Sources B and C. Compare the attitude of fascism to violence according to Sources B and C. How would you explain the differences?** **(40 marks)**

In Source B the attitude of fascism to violence can only be inferred from the charges brought by the deputy of Budrio against a specific 'fascist band'. From his description it appears that wide-spread use was made of terror and threats of death from clubs, revolvers and other weapons. Clearly the members of such fascist bands acted spontaneously and with little centralised control – except in their targeting of 'socialist clubs'. This is in complete contrast to Source C, in which official Fascist Party policy was to 'take steps to discipline' any 'disorderly struggles'.

This apparent contradiction was the essence of fascism. On the one hand, the *Fasci di Combatimento* were notoriously violent, especially in 1921, the year of the incident in Budrio. On the other hand, the Fascist Party (PNF) emphasised that it alone could keep law and order in a deteriorating situation. Usually the two were interlinked. The violence created by the squads could only be reined back by the Fascist Party, which meant that the PNF soon became seen as the only party which could maintain security. The Party Programme was careful to blame the violence not on the fascist squads but on ' disorderly struggles between classes and occupational interests' (Source C). In this way the squads were often justified by the party in taking defensive action against communists and socialists.

Because of their different nature the two sources would, in any case, be likely to show a very different slant on violence. A telegram from a provincial deputy to the Prime Minister would obviously need to convey a sense of urgency in order to explain the difficulty of handling the situation. A Party Programme, on the other hand would aim to be more detached, offering a solution to a more generalised problem.

c) **Use all the sources and your own knowledge. Explain whether you agree with the view that 'by 1923 fascism already had the support of all parts of the Italian population'.** **(60 marks)**

Total (120 marks)

As a set, these sources provide very different perspectives on the truth of this quotation. They range from the implication that fascism was a minority movement which was seeking to impose its will on the 'mass of the workers' (Source B) to statistical evidence that it was gaining support from a proportion of all parts of the population (Source A), with particular strength in some of these (Source D). Source C goes the whole way in anticipating broad support for fascism after the end of the 'disorderly struggles between classes'. Whether these views are accurate will depend on an analysis of the sources themselves in the light of additional material.

Any analysis of the sources has to bear in mind the distinction between the *Fasci di Combattimento*, formed in 1918, and the Fascist Party (PNF), set up in 1921. The former attracted violent activists (or *Squadristi*), the latter voters. Sources B and D focus very much on the violence of the activists, although in different ways. Since the purpose of Source B was to make a case for 'energetic measures' to protect 'freedom of association and personal safety', it was bound to stress that the *Squadristi* were in a minority. Source D, on the other hand, complements the descriptions of violence with a more considered analysis of the social origins of the activists ('these were the classes from which fascism drew its recruits'), suggesting that violence had a more popular base. Since this was admitted by a former communist, it is quite credible. Neither source, however, actually quantifies fascist support numerically. This is made up for in Source A, which shows, through percentages, the involvement of all parts of the population, from 'industrialists', through different categories of professionals to 'workers' and 'agricultural workers'. This information is, however, limited to the proportion of party membership from the different social groups, not the proportion of social groups belonging to the party. In any case, *membership* of the party did not necessarily reflect the extent of popular *support*; in the general election of 1923, Mussolini received 66 per cent of the total vote but most of this would have come from non-party members. Even so, Source A shows a degree of success for Mussolini's strategy of addressing separate policies to different classes and occupations, in contrast to the more sectoral approach of the Populists (PPI), Socialists (PSI) and Communists (PCI). The figures do tend to support De Grand's view that the fascist approach was quite flexible and that Mussolini promoted 'rural', 'urban', 'technocratic' and 'conservative' fascism.

It would therefore be true to say that fascism had support from *within* all parts of the population. But this support did not necessarily amount to a *majority* of each of these parts. Despite the confident assertions in Source C that the PNF would 'discipline the disorderly struggles between classes and occupational interests', there was still strong Catholic support for the PPI, while the clear majority of urban workers remained loyal to the PSI and PCI. In practice, exerting this 'discipline' meant creating disorderly struggles against those groups who rejected fascism. Just how many of these there were in 1923 – and remained after 1923 – is evident from the way in which Italians en masse turned against fascism 20 years later.

PARALLEL QUESTIONS WITHOUT WORKED ANSWERS

a) **Study Source C and use your own knowledge. Explain the meaning of
    the term 'National Fascist Party'.**   **(40 marks)**

   Advice: *Use your own knowledge to explain each of the three words, how the PNF was formed
   – and why.*

b) **Study Sources A and D. What similarities and differences are there between
    Sources A and D about the support for fascism? How would you explain
    the differences?**   **(60 marks)**

   Advice: *Avoid simply summarising Sources A and D. Find specific similarities first, then
   support brief quotations from Source D with a figure from Source A. Do the same for the
   differences. Explain the differences in terms of what the sources are actually dealing with:
   the attributions will help here.*

c) **Use all the sources and your own knowledge. Explain whether you agree
    with the view that 'fascism appealed only to those parts of the Italian
    population who were attracted by violence'.**   **(60 marks)**

                                                            Total (120 marks)

   Advice: *In the first paragraph explain that the sources as a set give a mixed response to the
   question – which reflects a broader debate. Then select criteria from your own knowledge
   and relate these back to specific examples from the sources. Remember to include comments
   on the usefulness of the sources in terms of content and reliability. Overall, you could distinguish between those who were attracted by the violence of the fascist movement and those
   who sought economic and political security by voting for the Fascist Party.*

2. Communism and fascism in theory and practice

This comparative exercise consists of three questions on two secondary sources, with a time allocation of 45 minutes.

Source A: Adapted from J. Laver, *Lenin: Liberator or Oppressor?* (1994). This
extract describes the basic principles of the communist society.

Lenin agreed with Marx that there would be a new 'Dictatorship of the Proletariat' after the
Revolution. Only after many years would oppression completely disappear, as the classless
society emerged. The Dictatorship of the Proletariat would be based upon the soviets. This for
Lenin solved the problem of how to involve the majority of the population in the running of the
State and ensured that abuses of power would be prevented. This system of government
would establish socialism. Eventually, under communism, social classes would disappear, along
with the State.

Source B: Adapted from S.J. Lee, *European Dictatorships* (2000). This extract describes the basic principles of the fascist society.

In 1932 Mussolini defined the basic ideas of the movement. Fascism, he said, was anti-communist, anti-socialist and strongly opposed to an economic conception of history. He denied that class war can be the major force in the transformation of society. Fascism was also anti-democratic, denouncing the whole complex system of democratic ideology. It was certainly authoritarian: 'The foundation of fascism is the conception of the State. Fascism conceives of the State as an absolute'. Finally, it promoted territorial expansion as an 'essential manifestation of vitality'.

QUESTIONS WITH WORKED ANSWERS

a) **Study Source A and use your own knowledge. Explain briefly the term 'classless society' as the long-term aim of communism.** **(3 marks)**

Marx and Engels believed that the 'classless society' was the long-term ideal of human development and change. It would see the harmonious coexistence of all members of society with few or no forms of political control. This would become possible as economic exploitation, based on class, was destroyed by the 'dictatorship of the proletariat'. Since all reasons for class conflict would have been removed, the coercive organs of the state would eventually be able to 'wither away'. This was the theory; whether it was ever seen as a practical proposition is another matter.

b) **Study Sources A and B and use your own knowledge. Explain the main differences between the ideologies of communism and Italian fascism.** **(7 marks)**

The most obvious difference is between the ideological structure of the two movements. The ideology of communism involved stages of development such as the 'dictatorship of the proletariat' and the classless society (Source A). These followed an earlier pattern of class conflict, which followed a dialectical approach borrowed by Marx and Engels from Hegel. Communism therefore had an infrastructure of philosophy and developmental logic. By contrast, fascism lacked any logical structure, and usually reacted against ideas – especially those of the left. If communism was a system of thought, Italian fascism was an anti-system: as Source B shows, it was 'anti-communist', 'anti-socialist' and 'anti-democratic'. Second, there was a difference in attitudes to social class. Communism was based on the concept of class struggle; the eventual victory of the proletariat – both urban and rural – would, in turn, remove class struggle in the future. Fascism, on the other hand, denied 'class war' as a factor in the 'transformation of society'; instead the different interests would be reconciled with each other because they would be bound together as in the symbol of the fasces.

This leads to a third contrast – in how the state was conceived. Under communism the state was a temporary necessity, which would eventually 'disappear' (Source A). The fascist conception was the exact opposite, with the emphasis, in the present and the future, on 'the state as an absolute' (Source B). The control of the state also differed. Lenin aimed to safeguard rule by 'the majority of the population' through the 'soviets' (Source A), whereas Mussolini's approach was uncompromisingly 'authoritarian' (Source B); in the fasces the rods which represented the classes were, after all, bound around the axe-head. Finally, the long-term future envisaged by communist theory was the end of conflict, whereas Mussolini saw expansion and war as an 'essential manifestation of vitality' (Source B).

c) **Refer to Sources A and B and use your own knowledge. To what extent did theory relate to practice in the case of either Marxism-Leninism under Lenin or fascism under Mussolini?**

(15 marks)

Total (25 marks)

Like any translation from theory into practice, Italian fascism was full of strong intentions but riddled with inconsistencies. This was because fascism emerged from two sources – the radical left and the far right. Usually the derivatives from the left were either ignored or only sporadically implemented. Influences from the right were applied more vigorously, but even these were undermined.

The left-wing derivatives, not referred to in Source B, entered fascism via Mussolini himself. The most important of these was the syndicalist ideas of the French socialist Georges Sorel. Most of these, however, faded during the 1920s as Mussolini became less concerned about economic and social theory and more interested in the practicalities of achieving and retaining power. This explains the absence of syndicalist theory from the definitions in Source B – which are really a *re*-statement of the meaning of fascism after a spell of ten years in power. The one major exception to this was the Corporate State, with its emphasis on corporations, syndicates, industrial harmony and state controls. But the structure of the Corporate State owed as much to traditional (in some cases, even medieval) ideas about guilds as it did to socialist theory. It certainly made little attempt to control big business or the larger industrial enterprises.

The right-wing derivatives were derived initially from D'Annunzio who, in turn, had been influenced by the French nationalist, Charles Maurras. During the 1920s the ideas of the right rapidly overtook those of the left, which explains the emphasis on them shown in Source B. In many ways they were less theoretical and could be seen as a justification for the political developments of the 1920s and a target for the 1930s. Hence it made sense to attack alternative systems of thought and to see 'the State as an absolute'. Mussolini did impose many of the controls associated with totalitarianism: a one-party system, a controlled media, the indoctrination of youth and a disciplined workforce. Similarly, the 'territorial expansion' got under way in 1935 with the conquest of Ethiopia, while the yardstick for the 'essential manifestation of vitality' was an emphasis on the power of ancient Rome. But even in these areas, fascist ideology fell well short in practice. Several historians have drawn a distinction between fascism and Mussolinianism, the latter based more strongly on the Cult of the *Duce* than upon any ideological principles. There was also some dilution of the theories of fascism to allow for a compromise with the Catholic Church. Even then, organisations like Catholic Action did a great deal to undermine the influence of fascism on a Catholic population. And, of course, there was contamination from Nazism, which pushed fascism towards anti-Semitic policies which it initially lacked.

The main problem was that if, in theory, fascism was an expression of untrammelled national power, Italy did not have the appropriate infrastructure to achieve it. Expansion was not really a 'manifestation' of 'vitality'; rather, it was an illusion which by 1943 had brought defeat and humiliation. Yet there is a final irony. Having failed with the policies of the far right, Mussolini returned fascism to the radical left in 1943 in the form of the Italian Social Republic.

PARALLEL QUESTIONS WITHOUT WORKED ANSWERS

a) **Study Source A and use your own knowledge. Explain briefly the term 'dictatorship of the proletariat' as applied to Russia between 1918 and 1924.**   (3 marks)

Advice: *Place 'dictatorship of the proletariat' within the context of the Russian experience, referring to the one-party system and the emphasis on egalitarianism.*

b) **Study Sources A and B. With reference to your own knowledge of the ideologies of communism and fascism, explain how the treatment of the Russian people in the 'dictatorship of the proletariat' and 'classless society' (Source A) differs in theory from the treatment of the Italian people in the fascist 'State' (Source B).**   (7 marks)

Advice: *Avoid a straight description or summary of the two sources. Think up two or three general issues for direct comparison and support with brief contrasting quotations from the two sources.*

c) **Refer to Sources A and B and use your own knowledge. When it came to putting theory into practice, who departed more from the theory: Stalin (by comparison with Source A) or Mussolini (by comparison with Source B)?**   (15 marks)

                                                            Total (25 marks)

Advice: *In this case you could safely argue that Stalin departed more from the theory than did Mussolini. The answer could therefore be based on brief quotations from the sources compared, in each case, with the practice.*

Part 4: Historical skills

Presentation by overhead projector

This section provides an introduction to the use of the overhead projector to make a presentation to the rest of the class. There are several advantages to this. A presentation can enhance a speech by sharpening the focus on the key points. The use of carefully chosen images can strengthen the impact of the argument in the presentation. And thinking about how the argument will be delivered should clarify the stages in the argument itself. The overhead projector (OHP) is particularly suited to this since it is versatile, readily available and easy to use.

For this exercise it is worth following the Key Skills programme, which contains a section on presentation, with criteria for assessment at the highest level.

'Make a presentation about a complex subject, using at least one image to illustrate complex points.'

A typical overhead projector

Advice: *In selecting a 'complex' subject you can opt for one which involves either the development of detail or the presentation of a more general interpretation. In each case, frame your presentation with a question or a controversial statement, either of which will force you to develop an answer.*

(i)   'Speak clearly and adapt your style of presentation to suit your purpose, subject, audience and situation.'

Advice: *Clear speaking usually means a slower delivery than normal, with careful voice projection and control of breathing.*
If you have a choice of seating, opt for a rectangle, which makes it easier to engage with every member of the group. Look around frequently and use whatever gestures you feel comfortable with. Do not simplify your vocabulary or sentence structure to the level of normal peer-group conversation. Keep them formal and to the standard of a good essay – but be prepared to explain the odd term if necessary. Remember to make the approach academic and avoid being too polemical (one-sided and confrontational). You are presenting a paper to make your audience think, not scoring debating points against them.

(ii)   'Structure what you say so that the sequence of information and ideas may be easily followed.'

Advice: *Most people find it more difficult to concentrate fully on an argument which is spoken rather than written. This means that a spoken presentation needs to have the different parts of the structure carefully highlighted. What is the overall theme that the audience needs to grasp? How is the audience to distinguish between the argument and the details supporting it? How is the overall structure of the presentation to be kept in mind throughout? When writing your notes for the presentation, be absolutely clear in your own mind what are the stages in the argument: you might write them in red. When delivering the presentation, you might include an overhead projection which reveals the stages of the argument as they develop. An example of this is given below, on pages 207–10.*

(iii)   'Use a range of techniques to engage the audience, including effective use of images.'

Advice: *Much of this relates to advice already given since techniques to engage the audience need to be part of the thinking and planning process. While speaking, try to vary the pace and give the audience clues about the structure from your delivery. Written essays have visual forms of emphasis. Presentations need an equivalent. Therefore, emphasise key points in the argument by going more slowly (imagine that you are underlining them). Pause between sections of the presentation to indicate a break (the equivalent of a new paragraph). Gestures can effectively convey a contrasting point ('on the other hand'). If there is a major change during the presentation, you could stand after sitting, or vice versa.*

Using images requires preliminary practice and the view foils for an overhead projector (OHP), which need to be prepared in advance. These can involve written text, diagrams and pictures but, to be effective, they need to be kept simple and directly relevant. While presenting them on a screen or whiteboard, stand sideways on so that all the audience can see the image and you at the same time. It is important to point to the image, possibly with an indicator of some sort.

OUTLINE OF A POSSIBLE PRESENTATION

Here are a few ideas about how to put together and deliver a presentation on Mussolini. These are in outline only and would need more detailed development.

Title:	'Releasing the devil from the pit'. The real effect of Mussolini's foreign policy.
Time available:	20 minutes.
Intention:	To provide an alternative slant on Mussolini's foreign policy during the 1930s by emphasising its importance as a catalyst for the growing confidence and aggression of Hitler's foreign policy.
Images:	Two cartoons (by David Low and Bernard Partridge); a photograph; a diagram of the ways in which Mussolini affected Hitler's foreign policy.

The historical material to be used in this presentation is based on the following argument. Mussolini's foreign policy from 1935 onwards created a major shift in the balance of power in Europe which did a great deal to help Hitler.

Until then, Mussolini had been suspicious of Germany, largely because he feared Germany's intentions towards Austria. He had therefore tended to side with Britain and France within the context of Collective Security (for example, the 1925 Locarno Pact was reinforced by the 1934 Stresa Front). Hitler, for his part, had to be very careful during his first two years in power not to provoke this combination through an aggressive foreign policy.

But Mussolini's invasion of Abyssinia in 1935 changed the whole situation. He antagonised Britain and France, who supported the imposition of sanctions on Italy through the League of Nations. Italy therefore moved closer to Germany, which changed the whole balance of power in Europe from 3:1 to 2:2. This released the constraints on Hitler by reducing the combination against him and, more specifically, by diverting Mussolini's attention away from Austria. Hence German policy became much more assertive, with the remilitarisation of the Rhineland (1936), the **Anschluss** with Austria (1938), the acquisition of the Sudetenland (1938) and Bohemia (1939), and pressure on Memel and Poland (1939). The absence of Italy from their side also helped condition the response of Britain and France to these developments: the policy of **appeasement**. The involvement of Italy and Germany in the Spanish Civil War (1936–9) gave appeasement a special mission, to prevent war from spilling out of Spain into Europe.

This meant that Hitler was able to pursue the sort of policy which led to the outbreak of war anyway.

THE PLAN FOR THE PRESENTATION

Requirements

Overhead projections to be used (Figures 5.6 to 5.9):

- *Figure 5.6*: Cartoon: 'The man who took the lid off' (Low)
- *Figure 5.7*: A series of view foils with text summarising the argument. Title: 'Releasing the devil from the pit': The real effect of Mussolini's foreign policy'. Summary of the argument entitled 'Releasing the devil from the pit'.
- *Figure 5.8*: Photograph: German troops in Austria 1938.
- *Figure 5.9*: Cartoon: 'In the melting pot again'. (Low)

Figures 5.6 to 5.9 can be used as follows:

- Start with Figure 5.6, explaining its meaning in general terms. You could include a few words about David Low. Indicate that it is one of those cartoons with a deep meaning, especially in retrospect.
- Use Figure 5.7 as the key OHP. Use the foils step by step, revealing them gradually, starting with the title only. Either cover the rest with a piece of paper or layer the OHP foils so that each one only has the amount of information needed at any one time. Use the information on the screen as a summary only: you need to go into more detail in what you actually say. This approach gives you the structure but prevents you from simply reading an essay from a sheet of paper. It will therefore be much more spontaneous and will hold attention.
- Refer back to Figure 5.6 as needed and introduce Figure 5.8 as you get to the right stages in the presentation. Explain the meaning of the images and the significance to the argument.
- Conclude by asking whether all this is reading too much into Low's cartoon. Perhaps: the cartoon, after all, looks forward, the analysis looks back. On the other hand, Low must have had a strong feeling about future trends. Show, explain and end on Figure 5.9.

Figure 5.6 **'The man who took the lid off' (Low), 1935**

THE MAN WHO TOOK THE LID OFF.

Figure 5.7 **View foils with text**

'Releasing the devil from the pit' **1**

The real effect of Mussolini's foreign policy

- Low's cartoon (October 1935) 'The man who took the lid off'
- My interpretation (a view of Low with hindsight)
- Mussolini's foreign policy from 1935 released Hitler from his early constraints and enabled him to become more aggressive.

Stage 1: Before 1935 Hitler was constrained by Collective Security **2**

Italy involved in this through:

- concern over Austria
- Locarno and Stresa

Hitler's foreign policy was therefore cautious.

Stage 2: From 1935 Mussolini removed constraints by changing balance of power **3**

He invaded Ethiopia 1935. This

- isolated Italy from Britain and France (sanctions)

He took part in the Spanish Civil War 1936–9. This pushed Italy towards Germany:

- Rome–Berlin Axis 1936
- Anti-Comintern Pact 1937
- Pact of Steel 1939

The result:

- Before 1935 the balance of power was 3:1
- After 1935 the balance of power was 2:2

Stage 3: From 1935 Hitler responded to the removal of constraints by becoming increasingly aggressive **4**

He accelerated his military and foreign policies:

- remilitarisation of the Rhineland 1936
- Anschluss 1938
- Sudetenland 1938
- Bohemia 1939
- Memel and Poland 1939

He was helped in this by:

- Anglo-French policy of appeasement (in response to 2:2)
- end of Italy's concern over Austria
- securing Italy's alliance 1939

Figure 5.8
German troops in Austria in 1938

Figure 5.9 **In the melting pot again (Low), 1936**

References

1. B. Mussolini, 'The Political and Social Doctrine of Fascism', in *International Conciliation*, 306, January 1935
2. A. de Grand, *Italian Fascism: Its Origins and Development* (Lincoln, NE 1982), Chapter 1
3. Sir I. Kirkpatrick, *Mussolini, Study of a Demagogue* (London 1964), Chapter 6
4. E. Tannenbaum, *Fascism in Italy: Society and Culture, 1922–1945* (London 1973), p. 73
5. M. Callo, *Mussolini's Italy* (New York 1973), Chapter 13
6. P.V. Cannistraro (ed.), *Historical Dictionary of Fascist Italy* (London 1982), entry for 'Anti-Semitism'
7. A. Cassells, *Fascist Italy* (London 1969), p. 58
8. J. Pollard, *The Fascist Experience in Italy* (London 1998), p. 84
9. E. Tannenbaum, op. cit., p. 100
10. J. Whittam, *Fascist Italy* (Manchester 1995), p. 122
11. C. Leeds, *Italy under Mussolini* (London 1968), Chapter 5
12. J. Pollard, op. cit., p. 109

Sources

1A. Adapted from J. Pollard, *The Fascist Experience in Italy* (London 1998), p. 34

1B. Ibid., p. 31

1C. C.F. Delzell (ed.), *Mediterranean Fascism 1919–1945* (London 1971), pp. 27–34, quoted in J. Pollard, op. cit., p. 42

1D. A. Rossi, *The Rise of Italian Fascism* (London 1938), pp. 94–7, quoted in J. Whittam, *Fascist Italy* (Manchester 1995), pp. 150–2

2A. J. Laver, *Lenin: Liberator or Oppressor?* (London 1994)

2B. S.J. Lee, *European Dictatorships 1918–1945*, second edition (London 2000), p. 112

Chapter 6

Nazi Germany, 1933–45

This chapter will consider the conversion of Germany from a falling democracy into a totalitarian dictatorship, initially through a 'legal revolution' but eventually more radical policies based on race and implementation of the *Volksgemeinschaft*. It also deals with the impact of foreign policy and war which is also discussed in Chapter 8.

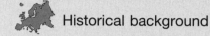 ## Historical background

Hitler's government and the
    consolidation of power,
    1933–4
Propaganda, terror, support and
    opposition
The Nazi economy
The *Volksgemeinschaft*, race and the
    Holocaust
Foreign policy and war, 1933–45

 ## Sources

1.   Nazi economic policy
2.   Nazi social policy

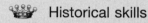 ## Historical skills

Presentation by PowerPoint

Essays

Hitler's government and the
    consolidation of power,
    1933–4
Propaganda, terror, support and
    opposition
The Nazi economy
The *Volksgemeinschaft*, race and the
    Holocaust
Foreign policy and war, 1933–45

Chronology

1933	Hitler appointed Chancellor (January)
	Last Reichstag election; Enabling Act (March)
	'Town hall revolutions'
	Law against the new formation of parties (July)
	Withdrawal of Germany from League of Nations
	Concordat with the pope
1934	Night of the Long Knives
	Death of President Hindenburg; Hitler as *Führer*
	Army's oath of allegiance to Hitler
	Nazi–Polish Non-Aggression Pact
	Schacht's New Plan
	Anglo-German Naval Agreement
1935	Nuremberg Laws
1936	Remilitarisation of the Rhineland
	Four Year Plan launched
	Rome–Berlin Axis
1938	*Kristallnacht*
	Anschluss (annexation of Austria)
	Sudeten Crisis and Munich agreement on Sudetenland (September)
1939	Occupation of rest of Bohemia (March)
	Pact of Steel with Italy
	Nazi–Soviet Non-Aggression Pact (August)
	Hitler's invasion of Poland
1940	Hitler's invasion of the Low Countries and France
	Battle of Britain
1941	Hitler's invasion of Soviet Union
	Wannsee Conference on the 'Final Solution'
1943	Battle for Stalingrad
1945	Allied invasion of Germany
	Hitler's suicide and surrender of Germany

Part 1: Historical background

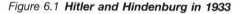

Hitler's government and the consolidation of power, 1933–4

Immediately after his appointment as Chancellor in January 1933, Hitler gave priority to strengthening the base of his political power in Germany. This involved a process which the Nazis called the 'legal revolution' (Essay 1a), whereby the constitution of the Weimar Republic was used against itself – to end the multi-party system and set up a dictatorship.

The method was a step-by-step consolidation of power, each step depending on the one immediately preceding it. The first was to launch a general election campaign to secure a two-thirds majority in the Reichstag which would enable Hitler to change the Constitution. Although the election results in March showed that the Nazis had fallen short, Hitler secured the majority he needed by doing a deal with the Centre Party and by expelling the newly elected communist deputies on a charge of subversion. Hitler then introduced the Enabling Act which authorised his government to introduce new legislation. Under its terms a new law was drawn up in July 1933 banning other political parties. Meanwhile, extensive changes occurred at the level of the individual states, as contingents of the SA forced a 'town hall revolution', forcing out existing administrations. Faced with constant pressure from the radical elements within the SA, Hitler ordered the purge of its leaders in the Night of the Long Knives in 1934. The army, grateful for being rescued from a possible takeover by the SA, swore an oath of personal allegiance to Hitler, who had now become Führer, adding the office of President to that of Chancellor. This was facilitated by the death of Hindenburg, the last remaining link with the former Weimar Republic.

Figure 6.1 **Hitler and Hindenburg in 1933**

These changes (covered in Essay 1b) effectively converted Germany from a democratic state (although democracy was in a state of collapse after 1930) to an authoritarian dictatorship. This meant a partial – but by no means total – alteration of Germany's political institutions (Essay 1c). Whether or not the changes amounted to a 'legal revolution' is open to question, depending very much on an analysis of the meaning of both words (Essay 2). There was certainly some confusion in the revised system, as a number of new Nazi institutions were supposed to coexist with institutions retained from the previous regime. It is debatable as to whether the overlapping of and confusion between political functions was deliberate or accidental (Essay 3). The theory was that the Führer was introducing *Gleichschaltung*, or co-ordination, which was based on his own personal overview and direction in terms of the *Führerprinzip* (Essay 13).

Propaganda, terror, support and opposition

It was never Hitler's intention to stop at the 'legal revolution'; this was merely a transitional stage into the 'national revolution' in which the German people would be brought to a true commitment to the ideology of national socialism. This, in turn, would transform an authoritarian regime into a totalitarian one. The two key channels for the 'national revolution' were propaganda and indoctrination on the one hand and terror on the other.

The main publicist of Nazi principles was Joseph Goebbels, Minister for People's Enlightenment and Propaganda (Essay 4a). His ministry, set up in 1933, comprised a series of Chambers for radio, films, the press, literature, music and the fine arts. Schools were controlled by the Ministry of Education, for a while under Robert Ley, while the **Hitler Youth**, made compulsory for boys and girls in 1935, was under the direction of the Reich Youth Leader, Baldur von Schirach. Details of these institutions are provided in Essay 4b. Whether or not these institutions and their methods succeeded in their objectives is discussed in Essay 4c.

The purpose of terror was to coerce or, as a last resort remove, anyone who had not been won over by propaganda (Essay 5a). The first of the three main organisations associated with terror (Essay 5b) was the *Sturm Abteilung* (SA), the mass movement of the party throughout the 1920s and 1930s which intimidated opponents and whipped up a combination of enthusiasm and fear. From this emerged an inner core, the *Schutzstaffeln* (SS), a more focused and disciplined force which, in turn, took over the *Geheime Staatspolizei* (**Gestapo**). Under the overall leadership of Heinrich Himmler the SS-Gestapo complex was responsible for surveillance, security, and the arrest of all forms of dissidents. The SS had another key function, which was to promote the 'purity' of the Aryan race. This involved systematic persecution of the Jews and, from 1941 onwards, a programme of genocide organised and administered by the SS (Essay 18). It has been argued that these organisations underpinned the Nazi regime, although the over-emphasis on terror can sometimes divert attention from the genuine popularity which the regime undoubtedly experienced (Essay 5c). Both the SS and the Gestapo developed a fearsome reputation. The SS expanded far beyond its original intentions and, during the Second World War, came close to taking over all the key administrative apparatus of the Nazi state. The Gestapo, however, were probably less numerous and effectively organised than is commonly supposed (Essay 6).

The extent to which these measures affected the German people can be assessed through the support for and opposition to the regime. Hitler was personally very popular with all sectors of the German population (Essay 7), partly because he projected a reassuring and moderate image by comparison with the rest of the Nazi leadership, and partly because he was credited with the improvements which occurred in the economy and with the successful steps in the demolition of the Treaty of Versailles. He also offered something to each class and social group, which meant that support came to be based on self-interest as well as on general adulation. At the same time, there was always an undercurrent of opposition (Essay 8). This took a variety of forms, ranging from everyday dissent and grumbling (which was very widespread) to targeted objections to specific measures (such as the Nazi policy on 'euthanasia') and political resistance (which occurred mainly during the Second World War). At no stage, however, was the Nazi regime ever seriously threatened and was ultimately destroyed only by military defeat.

 ## The Nazi economy

The main development in the economy during the 1930s was the gradual shift from a traditional mixed economy to one geared to military objectives (Essay 9a). Between 1933 and 1936 a policy of economic constraint was pursued by Schacht, based on the control of public expenditure and wages and the tightening of currency regulations (Essay 9b). His New Plan also promoted trade agreements with less developed countries in the Balkans and Latin America based on the exchange of German industrial credits for essential raw materials. From 1936, however, the economy was related more directly to military priorities (Essay 9c) in the form of the Four Year Plan (1936) which was intended to prepare Germany for war within four years. Under the direction of Goering, this placed emphasis on heavy industry, rearmament, autobahn construction and autarchy – or self-sufficiency.

The effects of these policies have been the subject of controversy. Essay 10 discusses the relative importance of rearmament and the standard of living in the development of government measures between 1933 and 1939. On the one hand, it has been argued that Hitler's overall objective was to break with all previous economic assumptions which had been based on boosting trade and increasing the prosperity of the German consumer. Instead, the consumer's interests would be subordinated to the pursuit of conquest and expansion. On the other hand, the way in which Hitler envisaged making these conquests – through a series of rapid campaigns based on **Blitzkrieg** – meant that the consumer would not be altogether ignored. *Blitzkrieg* was therefore an economic compromise as well as a military strategy, which meant that the German population in the 1930s suffered none of the economic hardships experienced by the Russian workforce under Stalin's Five Year Plans. Essay 11 analyses some of the statistical evidence to see in which areas German workers and consumers benefited, and in which areas their conditions deteriorated under Nazi rule.

The *Volksgemeinschaft*, race and the Holocaust

Whatever his policy, Hitler referred constantly to the *Volk*, or people. The **Volksgemeinschaft**, or people's community (Essay 14). The main asset of the *Volksgemeinschaft*, according to Hitler, was its racial composition. At the same time, the Aryan characteristics of the *Volk* had to be protected from the 'corrupting' Jewish influences, to which virtually every page of *Mein Kampf* makes direct reference. Racial theory was the core of Nazi ideology, expressing itself positively as the Aryan 'master race' and negatively in the form of extreme anti-Semitism (Essay 12a). Within the Nazi system race played a variety of roles, covered in Essay 12b. Anti-Semitic policies became more extreme over a period of time, although the underlying principles behind them remained the same (Essay 12c). Between 1933 and 1937 the emphasis was punitive legislation which gradually deprived Jews of their citizenship and rights, removed their presence from the professions and, through the 1935 Nuremberg Laws, prevented intermarriage with Germans. From 1938 onwards anti-Semitism became increasingly violent as Jews were denied any protection under the law. The process started with the smashing of Jewish property and the destruction of synagogues on *Kristallnacht* (1938). This was supposedly a spontaneous eruption of 'justified resentment' by the German people; actually it was carefully orchestrated by Goebbels and saw extensive involvement by the SA. Active persecution intensified with the Decrees for the compulsory marking and naming of Jews and for their confinement to specified ghettos. The invasion of Poland (1939) and the Soviet Union (1941) brought nearly 10 million more Jews under Nazi occupation. Special detachments of the *Wehrmacht* and *Einsatzgrüppen* squads of the SS began to shoot huge numbers of Jews, especially in the Ukraine. In the 1941 Wannsee Conference, however, the Nazi regime came up with a more 'efficient' method of genocide in the extermination camps of Auschwitz, Treblinka, Belzec, Maidanek and Sobibor; by 1945 the gas chambers had killed at least 6 million people. Although no reasonable historian questions the extent of this human catastrophe, there is a major debate as to why the earlier policies of Nazi anti-Semitism moved towards genocide in wartime (Essay 18). One theory is that war offered the opportunity to carry out a long-held objective which originated in the pages of *Mein Kampf*. The alternative is that the large Jewish population in eastern Europe were diverting German military resources at a time when they were needed against the Red Army; far from being planned in advance, systematic genocide therefore emerged as the response of a ruthless regime to a chaotic situation created by the new pressures of war.

 ## Foreign policy and war, 1933–45

Hitler's foreign policy was initially cautious, since he did not want to provoke a military revolt. Hence early measures were confined to withdrawal from the League of Nations in 1933 and illicit rearmament. At the same time Hitler tried, through the 1934 Non-Aggression Pact with Poland and Naval Agreement with Britain, to reassure the rest of Europe that he had no fundamentally hostile intentions. Hitler gradually became more assertive after 1935. The catalyst was probably Mussolini's invasion of Ethiopia, which diverted the attention of the powers from Germany, giving Hitler the opportunity to remilitarise the Rhineland in 1936 and, in the same year, to launch the Four Year Plan, a more explicit programme of rearmament and preparation for war. Encouraged by the Anglo-French policy of appeasement, he annexed Austria and the Sudetenland in 1938, along with Bohemia and Memel in 1939. He also sought to strengthen Germany's strategic position in 1939 by the Pact of Steel, an alliance with Italy, and a Non-Aggression Pact with the Soviet Union. Refusing to heed the reversal of appeasement by Britain and France, he invaded Poland in September 1939, thereby provoking declarations of war from London and Paris. Whether these developments were in line with a long-term programme, or whether they were the result of opportunism, trial and error, is discussed in Essay 15.

The initial reaction of the German people to war was apprehension. This, however, changed to euphoria with the apparently easy victories over Poland in 1939 and over the Low Countries and France in 1940 (Essay 16). Then, after equally rapid success against Russia in 1941, things became increasingly difficult. Goebbels had to accustom the population to the prospect of total war in 1943, while Allied bombing between 1943 and 1945 resulted in extensive destruction and heavy loss of life. Minority resistance groups tried to end the Nazi regime but, eventually, this could be accomplished only by Allied military victory. Essay 17 considers how the war affected the regime itself. Did the pressure of conflict make it even more extreme than it had been before? Or did the war provide an opportunity for the regime to carry out the sort of policies it had always intended? Nowhere is this debate more relevant than with the Holocaust, the worst atrocity of the Nazi period (Essay 18).

Part 2: Essays

Hitler's government and the consolidation of power, 1933–4

1. **'As a result of the "legal revolution" Hitler brought a complete transformation to the political system of Germany.'**

   a) **Explain briefly the meaning of the term 'legal revolution'.** (3 marks)

'Legal revolution' is a contradiction in terms, since the two words exclude each other. It is, however, a deliberate one as it describes the way in which Hitler used the Weimar Constitution against itself. He changed the political system in Germany through a series of 'legal' steps in the form of legislation. But the purpose of these steps was the destruction of democracy itself, a 'revolution' against what the Weimar Constitution stood for.

   b) **Explain the methods by which Hitler increased his political power between January 1933 and 1935.** (7 marks)

When he was appointed Chancellor on 30 January 1933, Hitler's power was still heavily constrained. He was one of only three Nazis in the Cabinet, he was still without a majority in the Reichstag, and he was subordinate to the President. By 1935 all of these constraints had been removed and Hitler now presided over a political dictatorship. His accumulation of power was carried out step by step.

The first step was taken within two days of his appointment as Chancellor. He requested a dissolution of the Reichstag so that he could increase the number of Nazi seats. During the election campaign he requested the use of emergency decrees, issued by President Hindenburg under Article 48 of the Constitution, to hamstring the other parties, especially the SPD and KPD. The reason given for this was the Reichstag fire, which was blamed on the Communists. Although the NSDAP did not achieve an overall majority in the election, they did succeed in increasing the number of their seats from 196 to 288.

The next stage was to use this increased presence in the Reichstag to change the Constitution; because of an entrenched clause this required a two-thirds majority. Hitler achieved this by banning of the KPD deputies from taking up their seats and by striking a deal with the Centre Party guaranteeing Catholic liberties in exchange for the absence of any opposition from the Centre Party to Hitler's measures. Hitler was therefore able to get the Enabling Act through the Reichstag in March 1933. This allowed the Chancellor as well as the Reichstag to issue legislation: in effect, it meant that the presidential decree powers were transferred to the Chancellor and that any pretence that they were emergency measures was dropped. These powers under the Enabling Act were used to extend Hitler's powers still further. In May 1933 trade unions were banned while, in June, the Law Against the New Formation of Parties was issued, declaring the NSDAP to be the only legally constituted party.

Hitler was, however, still vulnerable to possible dismissal by the President or removal by the army. This threat was increased by the declared intention of Röhm to absorb the army into the SA. Fearing that this would provoke the army into immediate action, Hitler used the SS to purge the leadership of the SA in the Night of the Long Knives (30 June). The army were now sufficiently grateful to Hitler to swear an oath of personal allegiance to him when, on the death of Hindenburg, Hitler added the presidency to his chancellorship.

By 1935, therefore, Hitler had become head of state and, as Führer, the focus of collective allegiance. He had taken over the legislative process, banned the opposition and assumed control over the army. The destruction of the Weimar system had been completed.

c) **'Germany's political institutions were completely changed after 1933.'**
Explain why you agree or disagree with this view. (15 marks)

Germany's political system experienced a transformation – the shift from a democratic Republic to the dictatorship of the Third Reich. In some cases the institutions themselves were changed. In others, they were put to a different use; here it was the powers which changed, not the institutions themselves.

In one respect the change in institutions was less than the change in their functions. This applied especially to the introduction of dictatorship through the weakening of the legislature and the strengthening and personalising of the executive powers. Although Germany retained the Reichstag, the Enabling Act of March 1933 deprived it of the exclusive right to legislation. Nor were elections continued beyond March 1933 since all parties other than the NSDAP were banned in July. Meanwhile, the executive powers were steadily increased. The chancellorship had the power to issue laws and, in 1934, was combined with the presidency. Both offices were centralised under Hitler as Führer. All the central government departments were kept – for example, the Ministries of Foreign Affairs, Interior and Education – as was the civil service. The paradox of the apparently seamless growth of democracy into dictatorship has been described as a 'legal revolution'.

In another respect, the institutional changes were more drastic; this is more a reflection of the violence of the 'town hall revolutions' conducted by the SA in 1933. Germany ceased to be a federal system: powers were no longer divided between the central government and the individual states, or **Länder**. Instead, the whole process was centralised. The state parliaments, or **Landtäge**, disappeared in 1934. The state prime ministers (or ministers president) remained, but they came under the direct control of the central government ministries.

In some cases there were indeed complete changes in institutions in the sense that the Nazi regime introduced a number of new offices. Yet, even here, there was an overlap with some of the traditional institutions. At the central level, there were new special deputies, such as the General Inspector for German Roads and the Youth Leader of the Reich. These were more distinctively Nazi organisations, often fulfilling similar functions to the departments. At local level the Gauleiters were given greater power as state governors, who often overlapped with the ministers president. Perhaps the most obvious examples of entirely new institutions were a third layer, which was independent of both the traditional ministries and the parallel offices. These included the Office of the Deputy Führer, the Four Year Plan Office (along, confusingly, with its six ministries), and the SS/Gestapo/SD complex under the authority of Himmler.

Hitler's own role represented a major – but not total – change. His power base was a strengthened presidency, which was merged with the chancellorship and given permanent use of emergency legislation. This was really a compression of several powers of the Weimar Constitution and the removal of the boundaries between them. What was entirely new was the *Führerprinzip* which enabled Hitler to personify the entire system. He became the embodiment of the state; oaths of allegiance were taken by the army and civil servants to him rather than the state; and his powers were enhanced by the development of personality cult. Unquestioning acceptance of his authority meant, ultimately, unquestioning acceptance of the ideology which went with it. This was a total departure from the principles upon which the Weimar Republic had been founded.

2. Assess the view that the way in which Hitler consolidated his power between 1933 and 1935 was a 'legal revolution'. (90 marks)

The term 'legal revolution' has been used to describe Hitler's overall approach to power in the opening two years of his regime. It is seen as an extension of the 'strategy of legality' which he pursued after the failure of the Munich Putsch in 1923.

At first sight the constitutional changes were made by observing stages of legality. Each step depended on the previous one taken and seemed to conform to the terms of the Weimar Constitution. Hence the Enabling Act of 24 March 1933 opened with the words 'The requirements of legal Constitutional change having been met'.[1] This made it clear that the Act had fulfilled the requirements for any measure altering the Constitution by being passed by a two-thirds majority in the Reichstag. In turn, the Enabling Act became the means whereby the Chancellor made increased use of executive powers to issue legislation in the future. The Law Against the New Formation of Parties (July 1933) therefore contained the preamble: 'The government has passed the following law, which is being proclaimed herewith.'[2] This was directly related to the Enabling Act, which had authorised the government to pass laws.

Legality was therefore claimed in the sense that each change was based logically on the step immediately preceding it. Yet the whole purpose of the changes can be seen as the very negation of legality. After all, the legal powers of the Constitution were being used to destroy any remaining influence the Constitution might have rather than to make it function more effectively. The Constitution was, in effect, turned against itself, thus the whole legality was therefore turned against itself, making the whole notion of legality nonsensical.

Indeed, Hitler's objective was the antithesis of legality – the total destruction of everything the Weimar Constitution stood for. Some of the results were paradoxical. For example, emergency powers were changed from an exceptional process to a normal one. The Enabling Act, in effect, turned Article 48 on its head by making permanent what had originally been intended as temporary. This destroyed the original purpose of Article 48, which had been to protect democracy against future enemies. By contrast, the basic assumption of the Enabling Act was that democracy itself was the enemy. Democracy was also damaged by the Law Against the New Formation of Parties. In eradicating the multi-party system, the Nazis removed any point in having an electoral system at all – the most basic principle enshrined in the original Constitution. Any use of 'legality' was therefore a mockery: a democratic Constitution was effectively turned by anti-democrats against itself.

If the notion of 'legal' was abused by Hitler's political changes, does this necessarily mean that there was a 'revolution'? The changes do not seem revolutionary when compared with the sweeping institutional changes made in Bolshevik Russia. After all, Hitler retained the Reichstag and the *Reichsrat* as legislative institutions, while Lenin set up an entirely different system based upon soviets. In Germany all the previous government ministries were retained; officials within Hitler's Cabinet, such as Foreign Minister, Interior Minister and Finance Minister, had all existed in the

Weimar Republic. By this analysis the institutions of the Weimar Republic were simply Nazified, not destroyed.

Again, however, this approach involves a misconception. 'Revolution' involves upheaval and mobilised pressure, both of which took place behind the facade of legality. This was apparent at the height of the so-called period of legality, especially in the town hall revolutions, by which the SA purged local governments and by the boycotting of Jewish stores from 1 April 1933. Indeed, such activities threatened to assume a momentum of its own as Röhm clearly intended to absorb the German army into the 'brown flood' of the SA. This all seemed to be pointing to a mass revolution – over which Hitler would probably lose control. This is why the most revolutionary of all the Nazi devices was introduced: the systematic expansion of terror. Hitler prevented a mass revolution by the SA by launching a more disciplined revolution based on the SS and Gestapo, which came to dominate the whole regime. This was as far removed from the constitutional apparatus of the Weimar Republic as it is possible to conceive. The period 1933–5 also saw the beginning of systematic indoctrination, organised by the new Ministry of People's Enlightenment and Propaganda, and launched a campaign of anti-Semitism which was based partly on physical intimidation and partly on measures such as the 1935 Nuremberg Laws. The changes in communications and racial policies were again a total departure from the human rights guaranteed by Part II of the Weimar Constitution.

In summary, the term 'legal revolution' makes sense only if it is understood as part of Hitler's step-by-step consolidation of power. His purpose was never to observe legality for its own sake. It was to avoid provoking any action against him while he turned legality against itself.

3. **How far do you agree that 'Germany between 1933 and 1939 had a chaotic system of government over which Hitler had no real control'?** (90 marks)

The traditional historical view is that the Nazi dictatorship was efficient and tightly organised, with Hitler in total control. This view has, however, recently been modified. It is now argued that the regime was far less orderly than was once thought and that there were examples of chaos.

First impressions seem to convey orderly control. The Nazi regime was based on a totalitarian format, which had been achieved rapidly and efficiently. The competing parties, coalition governments and political confusion of the Weimar Republic had been replaced, from July 1933, by a one-party system entirely dominated by Nazis. Legislation could now be carried out rapidly: the Enabling Act of March 1933 gave the Chancellor legislative powers with immediate effect. The government departments were headed by loyal Nazis and a new system of special deputies was established to ensure total conformity. The security of the state was guaranteed by the SS and Gestapo, while the loyalty of the population as a whole was gradually enhanced by the influence of Goebbels's Ministry of People's Enlightenment and Propaganda. As for Hitler's own role, this was never contested in any way. From 1934 onwards he was in overall control as Führer, having combined the positions of Chancellor and President and secured the oath of allegiance from the civil service and the army.

A second look, however, does reveal elements of chaos. The basic reason for this was that there were two trends operating which were in direct conflict with each other – the revolutionary dynamic of the Nazi movement and the persistence of traditional institutions. The consequences were duplication, overlapping and conflict, for which there was evidence in both central and local government.

At the level of central government this showed in the conflict between the traditional departments, which Hitler kept intact, and the new special deputies. The trouble was that these were basically 'parallel' institutions and fulfilled similar functions. For example, the newly created youth leader of the Reich had powers which encroached directly on those of the traditional Minister of Education. Such confusion was made even worse by the development of a third layer of officials who were connected neither to the traditional ministries nor to the new parallel structure. Examples were the Office of the Deputy Führer (Rudolf Hesse), the Four Year Plan Office (under Goering) and the SS/Gestapo complex, directed by Himmler. This produced incredible inefficiency. The duplication of functions between agencies inevitably meant conflict between officials. These, in turn, generated numerous appeals to the Führer for arbitration. But even here there was a difficulty. Which of Hitler's offices would make the decision? His chancellery actually contained six.

Similar problems appeared in local government. Here, too, there was a struggle for power between traditional authorities and new party functionaries. The former included the minister president of each state, the responsibilities of whom were redesignated. Although he was deprived of his former status as local premier, the minister president was still regarded as a useful official in the Nazi regime – this time as the local agent of the central government's Ministry of the Interior. Complications, however, ensued with the emergence of a new and largely parallel official, who was based more directly on the party. From the most senior party Gauleiters Hitler appointed ten Reich governors, who were given the explicit task of enforcing the Führer's edicts. Charged with similar responsibilities, the ministers president and the Reich governors were bound to clash and each appealed regularly to central government against interference by the other. Again, however, the question arose as to which part of central government would deal with the complaint. If it was a matter for a department, would it fall to a minister or a special deputy? If it went beyond this stage, which section of Hitler's chancellery would have the final say?

Hitler's role in all this chaos is the key to establishing whether or not he was ever really in 'control'. Two broad interpretations have been advanced which provide very different perspectives.

One might be termed 'controlled chaos'. Some historians, collectively described as 'intentionalists', have argued that Hitler deliberately set his officials against each other in order to guarantee his own position. Thus he held power precisely because of the 'confusion of conflicting power groups.'[3] By this analysis, chaos was an essential ingredient of Hitler's control. An alternative view, put forward by the 'structuralists',[4] is that the chaos resulted from confusion and neglect – and was therefore entirely unintended. By this argument, Hitler's power was incomplete because of the chaos – and the situation was chaotic because of the incomplete nature of his power.

An overall approach might be that the Nazi dictatorship was chaotic – as a result of the layers of administration which developed. This did not, however, mean that the chaos was total, since Nazi Germany continued to function as a dictatorship. Hitler's own involvement was indirect, his powers often exercised by competing subordinates. This is unlikely to have been set up as a deliberate policy of 'divide and rule' but, once established, it became a useful means of maintaining his power.

Propaganda, terror, support and opposition

4. **'With the special gifts of Joseph Goebbels, the Nazi regime perfected the use of indoctrination and propaganda in Germany.'**

   a) **What is meant by 'the special gifts of Joseph Goebbels'?** (3 marks)

Goebbels had an instinctive understanding of the means of effective communication. Like Hitler, he understood the mass psychology of the crowd and how to work on it. He was, however, more subtle than Hitler in his appreciation of the role of modern technology, especially the radio and cinema. He worked on the principle that it was not enough for people to be neutral; 'rather we want to work on people until they have capitulated to us'.

   b) **Explain the administrative methods used by the Nazi regime to control indoctrination and propaganda.** (7 marks)

Indoctrination refers to the process of creating permanent loyalty to a set of values by seeking to close off all other influences. Propaganda relates more to the systematic projection of ideas, particularly through the media. Vigorous attempts were made by the Nazi administration to achieve both.

The key to controlling indoctrination and propaganda was centralisation to ensure uniformity. Three institutions ensured this. The first was the Ministry of Education, which took over all the powers that had previously belonged to the *Länder*. This was responsible for all the changes to

Figure 6.2 **The systems of indoctrination and coercion in the Third Reich**

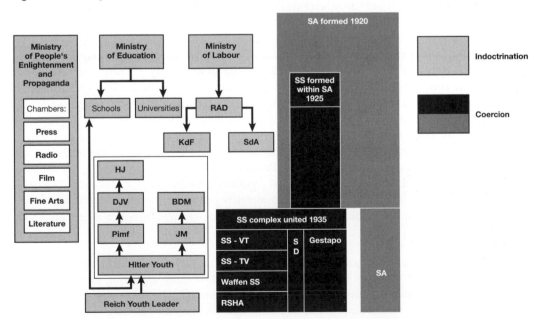

the school curriculum intended to strengthen Nazi ideology. A second, parallel, department was also set up. The Office of the Reich Youth Leader co-ordinated all the activities of young people outside the context of school. The third, and most important office, was the Ministry of People's Enlightenment and Propaganda, established in March 1933. Presided over by Goebbels, this aimed at the population at large. Through a series of sub-Chambers, it controlled all areas of propaganda through radio, films and the press, and influenced cultural output in the form of literature, music and the fine arts. In theory, at least, the regime had the power to apply negative censorship in whatever form it considered necessary and, more constructively, to shape the development of culture at all levels.

The loyalty of the population was ensured by administrative controls over specific groups. The workforce at large were part of the *Schönheit der Arbeit* (**SdA**) and *Kraft durch Freude* (**KdF**) which arranged a variety of activities to fill leisure time and to transmit the values of the regime. There were additional layers of control for the professions: teachers were required to belong to the *Nationalsozialistische Lehrerbund* (NSLB), while journalists received both guidelines and detailed instructions from the DNB. But the most famous example of regimentation was the Hitler Youth, which accounted for the large majority of the age group between 8 and 18. To ensure that the appropriate indoctrination and propaganda could be imparted, it was subdivided into four sections: the *Deutsches Jungvolk* (DJ), *Hitler Jugend* (HJ), *Jungmädel-Bund* (JM) and *Bund Deutscher Mädel* (BDM).

These institutions were designed to reach the entire population and to dominate its working and recreational life. They were therefore a key component of the totalitarian state.

c) **'The Nazi regime succeeded in the "total" indoctrination of the German people.' Explain why you agree or disagree with this view.** (15 marks)

As a totalitarian regime with a monopoly over the spread of ideas, the Nazis were bound to have widespread success in indoctrinating both youth and adults within the German population. Within each of these groups, however, there were enough exceptions to prevent the indoctrination from being 'total'.

From the start, Hitler emphasised the importance of youth. 'When an opponent says "I will not come over to your side" I calmly say "Your child belongs to us already."' There is no doubt that the new Nazi curriculum helped to close minds rather than to open them. The introduction of subjects such as race study, eugenics and health biology reinforced Nazi race policies and anti-Semitism, while the doctoring of traditional disciplines such as History and Mathematics prevented any questioning of the Nazi rationale. Another principle, affecting all youth, was the preparation of boys and girls for separate and obviously stereotyped roles. Yet, for all its thoroughness, the whole process was in many ways badly flawed. Because of administrative confusion, the Ministry of Education took until 1939 to produce detailed regulations for elementary education. The practical effect of this was that Nazi values were incompletely put across by teachers who were often uncertain about how it should be done. Hitler's 'new generation' was therefore never completely moulded.

More directly successful in indoctrinating the young was the Hitler Youth. The various subsections (DJ, HJ, JM and BDM) all carried widespread appeal, initially appearing as a challenge to more conservative forms of authority and giving youth a sense of collective power. But again the process suffered through administrative conflict, this time between the Ministry of Education and the Reich Youth Leadership, as to underlying objectives and overriding priorities. This meant that the Hitler Youth and the educational system often worked against each other. A substantial minority of young people managed to avoid involvement altogether. Some even established 'alternative' groups such as the Edelweiss Pirates, Kittelbach Pirates and Roving Dudes, whose purpose was to reject the official values of the Hitler Youth.

The rest of the population were affected by a wider variety of indoctrination techniques, geared to their particular roles in society. The most successful was the radio. This undoubtedly enhanced the Führer cult by giving the people regular contact with Hitler's speeches. Loudspeakers made possible communal listening in factories, an example of the way in which modern technology could be applied to create an illusion of the collective strength which was an essential part of Hitler's crowd psychology. Most of the population would also have witnessed key events such as the Nuremberg rallies of 1934 or the Berlin Olympics of 1936 through the films of Leni Riefenstahl. Yet the use of other forms of the media for indoctrination was more difficult. The regime was less successful in controlling minds and loyalties through print, whether through newspapers or officially approved novels. It took time to bring the 4,700 newspapers of the Republic fully under government control through the DNB – and then the result was a steady decline in readership. Germans, it seems, were less susceptible to being influenced through the printed word than across the airwaves or on the cinema screen.

It was also more difficult for the regime to indoctrinate through adult organisations than it was through the Hitler Youth. Although some of the benefits of the KdF and SdA were apparent to the workforce, there was much resentment at compulsory membership and the amount of time involved in the activities provided. Nor could the regime really expect to create a new cultural base for people who already had their own interests and conceptions. There was never a popular alternative to the more traditional art forms or literature. Instead, the regime had to settle for preventive censorship – never the most effective form of indoctrination. Attempts by Kampf and Ziegler to create a Nazi art form were also inept and the German public showed more interest in the 'degenerate art' exhibitions of banned artists.

Indoctrination was only partly successful. It did enhance Hitler's own popularity and managed to establish a form of control which reduced the necessity for terror. It also generated mass participation and, in many cases, commitment. At the same time, there is growing evidence that the population were never really committed to Nazi values, surely the ultimate test of success.

5. 'Nazi Germany was a state based on terror.'

a) What is meant by 'terror'? (3 marks)

'Terror' is a term often associated with revolution and the enforcement of massive changes within a short period of time. The Nazi Revolution was enforced by the calculated use of terror in the form of sudden arrest, torture, or processing through **concentration camps**. For much of the population, fear of the SA, SS and Gestapo was sufficient inducement to toe the official line.

b) Explain how 'terror' came to be organised in Nazi Germany. (7 marks)

In Nazi Germany the use of terror was based on four organisations. Although they were all interconnected, they arose for different reasons and each had a special function. Their responsibilities were also rearranged as the regime matured.

Figure 6.3
The SS/Gestapo

The earliest movement, the *Sturm Abteilung* (SA), had already brawled its way through the 1920s. From 1933 onwards it continued to be the most open form of intimidation, whether against local officials, as in the 'town hall revolutions', or against Jewish shops and department stores. They also provided the initial guards for concentration camps like Dachau and Oranienberg. From their ranks, however, had emerged the *Schutzstaffeln* (SS), with its distinctive black uniform and death's head device. Under Himmler's leadership, this carried out terror in a more disciplined way, focusing on targets which had been identified as a special threat to the Führer. By 1933 it had separated fully from the SA and, in the Night of the Long Knives (1934), implemented Hitler's orders to purge the SA of troublesome leaders like Ernst Röhm. The SS was therefore the means by which the Nazis fulfilled the habit revolutionaries have of 'devouring their own'.

The distinction was maintained between open coercion and disciplined terror in the form of the SA (beheaded of its troublesome leaders) and the SS–Gestapo–SD complex, entrusted with increased powers. Himmler became effective head of the Gestapo as well as *Reichsführer SS* and, in June 1936, Hitler issued a decree 'to unify the control of police duties in the Reich'. Under Himmler's overall command, the actual running of the Gestapo was carried out by Reynhard Heydrich and his deputy, Werner Best. Gestapo instructions epitomised the selective but ruthless use of terror. They were 'To discover the enemies of the state, watch them and render them harmless at the right moment.' Officials were able to use a variety of methods, usually including torture, to extract information and confessions. They targeted all types of dissidents, including Communists, Social Democrats and, during the late 1930s and early 1940s, alternative youth movements.

The SS expanded rapidly in other directions, combining terror with ideology. The army was controlled by the SS Special Service Troops (*SS-Verfugungstruppe – SS VT*), from which were eventually recruited the *Waffen SS*. The concentration camps were removed from the supervision of the SA and, instead, placed under *SS-Totenkopfverbande – SS-TV*, or Death's Head Formations, while the genocide programme from 1941 was organised by the Reich Security Main Office (*Reichssicherheitshauptamt* or RSHA). Although their target was restricted to a specific minority – the Jews – the RSHA introduced the most extreme form of terror known to the twentieth century.

c) 'Nazi Germany remained in existence because it was based on the threat of terror.' Explain why you agree or disagree with this view. **(15 marks)**

Nazi Germany certainly made use of terror in a widespread and systematic way. All classes and social groups were affected and the threat of reprisals was a strong argument for conformist behaviour. On the other hand, focusing entirely on 'terror' underestimates the attractions which the regime always held for a substantial proportion of its subjects.

These attractions were considerable. The *Führerprinzip* provided for highly effective personal leadership: Hitler was more genuinely popular in Germany than Stalin in Russia or Mussolini in Italy – without having to rely so much on a manufactured personality cult. Ironically, he was seen as a moderate in control of radicals and he was given personal credit for the recovery of the economy after 1933 and for the revival of Germany's strength through rearmament from 1934 and territorial acquisition from 1938. Many Germans therefore assumed that Hitler was controlling potential terror through his own moderation (as in the 1934 Night of the Long Knives), quite missing the point that his whole ideology represented the denial of moderation.

But this was the delusion behind the Third Reich. It meant that Germans were always aware of the terror lurking just below the surface, without really believing that it affected them personally. As far as Goebbels was concerned, the main purpose of the regime was to capture hearts and minds; the purpose of terror was to deal with those whom the regime had not reached or who had been cast out as an undesirable minority. This was an additional argument for conformity amongst the majority. As the SS became more and more concerned with the control of racial issues most people regarded themselves as safe so long as they were not associated with the racial minorities.

In other words, terror had provided an example for everyone of what happened to those beyond the scope of indoctrination.

6. **Assess the effectiveness of the SS and Gestapo as instruments of the Nazi regime?** **(90 marks)**

The SS and Gestapo were closely integrated and provided a powerful framework to reinforce Nazi policy, especially on terror, race and militarism. At the same time, however, the SS and Gestapo did suffer from a number of internal faults which reduced their operational efficiency.

The SS was the instrument by which the different elements of Nazism penetrated all parts of the German state. At first it provided security for Hitler against the more spontaneous eruptions of the SA: when the SS eliminated the SA leadership in the Night of the Long Knives (1934) it signalled the beginning of a more systematic, disciplined and targeted use of terror to uphold the regime. This was, in particular, the role of the SS Special Service Troops. Gradually this expanded into a military role. A key part of Hitler's policies was territorial expansion, or *Lebensraum*. The *Waffen SS* provided the military elite after the reorganisation of the *Wehrmacht* in 1938 and were at the forefront of the German advances into Poland in 1939 and Russia in 1941. In addition, the SS provided the administration of the conquered territories, through institutions such as the *Reichskommissariat* of Ostland.

The SS was also the means of radicalising Nazi race policies. It strengthened the racial basis of the *Volksgemeinschaft* far more completely than did any of the institutions of the Nazi state. It also weakened the ethical barrier of Christianity against racial legislation. Indeed, Himmler said in 1937 that 'It is part of the mission of the SS to give the German people over the next fifty years the non-Christian ideological foundations for a way of life appropriate to their character.' It was quite logical, therefore, that the SS should also become the main instrument of ethnic disposal in Nazi Germany. The genocide programme, drawn up in 1941, came under the control of the Reich Security Main Office (RSHA) and was actively implemented by SS officials such as Eichmann. The extermination camps were, in turn, manned by guards from the Death's Head Formations.

The impact of the SS was such that it came close to becoming the Nazi regime by 1944. By the criteria given it was, therefore, extremely influential. Yet, for all its impact, a number of deficiencies have been identified by historians. Höhne, for example, believes that 'the SS world was a bizarre nonsensical affair'.[5] More specific faults have also been identified. For example, there was a bitter rivalry between Himmler, *Reichsführer* SS, and other leading Nazis such as Goering and Bormann. Within the SS itself there were also growing differences between the racial 'idealism' of Himmler and the more ruthless and self-seeking opportunism of Heydrich. The SS structure could also be criticised for its increasing complexity, for its constant shifts, changes of shape and subdivisions – all of which were bound to reduce its practical efficiency.

Like the SS, the Gestapo has been seen as an example of sinister efficiency. Crankshaw, for example, considered them a 'highly professional corps'.[6] According to Schulz 'scarcely a politically significant initiative against the national socialist regime went undetected.'[7] The Gestapo performed two main functions – and seemed to perform them well. First, it was an instrument to ensure the success of the system of indoctrination by providing a sinister example to the German people of what was the alternative to their acceptance. If they were not convinced by Goebbels, they would fall prey to Heydrich and Best. Second, the Gestapo fulfilled the role of investigating and uprooting opposition and dissidents of all types, ranging from communists to rebellious youth groups. Together with the Soviet **NKVD**, the Gestapo has been seen as the twentieth century's most complete totalitarian police force, in control of an entire population.

This reputation was, however, less deserved even than that of the SS. It has been shown by recent historians that the reputation of the Gestapo was a myth arising out of its own propaganda. The reality was somewhat less impressive. Mallman and Paul argue that the Gestapo were insufficiently equipped to carry out the directives issued centrally and that they relied increasingly on information volunteered by members of the public.[8] This has been based largely on local studies which show that the Gestapo at local level was under-staffed, 'limping along behind the permanent inflation of its tasks.' This was particularly apparent in Stettin, Hanover, Bremen, Dortmund and Dusseldorf. The problem was increased by the war, which brought a further decline in the number of experienced officials as these were recruited into the *Waffen SS*. The Gestapo's total number fell to 32,000 of which only half were directly connected with police work. The organisation therefore became less proactive and depended increasingly on voluntary denunciations which poured in from the public. The Gestapo was therefore smaller – and less influential – than the KGB or the Stasi, which dominated the Soviet Union and East Germany in the post-war world.

And yet the all-embracing scope and purpose of the SS complex had no equivalent anywhere else. For all its practical deficiencies, the SS was the only organisation within any twentieth-century dictatorship which came close to absorbing the state itself.

7.   Assess the reasons for Hitler's widespread support in Germany between 1933 and 1939.   (90 marks)

'Support' can be explained in terms which are 'positive' and 'negative'. 'Positive' support, which tended to be open and active, was influenced by Hitler's personal appeal, his apparent ability to deliver results and his targeting of policies to each sector in Germany. A more 'negative' type of support would be compliance through necessity. Reasons for this included the removal of channels of opposition and Hitler's control over powers of coercion and terror.

The key factor in 'positive' support was Hitler's personal appeal. The extent of this was pointed out by Lloyd George, who wrote in the *Daily Express* after a visit to Germany in 1934 that, although Germans did express negative views about Nazi officials, he heard 'not a single word' ever uttered against Hitler personally. Even allowing for the possibility that a short visit could have created a distorted perspective, his view that Hitler was more popular than his movement has been shown to be correct. There was a widespread desire for strong personal control after the uncharismatic leadership of the Weimar Republic. Hitler's image undoubtedly benefited from the propaganda put out by Goebbels and his Ministry of People's Enlightenment. But it would be incorrect to see his popularity as an artificial creation. The main reason for his widespread acceptance by the German people was a strange one: he was seen by them as a moderate within a movement of radicals. His political changes were widely accepted as technically constitutional and many Germans were reassured by Hitler's constant emphasis on restoring traditional values. Until the late 1930s, he also professed to be deeply religious. In complete contrast, there was widespread unease about the rest of the Nazi movement, especially about the thuggish tendencies of some of it members like Röhm and Streicher. Hitler was perceived as the moderate who would tame the radicals; for this reason his reputation was enormously enhanced by the 'Night of the Long Knives' in 1934. In addition to controlling extremism, Hitler also appeared to guarantee peace, using it as a constant theme in his speeches until 1938. It could, therefore, be argued that Hitler's popularity was based partly on a misunderstanding of Hitler's real motives, a misunderstanding which he was willing enough to disseminate to stabilise his position in the 1930s.

Hitler's personal popularity preceded the outcome of many Nazi policies. His status with the population was, however, enhanced by an apparent ability to deliver results. In part, this was due to a series of opportunities on which he was able to capitalise. For example, the recovery of the economy after 1933 was projected to a grateful population as his doing rather than the result of the measures applied by Brüning and Schacht. His revisionist foreign policy was compared directly with the much slower developments made during the Stresemann era and he received popular adulation for remilitarising the Rhineland in 1936 and for taking over Austria and the Sudetenland in 1938 – all without the need for war. Even those with a vested interest in undermining his position were forced to concede the strength of Hitler's appeal: numerous reports produced for the SPD in exile (**SOPADE**) pointed to a steady increase in the Führer's popularity because he was achieving what he had set out to do.

Perceptions of this success were sharpened because Hitler deliberately offered something unique to each class within Germany while, at the same time, uniting all sectors within the *Volksgemeinschaft*. Specific sectors of the population therefore had specific reasons for supporting Hitler. Most of the business sector and industrialists were won over quickly by Hitler's measures against trade unions, which delivered to them a disciplined workforce. Major industrial enterprises such as Krupp and I.G. Farben were more fully involved in equipping the Nazi war machine and, from 1941, the forced labour and extermination programmes. Much of the middle class benefited from

substitutes. The Plan was also brought into line with Hitler's more aggressive foreign policy: the 1937 Hossbach Memorandum records that Hitler announced to his chiefs of staff that he was preparing for war. Goering was therefore placed in control of a new Four Year Plan Office and Schacht resigned in November 1937. Under the plan military expenditure grew rapidly, and there were huge increases in aircraft, tanks, heavy artillery, weapons and infantry divisions. By contrast with all of this, the German consumer appeared to be pushed into a subordinate position. Controls on working practices were increased through the DAF, KdF and SdA, working hours were increased, and lower priority was given to consumer goods.

And yet there is another side to the Four Year Plan. Although preparation for war was certainly its main objective, the ways in which that preparation was carried out indicates that it was not the only one. Hitler could not ignore altogether the interests of the German consumer, especially since a large measure of his popular appeal was his claim to have returned Germany to prosperity. Although some sacrifice was necessary, it should not be on the scale of Stalin's impoverishment of the Soviet workforce through the Five Year Plans. The answer was to prepare Germany for a series of swift and decisive campaigns based on the principle of 'lightning war'.

Blitzkrieg was therefore an economic as well as a military strategy. The intention was that Germany should conquer neighbouring countries without the necessity of total economic mobilisation. In this way, the German consumer would be spared the sacrifices demanded by a 'total war' economy and would be able to retain many of the economic advances which had occurred since 1933. At least, until 1940, Hitler was basing his policy on the need to prepare the consumer to accept war as well as on the needs of war itself.

10. Compare the relative importance of rearmament and the standard of living in the development of Nazi economic policy between 1933 and 1939. **(90 marks)**

While he was Economics Minister (1934–7), Schacht tried to pursue a policy which would ensure rapid recovery from the depression. Although this was not aimed specifically at raising the standard of living of the different classes, its main components were more likely to have that effect than a policy focusing on rearmament. Schacht's New Plan gave priority to restoring Germany's industrial and commercial capacity, both of which would improve the standard of living by creating genuine jobs and increasing the range of consumer goods. The trade agreements with the Balkans and Latin America were the first step in the recovery of Germany's collapsed foreign markets and the next logical step would have been the revival of consumerism. Although Schacht's currency controls initially allocated foreign exchange to key sectors of the German economy, subsequent commercial economic expansion would, again, have loosened the restrictions and broadened the range of both exports and imports. Schacht made it clear that the revival of key industries must come first – but that improved standards of living could well follow. What, in his view, would be most likely to disrupt the pattern of economic recovery would be a switch to rapid rearmament based on an economic policy of self-sufficiency, or autarky.

This is precisely what Hitler intended. While he was content, in the opening years of the Nazi regime, to let Schacht follow a conventional economic strategy, Hitler introduced a major change in 1936. In this he was following a series of long-held objectives in which he considered Germans not as consumers within an international commercial order but as components of a race community in an economic autarky which Germany would dominate. This meant controlling Europe, especially 'the lands to the east' through the conquest of *Lebensraum*. New communities would eventually be established on land carved out of Poland and Russia by the German army. Germany would also have self-sufficiency in raw materials and food as well as guaranteed outlets for its manufactured goods. All these goals would involve heavy rearmament. But this was to the benefit of the population, which would be prepared for its part in healthy conflict. By contrast, the consumer-orientated economies of Britain, France and the United States were bound to become effete and enfeebled. The Four Year Plan (1936–40) was therefore intended to redirect German expectations of living standards. They were to prepare for collective prosperity through conquest. In announcing the Plan, Hitler reasoned that since 'We are overpopulated and cannot feed ourselves from our own resources', the solution lay in 'extending our living space.' Hence 'The German economy must be fit for war within four years.'[9] Specific targets were set for armaments (aircraft, tanks and weapons) and also for key commodities (mineral oil, rubber, explosives, steel and coal). Goering, as head of the new Four Year Plan office, justified these measures in a radio speech: 'Guns will make us powerful; butter will only make us fat.'

We should not, however, go to the other extreme of assuming that the Nazi policies of autarky and rearmament discounted the needs of the German consumer altogether. Hitler was never able to depress German living standards in pursuit of his Four Year Plan to anything like the extent that Stalin could exploit the Soviet people in implementing his Five Year Plans. Indeed, there are two examples of the way in which the needs of German consumers actually forced Hitler's hand on rearmament. The first was the timing of the Four Year Plan itself, which was undoubtedly influenced by a food shortage between 1935 and 1936 affecting the entire German workforce. Hitler's solution was to accelerate rearmament to achieve *Lebensraum* – and prosperity – as quickly as possible. A second example relates to the type of war envisaged to achieve this. Hitler settled for the concept of swift but limited military strikes, part of an overall strategy of *Blitzkrieg*. But some historians have argued that *Blitzkrieg* was as much an economic device, forced upon Hitler by the need to compromise over the demands he could make of the German consumer. The only way in which Germany could expand through limited mobilisation was by steadily increasing her economic base through a series of rapid and specifically targeted conquests.

It therefore appears that Hitler did subordinate short-term aspirations for improved living standards to rearmament; this would achieve long-term collective prosperity in the form of *Lebensraum*. But, at the same time, the long-term objectives had to be modified by short-term consumer problems; the result was that rearmament was geared to *Blitzkrieg* rather than to total war.

11. How far did the German people benefit from Nazi economic policy between 1933 and 1939? (90 marks)

By 1939 Hitler was claiming credit for a transformation in standards of living in Germany. Superficially there appears to be much to support this. But closer analysis of the statistical trends shows that the achievements of the Nazi regime for the German people was actually very limited.

On the positive side, Germany seemed to be returning to prosperity after the bleak years of depression. Unemployment, for example, had declined from 4.8 million in 1933 to 0.1 million by 1939, a significantly faster decline than in the United States, France and Britain. The decline in unemployment was accompanied by an increase in wages, although these had by 1938 still reached only 85 per cent of their level in 1928. The German people were also part of a general increase in prosperity represented by a steady growth of Germany's national income. This had almost doubled from 44 billion marks (1933) to 80 billion (1938). In the process, the workforce benefited from being targeted by consumer goods such as radio sets and, more selectively, by Volkswagen cars. Bearing this in mind, it is easy to see why contemporaries should have considered that the German economy, along with the living standards of its people, had been transformed.

But we should not be too ready to assume that such improvements after 1933 were due directly and uniquely to Hitler. Many of the earlier policies of Schacht were directly influenced by those of Brüning between 1930 and 1932. Brüning actually benefited the Nazi regime. In ruthlessly taking control of the economy, Brüning intended to deal forcefully with the problems quickly and to enable Germany to come out of the crisis before its industrial competitors. In the process, Brüning's measures contributed to high levels of unemployment, which were already beginning to drop by the end of 1932. The worst was therefore over by the time that Hitler was appointed Chancellor in January 1933 which meant that Hitler was able to claim the credit for the accelerating recovery over the next two years.

Another possible reservation about the impact of Nazi policies is that any improvements which did occur to the economy were not automatically transmitted to the workforce. This is because the latter was not based on a consumer boom. Instead, the main priority was rearmament. The reduction in unemployment levels was the result less of new jobs in consumer industries than of the expansion of the armed forces and the use of the unemployed on public works schemes like the autobahns. Unlike the New Deal of Roosevelt, therefore, the Nazi regime used coercion and forced labour to reduce unemployment. Such measures also resulted in constraints on wage levels. Nor did the workforce as a whole benefit from the increase in national income, receiving an ever-decreasing proportion in the form of wages; whereas wages in 1933 had amounted to 63 per cent of the national income, the corresponding proportion by 1938 was 57 per cent. Over the same period the working week had been lengthened by an average of seven hours.

The German workforce were therefore putting in more effort for a declining financial return on its productivity. This was accompanied by a reduced priority afforded by the government to consumer needs. Although the production of consumables rose by 69 per cent between 1933 and 1938, this compared badly with the increase of industrial goods by 389 per cent over the same period. It therefore seems that German workers were subsidising rearmament by foregoing any significant improvement in their standard of living. Further evidence of this was the tightening of import controls and the substantial drop in consumer goods from abroad.

The Nazis claimed that the new organisations for employees in the form of the RAD, KdF and SdA, conferred real benefits upon the workforce and more than compensated for any shortages in consumer goods. But these institutions were actually part of the effort of a totalitarian regime to discipline that workforce. One of the main objectives was to prevent the revival of the consumer expectations of the Weimar period since this would divert economic resources from Hitler's main priority – rearmament.

Overall, the most positive economic features of the period were full employment and conditions of work which were far less oppressive than those in the Soviet Union under the Five Year Plans. Yet the German workforce suffered by comparison with those in other advanced economies which were pulling out of the depression. By 1938 the working week had increased considerably while, in terms of productivity, real wages had declined. The relationship between workers and the German economy was therefore one-way: they subsidised rearmament at the expense of any hope of improving their own living standards.

The *Volksgemeinschaft*, race and the Holocaust

12. 'Fundamental to the Nazi system were the twin influences of race and anti-Semitism.'

a) What, in this context, is meant by 'the twin influences of race and anti-Semitism'? (3 marks)

'Twin influences' refers to two connected but, at the same time, distinct factors. Their connection is identification of people on ethnic grounds. Their distinction in Germany was that 'race' was normally associated with positive 'Aryan' characteristics, while 'anti-Semitism' denoted the policies of persecution applied to the Jews.

b) Explain the role played by race in the Nazi system. (7 marks)

Nazi racial doctrine had three main roles. It provided the basic purpose for the Nazi regime; it established the main form of social cohesion; and it identified Germany's internal and external victims.

Unlike Italian fascism, which saw the nation state as the highest political form, Nazism aspired to the supremacy of the Aryan race, for which the existing German state was the starting point. The ultimate objectives were internal racial 'purification' and external 'conquest' – at the expense of the 'inferior' races of eastern Europe. Hence Aryanism and *Lebensraum* provided the basic rationale for the Nazi system. They also influenced the way the Nazi regime developed; the internal changes needed a totalitarian dictatorship, while external expansion assumed militarisation and acceptance of conflict as the highest human activity.

The Nazi emphasis on race also provided a new social cohesion in the form of the people's community, or *Volksgemeinschaft*. This was intended to replace the conflict between classes and other groups which had formed such a major part of Germany's recent history. Instead of fractured economic groups engaged in bitter struggle with each other, there would now be a single people united by its Aryan tradition and engaged in a common struggle with other races. The result would be conquest and supremacy. The corollary, however, was unquestioning loyalty to the regime and the sacrifice of individuality and consumerism. This meant that racial policies were closely connected with propaganda and indoctrination, especially in Germany's schools, and with the new work ethic implicit in organisations like the RAD, SdA and KdF.

Finally, race provided the Nazi system with its victims. These were identified as enemies to Aryanism, for reasons of ethnic origin, mental impairment, or social deviance. This turned the favoured majority against selected targets, providing the regime with a new dynamic based on targeted hatred. The largest and most consistent form of persecution was anti-Semitism, the most obsessive element of Nazi ideology. The stereotypes of Jewish 'conspiracy' and 'contamination' were used to justify the removal of legal and ethical norms in the treatment of a minority group. This made possible the notion of disposability, leading to genocide and the Holocaust.

c) 'There was a fundamental difference in the treatment of the Jews by
the Nazi regime before and after 1940.' Explain whether you agree or
disagree with this view. (15 marks)

Persecution of the Jews was endemic to the Nazi regime both before and after 1940; this was based
on ideas and principles which did not change. On the other hand, the measures actually introduced became more extreme after 1940, largely under the radicalising impact of war.

Nazi anti-Semitism was based on three propositions which were apparent in *Mein Kampf* and
from the very earliest stages of the regime – and which remained apparent to the end. The first
was alleged economic exploitation by the Jews. This was used to justify a whole range of measures
ranging from the SA boycott on Jewish shops in 1933 to the recycling of the property of
Jewish victims of the extermination camps from 1941. The second was the 'racial contamination'
resulting from Jewish contact with German 'blood'. The Nazi response was to use indoctrination
and race studies in the 1930s to protect Aryan racial 'purity', a process which was to underlie
virtually all the activities of the SS after 1940. Third, Jews were accused of moral and cultural
contamination of the *Volksgemeinschaft*, again resulting in a consistent campaign to expunge
Jewish influences.

There was, therefore, continuity of aim. Where differences arose was in the methods of achieving
the aim. The year 1940 is, in one sense, a clear dividing line between a policy based on exclusion
and one based on extermination. Before 1940 persecution focused on excluding Jews from German
life. Measures included removal from the civil service, judiciary and the medical profession in
1933. By the Nuremberg Laws (1935) Jews were deprived of German citizenship and prevented
from marrying Germans. From July 1938 they were prevented from participating in commerce,
their last preserve. By 1940 Jews were also compulsorily confined to ghettoes, ordered to wear the
Star of David; their movement was controlled by identity cards and passports. Hitler was also
considering schemes to exclude Jews from Germany altogether by compulsory deportation to
Madagascar.

These 'solutions' were a contrast to the 'Final Solution', drawn up in 1941. The latter removed
Jews in another sense – by extermination. The mass deportation of Jews to camps differed from
their earlier concentration in ghettoes. The calculated use of gas chambers at the extermination
camps at Chelmo, Auschwitz-Birkenau, Belzec, Sobibor, Treblinka and Maidenek also went far
beyond the earlier levels of persecution in the concentration camps. Yet, for all this, there was
also an element of continuity in the Holocaust. This was the perceived legitimacy of violence.
It was latent in the SA action against Jewish stores in 1933 and it surfaced in *Kristallnacht*
(9–10 November 1938). Above all, it was implicit in all the anti-Semitic statements in *Mein Kampf*.
It raises the suspicion that, although the Holocaust was signposted in 1941, the road to Auschwitz
actually started in 1933.

13. (a) What, in the context of Nazi Germany, was the *Führerprinzip*? (15 marks)

Führerprinzip meant the 'principle of leadership' – specifically of the personal power and cult of
Hitler as Führer, the title he adopted after the death of President Hindenburg in 1934. It was the
focal point of all other principles underlying the Nazi state, including *Volksgemeinschaft*,
Gleischaltung, *Aryanism* and *Lebensraum*.

In the first place, *Führerprinzip* was based on the acceptance that Hitler was the source of Nazi ideology. *Mein Kampf*, in particular, contained the definitive views on struggle, war, racism, anti-Semitism, conquest and *Lebensraum*. Although some of Hitler's ideas were derived from earlier influences, these were ignored: there was, therefore, no equivalent to Lenin's acknowledgement of Marx. *Führerprinzip* was also the acceptance of Hitler as the only true source of authority (*Führer-power*) in the Nazi system. It justified everything that Hitler did. This included the initial 'legal revolution', by which he converted the institutions of the Weimar Republic into those of the Third Reich, and the subsequent policy of *Gleichschaltung* (co-ordination), which combined the traditional and Nazi institutions. Yet *Führerprinzip* was not seen as the arbitrary exercise of tyranny. Although liberal democracy had been uprooted, it was replaced by a form of 'popular autocracy', or the people's will embodied in the Führer. As such, the role of the population was no longer to elect a fallible leader, but rather to obey and applaud one who had proved himself infallible.

Much the same demands of loyalty were placed on Hitler's subordinates. *Führerprinzip* involved no notion of 'collective leadership' or 'power-sharing' as happened from time to time in the Soviet system. All other Nazi leaders (for example, Goebbels, Himmler, Heydrich, Ley, Rust, von Schirach, Frank and Bormann) acted in his name, exercising whatever power he chose to delegate to them. In reality, this was considerable, since Hitler had little eye for administrative detail. His subordinates therefore added their own initiatives, taking care to justify them as being 'the will of the Führer'. Used in this way, *Führerprinzip* could therefore be an unquestionable sanction to action.

Finally, *Führerprinzip* also meant that Hitler was the focal point for popular support within the organic community, or *Volksgemeinschaft*. The Nazi system and Nazi ideology made frequent and sustained attacks on any reasoned justification for society. This meant that a complex set of principles, like those underlying communism, were unnecessary. Instead, Nazism projected a visionary appeal – which was much more closely associated with an individual than with an ideal. Hence the *Führerprinzip* was the only truly uniting force that Nazism had. Although in the end the issue hardly arose, establishing a succession to Hitler would have been exceptionally difficult.

b) How effective was the *Führerprinzip* in the Nazi system?   (15 marks)

The *Führerprinzip* had mixed effects. On the one hand it can be seen as highly successful. There is no doubt that the Führer achieved unprecedented levels of personal popularity in Germany; this applied to all classes. The propaganda media, especially the cinema and radio, built up the appeal of personal leadership and its interaction with the ranked masses. Germany's movement towards mobilisation, through the Four Year Plan (1936–40), and plunge into war in 1939 and 1941, were accepted without any real reservation by a population which had come to see the decisions taken under *Führerprinzip* as infallible.

Yet, in retrospect, there are serious reservations about the effectiveness of the principle in practice. The Führer State was projected as harmonious and efficient, largely because of the Führer's all-pervading will. In fact, the reverse was probably true. Hitler's personal power was possible only because of the untidiness of the political structure beneath him, which encouraged constant rivalry between his subordinates and their offices. The process of *Gleichschaltung* had been intended to harmonise new Nazi institutions with those traditional ones which had been kept. In practice, however, this bred in-fighting and delay – from which *Führerprinzip* promoted a lofty isolation. But the greatest danger of *Führerprinzip* was to be the lack of control over it in wartime. This resulted in disastrous mistakes in military strategy, including Hitler's decision to invade the Soviet Union in 1941 and his refusal to allow tactical retreat from Stalingrad in 1943. Both played a crucial part in the collapse of his whole system.

Hitler's vision of *Führerprinzip* was a totally personal one. When it came, destruction would therefore have to apply to the people as well as to their leader. Hence *Führerprinzip* eventually turned into *Gotterdammerung*.

14. Explain the purpose and structure of the *Volksgemeinschaft* in Nazi Germany. (90 marks)

Volksgemeinshaft meant 'people's community', a term which covered that part of the German population which was considered to be suitably 'Aryan'. It provided new criteria for social cohesion, based on race rather than class. Each social sector was considered to have its own place within the overall order, while the whole structure was upheld by propaganda and indoctrination from the centre.

The *Volksgemeinschaft* brought a changed relationship between the social classes. Industrialised countries like Germany had developed a large urban proletariat, or working class. These had been represented primarily by left-wing parties, in Germany by the SPD and KPD. Communism, especially, had been based on the Marxist principle of class conflict, which would lead eventually to the elimination of other classes and to the 'dictatorship of the proletariat'. The Nazis abandoned this notion of conflict in the 1920s, aiming to establish a community which would provide security for all classes. The *Volksgemeinshaft*, established from 1933, operated on the principle of providing each class with its place – and keeping it there. The working class was deprived of its political representation with the banning of the SPD and KPD; it also lost its right to belong to trade unions and to engage in strikes. Instead it was reorganised into the RAD, its working practices were regulated through the SdA and its recreation was controlled by the KdF. The *Mittelstand*, or middle classes, had already been attracted by the Nazi promise of a 'third way' between communism and capitalism and were kept under control from 1933 by economic policies like the New Plan (1934) and the Four Year Plan (1936). These promoted economic recovery, while concentrating initially on foreign exchange controls and then on rearmament. The middle classes therefore retained their social identity but lost their connection with consumerism. They also surrendered any professional independence. Teachers, for example, were expected to belong to the National Socialist Teachers' League, while lawyers were expected to follow a Nazified legal code. Farmers were more openly favoured by the emphasis on rural values and 'blood and soil', but were impeded by legislation like the Reich Entailed Farm Law (1933) restricting the subdivision of estates. The upper classes were allowed to keep the social predominance in Germany and gained the most economically from the Nazi system. Giant enterprises like I.G. Farben and Krupps flourished as never before and contributed to the repressive labour policies of the Reich.

In addition to settling the role of each class, the *Volksgemeinschaft* defined the relationship between different sectors of the population so as to cut across class boundaries. This was done by a centralised system of indoctrination and propaganda conducted by Gobbels's Ministry of People's Enlightenment and Propaganda. Most obviously affected were women, young people and religious groups. The roles of women were redefined as childbearing and homecare. Women were gradually removed from the professions and awards were provided for mothers of large families. Young people were to be reared as future Nazis through a restructured education system, which established different roles for boys and girls, and through the military emphasis of the Hitler Youth. Attempts were made to remove religion as a potential rival to Nazi ideology. Either it was depoliticised, as happened to the Catholic Church in the 1933 Concordat or it was brought under the control of the state itself, as occurred with the Protestant churches in July 1933. The

Volksgemeinschaft eventually saw the emergence of pagan movements as non-Christian alternatives more in tune with Nazi ideas. These, however, attracted little widespread support.

Removing the conflict between classes and other social sectors were therefore essential features of the *Volksgemeinschaft*. But there was a higher purpose behind this. The *Volksgemeinschaft* was, above all, a racial community, intended for external expansion and *Lebensraum*. Conquest was a logical result of this, since, to Hitler 'war is the father of all things'. Whereas Marxists believed that the history of societies was one of internal 'class struggle', the Nazi 'people's community' envisaged an external 'race war' against 'inferior' peoples to the east. This partly explains the creation of a *Blitzkrieg* economy based on the Four Year Plan.

In one very important respect the *Volksgemeinschaft* directed its focus of struggle inwards. The search for racial 'purity' produced policies of discrimination and violence against those groups which did not conform to the racial ideal. Measures were taken against minorities targeted for genetic, social or ethnic reasons. The task was carried out by the principal agents of coercion, the SS and the Gestapo, and was expanded from 1939 into a programme of 'euthanasia'. Social 'deviates', including tramps, homosexuals and alcoholics were sent to concentration camps. The main ethnic groups subject to persecution were the gypsies and Jews. The former were seen as a threat to the *Volksgemeinschaft* because of their mixed-race origin and their roving lifestyle. The hatred of the Jews was more fundamental, reflected by the numerous obsessive passages in *Mein Kampf* and by the vile material in Streicher's publication *Der Stürmer*. Anti-Semitism fulfilled two purposes for the *Volksgemeinschaft*. First, it provided a means of 'purification': the Nuremberg Laws (1935) prevented marriage or sexual relations with Aryans and were accompanied by a wide range of measures removing social benefits and legal rights. Second, it gave the Aryan community a target at which it could direct the blame for all of its problems. The ultimate result of both attitudes was physical removal through extermination by the SS in camps like Auschwitz-Birkenau, Treblinka, Maidanek and Sobibor.

The *Volksgemeinschaft* therefore gave each class and social group a place within an overall harmony. Dictatorship and race, however, added a destructive force. Externally the 'People's Community' sought expansion and *Lebenrsraum* through war and conquest. Internally it sought 'purity' and 'fulfilment' through repression and genocide.

 Foreign policy and war, 1933–45

15. How clear were the ideas and aims behind Hitler's foreign policy between 1933 and 1939? (90 marks)

See Chapter 8, Essay 16.

16. How did the German people react to the experience of war between 1939 and 1945? (90 marks)

The German people remained patriotic throughout the war but experienced a fundamental change in their reaction to the Nazi regime between 1939 and 1945.

When war broke out in September 1939, most people were apprehensive, fearing the possibility of defeat and humiliation as had happened in 1918–19. They had also hoped that Hitler would preserve the peace, as he had promised before 1936, and not involve Germany in a war which the Four Year Plan (1936) seemed to suggest. They had expected him to pull off a last-minute diplomatic solution to the Polish question, as he had in September 1938 to the crisis over Czechoslovakia. War, they feared, would be an altogether different experience.

But these reservations were reversed by the initial success of *Blitzkrieg* and the overwhelming success of German aircraft and tanks against Poland in 1939. The fall of France, after only a few weeks, in June 1940 caused another wave of euphoria. The population had been expecting a long, hard struggle similar to that experienced between 1914 and 1918. Instead it was given a series of easy victories, delivered without hardship and with very little change to the standard of living experienced before 1939. There was also pride that Hitler had managed to achieve German revenge for the surrender to the French army at Compiegne in 1918 and for the prominent role played by the French in the Versailles *diktat*. Almost certainly, the myths of the 'stab in the back' and the 'November Criminals' would have added hatred to victory. More than anything to date, victory in 1940 seemed to rationalise the Nazi regime to the German people. It seemed to justify the political and economic changes and to vindicate the whole principle of *Führerprinzip*. In the year 1940 Hitler had support with fewer reservations than ever before.

Yet this euphoria could not last indefinitely. Following the invasion of Russia in 1941, the style of conflict changed from *Blitzkrieg* to total war. It took some time, however, for the full implications of this to hit the population. It was not until 1943 that Goebbels announced, in a speech at the Berlin Sports Palace, the transition to an entirely different experience. 'I ask you: Do you want total war? Do you want it, if necessary, more total and more radical than we can even imagine it today?' This gave a hint of things to come. The change to total war had a complex effect on the German people. On the one hand, they responded with fortitude to a sudden increase in suffering. The Allied strategy of saturation bombing against Berlin, Munich, Essen, Dortmund, Cologne, Nuremberg, Hamburg and Dresden served only to stiffen civilian resistance. They experienced the full impact of blast, burns, suffocation and carbon monoxide poisoning, the survivors willingly helping to clear up afterwards. On the other hand, there was a creeping loss of morale caused by doubts about the reason for the war. The retreat in Russia raised doubts about the Führer's whole attitude to 'war as life' and 'life as war', which appealed only as a slogan only in victory. The later stages of the war also produced disturbing evidence about the evil deeds of a totalitarian regime – in the form of mass shootings on the eastern front. There may also have been widespread suspicions about mass extermination of Jews. Most Germans did not turn against the regime but there was a growing war weariness and a fundamental questioning of the whole Nazi rationale. But a significant minority were now taking active measures to try to end Hitler's dictatorship. Particularly important were resistance groups like the Kreisau Circle, which produced a programme entitled 'Principles for the New Order of Germany', and involvement in bomb plots by officials who had occupied high positions in the Third Reich, such as von Hassell (former German ambassador to Italy), Rommell (former commander-in-chief in North Africa), Goerdeler, von Koltke and von Wartenburg. They, too, must have become demoralised since there was very little they could do to ease the path back to democracy. The Allies were not open to any attempts to do a deal, as the resistance movement wanted; by insisting on unconditional surrender, they removed an important part of their programme.

All this points to a trauma. Externally there was the transition from easy victory to impossible defiance against overwhelming odds. Internally there was the transition from success, which had justified Hitler's earlier methods, to failure, which now highlighted the whole deficiency of Nazism.

Figure 6.4
The effect of bombing in the Second World War – the ruins of Hamburg

17. To what extent did war change the Nazi regime?   (90 marks)

At first sight it might seem that war would confirm the objectives of the Nazi regime, which seemed to have geared itself for struggle. On the other hand, the regime was complex and could therefore be affected in different ways by the war. The common factor, however, is that it was *radicalised*. After 1941, it became more extreme than ever.

The active pursuit of war would seem to suggest very few changes in the objectives of the Nazi regime. After all, Hitler had always seen 'struggle' as the natural human condition: 'All of nature is one great struggle between strength and weakness, an eternal victory of the strong over the weak.' In *Mein Kampf*, Hitler also made frequent and explicit references to conquest ('we turn our eyes to the lands of the East') and to *Lebensraum*. War would therefore seem to be the fulfilment of earlier aims. Hitler did, of course, emphasise the need for peace between 1933 and 1938. But he explained away this inconsistency in a secret speech to representatives of the German press in November 1938: 'Only by continually stressing Germany's desire for peace . . . could I provide the armaments which were always necessary before the next step could be taken.' By this time, the Four Year Plan had been in existence for two years, with the intention of 'preparing Germany for war'. The German invasion of Poland in September 1939 was therefore directly in line with the economic adjustment of the Nazi regime to the strategy of *Blitzkrieg*.

The pursuit of war seemed, therefore, to confirm, not change, fundamental Nazi policies. But the argument for continuity is not so clear-cut when we examine the impact of the war on the nature of the regime itself. One thing is clear: the regime became more extreme in its pursuit of policies such as genocide. What is not clear is whether, in becoming more extreme, the regime was actually changing.

On the one hand it could be argued that the potential for extreme policies already existed in Nazi Germany and that they were radicalised simply because war removed all the earlier constraints.

In other words, these changes amounted to the logical change for Nazism to take – and war made them possible. Alternatively, war could be seen as a destructive power – but against Nazism. It was more logical for Nazism to discover an equilibrium based on certain restraints – which is certainly what the German people wanted to see. What war did was to destroy this. Radicalisation was therefore a destructive, not a fulfilling process. These two perspectives can be seen in each of the following examples.

The German consumer was profoundly affected by the shift in the economic base from *Blitzkrieg* to Total War (announced by Goebbels in 1943). But it is still not entirely clear whether it was the regime's intention to build *Blitzkrieg* into ultimate Total War, or whether Total War was a basic change of direction – an admission that the earlier easy victories had given way to a struggle for survival against the Soviet Union. Either way, Germany was unable to match the production figures of its two main rivals, the Soviet Union and the United States.

The war certainly radicalised the regime politically. The SS, for example, expanded rapidly in importance, to the point where it is arguable that it had assumed many of the functions of the state itself. By 1944 it was running the army through the *Waffen SS*, the extermination programme through the RSHA, and the eastern occupied territories. It was also in charge of the Reich's racial policy through the RKFDV and had assumed virtual control over the industrial sector. By 1945, Himmler was being perceived by Hitler as a threat to his own political position. Again, this can be interpreted in two ways. Either it was a further stage in the growth of what had always been the regime's most powerful organisation, or the war provided a new departure, giving the SS the chance to move into military and administrative areas which would not have been open to them in peacetime.

The impact of war also had a profound effect on the official Nazi policy towards Christianity. During the 1930s the regime had recognised the need to maintain at least some contact with the Christian Churches. After 1939 this contact was rapidly eroded and Christianity came increasingly under attack. Martin Bormann, for example, said in 1941 that 'The concepts of national socialism and Christianity are irreconcilable.' But was this an acceleration or a change of direction? On the one hand, it could be argued that the Nazis were already moving in this direction, as shown by their undermining the 1933 Concordat and their attempts to Nazify the Church with organisations such as the Cross and Eagle League. All the war did was to accelerate the process. On the other hand, the regime abandoned any pretext to uphold Christianity as a direct result of the war and this radicalisation was sufficient reason for many Christian leaders to join the resistance movements against the regime.

The most important example of the war radicalising the Nazi regime was the implementation of the Holocaust. Before 1939 the conditions experienced by Jews in Nazi Germany had steadily deteriorated. But it was from 1940 and 1941 that mass killings were carried out in occupied territories in the east, initially by *Einsatzgrüppen*. The Wannsee Conference, called in December 1941 to implement the 'Final Solution', saw a deliberate move to industrialise genocide through gas chambers. This represents a new stage in anti-Semitism, which entirely transcended anything carried out in the 1930s. Whether or not this represented a 'change' of policy is the subject of the most active debate of all. One argument is that the war offered the Nazis the opportunity to implement the genocide they had always intended by suddenly putting huge numbers of potential victims in their power. The alternative is that the huge increase in extermination was largely the result of the chaotic situation produced by the war. This in no ways reduces the complicity of the regime, but it does indicate a change of direction.

The Nazi regime was destroyed by a war which it had created. In the process it became more extreme. But whether this meant that war released the constraints on earlier policies – or actually changed them – is still open to historical debate.

18. Assess the relative importance of any two reasons given for the introduction of the Holocaust from 1941.   (90 marks)

One reason which has been advanced by recent historians for the Holocaust is deliberate planning *by* the Nazi regime. Another is the pressure of circumstances *on* the regime. These are usually seen to be mutually exclusive. In fact, they can be associated and their relative importance directly compared.

The two possible reasons have been called Intentionalism and Structuralism. 'Intentionalist' historans (for example, Jäckel, Hillgruber and Goldhagen) attribute genocide to the calculated use of the power of a totalitarian regime to implement Hitler's own intentions. On the other hand, 'Structuralist' historians (such as Hilberg, Mommsen and Broszat) maintain that genocide was based not on a long-term plan but rather on the changing structure of circumstances and the way in which the state reacted to them. Intentionalism sees the Holocaust as the logical fulfilment of earlier anti-Semitic measures, whereas Structuralism regards the Holocaust as the last resort, following the failure of other policies.

The Intentionalist argument provides a stronger explanation of the powerful drive behind genocide. The origins of Holocaust have to be sought firmly in Hitler's own hatred of the Jews. Otherwise, there is a danger of making the gas chambers at Auschwitz, Treblinka and Maidanek seem unplanned and unpremeditated. As Goldhagen argues, there are four obvious stages in Hitler's move towards the Holocaust. The first was the publication of *Mein Kampf* in 1925; this contained an obsessive anti-Semitism which was clearly 'eliminationist'. Then, on coming to power, Hitler introduced a series of measures, including the 1935 Nuremberg Laws, which removed Jews from normal civic life and protection; from 1938 Jews were also subject to violence, as was shown in *Kristallnacht*. By 1939 'eliminationism' had moved into the area of physical removal. Hitler repeated in several speeches that war would provide the occasion for the death of European Jewry. And so it proved – but the initiative was taken by Hitler and the Nazi regime. The invasion and occupation of huge areas of Soviet Russia in 1941 provided the opportunity to implement the Final Solution, details of which were drawn up at the 1941 Wannsee Conference, convened by Eichmann on Heydrich's orders who, in turn, was acting on instructions from Goering. The strength of Hitler's obsession was such that it was still his main preoccupation while Germany faced imminent defeat in April and May 1945. Questioning this obsession has led at least one historian down a slippery slope: Irving first denied Hitler's direct connection with the Holocaust and then, notoriously, the existence of the gas chambers.

It is, however, possible to see pressures for genocide in addition to Hitler's obsession. The strength of the Structuralist argument is that it explains the way in which this obsession was allowed to become reality. Genocide was such a huge step, even for the Nazis, that an upheaval must have occurred in the state which administered it. It was the result of growing chaos and incompetence rather than of heightened efficiency. The original target had been resettlement, first to Madagascar, then to Siberia. The former had been made impractical by the outbreak of war, which had focused Germany's priorities on Europe itself. The latter was impeded by the nature of the war against Russia. Proposals to transport all Jews over the Urals were set in motion but were then blocked by the growth of Russian resistance to the German advance. This meant an accumulation of peoples in eastern Europe with no obvious long-term destination. The result was the search for a swift solution, first through the SS *Einsatzgrüppen* killings, then through the use of extermination camps equipped with gas chambers.

The type of genocide involved in the Holocaust was so radical that it is hard to envisage it without long-term inspiration from Hitler himself. Killings may happen spontaneously – even mass killings. But gas chambers do not. On the other hand, implementing the Holocaust was such a massive undertaking that it was a real departure from earlier policies. The descent of Nazi Germany into the abyss was therefore the result of extreme ideas being released by an increasingly chaotic situation.

Additional essay questions (with advice)

Each of these questions can be tackled as a single essay or as one of the answers to a question in several parts. Additional reading and research is desirable for each one.

19. In what ways did the Nazis transform Germany into a political dictatorship?

Advice: *Avoid simply describing the 'legal revolution'. Select some general components of 'dictatorship' and explain how these changed or 'transformed' Germany. Criteria could include: (1) the weakening of the legislature, (2) the banning of other parties, (3) the strengthening of the executive and head of state; and (4) the use of coercion to enforce this through new administrative structures.*

Essay plan

Para 1: Overall approach. 'Transformation' into 'political dictatorship' was accomplished by the conversion of democracy into dictatorship. This involved the erosion of the Weimar constitution through A to D.

Para 2: A. Weakening of the legislature – the basic component of any democracy. Enabling Act 1933 altering the 1919 Constitution.
- *End of principle of legislative control over the executive*
- *End of Ländtage.*

Most important to introduce dictatorship, although not of sustaining it.

Para 3: B. Strengthening of executive and especially head of state, counter to the basic principles of democracy. Enabling Act 1933 granting legislative powers to chancellor (supporting detail).
- *Combination of presidency with chancellorship as Führer 1934*
- *Oath of allegiance to Führer*
- *Nazi agencies added to traditional ministries.*

Most important method of sustaining dictatorship, although not of introducing it. Also – more elements of inefficiency than with changes to legislature.

Para 4: C. Use of coercion and indoctrination to undermine alternative viewpoints and basic rights guaranteed by the 1919 Constitution:

- *Ban on trade unions and on opposition parties in the Reichstag*
- *Development of coercive institutions – SS, Gestapo, concentration camps*
- *Intensification of indoctrination: Ministry of People's Enlightenment and Propaganda; Goebbels*
- *Persecution of minorities, especially Jews*

Most important method of ensuring compliance to the new institutions – but after dictatorship had been established. Effectiveness varied, as there were flaws.

Para 5: D. The promotion of Nazism as an anti-democratic ideology:
- *Concept of Führerprinzip*
- *Concept of Volksgemeinschaft*
- *Concept of Aryanism and anti-Semitism*

The theory upon which it was all based. But the theory could not by itself have established the dictatorship.

Para 6: Integrated prioritisation. Numerous possible combinations!

20. Assess the effectiveness of indoctrination and propaganda in Nazi Germany.

Advice: *Define both terms concisely and focus on their effect. To do this you will need to establish what the methods were – but this should be related directly to their impact. One example could be that the measures concerning the Hitler Youth created a largely compliant youth, accepting their future roles (elaborate on this). But there was also a significant backlash against gender stereotyping and mindless obedience (examine the significance of youth opposition groups).*

21. To what extent do you agree that 'it was really the SS which ran Germany'?

Advice: *Be careful – this is not just about the SS. You need to balance your answer between those areas in Nazi Germany which the SS did control (security, secret police, concentration camps) and those which were the responsibility of other sectors (propaganda, legislation, foreign policy). At the same time, you could argue that the war greatly expanded the scope of the responsibility of the SS (which now dominated the army through the Waffen SS, administered the occupied areas in the east, and implemented the 'Final Solution'). 'To what extent' needs to be quantified (i.e. 'partly' or 'largely' rather than 'entirely' or 'not at all'.*

22. Assess the reasons for and strength of opposition to the Nazi regime.

Advice: *Give equal time to the two parts of the question. Assess means two things: (1) explain and (2) prioritise. In relation to (2) you need to explain why some factors are more important than others and also why the latter are less important.*

23. 'The German people benefited from Nazi economic policies.'
Do you agree?

Advice: *Avoid describing the policies. Instead, establish criteria for 'benefited' and develop a mixed response which can go either way in the conclusion. Coverage needs to include the reduction of unemployment, the conditions of work, the treatment of the consumer and the focus on rearmament.*

24. Why did the Nazi regime place such a strong emphasis on anti-Semitic measures?

Advice: *Avoid a straight description of anti-Semitic policies, although the measures do need to be specified. Reasons could include: (1) Hitler's ideas; (2) the use of scapegoat; and (3) persecution of a minority to unite the majority within the Volksgemeinschaft. The radicalising impact of the war can also be covered. You could also prioritise the reasons, in line with the instructions for 'assess', although 'why' would not involve quite so much emphasis on this: perhaps this could be confined to the final paragraph?*

Part 3: Sources

1. Nazi economic policy

This exercise consists of three questions on four sources, with a time allocation of 60 minutes

Source A: Extracts from Hitler's announcement of the Four Year Plan (1936)

Germany's economic situation is in the briefest outline as follows:

1. We are overpopulated and cannot feed ourselves from our own resources
   . . .
6. The final solution lies in extending our living space, that is to say, extending the sources of raw materials and foodstuffs of our people. It is the task of the political leadership one day to solve this problem.

I thus set the following tasks:

I. The German armed forces must be operational within four years.
II. The German economy must be fit for war within four years.

Source B: Schacht's comment, written in his autobiography in 1949, on the management of the Four Year Plan by Goering

Goering set out, with all the folly and incompetence of the amateur, to carry out the programme of economic self-sufficiency, or autarky, envisaged in the Four Year Plan. Goering's policy of recklessly exploiting Germany's economic substance necessarily brought me into more and more open conflict with him, and for his part he exploited his powers, with Hitler and the Party behind him, to counter my activity as Minister of Economics to an ever-increasing extent.

Source C: N. Henderson, *Failure of a Mission* (1940)

The strain, both mental and material, under which the German people had been working since 1933 was immense. It was estimated in 1938 that sixty per cent, or more of the sum of its efforts in human beings, labour, and materials were destined for war. No people, even though disciplined and hard-working as are the Germans, would put up indefinitely with guns instead of butter, or endure an economic policy based solely on the control of the whole of a nation's economic output in the interests of military preparedness. There was always the question, therefore, whether Hitler would not feel obliged to seek to conquer by force the markets which Germany had lost by over-concentration on armaments, or, in other words, be compelled to follow the road of further adventure, either in order to forestall economic collapse or as the result of it.

Source D: Index of industrial and consumer goods (1928 = 100)

	1928	1934	1936	1938
Industrial goods	100	81	114	144
Consumer goods	100	91	100	116

QUESTIONS WITH WORKED ANSWERS

a) **Study Source A and use your own knowledge. Explain 'The final solution lies in extending our living space'.** (20 marks)

Hitler had used the term 'living space' or *Lebensraum* in his two main works, *Mein Kampf* and the *Second Book*. By this he had meant expansion well beyond Germany's frontiers; in *Mein Kampf* he had stated that 'Our eyes turn towards the lands in the East'. Source A places the emphasis on economic fulfilment through territorial expansion – providing new areas for access to 'raw materials'. The 'final solution' meant permanent conquest rather than temporary diplomacy, which meant a close link with rearmament. Because of the strong racial context of *Lebensraum*, eastward expansion, when it came, brought extermination as well as conquest.

b) **Study Sources B and C and use your own knowledge. Compare Sources B and C as interpretations of the development of the Four Year Plan.** (40 marks)

Both sources are highly critical of the development of the Four Year Plan, although in different ways. The nature of these criticisms is strongly influenced by the status and intention of the two authors.

Criticism of the Four Year Plan shown in the two extracts is based on a different premise. Schacht's complaints are directed against Goering's 'folly' and 'incompetence' and his deliberate campaign to undermine and discredit Schacht by exploiting 'his powers' and contacts with Hitler and the party. Source C, by contrast, is a more general criticism of the whole nature of the plan which, in its implementation, put immense strains on the people; they would be unable to 'put up indefinitely with guns instead of butter' or to endure the sacrifice of 'economic interests' to 'military preparedness'. It should, however, be pointed out that Schacht, too, was a critic of rearmament, believing that this would ruin all of the economic advances he had made in his New Plan, introduced in 1934; this is hinted at in his reference to Goering 'recklessly exploiting Germany's economic substance' to achieve 'autarky'.

The authors each have a reason for the slant of their criticism. Henderson provides a liberal perspective which criticises the plan as a closed system which would inevitably lead to conflict ('further adventure'). Schacht's criticism focuses more on Goering since if Schacht had to administer the plan in its opening months, it would reflect more positively on himself to blame his rival's 'incompetence' rather than his own reluctance to make it work.

c) **Study Sources A to D and use your own knowledge. How clear were Hitler's economic objectives between 1936 and 1939?**   **(60 marks)**

Total (120 marks)

The sources, taken as a set, provide a mixed answer. Sources A and D seem to indicate a clear priority, an itemised approach to fulfilling it and evidence of at least partial success. Sources B and C, on the other hand, focus more on the confusion in the plan, in terms both of its purpose and its execution. This contrast reflects both the nature of the sources and a more general historical debate on Hitler's economic policy.

The impression created by Source A is of a simple and overriding objective: to achieve specific economic objective through rearmament and expansion. But was Hitler's policy really that direct? Source A is, in a sense, misleading since it would have been the end result of previous thought and, because it was a directive, would have been expressed in simple terms. But how clear was the thought behind it? There are two possibilities.

One is that Hitler was deliberately turning economic policy inside out and implementing the ideas expressed in *Mein Kampf*. He was therefore integrating economics into the art of war. This seems to be supported by the switch in the whole emphasis of industry shown in Source D: industrial goods (associated mostly with rearmament) growing at a much faster pace than consumer goods. It would also help to explain Schacht's deep concern about the plan in Source B. Goering was seen as an 'amateur' because he was taken in by the whole approach to 'economic self-sufficiency and autarky'. Since Schacht did not want in 1949 to admit that he was unable to lead the Four Year Plan Office, he blamed Goering for intriguing against him. In reality, however, he was convinced that Hitler's whole policy was a departure from normal economic principles. Schacht had spent the previous three years as Minister of Finance pursuing tight but conventional economic controls (often referred to as 'partial fascism') but now had to try to implement something Hitler had always intended.

The alternative view is that Hitler was moving towards a policy which was more pragmatic and **reactive** to events. War and expansion had become priorities, despite the warnings of Schacht.

Source C provides a remarkably perceptive reason why: Hitler was moving towards conquest of the 'markets which Germany had lost through over-concentration of armaments'. Hitler, in other words, was by the late 1930s abandoning the more controlled economic policies he had earlier favoured to something which was radically different. He felt impelled to do this for one of two reasons, both contained in Source C – either to 'forestall economic collapse' or 'as a result of it'. The former is the more likely since the Four Year Plan seemed to offer a strategy which would satisfy both the German consumer and military aspirations. Historians like Sauer and Klein have argued that Hitler created a 'plunder economy' which involved the conquest and absorption of other economies to prevent the sort of economic hardship being experience by the Soviet people under Stalin's Five Year Plans. But this was arrived at as a result of the situation in the late 1930s, not as the implementation of a long-term strategy.

Clarity depends on perspective. These sources therefore open up two quite different approaches. By any conventional definition of economic policy, however, the more feasible interpretation is probably the second. Hitler, Goering and others were clearer about *other* priorities and often confused their 'economic objectives' with military ones.

PARALLEL QUESTIONS WITHOUT WORKED ANSWERS

a) **Study Source A and use your own knowledge. Explain why Schacht and Goering disagreed over Germany's economic policy.** **(20 marks)**

Advice: *Use your own knowledge to explain the differences in Source A. This will involve the fundamentally different objectives of Schacht and Goering, as well as their personal rivalry.*

b) **Study Sources A and C and use your own knowledge. In what ways do Sources A and C differ in their interpretation of the effect of rearmament on the prosperity of the German people? How would you explain these differences?** **(40 marks)**

Advice: *Avoid writing a summary of Source A followed by a summary of Source C. Instead, find specific points on which the sources disagree and use brief extracts in quotation marks. Explain the differences in terms of the type, purpose and reliability of the two sources.*

c) **Study Sources A to D and use your own knowledge. Assess the view of Henderson in Source C that Hitler's expansionist policies would be either 'to forestall economic collapse or as the result of it'.** **(60 marks)**

Total (120 marks)

Advice: *Explain the argument of Source C and consider how the sources as a set relate to this. Then extend the range of the discussion to include your own knowledge of rearmament, Blitzkrieg, Lebensraum, etc., including specific comments on the individual sources as appropriate. Try to include comments on reliability where relevant.*

2. Nazi social policy

This exercise consists of three questions on two sources, with a time allocation of 45 minutes.

Source A: Hitler's 'Address to Women' at the Nuremberg Party Rally, 8 September 1934

We do not consider it correct for the woman to interfere in the world of the man, in his main sphere. We consider it natural if these two worlds remain distinct.

The sacrifices which the man makes in the struggle of his nation, the woman makes in the preservation of that nation in individual cases. What the man gives in courage on the battlefield, the woman gives in eternal self-sacrifice, in eternal pain and suffering. Every child that a woman brings into the world is a battle, a battle waged for the existence of her people.

Source B: Hitler speaking on 26 January 1942, from Hitler's *Table-Talk* (1991)

I detest women who dabble in politics. And if their dabbling extends to military matters, it becomes utterly unendurable. In no local section of the Party has a woman ever had the right to hold even the smallest post. It has therefore often been said that we were a party of misogynists, who regarded a woman only as a machine for making children, or else as a plaything. That's far from being the case. I attached a lot of importance to women in the field of the training of youth, and that of good works ... Everything that entails combat is exclusively men's business. There are so many other fields in which one must rely upon women. Organising a house, for example.

QUESTIONS WITH WORKED ANSWERS

a) **Study Sources A and B. Compare what the sources reveal about the contrasting roles of men and women in the Nazi system.** **(5 marks)**

The main similarities between the two sources lie in the concepts of service and sacrifice. Both men and women serve the 'nation' and therefore have complementary roles. Both have to be prepared for sacrifices, or 'struggle', men through 'courage on the battlefield' and women through the 'battle' of childbearing (Source A). Both would also be involved in 'training of youth' – women explicitly in Source B, men by implication in both sources. The differences are more obvious. The two areas which should be the exclusive preserve of men are 'politics' and 'military matters' (Source B). Women should be excluded entirely from these since combat was 'exclusively a man's business'. The equivalent for women would be 'good works' and 'organising a house'.

Source B is simpler and more direct than Source A mainly because it is less crafted and more spontaneous. While Source A is addressed to women, and would therefore represent Nazi views as noble sentiments, Source B reveals them for the prejudices they actually were ('I detest women who ...').

b) **Use your own knowledge. In what ways did the Nazi regime try to promote greater social cohesion in Germany?** (7 marks)

The Nazi regime aimed to promote greater social cohesion through a variety of policies.

One was the ending of class struggle, replacing it with the People's Community (*Volksgemeinschaft*). This was held together by Aryanism, with its emphasis on racial superiority, and anti-Semitism, with former class hatreds now targeted against a persecuted minority. Also part of this community was a careful separation of the functions of men and women, partly to prevent rivalry between them and partly to ensure the continuing importance of the family as the basic social unit. Any 'undesirable' social influences would be forcibly removed and the more 'desirable' social norms would be expressed through the indoctrination and propaganda organised by the controlled media. Meanwhile, those consumer desires which promoted rivalry would be controlled through the KdF and SdA, reinforced by statements by Goering that 'guns' were preferable to 'butter'. Above all, social cohesion was to be maintained through the *Führerprinzip*, the personification of the collective good.

c) **Use your own knowledge. Did Nazi social policies 'unite' the German people? Explain your answer.** (18 marks)

Total (30 marks)

Social policies were those which related to the welfare of the German people; they therefore covered education, the family and the workplace. Unity can mean two things – uniting round the regime or developing greater internal harmony. Both types were emphasised in Hitler's speeches. But the effectiveness, in both senses, varied considerably.

Potentially the most effective target was youth. The Nazi regime certainly tried everything to mould it. It made the Hitler Youth, with its various movements (DJV, HJ, JM and BDM) compulsory in 1935. It tried to establish a uniform youth culture, combined with the extensive restructuring of education and the curriculum in schools. It could not, however, eradicate the growth of widespread alternative cultures and organisations – the Swing movement, the Edelweiss Pirates, the Kittelbach Pirates and the Navajos, to name a few. From the late 1930s and throughout the war period, youth was therefore split between the conforming majority and an increasingly rebellious minority, some of whom joined resistance movements.

The impact of Nazi policies on family life are more difficult to assess. On the surface, the family was strengthened. Because of the special emphasis on the family in the Nazi system, there were lower divorce rates than in the Weimar Republic. Radio also made the family the main vehicle for the transmission of the regime's values. But the process brought its own strains which fractured as much as it united. Men and boys were elevated at the expense of women, who were increasingly repressed. Recent research has pointed to the growth of female resentment, even among women who played an active part within the Nazi organisation. This could be a powerful destabilising influence.

The workforce was, in theory, united by the abolition of trade unions and their substitution by the RAD, KdF and SdA. SOPADE reports often despaired at the degree of support shown to Hitler by former members of the SPD and KPD. Yet even here there was extensive grumbling, fed by envy and aggravated by shortages of consumer goods and extensive hours spent at work or in KdF activities. The workforce was also targeted by secret cells of SPD and KDP, although these were far from united in their opposition. Taking these points together, it could be argued that the working classes were, despite efforts made to assimilate them to Nazism, as divided as ever.

The regime tried to ensure social cohesion through ideological conformity. Germany had always been divided between secular and religious interests, the latter mainly between Protestant and Catholic. But Nazi ideology never came close to replacing religion, even though the Protestant churches were extensively reorganised and most Protestants tended to conform. The Catholic Church at times provided a rival focus for ideological unity and became more and more outspoken in its criticism of Nazi policies over, for example, education and euthanasia. The Nazis never managed to provide an alternative religion to unite the people, least of all during the war years, when numbers of Catholics and Protestants combined in minority resistance groups such as White Rose.

More controversial is the effect on the population of coercion and terror. Recent research has indicated the dependence of the Gestapo on informers from members of the public. This might be seen as widespread acceptance of the regime and a unity of common purpose. Alternatively, it might indicate the fracturing of society, as people were prepared to inform on their neighbours for the most dubious of motives.

Finally, the Nazi concept of unity meant the exclusion of part of the population. Anti-Semitism was intended to pull Aryans together as part of the *Volksgemeinschaft*. Actually it had strong potential to divide German society. While there were many Germans who participated readily in anti-Semitic activities, others accepted it uncomfortably (as with *Kristallnacht*) or tried to evade it because it reminded them too much of the thuggish element of Nazism advanced by the likes of Streicher.

Overall, Nazi Germany created an illusion of social unity by removing the institutions, like trade unions, which had promoted class or sectoral interests. But, despite the obvious conformity and levels of support for Hitler himself, German society remained fractured and deeply disturbed.

PARALLEL QUESTIONS WITHOUT WORKED ANSWERS

a) **Study Sources A and B. What do the sources reveal about the different ways in which Hitler expected men and women to engage in 'struggle'?** **(5 marks)**

Advice: *'Reveal' means direct statement and indirect inference. Cover both.*

b) **Use your own knowledge. Explain the meaning and purpose of the *Volksgemeinschaft* (People's Community).** **(7 marks)**

Advice: *Make sure that 'meaning' and 'purpose' are both covered. 'Purpose' will probably involve the larger part of the answer.*

c) **Use your own knowledge. Did Nazi social policies 'unite' the German people? Explain your answer.**   **(18 marks)**

Total (30 marks)

Advice: *Avoid writing a description of Nazi social policies. Instead, establish criteria for 'unite'. Two sides are clearly discernible for gender policies, indoctrination, life at work and the treatment of minorities – in fact for the* Volksgemeinschaft *as a whole.*

Part 4: Historical skills

  ## Presentation by PowerPoint

The Skills section in Chapter 5 covered the use of the overhead projector (OHP) in a presentation. Preparing a presentation with PowerPoint is more complicated but can look much more polished and professional. It is, however, possible to go overboard with the special effects. Keeping these as simple as possible will keep the focus on the topic covered, not the way in which it is being presented.

This section provides an introduction to the use of PowerPoint to make a presentation to the rest of the class. There are several advantages to this. A presentation can enhance a speech by sharpening the focus on the key points. The use of carefully chosen images can strengthen the impact of the argument in the presentation. And thinking about how the argument will be delivered should clarify the stages in the argument itself. The purpose of a presentation, together with the best ways of interacting with the audience, are dealt with on pages 258–61.

Using images requires preliminary practice and the slides of PowerPoint need to be prepared in advance. This can be more time-consuming than preparing view foils for the OHP, so the best advice is to keep the individual slides simple. Slides could contain:

* a title;
* brief notes in bullet points. It is important to avoid reading from full sentences in the slide; instead, use the bullet points as indicators and talk around them; and
* an illustration from the Internet or a diagram or chart prepared on the computer.

PREPARING A POWERPOINT – THE TECHNICALITIES

Setting up the template:

* *Start > Programs > Office 2000 > Microsoft PowerPoint > Blank presentation > OK*
* **Choose an Auto Layout** > select top left-hand frame > **OK**
* First frame appears (for title); position cursor to right of small box on left; **Enter** 10 times for 10 text frames.

Preparing text for slides:

* Return cursor to first box (title); add title and sub-title; control size of letters in usual way.
* Return cursor to subsequent boxes; insert title and main text in boxes.

Using colour

- <u>A</u> controls colour of text; **paint can** (two to left of <u>A</u>) controls colour of background box.

Setting up diagrams

- Base any diagram on a series of boxes. Click ☐ on lower toolbar, position, adjust from corner, add text box (two to the right of ☐).
- Insert text and colour.
- Add links from *AutoShapes* > choose from selection.

Getting images from the Internet

- Go to a good Internet search engine > *Images* > enter your choice of topic
- Left click on selected Internet image to enlarge > Right click once on the enlarged image > *Save picture as* > scroll to selected area (*My Pictures* or whatever); change name of image > *Save*.

Adding images to the presentation

- Return to PowerPoint; go to chosen slide > *Insert* > *Picture* > *From File* > *My Pictures* (or whatever) > *Insert*
- Adjust location from inside image; adjust size from corner of image.

Preparing for display

To control speed: Click on text or image > *Slide Show* > *Preset Animation* > *Camera* (or whatever) for each item.

To set up display

Five options at top of lower toolbar:
- Far left: the one you are on: slide and text.
- Next right: mostly text.
- Next right: all slide.
- Next right: all the slides. To add one, click between two frames, click *Common Tasks* at top > *New Slide* > choose *Auto Layout* > *OK*. Return to 1 or 2 to work on it.

Far right: PowerPoint slide show. Double-click to start. To end, click left part of box in left hand corner > *End Show*. Takes you back to the five options.

OUTLINE OF A POSSIBLE PRESENTATION

The theme in this case is the way in which the Nazi regime destroyed the democratic system established by the Weimar Republic. There are ten slides altogether, each containing a combination of images and brief text. Each slide will have to be explained in further detail. Many people add too much text to each slide – and then proceed to read from it. Avoid this at all costs.

Slide title: From Democracy to Dictatorship

Find on the Internet an image which epitomises this – and insert above or below the title.

Slide title: Weimar democracy

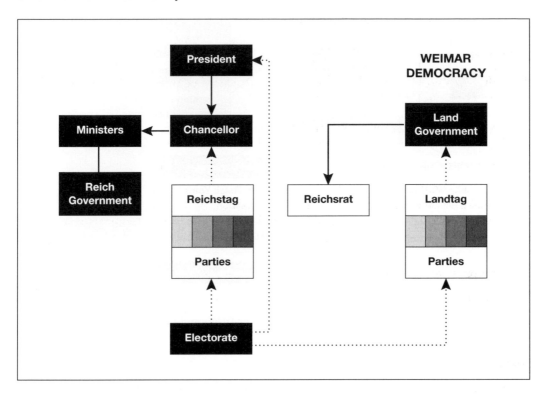

Commentary: Explain the key features of the Weimar democracy as shown in this diagram.

- There is a federal system with central (Reich) institutions and local (*Land*) government.
- There are executive powers (in black) and legislative powers (in white).
- Some of the institutions are elected (------➤), some are appointed (——➤).
- This all adds up to a democracy based on 'balanced powers' – until the balance stopped working in 1931.

Slide title: The importance of the Reichstag

Find on the Internet a photograph of the Reichstag in session. Insert into the slide and include a few key bullet points below it as to the importance of the Reichstag for democracy.

Slide title: Chancellors of the democratic Republic

Find on the Internet photographs of Scheidemann, Stresemann and Müller. Insert side by side on the slide and follow with a few bullet points on how democracy encouraged moderate policies.

Slide title: Nazi dictatorship

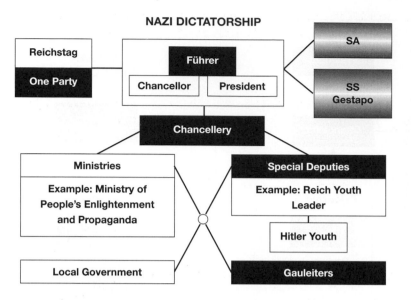

Commentary: Explain the key features of the Nazi dictatorship and the way in which it departed from Weimar democracy.

■ ■ ▦ Several new institutions were introduced.

▢ Several traditional institutions were retained but their powers were altered.

Dictatorship resulted from destroying the balance of democracy established by Weimar. The offices of Chancellor and President were merged into that of Führer. The Reichstag was weakened and made into a one-party chamber. Nazi agencies were set up alongside traditional ones. Special emphasis was given to:

■ terror (SA, SS, Gestapo) and

▦ indoctrination and propaganda

Refer to some of the details behind this interpretation – for example, the Enabling Act (1933), the Law Against the New Formation of Parties (1933), the merging of the chancellorship and presidency (1934), etc. A more advanced approach could explain the competing jurisdictions between the traditional institutions and the new agencies.

Slide title: The Führer in the Reichstag

Find on the Internet a photograph of Hitler as Führer speaking in the *Reichstag*. Follow this on the slide by a few bullet points explaining the change in the functions of the Reichstag.

Slide title: The *Führerprinzip*

Find on the Internet a propaganda image of Hitler which, in your view, epitomises the Hitler personality cult. Insert this into the slide and follow with bullet points on how leadership in the Nazi dictatorship differed from that in Weimar democracy.

Slide title: Indoctrination and propaganda

Find on the Internet a photograph of Goebbels and a propaganda poster for the Hitler Youth. Insert into the slide and follow with bullet points as to how indoctrination and propaganda negated democracy.

Slide title: Terror

Find on the Internet photographs of Himmler and Heydrich. Insert into the slide and follow with bullet points as to how terror underpinned dictatorship and destroyed democracy.

Slide title: Conclusion

Find an image and a quotation which aptly summarises the transition from democracy to dictatorship in Germany.

References

1. J. Remak (ed.), *The Nazi Years* (Englewood Cliffs, NJ 1969), p. 62
2. Ibid., p. 54
3. K.D. Bracher, *The German Dictatorship* (New York 1970)
4. M. Broszat, *Hitler and the Collapse of the Weimar Republic* (Oxford 1987)
5. S.H. Hoene, *The Order of the Death's Head* (London 1972), p. 12
6. Quoted in K.M. Mallman and G. Paul, 'Omniscient, Omnipotent, Omnipresent? Gestapo, society and resistance', in D.F. Crew (ed.), *Nazism and German Society 1933–1945* (London 1994), p. 169
7. Ibid., p. 169
8. K.M. Mallman and G. Paul, 'Omniscient, Omnipotent, Omnipresent? Gestapo, society and resistance', in D. Crew (ed.), *Nazism and German Society 1933–1945* (London 1994), p. 169
9. J. Noakes and G. Pridham, *Nazism* (Exeter 1996), p. 281

Sources

1A. Adapted from J. Noakes and G. Pridham, ibid. (Exeter 1996), p. 281–7
1B. Schacht's comment, written in his autobiography in 1949, on the management of the Four Year Plan by Goering. Source unavailable.
1C. N. Henderson, *Failure of a Mission* (London 1940), pp. 198–9
1D. Index of industrial and consumer goods. Source unavailable.
2A. Hitler's Address to Women, 1934, quoted in J. Laver: *Nazi Germany 1933–1945* (London 1991), p. 64
2B. From Hitler's *Table-Talk*, quoted in J. Laver: op. cit., p. 64

Chapter 7

Russia and the Soviet Union, 1918–53

This chapter will consider the regime of Lenin (1918–24), including its survival in the civil war and the implementation of political, social and economic changes. It will also deal with the succession to Lenin, the emergence of Stalin and the style of his dictatorship between 1929 and 1953.

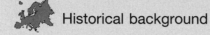 ## Historical background

Bolshevik rule, 1918–24
The rise of Stalin, 1924–29
Stalin's rule, 1929–41
Foreign policy and war
The period, 1945–53
After Stalin

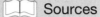 ## Sources

1. Life in the Soviet Union, 1928–41
2. Stalin's purges

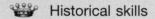 ## Historical skills

Coursework and individual studies

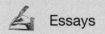 ## Essays

Bolshevik rule, 1918–24
The rise of Stalin, 1924–29
Stalin's rule, 1929–41
Foreign policy and war
The period, 1945–53

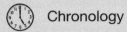 Chronology

1918	(January) Closing of the Constituent Assembly
	(March) Withdrawal from First World War at Brest-Litovsk
	Constitution of the RSFSR
1918–21	Russian Civil War
	War Communism
1921	Kronstadt uprising
	New Economic Policy
1924	Death of Lenin
	Triumvirate (Stalin, Kamenev, Zinoviev)
1927–7	Stalin vs Left Opposition (Trotsky, Kamenev, Zinoviev)
1927–9	Stalin vs Rightists (Bukharin, Rykov, Tomsky)
1928	Requisitioning Crisis
1929	Introduction of collectivisation
1928–33	First Five Year Plan
1934–38	Second Five Year Plan
1936	Constitution
1937–8	Peak of the Purges
1938–41	Third Five Year Plan
1939	Nazi–Soviet Non-Aggression Pact
1939–40	Russo-Finnish War
1941	Nazi invasion of USSR
1941–45	Great Patriotic War
1945	Yalta Conference (Stalin, Roosevelt, Churchill)
	Potsdam Conference (Stalin, Truman, Attlee)
1945–51	Fourth Five Year Plan
1947	Establishment of Comecon
1947	Zhdanov Decrees
1947–8	Berlin Crisis
1951	Leningrad affair
1953	Death of Stalin
	Collective leadership of Khrushchev, Malenkov, Bulganin
1956	Supremacy of Khrushchev
	Destalinisation policy

Part 1: Historical background

Bolshevik rule, 1918–24

Although the Bolsheviks had seized power from the Provisional Government in October 1917, the permanence of their regime was by no means a foregone conclusion. After all, two political systems had already collapsed, within seven months of each other: why should a third be any more successful? If anything, the situation faced by the Bolsheviks appeared even worse, since they soon faced a wider range of opposition than the Provisional Government.

Early in 1918 Lenin came to the conclusion that it was too dangerous for Russia to continue its role in the First World War. In March, therefore, Trotsky signed the Treaty of Brest-Litovsk, dictated to Russia by the victorious German armies. This resulted in a huge loss of territory, including Finland, Baltic States, Poland, Byelorussia and Ukraine. Trotsky justified this 'disgraceful settlement' on the grounds that it would save the new regime.

Even before the withdrawal from the war with Germany, the Bolsheviks were facing stiff internal resistance. Initially this was from the Socialist Revolutionaries, whose origins and development to 1917 are covered in Chapter 2. Aggrieved that they had won the elections for the Constituent Assembly, only to find that Lenin had dissolved the Assembly in January 1918, the Socialist Revolutionaries set up a series of rival governments to the west of the Bolshevik-controlled area. The early phase of the conflict was therefore between Bolsheviks (**Reds**) and other revolutionary groups (**Greens**). During the course of 1918 some of the rival governments were overthrown by counter-revolutionary groups (**Whites**), led by ex-tsarist officers; they aimed to restore the earlier system of government, although it was never quite clear precisely what this was to be. A number of powers provided military assistance to the Whites – especially Britain, the United States, France and Japan. Bolshevik Russia was therefore under attack from all directions. Yudenitch advanced along the Baltic coast to threaten Petrograd (which forced the Bolsheviks to transfer the capital to Moscow); Kolchak's armies moved westwards from Siberia and the Urals, while further east Semenov established control with the help of the Japanese. The most dangerous threat, however, came from the south, with offensives launched by Alexeyev, Deniken, Kornilov and Wrangel.

By 1922 most of the threats to the Bolshevik state had been overcome, as a result partly of the internal organisation created by Trotsky and partly of the deficiencies of the Greens and Whites (Essay 1b). In the process of conquering the whole of Russia, the Bolsheviks also won back Byelorussia and part of the Ukraine (although part of the latter was lost to Poland in the Russo-Polish War of 1920–1).

The Russian Civil War, meanwhile, acted as a catalyst for major social, political and economic changes. Socially, the main emphasis was on the promotion of equality through ending class differences and gender-based discrimination, and minimising wage differentials (Essay 2a). Politically, Russia became a monolithic dictatorship (Essay 2b). Lenin destroyed the possibility of any Western style of democracy by closing the Constituent Assembly in January 1918. He substituted a one-party system, which dominated the structure of soviets established throughout Russia. In 1918 he set up the Russian Federated Socialist Republic (**RSFSR**), which was followed by the Union of Soviet Socialist Republics (**USSR**), designed in 1922 and implemented in 1924. All other parties – the Constitutional Democrats, Socialist Revolutionaries and Mensheviks especially – were eliminated and, between 1918 and 1921, the Bolshevik-controlled areas came under the grip of the ***Cheka***

(Extraordinary Commission for the Suppression of Counter Revolution, Speculation and Sabotage). Attempts were also made to radicalise the economy (Essay 3a) through the introduction of **War Communism** in 1918. By 1921, however, this had been such a disastrous failure that Lenin was forced to make a strategic retreat into the New Economic Policy (**NEP**) which allowed for a mixture of private ownership and 'state capitalism'. Hence the economic changes between 1918 and 1924 proved to be far less extensive than the social and political (Essay 3b).

From 1922 onwards, Lenin ceased to be in effective political control, following a series of incapacitating strokes. In January 1924 the creator of the Bolshevik state died, leaving unsettled the whole issue of the succession.

Figure 7.1 *Lenin and Stalin together*

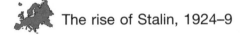

The rise of Stalin, 1924–9

In his *Political Will and Testament* (1922) and the Codicil added in 1923, Lenin passed over Trotsky and other contemporaries as his successor – and particularly warned against the elevation of Stalin. On the latter he went further, advising Stalin's dismissal from his post of general secretary of the Communist Party.

Yet, despite these recommendations, Stalin rose rapidly up the leadership hierarchy to establish supreme personal authority by 1929 (Essay 4a). He did this despite the strong claims of a variety of other candidates, especially Trotsky, Kamenev, Zinoviev, Bukharinn, Rykov and Tomsky. Between 1924 and 1925 Stalin became part of the Triumvirate, a collective leadership shared with Kamenev and Zinoviev. At this stage Trotsky was isolated. Between 1924 and 1927, however, he was joined by Kamenev and Zinoviev in the Left Opposition. Stalin, meanwhile had gained the support of the Rightists – Bukharin, Rykov and Tomsky – and, with their support, removed the Left from contention. Then, between 1927 and 1929, Stalin isolated and defeated the Rightists to emerge as the individual successor to Lenin. The reasons for this transformation and victory are covered in Essay 4b.

Stalin's rise was accompanied by some complex and important changes in policy. Whilst a member of the Triumvirate, Stalin had committed himself to **Socialism in One Country**, the key components of which were a domestic rather than an international focus and the continuation of the moderation of the New Economic Policy (NEP). Trotsky, by contrast, advocated **Permanent Revolution**; this involved spreading revolution abroad and, at home, reversing the NEP in favour of forced **collectivisation** and rapid industrialisation. By 1927, however, Stalin was changing part of the emphasis of Socialism in One Country. He maintained the domestic focus and was not interested in exporting revolution – but he had come to the conclusion that the NEP should be replaced by collectivisation and a centralised plan for industry. These details are explained in Essay 4a. In 1927 Stalin introduced the forced requisitioning of grain which he followed, in 1928 by a programme to replace the private ownership of land with collective farms (**Kolkhozy**). In 1929 he overlapped this with the First Five Year Plan, by which the Central Planning Bureau (**Gosplan**) set new targets for industrial production. Whether Stalin made these adjustments out of conviction, political expediency or the needs of the moment, is discussed in Essay 5.

By 1929 Stalin had removed all his rivals both from the **Politburo** and from the Central Committee of the Party. Bukharin predicted ominously that Stalin was a 'political intriguer' who 'will strangle us'.

 ## Stalin's rule, 1929–41

Stalin extended the regime of Lenin into a more systematic and ruthless dictatorship. He did this by personalising his control over the Communist Party, by instituting the most widespread terror the country had ever seen and by creating a command economy. The key to the early changes was rapid industrialisation, intended to build the Soviet Union into a superpower. The various reasons for this are discussed in Essay 6: the main priorities were the defence of the regime against external capitalist powers and the internal pursuit of socialism by the removal of all remaining class distinctions.

The most notorious of all of Stalin's policies was the spread of terror. This started at the beginning of the 1930s with the action taken against peasants who refused to join collective farms, as well as against managers in industry. The purges were then increasingly politicised from 1934 onwards as the NKVD (People's Commissariat for Internal Affairs) hunted down those accused of action against the state. These included prominent Bolsheviks who had played a major role in the Revolution: the 1936 show trial disposed of Kamenev and Zinoviev, Piatakov and Sokolnikov following in 1937 and Bukharin and Rykov in 1938. The purges also swept through the Party Central Committee, the army and navy, and all factories and collective farms. To some extent the terror was precautionary (Essay 7a). The reasons are controversial, ranging from interpretations based on Stalin's personal paranoia to his need for coercion to underpin the command economy (Essay 7b). The way in which this terror fitted into the rest of Stalin's system is analysed in Essay 7c.

Did all these measures actually work? The impact of the purges has been extensively debated, some historians seeing it as cataclysmic (Essay 8), others arguing that it may have been exaggerated. Stalin's industrialisation also attracts a split verdict (Essay 10). On the one hand, it has been argued that the Five Year Plans set up the infrastructure which enabled the Soviet Union to defeat Nazi Germany in the Second World War. On the other hand, there has been extensive criticism of Stalin's starving of the consumer sector – and some recent reconsideration of the effectiveness of the whole planning system. There has always been more uniformity about the impact of the agricultural policies, as is explained in Essay 9.

How did the Stalinist regime affect the Soviet people? Clearly they would have been extensively involved in the purges and in the economic changes. But they would also have been brought within the scope of a totalitarian regime (Essay 11a) which aimed to institutionalise the values of the Revolution through the establishment of cultural uniformity (Essay 11b). Social values were heavily underscored by Stalin's ideas, although whether Stalin was more revolutionary – or more traditional – than Lenin is now widely debated (Essay 11c). The whole system was enhanced by the personality cult which did much to keep Stalin's position intact between 1929 and 1941.

 Foreign policy and war

Stalin's main interest was in domestic issues; he did not share Trotsky's commitment to making the Soviet Union the centre of international revolutionary activity. Nevertheless, he could not avoid becoming actively involved in foreign policy between 1924 and 1941, the complexity of which is explained in Chapter 8, Essay 19.

The Bolshevik period (1917–24) had seen a shift from open revolutionary activity to coexistence with the West, based on the establishment of trading relations with selected capitalist states. This continued for a while under Stalin. Britain, for example, provided investments for the Soviet Union in 1924, along with diplomatic recognition – although both were subsequently withdrawn by Baldwin's Conservative government. The main connection was, however, with Germany, with whom the Soviet Union signed the Rapallo Agreement (1921) and the Treaty of Berlin (1926). Through the latter Stalin's regime secured German credits and investment in return for secret use of Russian territory for German military exercises. This approach seemed well established for the future.

Yet, between 1929 and 1933, Stalin seemed to undergo a major change of mind (Essay 12). He became increasingly suspicious of the West and was determined to avoid any dependence on Western funding for his Five Year Plans. In any case, he was convinced that the Great Depression indicated the crisis of capitalism and that it was time to isolate the Soviet Union from the source of infection. As for Germany, Stalin no longer valued the agreements of the 1920s. By 1932 he was actually contributing to the rise of Hitler by instructing the German Communist Party (KPD) not to collaborate with the moderate parties to keep the Republic afloat. Then, in 1935, he began to move back towards the democratic states by forming an alliance with France and Czechoslovakia and by assisting the Republican side in the Spanish Civil War. By 1939, however, the regime was once again in direct communication with Germany. In August 1939 the Russian Foreign Minister, Molotov, signed with his German counterpart, von Ribbentrop, the Nazi–Soviet Non-Aggression Pact. This guaranteed that each would remain neutral in the event of either being at war with a third power. A secret additional protocol also made possible the partition of Poland between Germany and Russia – which was actually carried out in September 1939. The reasons for these apparently inconsistent policies are dealt with in Essay 13.

Relations between the Soviet Union and Germany deteriorated between 1939 and 1941, leading to Hitler launching Operation Barbarossa on the Soviet Union. This attack came as a complete surprise to Stalin and Soviet forces were driven back. By 1942 Poland, Byelorussia, the Ukraine and part of Russia itself had been occupied by the German armies. The Soviet Union was in danger of total collapse (Essay 14). The year 1943, however, saw the beginning of a long recovery (Essay 15). Starting with the Battle for Stalingrad, this developed, via the Battle of Kursk, into the reoccupation of the western area of the Soviet Union and the invasion of other countries occupied by the Nazis. By 1945 Soviet troops had captured Berlin and Stalin was negotiating with Britain and the United States at Yalta and Potsdam over the future boundaries of central and eastern Europe.

The war with Germany had a huge impact. Essay 16 examines the Soviet Union's military collapse and revival, economic adjustments and social upheaval. Above all, the country experienced catastrophic losses and unprecedented levels of destruction, to which Stalin had to turn his attention in 1945.

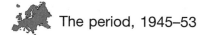 ## The period, 1945–53

Stalin emerged from the Second World War with his regime greatly strengthened. Or did he? The traditional view is that the period 1945–53 represents the peak of his personal power and security. It was also a vindication of all his earlier policies, which he was now able to resume after interruption by the war years. A more recent argument, however, is that Stalin was somewhat insecure during this period and that he was forced to reintroduce older policies to restore his position. Either view can be used to explain the main events which followed Soviet victory in 1945 (Essay 17).

Politically, Stalin restored the emphasis on personal rule which had characterised his pre-war regime, although whether this was motivated by security or insecurity is debatable. He wound up the wartime State Defence Committee (**GOKO**) through which he had shared the decision-making process with the military. He also revived his earlier policy of ignoring the party, rarely consulting the Politburo or summoning a Party Congress. A more sinister development was the revival of the purges through a new round of hectic activity by the NKVD under Beria. The Zhdanov Decrees of 1946, meanwhile, re-established tight ideological controls over Soviet culture.

The economy was also recentralised. The planning system, suspended after the German invasion of 1941, was restored with the introduction of the fourth and fifth Five Year Plans (1945–50 and 1950–5). Once again these emphasised collective farming and the promotion of heavy industry at the expense of consumerism. During the last phase of Stalin's leadership the Soviet economic infrastructure had to support the world's largest standing army and the emergence of a new nuclear capacity. Whether or not the economic policies were successful is examined in Essay 19.

Another vital component of the period was the development of the Cold War. Rivalries emerged between Stalin and Western leaders in 1945 at Yalta and Potsdam. The Soviet Union gained control over the eastern zone of Germany, along with Poland, Hungary, Czechoslovakia, Romania and Bulgaria; these were converted from broadly based regimes into Soviet puppets. To institutionalise Soviet hegemony Stalin ensured economic and ideological hegemony through the formation of **Comecon** and *Cominform*. At the same time, he applied pressure to the Western powers by blockading Berlin in 1948 and providing logistical support for communist North Korea in 1950. It appeared that Stalin had raised his sights and transformed himself from a class warrior into a Cold Warrior (Essay 18).

 ## After Stalin

On his death in 1953 Stalin had no obvious successor. For a time, therefore, the Soviet Union reverted to a period of collective leadership; there is therefore a parallel between the periods 1953–6 and 1924–9. From an initial Triumvirate which also included Bulganin and Malenkov, Khrushchev emerged supreme by 1956, just as Stalin had risen above Kamenev and Zinoviev to establish his own ascendancy by 1929.

There, however, the parallel ended. Whereas Stalin had derived legitimacy from Lenin as his predecessor, Khrushchev proceeded to denounce Stalin's record of leadership. From 1956 onwards he launched a campaign of **destalinisation**, which was intensified in 1960. By this, Stalin was associated with the capricious distortion of power which, it was claimed, distinguished his tyranny from the more legitimate 'dictatorship of the proletariat' set up by Lenin. In a way, Bukharin had anticipated this in the 1920s, accusing Stalin of 'confusing the dictatorship of the proletariat with dictatorship *over* the proletariat'.

Part 2: Essays

 Bolshevik rule, 1918–24

1. (a) What was the Russian Civil War (1918–22) about?   **(15 marks)**

The usual view of the Russian Civil War is that it was a struggle between the Reds, trying to save the Bolshevik Revolution, and the Whites, attempting to overthrow it. This is the truth – but not the whole truth. Also involved were other revolutionaries, generally known as the Greens, who had an influence on the outcome of the war.

The first challenge to the Bolsheviks came early in 1918 from other groups within Russia, especially the Socialist Revolutionaries and Mensheviks, collectively called by some historians the 'Greens'. These were aggrieved by Lenin's refusal to share power, even though the Socialist Revolutionaries had won the election to the Constituent Assembly in January. They therefore set up rival governments to the east of the area controlled by the Bolsheviks, especially in the Volga area, in the Urals at Omsk and the northern region of Ufa. These were, however, overthrown in mid-1918 by a series of military coups led by ex-tsarist officers like Kolchak, who then turned their attention on Lenin's regime.

This brought about the main conflict of the war which *was* between the Reds and the Whites. The issue was now simpler; from being what type of revolution would be permanent control, it was now whether any form of revolution would even survive. The Bolshevik area was surrounded by White offensives, led by former tsarist commanders like Kolchak, Kornilov, Deniken, Alexeyev and Wrangel. Their aim was to destroy communism and to substitute an alternative regime – although the execution of the Tsar and his family made it difficult for the Whites to agree on what type of regime this should be. Among the Whites were others who hoped for the establishment of a more progressive system along the lines of the Provisional Government. Also involved were a number of foreign powers (Britain, the United States, Canada, France and Italy) who hoped that a regime replacing the Bolsheviks would put Russia back into the First World War and undermine the German offensives being launched in 1918. There was also a general fear of the spread of communism to the rest of Europe, which sharpened the ideological focus of this stage of the Civil War. This involvement was, however, shortlived and the intervention was ended in 1919 as the failure of the Whites became increasingly likely.

The defeat of the Whites did not bring the end of the Civil War. Instead, the initiative returned in 1920 to the other, non-Bolshevik, revolutionaries. From that stage until its eventual victory in 1922, Lenin's regime was challenged in 36 provinces by 165 peasant armies, 140 of which were connected with the Socialist Revolutionaries. This is seen by some historians as a second 'Green' phase.[1] The insurgents aimed to destroy communism, which was seen as too repressive. The peasant armies used slogans such as 'Soviets without Communists' and demanded free elections and an end to enforced requisitioning of grain. Attempts were made by the Socialist Revolution-aries to co-ordinate the uprisings, but these resulted only in the ruthless elimination of all non-Bolshevik parties and the show-trials of Socialist Revolutionary and Menshevik leaders. By 1922 the regime was in full control, having weathered opposition both from White counter-revolutionaries and from alternative Green revolutionary strategies.

b) Why were the Bolsheviks able to beat off these challenges? (15 marks)

Two major reasons for the victory of the Bolsheviks were, first, the divided nature of the opposi-tion to them and, second, the effectiveness of the Bolshevik war effort. These were interdependent. The Bolsheviks were very much on the defensive and therefore were fortunate to have benefited greatly from the weakness of their enemies; at the same time, they were sufficiently well organ-ised to make their own luck at crucial moments.

The greatest threat to the Bolsheviks probably came in the first year of the Civil War – from the other revolutionary groups, especially the Socialist Revolutionaries. There was a real danger that these might displace the Bolshevik regime or at least prevent it from spreading much beyond the Russian heartland. The Bolsheviks were, however, reprieved by major divisions amongst their opponents. The Socialist Revolutionaries had administrations spread over a wide area, while the Mensheviks, also aiming for political control, had little in common with the Socialist Revolutionaries other than their opposition to Lenin's regime. But what really benefited the Bolsheviks were the military coups, organised by ex-tsarist officers, in the Socialist Revolutionary areas. Thus one anti-Bolshevik force disposed of another. At the same time, Lenin was well prepared to take on the White threat in the east. This was because he had ended Russia's partic-ipation in the First World War by the Treaty of Brest-Litovsk with Germany (March 1918). In August 1918 the Bolsheviks also drew up a trade agreement with Germany. As a result of these, the German military threat was removed from the west, enabling the Bolsheviks to concentrate on the situation developing to their east and to capture key areas like Kazan and Samara.

The main period of the White offensive against the Bolsheviks also showed a complete contrast between the two sides. Lenin was fortunate in facing an enemy which had no single political base, no common aim and a lack of military co-ordination. The lack of a single overall White regime was due largely to the way in which the Whites had emerged from the wreckage of Socialist Revolutionary governments. The Bolsheviks, on the other hand, tightened their political grip on their own area through political restructuring based on the soviets and Communist Party and reinforced with the use of the *Cheka*. The Whites also lacked any coherent ideology and made no attempt to persuade the people. This gave the Bolsheviks the opportunity to make effective use of their own measures, based on posters and leaflets which were distributed by *agitprop* trains. The Whites did have the theoretical military advantage of surrounding the Bolsheviks – but failed to develop an appropriate military strategy. The Bolsheviks were fortunate that the main White offen-sives occurred at different times to each other. Hence the campaigns of Yudenitch, threatening Petrograd from the west were not timed to link up with the invasion of Kolchak from the east or Deniken and Wrangel from the south. In these circumstance the Bolsheviks benefited from their control of Russia's industrial heartland and the main rail network, which radiated outwards from Moscow. They used the interior lines of communication for the rapid transfer of troops to deal with the White threats as they occurred. Instead of a weakness, therefore, being surrounded by their enemies was converted by the Bolsheviks into a positive advantage.

The contrasts between the divisions amongst the Whites and the co-ordination of the Reds became increasingly apparent in 1919. The Whites, for example, lost the support of the major powers, which decided to end their intervention. Not that this had counted for much in the first place: their role had been to protect supply lines, and none had participated in any of the battles. Governments had also come under pressure at home not to continue their support for right-wing groups which were known to be anti-democratic. Here the Bolsheviks ensured that they kept at least some contact with Western trade union movements and managed to earn considerable sympathy from them. Deprived of essential military supplies, the strength of the Whites drained away. At the very same time, the Bolsheviks steadily increased theirs, largely as a result of the measures taken by Trotsky to develop a new and powerful force. Using the Revolutionary Military Committee, or Red Guard, as the base, he established a Red Army of 5.5 million men. This was composed of recruits who were given a short period of intensive training and commanded by former tsarist officers whose loyalty to the new regime was guaranteed by political commissars.

As soon as the White threat had been disposed of, by 1920, the Bolsheviks were able to switch their attention to dealing with the revival of internal opposition. Although this was formidable, it was even more divided than the previous examples. There were over 150 peasant armies, some of which had effective leaders like Antonov. But there was virtually no co-ordination between them, or with their political supporters, the Socialist Revolutionaries who supported them. The Bolsheviks successfully used three strategies to overcome this last wave of opposition and to extend their control over the whole of Russia. The first was the type of military campaign which had been so successful against the Whites: swift and decisive. The second was the removal of any remaining political base by the ruthless suppression of the Mensheviks and Socialist Revolutionaries, thus depriving the peasant armies of any longer-term political aims. Finally, the regime aimed from 1921 to win over the peasantry, thereby preventing them from joining the insurgents. This was done through the introduction of the New Economic Policy (NEP) as a replacement for War Communism – which had done much to stir up the opposition in the first place.

2. (a) **How did the Bolsheviks change Russian society between 1918 and 1924?**   **(15 marks)**

The Bolshevik regime had an immense impact on Russian society, for reasons which were both intended and unintended.

Lenin intended nothing less than the social reorientation of all Russians. He was certainly influenced by the long-term Marxist vision of the 'classless society' and the preliminary stage necessary to reach it – the 'dictatorship of the proletariat'. To achieve both he identified the main priority as egalitarianism. The focus on social equality had the additional advantage of compensating for the obvious drift to political authoritarianism in politics – and for no obvious drift anywhere in the economy. Class distinctions were officially abolished by decree as early as November 1917 and replaced by a single citizenship. A particularly important change was the introduction of gender equality – for the first time in Russia's history. Women were given equal rights to men and were encouraged to join all sectors of the workforce. Equality of educational opportunity was guaranteed by the end of formal examinations, even for entry to higher education, and by the rapid spread of literacy by enthusiastic and committed volunteers. Wages, too, were brought into line with an industrial norm. Even culture was affected. Writers and painters were encouraged to avoid 'elitist' issues, while orchestras became more 'democratic' in the absence of conductors, who were seen as musical 'dictators'. In practice, of course, all this was intended to conceal the growth of political 'harmony', under a new 'conductor'.

The Bolshevik regime also reorientated Russia's key social institutions. Lenin downgraded the family, in line with the original Marxist view that the family was an institutionalised form of repression for women. Under the Bolsheviks, divorce and abortion were readily available and 'free love' given official sanction. The results, however, were social dislocation and juvenile delinquency on such a scale that later communist policy, starting with Stalin, made the family the key social institution within the state. Another target for the Bolsheviks was religion, once described by Marx as 'the opium of the masses'. Clearly it had no official place in a society now dominated by an ideology which was both atheistic and materialistic. In February 1918, therefore, the Church was separated from education and was no longer afforded any protection by the state. Meanwhile, education itself was given a more informal structure, with much less emphasis on formal class-rooms and uniforms. Again, this was something which Stalin later felt compelled to reverse – on the grounds that it had led directly to a fall in educational standards.

The unintended social dislocation which occurred during the Bolshevik regime was a direct result of the Civil War, the second most destructive in human history. At least 8.2 million civilians died, through atrocities, famine or disease. The survivors experienced – or participated – in widespread looting, which had an enormous impact on Russia's infrastructure. In some areas social order and convention broke down totally, resulting in the reversion to barbarism in its most basic form – killing other humans as a supply of food. In the final analysis, it is hard to assess whether the failure of some of the Bolshevik policies was due to unsound principles or to the disastrous circumstances in which they were introduced.

b) Why is it possible to call Bolshevik Russia (1918–24) a 'political dictatorship'?   **(15 marks)**

The term dictatorship is generally applicable to Russia between 1918 and 1924. Although mitigating explanations have been given for each step, the actual results still fulfilled all the criteria for dictatorship.

One of these is the removal of free elections and effective legislative powers. In January 1918, Lenin dissolved the Constituent Assembly and declared the elections to it void. Instead, he introduced a system of soviets as the main form of political representation. Lenin's justification for this was that Russia had to move away from Western institutions and that 'a republic of soviets is a higher form of democratic principle than the customary bourgeois republic with its Constituent Assembly'. But this was an excuse. The actual reason was that the Socialist Revolutionaries had scored a resounding victory in the elections to the Assembly and therefore had a strong democratic claim to have at least a share in government with the Bolsheviks. Lenin's refusal to let them do this was the first open sign of the Bolshevik move towards a post-revolutionary dictatorship.

A second component of dictatorship is the development of a one-party system. Lenin's actions here were quite uncompromising. Every effort was taken to remove opposition groups and to strengthen the Bolshevik (now Communist) Party so that it controlled all the soviets and also the government administration. To achieve this, 'the strictest centralism and the most severe discipline are an absolute necessity'. The key to this was the Central Committee, with its three specialist organs – the *Politburo*, *Orgburo* and Secretariat. Again, this process was defended as a form of democracy, although this was a new style labelled 'democratic centralism'. It would end the old conflicts between competing classes and economic interests in society, substituting a more disciplined harmony. This can, of course, be criticised on the grounds that the real aim was to remove any remaining influence of the other revolutionary groups, first by preventing their access to the various representative institutions and then by banning them altogether. The measures taken by Lenin between 1918 and 1924 were eventually to be tightened further by Stalin and converted into one of the most rigid dictatorships of the twentieth century.

Dictatorships also make use of propaganda and terror. Both were widely employed in the consolidation of Bolshevik power. There was a widespread poster campaign against all the enemies of communism, internal as well as external, along with the distribution of leaflets from *agitprop* trains. The *Cheka*, or secret police, was also established; by 1922, this had executed over 140,000 people, a tenfold increase on the victims of the tsarist equivalent, the *Okhrana*. The process was, of course, attributed to the emergency of the Civil War, as is suggested by the full name of the *Cheka* – the Extraordinary Commission for the Suppression of Counter Revolution, Speculation and Sabotage. Yet there was something more fundamental about the way in which terror was viewed. Trotsky, for example, famously said that 'we shall not enter into the kingdom of socialism in white gloves on a polished floor'. In its violence and its contempt for normal judicial processes, terror is nearly always the main factor in converting a revolutionary democracy into a revolutionary dictatorship.

The Bolshevik regime therefore fulfilled all the criteria for political dictatorship. It is true that it was not as extreme as it was later to become under Stalin and that it had not become fully totalitarian by 1924. It was, nevertheless, more authoritarian and ruthless than any other regime in Europe at the time.

3. (a) How did Lenin try to change Russia's economy between 1918 and 1921? (15 marks)

As a Marxist, Lenin initially hoped to transform Russia's economy by wiping out 'all exploitation of man by man' and eliminating the division of society into classes. But Lenin found that the theory could not be achieved in practice. Instead of a carefully planned transition from one type of economy to another, he had to follow a course which was dictated by the rapidly changing circumstances between 1918 and 1924. Hence his changes were often based on trial and error. At first he was cautious: until the middle of 1918 he nationalised only the banks, foreign trade and armaments works. He also avoided bringing the land under collective ownership, largely to try to win the peasantry away from the Socialist Revolutionaries. The Decree on Land therefore confirmed the individual ownership of property which had been taken from the nobility during the course of 1917.

From the middle of 1918, however, Lenin felt sufficiently confident to introduce more openly socialist principles. His policy of War Communism was intended to end the free market and to substitute state control over production and distribution. Any substantial industrial enterprise was brought within the scope of the Decree on Nationalisation, while the peasantry were now forced, under requisitioning orders, to hand over their grain to the state for distribution to the workers in the cities and the troops fighting the Whites. The problem with this approach is that it brought chaos rather than planned socialism. As the economy began to disintegrate, there was a decline in food production and the food shortages brought strikes and riots which threatened the very foundations of the Bolshevik regime.

In 1921, therefore, Lenin accepted that he had to change his strategy and restore to the economy a degree of capitalism and private enterprise. When he introduced the New Economic Policy

(NEP), he stressed that Russia could not move immediately to a socialist system; this was because of the severity of 'our poverty and ruin'. Hence it would take much longer than had previously been thought to 'transform the whole economic foundation'. Yielding to the inevitable, Lenin now allowed the peasantry to market their own produce under licence, while most industries were returned to private ownerships.

Lenin's motives in changing the economy therefore changed in essence – from hopes of creating a new system based on socialism to acceptance of a cautious evolution, with a burst of more frantic nationalisation and requisitioning between 1918 and 1921. This alternating approach was to become a common feature of Soviet economic policy in the future.

b) Why had fewer changes been made by the Bolsheviks to the Russian economy than to Russian government between 1918 and 1924? **(15 marks)**

As a Marxist, Lenin could have been expected to consider changes to the economy as an even greater priority than those to the political structure. After all, a key principle of Marxism was that any society consisted of a 'foundation' and a 'superstructure'. The foundation was the economic system upon which the society was based, the superstructure the political and social institutions which were created by the foundation. Any change of institutions needed therefore to be accompanied by a transformation of the economy. And yet Lenin approached the priorities in reverse order.

One reason is that Lenin had adapted Marxism to suit Russian conditions by emphasising the importance of structure and organisation within the Bolshevik revolutionary movement. This had played a key role in the October Revolution and was to be even more important in holding on to power between 1918 and 1921. Only by holding a monopoly of *political* power could the Bolsheviks hope initially to survive and eventually to introduce social and economic changes. Thus, rather than work on the 'foundation' through economic policy, he preferred to reverse the process and secure the 'superstructure'. He did so by ending the Constituent Assembly, extending the network of soviets, and introducing a new constitution in 1918. The whole structure was underpinned not by altered economic relationships but rather by a greatly strengthened and expanded party. The new party name, 'Communist', implied a recognition that economic issues would have to transformed – but not yet.

The speed with which the Bolsheviks consolidated their political control contrasted with their struggle even to control the economy – let alone change it. The main reason for this was the immediate need of their political position. The phases of economic policy reflected political need at any one time. Hence the initial caution between 1917 and 1918 was intended to keep the support of the peasantry and thereby prevent them from returning to the Socialist Revolutionaries. War Communism (1918–21) was, by contrast, a method of purging dissident rural elements and ensuring that the Bolsheviks retained the support of the urban workers by guaranteeing future supplies of food. When this proved widely unpopular, adjustments had to be made. The key point, however, is that now a hardened political structure made economic concessions in the form of the NEP. This was done to quieten dissent, without running the risk of allowing further opposition from emerging politically.

The relationship between the political and economic components of Russian communism was therefore the reverse of Marx's original intention. The basis of political power is what changed fundamentally, while the economy was pulled into different shapes to accommodate it. Later,

Stalin took the logical next step of the 'state-planned economy', using the 'superstructure' to 'redesign' the 'foundation'.

 ## The rise of Stalin, 1924–9

4. (a) Outline the stages in Stalin's rise to political power between 1924 and 1929 and the development of his economic ideas during this period. (15 marks)

There was a major contrast between Stalin's vulnerable position in 1924 and his complete supremacy by 1929. In the intervening period he overcame all the alternative contenders for power and, in the process, adapted his ideas about economic priorities.

His initial priority in 1924 was to persuade the rest of the Central Committee to set aside Lenin's Testament of December 1922 (which had criticised Stalin for 'concentrating limitless power in his hands') and of the Codicil of January 1923, which had advised the removal of Stalin from the post of secretary general. Crucially, Stalin managed to convince his colleagues that Lenin's fears had been ungrounded. Two of these, Kamenev and Zinoviev, felt that Trotsky presented a more serious threat and therefore pulled Stalin into a power-sharing Triumvirate. In the policy conflict which followed, Stalin rejected Trotsky's strategy of 'Permanent Revolution', which emphasised spreading revolution abroad and, at home, replacing the New Economic Policy (NEP) by forced industrialisation and collective farming. Instead, Stalin opted for 'Socialism in One Country', which would retain the NEP within Russia. If Stalin's priority here was to isolate Trotsky, he succeeded: the latter's proposals were defeated at the 1925 Party Congress.

By this stage, Kamenev and Zinoviev had woken up to Stalin's pursuit of personal power and switched their support to Trotsky, forming with them the 'Left Opposition' to Stalin. At the same time, Stalin enlisted the support of the 'Rightists' within the Party: Bukharin, Rykov and Tomsky. He continued to press for 'Socialism in One Country', which was formally adopted at the 1927 Party Conference. 'Permanent Revolution' was officially denounced and the 'Left Opposition' was expelled from both the Politburo and the party.

Between 1927 and 1929 Stalin completed his rise to power by turning against the 'Rightists'. He also began to harden his own economic ideas. 'Socialism in One Country' was now linked with rapid industrialisation and enforced collectivisation of agriculture which meant, in effect, that Stalin had adopted half of Trotsky's programme of 'Permanent Revolution'. In this he encountered opposition from Bukharin, Rykov and Tomsky, who had always supported a moderate policy towards the peasantry; this gave Stalin the excuse he needed to remove them from the Politburo and from their state functions. Stalin's reasoning was that the economic circumstances had changed and that the NEP should be replaced by state planning; the 'Rightists' were an obstacle which had to be removed.

Thus, by 1929 Stalin had achieved more complete political power than Lenin had ever had; he was also about to launch more radical economic measures than had even been considered before. The two developments were closely integrated.

(b) Why had Stalin been able to eliminate all his opponents by 1929? (15 marks)

Of all the possible candidates for future power Stalin was, in 1924, one of the least impressive. He was less experienced in military leadership than Trotsky and certainly had been less involved with the Bolshevik Revolution. Indeed, Trotsky openly despised him, calling him 'the party's most eminent mediocrity'. This was a view shared by others like Kamenev, Zinoviev and Bukharin. It was certainly a mistaken one and is one of the main reasons why Stalin was able to come to dominate the party so completely by 1929.

Although seemingly mediocre, Stalin had skills which were less obvious, but more deadly than those of Trotsky. He was adaptable and flexible, posing as a moderate in 1924 in order to gain acceptance from Kamenev and Zinoviev. He had a talent for making himself inconspicuous until he was ready to seize upon a weakness of his opponents and launch a surprise and devastating attack. This happened to Trotsky in 1925 and to Kamenev and Zinoviev the following year. The others were less effective politically. Trotsky was brilliant but arrogant and overbearing, incurring only suspicion from his colleagues, while Bukharin was a theorist who failed to convince others of practical implementation. Stalin, on the other hand, had gradually built up his position through the support of a newer generation of party members, such as Kalinin, Kuibyshev, Molotov and Voroshilov.

From this it becomes evident that Stalin's greatest strength was the security of his base within the Communist Party. As General Secretary from 1922, he effectively controlled the party's administration and, more importantly, its membership and promotion. This operated in the following way. The local branches of the party elected the Party Congress which, in turn, produced the membership of the Central Committee. From this was drawn the Politburo, the primary decision-making body. The membership composition of the local parties was determined by the Secretariat, which was under Stalin's control. He used his influence to build up a future base of personal support. Each time a top layer was removed the next moved up to take its place. Hence Stalin's nominees gradually became more and more prominent. This was sufficient to edge out Trotsky, Zinoviev and Kamenev by 1927, then the Rightists by 1929.

Stalin also benefited from the party's perception of the danger that Trotsky might become a military dictator, thus repeating Napoleon Bonaparte's career during the French Revolution. Suspecting Trotsky of having **Bonapartist** ambitions, they tended to side with Stalin whom they – mistakenly – saw as the safer option. In actual fact, Trotsky's power base was not that strong. The army had been politicised by the Bolshevik Revolution and the Civil War more completely any other army in any previous revolution. The party is therefore what really counted since it operated all the levers of power.

Finally, Stalin was able to shift his position on ideology and policy to adapt to changing circumstances, showing opportunism and great flexibility. Most of the other Bolsheviks had fixed positions. Trotsky was a radical. His policy of 'Permanent Revolution' envisaged replacing the New Economic Policy within Russia by rapid industrialisation and forced collectivisation, while abroad the focus would be on the spread of the communist style of revolution. Bukharin, Rykov and Tomsky were, by contrast, convinced moderates committed to maintaining the NEP as part of the strategy of 'Socialism in One Country'. Kamenev and Zinoviev, it is true, moved their position from the radical left to the centre during the period of the Triumvirate (1924–5) but they ended up by returning to their ideological roots and joining Trotsky in the 'Left Opposition' between 1925 and 1927. By contrast with all of these, Stalin was flexible enough to adapt his ideological stance to the apparent needs of the moment.

Whether Stalin changed his policies to seize the political initiative or was able to use his power to change his policies is still a matter for historical debate. Perhaps it is a false one. The two were

Stage 1 : 1924-5

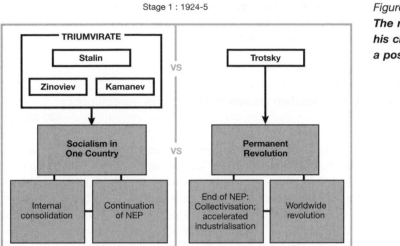

Stage 2 : 1925-7

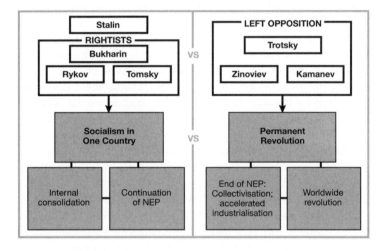

Stage 3 : 1927-9

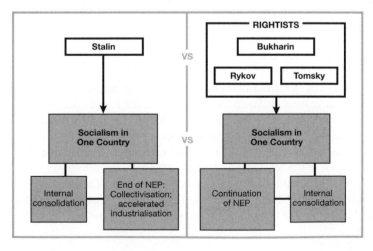

Figure 7.2
**The rise of Stalin and
his changing ideas:
a possible interpretation**

closely related, indicating how far Stalin had moved between 1924 and 1929. By the end of the decade, Bukharin warned that Stalin was a 'ruthless intriguer' and that he 'will strangle us with his power.' The 'eminent mediocrity' had therefore achieved the notoriety which Lenin had predicted in his *Political Testament*.

5.   Was Stalin's policy of collectivisation arrived at through his 'forethought and control'?   **(90 marks)**

The immediate origins of Stalin's agricultural changes lie in the period 1926–7. These years saw the 'procurement crisis', so called because less than 20 per cent of the grain harvested by the peasants was actually released for the industrial workers. Stalin immediately followed this up with the requisitioning of peasant grain, thus repeating the earlier measures taken by Lenin during the period of War Communism between 1918 and 1921. Step by step, requisitioning led to a more permanent policy of collectivisation. At first this was voluntary but, from 1929 onwards was ruthlessly enforced. Two possible reasons can be given for this decision. One is that, by this stage, Stalin was fully in control and that the procurement crisis was used as an excuse to introduce a carefully considered strategy for economic change. The alternative is that Stalin stumbled into collectivisation without planning or forethought – as a direct result of the procurement crisis.

The first view has much to commend it. Stalin was above all an opportunist, ready to seize upon anything which could be used to reinforce his policies. He was therefore fully capable of using a crisis as an excuse to bring the economy into line with his own ideas. The basic point is that he had become profoundly sceptical of the NEP. It did not fit into his scheme for a controlled economy and was hardly a relevant base for the stage that Soviet Russia had supposedly entered: 'the dictatorship of the proletariat'. In any case, the economy seemed to be based on split values – common ownership in the towns and private property in the rural areas. It was time to standardise the basic principle behind the economy and to bring the peasantry into line with the urban workers. At present the pattern of land ownership, which was based on fragmentation into small individual holdings, was entirely inappropriate to the needs of the cities. It led to a capitalist mentality which promoted individual rather than collective values; the procurement crisis was therefore the result of selfish hoarding – and the emergence of a new middle class of wealthy peasants, or kulaks. Everything fitted together. The NEP had outlived its usefulness; Stalin had an alternative scheme with which to replace it; and between 1926 and 1929 he had accumulated sufficient political power to see off attempts by Bukharin and the Right Opposition to restrain him. There was even an issue of national security. Stalin's expressed priority was to build up Soviet defences against hostile Western encirclement. The industrialisation needed to do this would have to be subsidised. In the absence of external sources, this would have to be done internally – by agriculture. The case for pressing on with the *kolkhozy* was complete.

This line of reasoning can, however, be criticised on the grounds that it attributes too much economic planning, forethought and control to Stalin at a time when his first priority was the elimination of political rivals to both his right and his left. The procurement crisis was not so much an opportunity seized by Stalin to implement his plans as the reason for sudden changes he might not otherwise have considered. Between 1924 and 1926 Stalin had identified Socialism in One Country with the continuation of the NEP and had attacked Trotsky's emphasis on forced industrialisation and collectivisation. The sudden switch was forced upon him. The procurement crisis was the direct result of the peasantry refusing to release their grain because industry had provided them with nothing to buy. This was likely to cause major disruption in the cities, up to that point the most solid supporters of the communist regime. Stalin adopted the only policy he felt would work – the forcible extraction of the grain from the peasantry in order to pacify the urban proletariat. The rest followed as, step by step, Stalin moved between 1926 and 1929 from requisitioning as a temporary expedient to collectivisation as a permanent solution. At the same time, he had to deflate those, like Bukharin, who still clung to the NEP. He also had to explain away his apparent movement towards the economic position held by his arch-rival, Trotsky. Fortunately, by 1929, his political power was sufficiently secure to enable him to construct a carefully considered ideological defence of collectivisation.

Few would deny that Stalin was committed to a command economy based on central planning for both industry and agriculture. But this commitment evolved as a result of the ending of the NEP. During the politically volatile period of the 1920s, Stalin took whatever course he considered necessary. When this opened up new possibilities for economic control he seized them and then – retrospectively – made everything appear logically planned.

Stalin's rule, 1929–41

6. Why did Stalin decide to force the pace of industrialisation at the end of the 1920s and the beginning of the 1930s?   **(90 marks)**

Stalin's decision to force the pace of Russia's industrial development was a major change from his earlier support for the New Economic Policy. There were several interconnected reasons for this: some were within his control, some due to pressures on him.

The most important of the pressures came from the industrial working class whose interests had become out of line with those of the peasantry. The workers needed guaranteed supplies of food which, of course, depended on the co-operation of the peasantry. It was therefore logical to accompany the campaign for collectivisation with major industrial changes which would benefit the workers. Indeed, the workers expected this to happen. Stalin was able to appear to take the initiative over this by justifying changes through ideological argument. He claimed that the only sure way of creating a socialist economy was through rapid industrialisation, under full state control. This had to mean a departure from the NEP, which was really based on the interests of the peasantry. It would also provide a better chance of success with the introduction of the Marxist phase of the 'dictatorship of the proletariat' and the triumph of the values and interests of the urban workforce over all other classes. This could not be accomplished if the priority continued to be given to fulfilling the needs of the peasantry.

During the period of his rise to power, especially between 1927 and 1929, forced industrialisation became a useful propaganda weapon against his political opponents. The idea of the command economy was used to justify his abandonment of the NEP which, in turn isolated those who were still committed to the NEP – such as Bukharin, Rykov and Tomsky. Introducing a command economy would also have certain political advantages for the future. New centralised institutions such as Gosplan could be controlled more easily and would be able to exert more control over local operations. Stalin intended to have ultimate control over all such institutions which would, in turn, reinforce his overall political authority.

Clearly, Stalin could hardly present his conversion to forced industrialisation in quite these terms. The argument he did put across was, however, persuasive. He stressed that Russia's very survival was threatened by capitalist encirclement by the West – and that the only way of combatting this was through self-sufficiency, or Socialism in One Country. The problem was immense and the solution uncompromising. 'We are,' he said in 1929, 'fifty to a hundred years behind the advanced countries. We must make good this distance in ten years. Either we do it or we shall be crushed.' This is a clear indication that Stalin was looking to give absolute priority to heavy industry rather than to the development of consumer goods, which explains the emphasis of the first three Five Year Plans on building new industrial complexes like Magnitogorsk, on developing engineering projects and on increasing the production of coal, steel, electricity and oil.

A major component of this whole policy was to move the Soviet economy on to a war footing, something which could not be achieved by continuing with the NEP. The engineering and steel industries were geared essentially to armaments production which, in turn, reflected changes in Soviet military strategy then taking place. The traditional ideas that Russia's best wartime strategy was defensive had been discredited by defeat in the First World War. Instead, the military theorists who most influenced Stalin were those who argued that Stalin should prepare for an offensive against the West at a time of his own choosing. This almost certainly meant that armaments were given far greater priority than would have been the case with a purely defensive production plan.

Pulling these points together reveals an aspiring dictator who was attempting to increase his political control by setting up a command economy in which industry would dominate agriculture. This would enable him to achieve the ideological target of the 'dictatorship of the proletariat' and prepare Russian armaments so thoroughly that the traditional defensive strategy could be replaced by one geared to an offensive. Stalin was nothing if not ambitious.

7. **'Through the purges Stalin inflicted on the Soviet people the most extreme example of precautionary terror to be found anywhere during the twentieth century.'**

    a) **In the context of the quotation, what is meant by 'precautionary terror'.** **(3 marks)**

Terror has formed a part, at some stage, of most political revolutions. But it is usually a reaction to opposition or directed against targeted enemies, as in Nazi Germany. Under Stalin, however, terror was taken a stage further and used to remove *potential* enemies; these were individuals and groups who had not yet emerged as a direct threat to the regime, but who might do so in the future. Most of Stalin's victims fell into this category and were usually part of 'quotas' for extermination or forced labour.

    b) **Explain why Stalin introduced the terror into the Soviet Union during the 1930s.** **(7 marks)**

Stalin had a number of reasons for introducing the purges during the 1930s. The first was to remove any possibility of political opposition to him within the party and state machinery. This explains the variety of methods used in the second half of the 1930s. The campaign started in 1934 with the assassination of Kirov, who had become Stalin's main potential rival. This was followed by the show trials of Kamenev and Zinoviev in 1936, Piatakov and Sokolnikov in 1937 and Bukharin and Rykov in 1938. They were all accused of plotting with Trotsky to destroy the communist regime; there were even allegations of collaboration with Nazi Germany in a 'fascist front'.

Second, he intended to create a disciplined workforce and a compliant peasantry, which would be capable of reaching the ambitious targets of the Five Year Plans. It is significant that the first victims were the managers in industry, of whom about 75 per cent were purged in the early 1930s. Then measures were taken to cut back the peasant kulaks and to provide industrial labour through the growth of the **gulag** system. Convicts, for example, built the Belomor Canal and mined diamonds in Siberia, particularly in the remote region of Kolyma. For Stalin, therefore, terror was closely linked to modernisation.

Stalin was also concerned to guarantee internal security by removing what he considered to be unreliable elements from the armed forces. The main casualties were the commissar for defence (Marshal Tukhachevsky) and all eleven deputy commissars, seventy-five of the eighty members of the Supreme Military Council, and all eight admirals from the navy. Stalin's reasoning was that in the event of a future invasion, possibly from Germany, there should be no threat of revolution as had occurred during the First World War. The best way of ensuring this was by removing the chance of any possible leadership emerging from within the armed forces.

Another reason has been suggested, which provides an overall link between all the others. This is the personality of Stalin. His obsession with opposition was unprecedented. He took action not only against suspects at the time but also against people who might emerge as opponents in the future, the latter accounting for the large majority of his victims. This might indicate calculation based on the utmost ruthlessness. The alternative is to see Stalin as personally unstable, even paranoid. Khrushchev, Stalin's successor, considered that Stalin had a disastrously flawed personality: he emphasised his brutality, vindictiveness, 'pathological distrust' and 'sickly suspicion'. Although Khrushchev had good reasons to want to discredit the memory of Stalin, he was not wrong in stressing the importance of personal factors in such organised brutality.

c) **'Terror did more than anything else to achieve what Stalin wanted in the Soviet Union before 1941.' Explain whether you agree or disagree with this view.** **(15 marks)**

Stalin wanted unchallenged power and the fullest possible implementation of all his policies. The extent of his ambitions required, in his view, drastic measures. The precise role played by terror in these measures is, however, debatable.

It is certainly true that terror played a major part in consolidating Stalin's power base and implementing his Five Year Plans. The purges created a slave-labour force, based on the gulag system, which accelerated the achievement of the Five Year Plan targets. The *Dekulakisation* squads of the NKVD ensured the rapid implementation of collectivisation and the created of Stalin's *kolkhozy* and *sovkozy*. Fear of the NKVD also ensured that Stalin's personality cult was openly supported: it was not safe merely to withhold opposition. It could even be said that terror played a larger part in achieving state policy in Russia than it did in any other dictatorship of the period. In Nazi Germany, for example, the use of terror was confined to opponents and 'race enemies'; otherwise, the emphasis of the regime was on the solidarity engendered by the *Volksgemeinschaft*. In Nazi Germany, terror was targeted outwards against those who were excluded from the community. In Stalinist Russia it was directed into the community itself.

Yet the extent of the use of terror did not by itself guarantee success. The notion that Stalin's policies were effective *because* they were ruthlessly applied can be challenged on three grounds. First, there was resistance to those policies which were enforced most ferociously. In the early attempts

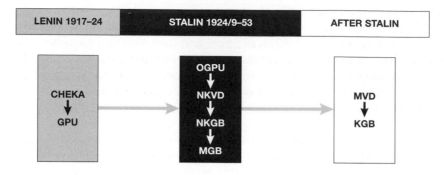

Figure 7.3 *The Soviet secret police*

to enforce collectivisation between 1930 and 1931, the Russian peasantry produced the greatest collective defiance experienced by any dictatorship between the wars. Despite the small chance they had of success, they deliberately destroyed the majority of their livestock and wiped out all the progress previously achieved under the NEP (1921–8). Second, the argument that state security was served by the purges is also specious: the capacity of the army was so badly affected by the sweep through the higher officer class that Russia had extreme difficulty in winning the Winter War against Finland (1939–40). And third, even Stalin was dismayed by the way in which terror spiralled out of control, magnified many times over through its local application by ruthless officials seeking to enhance their own interests.

This analysis suggests that terror was an essential part of achieving Stalin's objectives, but that it was counter-productive when it became too extreme. The logical conclusion, therefore, is that it was most effective when used along with other methods. It was the reverse side of the coin from incentives in industry: workers could either be exhorted to work harder through the propaganda about **Stakhanovites** or forced to work harder through the Gulag. It was the other side of the Stalinist cult: the Soviet people could either give their unqualified love to Stalin as a beneficent leader or feel his unqualified wrath as an avenging one. Terror and indoctrination lived in closer proximity in Russia than in Germany. In Germany the majority were indoctrinated, the minority intimidated – usually the latter were outside the scope of the former. In Russia indoctrination could give way to terror at any time for anyone. In Stalin's perspective this was probably necessary since the Russian people were expected to make greater sacrifices than the Germans in the establishment of industrial and military strength.

The nature of Stalin's regime is such that his policies cannot be imagined without a strong element of force behind them – nor without terror behind the force. At the same time, the policies were the priority. Terror worked most effectively where it remained the tool, used along with other tools, and not when it took over as the policy itself.

8. Assess the effects of Stalin's purges of the 1930s. (90 marks)

The Stalinist purges affected Russia in a paradoxical way. On the one hand, they extended the efficiency of Stalin's totalitarian dictatorship and control, while on the other spreading chaos. This contradiction can be seen in the politics, economy and security of the Soviet Union.

In the political sector, terror was the chief method by which the party machinery of the Bolshevik state was transformed into the personalised totalitarian dictatorship of Stalin. It enabled Stalin to create a regime which was as consistently ruthless and pervasive as that of Nazi Germany. The NKVD purged the CPSU of potential rivals for the leadership, thereby ensuring that Stalin remained the unchallenged successor to Lenin. The price, however, was widespread political chaos. The extent of the terror throughout the Soviet Union created wild oscillations as officials everywhere reacted to what they perceived to be Stalin's latest policies and requirements. This meant that agricultural and industrial policies were distorted and that the quotas for victims to be eliminated were usually exceeded in wild excesses at local level. This frequently meant that the central level of government had to intervene against local officials, thereby creating a new impetus to the purges and renewed examples of chaos.

A similar paradox applied to the economy. The purges certainly provided the momentum for the creation of a command economy, the development of a disciplined industrial workforce and the enforcement of a new system of land ownership on the peasantry. They also created a supplementary labour force as the Gulag system provided millions of slave workers to operate in the most hostile areas of the country, especially Kolyma. Yet the terror also did much to confuse the network through which the command economy operated, which partly undermined the effectiveness of state planning. The approach to collectivisation and 'de-kulakisation' was conducted with excessive zeal by local party officials and NKVD officials. In the rural areas the result was the mass disobedience of the peasantry – directed not so much at Stalin himself as at the officials interpreting his orders in their own way. In industry, plant managers were impeded by confused objectives and instructions along the command network, while the workforce itself was fundamentally destabilised by the pervasive atmosphere of fear and recrimination.

The third – and most obvious – example of the contradiction between Stalin's power and Soviet chaos concerns the impact of the purges on the armed forces. Stalin had always been obsessed by the possibility of being deposed by a military coup either in peacetime or as the result of the pressure of an external threat from Germany. His sweep through the high command of the Soviet army and navy certainly reduced the possibility of this happening and is a key factor in his survival after the German invasion in 1941. The side effect, however, was that the capacity of the Soviet Union to wage a successful war was, for a while, severely depleted. The wholesale execution or expulsion of officers brought a loss of experience at the highest level. This contributed to the poor performance of Soviet troops against Finland (1939–40) and the military collapse following the German invasion of 1941.

In one respect the impact of Stalin's purges seems to be clear and lacking in ambiguity. The sheer scale of the losses suffered throughout the Soviet Union as a result of organised terror was unparalleled elsewhere. The number of deaths has been calculated at 20 million by Robert Conquest, while figures in a recent Russian textbook are as high as 40 million. At any one time the population in the Gulag camps was about 10 million in the 1930s, reaching 12 million after the end of the Second World War. These statistics imply organisation on a massive scale. Or do they? Revisionist historians have pointed out that they can be interpreted as a loss of control at the centre and the proliferation of local initiatives as officials at all levels exceeded their quotas. This in no way exonerates Stalin or even reduces his responsibility for the brutality of the purges. It does, however, show that the unintended side effect of his terror was the emergence of a multitude of 'little Stalins', each of which negated the whole purpose of the terror itself and undermined central direction.

On balance, the political contradiction resolved itself in Stalin's favour, the purges and terror doing more to maintain him in power than to threaten his hold on it. Conversely, terror acted as a brake on effective economic growth by creating mass fear and paralysing initiative; this cancelled out much of the planning and logic behind the command economy. In the case of the military impact, terror almost brought defeat to the depleted armed forces. It may have saved Stalin from over-throw in 1941 – but would he have been so vulnerable had he not introduced the purges in the first place?

9. Were Stalin's agricultural policies between 1929 and 1941 a complete failure? (90 marks)

Stalin's agricultural policies can hardly be considered a complete success. The key issue is whether anything positive can be imputed to them to prevent them being considered a complete failure. This involves consideration of three key criteria – the speed with which they were implemented, the productivity which resulted, and the impact on the peasantry and the effect on other sectors of the economy.

The first criterion would suggest considerable success. Collectivisation was carried out with great speed, the proportion of collective farms increasing from 23.6 per cent in 1930 to 52.7 per cent (1931), 61.5 per cent (1932), 66.4 per cent (1933), 71.4 per cent (1934), 83.2 per cent (1935), 89.6 per cent (1936) and 98.0 per cent (1941). Yet this momentum was itself a problem. The process was so rapid that it spiralled out of control as Stalin himself lost the initiative to local officials and the NKVD. Indeed, he was so concerned about their frantic activities that he called a halt to collec-tivisation in 1931, accusing his officials of being 'dizzy with success'. The latter fell into line with this change but the result was inertia through fear. This, in turn, meant that Stalin felt obliged to restart the process and apply new pressure. Throughout the 1930s the pendulum swung violently backwards and forwards. Stalin introduced policies which became distorted as they were enforced locally. Every subsequent move Stalin made created an unintended backlash. The result, even in the most ruthless of authoritarian systems, was utter chaos.

Not surprisingly this had a serious effect on productivity, the second yardstick for assessing the effectiveness of collectivisation. Grain production fell from 73.3 million tons in 1928 to 71.7 million in 1929. A temporary recovery to 83.5 million (1930) was followed by a sharp reversal to 69.5 million (1931), 69.6 million (1932) and 67.6 million (1934). There was also a catastrophic decline in livestock: between 1928 and 1932 the number of cattle dropped from 70 million to 34 million, sheep and goats from 146 to 42 million and pigs from 26 to 9 million. These were not slight shifts or downturns: they represented an agricultural collapse on a scale which had been paralleled only in the bleakest months of the Russian Civil War.

The impact on the peasantry was therefore catastrophic. Admittedly the destruction was the result of a defiant resistance – and therefore self-inflicted. But this was made worse by the sacrifice of agricultural production to the hunt for kulaks by detachments of the NKVD. The result was the complete collapse in many localities of normal agricultural functions such as sowing, harvesting and breeding. The overall result was misery, especially in the Ukraine, which experienced a disas-trous famine between 1932 and 1933. There was also widespread social upheaval as peasants turned on each other, incited by officials to hunt down kulaks. This, in turn, affected the towns and cities, which were flooded with millions of desperate peasants seeking employment and survival. As a direct result, living conditions became ever more congested and squalid.

Figure 7.4
**A collective
farm in the 1930s**

There is one positive dimension which is often attributed to Stalin. It has been argued that he exploited agriculture to subsidise industrial growth. This may have been bad for agriculture, but at least it freed industry of any possible dependence on Western loans. Capital for industrialisation was generated internally – even if it did mean misery for the peasantry. This interpretation is now being strongly contested on the grounds that it would have been impossible to transfer such resources from the agricultural sector to industry. In fact, agriculture actually threatened to slow down the rate of industrial growth. The huge peasant migration was too much for industry to absorb, creating an administrative crisis and worsening social conditions. Besides, agriculture came to depend heavily on industry in the second and third Five Year Plans through the introduction of machine tractor stations (MTS). Instead of agriculture subsidising industry, therefore, industry came to subsidise agriculture.

Overall, it is hard to put any positive construction on Stalin's agricultural policies. Even arguments once made about the use of agriculture to subsidise industrial growth have now been closed off. The effects of collectivisation were uniformly catastrophic.

10. To what extent did Stalin's industrial policies have a positive impact on Russia? (90 marks)

Stalin's industrial policies were based on the first, second and third Five Year Plans (1928–33, 1934–8 and 1938–41 respectively). They had a very mixed impact on the economic base and well-being of the population of the Soviet Union.

In the first place, Stalin did not, as is often claimed, establish a new industrial base where none had existed before. There had been an extensive industrial infrastructure in Tsarist Russia, based on Moscow, Petrograd, the Donetz region, Baku and the Ukraine. To this Lenin had added electrification and plans to develop the Urals. What Stalin *did* do was to extend the scale of heavy industry through his emphasis on 'gigantomania'. This involved the building of new industrial cities such as Magnitogorsk and the expansion of heavy plant and steel production. The result, between 1928 and 1932, was an increase in the production of steel (from 3 million to 6 million tons), of coal (from 35 to 64 million) and of oil (from 12 to 21 million). During the second

Five Year Plan (1933–7) production climbed to 18 million tons for steel, 128 million for coal and 26 million for oil. By the time that the third Five Year Plan was interrupted by the 1941 German invasion the figures were 18 million, 150 million and 26 million.

This industrial expansion had both positive and negative perspectives. On the positive side, it has been seen as laying the base for the Soviet Union's survival in the Second World War. The focus on heavy industry had made it possible for the Soviet Union to rearm, the defence expenditure expanding from an initial 4 per cent of the budget to 33 per cent by 1940. There is, however, a more negative perspective. Such industrialisation may have contributed to the eventual military survival of the Soviet Union – but it had a bad effect on government. Recent research has shown that centralised state planning was often very inefficient. Setting targets through Gosplan was one thing but it was another to provide the necessary mechanism to achieve them. Indeed, so serious was the administrative chaos that the Five Year Plans had to be suspended between 1941 and 1945. As it turned out, the Soviet war effort was actually better off without them.

The effect of industrialisation of the workforce was also mixed. On the one hand, there was no unemployment after 1929, a direct contrast with the situation in the West. This was partly because the Soviet Union was insulated from the depression affecting the rest of the world and partly because the rapidly expanding base created millions of new jobs which absorbed both existing and new workers. On the other hand, the conditions in which people worked were often basic and very poor and there were no rewards in the form of consumer goods. There was serious congestion and squalor in the huge dormitories set up for workers. There was therefore an inherent contradiction. Although the intention of industrialisation was to modernise, the reality was that the changes tore apart the social fabric. This heightened people's suspicions of each other, which meant that they were prepared to denounce each other during the Stalinist purgees.

Overall, Stalin's industrialisation and its effects can be seen in two ways. Either it was a deliberate strategy to create an industrial superpower with an obedient workforce, or it was the result of inefficiency and chaos. If it was the former, then the harshness was part of the design and industrialisation was bought at a high price. But if it was the latter the approach to industrialisation was as badly flawed as that of agriculture – in which case the price was not only high, but unnecessary.

11. 'Stalin was typical of the inter-war dictators in using culture in the service of the revolutionary totalitarian state and in intensifying the degree of social control.'

   a) What is meant by 'the revolutionary totalitarian state'? (3 marks)

Totalitarian regimes aimed to establish complete control over political institutions in order to enforce their will on every area of the lives of the population. Totalitarianism was normally revolutionary since it involved new ideas and ideologies which swept away previous systems, often liberal, which had placed more emphasis on a balance of power within the state.

   b) How effectively did Stalin use culture in the service of the totalitarian state? (7 marks)

Stalin had a considerable impact on Soviet culture. He aimed to move artists of all kinds away from experimentation and individuality into a state-directed format. Art and literature were used directly to uphold Stalin's power and Stalin's policies. 'Artistic brigades' were established, along with the Russian Association of Proletarian Writers (RAPP) and the Union of Writers. These laid down cultural rules in accordance with 'Socialist Realism'; the purpose of literature was to 'mobilise the masses' and to act as 'engineers of the human soul'. At the same time, Stalin revived many of the traditional influences behind Russian culture, in effect making Socialist Realism 'national in form, socialist in content'. This enabled him to combine revolutionary Soviet communism with more traditional Russian nationalism – a vital ingredient for the endurance of morale during the 'Great Patriotic War'.

Culture was blatantly used as a tool of propaganda to support Stalin's power and policies. He succeeded in exerting control, but the resulting quality was often dubious. Painting, for example, served the purpose of political propaganda by showing contented collective farmers and prosperous workers. In two areas, however, Stalin promoted cultural changes of real quality. Soviet music was arguably the greatest of the twentieth century; the output of Prokofiev, Khachaturian, Kabalevsky and, above all, Shostakovich was impressive by any standard. The use of film was more subtle than in Germany; Eisenstein's *October, Battleship Potemkin* and *Ivan the Terrible*, are still considered masterpieces.

Stalin, like Hitler, attached more importance to culture as a form of totalitarian control than as an expression of quality. Russian culture proved more influential than German culture as an agent of government control, whilst in areas such as music the Soviet Union retained much higher levels of quality than Nazi Germany.

c) **'Stalin was more revolutionary than Lenin in imposing state control over all areas of society.' Explain whether you agree or disagree with this statement.**   **(15 marks)**

During his rule, Stalin (1929–53) had much longer than Lenin (1917–24) to make social changes and bring society more completely under state control. And yet the way in which he did this was not necessarily more revolutionary. As an overall pattern he started by trying to make Lenin's social changes even more radical, before discovering fairly quickly that the best way of imposing state control was actually by using more conservative and traditional devices.

The first example of this was his approach to social equality. Initially he took further the Bolshevik policy of removing all social distinction and wage differentials. During the early 1930s, however, he ended this radicalism and reintroduced privileges, which were conferred by the state as rewards for loyalty and service, Hence medals and decorations returned, as did ranks in the army and hierarchies in industry and the party. 'Wage equalisation' disappeared and differentials were introduced to encourage the labour force to follow the example of the *Stakhanovites* and exceed their production quotas.

Another sector of the population to feel the impact of Stalin's social changes was women. At first, he was content to extend the early Bolshevik policy of breaking down the family unit; yet, by the mid-1930s he had restored the family to its full status within society. Divorce was made more difficult from 1935, while abortion became illegal in 1936. Stalin also enforced a code of sexual conduct, in contrast to earlier libertarian attitudes. The underlying reason for these changes was that Stalin had come to realise that the family was the most effective channel for socialising political influence in a totalitarian state.

Education showed a similar pattern. Under Lenin discipline had been relaxed in schools and group activity increased, in line with Marxist ideas. Again, Stalin tried initially to maintain this. By 1934, however, he had reversed his approach by restoring the authority of the teacher and reintroducing formal learning and examinations. He had also restored school uniforms, including compulsory pigtails for girls. Subjects like History emphasised Russia's traditions as much as its revolutionary past, placing a positive slant on figures such as Ivan the Terrible and Peter the Great. Stalin also insisted that access to higher education should be based on academic suitability rather than – as under Lenin – on social class. Again, he had come to realise that the operation of indoctrination and propaganda operated more effectively through tightly organised institutions than through ones which had been shaken by revolutionary experimentation.

It is often said that there was a 'Stalinist Revolution'. If there was, this covered society in the way in which state control was exercised over society, not in the radicalisation over society itself. To achieve this, Stalin had to reverse some of the social initiatives of the 'Leninist Revolution'.

 Foreign policy and war

12. What were the main developments in Soviet foreign policy between 1921 and 1941? (90 marks)

See Chapter 8, Essay 17

13. 'Stalin's foreign policy had no clear direction between 1929 and 1941.' To what extent do you agree with this assessment? (90 marks)

See Chapter 8, Essay 18

14. Why was the Soviet Union defeated between 1941 and 1942? (90 marks)

The initial months of Operation Barbarossa, launched by Hitler on 22 June 1941, proved disastrous for the Soviet Union. In less than six months the Baltic provinces and the Ukraine had fallen and both Moscow and Leningrad were threatened. In 1942 the main advances were made in the south with the capture of the oilfields of the Caucasus and the threat to Stalingrad. During the first twelve months of the war Soviet resistance crumpled as the German armies killed one million Russians and took one million prisoners.

The reason for this defeat that first springs to mind is that the Germans must have had overwhelming superiority in armaments and size of forces. This is certainly maintained by Soviet historians. It is, however, simply not the case. Soviet troops outnumbered the Germans and the Soviet Union had 24,000 tanks – most of the world's supply. A much more likely explanation is the serious misjudgement shown by Stalin in his dealings with Germany since August 1939. He had completely misinterpreted Hitler's intentions, assuming that Hitler had logical objectives and a desire, above all, to avoid involving Germany in a war on two fronts. Stalin therefore expected some warning of a possible conflict with Germany, which would give him time to make concessions sufficient to prevent war from breaking out. He felt that the real danger was that the Soviet government might be duped by Western intelligence reports and tricked into a war with Hitler.

This whole approach was disastrously flawed. Hitler was not following a logical policy: everything about his plans for Operation Barbarossa defied military logic and incurred warnings from his generals. In the meantime, Stalin ignored warnings from British intelligence about German preparations to invade the Soviet Union. He even distrusted intelligence reports from Soviet sources such as General Golikov, the head of military intelligence, and Admiral Kuznetzov. Soviet agents in Tokyo and Berlin both gave the precise date of the intended attack – 22 June 1941 – but these warnings did not fit into the way in which Stalin had chosen to interpret Hitler's intentions. In ignoring them he delivered his country up to devastating defeat.

When it came, the German invasion was met by political and military paralysis. The impetus was too swift to allow for an orderly Soviet withdrawal. In any case, the Red Army had already been deprived of effective leadership by Stalin's purge of the officer class. This, in turn, reflected the chaos which had existed in all layers of Stalin's dictatorship during the 1930s. The planning system had been far from efficient and it simply folded up in 1941. Thus the first three Five Year Plans, which had been intended to prepare Russia for war, proved a serious obstacle when war broke out.

Another key factor in Soviet vulnerability was the huge potential for internal disintegration through mass discontent. This might have been through the resentment of millions of peasants who had been forced against their will into collective farms. Or it might have taken the form of resistance by ethnic groups to Russian domination. Thus the Germans were initially welcomed as liberators, especially by Belarussians, Ukrainians and Georgians, and by the peoples of the Baltic states. It has been estimated that about two million former Soviet citizens defected to the German armies.

Finally, initial Soviet defeat was due to German familiarity with the strategy of 'Blitzkrieg'. Taking advantage of Soviet indecision and inertia, the Wehrmacht attacked in strength, using armoured panzer divisions to advance in three prongs – against Leningrad in the north, Moscow in the centre and Kiev in the south. The element of surprise was rammed home by the Germans with devastating results: 57 per cent of all Soviet losses in the war were incurred in the opening campaign of 1941–2, and 17,500 of the 24,000 Soviet tanks were destroyed. This type of war was Germany's particular strength, although the longer term revealed the deficiencies of Blitzkrieg.

Overall, Soviet defeat seemed at the time to have been the result of an unexpected attack by an overwhelmingly superior military power. In fact, it was the reverse. It was widely expected, although Stalin chose to ignore warnings, and Germany was stretching its military resources to breaking point in launching it. Yet Stalin's blunders were sufficient to allow the German armies at least a temporary victory. Ultimately, therefore, much of the blame for the initial catastrophe must be laid at his door.

15. Why was the Soviet Union victorious in the war with Germany? (90 marks)

The victory of the Soviet forces against Germany between 1943 and 1945 was nothing short of remarkable, given the extent of Soviet collapse before that date. In many cases the reasons for recovery are the reverse of those for the original disasters. Several traditional assumptions have, however, been recently challenged by historians.

The first – and most obvious change – was Stalin's own recovery. After the initial shock of being on the receiving end of an invasion he had hoped to deliver, he began to implement a more appropriate administrative structure and military strategy. He established two new institutions – the *Stavka*, or general headquarters, and the GOKO, or State Defence Committee. The GOKO consisted of Molotov, Voroshilov, Malenkov and Beria and, under the overall authority of Stalin as people's commissar for defence, it replaced the usual party channels of communication. The whole administration was therefore streamlined, allowing the necessary military co-ordination to be fully effective. Similarly, the planning system was changed. The usual argument is that the Five Year Plans had built up the infrastructure which enabled Russia to outproduce Germany and to create new industrial centres in Siberia, beyond the reach of the German armies. This is true – but the planning system also had structural defects which slowed it down and rendered it inefficient. Stalin therefore decentralised production during the war years and allowed more local initiative and organisation. This was the reverse of what happened in capitalist states, whether democracies or dictatorships, since these imposed ever tighter centralised controls over production. According to one historian, the earlier '"mobilisation economy" had to be at least partially "demobilised" to achieve war mobilisation'.[2] It was, however, successful. The result was an even greater flow of weapons and parts which were deliberately simple, quick to assemble, easy to maintain and inexpensive to replace.

As a result of these changes, the Soviet Union was eventually able to overwhelm Germany with vast numbers of tanks, aircraft, artillery pieces and small weapons, all of which could be delivered to wherever they were needed. Soviet forces were provided with *Katyusha* rocket-launchers, the SUS (self-propelled artillery), heavy mortars, and the T-34, the best in use at the time. German vehicles were outnumbered and were not equipped for winter. The early German superiority in the air was soon reversed as the Soviet airforce was provided with fourteen new types of aircraft.

Accompanying the increase in weapons production was the emergence of a new military strategy. This abandoned the emphasis on 'offensive' warfare, developed during the 1930s, in favour of the more traditional combination of defence and counter-attack. This was used highly effectively by Zhukov. As a result there was close co-ordination between partisan warfare and the thrusts of the Soviet forces at Kursk in 1943, and the subsequent invasion of eastern Europe in 1944. In the process, the army was given more initiative than it had been in the 1930s and many of the deadening effects of the purges were now lifted. Men of real ability were promoted to supreme command, including Zhukov, Tolbukhin, Konev, Malinovsky, Vatutin and Rossakovsky. Stalin was much less inclined than Hitler to interfere in military decisions, allowing these to be taken at the front.

The participation of the Soviet people was an essential factor in the style of warfare conducted against the German armies. Stalin was therefore heavily dependent on patriotism. This was, to some extent, created through a massive propaganda campaign and through the forcible resettlement of any groups who were considered to be a possible security threat; this applied to the Balkars, Chechens, Karachais, Meskhetians, Crimean Tartars, Balts, Ukrainians and Cossacks. On the more positive side, connections were drawn with the Russian past – especially with the defeat of the French in 1812. The struggle against Hitler was labelled the 'Great Fatherland War', a replica of the 'Great Patriotic War' against Napoleon. There was also a great deal of spontaneous patriotism which showed remarkable levels of self-sacrifice and heroism – especially in the siege of Leningrad and the struggle for Stalingrad.

Yet the Soviet recovery and victory over Germany were not entirely self-generated. They were also helped by supplies and influences from outside. Essential back-up equipment was provided by US and British aid under the Lend-Lease programme: the import of trucks, jeeps and heavy rolling stock enabled Soviet factories to concentrate on producing armaments. By filling gaps in Soviet infrastructure, the Allies therefore made it possible for the Soviet Union to move more quickly than it could otherwise have done from the defensive to the offensive. Military developments were also crucial. British and American campaigns in North Africa (1942–3) drew off divisions vitally needed by the Germans for the Russian front. There is no coincidence about the similtaneous Soviet resistance at Stalingrad and the British victory at El Alamein.

The final factor in the Soviet victory was the collapse of the German offensive. To some extent this was self-inflicted. Hitler's strategy of maintaining the offensive was inappropriate for Russian conditions, as was to be proved at Stalingrad between 1942 and 1943. Atrocities committed by the *Wehrmacht* and *Waffen SS* also stiffened the resistance of the Soviet population, rendering the continuation of *Blitzkrieg* tactics impossible. Hitler, however, refused to accept this, insisting on impossible targets. Whereas Stalin learned the lessons of early defeat, Hitler had become unrealistic through initial victory.

16. What impact did the Second World War have on the Soviet Union?   (90 marks)

The impact of the Second World War on the Soviet Union was varied. The immediate result was military collapse. This, however, was followed by revival and victory, with the emergence of a strengthened and expanded superpower. During the war itself much of the previous administrative and economic structure was changed, although the previous pattern returned after the war had ended. All these effects were related to the most negative of all – the unprecedented levels of destruction.

The impact of the sudden German invasion in June 1941 was the most spectacular military collapse and the largest territorial losses in the whole of Russia's history. This meant that Belorussia, Ukraine and part of Russia itself all came under German administration and experienced the full rigours of Nazi labour regulations and anti-Semitic measures. Substantial minorities within these areas expressed their opposition to Stalin's regime by assisting the occupying forces. Hence the multi-ethnic nature of the Soviet Union was threatened even more fundamentally by the Second World War than it had been by the First World War. Except that, on this occasion, the situation changed fundamentally. For, in the longer term, the war resulted in military victory. With victory came expansion and domination, as the Soviet Union not only recovered the territories it had lost, but also recovered the area captured by Poland in 1920 and took the Baltic States and slices of Romania, Czechoslovakia and Finland. A Soviet presence remained in Poland, East Germany, Hungary, Czechoslovakia, Romania and Bulgaria, all of which became Soviet satellites and, from 1955, allies. The expansion of communism, which Trotsky had originally thought would be accomplished by revolution, was actually Soviet military domination in eastern Europe. The war also left the Soviet Union with the largest standing army in the world. This, along with the new control over eastern Europe, exacerbated poor relations with the West, especially Britain and the United States, thus initiating the Cold War. From 1945, therefore, the Soviet Union became the one of the two poles in a worldwide ideological and strategic confrontation.

Internal structures were also affected by the war, although in a strangely contradictory way. War normally tightens up the administration and increases centralised control over economic production. The reverse, however, happened in the Soviet Union between 1941 and 1945. During the late 1930s the purges and show trials had ensured Stalin's unquestioned control, while even the army and security forces of the NKVD had been fundamentally affected. The catastrophe of initial defeat brought major changes. For the first time in a decade there were no purges and Stalin was prepared to hand over unprecedented influence to his military command, especially Marshal Zhukov. He was also more willing, through the GOKO, to share the decision making and, surprisingly, provided a more genuine collective leadership than Hitler. Similarly, the economic planning system, tightly controlled by *Gosplan,* was abandoned. Initiatives and decisions on production were localised, which resulted in a vast increase in armaments production from 1942 onwards. And yet this did not last. Once the war had been won, Stalin returned to the system of the 1930s, reviving the command economy in the fourth and fifth Five Year Plans, increasing his own personal authority through another round of purges, and downgrading the influence of the military. Politically, it was as if the war had never been.

Economically, of course, the war had had a devastating impact, giving Stalin his justification to revive the planning system. This time, socialist construction would have to start with post-war reconstruction. Basically, the Soviet losses were the heaviest suffered by any country in history as the result of an invasion by another power. Something like 5.7 million soldiers died or disappeared while the total Soviet losses amounted to 23 million people, compared with 375,000 from Britain, 405,000 from the United States and 600,000 from France. This 23 million came on top of the 13.5 million deaths during the First World War and Civil War, and at least 7 million as a result of the famine and purges between 1931 and 1939. There was also massive destruction. The Germans had demolished 1,710 towns and 70,000 villages, 31,850 industrial enterprises and 98,000 collective farms. Two cities suffered particularly severely. Leningrad endured a 900-day siege which produced a casualty figure greater than that of all the Western Allies combined. Stalingrad was totally devastated as Russian and German troops fought over each street, and then in the ruins and rubble.

The effect of the Second World War was therefore paradoxical. It inflicted massive destruction on the Soviet Union and yet brought an immense increase in its power. It shook Stalin's regime and credibility as a leader, and yet enabled both to resume their pre-war pattern. The regime which entered the First World War was destroyed by it, while the reverse happened as a result of the Second World War.

 The period, 1945–53

17. Did Stalin reach the peak of his power in the Soviet Union between 1945 and 1953? (90 marks)

The last part of Stalin's period in power is often considered a bolt-on to the rest. In fact, it has more significance than this, although there is now some controversy as to whether it saw Stalin's dictatorship at its most mature and successful – or, alternatively, at its most vulnerable.

The argument for Stalin having reached the full extent of his dictatorship is a compelling one. The catalyst had been the victory in the Second World War, which had confirmed his personal prestige and authority, enabling him to strengthen the measures he had already taken to develop a totalitarian state and convert the Soviet Union into a dominant superpower. In political terms, Stalin was able to do without the assistance of the Central Committee of the Party, together with the Politburo, of which he called no meetings between 1945 and 1953. He even disbanded the State Defence Committee (GOKO) which had been the main form of government during the war years. To tighten his grip still further he introduced the Zhdanov Decrees in 1946 to control all forms of cultural activity and ensure that they were in line with Socialist Realism and the Stalinist personality cult. He was even confident enough to demote Marshal Zhukov and, in the Leningrad Affair, to criticise established war heroes of the famous siege. He was probably on the point of launching another major purge at the time of his death in 1953. Meanwhile, throughout the period 1945–53 he had resisted any pressure to introduce a different economic system: the fourth and fifth Five Year Plans (1946–50 and 1950–5) were therefore a continuation of those of the 1930s. In every way, therefore, Stalin had consolidated his earlier position and now presided over the world's most successful totalitarian system.

All this can, however, be seen as too simple. Another, very different version of the post-war Stalinist regime has been put forward by recent historians, who consider that Stalin was actually at his most vulnerable during the final period of his career. Instead of finding fulfilment between 1945 and 1953, Stalin had to deal again with all the problems he had managed to sort out before 1941. Far from confirming his power, therefore, the War actually loosened it.

This applied in all areas – military, political, social and economic. The very success of the Red Army in achieving victory over the Third Reich raised the threat in Stalin's mind of a military dictatorship. This went back to his earlier fears in the 1920s that power might be seized by Trotsky as a new Bonapartist figure. If he now demoted Zhukov, it was not because Stalin was strong – but because he was weak and vulnerable. He had to reduce the involvement of the military in any of the affairs of state, which also explains why he ended the State Defence Committee which had played such a vital administrative role during the war. If he refused also to consult the various organs of the party, especially the Politburo and the Central Committee, it was again through fear that they might produce a rival to challenge his supremacy. Of course, such actions carried dangers; they might actually provoke the sort of opposition that Stalin wanted to avoid. Hence he adopted the same approach that he had already used in the 1930s: a new round of purges. But these were for defensive reasons. Far from using his power to destroy opposition, Stalin was trying to destroy opposition to recover his power. The extent of his insecurity is shown by his victims. The heroes of Soviet resistance to the German invasion, including Voznesensky, were tried and executed during the notorious Leningrad Affair. Stalin's objection was that such heroism rivalled his own. He was also concerned that the years of war had weakened his hold on opinion and culture, which explains the renewed controls in the form of the Zhdanov Decrees. An indispensable feature of Stalin's renewed control was the revival of terror, with the resumption of police operations under the leadership and instigation of Beria. Terror, however, is the result of insecurity quite as much as it is the expression of power. Even Stalin's economic policies were an indication of his vulnerability. The planning system had been part of his command structure in the 1930s. Like his political authority, this had been loosened by the relaxed during the war. Stalin, however, now wanted its full return, not because he saw it as the only viable way of achieving reconstruction but because he was anxious above all to restore centralised control. The planning system had become more important than the plan itself.

Initial perspectives can therefore be misleading. The last word could go to Ward: 'This was no self-confident tyrant in charge of a smoothly functioning totalitarian machine, but a sickly old man; unpredictable, dangerous, lied to by terrified subordinates, presiding over a ramshackly bureaucracy'.[3]

18. Identify and explain the relative importance of two reasons for the development of Stalin's rivalry with the West between 1945 and 1953. (90 marks)

A range of specific reasons can be given for Stalin's growing rivalry with the West after 1945. These can, however, be grouped round two general factors. The first was the ideological antipathy between communism and capitalism; the second was the perceived need for Soviet security against renewed Western threats.

Ideological rivalry between the Soviet Union and the West had grown in intensity as a result of a simplification in the equation since the Second World War. From 1941 the main enemy of communism had been Nazism, not Western capitalism. But the defeat of Hitler restored the original conflict. Stalin now did whatever he could to strengthen the resistance of communism to any attempts of the West to influence eastern Europe. His response to the Truman Doctrine (1947) was to institutionalise Soviet communist control over not only the Soviet zone of Germany but also over Poland, Hungary, Czechoslovakia, Romania and Bulgaria. This was done through the establishment in 1947 of the Communist Information Bureau (*Cominform*), which would ensure Moscow's control over international communism and guarantee conformity to Stalinism in eastern Europe. This was followed in 1948 by the conversion of broad-front governments into monolithic communist regimes. These, in turn, were tied ideologically to the Soviet economic system by the Council for Mutual Economic Assistance (*Comecon*), set up in 1949. These methods ensured that the Soviet Union became the more powerful centre of an enlarged communist bloc. This enabled it to challenge more effectively the capitalist states which had, in turn, acquired a stronger core in the form of the United States.

Ideology is never an influence to be underestimated, but security was the ultimate factor in Stalin's policies, even if this was expressed in ideological terms. As far back as 1943 he was convinced that Britain and the United States were trying to weaken the Soviet Union by allowing it to take the brunt of the war against Germany whilst they delayed in opening a second front in the west. Fear about future Soviet security also underlay his assertiveness and inflexibility at the wartime conferences at Teheran in 1943, and at Yalta and Potsdam in 1945. At the same time, the US monopoly on the atomic bomb made him determined to keep intact the Soviet supremacy in terms of conventional military strength. Stalin's institutional arrangements, especially *Cominform* and the CMEA were established for security reasons, even if they were defended in the ringing ideological tones of the 1947 Zhdanov Line. In a speech Zhdanov warned of the new threat of the capitalist West. 'The cardinal purpose of the imperialist camp is to strengthen imperialism, to hatch a new imperialist war, to combat socialism and democracy, and to support reactionary and anti-democratic pro-fascist regimes and movements everywhere.' This could be prevented by linking the economies of eastern Europe with the Soviet planning system, keeping them out of the orbit of the Marshall Plan and providing controllable sources of raw materials and outlets for Soviet industrial goods. The next logical step was the establishment of a series of Soviet puppet regimes which would provide the Soviet Union with a glacis, or killing ground, in the event of a future offensive by a Western power.

The connection between ideology and security is apparent in the specific flashpoints between Stalin and the West. The first was the Iranian crisis (1945–6), in which the continued Soviet occupation of the northern part of Iran was challenged by the United States and Britain. The second – and more serious – was the 1948 Berlin Crisis. Stalin's attempts to squeeze out the Western presence from Berlin by closing off the access routes was defended on ideological grounds, even if the real motive was to secure the Soviet hold over the whole of the eastern zone of Germany. When this backfired on him, convincing the Western powers of the need for a defensive military alliance (NATO), Stalin exercised greater caution in the future. During the Korean War (1950–3) the Soviet Union confined itself to ideological invective at the United Nations in support of North Korea, along with the use of the Soviet veto in the Security Council. The problem Stalin now faced was the emergence of communist China as a new military rival in the Far East. This both constrained what he could do militarily and increased the need for strong messages of support for smaller communist regimes.

By 1953, therefore, Stalin was settling for a stand-off rivalry with the West, the main character-istic of the Cold War. Because he had satisfied Soviet security needs in Eastern Europe and had, by 1949, developed nuclear weapons, Stalin was at last prepared to focus mainly on ideological propaganda. Words were now speaking louder than actions.

19. Identify three aims Stalin had after 1945 and explain how effectively he achieved them. (90 marks)

Stalin's aims after the Second World War can be grouped into three overall categories. The first was to bring about recovery after the massive destruction which the Soviet Union had suffered since 1941. The second was to consolidate his own position in the Soviet Union, and the third was to consolidate the Soviet Union's position in Europe. These fitted closely together. Recovery was the pressing objective, requiring a massive injection of resources. His own position depended crucially on how this was to be accomplished; he had a similar personal interest in the way in which the Soviet Union fared against the Western powers. In every case he encountered mixed success.

Stalin assumed that reconstruction could succeed only if he reverted to the planning system of the 1930s. This explains why the fourth and fifth Five Year Plans (1946–50 and 1950–5) placed the focus on collective farming and the development of heavy industry at the expense of consumer goods. At first sight the results seem impressive. The *kolkhozy* were consolidated in size and reduced in number from 252,000 to 76,000. Heavy industry once again forged ahead, with the addition of considerable investment into Stalin's nuclear programme. By 1949 the Soviet Union possessed the atomic bomb and, by 1951, the hydrogen bomb; in 1950 it exceeded all the targets of the fourth Five Year Plan and, despite wartime destruction, had developed a larger industrial base than that of 1940. Yet this was at a huge cost. The Soviet consumer continued to be neglected, while the conditions of the workforce actually deteriorated. Even worse was the plight of agriculture, the 1946 harvest producing only 40 per cent of that of 1913. Stalin therefore produced a strange anomaly: a superpower with primitive living standards – an industrial giant with a shrinking agricultural base. Although recovery did occur between 1945 and 1953, it was much slower than that accomplished by western Germany or by Japan, both of which also experienced massive infra-structural damage. The most serious long-term problem was an economic system which had become so rigid that it could not adjust to the rapidly changing world economic climate of the 1970s and 1980s. Stalin's economic legacy was therefore a largely negative one.

His own position within the Soviet Union was similarly flawed. At first sight he appeared to have consolidated his power and introduced a new phase of 'developed' or 'mature' dictatorship. After all, he was able to disband the GOKO, which had assisted his wartime administration, and he dispensed almost entirely with the services of the CPSU Central Committee and Politburo. Instead, he increased the level of his personal supervision over the central administration and took many

Figure 7.5 **Map of the Soviet Union in 1950**

of the key decisions over the planning targets. He was also protected by the Zdhanov Decrees (1947), which controlled cultural output and taste, and continued to use the NKVD under Beria to eliminate actual and potential opposition. And yet all this can be seen as an indication of a sense of deep insecurity. Stalin may well have been struggling to regain the heights he had experienced in the 1930s. There were potential rivals within both the army and the party – both of which therefore had to be controlled. He lacked the confidence to experiment with new forms of economic development, despite the massive evidence from the 1930s that the Five Year Plans were deeply flawed. Instead, he had to revive old formulas and use old justifications for them. Although he kept the lid on opposition during his lifetime, there was an explosion of antipathy against his memory from 1956 onwards.

Stalin was, perhaps, more successful in achieving Soviet security in Europe. After 1945 it was a superpower with the world's largest standing army. It had achieved direct control over East Germany, Poland, Czechoslovakia, Hungary, Bulgaria and Romania, thereby increasing the security of Soviet territorial gains in the Baltic and the Ukraine. From 1949 and 1951, the extension of Soviet influence was given greater permanence by the protection of nuclear weapons. Thus, compared with Soviet insecurity in 1931, huge steps had been taken by the year of Stalin's death in 1953. On the other hand, such policies provoked a concerted response from the West against the Soviet Union, in the form of the Truman Doctrine and Marshall Plan (1948) and the establishment of NATO in 1949. In any case, Stalin had to back off over the Berlin blockade in 1948–9 and remain a virtual spectator in the Korean War (1950–3). The Cold War also had a serious internal impact on the Soviet Union, as the constant increase in defence expenditure caused an ever-increasing gap between the Soviet consumer and his counterpart in the West. This was to become a real problem during the 1970s and 1980s, as was the growth of protest in the Soviet Union's eastern European dependencies.

Most of Stalin's policies after 1945 proved a liability to the future development and growth of the Soviet Union. The effort he put into maintaining his dictatorship created a rigid system which could not adapt in the longer term. The first part of his legacy to go was his reputation, destroyed after 1956 by Khrushchev's destalinisation campaign. The second was the economy – by the 1970s it had become apparent that the rigid planning system could not compete with the west. This undermined the Soviet position in Europe, bringing an end to the Cold War in 1989 and the Soviet Union itself in 1991.

 Additional essay questions (with advice)

Each of these questions can be tackled as a single essay or as one of the answers to a question in several parts. Additional reading and research is desirable for each one.

20. Assess Lenin's achievement between 1918 and 1924.

Advice: *Avoid describing what Lenin did. Select criteria which enable you to 'assess' or 'weigh up' both positively and negatively. These might include: (1) overcoming opposition to the regime; (2) setting up a new system; and (3) managing the economy.*

21. 'Stalin rose to power between 1924 and 1929 because he was underestimated by his opponents.' How far do you agree with this view?

Advice: *Be careful how you argue this. Stalin's colleagues all underestimated him, especially Trotsky. But you need to explain: (1) in what ways he was underestimated; and (2) what his strengths actually were. That said, there were clearly other factors in his rise, including the vulnerability of his opponents. Include these in your coverage of 'how far', but find a way of bringing them back to Stalin being 'underestimated'.*

22. To what extent was Stalin's political power based on 'terror' before 1941?

Advice: *The 'terror' side of the answer clearly involves coverage of the purges. But you also need to deal with the other bases of his power – control over the party and the introduction of a new constitution. Think also in terms of indoctrination and the cult of personality.*

23. 'Ruthless but effective'. How far do you agree with this description of Stalin's economic policies before 1941?

Advice: *Give equal time to the two key words in the question. 'Ruthless' is easier to establish than 'effective', which may involve: (1) a split verdict between industry and agriculture; or (2) use of recent interpretations to downplay the effectiveness even of the industrial changes. Either will do.*

Essay plan (possibility 1)

Para 1: Overall approach. All areas of Stalin's economic policies were ruthless – but the degree of effectiveness varied:
- *between agriculture and industry*
- *between the different sectors of industry.*

Para 2: Stalin's ruthlessness is not in question:
- *Forced collectivisation, measures against the Kulaks and use of the NKVD (supporting detail).*
- *Industrialisation was accompanied by deteriorating living standards in the cities and indifference to consumer needs (supporting detail).*
- *Economic change enforced by purges and Gulag system, which provided additional labour (supporting detail).*

Para 3: Effectiveness varied in different sectors of the economy. In agriculture it was an unqualified failure:
- *Largescale resistance by peasantry to collectivisation, through destruction of livestock etc. (supporting detail).*
- *Long-term undermining of agriculture – which never recovered from Stalin's policy (supporting detail).*

Para 4: Industry was more varied:
- *Heavy industry was much more successful (supporting detail, including production figures for Five Year Plans).*
- *Importance of heavy industry in war with Germany 1941–5 (supporting detail).*

Para 5: On the other hand:
- *Consumer industry was neglected (supporting detail).*
- *This meant that, in the USSR, industrialisation did not bring improved living standards (supporting detail).*

Para 6: Integrated conclusion:

Stalin's policies were certainly ruthless.
- *This led to effectiveness where centralisation could be made to work (in industry) – but not in rural areas.*

Stalin set up the sort of economy which
- *could defeat Nazi Germany but could survive indefinitely in peacetime.*

Essay plan (possibility 2)

Para 1: Overall approach. All areas of Stalin's economic policies were ruthless but the degree of effectiveness has been variously interpreted.

Para 2: There is considerable evidence for the ruthlessness of Stalin's policies. As for possibility 1, paragraph 2.

Para 3: An argument has been advanced that his policies worked in industry. As for possibility 1, paragraph 4.

Para 4: On the other hand, the case against the effectiveness is overwhelming. In the case of agriculture his policy was disastrous. As for possibility 1, paragraph 3.

Para 5: Even the effectiveness of industrial change has been exaggerated:
- *The structure of the planning system was chaotic (supporting detail).*
- *Five Year Plans had to be suspended in wartime to release productive capacity.*

Para 6: Integrated conclusion. Stalin's economic changes were largely ineffective because of the structure of economic change. Ruthlessness contributed directly to this.

24. How far did Stalin modify the social changes made before 1924 by the Bolsheviks?

Advice: *Establish what the main social changes were – possibly: (1) egalitarianism; (2) the family, (3) values and discipline; and (4) religion. In each case the balance between continuity and change will be different, ranging from extensive change (the family) to very little (religion). Since there is no end date in the question, make sure you include some references to the period 1945–53.*

25. Was Stalin more effective as a leader in war (1941–5) or peace (1945–53)?

Advice: *Avoid a straight description of the events of the two periods. Select criteria and draw direct comparisons. Possibilities might be: (1) willingness to share power; (2) management of the economy; and (3) success in achieving objectives.*

Part 3: Sources

1. Life in the Soviet Union, 1928–41

This exercise consists of three questions on two sources, with a time allocation of 45 minutes.

Source A: Levels of agricultural production 1928–35

	1928	1929	1930	1931	1932	1933	1934	1935
Grain (million tons)	70.3	71.7	83.5	69.5	69.6	68.6	67.6	75.0
Cattle (million head)	70.5	67.1	52.5	47.9	40.7	38.4	42.4	49.3
Pigs (million head)	26.0	20.4	13.6	14.4	11.6	12.1	17.4	22.6
Sheep and goats (million head)	146.7	147.0	108.8	77.7	52.1	50.2	51.9	61.1

Source B: A report by a Reuters correspondent, 29 March 1932

Russia today is in the grip of famine. I walked alone through villages and twelve collective farms. Everywhere was the cry 'There is no bread; we are dying'. This cry came to me from every part of Russia. In a train a communist denied to me that there was a famine. I flung into the spittoon a crust of bread I had been eating from my own supply. The peasant, my fellow passenger, fished it out and ravenously ate it. I threw orange peel into the spittoon. The peasant again grabbed it and devoured it. The communist subsided.

QUESTIONS WITH WORKED ANSWERS

a) **Study Sources A and B. What do the sources reveal about the problems facing the implementation of collectivisation?** **(5 marks)**

Several problems are revealed by Sources A and B in the implementation of collective farming. The most serious was the uniform collapse in production. Livestock, for example, declined disastrously between 1928 and 1932, cattle from 70.5 million head to 40.7 million, pigs from 26 million to 11.6 million, sheep and goats from 146.7 million to 52.1 million. The decline in grain production after a temporary increase in 1930 overlapped the famine of 1931–2, described in graphic terms in Source B. This crisis was due partly to a second problem – the resistance of many of the peasantry to Stalin's policy; the sudden decline in livestock figures shows the impact of the mass slaughter carried out as an act of defiance. Stalin's response was mass requisitioning of grain, with the effects shown in Source B: 'There is no bread; we are dying'. Finally, the two sources provide clues as to the problems of effective central action to deal with the problem. Production figures remained variable until 1935, while the official line was clearly to ignore the social impact of food shortages rather than address them, as is shown by the attitude of the communist official in Source B.

b) Use your own knowledge. Why did Stalin introduce forced collectivisation?   **(7 marks)**

There were several interconnected factors involved in Stalin's decision to introduce collectivisation. One was a move away from the New Economic Policy, which had been introduced in 1921. By 1928 Stalin had come to oppose this form of 'state capitalism', with its special concessions to the peasantry. He considered that it was no longer appropriate to the real needs of the Soviet Union, especially since the 'procurement crisis' of 1927 left the country short of grain because the peasantry felt that there was little incentive to produce beyond their own needs. This intensified the pressure on the government from the industrial workers, who had never particularly benefited from the NEP.

Stalin was, in any case, moving towards a centralised planning system to accelerate industrial development since he saw this as the only way of guaranteeing the survival and security of the Soviet Union. Since he did not want to finance this by Western loans, the only method was to subsidise industrial growth through agriculture which, in turn, meant much tighter state controls and the end of private land ownership. In this sense, collectivisation was a step towards the Five Year Plans, and eventually came to be integrated into them.

What clinched the decision for collectivisation was Stalin's political position during the late 1920s. Between 1927 and 1929 he was involved in the final stage of his rise to power and was taking on the Rightists within the party, especially Bukharin, Rykov and Tomsky. Stalin underpinned his political attack with a public criticism of their continuing commitment to the NEP. He used his conversion to collectivisation and forced industrialisation to undermine their credibility within the Central Committee and to force a vote against them. It had all come together by 1929: the first Five Year Plan had been launched, Stalin had achieved uncontested supremacy – and the platform for both had been provided by collectivisation.

c) Use your own knowledge. How far was industry transformed by Stalin's first three Five Year Plans?   **(18 marks)**

Total (30 marks)

There is a strong argument for the transformation of industry during the first Five Year Plan (1928–32) as well as by the second (1933–7) and third (1937–41). Heavy industry grew rapidly, steel production increased over the period from 3 million tons to 18 million, coal from 35 million to 150 million and oil from 12 million to 26 million. There were also massive projects which showed an obsession with 'gigantomania', the most prestigious being the construction of a new industrial city at Magnitogorsk, the Dnieper hydro-electric dam, and the Belamor Canal linking the Baltic and White Seas. In addition, parts of Siberia were industrialised for the first time and the whole emphasis of the Five Year Plans was on over-fulfilling the targets of the plans: Stakhanovism became the main driving force behind growth in all areas.

The emphasis of the plans was on heavy industry and armaments. Again, a 'transformation' could be claimed. By 1941 the Soviet Union had developed a massive military capacity, which enabled it to survive a devastating German attack and eventually to outproduce and crush its rival. It could be argued that the difference between Russian defeat by Germany in the First World War and the Soviet victory over Germany in the Second World War was the size of its industrial infrastructure.

On the other hand, there are areas in which the extent of Stalin's industrialisation can be exaggerated. Emphasis on 'transformation' tends to overlook earlier contributions to Russia's industrial base by Witte in the 1890s. By 1914, there had already been an advanced network of industries based on textiles in the Moscow area, engineering around St Petersburg, coal in the Donets region, iron and steel in the Ukraine and oil in the Caspian Sea area. It is true that much of this had collapsed during the Civil War period (1918–21) but Lenin had begun the process of recovery and had initiated a programme of electrification. Any 'transformation' by Stalin should therefore be seen as 'restoration' and 'acceleration' rather than as 'innovation'.

In some ways, the impact of industrialisation was actually limited. Although the military implications were considerable, there was comparatively little effect on the standard of living. The vast majority of the population did not benefit materially since the advances in heavy industry were not accompanied by a similar increase in consumer goods. The Five Year Plans therefore failed to produce the 'social transformation' which normally accompanies an industrial revolution. It has also been argued that the whole administrative structure, based on *Gosplan* was inherently inefficient. The planning system was so difficult to control from the centre that it was actually dismantled during the war years; its revival after 1945 is now seen as a major error, condemning Soviet industry to long-term stagnation.

The verdict must therefore be a mixed one. The rapid emergence of a major industrial and military power from a base which was already there can be seen as a 'transformation'. The longer-term consumer deprivation and the structural inefficiency of the industrial planning system cannot.

PARALLEL QUESTIONS WITHOUT WORKED ANSWERS

a) **Study Sources A and B. What do the sources reveal about the effects of the policy of forced collectivisation?**   **(5 marks)**

Advice: *Cover (1) what is revealed directly and (2) what can be inferred, especially from the account of the Reuters correspondent.*

b) **Use Source B and your own knowledge. Why were the effects of the early years of collectivisation so severe?**   **(7 marks)**

Advice: *The focus of Source B is on starvation and the attitude of officialdom to it. This should suggest where to locate your additional knowledge.*

c) **Use your own knowledge. How far did Stalin transform Russian society between 1929 and 1941?**   **(18 marks)**

Total (30 marks)

Advice: *'How far' needs to be addressed. It should be possible to give an answer on an alternating scale, according to which area of society is being covered.*

2. Stalin's purges

This exercise consists of three questions on four sources, with a time allocation of 60 minutes.

Source A: An official Soviet cartoon of 1937 showing Trotsky washing his hands in the blood of Soviet Russia

Source B: The concluding speech of chief prosecutor Vyshinski at the show trial of 1938

Time will pass. The graves of the hateful traitors will grow over with weeds and thistle. But over us, over our happy country, our sun will shine with its luminous rays as bright and joyous as before. Over the road cleared of the last scum and filth of the past, we, our people, with our beloved leader and teacher, the great Stalin, at our head, will march onwards and onwards, towards communism!

Source C: Adapted from a speech by Khrushchev to the Twentieth Congress of the Communist Party in February 1956

It became apparent that many Party, Soviet and economic activists who were branded in 1937–1938 as 'enemies' were actually never enemies, spies, wreckers, etc., but were always honest communists.

Figure 7.6 ***An official Soviet cartoon of 1937 – Trotsky washing his hands in the blood of Soviet Russia***

Stalin was a very distrustful man, sickly suspicious; we know this from our work with him. The sickly suspicion created in him a general distrust even toward eminent Party workers whom he had known for years. Everywhere and in everything he saw 'enemies', 'two-facers' and 'spies'.

Possessing unlimited power, he indulged in great wilfulness and choked a person morally and physically. A situation was created where one could not express one's own will.

Source D: Adapted from R.W. Thurston, *Life and Terror in Stalin's Russia* (1996)

This book argues that Stalin was not guilty of mass first-degree murder from 1934 to 1941 and did not plan or carry out a systematic campaign to crush the nation. This view is not one of absolution, however: his policies did help to engender real plots, lies, and threats to his position. Then this fear-ridden man reacted, and over-reacted to events. All the while, he could not control the flow of people within the country, job turnover, or illegal acts by managers and many others. He was sitting at the peak of a pyramid of lies and incomplete information, and he must have known it.

QUESTIONS WITH WORKED ANSWERS

a) Study Source A and use your own knowledge. Explain why Trotsky was presented by Stalin as such a threat to his regime. **(20 marks)**

Source A depicts Trotsky as a traitor, washing his hands in the blood of the Soviet Union from a German helmet. His criminal activities are confirmed by the background clutter of bombs, pistols, daggers, letters and the towel hanging on the swastika. This was the public image of Trotsky presented by Stalin. During the show trials of the 1930s, prominent Bolsheviks like Bukharin were accused of being in league with him and the Gestapo. The charges were patently absurd and Stalin's real reason for fearing Trotsky was that the latter was a powerful critic from exile. By 1933 he was attacking Stalin's willingness to see the triumph of Nazism in Germany and was urging the formation of popular fronts against fascism. Stalin was also sensitive to Trotsky's criticism of his ruthlessness and the failure of his agricultural policies. But the most important factor all was that Stalin used Trotsky as an excuse for clearing out of the party a whole generation of Bolsheviks who had once been associated with Lenin and who might mount a future challenge to Stalin's leadership. The real conspiracy was not Trotsky's: it was Stalin's.

b) Study Sources B and C. Compare these sources as evidence for Stalin's personal control over the Soviet Union in the 1930s. **(40 marks)**

Both sources point directly to Stalin's enormous personal power in the Soviet Union. Source B, for example, refers to 'the great Stalin at our head', while C emphasises his possession of 'unlimited power'. Yet the way in which this argument is developed in the two sources is very different, largely because of the circumstances in which the sources were produced: B was a speech from a chief prosecutor upholding the Stalinist system against the 'scum and filth', while C was an attempt by Khrushchev to distance himself from the monster he had once served.

These motives are bound to affect the different ways in which Stalin is represented. The impression created by Source B is entirely positive, that in Source C totally negative. Contrast, for example, 'our beloved leader and teacher, the great Stalin' (Source B) with Source C's 'very distrustful man, sickly suspicious', or the altruistic use of power in the 'march' towards communism (Source B) with the 'great wilfulness' shown in Source C. The contrasting use of power is also revealed by the effects on those who felt it. In Source B these were 'hateful traitors', whose graves would 'grow over with weeds', while in Source B the victims were 'honest communists' and it was Stalin who 'choked' people 'morally and physically'.

These perceptions of Stalin went so far as to rewrite Soviet history to suit the image required by the present.

c) Study Sources A to D and use your own knowledge. Examine the view that Stalin's motives for the terror of the 1930s were entirely irrational. **(60 marks)**

Total (120 marks)

Taken as a set, these sources provide a very mixed answer to this question. Sources A and B strongly imply a properly functioning system taking entirely rational action against those seeking to destroy it through their treasonable activities. Sources C and D, by contrast, provide an explanation based much more on Stalin's irrational motives for a policy of terror.

To a large extent, Sources A and B can be discounted as direct evidence since they clearly distort for the purpose of propaganda. They are, however, useful in showing the enormous influence imposed by Stalin – which would strongly imply that the reason for the purges was systematic and rational. Source C presents the reverse picture and includes several words which would not normally be associated with rational behaviour – especially 'distrust' and 'sickly suspicion'. This might be considered formidable evidence since it comes from someone who had, as a prominent member of the party in Kiev and Moscow, been one of Stalin's most trusted lieutenants and must therefore have known Stalin well. Khrushchev could, however, have had a strong motive for exaggeration. The nature of the power base he was trying to build in 1956 meant that he needed to denounce the excesses of Stalin – but how? Since the system itself could not be blamed, the only alternative was to attribute them all to Stalin's paranoid personality. Much of what Khrushchev said about Stalin's instability was undoubtedly true – but probably went too far in the direction of irrationalism.

This imbalance is offset by Source D, a secondary source which reflects extensive research and therefore provides a clearer perspective. Unlike Source C, this sees a connection between the man and the system. Thurston argues that Stalin *was* fear-ridden and *did* implement a policy of terror. But the extent of this terror was due mainly to the loss of administrative control by central power over local officials. The conclusion which can be drawn from this view is that Stalin had motives which were both rational and irrational; these were, however, greatly distorted by a system operated by many 'little Stalins' over whom he had no effective control.

Additional knowledge tends to support this last view. Stalin was certainly ruthless but his commitment to implementing the 'Dictatorship of the proletariat' was ideological rather than paranoid. Terror had already been seen by Lenin and Trotsky as an essential part of building a new system and had been administered through the Cheka, the precedent for Stalin's NKVD. Stalin was now using terror on a larger scale to enforce his Five Year Plans and policy of collectivisation. At the same time, there was also a personal legacy of distrust, which made Stalin much more obsessive than the other Bolsheviks. Lenin had recognised this in his *Political Testament*, warning against the appointment of Stalin as his successor. The twists and turns of Stalin's rise to power between 1924 and 1929 confirmed his belief that he was surrounded by enemies – even if they had been of his own making. The personal involvement therefore interacted with the ideological use of terror. But it spiralled out of control – not just because of Stalin's irrational fears, but also because of major problems of communication and control within the administration of terror.

PARALLEL QUESTIONS WITHOUT WORKED ANSWERS

a) **Study Source B and use your own knowledge. Explain how Stalin built up his 'personality cult' during the 1930s.** (20 marks)

Advice: *Focus on what can be deduced from the prosecutor's address about the personality cult, using specific words in quotation marks. Extend this with your own knowledge.*

b) **Study Sources C and D. Compare these sources as evidence for Stalin's personal responsibility for the terror of the 1930s.** (40 marks)

Advice: *Cover two angles: (1) the views actually contained by the sources; and (2) the issue of usefulness and reliability – including any motives the author of each of the sources might have.*

c) Study Sources A to D and use your own knowledge. Examine the view that the impact of Stalin's terror in the 1930s was entirely destructive.   (60 marks)

Total (120 marks)

Advice: *In the first paragraph consider the variety of views offered by the sources as a set. Then use your knowledge of (1) the effects of the purges and (2) recent interpretations to provide a considered view. The word 'entirely' is particularly important.*

Part 4: Historical skills

Coursework and individual studies

PURPOSE

All A-Level History involves some coursework. Depending on the board and specifications, this may be for AS, A2 or both. The intention is to enable the student to produce a piece of individual writing under controlled conditions. For many it reduces the pressure by decreasing the number of examination papers which have to be taken, and for few, it leads to a permanent interest in a particular topic. The student probably does more reading for the coursework than for the examination topics and has the opportunity to do some genuine research work.

Unless it is done properly, however, coursework can be a liability: some students get their lowest marks for this component. There are several things to avoid at all costs. The first is the very common temptation to come up with a rehashed version of a topic covered previously – either for GCSE or for another subject. The second is descriptive narrative, although the emphasis of GCSE on argument makes this much less of a problem than it was twenty years ago. A third problem is plagiarism, which ranges from copying verbatim from books to downloading straight from the Internet.

Where there is scope for choice, it is therefore essential to go for a question or angle which is fresh and which will enable the development of interpretation rather than description. The preparation itself should be thorough and avoid lazy forms of research or the shortcuts which result in plagiarism.

PREPARATION

Answering the question

Almost all coursework is now based on a question rather than a title. The most important single factor in achieving a good result is answering this question as directly and as fully as possible. The technique for this will therefore be based on good practice for essays and source-based analysis. For advice on this, refer back to the Introduction, especially pages xii–xx.

It is also essential to keep to the word limit. For most people the problem is writing too much rather than too little. This can be prevented by careful planning – deciding in advance the number of words to be allocated to each section, and sticking to it.

Reading, note-taking and planning

All coursework for History involves extra reading; you will not, therefore, be able to rely on class notes or handouts. You should identify in advance all the books you need – probably about six. You will need to take notes on each one and to complete this process before you start writing the essay. Refer to pages 51–7 for advice on note-taking from books.

A good plan is essential for a coherent essay. This can be worked out and refined over a period of time, even while doing the reading. Base it on your own ideas, on your reading – and especially on the development of your own ideas as a result of your reading.

Checklist for drawing up a coursework plan

- Have you established an argument which answers the question directly, relevantly and completely?
- Does the argument fulfil all the criteria for AS or A2 specifications?
- Is the overall approach clearly stated in the first paragraph?
- Does each subsequent paragraph develop this approach step by step?
- Does the beginning of each paragraph give the reader a clue as to the stage reached? (see pages 311–12 below.)
- Is there sufficient historical (and, for A2, historiographical) support for each part of the argument?
- Have you avoided any straight narrative without argument?
- Is each part of the essay given appropriate weighting?
- Will the whole essay be within the word-total limits?

Throughout the preparation period, it is vital to avoid any form of plagiarism. This is usually the result of lazy research methods or poor note-taking skills. The most likely way in which plagiarism will occur is by copying your essay straight from the notes you have taken. If, on the other hand, you think about your notes critically, adapt them into your own approach or argument, and acknowledge any direct transfer in a footnote, you will avoid any hint of plagiarism. It is also important not to go too far in the opposite direction. Words and phrases used by authors can be transferred to your own work, as long as they are in the context of a different sentence. Doing this is actually recommended, since it will extend your vocabulary and upgrade your style.

The worst and most direct form of plagiarism in coursework is 'cutting and pasting' sections from articles downloaded from the Internet. This is equivalent to photocopying a page from a book, cutting out the paragraphs you want and sticking them in as your essay as your own work. Plagiarism from the Internet can be quite obvious and will usually produce work inferior to what you can provide yourself.

At what stage should the computer be used in coursework?

The use of a computer for coursework is strongly recommended. It enables you to make whatever changes you wish and to keep a copy as security. The main question, however, is *how* should it be used?

Possible uses of the computer in coursework

Possibility 1:   The notes, plans and essay are all handwritten. The computer is used to produce a final typed version.

Comment: The computer is being used essentially as a typewriter and many of its other functions are being missed.

Possibility 2:   The notes are handwritten. The computer is used to plan and write the essay from the outset to the final version.

Comment: Many of the computer functions are in use. Plans can be converted into detailed outlines, outlines into unrefined text, text into refined paragraphs.

Possibility 3:   The computer is used for note-taking, planning and writing.

Comment: Notes can be typed into a desktop or laptop computer if the books have been borrowed. Some libraries have facilities for use of a laptop, while a palmtop can be used anywhere. The main advantage of notes on the computer is that they can be converted into text much more quickly – but this greatly increases the chance of plagiarism. One way to avoid this is by using your own words as far as possible when you are using a book, putting any sentences by the author in quotation marks.

WRITING

Style

A lucid style is highly valued by historians. This takes time to develop and is always influenced by the styles and devices of others. In your reading, you should therefore be receptive to the author's style as well as the argument and details. The secret is to use words and phrases (but not whole sentences), preferably in other contexts.

Two particularly useful devices for improving style are rarely used by students – the semi-colon and the colon. These provide an alternative type of sentence structure, linking together two complete clauses.

Use of the semi-colon and colon

The semi-colon provides an alternative to the full-stop. For example:

Under Stalin the use of terror was permanently enshrined in the institutions of the OGPU and the NKVD; this was in contrast to Lenin's attempt to manage without terror when he abolished the *Cheka* in 1921.

The colon provides a link between two sentences where the second is really a continuation of the first. For example:

By 1927 Stalin had ended any remaining commitment to the NEP, opting instead for forced collectivisation: this was actually closer to the original policy of Trotsky.

Paragraphing

A piece of coursework can be seriously undermined by poor paragraphing. As an experiment, try scanning two or three pages from a History book you frequently use, remove the paragraphing indents and then insert your own paragraphing at random. With a few strokes of the keyboard you will have obscured the meaning and destroyed the flow of argument.

The purpose of paragraphs is to put breaks in the text, which would otherwise be solid and indigestible. But the breaks are an essential part of the structure; there is therefore no particular recommended length. To start with, work on the basis that each paragraph represents a stage in the overall argument and either complements the previous paragraph or contrasts with it. In most History essays it makes sense to start each paragraph with a sentence indicating which stage in the argument you have reached and make a general point which the rest of the paragraph covers in more detail. Most people instinctively read the opening of a paragraph more carefully than the rest of it. Take advantage of this. In a piece of coursework you have plenty of time to consider the overall structure, whereas you do not have this luxury in an exam. Ask yourself whether you could summarise your whole essay by putting together the opening sentences of all the paragraphs.

Examples of possible opening sentences and phrases for a new paragraph

Another essential factor in Stalin's rise to power by 1929 was his ability to use his control over the Party to outvote his rivals over key issues. This proved particularly important on three occasions. . . .

The traditional view of Stalin's purges, therefore, is that he was making ruthless and effective use of his power to eliminate possible opposition. But there is an alternative perspective, one which attributes the purges to confusion rather than to his control. There are several reasons for this . . .

Similarly . . . This can also be seen in . . . Much the same applies to . . . On the other hand . . . By contrast with this . . . Conversely . . . Alternatively . . . A different approach . . . The first . . . Second . . .

Paragraphing styles

The most common method (generally used in books) is indentation. Each new paragraph is indented on the line below the end of the previous paragraph. A space is not left between the paragraphs. The only paragraph which is not indented is the first paragraph below a heading or a table; this is always started at the margin.

Correct paragraphing. Option 1: indenting

. . . The industrialisation needed to do this would have to be subsidised. In the absence of external sources, this would have to be done internally – by agriculture. The case for pressing on with the *kolkhozy* was complete.

This line of reasoning can, however, be criticised on the grounds that it attributes too much economic planning, forethought and control to Stalin at a time when his first priority was the elimination of political rivals to both his right and his left. . . .

An alternative is to leave a line between paragraphs. In this case the first line of each new paragraph is not indented: it starts at the margin.

Correct paragraphing. Option 2: spacing

. . . The industrialisation needed to do this would have to be subsidised. In the absence of external sources, this would have to be done internally – by agriculture. The case for pressing on with the *kolkhozy* was complete.

This line of reasoning can, however, be criticised on the grounds that it attributes too much economic planning, forethought and control to Stalin at a time when his first priority was the elimination of political rivals to both his right and his left. . . .

Any combination of these methods is incorrect – and makes the work more difficult to read.

Incorrect paragraphing: example 1

. . . The industrialisation needed to do this would have to be subsidised. In the absence of external sources, this would have to be done internally – by agriculture. The case for pressing on with the *kolkhozy* was complete.
This line of reasoning can, however, be criticised on the grounds that it attributes too much economic planning, forethought and control to Stalin at a time when his first priority was the elimination of political rivals to both his right and his left. . . .

Incorrect paragraphing: example 2

. . . The industrialisation needed to do this would have to be subsidised. In the absence of external sources, this would have to be done internally – by agriculture. The case for pressing on with the *kolkhozy* was complete.

    This line of reasoning can, however, be criticised on the grounds that it attributes too much economic planning, forethought and control to Stalin at a time when his first priority was the elimination of political rivals to both his right and his left. . . .

Illustrations, maps, diagrams and appendices

Most people remember the first project they ever did – heavily plagiarised and profusely illustrated. The advice for A-level coursework is simple: do not include extra items unless there is a specific reason – in which case, they should be referred to in the text and form a part of the argument or support. An appendix may be necessary as a table of statistics, or a lengthy extract from a document, which again receives direct reference. Normally, this type of material does not form part of the word count.

Notes

It is now expected that any quotation is attributed or acknowledged in the Notes. These can be given at the bottom of each page or the end of the coursework. This is entirely a matter of individual preference and facilities for both are provided on computers. Try *Insert > Footnote >Footnote/Endnote* (choose). It is not necessary to attribute factual information, although you can make an exception if you are dealing with something unusual. Since your Bibliography will be based on books you have mentioned in the Notes, make sure you find a reason for including somewhere in the Notes anything you want included in the Bibliography.

When referring to a book for the first time, provide the details in full. The author goes in first, followed by the title, which is underlined. It is important that the complete title is included since many History books now have a title in two parts, often separated by a colon. The date of publication comes next (in brackets), followed by the page reference.

Example

 M. Lynch: <u>Stalin and Khrushchev: The USSR 1924–64</u> (1990), p. 34.

If you are quoting from an essay or chapter by one author contained in a book which is edited by another, the chapter is given quotation marks, while the book is <u>underlined</u>.

 R. Thurston: 'The Stakhanovite Movement: The Background to the Great Terror in the Factories, 1935–1938'; in J. Arch Getty and R.T. Manning (eds): <u>Stalinist Terror: New Perspectives</u> (1993), p.149.

The use of primary material follows the same pattern. The problem is that primary sources are often quoted by the author of one book from another. It is technically correct to provide the details of both, using whatever information is given in the footnotes of the book you are using. The secondary sources are underlined.

 Speech by Molotov, November 1938; in J. Degras (ed.): <u>Soviet Documents on Foreign Policy</u>, vol. III (1953), p. 360; quoted in S.J. Lee: <u>Stalin and the Soviet Union</u> (2000), p. 74.

If you have already referred to a book in the Notes, each subsequent mention can be abbreviated to the author's surname plus *op. cit.* and the page number. If one reference is immediately followed by another from the same book, abbreviate by *Ibid.* plus the page number.

1. I. Deutscher: Stalin: <u>A Political Biography</u> (1949), p. 332.
2. R. Thurston: 'The Stakhanovite Movement: The Background to the Great Terror in the Factories, 1935–1938'; in J. Arch Getty and R.T. Manning (eds.): <u>Stalinist Terror: New Perspectives</u> (1993), p.149.
3. M. Lynch: <u>Stalin and Khrushchev: The USSR 1924–64</u> (1990), p. 34.
4. Deutscher: op. cit., p. 346.
5. Ibid., p. 354.
6. Thurston: op. cit., p.165.
7. Ibid., p. 174.
8. Ibid., p. 186.
9. Deutscher: op. cit., p. 348.

Bibliography

The Bibliography is a list of all the books you have used in preparing the coursework. Normally the books listed are those referred to in the Notes. If you have omitted one from the Notes, go back and find a reason for including it there. The Bibliography is developed in two sections – primary and secondary sources.

Example

Primary sources

1.

2.

Secondary sources

3.   I. Deutscher: Stalin: <u>A Political Biography</u> (1949), p. 332.

4.

5.

6.

How it all fits together

See diagram on right.

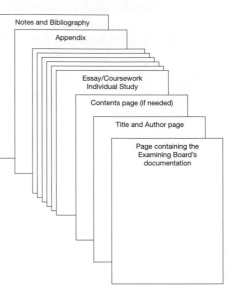

Presentation of the coursework

Notes and Bibliography

Appendix

Essay/Coursework Individual Study

Contents page (if needed)

Title and Author page

Page containing the Examining Board's documentation

References

1.   G. Swain, The Origins of the Russian Civil War (London 1996)
2.   J. Sapir, 'The economics of war in the Soviet Union during World War II', in I. Kershaw and M. Lewin (eds), *Stalinism and Nazism: Dictatorships in Comparison* (Cambridge 1997), p. 234
3.   C. Ward, *Stalin's Russia* (London 1993), p. 188

Sources

1A.   A.R. Wolfson, *Years of Change* (London 1978), p. 222
1B.   M. Lewin, *Russian Peasants and Soviet Power: A Study of Collectivization* (New York 1968), pp. 516–17
2A.   David King Collection
2B.   R.C. Tucker and S.F. Cohen (eds), *The Great Purge Trial* (New York 1965), p. 586
2C.   *The Anti-Stalin Campaign and International Communism: A Selection of Documents*, ed. by the Russian Institute, Columbia University (New York 1956), pp. 9–85
2D.   R.W. Thurston, *Life and Terror in Stalin's Russia* (London and New Haven 1996), p. 227

Chapter 8

International Relations, 1919–39

This chapter will resume the international focus of Chapter 2. It will consider the peace settlement, the establishment and problems of the League of Nations, the introduction of Collective Security and the subsequent switch to appeasement. It will also deal separately with the policies of the individual powers although the involvement of Italy, Germany and the Soviet Union in the Second World War is covered in Chapters 5–7.

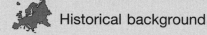 ## Historical background

The creation of a problem, 1919–23
The search for solutions, 1923–9
The solutions threatened, 1929–33
The foreign policies of the individual
    powers

 ## Sources

Germany and the Treaty of Versailles

Historical skills

Concentration, time-management and revision

 ## Essays

The creation of a problem, 1919–23
The search for solutions, 1923–9
The solutions threatened, 1929–33
The foreign policies of the individual
    powers

Chronology

1918	Wilson's Fourteen Points
1919	Paris Peace settlement, including Treaty of Versailles
	Formation of the League of Nations
1920–1	Russo-Polish War
1922	Washington Conference
1923	French occupation of Ruhr
	Corfu Crisis
1924	Dawes Plan
1925	Locarno Pact
1926	Treaty of Berlin
1928	Kellogg–Briand Pact
1929	Young Plan
1930	London Conference
1931	Japanese invasion of Manchuria
1931–3	Geneva Disarmament Conference
1933	Germany's withdrawal from League of Nations
1934	Nazi-Polish Non-Aggression Pact
1935	Mussolini's invasion of Ethiopia
	Hitler's remilitarisation of the Rhineland
	Franco-Soviet Pact
1936	Anti-Comintern Pact
	Rome–Berlin Axis
1936–9	Spanish Civil War
1937	Italy's accession to Anti-Comintern Pact
1938	*Anschluss* (annexation of Austria by Germany)
	Sudeten crisis and Munich agreement
1939	German occupation of Bohemia
	Pact of Steel (Italy and Germany)
	Italian invasion of Albania
	Nazi–Soviet Non-Aggression Pact
	Hitler's invasion of Poland
	Outbreak of the Second World War

Part 1: Historical background

The creation of a problem, 1919–23?

When they met in Paris in January 1919 the leaders of the victorious Allies intended to lay down a peace settlement which would prevent any future repetition of the Great War. The Council of Four, which carried out the bulk of the work, consisted of President Wilson of the United States and the Prime Ministers of Britain (Lloyd George), France (Clemenceau) and Italy (Orlando). None of the defeated powers – Germany, Austria-Hungary, Bulgaria and Turkey – was invited to send representatives.

The main problem arising at the preliminary discussions was the wide range of influences behind the policies of the individual statesmen. Clemenceau was concerned mainly about future French security and therefore placed the emphasis firmly on a punitive settlement which would reduce German power as much as possible. Orlando pressed for the territorial reward of Italy promised by the Secret Treaty of London (1915) by which Italy had entered the war on the side of the Allies. President Wilson, by contrast, appeared more concerned with establishing the principle of national self-determination, which had played such a prominent part in his Fourteen Points, issued in January 1918. Finally, Lloyd George aimed to establish a settlement which would prevent the resurgence of any future German threat without destroying the balance of power in Europe. The result of these contrasting aims was the hybrid settlement of 1919–20.

Generally known as the Paris Settlement, this comprised five specific treaties. The first was the Treaty of Versailles (28 June 1919), which dealt with Germany. This was followed by the Treaties of St Germain (September 1919), Neuilly (November 1919) and Trianon (June 1920), which concerned Austria, Bulgaria and Hungary respectively. Turkey was the subject of the Treaty of Sèvres (October 1920), although this was subsequently amended in July 1923 by the Treaty of Lausanne.

In terms of issues raised in the future, the terms of the Treaty of Versailles were the most contentious. Article 231 affirmed the 'responsibility of Germany and her allies' for the outbreak of war and made provision for appropriate territorial adjustments, demilitarisation and economic compensation for the losses incurred. Accordingly, Germany was deprived of Alsace-Lorraine, Eupen and Malmédy, Posen, West Prussia and all her overseas colonies (Togo, Kamerun, South West Africa, Tanganyika, Rwanda, Burundi, the Solomon Islands, German New Guinea and the Mariana Islands). Further areas, including Northern Schleswig and Upper Silesia were lost after plebiscites. The military clauses imposed restrictions on Germany's navy, confined its army to 100,000 volunteers and demilitarised the Rhineland. Finally, compensation and reparations were payable to the Allies in terms of rolling stock and merchant shipping, while in 1921 the Reparations Commission fixed the total amount payable at 136,000 million gold marks.

Since the dual state of Austria-Hungary had already broken up, the two main components were treated separately. The Treaty of St Germain confirmed the independence of the new Czech state and transferred Galicia to Poland and Dalmatia to Yugoslavia, while Italy received South Tyrol, Trentino, Istria and Trieste. Hungary was even more severely depleted by the Treaty of Trianon, losing about 75 per cent of its area and population. Slovakia was transferred to Czechoslovakia, Transylvania to Romania and Croatia to Yugoslavia. Meanwhile, the Treaty of Neuilly had already transferred Dobrudja from Bulgaria to Romania, and eastern Thrace to Greece. By the Treaty of

Sèvres, Turkey lost all its Arab areas (Iraq, Syria, Palestine, parts of Arabia and Yemen) and eastern Thrace was handed to Greece. The last of these changes was, however, subsequently reversed by the Treaty of Lausanne.

These terms were bound to be highly controversial and it would clearly be difficult to enforce them. Certainly there were immediate complications. Germany remained deeply resentful about the War Guilt Clause of the Treaty of Versailles and the size of the reparations bill (see Essays 1 and 2). The German government was unwilling to co-operate at this stage, which resulted in the French invasion of the Ruhr in 1923 and the collapse of the German mark. The Italian government complained about the limited nature of its gains from the Treaty of St Germain, referring to it as a 'mutilated settlement' (Essay 3). Greece and Turkey were at war until 1923, which complicated the diplomacy of British and French politicians. Eastern Europe was also experiencing major crises. Russia was involved in civil war between 1918 and 1921 and a border conflict with Poland (1920–1). It must have appeared that the entire post-war settlement was beginning to break up. Even the stabilising influence expected from the United States did not materialise since the new Republican majority in the Congress took the decision to withdraw altogether from European commitments.

Everything now depended on whether a framework could be established to enforce the peace settlement without further conflict and chaos. Hope was placed partly in the League of Nations, embedded in the terms of the Treaty of Versailles, and partly in special arrangements to deal with individual problems.

 The search for solutions, 1923–9

The problems between 1919 and 1923 culminated in the French invasion of the Ruhr (1923) and the collapse of the mark in Germany. These crises showed the need for a solution which would deal effectively with both economic and diplomatic challenges. These would have to be addressed multilaterally and within an agreed overall structure; economic issues would need to involve the stabilising influence of the United States, while problems of aggression would have to be dealt with by agreements sanctioned by the League of Nations.

The first example of the economic settlement was the Dawes Plan (1924), which was drawn up between Germany, the United States, Britain and France. It provided for the withdrawal of French troops from the Ruhr, in return for Germany's undertaking to pay reparations in line with an annual 'index of prosperity'. This was accompanied by a series of loans to provide stability for the German economy and to prevent the future recurrence of hyperinflation. American investment seemed to provide the answer to Europe's debt problems generally since, with the help of US investment, Germany could pay reparations to Britain, France and Belgium, while these three recipients could, in turn, repay war debts to the United States. Further adjustments, under the Young Plan (1929) transferred the payment of reparations to German control, extended the deadline for the final payment by a further fifty-seven years and removed allied troops from the Rhineland five years ahead of schedule. Between 1924 and 1929, Germany actually received more through investments than it paid out in reparations. As a result, it was able to develop a more stable economic infrastructure; by 1929 German industrial production was higher than its previous record level of 1913. To the Allies this had the additional advantage of making political stability in Germany more likely, along with which would possibly come eventual acceptance of the Versailles Settlement.

Along with the economic settlement, the powers tried to resolve by diplomatic means the tensions which had built up between 1919 and 1923. This took the form of Collective Security (Essay 4), which had three main purposes. The first was to contain the possibility of German revisionism and to uphold at least some of the boundaries laid down by the Treaty of Versailles; this can be seen as the defensive element and was of particular concern to the French. The second was to rehabilitate Germany to enable it to re-enter the mainstream of European diplomacy. This was due largely to the conciliatory policies of the German Foreign Minister, Gustav Stresemann, who saw Germany as 'the bridge which would bring East and West together in the development of Europe'. The third was to provide a method for the settlement of disputes which would involve the League of Nations; multilateralism was therefore to replace bilateralism and, more particularly, unilateralism.

One example of Collective Security was the Locarno Pact (1925), a series of five agreements between Germany and its neighbours. The most important of these was the Treaty of Mutual Guarantee, which involved Britain, France, Germany, Belgium and Italy. Article 1 guaranteed the frontiers between Belgium and Germany and between France and Germany. Under Article 2, any disputes would be settled by 'peaceful means' and, if necessary, submitted to a Conciliation Commission or the Council of the League of Nations. If authorised by the League Council, the signatory powers would then 'come immediately to the assistance of the Power against whom the act complained of is directed' (Article 4). Although Britain and Italy had no direct stake in the boundary question, they clearly saw the Locarno Pact as a means of regularising the channels for diplomatic pressure should anything untoward happen in the defined area. The remaining four agreements were **bilateral** – a series of arbitration treaties between Germany and each of France, Belgium, Poland and Czechoslovakia. These contained assurances that each frontier would not be adjusted, but the agreements with Poland and Czechoslovakia lacked the guarantee of intervention by the Western powers if they were.

During the diplomatic atmosphere of the 1920s, further progress was made. Germany was admitted to the League of Nations in 1926, Stresemann emphasising that this was a direct follow-up to the Locarno Pact and that it completed Germany's rehabilitation. 'The German Government is resolved to persevere unswervingly in this line of policy and is glad to see that these ideas, which at first met with lively opposition in Germany, are now becoming more and more deeply rooted in the conscience of the German people.' Collective security reached an idealist peak in the Kellogg–Briand Pact or the Pact of Paris (1928), when the sixty-five signatory states condemned 'recourse to war for the solution of international controversies' and renounced it 'as an instrument of national policy in their relations with one another'.

What part did the League of Nations play in Collective Security? (Essay 5) Article 10 of the Covenant obliged member states 'to respect and preserve as against external aggression the territorial integrity and existing political independence of all members of the League'. Yet there were no precise procedures for taking action over potential crises, which meant that complementary arrangements, such as the Locarno Pact, had to be made in its name to deal with specific issues. Another example of this was the use of the Conference of Ambassadors in 1923 to resolve the conflict between Italy and Greece which had led to Mussolini's seizure of Corfu. Although the League was the sanctioning authority, the action was sometimes taken by other bodies on its behalf. Direct involvement by the League tended to be confined to cases not involving a major power – such as the resolution of territorial disputes between Sweden and Finland, Iraq and Turkey, Greece and Bulgaria, and Albania and Yugoslavia.

Figure 8.1
**The League
of Nations
in session**

During the period 1923–9 there was much to applaud in international diplomacy and it appeared that the initial problems which had become apparent between 1919 and 1923 were on the way to being resolved. There were, however, three remaining problems. One was the force of political revisionism in Fascist Italy and also among the leadership in the army in Weimar Germany. It would not take much to activate this in the future as a direct challenge to the whole Versailles settlement and Collective Security. Second, the area most vulnerable to future upheaval was Eastern Europe, which was not covered by any form of Collective Security. A more aggressive German government could press for frontier changes there. Third, this area was rendered particularly unstable by the unpredictable nature of Soviet foreign policy. Fundamentally suspicious of capitalist states, it was nevertheless allowing secret German military exercises on the Soviet soil, a by-product of the Treaty of Berlin between the two countries in 1926. The newly emergent regime of Stalin could stir the waters any time it chose. Even if it did not, the profound suspicion with which Britain treated it would be sufficient to prevent any meaningful extension of Collective Security to the area.

Calmness lay on the surface – but volatility seethed beneath it.

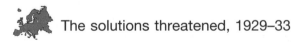 The solutions threatened, 1929–33

Europe and the world entered a period of profound uncertainty after 1929. The immediate reason for the downturn was the collapse of economic stability which, in turn, threatened the political and diplomatic settlement in Europe. The origins of the depression were the Wall Street Crash (1929) and the collapse of *Kreditanstalt* (1931). Attempts were made to deal with reparations and shrinking international trade. In 1931, for example, President Hoover proposed a one-year moratorium on reparations and war debts. This was followed at Lausanne by the virtual end of reparations. By this stage, however, the damage had been done. The main components of the economic crisis were the destabilising of Germany and Italy, and the emergence of tariff barriers.

These were bound to have a negative impact on international relations at all levels (Essay 6). For one thing, the experience of economic crisis radicalised three regimes. In the case of Japan and Italy existing regimes, threatened with internal instability, sought an external outlet in the form of aggression abroad. This partially explains the Japanese attack on Manchuria in 1931 and Italy's invasion of Ethiopia in 1935. Germany emerged from economic chaos with an entirely new regime, which became increasingly committed to rearmament and expansion. In defiance of the Treaty of Versailles, Hitler remilitarised the Rhineland in 1935, annexed Austria in the *Anschluss* of 1938, incorporated the Sudetenland from Czechoslovakia (1938) and annexed the rest of Bohemia (1939).

This, in turn, destroyed the atmosphere of internationalism which had existed during the 1920s. Many of the powers moved away from a **multilateral** approach in favour of **unilateral action**. This had a profound impact on the League of Nations (Essay 7), which found itself faced with serious crises like the invasion of Ethiopia (1935) and the Spanish Civil War (1936–9) at the very time that it was losing some of its members and seeing the destruction of parallel systems such as Collective Security. The League tried, but failed, to reassert its influence. Sanctions on Italy had no effect and the Non-Intervention Committees, designed to prevent other powers becoming involved in Spain, were ignored by Germany and Italy.

The collapse of Collective Security and the enfeeblement of the League of Nations meant that Britain and France increasingly resorted to their own methods of dealing with the aggression of Italy and Germany. France initially tried to strengthen its own system of alliances in eastern Europe through the Franco-Soviet Pact of 1935, before coming under the influence of Britain's preferred option between 1936 and 1938 – appeasement. This was an acknowledgement that the Treaty of Versailles could no longer be enforced by Collective Security; instead, it would make more sense to allow Germany some scope to revise the Treaty. This explains Anglo-French willingness to allow Hitler to annex Austria in 1938 and to absorb part of Czechoslovakia into the Reich. Appeasement (Essay 8) was therefore a response to the collapse of the various expedients which seemed to have worked in the 1920s. It contained a misdirected faith in Germany conducting a limited revisionist programme, but was also a more pragmatic search for time.

This brings us to the most important destabilising development of the 1930s – general rearmament. The League of Nations failed between 1930 and 1934 to produce an agreement from the Geneva Disarmament Conference. Hitler withdrew Germany from both the Conference and the League in 1933, ignored all the arms restrictions clauses of the Treaty of Versailles and introduced the Four Year Plan in 1936 to prepare the German economy for war. Meanwhile, the basis of Stalin's Five Year Plans was the development of heavy industry, tanks and aircraft, while Mussolini's Corporate State was gearing the Italian population to accepting a decade of war. Japan was already fully mobilised during the 1930s and in occupation of substantial areas of China. From 1937 onwards Britain and France accepted the inevitable and rearmed rapidly to meet the German and Italian threat.

In these circumstances the outbreak of general war was never out of politicians' minds. There was, however, an additional source of international tension, the Spanish Civil War (Essay 9). The sides involved were the Republicans and the Nationalists. The former consisted of liberals, republicans, socialists, communists and anarchists, while the Nationalists, who aimed to overthrow the Republic, were a coalition of monarchists, conservatives, the Catholic leadership, and Spanish fascists. The Nationalists, under the leadership of Franco, were helped to eventual victory by extensive support from Nazi Germany and Fascist Italy. Although the Soviet Union provided temporary assistance to the Republicans, Britain and France unsuccessfully attempted, through the Non-Intervention Committee of the League of Nations, to prevent arms being sent to either side. The impact of the Spanish Civil War was considerable. It increased the confidence and aggression of Europe's fascist powers and brought together Italy and Germany in the Rome–Berlin Axis (1936) and the Pact of Steel (1939). It also influenced the development of the Anglo-French policy of appeasement – through fear that the civil war would flare up into a general European war.

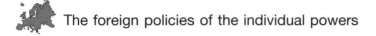 ## The foreign policies of the individual powers

International relations are largely the result of the impact of the foreign policies pursued by individual governments and of the reaction of governments to each others' policies. The remainder of the essays in this Chapter therefore focus on specific countries, although the issues involved all overlap with previous sections.

Although not the strongest of the major powers, Italy's foreign policy was one of the most important as a catalyst for other developments. Mussolini's aims appeared to vary considerably (Essay 10); during the 1920s his emphasis was primarily on diplomacy, which meant that he had an important input into the Locarno Pact (1925) and the Kellogg–Briand Pact (1928). In the 1930s, however, his approach became more aggressive and adventurist, resulting in the invasion of Ethiopia (1935), intervention in the Spanish Civil War (1936–9) and the annexation of Albania (1939). In the process, Italy became increasingly committed to Nazi Germany, through the Rome–Berlin Axis (1936) and Pact of Steel (1939). Mussolini's successes and failures during the period (Essay 11) depended very much on how effectively he used Italy's limited resources; this meant that the role he played as the diplomat during the 1920s was more successful than that as a conqueror in the 1930s. This, of course, raises the crucial question of why he committed Italy to tasks beyond her compass, especially the invasion of Ethiopia and heavy support for the Nationalists in the Spanish Civil War (Essay 12); the answers have much to do with the nature of the fascist regime itself and of Italy's internal contradictions. Despite temporary benefits, the impact of these two wars on the Italian economy and whole industrial infrastructure were ultimately disastrous (Essay 13). Although Italy had become ever more closely committed to Germany, Mussolini was unable to honour the Pact of Steel in September 1939 (Essay 14). When, however, Hitler seemed to have conquered Europe, Mussolini took Italy into the Second World War, with fatal consequences for the fascist regime.

Of all the European powers, Germany pursued the most successful during the period 1933–5, as is shown by the outline of Hitler's achievements (Essay 15). Initially cautious between 1933 and 1935, Hitler confined himself to undermining the armaments limitations of the Treaty of Versailles and removing Germany from the Geneva Disarmament Conference and the League of Nations. Between 1935 and 1938, however, Hitler benefited from the diversion of British and French attention to Mussolini's aggression in Ethiopia. He was therefore able to remilitarise the Rhineland in 1935 and annex Austria and the Sudetenland in 1938. By this stage Britain and France were responding with a policy of appeasement. When this was reversed in March 1939, following the annexation of the rest of Bohemia, Hitler wrongly interpreted this as a bluff and his subsequent attack on Poland resulted in the outbreak of general war in September. Behind all this is the key issue of Hitler's motives (Essay 16); did he have long-term aims, including German expansion and *Lebensraum* – or was he primarily an opportunist responding to the measures taken by other powers? And, bearing these in mind, was he alone responsible for the outbreak of the Second World War?

The policies of the other powers were largely in response to those of Italy and Germany. France, never fully convinced about the effectiveness of Collective Security, attempted during the 1920s to build up a network of alliances involving Eastern European countries such as Poland, Czechoslovakia, Romania and Yugoslavia. Although most of these did not survive the destabilising influence of the depression, a new alliance was built with Czechoslovakia and the Soviet Union in 1935. This might possibly have been a means of containing Germany in the future – but it was considered obstructive by Britain, which pursued a separate line. British foreign policy combined the elements of minimal involvement in Europe, a revisionist approach to the Treaty of Versailles and – eventually – a search for time to rearm against the growing threat of Germany. Since successive British governments were as anti-Soviet as they were anti-Nazi, they aimed to detach France from the Franco-Soviet Pact and involve it in the policy of appeasement instead. When this failed in 1939, the British line switched to guarantees to Poland, by which time the possibility of a broad alliance against Germany had disappeared.

By far the most changeable policy was pursued by the Soviet Union. The outline (Essay 17) shows that Stalin deliberately assisted the rise of Hitler to power in Germany between 1932 and 1933; he then switched to an anti-Hitler policy which included an alliance in 1935 with France and Czechoslovakia. In 1939 he followed a dual approach, before opting eventually for the Nazi–Soviet Non-Aggression Pact in August 1939. The reasons for this inconsistency are controversial; it could be argued either that Stalin lacked any real control over the way in which his policy was developing or, alternatively, that he had a fixed objective and that the means of achieving it altered as circumstances required (Essay 18).

Finally, the way in which the policies influenced each other provides some intriguing questions and combinations, which are considered in Essay 19. Did Italian foreign policy in the 1930s liberate Germany's? Did Germany's destroy Italy? Did the Soviet Union's exploit Germany – or Germany's the Soviet Union? Did French foreign policy undermine Britain's – or did Britain's destroy French security?

Part 2: Essays

The creation of a problem, 1919–23?

1. **With what justification can the Treaty of Versailles be considered a 'harsh settlement' for Germany?** (90 marks)

See Chapter 2, Essay 18.

2. **How serious was the effect of the Treaty of Versailles on Germany?** (90 marks)

See Chapter 4, Essay 10.

3. **Why and with what results were the Italians so resentful of the peace settlement of 1919?** (90 marks)

See Chapter 5, Essay 2b.

The search for solutions, 1923–9

4. How effective was Collective Security during the 1920s? **(90 marks)**

Collective Security was the means whereby the European powers tried to make up for the procedural deficiencies of the League of Nations when dealing with threats to the peace or to the Versailles Settlement. At the same time, Collective Security was under the official umbrella of the League, intended to complement it rather than to compete with it. Its benefits and shortcomings need to be considered in this light.

The benefits were considerable. The Locarno Treaties of 1925 openly acknowledged the tensions inherent in the Versailles Settlement and gave the League of Nations a structure through which these could be resolved. For example, the Treaty of Mutual Guarantee, involving France, Germany, Belgium, Italy and Britain, guaranteed the frontiers between the first three, making provision for collective action against any aggressor with the approval of the League Council. This effectively reconciled Germany with those clauses of the Treaty of Versailles which concerned western Europe, while France and Belgium felt more secure than at any time since 1870. As a result, there was scope for a great deal of positive diplomacy between Stresemann and his counterparts, with Germany becoming fully reconciled and rehabilitated. It is no coincidence that Germany's accession to the Locarno Treaties in 1925 was followed a year later by full membership of the League of Nations. By 1928 Collective Security was being associated with another means of defusing tension in Europe; again under the League of Nations umbrella, talks were under way to control levels of armaments and, in the 1928 Kellogg–Briand Pact, over fifty countries agreed to renounce 'recourse to war' in settling their relations with each other.

Collective Security had another advantage. It was more flexible than the League of Nations in enabling individual powers to contribute what they felt was appropriate to international diplomacy. The United States had withdrawn from the League in 1920, yet Collective Security enabled it to play a key role in the Washington and London naval conferences of 1922 and 1930. Britain, which remained a member, nevertheless had reservations about too close a commitment to the defence of France. Collective Security was for Chamberlain and Baldwin the ideal compromise: Britain would act only in concert – and with the further proviso that the League agreed in principle. It is not surprising that contemporary views were favourable. According to Churchill, 'At the end of the second Baldwin administration the state of Europe was tranquil, as it had not been for 20 years, and was not to be for at least another 20.' He added that 'A friendly feeling existed towards Germany following upon our Treaty of Locarno.' Austen Chamberlain saw the Locarno Pact as 'the real dividing line between the years of war and the years of peace'.

But this is only a partial perspective. In some ways Collective Security was deeply flawed.

One problem was that it was not a permanent answer to underlying German resentment against the majority of the terms of the Treaty of Versailles. Anxious as he was to project himself as the 'good European', Stresemann in fact had a double agenda which also involved being a 'good German'. Openly he sought 'reconciliation between Germany and the other powers through open agreements openly arrived at'. Secretly, however, he was convinced that the Treaty of Versailles should eventually be revised' the only issue was how long this needed to be deferred. Much of his diplomacy was double-edged. Hence he believed that 'German policy . . . will have to be one of finesse'. The conclusion from this has to be that Collective Security involved no fundamental commitment from Germany. It provided a new set of rules by which Germany could play along with the other nations – until more favourable opportunities presented themselves.

The most likely area for these was eastern Europe. This represented a serious gap in the whole system of Collective Security, which ultimately caused its collapse in the 1930s to the concerted onslaught of a revitalised Germany. Quite simply, there were no collective guarantees for the boundaries of new eastern European states such as Poland and Czechoslovakia. Stresemann was careful to avoid bringing their frontiers within the scope of the Treaty of Mutual Guarantee, agreeing instead to sign separate arbitration treaties of mutual guarantee with the two countries concerned. This made it far easier for Germany in the future to unpick bilateral agreements of this kind than to defy a multilateral one. Poland and Czechoslovakia never felt secure because they were not collectively secured in the way that Belgium and France were. Even France sensed a problem. Collective Security in the west could easily be undermined by German pressure in the east. This explains why France felt it necessary to compensate for the deficiencies of the Locarno treaties by developing her own system of alliances with Poland (1925), Czechoslovakia (1925 and 1935), Yugoslavia (1927) and the Soviet Union (1935). Even a state which *was* collectively secured felt the need to seek extra security.

Finally, there remains a strong suspicion that two states were seeking only a minimal involvement in Collective Security. The United States clearly wanted no obligations in Europe – and certainly none which would be connected with a line of approval from the League of Nations. It did not, therefore subscribe to any of the 1925 Locarno Treaties, even though it had underwritten the new economic arrangements affecting Germany in 1924. Britain also had reservations. Although involved as one of the guarantors behind the Locarno Pact, Chamberlain was certainly not in favour of extending Collective Security to eastern Europe, one of the main reasons why Stresemann was allowed to keep Germany's loophole within the new arrangements. This was to be exploited fully by Hitler in the late 1930s.

Collective Security was essentially a fair weather system. Although it contributed much to the improvement of international relations after 1923, its continuation came to depend on this improvement. The 1930s, however, showed up its underlying deficiencies and eventually saw its replacement by appeasement.

5. How much did the League of Nations achieve between 1919 and 1930? (90 marks)

In some respects the League achieved a great deal. Its very existence was a major step forward. Although there had been international organisations in the nineteenth century – such as the International Telegraphic Union and the Universal Postal Union – the League of Nations was the first permanent institution to provide overall co-ordination between ad hoc bodies.

It also enabled the Allies to carry out some of the more complex terms of the Treaty of Versailles. The League, for example, provided the Governing Commission for the Saar region, as well as the High Commissariat for Danzig. It provided the means whereby the principle of national self-determination could be implemented; in 1921 it organised plebiscites in Schleswig, Upper Silesia and East Prussia. Continuing success was achieved with the settlement of border disputes between Turkey and Iraq over the Mosul region, as well as between Bulgaria and Greece and between Albania and Yugoslavia. The longstanding dispute between Sweden and Finland over the Aaland Islands was submitted for arbitration to the League, which awarded sovereignty to Finland.

The League was also of vital importance in the non-political field. For example, the Health Organisation supervised research into vaccines and drugs to treat major diseases such as leprosy and malaria, while the Epidemics Commission focused on typhus and cholera in eastern Europe – the legacy of mass movements of people following the collapse of Austria-Hungary. This disruption was also alleviated by the Nansen Report on refugees, sponsored by the League. The continuing traffic in women and children was investigated, as was the exploitation of child labour in the Persian carpet industry. The International Labour Organisation, one of the League's specialist committees made progress towards standardising working practices and conditions in member states. The League even became involved in issues of national and international transport and electrical power. The very expansion of the League's activities in these areas indicates an unprecedented degree of success between 1919 and 1930.

There were, however, areas in which the League was vulnerable to criticism, even during these halcyon years.

One was the substantial gap between theory and practice when it came to peacekeeping. According to Article 10, the members of the League undertook to 'respect and preserve as against external aggression the territorial integrity and existing political independence of all members of the League'. Article 11 stated that the League should 'take any action that may be deemed wise and effectual to safeguard the peace of nations'. The problem of delivering these became notorious, given the absence of the United States after 1920 and the 'unanimity clause' (Article 5) which required 'the agreement of all the members of the League represented at the meeting'.[1]

The 1920s saw various attempts to tighten up this deficiency. The most promising means of guaranteeing effective concerted action were the Draft Treaty of Mutual Assistance and the Geneva Protocol. Neither, however, materialised, largely because of British opposition to such extensive involvement. The other – and more successful – development was Collective Security, which embodied specific agreements like the Locarno Pact. But this was also an acknowledgement that the League could not work effectively through its own organs to enforce peace; Collective Security

Figure 8.2
Signing the Locarno Pact of 1925 – Austen Chamberlain, Gustav Stresemann and Monsieur Briand are present

was a system which ran parallel to the League, acting on its behalf and with its approval – but not actually contained within it. Similarly, ad hoc institutions sometimes had to be established to deal with specific crises. When Mussolini took Corfu in 1923 the League Council had to recommend the use of the Conference of Ambassadors to negotiate a solution; this was a clear indication that the League's unwieldy framework was preventing swift treatment of any crisis.

More serious was the failure to make any real headway over disarmament in line with the objectives set out in Article 8 of the Covenant. From 1926 onwards the League attempted to establish procedures for a general reduction of armaments by the powers but, by 1930, had made no real impact. The only genuine agreements were those drawn up in Washington (1922) and London (1930) involving voluntary agreements on the ratio of naval shipbuilding by the United States, Britain and Japan. These were, however, only indirectly connected to the League since the United States had withdrawn from the League in 1920.

The League of Nations was certainly more successful during the 1920s than in the 1930s. Even so, it was impeded by the grandeur of its own vision. It was set up to guarantee the peace settlement, which immediately stored up major problems for the future. It aimed to satisfy all member states but the unanimity clause meant that it was helpless to take action in particular crises. This meant that it succeeded either when dealing with non-contentious social and economic issues or with those political disputes in which both parties were prepared to recognise the League's jurisdiction. In all other cases it had to concede a series of overlapping systems such as Collective Security. These did at least hide the League's basic vulnerability even before the 1930s.

The solutions threatened, 1929–33

6. Assess the impact of the Great Depression on international relations between 1929 and 1939. **(90 marks)**

Economic upheavals are often a catalyst for political and economic change, although they generally release tensions which already exist but which have been restrained by economic prosperity. The Great Depression certainly accelerated international instability – but it did not necessarily *create* it.

The first major impact of the depression was the radicalisation of the three regimes which subsequently did more than any others to destabilise the international scene. Two of these were already in existence by the time of the depression – and were already committed to long-term expansion. The onset of depression, however, propelled them into aggression. Japanese militarism increased rapidly from 1930 and the army became increasingly involved in Japanese politics following the assassination of the Prime Minister, Hamaguchi Yuko. The Japanese occupation of Manchuria had long been on the cards but was brought forward to 1931 to control the outlet of raw materials which would sustain Japan's industrial base. The depression did not forge the link between industrialisation and militarism – but it did influence the use of this link for actual conquest. Similarly, Mussolini's fascist regime had long-term ambitions of extending the Italian empire. During the 1920s, however, Mussolini had focused on diplomacy rather than aggression. This began to change during the 1930s as the depression undermined the Italian economy and created the danger of a popular backlash; this was diverted by the invasion of Ethiopia in 1935. Germany experienced an actual change of regime as Hitler was helped into power by the economic chaos caused by the depression. After two years of initial caution, the new Reich completely transformed

Germany's foreign policy, especially since Hitler's economic theories were based largely on the absorption of the resources of Germany's neighbours. In his eyes, economic recovery involved the expansion which he had always favoured anyway.

In addition to radicalising regimes already inclined to aggression, the depression undermined the international constraints which had so far *discouraged* aggression. Internationalism, an essential principle behind the League of Nations, Collective Security and disarmament proposals were all damaged by the unilateral imposition of tariff barriers despite the attempts of the World Economic Conference in 1933 to maintain open trade. Nor was there any longer the boost given by the United States, which had been so important in underpinning economic agreements in the 1920s. After 1931 the United States cut economic as well as political commitments to Europe, a decision which further undermined international perspectives and solutions. Heightened national suspicions led to the collapse of the Geneva Disarmament Conference in 1933; this was partly because several of the states involved intended to move in the opposite direction and use rearmament to promote economic recovery. This, of course, led directly to increased aggression – at the very time that the League of Nations was least able to deal with it. It is true that some powers, including Britain and France, attempted to use economic sanctions to force Italian withdrawal from Ethiopia; this was actually an attempt to strengthen the impact of the depression in order to *end* aggression. In practice, however, it had the reverse effect – of strengthening Mussolini's commitment to aggression and pushing Italy towards Germany. The failure of sanctions virtually doomed the League of Nations as an effective international influence, giving rise to alternative strategies such as appeasement and the Non-Intervention Committees.

During the 1920s, therefore, there had always been the latent threat of national aggression, but this had been controlled by international solutions expedients. The depression reversed the relationship between the two. Nationalism became powerful enough to break through the constraints, while internationalism rapidly lost the means to prevent this from happening. The influence for radicalising nationalism was therefore the key to the dangerous world of the 1930s; the weakening of internationalism simply accelerated the process.

7. **Assess the reasons for the failure of the League of Nations during the 1930s.** (90 marks)

After a great deal of favourable publicity and relative success during the 1920s, the League of Nations entered a prolonged crisis during the 1930s from which it never recovered. The reasons for this were partly internal structural weaknesses and partly a unique succession of external blows delivered by no fewer than four major powers – Japan, Italy, Germany and the Soviet Union.

The League was never equipped to deal with prolonged international upheaval. It had been set up in 1919 on the premise that such an upheaval had already been resolved and that, in the words of H.G. Wells, the Great War had been the 'war to end wars'. The League was always seen as a means of keeping the peace by upholding the status quo of 1919, which is why the League Covenant was an integral part of the Treaty of Versailles. From the outset, however, its effectiveness had been undermined by the Anglo-American understanding of its purpose. Based on a preference for liberal democracy – and minimal practical involvement – this meant that the League should operate on voluntary agreement and consensus. Hence, although Article 11 authorised the League to take necessary action, Article 5 imposed the need for unanimity which made it impossible to deal quickly or effectively with subsequent large-scale aggression. The French preference for an army with coercive powers was not implemented. Instead, the League proceeded on the assumption that the great powers would wish to co-operate with the Covenant, not to defy it. By 1931, however, the possibility of amicable agreement between the powers had ended, with the death of Stresemann in 1929 and the radicalisation of Japan, Italy and Germany by the economic depression which followed the Wall Street Crash.

The deficiencies of the League could more or less be disguised in the 1920s by the existence of parallel systems such as Collective Security. But, because of its structural weakness, the League was helpless against the onslaught of Japan on Manchuria (1931), the Italian invasion of Ethiopia (1935) and Hitler's aggression against Czechoslovakia and Poland (1938–9). Even the Soviet Union became involved, launching a border war with Finland at the end of 1939. Behind these incursions were aggressive ideologies, based on militarism and the pursuit of territorial conquest which no international system could have withstood. The League had very little to offer as the alternative to the earlier more gentlemanly diplomacy of Stresemann, Briand and Austen Chamberlain. The absence of the United States from the political scene since 1920 had always been keenly felt but the 1930s saw the world's most influential power withdraw into economic isolation as well. This left France, which placed more faith in its own bilateral diplomacy with the Soviet Union (1935), and Britain, which constructed a policy of appeasement on the premise that the League might still prevent open war. As British Foreign Secretary, Eden, observed in 1937 of the Non-Intervention Committee, 'even a leaking dam can serve its purpose'.

Faced with the combination of heavy blows against a soft target, the League gave the impression of going through the motions in trying to deal with aggression. The Lytton Commission created an impeccably two-sided assessment of the situation in Manchuria in 1931, which the Japanese subsequently rejected and, after establishing the puppet state of Manchukuo, pulled out of the League. The League could have done little more especially since (as Chamberlain pointed out) the United States would not help resist 'any action of Japan short of an attack on Hawaii or Honolulu'. It was also highly unlikely that the League could ever have moderated the policy of Nazi Germany; Hitler was bound to object to the Disarmament Conference proposals since these would certainly have prevented his revisionist intentions against the Treaty of Versailles. Germany's withdrawal in 1933 from both the Conference and the League was even given overwhelming plebiscitary approval by the German people. What could the League have done here? A stand was, it is true, taken over the Italian aggression in Ethiopia, with the imposition of partial sanctions. These proved, however, to be a gesture which lacked any means of enforcement and were, in any case, abandoned in July 1936. Italy was even allowed the face-saving device of voluntary withdrawal, rather than expulsion, from the League in the same year. Britain and France were, by this stage, trying to win back the diplomatic support of Mussolini as a means of moderating the growing threat of Germany. By 1939 the League had become virtually defunct although, like a dying candle, it flared up in a final and futile gesture – the expulsion of the Soviet Union for aggression against Finland. When internationalism was revived in 1945, the key lessons learned by the United Nations were that it should try to restrain the powers without losing their membership.

Historian Sally Marks maintained that 'In its larger role the League foundered on the twin rocks of the unanimity clause and the absence of America.'[2] This aptly summarises the League's structural deficiencies. It should, however, be added that the League was driven on to these rocks between 1931 and 1939 by the aggressive policies of four powers. While the propensity for collapse was internal, the impetus was certainly external. The League could have survived without these attacks; it is difficult to see what else could have survived *against* them.

8. Assess the reasons for and results of the British policy of appeasement. (90 marks)

The reasons for the development of appeasement by successive British governments can be grouped into two categories: principled and pragmatic. The former was more important during the earlier stages, giving way later to more explicit self-interest.

The principles behind appeasement tend to give a more positive impression to an otherwise much vilified form of diplomacy. They can be summarised as equity and justice in the treatment of other peoples and countries, along with an underlying commitment to a peaceful resolution of disagreements. These were already apparent before the heyday of appeasement in the 1930s, although they were initially articulated by opposition groups; these included the Union of Democratic Control, comprising Liberal and Labour MPs, and critics of the Treaty of Versailles, such as Harold Nicholson and J.M. Keynes. By the early 1930s they had entered the political mainstream, showing that government ministers and spokesmen were more receptive to the idea that the Treaty of Versailles might be revised – provided that this was approached rationally and peacefully. This explains why, for example, Neville Chamberlain was prepared to put pressure on Daladier's French government to join British recognition of Hitler's *Anschluss* and annexation of the Sudetenland (1938).

This line of argument has been seen by many as disingenuous. What really counted was the prevailing circumstances: the threat of general war which would arise from assisting the Spanish Republic against fascism after 1936, or from preventing Hitler making unilateral changes to Germany's frontiers from 1938. In part, this was due to fear of the huge commitments Britain would have to make to a continental war – always a difficult decision for a power with predominantly maritime interests. This was intensified in 1938 by the fear of mass destruction which would, Chamberlain thought, inevitably be delivered by the *Luftwaffe*. This makes some sense of his reference in September 1938 to the perils of supporting Czechoslovakia, 'a remote state in eastern Europe about which we know so little'. He was trying to disentangle Britain from any continental commitments, at the same time, rescuing the French from their obligations under the Franco-Czechoslovak Treaty (1935). Lest Chamberlain should be seen as a coward (a popular, but mistaken view), it should also be accepted that appeasement was also a tactic to gain time for British rearmament. This approach had been started by Baldwin as early as 1936 and Chamberlain placed priority on building up Britain's air defences. Time was also needed to prepare the British Dominions, especially South Africa and Canada, for the possibility of war in the longer term. This rather hard-headed approach to appeasement would appear to be supported by Chamberlain's willingness to reverse it in March 1939 by guaranteeing the future of Poland against German aggression. Principle to justify inaction, or inaction to allow preparation for future action? The former probably led gradually but inexorably to the latter.

Very much the same focus can be given to the effects of appeasement, although with more controversy. Principle is the reverse of one perception of appeasement, especially in 1938: the betrayal of a minor state and weakening of an ally. Telford Taylor, for example, argues that Chamberlain 'undermined the Czechs' will to resist' and followed a policy which was inherently dishonourable. A.J.P. Taylor, by contrast, refers to the 1938 Munich settlement as a 'triumph' for all that was 'best and most enlightened' in British policy. Chamberlain served the interests of both the Sudeten Germans, allowing the national self-determination denied by the 1919 Versailles Settlement, and the Czechs, rescuing them from a bloodbath. After all: 'In 1938 Czechoslovakia was betrayed. In 1939 Poland was saved.' Since 100,000 Czechs subsequently died, compared with over 6 million Poles, 'Which was better – to be a betrayed Czech or a saved Pole?'[3] An interesting argument, although not one of A.J.P. Taylor's stronger ones.

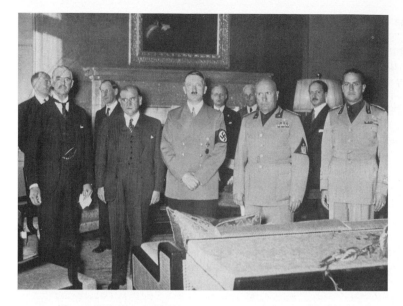

Figure 8.3
Neville Chamberlain at Munich, 1938

When it comes to pragmatic consequences there is a more genuine, and finely balanced, debate. Telford Taylor maintains that appeasement 'shattered the Czech-Franco-Russian defensive alliances'[4] and doomed France to defeat by Germany in 1940. There is much to be said for this. Had Britain and France stood by Czechoslovakia in 1938 they could have enlisted Soviet aid. German forces, including the *Luftwaffe*, would have been completely outnumbered and confronted by enemies on all sides. This would have made for a war which Germany would have found difficult to win. By 1939, when war actually broke out, appeasement had given Germany a further year to rearm, while the Soviet Union had reacted against Chamberlain and Daladier by drawing up the Nazi–Soviet Non-Aggression Pact in August. This enabled Hitler to carry out his *Blitzkrieg* strategy in two separate and successful stages – first against Poland in 1939, then against France in 1940. Significantly, he experienced his first major land defeats when he invaded Russia, but not before. The alternative perspective is that Britain was seriously unprepared for war in 1938. Appeasement bought an extra year in which the RAF was sufficiently strengthened to enable it to win the Battle of Britain in 1940 and to survive the bleakest period of the entire war. But this survival was not in itself sufficient to defeat Germany, since appeasement had helped destroy the feasibility of a continental offensive.

From the point of view of French security, therefore, the effects of appeasement were disastrous, whereas there is a strong case for its having saved Britain. It could even be said that if appeasement bought time for Britain, it was at the expense of France. It was not until Hitler launched Operation Barbarossa on the Soviet Union in 1941 that appeasement ceased to have a direct effect on the course of the war.

9.   To what extent was the Spanish Civil War an 'international' issue?   (90 marks)

The Spanish Civil War was a domestic issue which developed serious international implications. It involved internal tensions going back to 1931 but, between 1936 and 1939 it overlapped and exacerbated the tensions between the major powers and their opposing ideologies. There are, therefore, internal and international perspectives.

The origins of the conflict between the Republicans and Nationalists were entirely Spanish in origin. The dispute concerned the policies of the Second Republic which had replaced the monarchy after the abdication of Alfonso XIII. The Nationalists, comprising conservatives, clerical leaders and Spanish fascists from the **Falange**, objected to the liberalising measures of the 1931 constitution along with the reform of the army, the reduction of the social and political influence of the Catholic Church, the introduction of regional autonomy to Catalonia and the increase of land available to the peasantry. The Republicans, a broad coalition of liberals, socialists, communists and anarchists, aimed to build upon these measures in the future. What developed was a clash between the right, fighting to maintain traditional Spanish institutions and influences, and the left, who aimed to modernise them. Spanish society was divided in its preferences, the industrial workers and most of the peasantry opting for the Republicans, while the upper classes and the upper clergy of the Catholic Church supported the Nationalists. The professional middle classes were evenly divided between the two. The campaigns, which followed the military revolt of Franco and Mola in 1936, were also planned, directed and led by Spanish commanders; the casualties were inflicted on and by Spanish conscripts; and most of the atrocities were committed by Spaniards on Spaniards – in the name of Spain.

But, although the war was unquestionably fought on domestic issues, it rapidly developed a much wider dimension. There were, indeed, two international issues. One concerned the involvement of powers such as Germany, Italy and the Soviet Union, thus making Spain a focal point of rivalries between other European powers. The other was the threat that, because of this involvement, the Spanish Civil War might spread into the rest of Europe. This was particularly an issue with Britain and France, helping to shape their policy of appeasement.

Foreign intervention in the Spanish Civil War brought out into the open the intentions of Germany, Italy and the Soviet Union. Hitler saw Spain as a useful testing ground for German rearmament being developed under his Four Year Plan (1936–40), especially for the newly formed *Luftwaffe*. This explains why he provided Franco and the Nationalists with 16,000 German military advisers and the services of the *Kondor* Legion. In return, Germany learned a great deal from the experience, especially the effectiveness of the *Blitzkrieg* strategy which was later to be used to such effect against Poland in 1939 and Norway, the Low Countries and France in 1940. Mussolini's aims – and contributions – were more extensive. He hoped to spread Italian influence across the Mediterranean and to sustain the martial spirit apparently induced in Italy by the invasion of Ethiopia. To this effect, he provided the Nationalists with 50,000 Italian troops, 950 tanks, 763 aircraft and the use of 91 warships. Within this context, Germany and Italy became more closely involved in the form of the Rome–Berlin Axis (1936) and the Pact of Steel (1939). The Soviet Union, meanwhile, sponsored agreements between the different brands of socialism and communism in order to maintain a popular front against fascism. The war therefore increased the ideological antipathy in Europe. Fascism was seen as a source of military aggression, while communism was increasingly condemned by the Catholic Church (which therefore sided with Mussolini and Franco).

The Spanish Civil War also influenced the development of the policy of appeasement. Fearing that the war would overspill into the rest of Europe, Britain and France tried to contain it within Spain through international bodies like the Non-Intervention Committee. When this was ignored by Germany and Italy, Britain sought to accommodate Hitler's increasing demands in Europe, recognising in 1938 his annexations of Austria and the Sudetenland. One of the key influences behind appeasement at this stage was the fear of the possible impact of aerial bombing, as demonstrated by the *Luftwaffe* in Spain; in 1938 the *Kondor* Legion bombed the Basque city of Guernica, a communications centre for the Republicans. Chamberlain, in particular, was convinced that the outbreak of general war would result in the destruction of cities like London and Paris within days. This fear proved to be greatly exaggerated, the type of destruction envisaged by Chamberlain occurring only in 1944 as a result of sustained round-the-clock bombing by the RAF and USAF over Germany. There is, however, no doubt that the use of the *Luftwaffe* in the Spanish Civil War was a powerful weapon of propaganda and diplomatic intimidation which hastened the decision to allow Hitler to annex the Sudetenland in September 1938.

The Spanish Civil War was, therefore, an internal conflict between contrasting ideologies within Spain, with liberal democracy, socialism and communism polarising, on one side, against conservatism, nationalism and fascism on the other. This overlapped into the European context, although the latter developed a three-way antipathy between communism and fascism (which became actively involved in Spain) and the liberal democracies (which followed a pacific line). This carried huge international dangers which resulted in the Spanish Civil War being called a 'European civil war fought in Spain'.

The foreign policies of the individual powers

10. What were the main aims of Italian foreign policy between 1923 and 1940?   (90 marks)

Mussolini's main aim in foreign policy was, in his own words, to 'make Italy great, respected and feared'. This involved the more specific aims of expanding Italy's frontiers and military power, seizing the diplomatic initiative and creating fascist solidarity in Europe. Prioritising meant bringing one or more of these aims to the forefront. Between 1922 and 1940 the aims remained fairly constant, although the priorities changed.

The expansion of Italy was intended partly to revise the post-First World War settlement, the 'mutilated victory' which had left Italy short of the areas promised by the Secret Treaty of London (1915). This explains Mussolini's action in seizing Corfu in 1923, occupying Fiume (1923–4) and invading Albania in 1939. He also aimed to create an overseas empire, largely through the invasion of Ethiopia in 1935; in this he was influenced by the Roman past and also by the desire to avenge earlier Italian defeats, such as Adowa. In both cases expansion would involve a build-up of Italy's military power and infrastructure.

In terms of diplomacy, Mussolini aimed to gain the respect of other European statesmen, who would acknowledge Italy as the central point of the balance of power. In the process, Italy would be able to join whichever combination most suited its intentions at a particular time. This would mean that Italy would exploit other powers – instead of being exploited by them. Mussolini was therefore willing to experiment with a wide range of diplomatic initiatives. He signed the Locarno Pact (1925) and the Kellogg–Briand Pact (1928), attempted to destabilise France in eastern Europe by breaking the Little Entente, joined the Stresa Front with Britain and France to control Germany, and finally established a closer connection with Germany through the Rome–Berlin Axis (1936) and the Pact of Steel (1939).

Mussolini also had two stated ideological aims. One was to promote fascism as a force to defend Europe from the spread of communism. This is a reason for involving Italy in the Spanish Civil

War (1936–9) and for signing the Anti-Comintern Pact with Germany and Japan in 1937. The other was to launch a 'Crusade' on behalf of Catholicism; this was used to justify the invasion of Ethiopia in 1936 against 'paganism' and intervention in Spain against 'atheism' (both allegations were untrue).

Mussolini's priorities differed at various stages of his administration. Between 1922 and 1935 the main priorities were diplomacy and strategic security, as illustrated by the Locarno Pact of 1925 and the Stresa Front in 1934. These, however, alternated with bursts of limited expansionism – such as the seizure of Corfu in 1923 and Fiume in 1924 – and also attempts to disrupt the French system of alliances in eastern Europe. Between 1935 and 1940, however, he had three quite different priorities. One was more rapid expansionism, including the conquest of Ethiopia, intervention in the Spanish Civil War and the invasion of Albania in 1939. Another was the search for strategic security, leading to the Rome–Berlin Axis (1936) and military alliance with Germany in the form of the 1939 Pact of Steel. The third was rearmament and militarism, which eventually led Mussolini into 'parallel war' in 1940.

There were good reasons for this variation in priorities. The period 1922–35 involved the consolidation of Mussolini's power within Italy and a strong focus on domestic issues. Italy's role in Europe therefore was inclined to caution until Mussolini's position was fully secure. At this stage he was also influenced by the traditional career officials and diplomats in his foreign ministry; most had served in previous governments during the pre-fascist era and were still able to bring some liberal influences to bear on Italian diplomacy. Mussolini was at this stage biding his time, waiting for the right moment to begin his preferred expansionist and militarist approach. The period after 1935, by contrast, switched the priority to 'fulfilment' since the Cult of the *Duce* now needed to produce results. It has also been argued that, by this time, Italy needed a diversion abroad from its slow economic recovery from the effects of depression. Mussolini therefore threw caution away, especially when Britain and France reacted with hostility over the Italian invasion of Ethiopia in 1935. He also took a chance on a closer attachment with Germany, thus reversing all his earlier concerns about Austria.

From 1936 onwards, therefore, Mussolini subordinated everything to his quest for land and glory in imitation of ancient Rome. In the process he forgot about his more moderate – and modern – aspirations of being 'arbiter' of Europe. It is no coincidence that the civilian suit had given way to the military uniform.

11. Examine the successes and failures of Mussolini's foreign policy between 1922 and 1940. (90 marks)

Since Italy had such a limited economic, industrial and military infrastructure, success in foreign policy tended to accompany limited measures, while failures were usually associated with more ambitious schemes.

Mussolini's most enduring successes were diplomatic, mainly in the 1920s. The main example was participation in Collective Security, along with Austen Chamberlain, Briand and Stresemann, to form the Locarno Pact in 1925, the Kellogg–Briand Pact (1928) and the Stresa Front (1934). In the process, he earned the respect of other statesmen; Churchill called him 'Roman genius in person', while Chamberlain said: 'I trust his word when given and think we might easily go far before finding an Italian with whom it would be as easy for the British Government to work.'

Between 1930 and 1934 Mussolini added another dimension in a policy of 'equidistance' between Britain, France and Germany. These policies generally succeeded because the times and circumstances in Europe favoured conciliatory diplomacy. Mussolini therefore had an appropriate national response to an international situation.

Partial success accompanied some of his more aggressive policies. In the 1920s he aimed at the pursuit of specific objectives, without antagonising the other powers and upsetting the diplomatic achievements. One example was the seizure of Corfu in 1923 after the assassination by terrorists of General Tellini and other members of a boundary commission on the border between Greece and Albania. Mussolini demanded compensation of 50 million lire and an official apology from the Greek government. When these did not materialise, he seized Corfu, clearly his original intention. He was partially successful in that the Greek government paid compensation of 50 million lire, but the Italians withdrew from Corfu. Similarly, Mussolini successfully installed an Italian commandant in Fiume, and Yugoslavia had to recognise Italian administration of the enclave in the 1924 Pact of Rome. These policies generally succeeded because Mussolini was making realistic use of Italy's very limited infrastructure and power base.

Some policies were spectacular and initially successful, but resulted in the longer-term destabilisation of the regime. The invasion of Ethiopia in 1935 achieved the 'imperium' for which Mussolini had striven, considerably extending Italy's African empire. It resulted in victory (by contrast with the Italian defeat at Adowa in 1895) and was popular within Italy, enhancing Mussolini's prestige and winning the regime open support from the Catholic Church. The Rome–Berlin Axis of 1936 compensated Italy for the alienation of Britain and France and seemed to extend Italy's future military prospects. Assisting Franco's victory in the Spanish Civil War (1936–9) appeared to outflank France with three fascist powers. The invasion of Albania in 1939 resulted in the addition of territory on the Adriatic, a compensation for the territory Italy had not been given in the 1919 peace settlement. These policies were, however, carried out at immense cost, which eventually shattered the regime's limited infrastructure.

There are also examples of direct failures. During the 1920s he did not succeed in his attempts to destabilise the French pattern of alliances in Eastern Europe. He tried, for example, to break the pro-French Little Entente, which comprised Yugoslavia, Rumania and Czechoslovakia. It seemed at first that he might undermine this by separate agreements with Czechoslovakia and Yugoslavia. But his involvement in the Albanian Civil War encouraged the Little Entente to tighten up in reaction. He also failed to achieve his objectives in the Albanian Civil War. He supported the rebel Noli against Zogu – but the latter won and proclaimed himself King Zog. Mussolini therefore remained largely outflanked in eastern Europe. These policies were too ambitious for Italy's limited resources. But at least failure was not turned into disaster at this stage because Mussolini avoided becoming involved in any large-scale war.

The 1930s brought a different kind of failure. It was not that Mussolini's policies did not achieve their objectives (for they did). They were, however, failures in the impact they had on the regime. They were too ambitious for Italy's limited economic and military infrastructure and resulted in total exhaustion by 1939. For example, the invasion of Ethiopia, although successfully completed by 1936, had serious side-effects: Britain and France were alienated and economic sanctions were imposed against Italy by the League of Nations, from which Italy had to withdraw. Hitler was able to take Austria in 1938 (which Mussolini had originally wanted to prevent). Italy fell under increasing German influence through the Rome–Berlin Axis (1936), the Anti-Comintern Pact (1937) and the Pact of Steel (1939). Meanwhile, assembling the largest army ever to enter

Africa wrecked any chances for the recovery of the Italian economy, while involvement in the Spanish Civil War may have helped Franco to achieve power but used up huge amounts of Italian war materials in the process. The invasion of Albania was accomplished in 1939 only after some difficulty, a clear indication that the other involvements of Mussolini had already drained Italy's strength.

Overall, Mussolini tended to succeed in his foreign policy when they were limited and in line with Italy's economic and industrial infrastructure. These generally worked. When he became more ambitious, however, Mussolini bought short-term achievement at the cost of long-term disaster.

12. Assess the reasons for Mussolini's invasion of Ethiopia in 1935 and for his intervention in the Spanish Civil War (1936–9). (90 marks)

Mussolini's foreign policy underwent a sudden increase in momentum between 1935 and 1939, resulting in the launching of one war and involvement in another. In both cases the three main factors to consider are Mussolini's long-term aspirations, short-term necessity and favourable external factors. The order of these priorities was not the same.

The underlying motives behind Mussolini's decision to launch an invasion of Ethiopia were particularly strong. Italy had already attempted a conquest in 1896 but had been defeated at Adowa. Mussolini aimed to avenge this defeat and, in the process, create an African empire. Ethiopia would be added to Italy's existing colonies – Eritrea, Somaliland and Libya. This, in turn, would begin the revival of Mussolini's 'Roman Empire'. Ethiopia, as the richest of Italy's colonies, would provide resources for the 'growing economy' and accommodate Italy's surplus population, which would result from the 'Battle for Births'. There was also a powerful ideological impetus: a fascist yearning for expansion and conquest.

The decision had, therefore, long since been taken. But there was a more immediate and pressing reason for the actual timing: domestic pressures were forcing a change of foreign policy in 1935. Carocci argues that the economic situation had deteriorated during the 1930s as Italy was taking a long time to emerge from depression. By 1935: 'People all over the country felt indifferent to the regime, detached from it. In order to overcome these feelings, in order to galvanise the masses and try to break the vicious circle of economic crisis, more drastic and more attractive measures were needed.' The invasion was therefore intended to generate a new spirit and mobilise support behind Mussolini. It was a propaganda device to reinforce the cult of the Duce. A 'crusade' in Ethiopia would also ensure the loyalty of the Catholic Church to the regime. It would therefore reinforce the Lateran agreements of 1929.

External factors reinforced the timing of the invasion, although they were less important than domestic pressures in deciding it. The diplomatic situation seemed to support the idea of a swift and decisive stroke. Britain had acknowledged an Italian role in the Horn of Africa ever since 1906 and the French appeared willing in 1935 to allow Italy freedom of action. As far as the German threat was concerned, an Italian victory in Africa would deter Hitler from any further action over Austria and could be accomplished sufficiently rapidly to restore an Italian military presence in the Danube area. Even though the Hoare–Laval Pact was subsequently renounced by the British and French governments, Mussolini was determined to press on with his long-term ambition in an attempt to stabilise his domestic position.

The reasons for Mussolini's involvement in the Spanish Civil War were less clear cut. Why should he want to side with the Nationalists, thereby enabling Franco to overthrow the Spanish Republic and establish a right-wing regime? In this case, the long-term objectives, domestic influences and favourable circumstances assume a different relationship.

Indeed, the last of these was the most important, since without it the other two would have had no scope for involvement. To Mussolini, the outbreak of war in 1936 offered the sudden prospect of backing a right-wing military campaign against a weakened and isolated left-wing republic. This would carry immediate diplomatic and strategic benefits. Mussolini could reverse Italy's vulnerability to Anglo-French pressures over Ethiopia by establishing a new alliance with Spain and Germany, also involved on the side of Franco. A Fascist Spain would weaken Britain's naval position in the western Mediterranean by threatening Gibraltar, while France would now be outflanked by three hostile states – Spain, Italy and Germany. The only other possible threat, the Soviet Union, would also be neutralised. Stalin would lose the Spanish Republic as a potential ally and hence any possibility of communism establishing itself in the western Mediterranean. Hence the opportunity which suddenly arose from Spain's internal crisis appeared too good for Mussolini to miss.

It also fitted well with Mussolini's longer-term objectives of spreading Italian power throughout the Mediterranean to offset the humiliating treatment received under the 'mutilated' territorial settlement of 1919–20. This would, in turn, link up with the spread of Italian imperialism in Africa, offering the real prospect of converting the Mediterranean into a new 'Roman sea'. Mussolini could also establish a series of puppet regimes of the type which had eluded him in the 1920s. Earlier intervention in Albania had failed, but influence over a new Francoist Spain could also lead to the fascistisation of Salazar's Portugal. Intervention in Spain therefore provided sudden focus to one of Mussolini's more nebulous visions – the new 'Fascist Century'. Without this special situation it is difficult to see how this could have happened.

Domestic factors also featured in Italian intervention in the Spanish Civil War, although their real impetus had already been felt in the invasion of Ethiopia. They therefore exerted a continuing, not an initiating, influence. Victory in Ethiopia had provided Mussolini with a boost to his popularity, but this needed to be sustained by success in Europe. Similarly, support from the Catholic Church had begun to wear thin during the later stages of the Ethiopian campaign but could now be revived by the support given to the campaign against 'atheistic communism'. This time the 'crusade' was Franco's, but Mussolini prolonged his credit with the Vatican by supporting it. This was probably not a direct consideration in Mussolini's decision to intervene – but it would have been seen as a definite bonus.

13. **'For Italy, the negative effects far outweighed the positive.' To what extent do you agree with this view of Mussolini's invasion of Ethiopia (1935) and involvement in the Spanish Civil War (1936–9)?**   **(90 marks)**

The effects of this period of hectic activity were momentous. Mussolini claimed that involvement in these ventures brought enormous benefits to Italy. From a partial perspective this may appear true. Through the 1935 invasion, Italy avenged its defeat at Adowa (1895) and added Ethiopia to its existing colonies (Somaliland, Eritrea and Libya) to consolidate its African empire. As a direct result of co-operating with Hitler in the Spanish Civil War, Mussolini established a military link between Italy and Germany through the Rome–Berlin Axis (1936) and the Pact of Steel (1939). This more than offset the loss of the Anglo-French connection and the collapse of the Stresa Front.

Italy also became part of a broader fascist front which outflanked France on three frontiers and also removed any remaining Soviet influence in the western Mediterranean. Mussolini had therefore achieved success in three ways. He had extended Italian imperialism and revived the dream of naval control over the Mediterranean. He had proved Italy's military strength in Africa and in Europe – which he confirmed by the occupation of Albania in 1939. And he was at the centre of a formidable ideological system.

Events, however, proved that these effects were transient. A much stronger case can be made for the serious damage inflicted by Mussolini's ventures on Italy's position in Europe. Between them, the Ethiopian and Spanish wars were a major catalyst for change in Italian policies and interests, narrowing the range of Mussolini's future diplomatic options. Given Italy's limited industrial infrastructure, Mussolini's greatest chance of success on the international stage was through flexible diplomacy rather than military commitment. He had already shown this in two earlier periods. During the 1920s he had alternated between limited and targeted bouts of aggression (such as the occupation of Corfu in 1923 and of Fiume in 1925) and involvement in mainstream diplomacy (as at Locarno in 1925). Between 1930 and 1935, he had successfully implemented a policy of 'equidistance' between France and Germany on the one hand and Germany on the other. But the invasion of Ethiopia alienated Italy from Britain and France, while the Spanish Civil War confirmed the new connection with Germany. The latter ultimately proved disastrous, committing Italy to a war in the Balkans and North Africa which, by 1943, was to destroy Mussolini's regime. Nor was Italy to receive any help from Nationalist Spain. Franco proved eventually to be the survivor that Mussolini could have been – but only because he recognised the limitations of Spain's infrastructure and therefore remained neutral.

The domestic impact of Mussolini's more dynamic foreign policy was also mixed. On the one hand, there were certain benefits. The Ethiopian and Spanish conflicts temporarily increased Mussolini's popularity at home and strengthened the Cult of the *Duce*. Mussolini was projected increasingly as the new 'Caesar', who was reviving Roman power. This was a temporary diversion from economic hardship and war was used deliberately by the fascist regime to control consumer expectations which the economy could not possibly satisfy. Mussolini could also justify the increased complexity of the Corporate State as the necessary administrative structure of an enlarged empire. Quite simply, potential criticism of the regime's internal deficiencies were for the moment stifled by the powerful appeal to a unifying patriotism. To this was added the official sanction of the Catholic Church, which was won over to Mussolini's regime, partly because of the Lateran Agreements of 1929 but also because of Mussolini's apparent stand against 'atheistic communism'.

Again, however, such benefits were short-term. Mussolini's foreign policy after 1935 eventually weakened the regime internally, made Italy vulnerable to external defeat and alienated most of the population. This was a huge price to pay for a few years of salvaged prestige. The commitments involved in the invasion of Ethiopia and the Spanish Civil War had a serious impact on the Italian economy. They severely undermined the whole programme of Italian industrialisation, including the channelling of state investment through the IRI (*Istituto per la recostruzione industriale*), set up in 1933. They also distorted the industrial base by forcing it to concentrate on the development of armaments. These, in turn, were wasted at a profligate rate. The invasion of Ethiopia involved 1.5 million troops, along with massive technological support, while involvement in the Spanish Civil War cost Italy 763 aircraft, 950 tanks and 14 billion lire. Mussolini was unable to make up the loss of equipment before the outbreak of the Second World War. This was to prove particularly serious since Britain and France, convinced that Italy was now irrevocably hostile, began from 1937 to rearm at a pace which Italy, with her smaller industrial base, could not match. While all the other major powers were stronger in 1939 than they had been in 1936, Italy was therefore undeniably weaker. The Italian population were also becoming increasingly suspicious of a regime which had bound itself irrevocably to Germany. Mussolini's anti-Semitic policies, introduced in 1938 by the Manifesto on Race, were particularly resented and undermined much of the goodwill which the regime had previously earned from the Catholic Church. By 1939 it was clear that Italy was once again a society in crisis.

Despite the devastating impact of Mussolini's foreign policy between 1935 and 1939, there was still a possibility that his regime might have survived. Mussolini accepted reality in failing to support Hitler in September 1939. Yet this could only be an attempt to recover rather than a reversion to earlier caution. The period 1935–9 had set an agenda which meant fascism's victory or destruction. The cost of this agenda before 1939 meant the latter.

14. Why did Italy enter the Second World War on the side of Germany – but in 1940 rather than in 1939? (90 marks)

Mussolini entered the Second World War on the side of Germany because of the growth of diplomatic agreements between Mussolini and Hitler, culminating in a full-scale military alliance in 1939. Although Mussolini had originally distrusted Hitler, especially over the latter's hopes of achieving an *Anschluss* with Austria, the effects of Mussolini's own actions abroad increasingly drew him into what F.W. Deakin has termed a 'Brutal Friendship' with Germany.[5]

This commitment involved two distinct, but interconnected, stages: the alienation of Italy from France and Britain, and the move towards Germany. Mussolini's invasion of Ethiopia in 1935 broke the close diplomatic connection between Italy, Britain and France, which had been formalised in the Stresa Front. Their attempts to impose economic sanctions through the League of Nations convinced him that there was no longer any point in maintaining the connection. Since he had already sought to eradicate western democracy within Italy, it now made more ideological sense to do a deal with a fellow-totalitarian regime. The involvement of both Italy and Germany on the side of Franco in the Spanish Civil War (1936–9) accelerated the 'Brutal Friendship' in the form of the 1936 Rome–Berlin Axis; according to von Hassell, German ambassador in Rome, Italy was now realising 'the advisability of confronting the western powers shoulder-to-shoulder with Germany'. The Axis was given an ideological base with the signing of the Anti-Comintern Pact with Germany and Japan in November 1937, while the military connection followed in May 1939: the Pact of Steel committed Italy and Germany to mutual military support in any offensive or defensive war involving either country. It was this final obligation, following on from three years of diplomatic change, which eventually brought Italy into the Second World War.

Yet the outbreak of war in September 1939 caught Mussolini unprepared and unable to participate. When Germany invaded Poland in September 1939, Mussolini was severely embarrassed. He could not claim that this did not involve Italy since the Pact of Steel specified support for offensive as well as defensive campaigns. Ciano had given von Ribbentrop what amounted to a blank cheque and Mussolini had not properly monitored it since he had assumed that Hitler would not go to war before 1943. The problem with any earlier commitment was that Italy's military capacity had been weakened by half a decade of war in Ethiopia and Spain, her resources further extended by Mussolini's attack on Albania in April. Mussolini simply could not afford now to rush into a conflict with France and Britain, which Hitler had so inconveniently provoked in September 1939. The Italian government therefore sent Berlin a list of strategic materials it needed to enable it to go to war in support of Germany. Failing to obtain these, Mussolini had to secure from Hitler a temporary release from Italy's obligations under the Pact of Steel.

There were several reasons why Mussolini changed his mind and declared war on Britain and France in June 1940. In the first place, the situation in Europe had changed considerably since September 1939. With the collapse of Poland, Norway, the Low Countries and France, the war seemed all but over and Mussolini had little to fear. Since France was on the point of surrender Italy would not be committing itself to a prolonged struggle. Here was a chance for a quick round of hostilities which would reverse the humiliating experience of Italian neutrality in 1939 and enable Mussolini to take part in a conference to receive the spoils due to a victorious power. If, on the other hand, he did not participate, he would have no claims to territory in southern France or the Balkans. There was a unique chance to make up for Italy's humiliating treatment at St Germain (1919) in a new settlement in 1940 – and with far less expenditure of effort and resources.

The whole process shows a series of miscalculations and misjudgement which eventually destroyed his rule and his regime.

15. What were the main stages of German foreign policy between 1933 and 1939? (90 marks)

Hitler's foreign policy went through several stages between his appointment as Chancellor in January 1933 and the outbreak of war in September 1939. These were influenced by opportunities and external factors as well as by his own intentions.

The first stage, between 1933 and 1935, was a cautious and gradual repudiation of the Versailles Settlement. At this stage caution was dictated by Germany's vulnerability in Europe; Hitler therefore alternated between conciliatory diplomatic gestures and specific measures to rebuild Germany's military power. An example of his diplomacy was the way in which he used the Geneva Disarmament Conference to Germany's benefit in 1933. Looking for an opportunity to withdraw from any future constraints on armaments, Hitler backed MacDonald's proposal to allow parity between Germany and France in troop levels, knowing that France would reject this. When he was proved correct, he had a reason to withdraw Germany from the Conference and from the League itself. At the same time, he allayed fears of future aggression by drawing up in 1934 a Non-Aggression Pact with Poland. While the League was uncertain about what to do, Hitler gradually repudiated the military clauses of the Treaty of Versailles. By the middle of 1934 he had increased the German army to 240,000 men, more than twice the number allowed by Versailles, while in March 1935 he introduced conscription and announced the formation of the *Luftwaffe*.

Even so, Germany remained isolated at this stage and Hitler had to be careful not to provoke retaliation. France had an extensive network of alliances in eastern Europe, while Italy's suspicions that Germany had designs on Austria were greatly increased by the assassination of President Dollfuss by Austrian Nazis in 1934. Mussolini was sufficiently outraged by this to form the Stresa Front (1935) with Britain and France. Meanwhile, France strengthened her Eastern alliances by drawing up the Franco-Soviet Pact in the same year. Despite Hitler's diplomacy and phased rearmament, it seemed that Germany was as vulnerable as ever.

The second stage, between 1935 and 1937, brought changes in the international scene, which offered Hitler a series of opportunities to end German isolation, put pressure on Britain and France and close ranks with Italy. He was assisted initially by the determination of the British government to keep out of continental commitments, which meant that it was always willing to sign agreements to control the level of armaments. The result was the 1935 Anglo-German Naval Pact, in which Hitler received what was virtually a *carte blanche* to resume naval construction, provided that Germany did not exceed 35 per cent of the total British strength. Hitler also benefited from Mussolini's decision to launch an Italian invasion of Ethiopia in 1935. This diverted Italian attention from Austria and, when Britain and France applied sanctions against Italy, broke up the Stresa Front against Germany. Confident that further breaches of the Treaty of Versailles would not now provoke Anglo-French intervention, Hitler was able to remilitarise the Rhineland in 1936. He was also able to draw Italy into a 'Rome–Berlin Axis', assist in the creation of the Nationalist regime in Spain, and put together an Anti-Comintern Pact against Russia, comprising Germany, Japan and Italy. From 1936 onwards, Germany was also gaining economic and diplomatic control over Rumania, Yugoslavia, Bulgaria and Greece.

By 1937, therefore, Hitler was ready for the next stage – one of more targeted aggression. This was initiated in November 1937 when, according to the Hossbach Memorandum, Hitler showed his chiefs of staff his schemes for the future expansion of Germany. This clearly indicated a change in the pace of Hitler's diplomacy and indicated he was now much more willing to run high risks to achieve his aims. Indeed, he scored two major successes in 1938. In March he defied the Treaty of Versailles to incorporate Austria into Germany through the *Anschluss*. The ease with which this was accomplished encouraged his second undertaking in 1938, the incorporation of the Czech border province of the Sudetenland into the Reich. Hitler made use of the Sudeten Nazis to stir up the German population, relying on the unwillingness of Chamberlain and Daladier to assist the Czech President, Benes. The result was the Munich Agreement (29 September 1938) which enabled Hitler to annex the Sudetenland without a war with Czechoslovakia.

Hitler was sufficiently encouraged by this to enter the next stage of his foreign policy: a series of limited military engagements against Germany's neighbours in 1939. The first was the occupation of Bohemia and Moravia, which were incorporated into the Reich in March. Having accomplished his objectives in central Europe, Hitler turned his attention eastwards, gaining Memel from Lithuania. His third victim was Poland, from which he demanded Danzig and a corridor to link Germany with East Prussia. Hitler swiftly stepped up the pressure by demanding Danzig and the Polish corridor. Although Britain and France changed their policy in March from appeasement to a guarantee for Poland, Hitler was convinced that this would never be implemented. However, to secure Germany's position, Hitler drew up two major agreements in 1939. One was the Pact of Steel, a full military alliance agreed with Italy in May. The other was the Non-Aggression Pact with the Soviet Union in August. This was a major diplomatic turnabout which made a nonsense of any undertaking by the West to protect Poland. It also meant that Hitler's conquest of Poland could go ahead unimpeded in September 1939, unaffected by the declaration of war on Germany by Britain and France.

Germany's foreign policy therefore underwent a major transformation between 1933 and 1939, the overall pattern changing gradually from cautious assertiveness to defiant aggression.

16. How clear were the ideas and aims behind Hitler's foreign policy between 1933 and 1939? (90 marks)

Hitler's foreign policy was certainly based on ideas which he had developed before he came to power in 1933. But whether these ideas were ever converted into clearly defined aims has been the subject of major controversy. The aims were either a focused or a blurred version of the ideas.

Hitler's ideas on foreign policy are clearly set out in three main sources: *Mein Kampf*, *Zweites Buch*, and *Tischgespräche*. From a combination of the three several priorities can be deduced. Hitler believed that previous German governments had concentrated too much on the 'fixed frontier'. Instead, the Nazis would follow a 'territorial one', the purpose of which would be 'to secure the space necessary to the life of our people'. Earlier mistakes would be rectified and *Lebensraum* would be achieved by depriving the 'inferior races' of their territory. This would be in accordance with 'an eternal law of Nature', by which 'the right to the land belongs to the one who conquers'. Indeed, 'Every healthy, vigorous people sees nothing sinful in territorial acquisition, but something quite in keeping with its nature.' In carrying out this expansion, Hitler wrote in *Mein Kampf*: 'we turn our eyes to the land in the East'. In particular, he had in mind 'Russia and its subjugated border states'.

Whether these ideas grew into specific foreign-policy aims has been the subject of a major historical controversy.

On the one hand, there is much to be said for the view that Hitler had a clear programme in mind. Trevor-Roper, for example, saw *Mein Kampf* as 'a complete blueprint of his intended achievements'.[6] The German historian, Hillgruber, argued that Hitler's 'programme of foreign policy' can be divided into three phases.[7] During the first, Germany achieved internal consolidation and rearmament and concluded agreements with Britain and Italy. This seems to correspond to the development of the Four Year Plan (1936–40), the Anglo-German Naval Agreement (1935), the Rome–Berlin Axis (1936) and the Pact of Steel (1939). In the second phase, Germany would need to defeat France in a preliminary engagement; this was actually achieved in 1940. Then 'the great war of conquest against Russia could take place during the third and final phase'. This seems to have been the main motive behind the invasion of the Soviet Union in 1941. An alternative, but overlapping programme is also possible. Hitler's first priority was to destroy the Versailles Settlement and rearm Germany: this started with the withdrawal from the League of Nations and the announcement of conscription in 1934 through to the remilitarisation of the Rhineland in 1936. The enlargement of the Reich would come next (accomplished in 1938 by the *Anschluss* and the inclusion of the Sudetenland) and then the achievement of *Lebensraum* (through the invasion of Poland in 1939 and Russia in 1941).

All this provides a logical explanation as to how Hitler could build Germany up to achieve the ultimate aim of *Lebensraum* which he had already conceived as his principal idea. But what if this idea had not been intended for realisation? A.J.P. Taylor, for example, argued that Hitler's projects were 'in large part daydreaming, unrelated to what followed in real life'. In his opinion, 'Hitler was gambling on some twist of fortune which would present him with success in foreign affairs'.[8] Again, a British historian has been supported by a German. Mommsen argued that Hitler's foreign policy was a series of responses to specific events rather than a preconceived plan. He added: 'hindsight alone gives them some air of consistency'.[9]

This line also makes sense. Virtually all Hitler's actions could be seen as a reaction to developments which he did not initiate. His withdrawal from the League of Nations Disarmament Conference in 1934 was a reaction to MacDonald's failure to get French agreement to armaments parity with Germany. The subsequent Nazi–Polish Non-Aggression Pact was simply an expedient to protect Germany's eastern frontier against a still powerful state. The remilitarisation of the Rhineland (1936) was an opportunity presented by Mussolini: his invasion of Ethiopia destroyed the Stresa Front between Britain, France and Italy, and hence made any counter-measures against Germany much more difficult. Similarly, Italy's isolation suggested the formation of the

Rome–Berlin Axis, which was tightened into the 1939 Pact of Steel. Mussolini's problems also diverted Italy's attention from Austria, which Hitler hastened to annex in the *Anschluss* of 1938; his timing was decided by the preoccupation of both the French and the British governments with internal crises. Hitler was also able to take advantage of the Anglo-French policy of appeasement to annex the Sudetenland later in the same year. Overall, Hitler went with the diplomatic trends in Europe and actually did little more than dictate their pace. This amounts to piecemeal opportunism rather than consistent policy.

These interpretations are equally valid, depending on which perspective is adopted. A limited synthesis is, however, also possible. Like most radicals, Hitler had ideas which he committed to paper and articulated in his speeches. Between 1933 and 1936 Germany's vulnerability in Europe meant that he was in no position to convert these into policies. Changes in the diplomatic scene, however, favoured unscrupulous opportunism. This began to move into line with the ideas so that a programme began to emerge at the end of 1937 with the Hossbach Memorandum. In 1938 the opportunism over Austria and Czechoslovakia now seemed to be based on more obvious policies while, in 1939, policy took over from opportunism: this is why Hitler took the fateful decision to ignore the Anglo-French guarantee and invade Poland.

17. What were the main stages of Soviet foreign policy between 1921 and 1941? (90 marks)

Soviet foreign policy underwent a number of major changes during the 1920s and 1930s. At times these were so pronounced that they resembled a zig-zag and appeared to be bouncing from one expedient to another.

The first major example of Soviet diplomacy came with the Rapallo Agreement of 1922. This was a settlement with Europe's other pariah power, Germany, and came as a shock to the Western states who were at the time trying at Genoa to sort out a solution to current German and Soviet debts. After Lenin's death in 1924 the focus of the new Soviet leadership (the Triumvirate of Kamenev, Zinoviev and Stalin) was on improving relations with the West. During this period, diplomatic recognition came from Britain, France, Italy and Japan. In 1926, however, Stalin began to show a preference for Germany, strengthening Soviet links through the Berlin Treaty which, among other things, opened the way for secret German rearmament with Soviet connivance. Meanwhile, relations deteriorated with Britain to the point of a diplomatic break in 1927. By the end of the 1920s Stalin was arguing that the Soviet Union no longer needed any form of Western economic assistance and that, in any case, capitalism was about to be destroyed by economic crisis. For the moment, the future lay with renewing, in 1931, the Treaty of Berlin.

From this stage onwards the swings in policy intensified. Despite his diplomacy with Germany, he made no attempt to assist it in preventing the rise of Hitler between 1931 and 1933; indeed, he even ordered the KPD under Thälmann not to co-operate with the SPD. Stalin considered that Nazism was a lesser evil than social democracy and that, in any case, it would soon collapse, allowing communism to rise from the wreckage. As it became clear, between 1933 and 1935, that this was not going to happen, Stalin became actively involved in diplomacy to contain Germany. This involved re-establishing contacts with states he had previously rejected. In 1935, for example, he drew up the Soviet–French and Soviet–Czechoslovak Treaties of Mutual Assistance. In the same year, he took the Soviet Union into the League of Nations and, from 1936, he actively encouraged the establishment of popular fronts throughout Europe – especially in Spain – to encourage the co-operation between communists, socialists and liberals against fascism. This was in direct contrast to his earlier rejection of any agreement with the German Social Democrats.

Yet, by 1938, Stalin was making further changes to Soviet policy. In 1939 he entered separate negotiations with Britain and France, on the one hand, and with Nazi Germany on the other. In August 1939 he appeared to have returned to the German track in the form of the Nazi–Soviet Non-Aggression Pact, signed by the Soviet and German Foreign Ministers, Molotov and von Ribbentrop. By this each of the powers undertook neutrality in the event of the other being involved in a war, while the Secret Additional Protocol established the principle that eastern Europe should be divided into German and Soviet spheres of influence. This opened the way to the conquest of Poland from both east and west. Yet, from September onwards, Stalin became increasingly insistent that the Soviet sphere should be enlarged by the inclusion of the greater part of the Baltic states and by a slice of Romania, thus running the risk of alienating his new ally. Meanwhile, Soviet involvement in the Winter War with Finland resulted in its expulsion from the League of Nations and the lowest point in Stalin's relations with the West. It was at this point that Hitler launched Operation Barbarossa on the Soviet Union in June 1941.

18. 'Stalin's foreign policy had no clear direction between 1929 and 1941.' To what extent do you agree with this assessment? (90 marks)

Soviet foreign policy followed such a tortuous route between 1921 and 1941 that two main interpretations have been applied to it. One is that it lacked overall direction, even though it did possess individual aims. The other is that its strange inconsistencies should not detract from an underlying and farsighted logic. Neither of these views are conclusive, although each contains elements for a third and more convincing alternative.

On the one hand, Stalin has been seen as fundamentally out of control of Soviet foreign policy, the various stages showing alarming inconsistency. Between 1932 and 1933, for example, he instructed the German Communist Party (KPD) not to collaborate with the SPD to prevent the rise of the Nazis; his assumption was that the latter could subsequently be overthrown and a German communist regime established. When this did not occur, Stalin took measures to contain Germany in Europe by drawing up alliances with France and Czechoslovakia and by promoting in Spain the very idea of the popular front against fascism which he had forbidden in Germany. Then, in 1938, he was arguing that Western appeasement had shown that France was a broken reed and that the only sensible option was the 1939 Non-Aggression Pact with Germany. Two years later he was caught spectacularly off-balance by Hitler's invasion of Russia. Churchill later regarded Stalin as one of the greatest bunglers of 1941; this might actually be given a pedigree going back at least to 1933.

An alternative interpretation is that Stalin's error of judgement in 1941 was out of character with a much more successful earlier phase. It has been argued that Stalin's long-term objective had always been an alliance between Germany and the Soviet Union, which would guarantee Soviet security in Eastern Europe, especially against Poland. This had been the original intention of helping Hitler into power, since a radicalised Germany would be much less likely to find favour with the Western powers. At the same time, Hitler had to be shown the importance of recognising the damage that the hostility of the Soviet Union could do; this explains Stalin's bout of apparently anti-German diplomacy between 1935 and 1937. By 1939, however, it was clear that Germany was making stronger approaches, through Ribbentrop, for a deal. The Nazi–Soviet Non-Aggression

Pact was therefore the logical outcome of Stalin's original objective. The fact that Stalin was wrong to trust Hitler to abide by it does not affect the argument that Stalin had planned for something like it.

It is, however, difficult to see Stalin either as the total bungler suggested by the first scenario or as the far-sighted schemer depicted in the second. Yet *elements* of each would certainly apply. Stalin did not, it should be said at the outset, have a long-term commitment to Nazi Germany, which would rule out any aim for an ultimate German alliance. He did, however, have a funda-mental antipathy towards the West, shown in his speech of 1931: 'We are fifty to a hundred years behind the west and must make good that gap within ten; either we do it or they crush us.' This dictated the whole direction of his economic policy, the Five Year Plans (1928–33, 1933–7 and 1938–41) being aimed at developing heavy industry and armaments in particular. Since the West represented two ideologies hostile to communism – fascism and liberal democracy – it made sense to manoeuvre freely between them. This explains why, for example, he switched from supporting Hitler's rise to power (1922–3) to an alliance with France (1935) and back to a non-aggression Pact with Germany (1941). His aim was to strengthen Soviet security by promoting divisions else-where. This was not, however, based merely on an analysis of shifting balances of power. Recent historians have shown that Stalin had developed a military strategy which was moving away from its traditional emphasis on defensive warfare towards the principle of the pre-emptive strike. It could well be that, by 1939, Stalin had come to the conclusion that a deal with Germany was the only way of keeping the peace until he was ready for war.

Ironically, of course, Stalin placed too much faith in his own assessment of Hitler's motives. He rightly assumed that any German invasion of Russia would be an irrational act while a front was still open in the West. This judgement, although proved wrong by Hitler's invasion in 1941, is clear evidence that Stalin's switches and changes were based on an assessment of probabilities. His foreign policy had no long-term plan beyond Soviet security against the west. It did, however, show an ultimate sense of direction and at least some method in his short-term changes in course.

19. How far did the foreign policies of the European powers affect each other between 1931 and 1939? (90 marks)

The key issue affecting the major powers was the implementation of the Versailles settlement and the extent of Germany's reconciliation to it. Major changes occurred from 1929 onwards as a result of the international economic crisis, the rise of Hitler within Germany and the growing divergence of the policies of the powers away from the multilateral base. Even so, there was a final period of uneasy international stability in Europe between 1929 and 1935. This was upset by Italy.

Italian foreign policy has been much underrated in terms of its importance. The policies of Mussolini seem to have gone through two quite distinct periods. The first, which might be seen as having had a limited etatist base between 1922 and 1935, enabled Italy to coexist more or less harmoniously with the Western powers. In the 1920s Mussolini was seen as a major statesman and Italy as an important part of Collective Security. In the early 1930s Mussolini's main concern was Germany's growing interest in Austria and he was especially worried about Hitler's ambitions in that direction from 1933 to 1935. This made Italy a stabilising influence. Then came the second phase, started by the invasion of Abyssinia in 1935. This had a huge impact on the international scene. It broke the Italian connection with Britain and France (both of whom imposed sanctions) and drove Italy into the Rome–Berlin Axis with Germany which culminated in the 1939 Pact of

Steel. The effect was to release the constraints on Hitler. Collective Security was weakened; Britain and France had two potential enemies; Germany was no longer in isolation; and Italy's attention was fixed on Africa and Spain, not on Austria.

The result was a rapid acceleration in German foreign policy. Between 1933 and 1935 Hitler had had to be cautious and to avoid antagonising the stronger Anglo-French combination. The change of Italian orientation meant that he could remilitarise the Rhineland in 1936, annex Austria in 1938 and press for the Sudetenland in September 1938. The following year he extended his scope to include Bohemia (March) and Poland (September). Whether he was following a blue-print or simply reacting to events as they occurred is a matter of interpretation: the original debate between Trevor-Roper and A.J.P. Taylor has since acquired several subsequent layers of historiography.

The momentum of Hitler's changes – for whatever reason – was conditioned partly by the response of other countries. Here, British foreign policy was especially important. The switch from Collective Security to appeasement may be over-dramatic as an interpretation: the process may have been more gradual, with Collective Security always having elements of appeasement and appeasement retaining at least some Collective Security. Nevertheless, Baldwin and Chamberlain did give a high priority to keeping Britain out of any conflict in Europe. This meant pursuing a policy on non-intervention in the Spanish Civil War (1936–9) and allowing Hitler to pursue what Britain saw as a policy of revisionism over the Rhineland, Austria and the Sudetenland. This, too raises a controversy. Did Chamberlain actually believe in appeasement? Was this a policy based on convic-tion or was Chamberlain buying time for the proper preparation of Britain's defences? In March 1939 Britain guaranteed Poland's integrity, a policy which culminated in Britain's declaration of war on Germany in September. Was this a reversal of appeasement? Or was there actually contin-uity in what Chamberlain was trying to do? Whichever is the case, it certainly seems as though Hitler misread Chamberlain's intentions. But there is a parallel debate as to whether Hitler was actually looking for war at this stage, or whether he stumbled into it by accident.

It could also be said that Chamberlain failed to exploit the counterbalancing potential of the Soviet Union, through his longstanding mistrust of communism. Did this make a difference? It depends on what Stalin had in mind. Soviet foreign policy is highly controversial – partly because there is so little available documentary evidence. This allows for a greater degree of 'creative' historiog-raphy, as can be seen in the contrasting views of Deutscher and Tucker over the priorities of Stalin. Did Stalin fumble his way from one expedient to another, having to correct earlier mistakes by radical changes of course, as Deutscher argues?[10] Or was Stalin moving towards the long-term objective of association with Germany, as Tucker believes?[11] The answer to this affects the way in which we might perceive the Soviet influence on European international relations. Was the Soviet Union alienated in 1938 by the Anglo-French policy of appeasement in connection with Czechoslovakia and by Chamberlain's persistent and open anti-communism? Or was the Nazi–Soviet Non-Aggression Pact of August 1939 the inevitable outcome of Stalin's policies – quite irrespective of what Chamberlain thought or did?

French foreign policy has certain tragic connotations – or does it? France was above all concerned with its own security, which was a key factor in its attempt to cut Germany down to size by the Treaty of Versailles. Whether France went too far in this direction has become the subject of debate: according to Trachtenberg[12] and McDougall,[13] France was being entirely reasonable. French security was badly affected by the withdrawal of the United States from the European scene and from the League of Nations, which meant that Britain was less willing to become involved in guaranteeing France. Hence France took its own measures. These included a unilateral attempt to collect reparations in the invasion of the Ruhr in 1923. When Collective Security was introduced, France was unable to secure its extension to Germany's eastern frontiers; hence France made its own arrangements and plugged into an Eastern European security system involving Poland, Romania, Czechoslovakia and Yugoslavia. Friendship with Russia was difficult because of French support for Poland 1920–1. The 1930s saw further adjustments in French policies, including the formation of the Franco-Soviet Pact in 1935. But the growth of appeasement had a devastating effect on French security by breaking up any connection with Eastern Europe and undermining the Franco-Soviet connection, while the guarantee to Poland in 1939 was an obligation without any military return. The defeat of France in 1940 was partly a result of the collapse of French alliances and security networks. It is a debatable point as to who or what was most responsible for this.

Additional essay questions (with advice)

Each of these questions can be tackled as a single essay or as one of the answers to a question in several parts. Additional reading and research is desirable for each one.

20. **Assess the reasons for the treatment of Germany and Austria-Hungary by the peace settlement of 1919–20.**

   Advice: *Focus on the* reasons, *which can be deduced from the* treatment. *For example, Germany was constrained in various ways because, although defeated, it was still considered a potential threat. The break-up of Austria-Hungary was confirmed because it had already happened and national self-determination needed to be accommodated. Relate these general points back to the aims of statesman like Wilson, Clemenceau and Lloyd George. Try to prioritise the importance of these issues.*

21. **'The League of Nations failed because the major powers refused to take it seriously.' Do you agree with this view?**

   Advice: *There are two issues here: (1) Did the powers refuse to take the League seriously? (2) If they did refuse, was this the key factor in the League's failure? You could argue that the perception of some of the powers changed during the 1930s because they became more aggressive and that this badly affected the League's ability to exert a direct influence. On the other hand, some powers continued to take it seriously enough to try to impose sanctions on Italy. The declining credibility of the League was, however, directly linked to the aggression of Japan, Italy and Germany and – of course – vice versa.*

22. **Explain why Collective Security gave way in the 1930s to appeasement.**

   Advice: *Consider: (1) the changing circumstances in which Germany and Italy, two powers linked with Collective Diplomacy, drifted away from it; and (2) why Britain and France switched their response to appeasement. There is also a case for seeing some of the roots of appeasement in Collective Security, which might establish a degree of continuity as well as change.*

23. **'Mussolini's foreign policy between 1935 and 1939 had much more benefit for Germany than it did for Italy.' How far do you agree?**

Advice: *Avoid a description of Mussolini's foreign policy. Instead, focus on the effects on Italy (which were mixed) and on Germany (which were uniformly favourable to Hitler's aims in Europe).*

24. **Assess the interest of the European powers in the Spanish Civil War (1936–9)?**

Advice: *Consider the war from the point of view of the attitudes of the various powers, not as an internal issue for Spain. You could cover: (1) the ideological conflict between left and right; (2) the opportunity for the USSR and Italy to set up a satellite state of strategic importance; (3) the chance for Germany to test the effectiveness of its rearmament; and (4) the fears of Britain and France about the spread of the war to the rest of Europe.*

Essay plan

Para 1: Overall approach. The Spanish Civil War interacted with issues and problems affecting the rest of Europe. 'Interest' in this case meant:
- *either seeing the war as an opportunity for action*
- *or seeing the war as a threat to stability and trying to prevent action.*

Paras 2 and 3: 'Interest' in the sense of 'opportunity':
- *Strategic possibilities for Soviet Union and Italy converting Spain into a communist or fascist state (supporting detail).*
- *Opportunities for Soviet Union, Italy and Germany to test arms and equipment for possible use in a future European conflict (details and figures).*
- *Opportunities for Hitler to destabilise the European international scene and pursue German revisionism against Versailles (supporting detail).*

Paras 4 and 5: 'Interest' in the sense of 'concern' about the extension of the Spanish Civil War into a more general European conflict:
- *Concerns of Britain and France – part of growing policy of appeasement (supporting detail).*
- *Concerns of international bodies – League of Nations and Non-Intervention Committee (supporting detail).*

Para 6: All the powers had a heightened perception of their interest because of the ideological nature of the conflict:
- *Fascism vs communism (supporting detail).*
- *Liberal democracy vs both (supporting detail).*

Para 7: Integrated conclusion. 'Interest' in the sense of exploitation provoked 'interest' as concern. This led to a vicious circle.

25. To what extent was Hitler responsible for the outbreak of the Second World War?

Advice: *Focus on the 'extent'. The answer is likely to be 'largely', given his intentions and policies, especially in 1938 and 1939. On the other hand, also consider the contributions of Britain and France (especially the sudden ending of appeasement in March 1939), of Italy (which helped free German foreign policy from its earlier constraints) and of the USSR (which removed the threat against Germany from the East in 1939 and made an agreement to partition Poland.*

Part 3: Sources

📖 Germany and the Treaty of Versailles

This exercise consists of three questions on three sources, with a time allocation of 45 minutes.

Source A: A German cartoon: Versailles sends Germany to the Guillotine

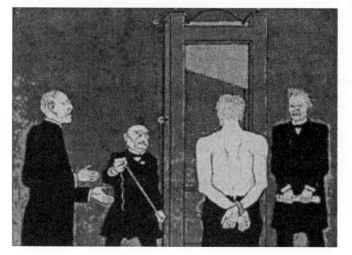

Figure 8.4
The Treaty of Versailles sends Germany to the Guillotine (unknown source)

Source B: Adapted from the British economist, J.M. Keynes, *The Economic Consequences of the Peace* (1919)

It is evident that Germany's pre-war capacity to pay an annual foreign tribute has not been unaffected by the almost total loss of her colonies, her overseas connections, her mercantile marine, and her foreign properties; by the cession of ten per cent of her territory and population, of one-third of her coal and of three-quarters of her iron ore; by two million casualties among men in the prime of life; by the starvation of her people for four years; by the burden of a vast war debt.

I believe that the campaign for securing out of Germany the general costs of the War was one of the most serious acts of political unwisdom for which our statesmen have been responsible.

Source C: Adapted from E. Kolb, a German historian, *The Weimar Republic* (1988)

But, severe though the terms were, in some respects they were less so than might have been expected from the course of the negotiations. The Treaty did have the nature of a compromise: it was not the generous 'Wilsonian peace' that the Germans had fondly hoped for (but that Wilson had never intended in such a form), yet neither was it a 'Carthaginian peace' such as had been demanded by influential statesmen and large parts of public opinion in the victorious countries. Moreover, despite the Treaty of Versailles, Germany continued to be a great power with the longer term prospect of again playing an active part in European affairs.

QUESTIONS WITH WORKED ANSWERS

a) **Study Source A and use your own knowledge. Identify the three figures in front of the guillotine in Source A and briefly explain why they are depicted as executioners.** (3 marks)

The three figures are President of the United States (left), Woodrow Wilson, French Premier, Georges Clemenceau (centre) and British Prime Minister, David Lloyd George (right). They are represented as executioners because the cartoonist is reflecting German opinion that the Treaty of Versailles was the harshest of punishments, imposed as a sentence or *diktat*. Clemenceau was seen as particularly vindictive; it is, therefore, appropriate that he is holding the rope which controls the guillotine blade.

b) **Study Sources B and C. Compare Sources B and C as comments on the Treaty of Versailles.** (7 marks)

The two sources contain both similarities and contrasts. The main similarity is that they both express views which run counter to national stereotypes: the Treaty of Versailles is strongly attacked by a British observer and partially defended by a German.

The differences, however, are more obvious. The basic argument of Source B is that Germany was punished beyond her capacity, while Source C maintains that the treatment could have been a great deal worse. Source B considers it the harshest of acts, itemising the loss of territory and resources; the Treaty also ignored the 'two million casualties', the 'starvation of her people' and the 'burden of her vast war debt'. In contrast, Source C plays down the losses by stating that it was not a 'Carthaginian peace' aiming at the destruction of Germany's power – even if it was not as lenient as 'the Germans had fondly hoped for'. Source B blames the architects of the Treaty for the ultimate in 'political unwisdom', while Source C suggests that the statesmen had been quite reasonable, holding out against the harsher terms demanded by 'influential statesmen' and public opinion.

A final difference between the sources is their timescale. Source B is from the time: its comments therefore reflect the fears many contemporaries would have held for the future. For Source C, however, this future is in the past, which means that the analysis has more perspective – and detachment.

c) **Study Sources A, B and C and use your own knowledge. 'The argument that the Treaty of Versailles was unduly harsh on Germany is more convincing than the argument that its harshness has been overstated.' Do you agree?** (15 marks)

Total (25 marks)

The argument for the harshness of the Treaty of Versailles is put in Sources A and B, as well as by a number of inter-war historians. Within the past three decades, however, there has been a tendency to vindicate parts of the Treaty and to consider some of the original arguments as 'overstated'.

Much has been written about the conditions in which the settlement was drawn up. The government of the new German Republic, struggling to moderate popular nationalism, was appalled by the injustice of having to accept the 'War Guilt Clause' and by the insistence on compensation. Germany had played no part in drawing up the peace settlement, which was imposed as a diktat, It is hardly surprising that this should have produced comparisons with the 'execution' and 'victim' depicted in Source A. Yet, although insisting on Germany's responsibility for the war was probably a political mistake, a wave of recent historians (many of them German) have established that German policy did contribute substantially to the outbreak of war in 1914. Moreover, had Germany succeeded in its war aims, it would have established direct control over eastern Europe and economic ascendancy over most of the rest. In this light. the Treaty of Versailles was a restraining influence which, in the words of Source C, enabled Germany to continue to be 'a great power' with the prospect of 'again playing an active part in European affairs'.

The territorial clauses of the Treaty have been considered excessively harsh. Source B refers to 'the almost total loss of her colonies', of her 'foreign properties' and of 'ten per cent of her territory and population'. The colonies, which constituted the world's third largest colonial empire in 1914, had included such diverse areas as Togo, Kamerun, South West Africa, Tanganyika, Rwanda, Burundi, part of New Guinea, the Solomon Islands and the Mariana Islands. As for the territorial losses in Europe, the cession of Alsace-Lorraine, Eupen-Malmédy, Northern Schlewig, Posen, West Prussia and Morava-Ostrave left large German minorities in other countries at a time when Wilsonian idealism was supposed to be producing a settlement based on national self-determination.

Some of this is certainly true, but much is 'overstated'. Germany's territorial losses were far from arbitrary. In some cases they were a redress of past grievances. The obvious example is the return to France of Alsace-Lorraine, taken by Prussia in 1871. Similarly, Northern Schleswig's return to Denmark (after a plebiscite) partially reversed Prussia's seizure of Schleswig and Holstein from Denmark in 1864. Posen and West Prussia had been part of the historic Kingdom of Poland, the revival of which had, incidentally, come most from Russian territory given up by the Treaty of Brest-Litovsk in 1918. These changes did, it is true, leave 'bleeding frontiers'. But the German minority which later caused the most intense criticism of the Treaty – the Sudeten Germans – had never been part of Germany at all. The loss of all overseas colonies was certainly more difficult to justify but it is by no means clear that colonial empires conferred much economic benefit after the First World War. Probably more significant was the surrender of Germany's overseas investments; but even these were very much a remnant of what had already been used up in fighting the war.

The military and economic clauses have been condemned as overbearing and excessive. The demilitarisation of the Rhineland, the reduction of the armed forces to 100,000 volunteers, the massive naval cuts and the abolition of the airforce, all removed Germany's chance of defending itself against new and resentful neighbours. The case for Allied economic injustice was best put by J.M. Keynes. Elsewhere in his *Economic Consequences of the Peace*, he had argued that, contrary to the usual view, Germany had been united 'not by blood and iron but by coal and iron'. Depriving Germany of this base through the cession of 'one third of her coal and of three-quarters of her iron ore' made it impossible to pay 'the general costs of the War' (Source B). Above all, the final reparations figure of 136,000 million gold marks was well beyond Germany's capacity and contributed to the hyperinflation of 1921–3.

Again, however, allowance needs to be made for 'overstatement'. The armaments clauses were, it could be argued, necessary for the future protection of Belgium and France. Events were later to show that the remilitarisation of the Rhineland in 1935 was the first step towards a revival and refinement of the Schlieffen Plan against France and the Low Countries in 1940. The 100,000 volunteers allowed to the army actually worked in Germany's favour since it produced a highly professional core for the future *Wehrmacht*. As for the transfer of resources, Germany had suffered little infrastructural damage compared with Belgium and north eastern France, where the war on the western front had been fought. Some transfer of resources was therefore to be expected. The reparations figure was of late universally acknowledged to be a mistake. But the effects even of this has been overstated. The Weimar Republic recovered from reparations-induced inflation. It later succumbed to economic depression, by which time reparations were no longer an issue.

PARALLEL QUESTIONS WITHOUT WORKED ANSWERS

a) **Study Source A and use your own knowledge. Explain how Source A shows German resentment against the Treaty of Versailles.** (3 marks)

Advice: *Pick out specific details from Source A and use your own knowledge to explain the reference and why it caused resentment.*

b) **Study Sources B and C and use your own knowledge of the Treaty of Versailles. Explain the difference in interpretation between Sources B and C.** (7 marks)

Advice: *Explaining the difference in interpretation needs to be done with reference to the content of the sources and the types of source. Avoid a simple dismissal of Source C as a 'secondary source': consider the scholarship behind such works.*

c) **Study Sources A, B and C and use your own knowledge. Compare the specific terms of the Treaty of Versailles with the arguments advanced in Sources A, B and C.** (15 marks)

Total (25 marks)

Advice: *Between them, the three sources cover all the major aspects of the Treaty of Versailles. You could therefore look at the terms, based on your own knowledge, and make direct references in each case to the relevant parts of the sources. Draw attention to any discrepancies or differences between the sources.*

Part 4: Historical skills

Concentration, time-management and revision

This section deals with the main pressures faced by sixth-form students, ranging from the day-to-day issue of concentration, the weekly use of time and, above all, the preparation for the end-of-course examination.

CONCENTRATION

Concentration means being able to give most of your attention to a particular task for a specified period. This means total involvement and commitment, without being resentful at having to spend time on the task. There has to be determination to complete the task, or the stage decided on, and in the process to overcome distractions. Concentration should not be taken for granted: it has to be developed through regular use.

A typical situation can be seen in the figure below. The source of the concentration may be an essay or an examination. We can assume three main types of awareness:

1. The main focus of concentration; the more concentrated it is, the more likely it is that the task will be completed.
2. An awareness which may assist the task but is not actually part of it. An example would be background music, which many people find helps concentration.
3. An awareness of surroundings which do not have a part in the task.

There will obviously be a difference between writing an essay in normal circumstances and writing an essay in an examination room. The former will involve 1, 2 and 3 in similar proportions. The secret is to keep the focus of 1 as sharp as possible. Exam conditions are much more likely to expand 1 at the expense of 2 and 3. Some people find this quite uncomfortable and exam conditions do need to be rehearsed.

What interferes with concentration? Distractions come from two sources – external and internal. External distractions are usually noise, alternative attractions or friends competing for your intention. Internal distractions, on the other hand, are self-induced. You put off getting down to work; you do not know precisely what you are going to do; you interrupt yourself; you get bored and you make excuses for giving up.

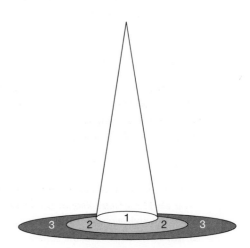

Types of awareness while working at an academic task

Overcoming distractions

External distractions

*   Start your work at the time decided. Do not be deflected by something else which is on. This applies especially to television programmes: build these into your planning in advance. Delayed start can be the worst form of external distraction.

- Force yourself to ignore external noise. This takes practice.
- Experiment with earplugs. These can sometimes have the effect of removing internal distractions as well.
- Make it clear that you do not want to be disturbed – by anyone. Be abrupt with anyone who does.
- Make a pact with people who share your work area. This can mean either working together or leaving them alone.
- Look at this as training for the future. You may well have to work in waiting rooms, on trains, in cars, or at airports. Try this now.

Internal distractions

This means removing whatever is likely to slow you down.

- Expect to concentrate. Rid yourself of any feeling of resentment at having to do the work. This means advance anticipation.
- Focus on your work. Do not look up or round. A reading lamp in an otherwise dark room can help.
- Have everything you need: books, papers, instructions, pens, pencils. Looking for these once you have started will destroy concentration.
- Work quickly and put yourself under pressure. Do not give yourself a chance to become distracted. Persevere.
- Use whatever external factors help concentration. Remove anything which does not. Music helps some tasks but not others. Learn to discriminate.

How can concentration be helped?

1. *Through involvement and commitment*

   These can be achieved by:

   - Regular work habits. Concentration has to be trained and can gradually be built up. It will not happen straight away.
   - Spaced working sessions to maximise efficiency. Plan and anticipate.
   - Breaks long enough for recovery but not long enough to distract.
   - Comfortable work surroundings: somewhere appropriate to your needs.

2. *By completing a task*

   This can be helped by:

   - Realistic targets. They must be specific and achievable within the time allocated.
   - Working against a clock or watch. This eventually speeds up the process by adding a sense of urgency.

TIME-MANAGEMENT

How many hours should an A-level student spend per week on work outside the classroom? The recommended weekly average is 4 hours 30 minutes for each AS subject and 6 hours for each A2 subject. This means an overall average of 18 hours. These figures do not include General Studies or an extra AS or A2.

This may seem a large total, but it is worth bearing in mind that, with 4 AS Levels the total class contact time will be about 28 periods per week (or 19 hours). This means an overall total on academic work of 37 hours per week. You will probably be working longer hours than this in your future job. Admittedly you now have extra commitments during a demanding school or college day. But these can be offset against future job commitments and work which has to be taken home.

The time expectation is therefore demanding – but realistic. How should this time be distributed? As a general principle it makes sense to do as much as possible at school, the rest at home.

Finding 20 hours per week

Allocation of time for academic work (assuming 4 hours 30 minutes per week per AS Level and 2 hours for other academic commitments)	At school or college	Outside school or college
Most study (free) periods	6 hours	–
30 minutes from each of 2 lunchtimes	1 hour	–
4 evenings for 2 hours each	–	8 hours
5 hours at the weekend	–	5 hours
	Total	20 hours

Subtract from the above:
- any time spent reading while travelling (e.g. 30 minutes each way gives 6 hours per week)
- use of the early morning (e.g. one hour per day for 6 days gives 6 hours)

Common problems – and possible solutions

'I can't work in school.'
Make yourself. Go to the Library. Concentrate. Develop a work habit. Plan ahead and use your study periods. One advantage of study periods is that you can end what you are doing by the time your concentration begins to wander. The important thing is to have your materials organised so that you can start immediately. Finish in time to prepare for the next session of private study. This helps you wind down, which is far better at the end of a study session than at the beginning.

'I need to relax in my free periods.'
Why? You didn't have any last year. Are you becoming less efficient in the sixth form?

'I can't work in the evening.'
Tiredness can be an important disincentive. Decide yourself what is reasonable and achievable – and stick to it. Avoid delayed starts. Use of study periods can reduce pressure in the evenings.

'I can't work in the early morning.'

The ability to do this generally comes with age. But capitalise on it if you can do this now. You could manage up to 6 hours per week. It might be an alternative to working late at night.

'I can't work while travelling.'

If the reason is that you can't concentrate, then try to develop the habit of reading, learning or reviewing. If the reason is physical, there is not much you can do about reading (but try thinking).

'I don't need to put in all that time: I can do the work set in less.'

This is very unlikely. Subject teachers all work on the assumption that an AS and A2 subject requires the full-time allocation. History is one of the most time-intensive of all sixth-form subjects.

'I only work when deadlines come up. This makes some weeks heavier than others.'

Try to anticipate and spread the load. This means anticipating and planning ahead.

'I need to be made to work.'

Why?

- You have opted for an A-Level course.
- You expect to go on to higher education.
- You intend to have a career with some responsibility.

These all depend on what you do with your time.

REVISION

History contains a larger content than many other AS or A2 subjects. When it comes to examinations, therefore, revision for History is often seen as particularly difficult. Some students work on the assumption that the only realistic way to learn the material is to leave it until shortly before the exam and to be selective in their coverage of the topics; earlier revision is a waste of time since much of it will be forgotten by the time of the exam.

This is bad strategy for two reasons. First, there is very little choice on the AS and A2 exam papers. Selecting topics is therefore highly risky and removes any possibility of choosing a question on the basis of the wording. Second, the memory operates far more effectively when revision is set up well in advance and repeated in three phases. During the first phase, which is the longest, the best approach is to work systematically through all your material, supplementing it as necessary through extra reading; you should also prepare any revision notes which will be needed in the longer term. The second stage involves a greater commitment to learning the factual details, which is best done through revision summaries. The third phase takes place during the examination period and involves bringing your material back to the surface of your memory; the ideal is to peak at the time of the paper.

The figure on the next page shows the three phases. The vertical axis indicates the amount remembered and the horizontal axis the amount of time after learning. It is natural to remember less and less as the time increases after learning. It is, however, encouraging that the amount remembered becomes progressively greater in the second and third phases. This is because you are building on earlier revision, which can quickly be reactivated.

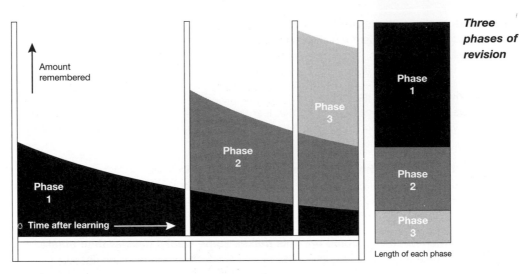

Three phases of revision

This approach needs careful planning and it is important to calculate precisely what needs to be covered in the short term (daily or weekly) and the long term (weekly or monthly). Planning can be done on paper, on a computer or in one of the many types of organiser on the market. Experiment, establish a method and stick to it.

Revision notes

Not everyone is convinced about the need for making revision notes – but there is one simple test. Imagine yourself the night before the History paper. What will you want to be looking through: your complete set of notes or a set of summaries? Then imagine yourself in the exam answering a question which overlaps a number of sections. Which type of notes would you rather have concentrated on the night before?

Assuming that you would find revision summaries useful, there are three main ways of going about making them as shown below.

The three main types of revision notes

Linear notes: These are simply summaries on file paper, substantially reducing the volume of the original notes. The key is to use as few words as possible and concentrate on the concepts or details that have to be remembered. Focus on the middle of the page rather than the edges, so that when you read the summaries you can take a whole page in at a glance.

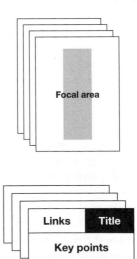

Cards: These distribute the information over a smaller area, which means that there will be more of them. They are easier to handle, can be looked at very quickly and shuffled into different orders. Try leaving space at the top for the title and for links between topics.

Charts: Some students prefer to use summaries in diagrammatic form. These have been variously described as spidergrams, mindmaps or flow charts. They have the advantage of reducing the number of words even further. Further details are provided below.

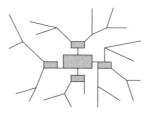

In all these types of revision notes, the use of different colours can be very helpful, especially for the night-before review. It is, however, essential to use colour consistently. You could start by trying out the suggestions below and then come up with your own scheme.

Red	Dates	**Purple**	?
Blue	Names	**Brown**	?
Green	Treaties or Statutes	**Grey**	?
Yellow underlining	Quotations	**Black**	Normal medium

Charts

A great deal of research has been done in connection with the impact of visual stimuli on the brain. A substantial minority of students find it much easier to learn from 'spidergrams' or 'mindmaps'. The theory on which this is based is the different functions of the two hemispheres of the human brain.

The hemispheres of the brain

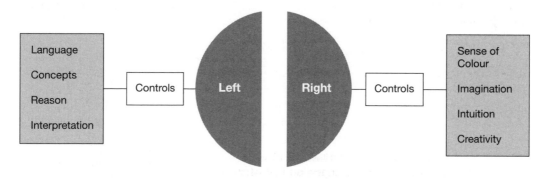

A possible deduction from this is that learning is more successful when both hemispheres are involved, rather than the left hemisphere alone. A possible clue to right-hemisphere activity is the amount of doodling you normally do. This could be used more constructively to reinforce the involvement of the left hemisphere.

The method normally suggested is the replacement of many of the words by signs and symbols and a change in the eye movement. The figures below show the basic difference between the linear page and the diagrammatic page.

Linear page   *Diagrammatic page*

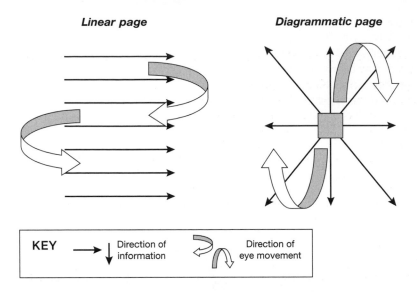

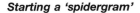

Developing a 'spidergram' or 'mindmap' takes a little practice but can be done quite quickly: 20 minutes per page is a reasonable target. Everything should be drawn freehand since rulers only slow the process down. Start in the middle of the page with a topic box. Then insert the main sub-heading boxes. After these have been done, summarise the rest of the topic by working outwards towards the edge of the page. Colours – as suggested earlier – help to complete the visual effect.

Starting a 'spidergram'

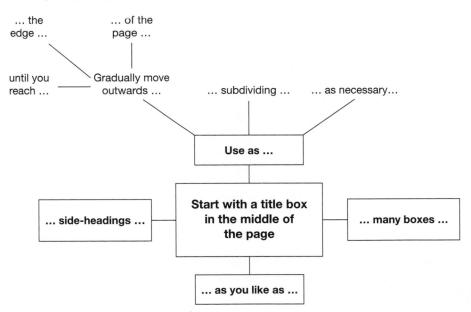

Using these methods will certainly make the third phase of revision less frantic. They might even make the first phase more interesting.

References

1. Extracts from J.A.S. Grenville (ed.), *The Major International Treaties 1914–1973* (London 1974), pp. 59–64
2. S. Marks, *The Illusion of Peace* (London 1976), Chapter 1
3. A.J.P. Taylor, *The Origins of the Second World War* (Harmondsworth 1963), p. 26
4. Telford Taylor, *Munich: The Price of Peace* (London 1979), p. xiv
5. F.W. Deakin, *The Brutal Friendship*, 2 vols (London 1962)
6. Quoted in D.G. Williamson, *The Third Reich* (Harlow 1992), op. cit., Chapter 9
7. A. Hillgruber, *Germany and the Two World Wars* (trans. W.C. Kirby; Cambridge, MA and London 1981), Chapter 5
8. A.J.P. Taylor, *The Origins of the Second World War* (London 1961), Chapter 7
9. Quoted in K.H. Jarausch, 'From Second to Third Reich: the problem of continuity in German foreign policy', *Central European History*, 12, 1979
10. I. Deutscher, *Stalin: A Political Biography* (Oxford 1949)
11. R.C. Tucker, 'The emergence of Stalin's foreign policy', in *Slavic Review*, xxxvi, 4 Dec. 1977
12. M. Trachtenberg, *Reparation in World Politics* (New York 1980)
13. W.A. McDougall, 'Political Economy vs National Sovereignty: French Structures for German Economic Integration after Versailles', *Journal of Modern History* (1979)

Sources

1A. Cartoon, 'The Treaty of Versailles sends Germany to the Guillotine' (source unknown)
1B. Adapted from J.M. Keynes, *The Economic Consequences of the Peace* (New York 1920)
1C. Adapted from E. Kolb, *The Weimar Republic* (trans. P.S. Falla; London 1988), p. 33

Chapter 9

General Conclusion: From AS to A2

The purpose of this book has been to prepare for essays and examinations at AS rather than A2, which has a different approach. But some of the topics studied and all of the historical skills acquired at AS lead naturally and logically to the next conceptual stage represented by A2. This includes two approaches which are rooted in AS but grow beyond it. One is Historical Interpretation, with an emphasis on historiography or the study of different historical viewpoints. The other is a Synoptic Study of a period of about 100 years. These are common to all the Examination Boards.

AS to A2: Historical Interpretation

An example of the approach to Historical Interpretation at A2 can be seen in the OCR Specifications for the paper entitled *Historical Investigations.*

Investigations are built around topics of current interests to historians and the specific aim is to develop an understanding of how the past has been interpreted and represented, and how historical research generates controversies over interpretation. Candidates are expected to understand the principal arguments surrounding their chosen topic and to be able to offer their own explanations and interpretations.

Extract from OCR Specifications for A2 History: Historical Investigations

One dimension of this has already been extensively covered. All AS students are familiar with at least one historical issue which is inherently controversial. They know how to interpret this issue in response to a specific question about it, making selective and creative use of the factual material relating to the topic.

The AS approach to Historical Interpretation

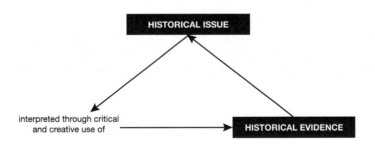

This has been the whole point of answering questions which begin with '*Why . . . ?*', '*How far . . . ?*', '*To what extent . . . ?*', '*Assess the reasons for . . .*' and many others. Use has been made of evidence from the period (factual knowledge) to consider possible reasons, to explain how these fit together and to weigh up which are the most valid.

This is the starting point for the A2 approach, which adds the extra dimension of assessing other *views* which have been put forward by different historians and groups of historians (who are part of 'schools of thought'). At A2 students have to be aware of the *real* controversy behind the issue as well as the *possible* interpretations which will have occurred to them at AS. Historiography is therefore added to History. But the whole process still has to take account of the historical evidence. Historiography does not replace History – it provides additional perspectives and further opportunities for creative and original thought.

The A2 approach to Historical Interpretation

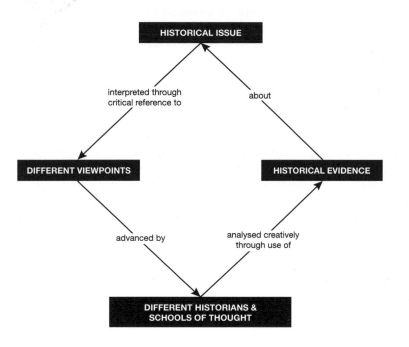

To give a practical example, an AS task might involve assessing the reasons for the success of Lenin and the Bolsheviks in October 1917. At A2 the emphasis would be more on explaining why there is a major controversy about October 1917 and assessing the reasons given for Bolshevik success.

AS to A2: Synoptic Study

'Synoptic' in the context of A2 History has two possible meanings. The first is the connection *between* some of the different topics covered at AS and A2 to create a broader perspective on another paper; this is required by some specifications but not by others. The second is an approach *within* an A2 paper (whether or not it involves areas previously studied) which requires an analysis of the broad sweep of change over a period of approximately 100 years. The OCR Specifications, for example, refer to the Synoptic Study as *Themes in History*, which:

develop understanding of connections between different elements of the subject. They draw together knowledge, understanding and the values of diverse issues centred on Key Themes. The topics are based on Key Themes covering an extended period of approximately a hundred years with an emphasis on continuity and change within the topic. The emphasis is on developing a broad overview of the period studied. They are historical perspectives modules, so concern is centred on links and comparison between different aspects of the topics studied.

Extract from OCR Specifications for A2 History: Themes in History

As with the Historical Interpretation, the skills developed at AS lead to those needed at AS. This time, the change concerns the way in which perspectives are viewed. At AS the approach was to analyse a specific topic in a broad sweep (for example, the reasons for the failure of the 1905 Revolution). At A2 the perspective is considerably extended, but the topic becomes much more selective. The contrasting approaches can be seen as an open pair of scissors.

The A2 Synoptic approach and how it compares to AS

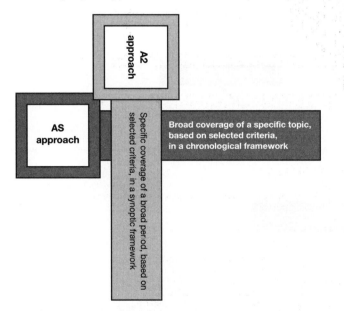

Typical A2 topics would cover Russia 1855–1956, Russia 1894–1993, Germany 1815–1918 and Germany 1890–1991. Coverage at A2 is based on 'themes', some of which cover the whole period; an example of a 'theme' might be political repression in Russia 1855–1956. It also takes in comparisons – possibly between individuals and certainly between periods, for example between the Russian tsars and the Soviet leaders. This is an extension of AS-style questions based on the instructions '*Compare and contrast . . .*'. At A2, however, the range of coverage is so extensive that careful selection has to be made of criteria for discussion. Again, this will not be entirely new, since one of the AS styles of question requires the student to '*Identify and explain three reasons for . . .*'. At A2 this is extended to identifying the subject matter itself. Finally, A2 coverage of this subject matter is less likely to be chronological than at AS: different periods are considered quickly and without necessarily looking at the connecting phases. Even this, however, will not be completely unexpected, since any AS essay depending strictly on chronology always runs the risk of narrative.

The Synoptic Study is so complex that it really needs a specific example of how it works and how it builds on the AS approach. Here are the stages by which an answer to a typical A2 question might be built up.

Stage 1: A2 essay identifying the periods for coverage

During the period 1855–1956 were the Russian tsars more repressive politically than the Soviet leaders?

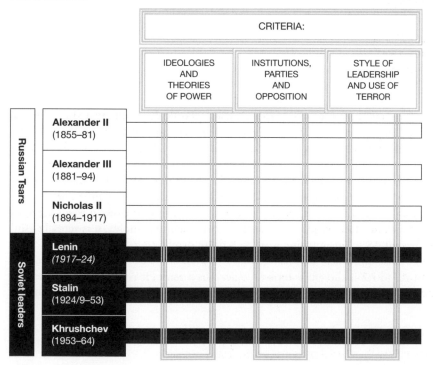

Stage 2: A2 essay identifying criteria for analysis

During the period 1855–1956 were the Russian tsars more repressive politically than the Soviet leaders?

Stage 3: A2 essay making comparisons through the whole period, using the criteria

During the period 1855–1956 were the Russian tsars more repressive politically than the Soviet leaders?

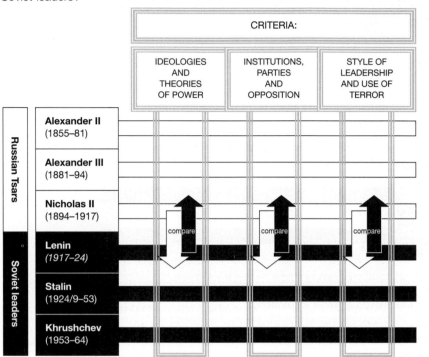

The first preparatory stage is to identify the people involved and then to distinguish between 'Russian tsars' and 'Soviet leaders'. This is one of the simpler AS skills.

The second stage (see Stage 2, p. 367) is to select three or four key criteria for assessing the political systems of the Russian tsars and Soviet leaders. These should be distinctive and examples should be drawn – overall – from the full time span 1855–1956. Again, this approach is reasonably familiar to AS students used to choosing criteria.

In terms of technique – if not of content – this could still be an AS essay. Many students would tend to use the criteria by working *chronologically* through the Russian tsars and Soviet leaders. What would convert this into a full A2 approach is a direct comparison between them acting as the basic structure of the essay (see Stage 3). Although this may sound complex, it is actually using a skill already acquired at AS – but notching it up to a more demanding A2 approach.

The transition from AS to A2 is therefore entirely logical. In a sense, it represents the two main dimensions of History – the study of the past and an enquiry into methods used for that study.

Biographies of Important Personalities

(* before a word indicates a further reference in the Glossary of Key Terms, * after a word indicates a further reference in the Biographies.)

Alexander II (r. 1855–81)

Son of Nicholas I*, Alexander II* became Tsar during the Crimean War. His immediate priority was to modernise the country, which he attempted to do through a series of reforms issued in the form of *Edicts. These included the emancipation of the serfs (1861), reforms of universities and schools (1863–4), the introduction of rural and urban governing bodies (1864 and 1870) and an overhaul of the army (1874). Conversely, Alexander also presided over a number of repressive policies, sparked partly by the Polish revolt (1863) and partly by an attempt on his life in 1866. His reign certainly saw the development of the *Populist revolutionary movement, the militant branch of which assassinated him in 1881.

Alexander III (r. 1881–94)

Profoundly affected by his father's assassination, Alexander III turned resolutely against any policy of reform and, under the influence of Pobedonostsev*, did whatever he could to uphold *autocracy. His measures included the Statute of State Security (1881), the restriction of freedom of expression and a severe tightening of censorship. Towards the end of his reign he did, however, recognise the importance of economic reform and his Finance Minister, Vyshnegradsky, provided the basis for the subsequent economic development pursued by Sergei Witte* during the reign of Nicholas II*.

Briand, Aristide (1862–1932)

A politician of the left, Briand was elected Prime Minister of France no fewer than 11 times. As important, however, was his role as Foreign Minister between 1925 and 1932. This period saw a considerable improvement in relations between Germany and France, for which Briand was partly responsible, along with the German Foreign Minister, Stresemann*. A similar process of *detente was taking place between Stresemann and the British Foreign Secretary, Austen Chamberlain. The practical results of this three-way relationship were the Locarno Pact (1925), Germany's entry into the League of Nations (1926) and the Kellogg–Briand Pact (1928). Briand received recognition for his diplomatic contributions when he shared the 1926 Nobel Peace Prize with Stresemann.

Brüning, Heinrich (1885–1970)

Elected to the *Reichstag in 1924, Brüning took over the leadership of the *Centre Party (Z) in the late 1920s, also joining the Grand Coalition led by Hermann Müller* between 1928 and 1930. When Brüning held out in favour of cutting unemployment benefit in 1930, Müller resigned and removed his party, the *SPD, from the coalition. Without a majority in the Reichstag, Brüning was forced to rely on the use of presidential decrees under Article 48 of the *Constitution. He also introduced tough deflationary measures to deal with the Depression and managed to convince Britain and the United States that Germany was no longer capable of paying *reparations. He was replaced as Chancellor by von Papen* in 1932 and, a year after the appointment of Hitler* in 1933, emigrated to the United States.

Bukharin, Nikolai (1888–1938)

Initially on the left of the *Bolshevik Party, Bukharin was strongly in favour of spreading revolution beyond Russia in 1918. Gradually, however, he adopted a more moderate stance and, as a firm supporter of the *New Economic Policy from 1921, he went along with the Stalinist strategy of *Socialism in One Country after 1924, rejecting the formula of Trotsky* for *Permanent Revolution. By 1929, however, he had come to oppose the introduction by Stalin* of *collectivisation and forced industrialisation through central planning. During the 1930s his great achievement was the 1936 Constitution, for which he was largely responsible. This did not, however, save him from Stalin's accusation that he was plotting against the regime and he was shot after the *show trial of 1938.

Ciano, Galeazzo (1903–44)

Rising rapidly up the Italian fascist hierarchy during the 1930s, Ciano was given responsibility for the press and foreign affairs. He also became part of the family, as Mussolini's son-in-law and designated successor. As Mussolini's Foreign Minister between 1936 and 1943, Ciano was responsible for signing the Pact of Steel with Germany in May 1939. But he subsequently persuaded Mussolini not to go to war alongside Germany in September, a decision which was reversed the following year. As Italy faced imminent defeat from the British and American invasion in the south, Ciano – along with Grandi* and Bottai – used the Fascist Grand Council to secure the dismissal of Mussolini by the King. After his establishment of the Italian Social Republic (*RSI) in the north of Italy, Mussolini ordered the trial and execution of Ciano and others in 1944.

Clemenceau, Georges (1841–1929)

Twice French Prime Minister (1906–9 and 1917–20), Clemenceau combined the politics of the socialist left within France with a strong nationalist stance in Europe which was more commonly associated with the right. He was especially influential at the Peace Conference in 1919, his anti-German stance confirming his nickname of 'Tiger'. Other French statesmen, such as Aristide Briand*, were more prepared to see diplomacy as the art of reaching a compromise as well as the science of extracting concessions.

D'Annunzio, Gabriele (1863–1938)

Author and man of action, D'Annunzio was admired in Italy for his flair and sense of adventure; during the First World War he served in all three branches of Italy's armed services. After the war he captured the public's imagination by seizing Fiume, which the Allies had refused Italy in 1919, holding it until he was forced out in 1920. His main importance, however, was in providing the nationalist link to fascism. Mussolini* borrowed many of D'Annunzio's right-wing ideas and theatrical devices, grafting them on to his own contributions from the *syndicalist left to form *fascism.

Dollfuss, Engelbert (1892–1934)

As Austrian Chancellor from 1934, Dollfuss established a right-wing dictatorship and suspended parliamentary rule. He was, however, strongly opposed to suggestions for an *Anschluss (union with Germany), which was probably a key factor in his assassination in 1934 by Austrian Nazis. He was a close friend of Mussolini*, who reacted to his death by a period of strong anti-German diplomacy.

Ebert, Friedrich (1871–1925)

Elected to the *Reichstag in 1912 and President of the *SPD the following year, Ebert managed to hold the majority of his party together after the secession of its far left in 1917. At the end of 1918 he collaborated with the remnants of the German army under Groener to suppress the attempts of the *Spartacists to seize control in Berlin and to take back Munich from the *Independent Socialists. After the formation of the new constitution of the Weimar Republic, he was elected President. Until his death in 1925, he used his office to promote coalitions between the moderate parties (usually the *SPD, *DDP and *Centre). When necessary, however, he also took firm action, under Article 48 of the *Constitution, to meet threats to the Republic from the far right and far left.

Farinacci, Roberto (1892–1945)

Farinacci was the Fascist Party secretary between 1924 and 1926 and later a member of the Fascist Grand Council, in which he supported Mussolini* against the vote of no confidence introduced in 1943 by Grandi* and Ciano*. Farinacci was more extreme in his views than most of the other fascist leaders, playing an important role in introducing racism and anti-Semitism to Italy. He was also an admirer of the Nazi regime in Germany. He was shot by Italian partisans in 1945.

Franco, Fancisco (1892–1975)

A right-wing Spanish general, Franco led the Nationalist campaign to replace the government of the Second Republic. The Spanish Civil War (1936–9) saw the eventual victory of the Nationalists over the Republicans, Franco establishing an authoritarian and anti-democratic regime which he led until his death in 1975. Franco's importance also had a European dimension. He allowed Hitler* and Mussolini* to bolster Nazism and fascism through their involvement in the Spanish

Civil War and Germany, in particular, gained valuable military experience. In the long run, however, Franco exploited his two allies. Despite their obvious importance in the victory of the Nationalists in Spain, Franco refused to commit Spain to the cause of Hitler and Mussolini in Europe. This is why he survived – and they did not.

Giolitti, Giovanni (1842–1928)

The best example of a politician from Italy's 'liberal' pre-fascist era, Giolitti served as Prime Minister no fewer than five times (1892–3, 1903–5, 1906–9, 1911–14 and 1920–1). He was opposed to Italy's entry into the First World War and tried in 1920 to deal with the war's social and economic backlash on Italy through measured reform. By 1921, however, he had lost the struggle to maintain political moderation in Italy and was unable to cope with the alternative – the politics of violence now on offer from the *fascist movement.

Goebbels, Paul Joseph (1897–1945)

Goebbels joined the *NSDAP in 1924. From his base in the Rhineland, he was initially sceptical of Hitler's* strategy and leadership, especially in view of the failure of the 1923 Munich Putsch. But, from the time of the 1926 Bamberg Conference, Goebbels became Hitler's most consistent and loyal supporter, providing a contrast to the growing ideological challenge of the Strasser brothers, Gregor* and Otto. Hitler rewarded Goebbels with the party offices of *Gauleiter of Berlin (1926) and propaganda director (1929). In 1933 Goebbels was elected to the *Reichstag and was appointed Minister of People's Enlightenment and Propaganda. In this role he exercised enormous influence over all parts of the population. He was also partly responsible for the personal popularity of Hitler, ensuring that all his main speeches were broadcast on radio. During the Second World War he sought to maintain a balance between morale and sacrifice by a combination of propaganda and increasing austerity. In 1944 he became Reich Plenipotentiary for Total War, but continued to invest heavily in feature films such as *Kolberg*, a Napoleonic period piece which drew off German troops from the eastern front. He assisted Hitler's suicide plans in April 1945, before killing his family and himself on 1 May.

Goering, Hermann (1893–1946)

He had a distinguished record as a pilot in the First World War, before joining the Nazis in 1922 and taking part in the Munich Putsch the following year. He was elected to the *Reichstag in 1928 and became President of the Reichstag in 1932. After Hitler* had become Chancellor in 1933, Goering was appointed Prime Minister of Prussia; in this capacity, he established the Gestapo in 1933, although this subsequently came under the control of the *SS under Himmler*. His other positions in the Third Reich included Minister for Aviation (which he used to create the *Luftwaffe*), Minister for the Four Year Plan and Reich Marshal in 1940. He was implicated in the *Nazi policies of *anti-Semitism, announcing the Nuremberg Laws in the Reichstag in 1935 and issuing the instructions for the *Wannsee Conference (1941) to consider a *'Final Solution'. He was tried at Nuremberg in 1946 but escaped his death sentence by committing suicide. He is a good example of a ruthless – and often inefficient – pragmatist operating within the Nazi system and contributing to its internal confusion.

Grandi, Dino (1895–1988)

Grandi played a prominent part in Mussolini's* *fascist movement from 1922 onwards. He was particularly important in foreign affairs, as Foreign Minister (1929–32) and ambassador to Britain (1932–9). As an aristocrat, he saw the advantages fascism offered in fending off the far left and delivering a compliant workforce. On the other hand, he was quick to act when Musslolini lost credibility as a result of military defeat in the Second World War. At the Fascist Grand Council meeting in 1943 he forced Mussolini's resignation, avoiding Mussolini's subsequent revenge in 1944 by fleeing to Portugal. He lived in exile in Brazil until 1973.

Heydrich, Reinhard (1904–42)

Heydrich joined the Nazi movement in 1931 via the *SS, within which he rose rapidly. He became Himmler's* deputy and effective head of the *Gestapo. From 1939 onwards he became head of the RSHA and, in 1941, he co-ordinated the *'Final Solution' decided on at the *Wannsee Conference. His other responsibilities, however, caught up with him. As Reich Protector of Bohemia and Moravia, he aroused considerable resentment through his brutality and was assassinated by a resistance group in 1942. Heydrich is often considered one of the most ruthless of the Nazi leaders; certainly there was considerable tension between his cynical pragmatism and Himmler's mystical race theories.

Himmler, Heinrich (1900–45)

Himmler took part in the 1923 Munich *Putsch. He was appointed head of the *SS in 1929 and, in 1934, took over command of the Gestapo as well. *Reichsführer SS* and head of the *Gestapo; his other positions in the Third Reich included Minister of the Interior (1943–5). Himmler's principal contribution to the Nazi system was his vigorous prosecution of Aryanism and the *'Final Solution'. He was firmly committed to the race theories of Hitler*, adding his own ideas on natural selection based on his earlier experience as a poultry farmer. In addition to its security dimension, he used the SS to propagate a future *Aryan stereotype through 'race farms' and to implement the 'Final Solution' through the extermination camps which were run by SS guards. During the Second World War, Himmler's SS came close to replacing Hitler's regime as the main organ of the state, although Himmler himself remained too imbued with race theory to control it effectively. He lost Hitler's confidence in 1945 and committed suicide when he was captured by British troops.

Hindenburg, Paul von (1847–1934)

Even before the outbreak of the First World War, Hindenburg had already had an extensive career. He had been involved in the Austro-Prussian War (1866) and the Franco-Prussian War (1870–1), before retiring from active service, as a general, in 1911. During the First World War, he was recalled, as field marshal, to repel the Russian invasion on the eastern front. His success enabled him, along with Ludendorff, to substitute the normal political system with a military dictatorship. By October 1918, however, it had become clear that Germany was facing imminent military defeat; Hindenburg therefore advised negotiation with the Allies. After the Armistice of November 1918, however, Hindenburg initiated the 'stab in the back' myth, placing the blame for the surrender firmly on the civilian government and reprieving the reputation of the army. This enhanced his popularity amongst the substantial portion of the electorate which was profoundly suspicious of the Weimar Republic. The result was his election as President in 1925 – and his re-election in 1932. Between 1930 and 1932 he showed his suspicion of parliamentary democracy by allowing three chancellors (Brüning*, von Papen* and von Schleicher) to make full use of Article 48 of the *Constitution to bypass the normal *Reichstag legislative process and, in effect, to rule by presidential *decree. Hindenburg also agreed to appoint Hitler as Chancellor on 30 January 1933, to his request for the dissolution of the Reichstag the following day and to special decrees under Article 48 to hamstring the opposition parties in the subsequent election campaign. Following Hitler's confirmation as Chancellor in March 1933, Hindenburg appeared to have become too senile to offer any effective control and, on his death in 1934, his powers were effectively subsumed into Hitler's new appellation – Führer.

Hitler, Adolf (1899–1945)

Rejected by the Vienna Academy of Arts for his preferred career, Hitler lived as a vagrant before joining a Bavarian regiment in 1914. He served as a corporal in the First World War and, after its conclusion, became a member of Drexler's German Workers' Party (DAP). This was reformed as the *NSDAP in 1920 and given a Twenty-Three Point Programme. In 1921 Hitler ousted Drexler, assuming the leadership himself. In the meantime he had acquired a propaganda mouthpiece, the *Völkischer Beobachter*, and a paramilitary base in the form of the *Sturm Abteilung* (*SA). At this stage Hitler aimed to place the *Nazi movement in power through revolution and made a bid in the Munich *Putsch of 1923. When this failed, Hitler used his time in Landsberg prison to write the first part of *Mein Kampf* and to reformulate his whole approach. Adopting a 'strategy of legality', he aimed to achieve power constitutionally, but also to introduce a subsequent revolution from above. Initially unsuccessful, Hitler benefited from an upsurge of popular support following the onset of *depression in Germany in 1929 and, with the collaboration of the conservative right, was appointed Chancellor in January 1933.

Once in power, Hitler employed the measures of his *'legal revolution' to destroy the democratic process of the Weimar Constitution and to accumulate personal authority. This removed the *Reichstag's monopoly on legislation, banned trade unions and opposition parties, and combined the presidency with the chancellorship. This was accompanied by other measures to institute a *totalitarian regime – the *SS and *Gestapo under Himmler* and Heydrich*, the regulation of the workforce through the *RAD, *SdA and *KdF, and the control of propaganda, education and youth movements by Goebbels*. The economy, meanwhile was reorganised under the Four Year Plan (1936–40), which was placed under the control of Goering*. Through the use of the *Führerprinzip*, Hitler emphasised the creation of a new type of community which transcended the state – the *Volksgemeinschaft*. An integral part of the whole system was a policy of *anti-Semitism, which was embedded in Nazi ideology and was practised through the virulent propaganda of Julius Streicher and through official legislation such as the Nuremberg Laws (1935).

By 1939 Hitler had also made considerable strides in foreign policy, remilitarising the Rhineland in 1936 and annexing Austria and the Sudetenland (1938) and the rest of Bohemia (1939). Following the outbreak of war, Hitler's *Blitzkrieg* strategy brought the rapid conquest of Poland (1939) and of Norway, the Low Countries and France (1940). Failure to invade Britain (1940–1) and the overwhelming cost incurred by the invasion of Russia from 1941, meant that Hitler had to approve the switch from *Blitzkrieg* to Total War, although this failed to prevent Germany from being overwhelmed by 1945 by invasion of the Red Army in the east and by the western allies in Italy and France. Reduced to taking refuge in a bunker under the chancellery, Hitler committed suicide in May 1945 as Soviet forces entered Berlin. Allied armies uncovered evidence of genocide, as extermination camps all over the Third Reich bore witness to the Nazi Holocaust.

Nazi ideology was very much a personal creation of Hitler. It was a loosely assembled and *eclectic mish-mash of *anti-Semitism, Social Darwinism and nineteenth-century ideas, all given a savage twist by Hitler himself. His control over the institutions of the Reich were, however, less obvious. Far from making a clean sweep of the political system of the Weimar Republic, Hitler retained virtually all of the previous institutions, although he did establish parallel Nazi organisations. The result was often administrative chaos, although whether or not Hitler intended this is a matter for historical debate, as is the question as to whether or not Hitler planned the extermination of the Jews from the outset.

Kerensky, Aleksandr Fedorovich (1881–1970)

A Socialist Revolutionary, who was elected to the Russian *Duma in 1912, Kerensky played a vital role in Russian politics during the course of 1917. A member of the Petrograd *Soviet, he also joined the *Provisional Government after the March Revolution, serving as Minister of Justice in the coalition under Prince Lvov. When this coalition collapsed in July, Kerensky became Prime Minister. But from this time onwards his power base declined rapidly. The threat from General Kornilov on Petrograd in August forced Kerensky to accept *Bolshevik support in defending the capital and to reverse some of the punitive measures he had already taken against them. His coalition narrowed with the withdrawal of the Liberals, or *Constitutional Democrats while, at the same time the Bolsheviks were pressing strongly for the establishment of an alternative regime. Kerensky lost the battle for popular support when he insisted on maintaining the war effort, postponing elections for a permanent *Constituent Assembly and sending troops to prevent the peasantry from taking possession of the land from the aristocracy. On the night of 24–25 October, Kerensky's Provisional Government was overthrown with the Bolshevik capture of the Winter Palace and the Admiralty Buildings. Kerensky escaped in the disguise of a nurse and went into permanent exile, mainly in New York, until his death in 1970.

Lenin, Vladimir Ilich (1870–1924)

Co-founder, with Martov* and Plekhanov, of the Russian Social Democrats (*RSDLP) in 1898, Lenin consistently followed a more radical line of Marxism, abandoning ideological conformity to adapt Marxism to Russian conditions. This became clear in his major works on revolutionary strategy – *What Is To Be Done?* (1902) and *Two Tactics* (1905). His main contribution to revolutionary theory was to insist on a tight and conspiratorial structure for the party and to accelerate the whole revolutionary process. This brought a major rift with Martov and Plekhanov at the 1903 Congress of the *RSDLP and a split between the *Bolshevik and *Menshevik factions. Lenin's intransigence and dictatorial style prevented subsequent reconciliation and the split within the RSDLP remained permanent. Lenin and the Bolsheviks had comparatively little direct influence before 1916. They played no part in the 1905 Revolution and were no more influential than the other revolutionary groups during the First World War. Although he aimed to convert the 'capitalist war' into a 'civil war' to bring down the regime, Lenin spent almost the whole time between 1914 and early 1917 in exile.

Lenin's chance came during the course of 1917 and his target was the *Provisional Government which had replaced the tsarist regime in March. His arrival in Petrograd was immediately followed by his *April Theses*, in which he showed a large degree of pragmatism by promising to meet many of the demands of the industrial workers and peasantry in exchange for their support. The Bolsheviks made an abortive attempt to seize power in July, after which Lenin was forced into hiding in Finland. The decline of Kerensky's government, however, enabled Lenin to make a come-back and, once the Bolsheviks had secured a majority in the Petrograd *Soviet, he urged the Party's Central Committee to seize power in its name. This transfer was carried out on the night of the 24–25 October, largely through the *Revolutionary Military Committee organised by Trotsky*.

Between 1918 and 1924 Lenin led the first *communist regime ever established. In the Civil War, which followed the seizure of power, this overcame the opposition of other revolutionary parties and of the *White counter-revolutionaries. Lenin also took the decision to close the newly elected Constituent Assembly in January 1918 and to substitute a one-party state acting through the theoretical legitimacy of a new system of soviets. He proved utterly ruthless in eradicating dissent and fully approved the systematic terror established by Trotsky and Dzerzhinsky. He was, however, less successful in bringing about economic change. His policy of *War Communism, introduced in 1918, proved a ruinous failure and had to be reversed by the more moderate *New Economic Policy in 1921. For the last two years of his life Lenin was incapacitated by illness and lost direct control of political power to his subordinates. Two of these – Trotsky and Stalin* – he named in his *Political Testament* as unsuited to the succession. After his death in January 1924 he became embodied in official theory as the inspiration behind, and founder of, the Soviet state.

Non-Soviet views have always been more critical of Lenin, seeing him as being guided as much by opportunism as by ideology. Recently, however, a division of opinion has emerged between historians who continue to see him as an effective organiser, strategist and leader and those who point to a fundamental uncertainty and inconsistency. There is, therefore, also an alternative to the traditional view that he imposed his views and power from above; revisionist historians now see Bolshevik success – at least until the end of 1917 – as due to a powerful surge of popular opinion disillusioned with the failed alternatives of 1917.

Lloyd George, David (1863–1945)

Prime Minister between 1916 and 1922, Lloyd George played a key role in the First World War – and in the peace which followed. He led the British war effort between 1916 and 1918 and was responsible for many of the measures covered in Chapter 2, Essay 15. Along with President Wilson* and Georges Clemenceau*, he drew up the Paris settlement which dealt with Germany and its allies. In the context of the Treaty of Versailles he is often seen as a moderating and pragmatic influence between the idealism of Wilson and the *revanchism of Clemenceau. Revisionist views, however, suggest that he was the most important influence behind the imposition of heavy reparations on Germany. After 1922 he no longer had any influence on the European situation. As leader of one part of a fragmented Liberal Party, his lack of power enabled him to reflect on the peace settlement and, by the early 1930s, to concede that an injustice had been committed. This may explain his strange admiration for Hitler's regime after 1933, which contributed to one of the strands of the British policy of appeasement.

Luxemburg, Rosa (1870–1919)

Originally Polish, Rosa Luxemburg acquired German citizenship through marriage. She was on the far left of the SPD and, along with Karl Liebknecht, formed the break-away Spartacus League, which eventually became the Communist Party (*KPD). They were both involved in the Spartacist uprising in Berlin in January 1919. This was put down by the remnants of the German army and both Luxemburg and Liebknecht were shot, probably in cold blood, by members of the *Freikorps.

Martov, Julius (1873–1923)

A co-founder with Lenin* of the Russian Social Democrats (*RSDLP) in 1898, Martov followed a more moderate form of Marxism based on a long-term approach to revolution. He believed that it was necessary first to win the support of the middle classes to overthrow the tsarist system, after which there would be a period of evolution towards a socialist system. He clashed with Lenin in 1903 over future strategy, as well as over the composition and leadership of the party. Despite subsequent attempts to reunite the Social Democrats, Martov's wing remained separate from Lenin's. His more moderate *Mensheviks remained in existence until they – along with Martov himself – were finally purged by the *Bolshevik regime between 1921 and 1923.

Müller, Hermann (1876–1931)

Müller was leader of the Social Democratic Party (*SPD) and German Chancellor in 1920 and again between 1929 and 1930. He is generally seen as a moderate reformer, strongly committed to maintaining the democratic foundations of the Weimar Republic and its welfare provisions. For this reason he fell out in 1930 with his partner in the Grand Coalition, the Centre Party leader Heinrich Brüning*. Müller held out against Brüning's proposals to cut unemployment benefit as a means of reducing public expenditure in the wake of the Great Depression. His resignation brought the collapse of the coalition – and of democracy in Germany.

Mussolini, Benito (1883–1945)

Originally a socialist, Mussolini was particularly influenced by *syndicalism and the ideas of Georges Sorel. In 1912 he became editor of *Avanti*, a socialist (*PSI) newspaper, but was removed from this post when he campaigned for Italy's involvement in the First World War. Towards the end of 1914 he founded his own newspaper, *Popolo d'Italia*. By 1918 Mussolini had formed an alternative both to the socialist left and to the capitalist right. He had developed a compound of nationalism (derived partly from the flamboyance of D'Annunzio*) and syndicalism. Given a strong populist and paramilitary stir, the mixture was exceptionally volatile in the chaotic conditions of post-war Italy. Yet Mussolini was careful to project fascism as both a movement (based on the *Fasci di Combattimento*) and a parliamentary party, the *PNF. The movement stirred up violence which the party blamed on others, at the same time promising a practical solution. This was the way in which Mussolini rose to power. The 'March on Rome' in 1923 induced King Victor Emmanuel III* to appoint Mussolini as Prime Minister over a coalition government.

Mussolini considerably extended his political power during the 1920s. He changed the electoral system to ensure a fascist majority in the Chamber, banned the opposition after the Matteotti affair and enhanced his own role in government to an unprecedented degree. He developed a personality cult, based on his new title of *Duce, although some historians draw a distinction between the implementation of 'fascist' policies and the 'Mussolinian' quest for power for its own sake. Whatever the motive, Mussolini attempted to establish a *totalitarian state, using a combination of indoctrination and force. Never one for religious belief, Mussolini nevertheless saw the sense in reaching an agreement with the Catholic Church in 1929 through the Lateran Treaty, thus weakening the likelihood of any ideological opposition. All this worked only to an extent. Internal problems began to surface as a result of the disastrous combination of Mussolini's economic policies, war and commitment to Nazi Germany.

Mussolini based his economic policy on his own vision of syndicalism. The resulting *Corporate State caused confusion and chaos, which delayed Italy's emergence from the depression. To make matters worse, Mussolini switched from a realistic diplomacy in the 1920s to an attempt in the 1930s to revive the glories of the Roman Empire. The result was Italian involvement in a ruinous sequence of warfare between 1936 and 1939. At the same time, Mussolini made the ultimately fatal decision to commit Fascist Italy to Nazi Germany. This involved the introduction of widely unpopular anti-Semitic policies in Italy and, by 1943, disastrous military failure. In 1943 Mussolini experienced the humiliation of being outvoted in the Fascist Grand Council and dismissed by the King who had appointed him in 1923. From 1943 onwards Mussolini became, more than ever, a puppet of Hitler. His new Salo Republic (*RSI) in northern Italy was in reality controlled by the SS and defended by the German army. When the latter withdrew in 1945, Mussolini was caught and shot by Italian partisans.

Nicholas II (r. 1894–1917)

Although milder than his father, Alexander III*, Tsar Nicholas II ruled as a confirmed *autocrat and was heavily influenced by the ideas of Konstantin Pobedonostsev*and by the forceful personality of the Empress Alexandra. His reign divides into four main phases. Between 1894 and 1904 he embraced the economic modernisation offered by Sergei Witte*, but used it to intensify Russia's expansion in the Far East. Between 1904 and 1905 this resulted in a disastrous war with Japan, defeat in which precipitated the 1905 Revolution, which shook the regime to its foundations. In conceding a new constitution Nicholas II was given a second chance between 1906 and 1914, although this had mixed results. His refusal to implement the constitutional experiment properly led to growing political tension and pressures from revolutionary organisations, although these were partially concealed by renewed economic growth. The final period (1914–17) was heavily influenced by Russia's poor performance during the First World War. Following initial Russian reverses in 1914 and 1915, he left Petrograd to lead the army in person. The result was the distortion of the functions of central government by the empress, who was under the influence of Rasputin*. This discredited any remaining reputation of the Tsar himself and, following the March uprising in 1917, a committee of the *Duma forced him to abdicate. Nicholas and his family lived in internal exile until they were shot by the *Bolsheviks at Ekaterinburg in 1918.

Papen, Franz von (1879–1969)

Chancellor in 1932, Papen delivered the deathblow to Weimar democracy by ruling permanently with the aid of Article 48 of the Constitution and by persuading President Hindenburg* to appoint Hitler* as Chancellor in January 1933. Papen was Vice-chancellor until 1934 when he became ambassador to Vienna. Between 1938 and 1944, he was ambassador to Turkey. He was sentenced to a term of imprisonment in a west German de-Nazification court in 1947.

Pobedonostsev, Konstantin Petrovich (1827–1907)

Probably the most important theorist behind late tsarist autocracy, Pobedonostsev had a profound influence on the last two Tsars. He was tutor, in their early years, to Alexander III* (r. 1881–94) and Nicholas II* (r. 1894–1917), helping to embed within both a profound suspicion of liberal democracy and of parliamentary institutions. As procurator of the Holy Synod (1880–1905) he was the strongest force for *conservatism – and against reform – within Russia. His influence survived his death in 1907 and was an important factor in Nicholas II's inability to show genuine commitment to the constitutional experiment after 1905.

Rasputin, Grigory Efimovich (c.1864–1916)

A monk and faith healer of peasant origin, Rasputin established a strong influence over the Empress Alexandra through his ability to alleviate the symptoms of haemophilia suffered by the Tsarevich Alexis. When Nicholas II left Petrograd for the front in 1915, the empress filled the political vacuum left in Petrograd and greatly increased the political power of Rasputin. This alienated much of the bureaucracy, the *Duma and most of the nobility, contributing greatly to the decline in the Tsar's reputation. Rasputin was assassinated in December 1916 by members of the nobility who included Iusupov, Pavolovich and Purishkevich. Rasputin probably did not exercise much direct influence – but was perceived to be doing so. His notoriety certainly contributed to the Duma's willingness to pronounce the Tsar unfit for government and to demand his abdication during the revolution of March 1917.

Röhm, Ernst (1887–1934)

A Nazi activist and organiser of street battles, Röhm took part in the Munich Putsch in 1923, after which he became increasingly committed to the *Sturm Abteilung* (*SA) – and was appointed its leader in 1930. Shortly after Hitler's* appointment as Chancellor (30 January 1933), Röhm accused the Nazi leadership of allowing the Nazi revolution to 'go to sleep'. In pressing for an acceleration of radicalism, however, Röhm trod on dangerous ground, especially when he expressed his desire to merge the German army into the SA. Becoming increasingly alarmed that Röhm's pressure might pre-empt a military coup against the Nazi regime, Hitler ordered his elimination, along with that of other leading Nazi dissidents, in the Night of the Long Knives in 1934. The orders were carried out by the *SS, which subsequently replaced the SA as the leading paramilitary organisation of the *Nazi movement.

Stalin, Josif Vissarionovich (1879–1953)

Of peasant origin, Stalin gravitated rapidly to the radical wing of the RSDLP. He played a significant role in Bolshevik victory during the Civil War, although not as great as he later claimed. His main influence was in his homeland, Georgia, and in the Bolshevik Party (renamed the CPSU), which he used increasingly to further his own position. Before Lenin's* death in 1924, he had already accumulated key positions such as commissar for nationalities and general secretary of the party. As significant, however, was his power within the recruiting and firing sections of the CPSU, Orgburo and the Control Commission. Lenin became so concerned about Stalin's power base that he added a codicil to his Political Testament in 1923, recommending the immediate demotion of Stalin.

This, however, did not happen and, after Lenin's death Stalin was reprieved. This was largely because the other key Bolsheviks regarded Trotsky* as the main threat; Stalin, by comparison, was seen as a relatively harmless mediocrity. Hence he was included in the Triumvirate with Kamenev and Zinoviev*. Gradually, however, Stalin outmanoeuvred his rivals, starting with his isolation of Trotsky, Kamenev and Zinoviev and completing the process by 1928 with the demotion of Bukharin*, Rykov and Tomsky. By 1929 he had also changed his earlier commitment to the *New Economic Policy to enforced collective farming and rapid industrialisation through the Five Year Plans which ran through the 1930s until their interruption by the German invasion of the Soviet Union in 1941. When *collective farming was fiercely resisted by a substantial proportion of the peasantry, Stalin responded with characteristic ruthlessness, ordering widespread shootings and deportations. From 1934 onwards he also imposed his personal stamp on the *totalitarian dictatorship and launched a series of *show trials to remove the remaining Bolsheviks who had been involved in the October Revolution. Between 1936 and 1938 he secured the condemnation and execution of the likes of Zinoviev and Bukharin while, at the same time, drawing up quotas for the processing of millions of ordinary Russians through the *Gulag system operated by the *NKVD. He also purged the armed forces and the Central Committee of the Party itself.

Following a strangely inconsistent foreign policy during the 1930s, Stalin drew up a Non-Aggression Pact with Germany in August 1939. This lulled him into a false sense of security, so that he ignored warnings of an impending attack by Hitler in 1941. It is not, therefore, surprising that the initial Soviet resistance to the Nazi invasion folded up. By 1942, however, Stalin had succeeded in reimposing his leadership. With the help of a very able High Command, led by Marshal Zhukov*, Stalin presided over a major Soviet recovery which eventually led, via victories at Stalingrad and Kursk, to the occupation of eastern Europe, the invasion of Germany and the fall of Berlin.

Gradually, however, relations between Stalin and the Western leaders (initially Roosevelt and Churchill, then Truman and Attlee) worsened. The most contentious issues were the post-war boundaries and the types of regime. Stalin tightened his control over eastern Europe, which precipitated a series of US responses within the framework of the Cold War. At the same time, Stalin renewed his iron grip on the Soviet Union itself after having relaxed his centralisation during the war years. He restored the Five Year Plans from 1945 and the Zhdanov* Decrees introduced new regulations for the control of all forms of culture and thought. By the time of his death in 1953 he was probably on the point of introducing a new round of purges. His eventual successor, Nikita Khrushchev, launched a 'destalinisation' campaign in 1956 which revealed something like the true extent of Stalin's excesses.

Like Lenin and Hitler, Stalin is now the subject of differing historical viewpoints. Very few question that he was one of the most ruthless leaders of the twentieth century. But some revisionists now doubt whether this ruthlessness was either the result of, or precondition for, efficiency. Similarly, the period of Stalinist rule between 1945 and 1953 has been seen either as a period of 'mature dictatorship', in which Stalin was at the peak of his power or as a period of frustration in which he desperately tried to recover the authority which he had lost through the sudden intervention of war.

Stolypin, Petr Arkadevich (1862–1911)

One of the most important officials of Nicholas II*, Stolypin served as governor of the provinces of Grodno and Saratov (1903–6). Following the introduction of the 1906 Constitution he became chairman of the Council of Ministers. He clashed frequently with the new *Duma, securing the dissolution of the first and second, and providing for an amended electoral law in 1907. He also made extensive use of Article 87 of the Constitution to impose emergency decrees. Stolypin did, however, have a significant reforming role: he sought to create a prosperous layer within the peasantry who would be committed to the regime. To this end he encouraged land-ownership and agricultural improvements. These were not acceptable to the majority of the peasantry and, in 1911, he was assassinated at the opera in Kiev by a Socialist Revolutionary activist.

Strasser, Gregor (1892–1934)

Although he was involved in the Munich *Putsch, Gregor Strasser drifted apart from Hitler during the later 1920s and early 1930s. There were two reasons for this. One was Strasser's preference for the 'socialist' components of Nazism, in contrast to Hitler's emphasis on nationalism and racism. The other was Strasser's negotiation to join Schleicher's government in 1932. When he became Chancellor in January 1933, Hitler immediately sidelined Strasser, eventually including him in the list of victims in the Night of the Long Knives in 1934.

Stresemann, Gustav (1878–1929)

A leading German politician, Stresemann represented the National Liberals in the Reichstag until the party's dissolution in 1918. He then established the National People's Party (*DVP), which he led until his death in 1929. A member of many of the coalition governments of the Weimar Republic, Stresemann was also Chancellor in 1923 and Foreign Minister between 1923 and 1929. During this period he introduced the *Rentenmark* (November 1923); agreed to the Dawes and Young Plans (1924 and 1929) on the rescheduling of reparations payments; signed the Locarno Pact (1925) and the Treaty of Berlin with the Soviet Union (1926); and took Germany into the League of Nations (1926). He also received the Nobel Peace Prize. Two controversies are usually associated with his role in German politics and international relations. To what extent was he responsible for a period of 'recovery' in the Weimar Republic between 1923 and 1929? And was it really his intention to 'reconcile Germany with Europe – or rather to initiate a policy of territorial revisionism? (See Chapter 4.)

Trotsky, Lev Davidovich (1879–1940)

Eventually to be one of the most influential of all the Russian revolutionaries, Trotsky neverthe-less took some time to make up his mind which faction he really supported. During the splitting of the Social Democrats (*RSDLP) in 1903, he was critical of Lenin's approach and remained more favourable to the *Mensheviks – without committing himself to the ideas of Martov*. He played an individual role in the 1905 Revolution, establishing and leading the St Petersburg *Soviet, until this was broken up by Russian troops in November. Trotsky spent most of the next twelve years in exile, returning to Russia shortly after the Revolution of March 1917. In May he brought his faction – the Menshevik Internationalists – behind Lenin's Bolsheviks for the first time. Trotsky then played a key role in the overthrow of the *Provisional Government. Elected President of the Petrograd Soviet, he established the *Revolutionary Military Committee (or Red Guard) to seize power in accordance with the instructions given by Lenin in October. During the Civil War which followed the Bolshevik Revolution, Trotsky became war commissar. In this role he co-ordinated the war effort against both the *Socialist Revolutionaries and the *Whites, expanding the Red Guard into a Red Army numbering over 5 million. He also justified the introduction of the Terror between 1918 and 1921 and, as commissar for foreign affairs, pursued a policy of promoting revolutionary movements abroad, especially in Hungary, Italy and Germany.

The early 1920s proved to be a turning point in Trotsky's career. Following Lenin's death in 1924, he became involved in a power struggle with Stalin for the future leadership of Soviet Russia. In part, this was ideological, based on the conflict between Trotsky's *Permanent Revolution and Stalin's *Socialism in One Country. But it was also about personal power, with Trotsky's hold on some of the key offices of state being challenged by Stalin's control over the Communist Party. By 1928 Trotsky had been politically isolated, expelled from the Politburo and exiled. During the next decade he refined his ideas, adopting approaches which still influence some of the far left in the West. He argued for a common front against fascism and, instead of a direct approach to international revolution, substituted a strategy on entryism – penetrating and gradually taking over an already established party of the left. Above all, he turned against Stalin, whom he accused of perverting communism and of establishing a bureaucratic and personalised dictatorship. Stalin returned the compliment by accusing Trotsky of collaborating with Nazi Germany and of being the mastermind of anti-Soviet subversion for which many millions of Russians were purged. By 1940 Stalin had convinced himself that Trotsky was an actual threat and therefore had him tracked down to his retreat in Mexico and assassinated.

Victor Emmanuel III (1869–1947)

Although in theory a constitutional monarch, Victor Emmanuel preferred to make his own decisions without parliamentary authorisation. Two examples of this were his involvement of Italy in the First World War (1915) and his appointment of Mussolini* as Prime Minister in 1922, despite the advice of the incumbent (Nitti) that the *fascist threat should be dealt with by martial law instead. Although Mussolini subsequently extended his own powers as *dictator, Victor Emmanuel insisted on remaining head of state and commander-chief. This was to prove crucial. Although he rarely interfered with the *fascist regime during the 1920s and 1930s, defeat in war was a very different matter. He used his royal prerogative in 1943 to dismiss Mussolini after the attack on the latter by the Fascist Grand Council.

Wilson, Thomas Woodrow (1856–1924)

Elected President in 1912 – and re-elected in 1916 – Woodrow Wilson led the United States into the First World War in April 1917, enabling the Allies to grind Germany into defeat on the western front. His Fourteen Points provided the basic principles upon which a post-war settlement was to be based, most finding their way into the various Paris treaties between 1919 and 1920. His ideals were, however, watered down by the more hard-headed approach of Lloyd George* and Clemenceau*. Ironically, everything he campaigned for was subsequently disowned by the United States Congress, which refused to ratify the Treaty of Versailles. Because this also contained the Covenant of the League of Nations, a veto was in effect placed on US membership, to the extreme detriment of international diplomacy during the inter-war period.

Witte, Sergei Iulevich (1849–1915)

As Minister of Finance between 1892 and 1903 – first to Alexander III*, then to Nicholas II* – Witte presided over the most extensive economic change experienced by Russia since the reign of Peter the Great. Like Vyzhnegradskii, whom he succeeded, he aimed to establish a system of state-controlled capitalism, financed partly by foreign loans and devoted to intensive industrialisation. Witte believed that this type of economic reform would help to underpin tsarist autocracy. He was, however, dubious about the increasingly assertive foreign policy pursued by Nicholas II after 1900 and opposed the drift towards war with Japan in 1904. During the 1905 Revolution, which accompanied Russia's defeat, he advised the Tsar to agree to political concessions and briefly served as chairman of the Council of Ministers between 1905 and 1906. Along with Petr Stolypin*, he is considered one of the key influences behind economic developments during the reign of Nicholas II, although he had little control of the way in which economic change affected political decisions.

Zhdanov, Andrei Aleksandrovich (1896–1948)

One of the key party leaders from 1934 onwards, Zhdanov became the main organiser of cultural ideas and norms during the Stalin* period. Under Stalin's direction, he established the principles of Socialist Realism during the 1930s and introduced a second wave of cultural constraints between 1946 and 1948, based on the Zhdanov Decrees. These were eventually reversed during Khrushchev's destalinisation campaign.

Zhukov, Georgy Konstantinovich (1896–1974)

The most successful of all the Soviet military commanders in the Second World War, Marshal Zhukov was responsible for the Soviet victories over the *Wehrmacht* at Stalingrad (1942) and Kursk (1943). He subsequently led the assault on German-occupied Poland, before entering Germany itself and capturing Berlin in 1945. Stalin demoted him after the end of the war, largely because of his widespread personal popularity. After Stalin's death in 1953, Zhukov played an important part in the emergence of Khrushchev – and in the removal of one of the main alternatives, the *NKVD leader, Beria. Khrushchev made him Minister of Defence until 1957.

Zinoviev, Grigory Evseevich (1883–1936)

Along with Kamenev, Zinoviev* expressed strong reservations about Lenin's* call for a *Bolshevik uprising in October 1917. His main influence after October was as chairman of the Communist International (Comintern). After Lenin's death in 1924, Zinoviev joined with Stalin* and Kamenev in the Triumvirate. By 1926, Zinoviev and Kamenev had awakened to the threat posed by Stalin to their position and both joined Trotsky* in the Left Opposition. They were subsequently expelled from the Politburo and, in the 1936 show trial, Zinoviev was sentenced to death.

Glossary of Key Terms

(* before a word indicates another reference in this Glossary, * after a word indicates a reference in the Biographies.)

Alliance A binding agreement between two or more countries. It is tighter than an *Entente or *Non-aggression Pact since it usually involves military commitments in the event of war. Most alliances are 'defensive' (for example the Dual Alliance of 1879), although some, like the Pact of Steel (1939) can be more open-ended.

Anschluss Unification between Austria and Germany, carried out by Hitler* in 1938.

Anti-Semitism Hatred of the Jews, shown either as prejudice among the population or as deliberate government policy (as in Tsarist Russia under Alexander III*, Nazi Germany between 1943 and 1945 or in Fascist Italy from 1938).

Appeasement A style of foreign policy followed during the 1930s, mainly by Britain and France, to avoid the outbreak of war by making measured concessions to Hitler*.

Aryan According to Hitler*, the 'purest' race, primarily German and responsible for most of human 'culture'. Under his leadership the Germans were 'destined' to convert the Aryans into the 'master race'.

Ausgleich The 'compromise' of 1867. Following its defeat by Prussia in 1866, Austria gave autonomy to Hungary to prevent the possibility of break-up. There were, in effect, two states which were joined to each other by the sovereign (emperor of Austria and king of Hungary). There were two capitals (Vienna and Budapest) and two governments. The name of the country was changed to Austria-Hungary.

Autarky (or autarchy) Economic self-sufficiency, a policy pursued especially in Fascist Italy and Nazi Germany. Mussolini* saw it as one of the objectives of the Corporate State and tried to implement it through a series of 'Battles' (for example the Battle of Grain). Hitler* made it an essential component of the Four Year Plan in 1936 and associated it with the eventual target of *Lebensraum.*

Authoritarian A style of regime which is either anti-democratic from the start (for example, Franco's* Spain after 1939) or has emerged from a democracy which is no longer functioning properly (for example, Germany under Hindenburg* between 1931 and 1932). It contrasts with *autocracy in not usually being based on nineteenth-century dynastic rule and with *totalitarian in not attempting to stir up the masses with ideology.

Autocracy A style of rule associated with the absolute power of hereditary monarchs. The main example within the scope of this book is Tsarist Russia. Alexander III* (1881–94) insisted that this was the only feasible system and was influenced by the ideas of Konstantin Pobedonostsev*.

Bilateral In diplomacy, the involvement of two states, either in negotiation or agreement. It contrasts with *unilateral and *multilateral.

Blitzkrieg ('Lightning War') In military terms this means rapid German attacks on limited fronts, using aircraft, tanks and armoured divisions; examples include the invasions of Poland (1939) and France (1940). Some historians have argued that Hitler* used this method between 1939 and 1941 to avoid having to commit Germany to *Total War, which would place more strains on the economy and on the German consumer.

Bolshevik A radical group within the Russian Social Democrats (*RSDLP) who separated from the moderate Mensheviks at the 1903 Congress over the questions of organisation and strategy. Under the leadership of Lenin* the Bolsheviks (meaning literally 'the majority') seized power in October 1917 and established a communist regime. The name Bolshevik was replaced by *Communist between 1918 and 1924.

Bonapartist A derogatory term to describe a military commander with aspirations to establish a military dictatorship and to turn a revolution into a personal regime. It was based on the career of Napoleon Bonaparte, who seized power in France, converting the French Revolution into an Empire ruled by himself between 1804 and 1815. Stalin* and others applied it to describe the threat they perceived from Trotsky* after 1924.

Bundesrat The upper chamber of the *legislature of the German *Reich between 1871 and 1918. It consisted of delegates appointed by the governments of the individual German states and was empowered to approve or block legislation from the *Reichstag, or lower chamber. Prussia contained a permanent blocking vote within the *Bundesrat*.

Bureaucracy A general term to describe government administration, from the government departments and their ministers down to the civil servants who implemented government policy. Although it can be used of any system, it is often critical in tone, implying complexity or inefficiency. In the scope of this book, it applies most commonly to the administration of Tsarist Russia.

Cheka (Extraordinary Commission for the Suppression of Counter-Revolution, Speculation and Sabotage) Headed by Dzerzhinsky, it was the Bolshevik secret police force during the Civil War period until its abolition in 1921. It was the forerunner of the *NKVD.

'Classless Society' The ultimate target of political and economic change, according to Marxist analysis. Marx and Engels argued that all history is based on 'class conflict'. After the overthrow of the bourgeoisie, the *proletariat would set up a temporary phase known as the *'dictatorship of the proletariat': this, in turn, would evolve over time into the 'classless society', in which there would be no need for coercive institutions and the state could 'wither away'.

Collective Security A diplomatic term used during the 1920s and early 1930s to describe the prevention of conflict by upholding the boundaries established by the 1919–20 peace settlement. The most specific part of collective security was the 1925 Locarno Pact and its most idealistic form was the 1928 Kellogg–Briand Pact. During the 1930s collective security gave way to *appeasement.

Collectivisation A policy pursued in the Soviet Union to end private ownership of land. Introduced in 1928 by Stalin*, collective farms (*Kolkhozy) were organised jointly by large groups of peasants, while state farms (*Sovkhozy*) were owned more directly by the state. The latter gradually became the main form of collective farming.

Comecon (Council for Mutual Economic Assistance (CMEA)) Set up in 1949 by Stalin*, this co-ordinated the economic planning of the eastern European states brought under Soviet control after 1945.

Communism An ideology based on *Marxism, as adapted by Lenin to form Marxism Leninism. It was introduced into Russia by the *Bolsheviks, from where it spread to eastern Europe after 1945. In 1949 it took control of China, as adapted by Mao Zedong. It was also established in a number of third world countries, especially North Korea, Cuba and Vietnam. In its Russian form communism stood for a one-party state, an economy planned and directed by the state and the elimination of class interests.

Concentration camp Originally used by the British in the Boer War to concentrate large numbers of detainees where they could be guarded. In Nazi Germany a more notorious form developed, initially at Dachau and Oranienberg. By the late 1930s concentration camps had been set up throughout Germany for political opponents, 'social undesirables' and Jews. During the Second World War some were equipped with gas chambers in imitation of the *extermination camps.

Concordat (see also **Lateran**) An agreement or treaty between a state and the pope, defining areas of respective authority and interest. During the period of this book there were two examples. The first was part of Mussolini's* Lateran Treaty (1929), the second the Concordat signed by Nazi Germany in 1933.

Constitution A set of basic rules by which a country's political system operates. Examples include the 1871 Constitution of the German Reich, the 1906 Russian Constitution, the 1918 Constitution of the *RSFSR, the 1919 Constitution of the Weimar Republic and the 1936 Constitution of the *USSR.

Constitutional Democrats (Kadets or Cadets) A party which was legalised in 1905–6 and adopted a programme based on liberal democracy. It aimed for full parliamentary sovereignty based on universal suffrage and full guarantees of civil rights. It played an important part in the 1917 Provisional Government but was eventually wiped out by the Bolsheviks between 1921 and 1922.

Corporate State Mussolini's* restructuring of Italy, especially of the economy, into a series of syndicates and corporations. The details are provided in Chapter 5.

DDP (German Democratic Party) Germany's Liberal Party of the left, which played an important part in drawing up the Constitution of the Weimar Republic and in the coalition governments. It suffered heavy loss in support to the Nazis from 1930.

DNVP (German National People's Party, or National Party) The main party of the conservative right, it opposed the democratic principles of the Weimar Republic, preferring the more authoritarian base of the former Reich. It collaborated with the NSDAP between 1928 and 1933.

DVP (German People's Party) Germany's Liberal Party of the right and successor to the National Liberals in the Reich period. It was led by Stresemann* but, after his death in 1929, it suffered loss of support to the Nazis.

Destalinisation A policy pursued by Khrushchev from 1956 onwards which denounced Stalin* and the regime of terror which he had imposed. Stalin was subsequently 'written out' of official Soviet histories on Khrushchev's order.

Dictatorship (see also **Autocracy**) A general term applying to the unlimited use of power by the leadership (usually) of a twentieth-century state. A dictatorship can be *authoritarian or *totalitarian.

'Dictatorship of the Proletariat' (see also **'Classless Society'**) A theoretical construction of Marx and Engels, this was a period, immediately following the proletarian revolution, in which other classes are eliminated in economic terms. As applied in practice in Russia, it came to mean a one-party political dictatorship.

Dual Monarchy Austria-Hungary from the time of the *Ausgleich* (1867) to its break-up 1918–19.

Duce Meaning 'leader', this was the title assumed by Mussolini* in addition to that of Prime Minister. Unlike Hitler, Mussolini never became head of state as Italy retained its monarchy. The cult of the *Duce* refers to the projection of Mussolini's personal popularity (see also *Mussolinianism).

Duma This has two meanings: (1) an elected town council of the type introduced by Alexander II in 1870 and (2) an elected central parliament, introduced in Russia in 1906.

Eclectic A combination of different components and ideas which are loosely joined together, leaving the original parts clearly distinguishable. Fascism is a good example of an eclectic ideology.

Edict A law issued by the government or head of state instead of being passed by a legislature. Examples include the Alexander II's* Edict of Emancipation (1861) and the emergency edicts issued by the president of the Weimar Republic under Article 48 of the Constitution.

Encyclical A statement on Catholic doctrine issued by the pope and requiring observance by all Catholics.

Entente An agreement between two countries to resolve differences and develop friendly relations – but not going as far as a military alliance. The main example is the 1904 Anglo-French Entente.

Etatist A term used to describe a political system wherever the state is the highest form of organisation. This applied more to Fascist Italy than to Nazi Germany (where the highest form was the 'race').

Executive The part of the constitution which carries out the laws, this usually includes ministers, government departments and civil servants.

Extermination Camp Developed after the Wannsee Conference (1941) from earlier concentration camps, the extermination camps were equipped with gas chambers for the killing of Jews. The main examples were Auschwitz, Treblinka, Sobibor, Chelmo and Maidanek.

Falange Spanish fascist organisation within the broader Nationalist movement of General Franco.

Fascism An ideology originating at the turn of the nineteenth century in France with the convergence of ideas of the extreme left and extreme right. It developed into a political system in Italy under the leadership of Mussolini* and appeared as movements in other European states. In Italy it was characterised by anti-communism, anti-liberal democracy, authoritarianism, militarism and expansion. In Germany it influenced the development of Nazism, although Hitler's ideas were based more on race than on the state.

Fasci di Combattimento The squads of the fascist movement, set up in 1918. They were responsible for the early fascist violence.

Freikorps Some of the remnants of the German army after the armistice, which operated as paramilitary units and influenced by right-wing ideas. They were used to suppress the initial communist threats to the Republic. Many later joined the Nazis via the *SA.

Führer The 'leader' of the Nazi movement during the 1920s and the official title of Hitler* when he assumed the presidency on Hindenburg's* death in 1934.

GOKO (or **GKO**) State Committee for Defence, the central government used by Stalin* during the course of the war with Germany between 1941 and 1945.

Gauleiter A leader of a Gau, a territorial division of the NSDAP. Each Gauleiter was responsible directly to Hitler*. An example was Goebbels* who was appointed Gauleiter of Berlin in 1926.

Gestapo (**Geheime Staatspolizei**) Secret state police, set up by Goering in 1933 to cover the state of Prussia, it was brought into the SS and placed under the overall control of Himmler*. The effective head of the Gestapo from 1934 was Heydrich*.

Gosplan The department responsible for drafting the Five Year Plans within the *USSR.

Greens The term has two meanings: (1) the peasant armies during the Russian Civil War and (2) the non-Bolshevik revolutionary movement in Russia to 1921. Some historians now refer to the Civil War as a three-sided conflict which involved the Greens (in both senses) as well as the *Reds and the *Whites.

Gulag The administration for the labour camps in the Soviet Union, established by Stalin* and abolished by Khrushchev in 1956.

Hereditary Tenure In connection with the emancipation of the serfs in Russia, land was made available to the peasantry under the direction of the village commune. In some areas land ownership was permanent, or hereditary, while in others it was periodically redistributed.

Hitler Youth Part of the Nazi movement in the 1920s, it was made compulsory in 1935. It comprised three sections for boys (the *Pimpf, Deutsches Jungvolk* and *Hitler Jugend*) and two for girls (the *Jungmädel-Bund* and the *Bund Deutscher Mädel*).

Irredentism A commitment to regaining territory considered to be essential for the completion of a nation state. Examples are French irredentism over Alsace-Lorraine and Serb irredentism over Bosnia and Herzegovina.

Judiciary The part of a constitution concerned with the administration of justice.

KdF (*Kraft durch Freude*) 'Strength through Joy', the Nazi organisation which organised the leisure activities of the German labour force.

KPD German Communist Party, which originated as the Spartacus League and was joined by most of the USPD (Independent Socialists). Both came from the radical wing of the *SPD, which broke away during the First World War. The KPD was opposed to the Weimar Republic and, under the instructions of Stalin, refused to co-operate with the other parties to try to prevent the rise of Hitler and the Nazis. The KPD increased its electoral support after 1928 but was banned in 1933.

Kolkhoz (plural *Kolkhozy*) Collective farm of the type established by Stalin* in the Soviet Union.

Kulak The wealthier members of the Russian peasantry. The official policy of Stolypin* was to promote a peasant elite which would remain loyal to the tsarist system. When the Bolsheviks came to power, Lenin* initially put pressure on the Kulaks through *War Communism but had to reverse this through the *NEP. The Kulaks therefore experienced a second period of relative prosperity. Stalin, however, saw them as 'class enemies' and made them his main target in his programme of *collectivisation. Hundreds of thousands of Kulaks were executed or sent to labour camps.

Kulturkampf The conflict during the 1870s between the Catholic Church and the German state over the issue of control over education and other social issues.

Laissez-faire A term used mainly in the nineteenth century to indicate the absence of state control over the economy. It literally means 'leave alone'.

Land (plural *Länder*) A federal state within Germany (for example, Prussia and Bavaria).

Landtag (plural *Landtäge*) The state assembly or parliament.

Lateran Relating to the papacy (for example the 1929 Lateran Treaty between Mussolini and the pope).

Lebensraum Hitler's* concept, expressed in *Mein Kampf* and the *Second Book*, of 'living space'. This would involve the future expansion of Germany's frontiers eastwards to settle Germany's surplus population. *Lebensraum* was closely connected with the belief in the 'supremacy' of the *Aryan race.

Legislature The part of a constitution concerned with drawing up laws. Examples were the Reichstag in Germany, the Duma in Tsarist Russia and the Supreme Soviet in the USSR.

Luftwaffe German airforce, banned by the Treaty of Versailles but re-established by Hitler.

Lumpenproletariat (see also **Proletariat**) The lowest level of the working class, usually unemployed or casual labourers.

Mandate In general political terms, a 'mandate' usually refers to electoral approval for a certain government policy. A more specific context, however, is the removal of overseas colonies from Germany by the Treaty of Versailles; these were entrusted as 'mandates' to another power. For example, Kamerun was mandated to Britain and France (as the Cameroons).

Manifesto A widely publicised statement of policy.

Marxist A follower of the ideas of Marx and Engels. The basic components of Marxism are (1) an approach to history which is based on class conflict, (2) a belief in the necessity of the end of capitalism and (3) a view of the future moving via the *'dictatorship of the proletariat' to the *'classless society'. Since Marxism was not at all clear about the practicalities of change, different approaches emerged in Europe, usually comprising evolutionary and revolutionary strategies. This applied in Germany, where the SPD, originally a Marxist party, split between the SPD moderates and the KPD radicals, or communists. Similarly, the *RSDLP, or Russian Social Democratic Labour Party, established as a Marxist organisation, split in 1903 between the moderate Mensheviks and the Bolsheviks, later known as communists. It could be said that all communists are Marxists, but not all Marxists are communists.

Mensheviks The moderate faction within the RSDLP which believed in co-operating with the bourgeoisie to bring down the tsarist system. Under Martov*, it broke with the more radical *Bolsheviks. The Mensheviks played an important role in the Petrograd Soviet and the Provisional Government (1917) but opposed the monopoly of power held by the Bolsheviks from October 1917. They had been largely eliminated by 1922.

Menshevik Internationalists The more radical wing which developed within the Mensheviks, stressing the need for international revolution. Their main spokesman was Trotsky*, who took most of them over to the Bolsheviks in 1917.

Mobilisation Within the context of Chapter 2, preparation for war by calling up all troop formations and moving them towards the designated front in accordance with a war plan based on a special railway timetable. It is often argued that the timetables were so inflexible that mobilisation led inevitably to the outbreak of war.

Multilateral Involving a number of powers, either in negotiation or agreement. See also *bilateral and *unilateral.

Mussolinianism (see also *Duce*) A term used by some historians to distinguish between the ideas and institutions of fascism and the glorification of Mussolini* himself. This is a useful distinction since it avoids the oversimplification of fascism as the personal creation of Mussolini himself.

NEP (New Economic Policy) Introduced by Lenin* in 1921 to reverse the previous attempt at War Communism. The NEP allowed (1) the return of most industries to private ownership or trusts and (2) the peasantry to sell their produce subject to a state licence. The policy is sometimes seen as 'state capitalism'. After Lenin's death there was a major controversy over its future, which ended with Stalin's* decision to introduce *collectivisation and state planning.

NKVD (People's Commissariat for Internal Affairs) Stalin's* secret police which was responsible for implementing most of the terror of the 1930s.

NSDAP National Socialist German Workers' Party, the full name of the Nazi Party from 1920.

Narodniya Voliya (People's Will) The radical wing of the Russian Populist movement which followed a strategy of violence and assassination. It was responsible for the death of Alexander II* in 1881.

OVRA (*Opera Voluntaria per la Repressione Antifascista*) Mussolini's* secret police force.

October Manifesto Issued by Nicholas II* in October 1905, this promised basic liberties and the summoning of a representative assembly.

Octobrists A moderate conservative party in Russia. It took its stand on the principles of the October Manifesto and at first strongly supported the tsarist system. From 1915, however, some Octobrists joined the Progressive Bloc in the *Duma in protest against arbitrary despotism.

Okhrana Tsarist secret police.

PCI Italian Communist Party.

PNF (*Partito Nazionale Fascista*) Italian Fascist Party, set up by Mussolini* in 1921 in an attempt to widen the appeal of fascism and win votes from the electorate.

PSI Italian Socialist Party.

Permanent Revolution The programme followed by Trotsky* after Lenin's* death and opposed to *Socialism in One Country. It emphasised (1) the need to spread revolution to other countries and (2) to end the NEP, collectivise agriculture and accelerate industrialisation.

Plebiscite A popular vote. Two examples are the plebiscite held by the League of Nations to decide the future of Schleswig (1920) and the plebiscite held in Austria and Germany in 1938 to seek popular approval for Hitler's *Anschluss*.

Pogroms Violent persecutions, especially of Jews in Tsarist Russia.

Politburo Political Bureau, formally established within the Central Committee of the Communist Party in 1919. It consisted of the ten top Bolsheviks. Stalin* tended to bypass it in favour of smaller groups. Between 1952 and 1964 it was renamed the Praesidium, but Khrushchev's successors reverted to the original name.

Populists One of the two main branches of Russian revolutionaries, the other being Marxist. The Populists were supported mainly by the peasantry and followed a programme based on rural socialism. They divided into different groups which included moderate organisations like Black Partition and radicals like *Narodniya Voliya* (People's Will). In 1900 the Populist groups united to form the *Socialist Revolutionaries.

Procurator-General of the Holy Synod The Russian minister (a member of the tsarist government) responsible for the Russian Orthodox Church, the clerical head being the patriarch. This could be a highly influential post in the hands of a man with strong conservative views and a determination to control the country's progressive influences. Pobedonostsev*, who served as procurator-general under Alexander III and Nicholas II, was just such a person.

Progressive Bloc A group of members in the Duma comprising mainly *Constitutional Democrats and *Octobrists who, from 1915, tried to put pressure on the Tsar to consult the Duma and abandon his attempted return to autocratic rule under the impetus of the First World War. From the Progressive Bloc eventually emerged those who put pressure on the Tsar to abdicate in March 1917 and who set up the Provisional Government in his place.

Proletariat (see also *Lumpenproletariat*) A term normally associated with Marxism, but actually a neutral reference to the working class.

Provisional Government The government which replaced the Tsar on his abdication on 15 March 1917. It emerged from the Provisional Committee of the Duma in response to the growing political emergency at the end of 1916. The Provisional Government was initially led by Prince Lvov and, from July 1917, by Alexander Kerensky*, a Socialist Revolutionary. It was increasingly challenged by the Petrograd Soviet and overthrown by the Bolshevik Revolution in October 1917.

Putsch A German revolt (equivalent to the French coup). Examples include the Kapp Putsch of 1920 and Hitler's* Munich Putsch of 1923.

RSDLP (Russian Social Democratic Labour Party) Formed in 1898, this united the various Marxist organisations which had sprung up during the last two decades of the nineteenth century. Since it included moderates and radicals, the RSDLP split in 1903 between the Mensheviks, led by Martov*, and the Bolsheviks under Lenin*. Subsequent attempts at reunification failed.

RSFSR (The Russian Soviet Federated Socialist Republic) Set up by Lenin's* 1918 Constitution, it was intended to be a federal system representing the different regions of Russia. The later Constitutions of 1922 and 1936 added the *USSR to include the other, non-Russian parts of the former Russian Empire. The RSFSR (or Russia) therefore came to exist as one of the Republics of the USSR (or Soviet Union). After the break-up of the USSR in 1991, the RSFSR separated from the other Republics and became the Russian Federation.

RSI (*Repubblica Sociale Italiana*) The Italian Social Republic was set up by Mussolini* after his rescue from captivity from Gran Sasso by the Germans. Northern Italy was still under Nazi control and the RSI became a puppet fascist regime, largely under SS control. It was administered from Salo, on Lake Garda, despite fierce resistance from Italian partisans. It collapsed with the retreat of German troops in 1945 and Mussolini was captured and shot.

Radical In its political context, a term meaning extreme – either on the left or on the right. Hence communists usually started as radical socialists or Marxists.

Reaction In political terms, a strong resistance to progressive change. In the period of this book, reactionary policies were most common in Tsarist Russia, especially under Alexander III* (1881–94).

Reactive Frequently confused with 'reaction' but actually quite different, 'reactive' means responding to a situation and hence being influenced by it. An example of a 'reactive' measure was the October Manifesto, issued by Nicholas II* to try to end the 1905 Revolution.

Reds (Bolsheviks) The term 'Reds' was used most frequently during the Russian Civil War to distinguish the Bolsheviks from the counter-revolutionary *Whites. The Revolutionary Military Committee, which seized power in October 1917, organised the Red Guard which, in turn was expanded into the Red Army. Red is, of course, the colour of both revolution and the working class.

Red Guard See *Reds.

Reich (German Empire) Usually the term 'Reich' applies to the periods 1871–1918 (sometimes known as the 'Second Reich' or *Kasierreich*) and 1933–45 (referred to by the Nazis as the 'Third Reich'). Confusingly, it was also used in the 1919 Constitution as a reference to the central system in Germany (for example, 'Reich government', 'Reich laws' and, of course, 'Reichstag'), even though the Empire had been replaced by a Republic. The term 'Reich' was abandoned in 1945.

Reichsrat The second chamber in the *legislature of the Weimar Republic, which replaced the *Bundesrat* of the Second Reich, represented the states of the federal system. The representatives in the *Reichsrat* were appointed by the state governments.

Reichstag The elected chamber of the legislature of imperial Germany (1871–1918) and the Weimar Republic (1919–33). It also continued through the Nazi period (1933–45), although the last multi-party Reichstag election was held in March 1933. Thereafter many of its functions passed to the Chancellor and *Führer.

Reichswehr The German army – until its reorganisation in 1938 into the *Wehrmacht.*

Rentenmark The currency, issued in November 1923 by the *Rentenbank,* to replace the *Reichsmark,* which had been devalued by hyperinflation.

Reparations In the context of Chapter 4, the charge placed on Germany by the Allies for the cost of the war. Payment was made in two ways – in kind (by infrastructure, moveable assets, etc.) and in money. The total reparations bill was fixed in 1921, by the Allied Reparations Commission, at 136,000 million gold marks.

Repartitional Tenure A form of land tenure among the Russian peasantry after 1861 which was subject to redistributed ownership on the decision of the local commune. It was the alternative to the more common *hereditary tenure.

Revanchism A desire for revenge transformed into political pressure.

Romanov Since the seventeenth century, the dynasty of the royal family in Tsarist Russia.

Russification The imposition of Russian culture, language and institutions on minority groups or non-Russian provinces. This was a policy deliberately pursued by Alexander III* and Nicholas II*.

SA (*Sturm Abteilung*) The brown-shirted stormtroopers were established in 1920 as the para-military units of the Nazi movement. They were notorious for their violence, especially against communists and Jews, and indiscipline. Their leadership, including Röhm, was killed by the SS in the Night of the Long Knives (1934) but the movement remained in existence throughout the Third Reich.

SdA (*Schönheit der Arbeit* (the 'beauty of labour')) An organisation responsible for working conditions in Nazi Germany.

SOPADE The SPD in exile. SOPADE tried to co-ordinate opposition in factories to the Nazi regime but often had to compete with rival communist cells. The main importance of SOPADE to the modern historian is the extensive reports written by its agents on conditions and attitudes in the Third Reich.

SPD (German Social Democratic Party) This was formed on Marxist principles in the early 1870s. Bismarck sought to undermine it but succeeded only in extending its popularity. By 1914 the SPD was the largest party in Germany. In 1917 the radical left broke away, eventually becoming the *KPD. The SPD were the leading democratic party of the entire period of the Weimar Republic and the one which stood up to the Nazis until it was banned in July 1933.

SS (*Schutzstaffeln*) Black-shirted security squads, which grew out of the SA as a more disciplined elite under Himmler*. Their development and importance to the Nazi system are covered in Chapter 6.

Slavs A broad ethnic term for the inhabitants of eastern Europe, especially the Russians, Poles, Czechs, Slovaks, Slovenes, Serbs and Croats. The northern and southern Slavs formed at least 50 per cent of the population of Austria-Hungary, which they broke up in 1918 to form successor states such as Czechoslovakia and Yugoslavia.

Socialism in One Country The strategy pursued after 1924 by the Stalin* faction – in opposition to Trotsky's* focus on *Permanent Revolution.

Socialist Revolutionaries The unification of the various Populist groups in Russia in 1900. The SRs were the main revolutionary alternative to the Marxists and, because their main support came from the peasantry, they were more widely popular than either the Bolsheviks or the Mensheviks. In 1917 the right SRs (for example, Kerensky*) supported the Provisional Government, while the left SRs broke away and collaborated with the Bolsheviks. The right SRs formed the main revolutionary opposition to the Bolsheviks in 1919. They won the election to the Constituent Assembly and, when Lenin* closed the Assembly in January 1919, the SRs established their own government to the east of the area controlled by the Bolsheviks. The Right SRs were eventually eliminated by the Bolsheviks in 1921 and 1922.

Soviets Councils of Workers' and Soldiers' Deputies. The first of these was set up in St Petersburg in the 1905 Revolution, headed by Trotsky*. It was reconstituted in Petrograd during the Revolution of March 1917 and, by October, had a Bolshevik majority. Lenin* made the soviets the basic form of *legislature in preference to the Western style of parliament. The term is sometimes used (inaccurately) to denote the inhabitants of the Soviet Union.

Spartacus League The radical offshoot from the left wing of the SPD, led by Karl Liebknecht and Rosa Luxemburg*, both of whom knew Lenin* and hoped to set up a communist regime in Germany. The Spartacists failed in an attempt to seize power early in 1919, in which Liebknecht and Luxemburg were both shot by the *Freikorps. The Spartacus League reconstituted itself as the *KPD.

Stakhanovites 'Shock workers' in Stalinist Russia who were renowned for exceeding their production quotas and were therefore made an official model for the rest of the workforce. Needless to say, they were not popular.

Syndicalism A form of radical socialism in France at the turn of the nineteenth century, particularly influenced by the ideas of Georges Sorel. One of its aims was to use the power of the strike for political purposes. Mussolini* was strongly influenced by syndicalism, which he later adapted to radical nationalism to form the Italian variant of *fascism.

Totalitarian (see also **Authoritarian**) A style of dictatorship which aimed at establishing total control over the population by activating the masses through propaganda and indoctrination. It was based on a one-party system and a head of state who was usually the focus of a personality cult. The overall system was based on an ideology. Mussolini claimed that Fascist Italy was the most genuine totalitarian regime but, in reality, the description was more appropriate to Nazi Germany and Stalinist Russia.

USPD Independent Socialists, who broke away from the *SPD at the end of the First World War. After a brief period as a separate party, most of them merged with the *KPD.

USSR (Union of Soviet Socialist Republics) A federal system linking the *RSFSR (Russia) with the other parts of the former Russian Empire. The USSR collapsed in 1991.

Unilateral Action by one side without reference to any other (in contrast to *bilateral and *multilateral).

Volksgemeinschaft The People's Community, explained in detail in Chapter 6.

War Communism An attempt by Lenin's* regime in 1918 to accelerate the growth of state control over industry and to requisition the grain of the peasantry. It resulted in starvation and widespread opposition, in the face of which the *Bolsheviks had to backtrack into the *NEP in 1921.

Weltpolitik Kaiser Wilhelm II's policy during the 1890s of converting Germany from a European into a world power through colonial expansion and a naval-building programme.

Whites Opposition to the *Reds in the Russian Civil War. They aimed to overthrow the regime established in the October Revolution, although they were not agreed on what should replace it.

Z (*Zentrum* or Centre) The party in imperial Germany and the Weimar Republic which received a large proportion of the Catholic vote.

Zemstvo (plural zemstva) Elected local governments set up by Alexander II* in 1864.

Select Bibliography

The era of the First World War, 1890–1919

The following are recommended as basic reading for this topic:

I. Cawood and D. McKinnon-Bell, *The First World War* (London 2001); *Questions and Analysis in History* series
R. Henig, *The Origins of the First World War* (London 1985); *Lancaster Pamphlet* series
R. Henig, *Versailles and After: Europe 1919–1933* (London 1995); *Lancaster Pamphlet* series
J. Lowe, *Rivalry and Accord. International Relations 1870–1914* (London 1988); *Access to History* series
A.J.P. Taylor, *War by Timetable* (London 1969)
L.C.F. Turner, *Origins of the First World War* (London 1972)

Sources are included in:

I. Cawood and D. McKinnon-Bell, op. cit.
M. Hurst (ed.), *Key Treaties for the Great Powers, Vol. 2: 1871–1914* (Newton Abbott 1971)
J.A.S. Grenville (ed.), *The Major International Treaties 1914–1973* (London 1974)

As a link between AS and the methodology of A2 the following titles are recommended:

D.E. Lee, *The Outbreak of the First World War: Who Was Responsible?* (Boston 1963); *Problems in European Civilization* series
J. Remak, *The First World War: Causes, Conduct, Consequences* (New York 1971); *Major Issues in History* series

Russia 1855–1917

The following are recommended as basic reading for this topic:

S.J. Lee, *Lenin and Revolutionary Russia 1900–1924* (London 2003); *Questions and Analysis in History* series
A. Wood, *The Russian Revolution* (London 1979); *Seminar Studies in History* series
A. Wood, *The Origins of the Russian Revolution* (London 1994); *Lancaster Pamphlet* series
R. Sherman, *Russia 1815–81* (London 1992); *Access to History* series
M. Lynch, *Reaction and Revolutions: Russia 1881–1924* (London 1992); *Access to History* series

Sources are included in:

S.J. Lee, op. cit.
A. Wood, op. cit.
B. Dmytryshyn, *Imperial Russia. A Source Book* (Hinsdale, IL 1974)
J. Daborn: *Russia, Revolution and Counter-Revolution 1917–1924* (Cambridge 1991); *Cambridge Topics in History* series.
N. Rothnie, *The Russian Revolution* (London 1990); *Documents and Debates* series.
M. McCaulay, *The Russian Revolution and the Soviet State 1917–1921* (Basingstoke 1980)

As a link between AS and the methodology of A2 the following titles are recommended:

A. E. Adams, *Imperial Russia After 1861* (Boston 1965); *Problems in European Civilization* series
R.V. Daniels, *The Russian Revolution* (Boston 1972); *Problems in European Civilization* series
E. Acton, *Rethinking the Russian Revolution* (London 1996)

Imperial and Weimar Germany 1890–1933

The following are recommended as basic reading for this topic:

S.J. Lee, *Imperial Germany 1871–1918* (London 1999); *Questions and Analysis in History* series
S.J. Lee, *The Weimar Republic* (London 1998); *Questions and Analysis in History* series
G. Layton, *From Bismarck to Hitler 1890–1933* (London 1995); *Access to History* series
L. Abrams, *Bismarck and the German Empire, 1871–1918* (London 1998); *Lancaster Pamphlet* series
R. Henig, *The Weimar Republic 1919–1933* (London 1998); *Lancaster Pamphlet* series
J. Hiden, *The Weimar Republic* (London 1974); *Seminar Studies in History* series
J. Hiden, *Republican and Fascist Germany* (London 1996)
C. Fischer, *The Rise of the Nazis* (Manchester 1995)

Sources are included in:

S.J. Lee, op. cit.
J. Hiden, op. cit.
C. Lodge, *From Confederation to Empire: Germany 1848–1914* (London 1997); *History at Source* series
J. Laver, *Imperial and Weimar Germany 1890–1933* (London 1992); *History at Source* series
A. Kaes, M. Jay and E. Dimendberg, *The Weimar Republic Sourcebook* (Berkeley 1994)
L. Snyder, *The Weimar Republic* (Princeton, NJ 1966)

Italy 1918–45

The following are recommended as basic reading for this topic:

M. Blinkhorn, *Mussolini and Fascist Italy* (London 1994); *Lancaster Pamphlet* series
M. Robson, *Italy: Liberalism and Fascism 1870–1914* (London 2000); *Access to History* series
A. Cassels, *Fascist Italy* (London 1969)
J. Pollard, *The Fascist Experience in Italy* (London 1998)
J. Whittam, *Fascist Italy* (Manchester 1995)
P. Morgan, *Italian Fascism 1919–1945* (London 1995)

Sources are included in:

J. Whittam, *Fascist Italy* (Manchester 1995)

Nazi Germany 1933–45

The following are recommended as basic reading for this topic:

S.J. Lee, *Hitler and Nazi Germany* (London 1998); *Questions and Analysis in History* series
D.G. Williamson, *The Third Reich* (London 1982); *Seminar Studies in History* series
R. Geary, *Hitler and Nazism* (London 1994); *Lancaster Pamphlet* series
N. Stone, *Hitler* (London 1980)
A.J. Nicholls, *Weimar and the Rise of Hitler* (London 1968)

Index